D0072703

AN UNEASY SOLITUDE

Not only does democracy make every man forget his ancestors, but it hides his descendants, and separates his contemporaries, from him; it throws him back for ever upon himself alone, and threatens in the end to confine him entirely within the solitude of his own heart.

—Tocqueville

AN UNEASY SOLITUDE

Individual and Society in the Work of Ralph Waldo Emerson

~ BY ~

MAURICE GONNAUD

TRANSLATED BY

LAWRENCE ROSENWALD

PRINCETON UNIVERSITY PRESS

PRINCETON, NEW JERSEY

Published by Princeton University Press, 41 William Street,
Princeton, New Jersey 08540
In the United Kingdom: Princeton University Press,
Guildford, Surrey

Library of Congress Cataloging in Publication Data will be found on the last printed page of this book

ISBN 0-691-06718-X

Publication of this book has been aided by a grant from the Paul Mellon Fund of Princeton University Press

This book has been composed in Linotron Monticello

Clothbound editions of Princeton University Press books are printed on acid-free paper, and binding materials are chosen for strength and durability. Paperbacks, although satisfactory for personal collections, are not usually suitable for library rebinding

Printed in the United States of America by Princeton University Press
Princeton, New Jersey

The preparation of this volume was made possible by a grant from the Translations Program of the National Endowment for the Humanities, an independent Federal agency.

CONTENTS

PART IV
Individual *and* Citizen

FOREWORD

WHEN Maurice Gonnaud's *Individu et société dans l'oeuvre de Ralph Waldo Emerson* was published in 1964, the figure of Emerson that dominated American literary history was resolutely disembodied, a quite literally antisocial Emerson, who transcended or repressed (depending on one's point of view) the forces of history and politics. This was the "optimistic" Emerson projected by F. O. Matthiessen in his extraordinarily influential *American Renaissance* (1941): a "transcendental idealist," who, although "the Yankee in his make-up kept pulling him back to a grounding in common fact" (43), could not, like "the Vedantist" (52), finally resist "the sweep of the divine mind" "in which all the severing details of man's existence . . . are caught up and reconciled and obliterated" (44).[1]

In 1953 Stephen Whicher published *Freedom and Fate: An Inner Life of Ralph Waldo Emerson*, which—until now, perhaps—has been the single most influential book in Emerson studies. What Whicher achieved in his book was a certain translation of Matthiessen's Emerson, which transformed the synchronic tension between Yankee and Vedantist (always finally overcome by the Vedantist, much to Matthiessen's overt dismay) into a diachronic trajectory from Vedantist to Yankee, or, to use figures proper to Whicher, from "transcendentalism . . . to a basic empiricism" (97).

So, as Whicher's story of Emerson goes, in the 1830s—the decade of *Nature* (1836), "The American Scholar" (1837), and the Harvard Divinity School address (1838)—Emerson's radically optimistic thought

[1] In addition to Maurice Gonnaud's *Uneasy Solitude*, citations from the following books will be found in this Foreword: F. O. Matthiessen, *American Renaissance: Art and Expression in the Age of Emerson and Whitman* (1941, repr. New York, 1968); Stephen E. Whicher, *Freedom and Fate: An Inner Life of Ralph Waldo Emerson* (Philadelphia, 1953); Carolyn Porter, *Seeing and Being: The Plight of the Participant Observer in Emerson, James, Adams, and Faulkner* (Middletown, Conn., 1981); Quentin Anderson, *The Imperial Self: An Essay in American Literary and Cultural History* (New York, 1971); and Harold Bloom, *Poetry and Repression: Revisionism from Blake to Stevens* (New Haven, 1976). Page numbers to the material cited from these books appear directly following the citation in the body of my text.

(optimistic because, as in Matthiessen's Emerson, his thought is "immune to experience" [Whicher, 154]) is in "revolt against tradition . . . designed to cut the traces that bound him to history" (98). But "[i]n the 1840's he [Emerson] more and more often ascribes the power of performance, not to an influx of the divine, but to animal spirits; and, whereas he speaks of the first with hope, of the last he uses almost a valetudinarian tone" (100). Thus, what Whicher refers to as Emerson's "romance of self-union" (109), his dream of the limitlessness of a pure disembodiment, becomes in a short period of time a realistic tale of self-division. For Emerson "came to recognize that his real self was his whole contradictory nature, divine potentiality and mortal limits together" (103). Near the end of Whicher's "inner life" of Emerson, a life that appears to reproduce the trajectory from romance to realism of traditional American literary history, the figure of Emerson returns for a moment to the tension between embodiment and disembodiment that momentarily characterizes Matthiessen's Emerson.

Yet both in Matthiessen and Whicher and in the discourses on Emerson and American literature that have followed them and accepted the terms of their discussions (the terms of embodiment and disembodiment), the tension is finally not a tension, so overdetermined does the figure of disembodiment appear. Thus, in the case of Matthiessen's canon, of which Emerson is the founder, although "[h]e wrote no masterpiece" (xii), Emerson's disembodiment establishes, inasmuch as it allows or makes visible, what is for Matthiessen the progressive movement that culminates in the embodiments of Melville and Whitman, a union of ideality and materiality (or sensuality, or sexuality) that Matthiessen refers to at one point as the "male principle in our literature" (524). For Matthiessen, Emerson's disembodiment is a loss of (male) power, which, paradoxically, is the power that founds a (white, patrician, Christian) tradition (I put these terms in parentheses to mark their implicit circulation in *American Renaissance* rather than their explicit examination by Matthiessen). This paradox emerges with particular force in Matthiessen's methodological introduction to *American Renaissance*, where—borrowing a figure from Emerson himself—Matthiessen describes Emerson as "the cow from which the rest [Thoreau, Hawthorne, Melville, and Whitman] drew their milk" (xii), thus inscribing the founding father as a female figure, nourishing the male figures who were to complete her.

For Whicher, on the other hand, it is embodiment, the force of experience, that marks the decisive loss of power in Emerson. For Emerson's revolutionary or originary power resides in his disembodiment (and this is also true of Matthiessen's Emerson, though as I have just suggested, in a decidedly ambivalent way): "If the keynote of his early thought is revolution, that of his later thought is acquiescence and optimism. From an intense rebellion against the world in the name of the Soul, he moved to a relative acceptance of things as they are, world and Soul together; from teaching men their power to rise above fate, he turned to teaching them how to make the best of it" (124–25). Yet, Whicher acknowledges, there was always a "basic complacence [that] underlay and qualified" (ibid.) Emerson's revolutionary inner vision, a complacence, Whicher suggests, firmly based in Emerson's comparatively fortunate middle-class outer life: "His release from his profession [of clergyman], his inheritance [from his first wife, Ellen, which enabled this release], his marriage [to his second wife, Lydia], his country home, and his success as a lecturer and author" (ibid.). In the 1840s, then, what we see, according to Whicher, is the "emergence" of this complacence as Emerson's "primary attitude," an attitude that entails "a dwindling of his first hostility to society" and a "com[ing] to terms with the outside world" (ibid.). Now Emerson's "thought is characteristically an affirmation of a *second best*," a strategy that, having seen that "a perfect freedom [of disembodiment] was clearly out of reach," tried to articulate a freedom within the confines of the body (126). Whicher's Emerson has moved from a revolutionary individualism of the disembodied self to a conservative corporatism (130) of the body politic. And as we can read in Whicher's description of this movement of embodiment—a movement Whicher describes in terms of "acquiescence," "complacence," "dwindling," and "*second best*"—this movement is definitely a diminishment of his figure of Emerson, a shrinking of "the infinitude of the private man" (25) to the finitude of the public, a fall from the "air of high romance" (155) to the ground of realism. And even as Whicher wonders whether or not this fall represents a "loss," he describes it in precisely those terms (ibid.).

Neither the part of Matthiessen's Emerson that is Yankee nor the part of Whicher's that is corporate survived the work of these two scholars. Rather, as I have suggested, what emerged into the memory of American literary history was a wholly disembodied Emerson: Emerson the Idealist, the Romantic, the Transcendentalist. This particular survival is due to the fact that neither Matthiessen nor Whicher appears, finally, to believe in a sensuous Emerson. Matthiessen agrees in effect with Carlyle, whom he quotes early in *American Renaissance*, that Emerson's voice was " '*un*embodied,' " removed from his " 'own poor nineteenth century' " (10). And thus when Matthiessen thinks of Emerson he barely thinks of this figure woven into or weaving the figuration of an American history. It seems to me, following the cogent suggestions of Jonathan Arac, that Matthiessen is struggling, more or less successfully, to repress numerous American histories of class, gender, and race disruptive of the *organic whole* he wants the American Renaissance to be. And this may account for the fact that he refuses to read in any but the most fragmentary way Emerson's prose, which in the figures of its rhetoric is precisely composed of these disruptive histories. So while Matthiessen at the beginning of *American Renaissance* accurately sees that "[t]he problem that confronts us in dealing with Emerson [is] his inveterate habit of stating things in opposites," he also immediately displaces or misplaces the problem from the actual space of Emerson's language to the hypothetical space "lying behind" that language: "But the danger now is that in the multiplicity of his conflicting statements, we shall miss the wholeness of character lying behind them" (3). In fact the danger was, and is, just the opposite: that in our misplaced desire for some hypothetical unity beyond the text, we will miss the conflictive actuality of Emerson's language. And we can, perhaps, glimpse or grasp here in Matthiessen's initiatory gestures a habit of reading that does not comprehend what it posits as Emerson's profound disembodiment as much as it projects it, disembodying Emerson from the figures of his prose even as it goes on to lament or celebrate what it takes to be Emerson's self-disembodiment.

Whicher's habit of reading Emerson follows Matthiessen's closely. The figure of this habit is articulated for us in his subtitle, *An Inner Life of Ralph Waldo Emerson*. What this subtitle implicitly insists on is an old metaphysical dictum: that *inner* life and *outer*, *private* and *public*, *mind* and *body* are separable and that this separation represents a hierarchical relationship between the two spheres, in which the *inner* is privileged (the *outer* always being the space where the *inner* falls, when and if it falls). This metaphysical privilege, which masks, or purifies, political privileges and the conflicts arising from them of race, gender, and class, structures his view of Emerson. The result of this structuring is that what Whicher terms Emerson's "radical self-reliance" (25) becomes—both in *Freedom and Fate* and in the literary history that *Freedom and Fate* helps inscribe—the central trope for Emerson's writing life, almost naturally, as if Emerson himself had centered this trope. And this centering of self-reliance requires only a footnote of justification: "I am speaking here, of course, of the aims of his [Emerson's] private thoughts. Personally, though not gregarious, he was always a man of a few strong attachments and deep affections, a temperamentally domestic soul, and one generally careful to give the community its due and more" (25). This literal marginalization of the figures of the domestic and the communal in Emerson (figures that I have argued in my work on Emerson radically compromise the metaphysical privilege of Emerson's self-reliance) points to their ideological marginalization in traditional American literary history. This is a literary history in which these figures of the communal and the domestic—the primary figures of history, after all—have either been erased or displaced, so that they cannot energetically call into question the autonomy ascribed to Emersonian self-reliance in this history, but only appear as its exhausted remains.

Since about the mid-1960s or so, another literary history has begun to emerge. Principally under the influence of feminist and ethnic studies, often but not necessarily angled from Marxist and/or the post-structuralist perspectives of Derrida and Foucault, this other literary history is centrally interested in *re*placing figures of the communal and the domestic in the literary history that has sought to displace them. How this replacement, or rewriting, should take place is by no means a matter of unanimity, as ideologies compete to redraw the critical map. And so I would be more accurate in speaking of the emergence of other American literary histories, rather than simply of another history. But whatever the conflicts between these histories, whatever their similarities and differences, however distinct or blurred their boundaries, they all share a central interest in what they term *history*, the representation, or embodiment, of power and authority in that sphere in which social, cultural, economic, and political forces interplay and from which literary representation, so these histories insist, cannot be separated. Purely formalist studies or a purely literary history are forbidden here, because here literary value cannot be separated from political value. We seem to have returned, in fact, to the realm of rhetorical studies, in the classical sense, where questions of power, authority, and literary value (the value of all forms of letters, written and spoken) were inseparable. What rhetorical studies always problematized, however, and what in this new longing for history has not been sufficiently problematized (when it is brought up at all) is the term *history* itself. For *history* cannot escape the questions of power and authority, that is, of its own rhetorical force, which it is being used to represent.

At the present critical moment, then, the figure of Emerson is becoming associated more and more with this term *history*. This figure, I would say, is finally beginning to be located in some of its possible figurations (the sexual–political, for example, and the economic). The following passage from Carolyn Porter's recent *Seeing and Being* suggests both how this present intense interest in history is translating the traditionally self-reliant, or disembodied, Emerson, and how Maurice Gonnaud's Emerson has a most valuable contribution to make to this translation process: "Emerson's reputation as a subjective idealist, intent upon 'coming out of culture,' and irremediably hostile to society . . . has grown out of the failure to appreciate the fact that Emerson's revolt occurred within a particular society; it was not Society in the abstract, but *this* society which he attacked" (61).

The opposition between individual and society implied in the original title of Maurice Gonnaud's book is not the traditional opposition between Emerson as "subjective idealist" (the disembodied Emerson I have been describing) and "Society in the abstract," which Porter rightly sees as comprising "Emerson's reputation." Gonnaud's Emerson is resolutely *not* Matthiessen's Emerson, torn between Yankee and Vedantist, with, nevertheless, the Vedantist always triumphing. Neither is Gonnaud's Emerson Whicher's, who travels from the revolutionary freedom of the disembodied soul downward to the fleshy constraints of fate. Yet there are, certainly, marks that suggest a commonality between the Emersons of Matthiessen and Whicher and that of Gonnaud. And we would do well to attend briefly to a primary mark, Emersonian "optimism," as a way to begin to distinguish Gonnaud's Emerson.

Gonnaud's Emerson, following both Matthiessen's and Whicher's, is optimistic. Yet, we might note initially, the optimism of Gonnaud's Emerson is not founded on an immunity to experience, but on a certain openness to it: "The particular mark of Emersonian optimism" is that in its grip "Emerson renounces nothing; he neither abuses nor represses any of his faculties. Rather, he indulges in [*jouit de*] their surprising elasticity, which permits them to turn with equal pleasure toward the infinity of the Spirit and the diversity of beings and objects" (chapter 6). What is translated as "pleasure" is the French *bonheur*, for which "happiness" might be another translation. And, indeed, Gonnaud's description of Emersonian optimism here might seem to a modern temperament too happy, too open, too resilient, too Chaplinesque. Such a temperament might see Emersonian optimism more in the figure of a darker comedian, Buster Keaton, for example. In this figure we have a deadpan Emerson, tinging the acrobatic play of language with melancholy, despair, or even indifference.

But Gonnaud's prose is supple, both in the original and in the translation; capable of the second thought, of revision, of doubling back, it is the kind of prose useful in reading Emerson. And so Gonnaud is continually rethinking this problem of Emersonian optimism (indeed, he implicitly and explicitly makes it much more a problem than either Matthiessen or Whicher and the tradition that follows them). We can find, then, in Gonnaud's pursuit of the problem a less happy, more contradictory optimism than might at first appear: "an optimism whose resilience [*robustesse*] is due to its acceptance [*acceptation*] of ignorance, of error, and even . . . of contradiction immediately experienced" (chapter 7). In the space between "resilience" and "acceptance," where each term becomes a translation of the other, Gonnaud's prose registers the possibility of irony or paradox in the contradictions that comprise Emersonian optimism. For how can acceptance of ignorance and error, which suggests, albeit ambiguously, a stasis or passivity in relation to the unhappy facts of life, result in a resilience, which suggests a positive dynamism?

However, although Gonnaud momentarily entertains the possibility of an Emersonian irony arising from the contradictory movement of Emerson's prose, he just as quickly dismisses it. For

> the problem [in establishing such an irony] is with the *form* of his work; fragmented into journal paragraphs, or letters, or essays, which are themselves patchworks of fragments, the form hardly allows that juxtaposition of opposites which is irony's prerequisite. That such diffuseness is unfortunate no one would deny; but it seems to me that it can be partially overcome if attention is directed to the various lecture series, which are better organized and more solidly articulated than is generally admitted. (chapter 10)

Gonnaud's need for a certain kind of traditional coherence, a need Gonnaud shares with some of Emerson's most important critics (Matthiessen and Whicher among them) even as he recognizes with these critics that Emerson's prose does not move dialectically but by "contradictions, . . . second thoughts, [and] non sequiturs" (Author's Preface) leads him to mistake, along with these critics, a lack of dialectical form for a lack of form. This habit of mind takes Gonnaud for the most part away from a close inspection of the essays, though it does lead him to give us the most important and thorough account of the lectures that we have to date. But more significantly, in the case of Emerson's prose generally it takes him away from a consideration of its ironic possibilities, that is, of its dramatic or figurative form. We go wrong, as Henry Nash Smith suggested in 1939, if we try to read Emerson as a proper essayist, concerned with the elaboration of logical, or dialectical, meaning. And Emerson's own central interest in figurative language, elaborated first and most extensively in *Nature*, coupled with his emphasis on the poet/orator as the prime maker and user of this language, suggests the same. Emerson is a rhetorician, in the subversive Socratic sense, not a dialectician.

This need to supply Emerson with a *sens propre*, which places Gonnaud at moments in the tradition of Matthiessen and Whicher, affirms the need Matthiessen expresses to get beyond "the multiplicity of

[Emerson's] conflicting statements [to] the wholeness of character lying behind them." This essentializing need to define *the* Emerson (as if "*the* Emerson" were not itself a figure of speech) is intimately connected, I believe, with the positing of an Emersonian optimism. Such a position treats Emerson's language as if, to quote Gonnaud, it were not only "profoundly innocent [étrangère] of any dialectical construction" (chapter 7)—which it is—but also as if it were profoundly innocent of any figurative language, in the sense that within the whole Western rhetorical tradition from Aristotle to Freud, figurative language—for the European, literate, masculine mind obsessed with it—has been the sign of a fall from pure thought to language itself (from self to otherness, from mind to body, from the masculine to the feminine, from the civilized to the savage, and from the national to the foreign, to cite some examples of a classic declension).

For Emerson, the space of this fall into otherness, what he calls in *Nature* "the NOT ME, that is, both nature and art, all other men and my own body," is precisely the space of figurative language. And Emerson's first book records the struggle of its narrative voice(s) both to settle, domesticate, or dominate this space, which it variously identifies with the "feminine," the "savage," and the democratic "mob," and to relinquish this space to the very forces it is apparently seeking to dominate. This struggle, which is endlessly ironic in Emerson (hence the often observed oscillating play of his language), *is* the relinquishment, the acknowledgment of the self's dependence on the other, even as it seeks to repress this dependency. What the traditional optimistic viewpoint of American literary history misses in Emerson is the central function of otherness, or the figure of what Emerson calls in *Nature* "actual life"; as Quentin Anderson tells us in one extreme yet exemplary view of Emersonian optimism:

> An emotional constitution such as this, whose triumphs, momentary though they are, had a psychotic completeness, could no more reckon with the dramatically opposed strands in daily experience than it could conceive the funded otherness of sexuality, parenthood, death, or simple heroism. . . . To read Emerson is to find that associated life has become almost unreal, that the middle ground is filled, insofar as it is filled, with projections out of the self. (57)

What Anderson denounces in Emersonian optimism as "psychotic," Emerson's wanton projection of an "imperial," or dissociated, self onto a middle ground where history, society, and culture should normally stand embodied, Harold Bloom applauds in his hero of Identity as "healthy-minded." In *Poetry and Repression*, Bloom tells us that "Emerson had nothing to say about two subjects and two subjects only, sex and death, because he was too healthy-minded to believe that there was much to say about either. Emerson had no sexual problems, and was a Stoic about death" (257). And more recently, in the *New York Review of Books* (November 22, 1984), Bloom has reasserted Emerson's lack of interest in anything but the disembodied Self: "Sin, error, time, history, a God external to the self, the visiting of the crimes of the fathers upon the sons . . . were precisely of no interest whatsoever to Ralph Waldo Emerson" (19). This is, of course, the dead end of Emersonian optimism: Emerson embalmed in the completely proper—sexless, sinless, deathless. And why should we have any interest in this optimism, since it has no interest in us?

I describe the extremes of Emersonian optimism, the psychotic purity of Anderson's Emerson and the pure health of Bloom's, in order to focus more sharply on the center. For it is to these extremes that the experientially immune Emerson of Matthiessen and Whicher inevitably leads. Gonnaud's Emerson, as I have suggested, is optimistic, but not immune. Indeed, if we must have an optimistic Emerson—and I hope that we might be able to relinquish this figure—I recommend Gonnaud's. For the split between individual and society that Gonnaud chronicles in his Emerson is not the split between a disembodied and an embodied self. As Gonnaud puts it at a point in his book that examines Emerson's disturbing relation to dreams, Emerson is an "idealist obliged to consider his body, bound to endure its caprices without understanding them" (chapter 7). (I would only dissent from the latter part of this statement somewhat by noting that in Emerson understanding is evocation and that his prose is precisely evocative of the body's caprices.)

For Gonnaud, then, Emerson has a body; and this body, as Gonnaud narrates the well-known story of Emerson's brushes with blindness and tuberculosis while he was at the Harvard Divinity School (1825–1826), is the source of Emerson's enduring social sense: "Born, one might say, of Emerson's sickness, it [Emerson's social sense] receives from that sickness an equivocal character and provokes, at a level Emerson's consciousness is hardly aware of, a violent and troubled reaction" (chapter 4). Thus, in Gonnaud's insightful reading, Emerson's vulnerable body—and here we must remember all the family deaths he suffered through—becomes a figure for his social being. It would be accurate to say, then, that far from being immune to experience Emersonian optimism represents a *desire* to be immune from it, a desire provoked by the sharp experience of the infection itself.

Gonnaud's book gives one of the richest and most original accounts we have of the trajectory of this infection, which is, as he devotedly describes it, political in nature. So, to use Carolyn Porter's words, Gonnaud's book is a fine appreciation of "the fact that Emerson's revolt occurred within a particular society" (61). And although Gonnaud's Emerson, following Whicher's, undergoes a crisis around 1840 in which "the absolute prerogatives of the Oversoul" must accommodate "those realities of fact which seemed at every instant to contradict them" (518), Gonnaud's profoundly researched account of Emerson's persistent interest *in* society testifies to the fact that the Oversoul never had any absolute prerogatives, precisely because it was the notional product of Emerson's troubled interaction with certain mid-nineteenth-century American political forces.

Of these forces, two emerge with particular power in Gonnaud's Emerson: race and property, which entail questions of class and community that this Emerson must continually face. The Emerson that emerges from what Gonnaud terms at one moment "this incessant confrontation with history, with the economic and political forces of his country, with slavery, 'the special enigma of the time' " (chapter 3) is a more disturbing, because more embodied, Emerson than the figure that grounds traditional American literary history. Gonnaud's Emerson, even in spite of Gonnaud himself at times, will not be contained within the symmetrical form of Whicher's Emerson, who moves from revolutionary Soul to conservative body. Between 1829 and 1832, the years of Emerson's tenure at the Second Church of Boston, the traditional Emerson is fomenting the spiritual revolution that will eventuate in the notion of the democratization of God, found fully developed first in both *Nature* and the Divinity School address. And Gonnaud traces this particular foment through careful analyses of select sermons from these years. But next to this traditionally perceived Emersonian revolt against the institutionalization of Spirit, Gonnaud places—and herein lies the powerful originality of his book—another strain of Emerson's thought, a strain that in the same series of proto-revolutionary sermons "emphatically denounces the projects of European revolutionaries" (chapter 4) for the redistribution of property. This strain of thought, while intellectually opposed to slavery, confides to the journal of the 1820s a belief in the "natural" racial hierarchy of white over black that rationalizes the institution. Gonnaud rightly finds in this juxtaposition of Emerson's revolutionary spiritual thinking and his social "Federalist habits of thought" (for it is in this particular source of elitism that Gonnaud locates Emerson's ideas of race and property) a "contrast . . . so sharp as to make his personality seem almost incoherent" (chapter 4).

The force of Gonnaud's book is that it gives us the material and challenges us to face this incoherence, this *continual* juxtaposition of revolution and reaction, in the figure of Emerson. What, for example, do we make of an Emerson who in 1837 (the year of "The American Scholar," the intellectual's "declaration of independence") was, as Gonnaud tells us, "dissuaded . . . from supporting militant abolitionism" because of, among other reasons, "his belief in the natural inequality of races, which justified in his eyes the de facto supremacy then held by whites" (chapter 11)? In 1840, this Emerson says of the Negro in a journal entry cited by Gonnaud: "It is plain that so inferior a race must perish shortly like the poor Indians" (ibid.). Not to mitigate matters but to complicate them, we might remember here, in the face of such complacence, Emerson's impassioned defense in 1838 of the "poor" Cherokee Indians. Gonnaud describes the affair in traditional terms, as representative of a conflict in Emerson between "civic obligations" and "personal integrity" (chapter 8; Emerson seems to have felt himself compromised, even sullied, in writing the letter to President Van Buren defending the Cherokee's land rights). Yet—which is admirably typical of this book—the way Gonnaud develops the material leading up to and surrounding the Cherokee affair, including Emerson's response to the economic crisis of 1837, asks us to question the coherence of the opposition "civic obligations" versus "personal integrity"; for so committed is Gonnaud to placing his Emerson in a "social context" and in "the historical milieu in which his long career took place" (Author's Preface) that the notion of Emerson's "personal integrity" cannot help but become entangled with a certain middle-class complacence, the desire for comfort and control that characterizes striking aspects of this representative man.

His inheritance from his first wife, Ellen, enabled one particular realization of this desire, his permanent, gentlemanly life in Concord. Gonnaud describes Emerson's move there from Boston in 1834 in ways that suggest it as a suburban retreat from what Emerson perceived as the increasing urban incoherence of the Jacksonian "mob." His prose (especially *Nature*, the major addresses, and the essays) is both a retreat from and a registering of these perceived incoherencies, which makes it doubly incoherent; its tone is one of mixed ease and dis-ease. In a journal entry of 1840 cited by Gonnaud (the same year that Emerson made his terribly complacent comment on race noted previously), he can say, "whilst another man has no land, my title to mine is at once vitiated" (chapter 9). And yet this same Emerson, as Gonnaud points out, can maintain an "attitude of distant indifference to the [landless] situation of the working class" (ibid.).

Under Gonnaud's rigorous yet sympathetic charting of these incoherencies, we encounter a different Emerson, one who escapes any simply revolutionary or reactionary image, one who is, indeed, like the bulk of his readers, deeply middle-class, not simply in his social image but in the range of his prose, which is constantly seeking a balance between the extremes it is both attracted to and retreating from. However, this search for balance unbalances. For there is no middle ground between the landed and the landless, between the master and the slave. In this Emerson's defense it may be said that in 1844, at the time of his speech commemorating British West Indian emancipation, he ameliorated his views on racial hierarchy and began to espouse abolitionism, although, Gonnaud cautions, his "position on the issue remained loftily abstract; what he valued in abolitionism was the affirmation of a moral principle, and he was little troubled with the situation of the slaves themselves" (chapter 12). This qualification may be countered with Emerson's strong public stand against the Fugitive Slave Law in the early 1850s, of which Gonnaud gives us a searching account; but he also suggests that Emerson was developing at the same time a renewed vision of racial hierarchy, "ascribing to race—to *his* race—the triumphs he had once dreamed of for himself" (chapter 13).

I believe this type of the *translatio imperii et studii* (which Gonnaud, anticipating in a way the work of Sacvan Bercovitch, locates in the Puritan vision of America as New Jerusalem) appears much earlier in Emerson's work; in its earliest published form in fact, that is, in *Nature*. Here, I would suggest, in a book that quotes from Shakespeare's *The Tempest*—which gives us a late Renaissance vision of the *translatio*—we find the violent force of Manifest Destiny in the Emersonian embodiment of Spirit, the "FATHER." Here also social forces, which Emerson marshalls under the figure of nature, the "beautiful mother," are moving against this force. Although Gonnaud reads *Nature* in a traditional way, as a "manifesto consecrated to the genius of solitude" (chapter 7), the rich, volatile material he develops throughout his book on Emerson's attitudes to race and property encourages us to read *Nature*, the major addresses, and the essays as a manifesto consecrated to the political conflicts and drives, the incoherencies, of nineteenth-century American life.

Maurice Gonnaud's valuable Emerson is, like the present moment, in conflictive transition between two American literary histories. One history is white, male, and middle-class. And this history represses these political signs of its gender, race, and class in order to see itself as transcendent, as truly universal; while through the gaze of another history, of other histories of race, gender, and class, this first history is being translated down to the radical relativities of earth, where it is beginning to see itself to be acutely marginal in the eyes of others.

Eric Cheyfitz

TRANSLATOR'S PREFACE

MAURICE GONNAUD'S *Individu et société dans l'oeuvre de Ralph Waldo Emerson* was published in 1964, and in the ensuing twenty years knowledge and understanding of Emerson have undergone large changes. Professor Gonnaud and I had therefore to consider to what extent the present translation could or should take account of them.

Our answer for the most part has been: not at all. The text of the book has not been altered to address issues raised by recent works of interpretive scholarship, or the notes altered to cite them. This is a book very much *of* its moment, and the scholarly world it inhabits is that of Stephen Whicher and F. O. Matthiessen and Perry Miller, not that of Joel Porte and Sacvan Bercovitch and Stanley Cavell. Few works on Emerson are more vividly, committedly aware of their predecessors, sources, and antagonists than is Professor Gonnaud's, and to set it even bibliographically in another world than its own would be to remake its character altogether. This is, of course, not to say that it has nothing to contribute to the current discussions of Emerson; indeed its power to address them is to some extent a *consequence* of its rootedness in its own moment. But the proper place for beginning to outline that contribution is Professor Cheyfitz's Foreword, not the text of the translation itself.

Three changes, however, were required to make the text usable. The first is that all references to manuscript material published since 1964 have been keyed to the published editions, and the material itself adjusted to the published versions. (Some few bibliographical footnotes have accordingly been deleted or rewritten.) The second is that all references to material drawn from the 1909–1914 editions of Emerson's journals have been keyed to the monumental 1960–1981 *Journals and Miscellaneous Notebooks of Ralph Waldo Emerson* (JMN), and the material itself, again, adjusted to the more recent version. (It is no disparagement of JMN to note with pleasure that in no case did its readings undermine Professor Gonnaud's arguments.) The last change is that made in the bibliography: the list of secondary sources has simply been omitted, the list of Emerson's own works updated.

In other respects I have done what I take it translators of scholarly works ought to do, namely, adapt the scholarly conventions of one language to those of another. Thus the French text reduces the first names of cited scholars to their initials; the English text does not. French sentences beginning with long subordinate clauses, exquisitely retarding the entrance of the principal verb, have sometimes been reorganized into two independent clauses, in deference to what one might consider to be the faster tempo of American scholarly prose. I have throughout kept in mind Ernest Jones's description of Freud's procedure in translating John Stuart Mill: "he would read a passage, close the book, and consider how a German writer would have clothed the same thoughts." That policy has been prevented from distorting the French text by Professor Gonnaud's indefatigably scrupulous reading of the translation.

Lawrence Rosenwald

AUTHOR'S PREFACE TO THE FRENCH EDITION

DEALING with an author whom T. S. Eliot pronounced useless baggage forty years ago, and following an efflorescence of studies remarkable in some cases for their wealth of information and in others for the profundity or the boldness of their thought, this study requires some preliminary justification. Emerson is not, one must concede, the bedside book for the young that he was for several decades, indeed for several generations. The inward experience of our century is not in harmony with his intuitions; and in a number of respects the nineteenth century, and above all the American nineteenth century, seems more distant from us than do those older periods that share with ours a common anxiety and insecurity. And one might add that a French mind, however open or unprejudiced it may be, is hardly ever comfortable with Emerson's thought: fragmentary in the extreme, weak in structure even when striving for order, fertile in contradictions, in second thoughts, in non sequiturs, and so indifferent to logical rigor as to seem positively unsound. Pascal is the implicit point of comparison, and we bear some resentment toward Emerson for not having been able, as was Pascal, to constrain us with logic even when charming us by the force and the vivacity of his insights.

But the kinship that certain formal similarities suggest between the two authors is illusory. One has to try to read Emerson with a virgin mind, so to speak—following the movement of his thought, experiencing the alternation of his inward tides—if one wants to catch the original quality of the work. To sharpen the terms of contrast, one might say that Pascal, quick despite all appearances to efface his particular self, asks to be read in the classic mode; and that Emerson, conscious of having no other wealth than that particular self and constantly occupied with generalizing from his individual experience, demands to be read in the romantic one. It is by accident that Pascal left us *disjecta membra* in place of the book he did not have the time to assemble. For Emerson, by contrast, to assemble, to compose, to construct was to tarnish the freshness of his inspiration, to substitute lies for spontaneity; and posterity has in one sense declared him right, since the journal in which he noted his ideas in bulk, day after day, is currently considered his most valuable work, or in any case that in which the artist expresses himself most distinctly and with the greatest felicity. In consequence, Emerson becomes choice prey for research and scholarly criticism because of, rather than in spite of, his literary negligence. Criticism's task, then, is to investigate as closely as possible the birth of ideas and feelings, to follow their development, to distinguish the crises they pass through, to describe their transformations—to trace, in short, with all the fidelity our distance in time permits, the line of development of an intelligence, a sensibility, an imagination of singular originality and inexhaustible activity. One might in the end maintain that with Emerson the work of the artist cannot be distinguished from the totality of his written utterances, and correspondingly that the enterprise of critical interpretation cannot be accomplished except by integrating into an adequate structure every sentence and verse he wrote.

The accomplishment of this herculean task is not as utopian a prospect as it may seem. Criticism of Emerson, like that of a good number of other authors, has made extraordinary progress in the past thirty years—progress that, on the whole, is along the lines I have just indicated. We owe to Ralph L. Rusk a biography as complete and exact as we could wish and an almost exhaustive edition of the letters. The publication of the whole journal is in progress; a volume of hitherto unpublished early lectures has appeared, and two others are promised. At the same time, critics are more and more often basing their interpretations on studies of the manuscripts. Kenneth Cameron, Carl F. Strauch, and the late Stephen Whicher—to cite only three names among many worthy of mention—have contributed to a decisive transformation of our knowledge about and our understanding of Emerson. By a series of close collations between unpublished and published texts—by an auscultation, so to speak, of Emerson's thought at every step of its course—they have recreated the debates, the uncertainties, the victories, the renunciations that marked its path. The great texts themselves, read in the light these researches offer, lose their *silex scintillans* quality and turn out more often than one would have expected to be the fragile expression of a dynamic equilibrium attained only with difficulty. In general, that is, the service rendered by this recent criticism is that it has done away with the illusion, which Emerson himself worked hard to sustain, of being not of an age but for all time. For a long while this illusion had masked for us the fluctuations of a supple and extraordinarily reactive thought.

I am conscious of having benefited, in composing the following study, from all these researches, probably to an extent beyond that indicated in the explicit acknowledgments of the notes. But it seemed to me that not enough attention had been paid to an aspect of Emerson's work that though secondary—some would say marginal—nonetheless resonates throughout the whole and affects its meaning. The literary and philosophical influences affecting Emerson had been measured and classified. But little study had been made of his social context, either the general and impersonal context or the detailed, particular context, variable not only in extent but also in nature, to which Emerson's reflections fitted themselves day after day. Between the cloistered life of the thinker and artist, living in the companionship of his books (and chiefly in that of the best of them, Nature) and the life of the pastor, the citizen, the "intellectual," subject to a complex and delicate play of outer pressures, there are complicities more profound and more essential than is generally admitted. How can one explain Emerson's taste for solitude, the lyric ardor it awakens in him, without exploring in some detail the diverse reasons that turned him away from a society poor in the substantial nourishment he craved? And then one must explain why after his fortieth year he relaxed that hostility (but is it still the same society that is its object?), and seek to understand the consequences, intellectual and otherwise, of that change. Similarly, in tracing the path of Emerson's lived experience, it is no longer possible to ignore the development of the historical milieu in which his long career took place. The America of his birth is still that of the Founding Fathers; but he dies seventeen years after the end of the Civil War, at the height of the Gilded Age. Of the events that marked the passage from the age of Jefferson to the age of capitalism Emerson was the witness—and a more attentive, certainly a more responsive witness, than has commonly been discerned. In particular, the growth of egalitarianism over the three decades that preceded the Civil War found in Emerson an observer whom even our age might easily call *engagé*—for America in those crucial years was busy trying out certain of the ideas of which he was, in a small, enlightened elite, the advocate: "*Individualism* is a novel expression, to which a novel idea has given birth," wrote Tocqueville in 1840; and opposing individualism to *égoïsme*, which he characterized as intrinsically harmful, he added, "Individualism is a mature and calm feeling, which disposes each member of the community to sever himself from the mass of his fellow-creatures; and to draw apart with his family and his friends; so that, after he has thus formed a little circle of his own, he willingly leaves society at large to itself."[1]

[1] Alexis de Tocqueville, *Democracy in America*, trans. Henry Reeve (New York, 1961), II.118.

As is suggested by the title of this study, I have attempted throughout to grasp the reciprocal influence of these two factors—the individual and the social, the personal and the collective—and thereby to bring out the originality of a thought that though indebted to its time was never subject to it. In directing attention to a particular aspect of a remarkable body of work, I have not excluded the larger, "representative" meaning, in the Emersonian sense of the term, that that work can bear. I had thought for a time of enlarging this study so as to include in it most of the authors normally called Transcendentalists; but we have no solid bases for carrying out such an enterprise successfully, and judicious advice dissuaded me from it before it was too late. But if Emerson remains my subject throughout, I hope that he will appear to the readers of these pages somewhat different from the Emerson they already know—which is not to claim that this Emerson is truer.

There remains only the agreeable task of acknowledging all the assistance that has made this book possible. Professor Maurice Le Breton, of the Sorbonne, directed its writing with the authority and surehandedness of a master; he has my profound gratitude for the indefatigable attention he has given this work since its first beginnings. The debt of gratitude owed to Professor Louis Landré, also of the Sorbonne, goes back to my years at the École Normale; my thanks to him for a friendship that held fast even in times of difficulty. At Dijon, while I was pursuing my researches, I had many stimulating conversations with colleagues both American and French; in particular Professor Henri Talon, of the Faculté des Lettres, was good enough to draw up for me the list of Emersoniana in the Huntington Library. At Lyons, where the work was finished, I found in Pierre Fruchon, *maître-assistant* in Philosophy of the Faculté des Lettres, the informed and sympathetic reader I needed for a final polishing of the text.

In the course of my stays in the United States, I received a cordial reception and generous assistance from Professor Robert Spiller, of the University of Pennsylvania, and from the late Stephen Whicher, of Cornell University. Professor Kenneth Walter Cameron, of Trinity College, Hartford, offered the infinitely precious assistance of his expertise and his untiring graciousness. To Professor Warner Berthoff, of Bryn Mawr College, who was first my initiator into American literature and later my good friend, I wish to express here my affectionate gratitude. I am in no danger of forgetting those librarians in France, England, and the United States who worked so hard to make my work easier; in particular I should like to thank Professor William A. Jackson and Carolyn Jakeman, of the Houghton Library at Harvard University, for providing access to the manuscript sources of Emerson's work, and also the

Ralph Waldo Emerson Memorial Association for the generosity with which it permitted me in this work to make use of them.

On more than one occasion I have received financial aid from the governments of the United States (the Smith-Mundt Fund) and France (the Ministry of Cultural Relations). And when the work was ready for publication, the French Ministry of Higher Education awarded me a grant covering part of the expenses entailed by publication. Without such abundant and varied help, and without two years' leave at the Centre National de la Recherche Scientifique, quite possibly this book would never have come into being.

Maurice Gonnaud

ABBREVIATIONS

Primary Sources

CEC	*The Correspondence of Emerson and Carlyle*, ed. Joseph Slater (New York, 1964)
EL	*Emerson, Essays and Lectures*, ed. Joel Porte (New York, 1983)
H	manuscripts in the Houghton Library, Harvard University (manuscript journals are abbreviated JMS, H)
J	*The Journals of Ralph Waldo Emerson*, ed. Edward Waldo Emerson and Waldo Emerson Forbes, 10 vols. (Boston, 1909–1914)
JMN	*Journals and Miscellaneous Notebooks of Ralph Waldo Emerson*, ed. William H. Gilman et al., 16 vols. (Cambridge, Mass., 1960–1982)
L	*The Letters of Ralph Waldo Emerson*, ed. Ralph L. Rusk, 6 vols. (New York, 1939)
W	*The Collected Works of Ralph Waldo Emerson*, 12 vols. (Boston, 1903–1904)

Secondary Works

AL	*American Literature*
Cabot, *Memoir*	James Eliot Cabot, *A Memoir of Ralph Waldo Emerson*, 2 vols. (Boston, 1887)
ESQ	*Emerson Society Quarterly*
NEQ	*New England Quarterly*
Rusk, *Life*	Ralph L. Rusk, *The Life of Ralph Waldo Emerson* (New York, 1949)
Whicher, *Freedom and Fate*	Stephen Whicher, *Freedom and Fate: An Inner Life of Ralph Waldo Emerson* (Philadelphia, 1953)

PART I

The Uncertainties of a Vocation

1

~ ~ ~ ~

THE FAMILY MILIEU

TWO YEARS after the Civil War, Emerson noted in his journal that "in old Boston, a feature not be [sic] forgotten was John Wilson, the town crier, who rung his bell at each street corner,—'*Lost*! A child strayed this morning from 49 Marlborough Street; four years old; had on check apron, . . .' He cried so loud, that you could not hear what he said, if you stood near."[1] As coming from the pen of a venerated and supposedly austere man, the anecdote has all the charm of the unexpected; but at the same time it disorients us and stimulates our imagination. Boston at the beginning of the nineteenth century was still Arcadia. Biographers of Emerson have taken pleasure in describing that city of thirty thousand inhabitants, ranged upon its three hills, with its streets interspersed with green spaces, charmingly provincial and yet, from another point of view, open to the sea and to adventure.[2] Schooners and brigs came to anchor along its docks, with their freights of Antilles rum, Burgundy and Spanish wines, Georgia and South Carolina cotton. To be sure, the port and the city were not to be confused—nothing could be less like the motley crowd around the warehouses than the bourgeois elite established on the slopes of Beacon Hill. But aside from the fact that merchants and shipowners constituted by profession the necessary link between the two classes, people knew perfectly well that Boston's fortunes and its commerce were strictly linked.

There had been a period of difficulty; but the future now looked clear

[1] JMN 16.63 (1867).

[2] See particularly Cabot, *Memoir*, 1.4, and Rusk, *Life*, chapter 2.

and bright. The violence that in 1786 had accompanied the protest of Shays' Rebellion had had no sequel. The Revolution itself had after all been political and not social, and the few years between the Declaration of Independence and the Constitution of 1787 were enough to efface any influence of the ideas of Thomas Paine.[3] The establishment of a second legislative chamber, not only at Washington but also in each of the individual states, sanctioned the predominance of an elite minority at the exact moment at which Hamilton, in the *Federalist Papers*, was elaborating the doctrine according to which the government belonged by right to the rich, the just, and the wise. The task was to set limits on the Revolution; and by the beginning of the nineteenth century the limits were set. If on every Fourth of July the lovers of oratory made the Revolution the theme of their discourse, its heroes for the most part—official celebrations excepted, of course—remained within their shrines.

By 1805 the danger, if danger there was, came from the White House; Jefferson's expansionist politics were judged imprudent and their financial consequences feared. But in the eyes of most Americans, such fears were exaggerated; and for Bostonians in particular, there was no doubt that the dawn of a new era, an era both rational and prosperous, had appeared on the banks of the Charles River. The destiny of the city was in the hands of a solid phalanx of merchants who joined a sense of order to a taste for enterprise and considered success to be a providential acknowledgment of their diligence. Already their ships cut through the China Sea and the Indian Ocean, carrying the standard of their might as far as the antipodes. How could such men not have been by natural extension also the leaders of their city?

One has to evoke an image of these substantial men when one attempts to understand the personality of William Emerson, Unitarian minister of the First Church of Boston, and not take at their face value the judgments—not numerous in any case—that his son has left us.[4] That on occasion William preferred the pleasures of conversation to the care of his ministry no one will deny. But one should also note that the religion he had the mission to preach and, if need be, to defend, was itself neither rigid nor especially rigorous. James Eliot Cabot wondered

[3] Paine's name seldom appears in Emerson's journal. A reference dated September 23, 1836 (JMN 5.302) indicates that in the author's judgment Paine belongs to an age gone by.

[4] See particularly a letter to his brother William, dated February 10, 1850 (L 4.178–179): "I was eight years old when he died, & only remember a somewhat social gentleman, but severe to us children. . . . I have never heard any sentence or sentiment of his repeated by Mother or Aunt, and his printed or written papers, as far I know, only show candour & taste, or I should almost say, docility, the principal merit possible to that early ignorant & transitional *Month-of-March*, in our New England culture."

in this regard, not without humor, whether a Unitarian minister's most efficacious tactic in resisting the increasing laxity was not in fact to loosen the bonds of orthodoxy still further. [5] Let us say only that in dealing with the men and women of principle who made up his congregation William did not burn with apostolic zeal. His calling (for it would be unjust to count him as not having had one) led him elsewhere, toward something whose absence from the Boston of 1800 he felt acutely: that taste for the things of the mind and that intellectual curiosity which are the source and condition of culture.

In the letter cited before, Emerson mollifies somewhat the severity of his assessment by adding that William's "literary merits really [were] that he fostered the Anthology & the Athenaeum." The account is incomplete—William Emerson was also one of the first members of the Massachusetts Historical Society [6]—but above all it lacks warmth. Certain critics, and not all of them minor critics, have adopted Emerson's reservations uncritically, and indeed have suggested on the basis of them that from 1790 to 1820 New England was an almost perfect intellectual vacuum.[7] The reality was more varied.[8] On the morrow of the Revolution—as the counterpart, so to speak, of political emancipation—there begins to manifest itself in Boston a desire for an independent intellectual life; and the Unitarian church, still fresh from the schism that had cut it off from the Congregationalist tree but not yet having adopted any doctrine in the strict sense of the term,[9] becomes the avant-garde in the first and timid American Renaissance. The *Monthly An-*

[5] Cabot, *Memoir*, 1.19, partially reproduces the letter in which the members of the First Church of Boston asked William Emerson to become their pastor, or more precisely justified their request to the rural congregation he was then serving: in particular they declared that "the alarming attacks upon our holy religion, by the Learned, the Witty, and the Wicked, especially in populous and seaport towns, call aloud to invite and support, in the places of most eminence, such spiritual workmen as are endowed with talents to convince and confound the Wicked by their arguments, *and allure them by their amiable behavior*" (my italics).

[6] Cabot, *Memoir*, 1.23.

[7] For example, Vernon Louis Parrington, in *Main Currents in American Thought*, 3 vols. (New York, 1927–1930), 2:317: "The utter sterility of those old times Emerson understood only too well. It was the world of his own youth, whose pale negations he had come to hate. The creative impulse was stifled, the mind had grown stale from tedious iteration."

[8] See on this subject Lewis P. Simpson, "Emerson and the Myth of New England's Intellectual Lapse" (ESQ 10.1 [1958], pp. 28–31).

[9] It is generally admitted that not till 1819 and "Unitarian Christianity," a sermon preached in Baltimore by William Ellery Channing for the ordination of Jared Sparks, does one get the classic formulation of Unitarian belief. Cf. on this point Henry Adams, *History of the United States in the Administrations of Jefferson and Madison*, 9 vols. (New York, 1890), 9:182, and *The Transcendentalists: An Anthology*, ed. Perry Miller (Cambridge, Mass., 1950), pp. 21–25.

thology, founded in 1805, makes us smile today with its 450 subscribers, its conservative good tone, and its fears regarding France. It is nonetheless true that "the Review far surpassed any literary standards then existing in the United States, and was not inferior to any in England; for neither the Edinburgh nor the Quarterly Review was established until several years later."[10]

The distance is thus less than it seems between William Emerson, first chief editor of the *Monthly Anthology* and fervent book-collector for the Boston Athenaeum, and his son Ralph Waldo, widely known for his efforts to enrich the city library of Concord and responsible, at a certain moment, for tasks strikingly analogous to his father's editorship.[11] The resemblance becomes still more prominent[12] when for the image of the fervid Transcendentalist one substitutes that equally authentic image of the Saturday Club regular.[13] All in all, the contrast between father and son preserved in literary history derives less from taste or inclination than from temperament. There was in Ralph Waldo Emerson a demand for integrity that was to lead him, at the end of a long and difficult evolution, to a brutal rejection of the humanitarianism of the previous generation. A culture devoted entirely to the graces could not satisfy him even if the life of the mind was stimulated by it. He needed a stronger intellectual sustenance: and is that not as much as to say that for the son of the enlightened minister the atavistic Puritan strain had retained its virulence?

There is hardly any American writer who evokes as powerfully as does Emerson the idea of rootedness.[14] On his father's side, his ancestors are among the immigrants who fled England during the persecutions of Archbishop Laud. Thus one Thomas Emerson, originally of the County of York or of Durham, established himself at Ipswich, Massachusetts in 1635 as farmer and baker.[15] His son Joseph began an impressive line of ministers, interrupted only once[16] between the end of

[10] Henry Adams, *History*, 9:201.

[11] On Emerson's role in publishing the *Dial* see Rusk, *Life*, chap. 17, and infra, chapter 9.

[12] Oliver Wendell Holmes, in *Ralph Waldo Emerson* (Boston, 1884), p. 13, reports the opinion of the Reverend Dr. Furness of Philadelphia that Ralph Waldo resembled his father, his brothers their mother.

[13] On the Saturday Club, see the notes furnished by the editor of W in the appendix to "Clubs" (W 7.415–418), and also infra, chapter 13.

[14] Numerous studies linger over Emerson's origins, so it is unnecessary for us to go into detail here. See especially, in addition to the works of Rusk, Cabot, and Holmes already cited, Moncure D. Conway, *Emerson at Home and Abroad* (Boston, 1882), and Marie Dugard, *Emerson, sa vie et son oeuvre* (Paris, 1907).

[15] Cf. Conway, *Emerson*, p. 31.

[16] The continuity was broken by Joseph's son Edward, who chose to become a merchant. But he was for some time deacon of the First Church of Newbury. Cf. ibid.

the seventeenth century and the beginning of the nineteenth. Often these ministers married the daughters of ministers, so that there gradually constituted itself a sort of intellectual caste, joining the care of souls to a taste for reading and study. This same Joseph Emerson, for example, married the granddaughter of Peter Bulkeley, who had himself crossed the Atlantic to escape Laud's vexations and had distinguished himself as pioneer (founder in 1635 of the village of Concord on the banks of the Musketaquid),[17] as theologian (author of the robust and ponderously scholastic treatise *The Gospel Covenant*) and as church dignitary (moderator of the synod that exiled Ann Hutchinson from Boston).[18]

Emerson never denied his descent. It filled him in fact with a sort of patrician pride, which echoes here and there throughout his work. Thus an unpublished quatrain of his, undated and untitled, opposes the aristocratic blood inherited from the Bulkeleys to the more ample stream of his more democratic ancestors.[19] One ought also to look in this connection at the only sermon Emerson thought fit to publish[20] before the famous communion sermon of 1832. The circumstances made for solemnity: a young man Emerson had known at the Divinity School was being ordained as assistant pastor of the Congregational Church of Concord. Now Emerson's grandfather William Emerson had been minister at Concord during the Revolution, and then army chaplain (he was to die at thirty-three of the consequences of a fever contracted during a campaign); moreover his widow had married the minister named to succeed him, Ezra Ripley. In the fifty years he ministered to his congregation, Ripley had won everyone's respect. Emerson for his part had had occasion to be much in his company and had considerable affection for him. The task that devolved on him that day—to offer his sympathy to a young colleague he esteemed in the presence of an aged ancestor he revered—was entirely to his taste. The sermon develops the theme of the unity of good men. Though men remain divided in the shadow of sin, hostile to one another, they are rejoined and reunited to the extent

[17] See the story of the founding in the speech Emerson gave on the occasion of the town's bicentennial anniversary (W 11.31–39).

[18] Cf. Conway, *Emerson*, p. 31.

[19] An ancient drop of feudal blood
From the high line of Bulkeley-Mere
Mixed with the democratic flood
Of sires to Yankee freedom dear.

(H.136, "Poetry," p. 247.)

[20] "A sermon delivered at the Ordination of Hersey Bradford Goodwin, as Colleague Pastor with Ezra Ripley, D.D., of the Congregational Church and Society in Concord, Mass., Feb. 17, 1830." The text is scarce, but is reprinted in ESQ 12.3 (1958), pp. . 39–40.

that they can see the truth; and the object of the ceremony that is the speech's occasion is precisely to symbolize the solidarity of the just. The text lacks neither solidity nor nobility, but Emerson, who considers himself as the "organ [of] the Christian churches," subjects himself to the constraints of strict impersonality; the effect is thus very powerful when just at the end, stripping away the anonymity he has thus far maintained, he takes on the role of special heir:

> I feel a peculiar, a personal right to welcome you hither to the home and the temple of my fathers. I believe the church whose pastor you are will forgive me the allusion, if I express the extreme interest which every man feels in the scene of the trials and labors of his ancestors. Five out of seven of your predecessors are my kindred. They are in the dust, who bind my attachment to this place; but not all. I cannot help congratulating you that one survives, to be to you the true friend and venerable counselor he has ever been to me.[21]

Far from making the peroration familiar, this transition to the first person endows it with an increased dignity, as if Emerson were acknowledging and proclaiming an inheritance received from his minister ancestors.

One should not of course see that inheritance as an unrelievedly somber one. Serious as are all men who believe in the importance of their tasks, the pastors of the seventeenth and eighteenth centuries were delivered by the often precarious conditions of their existence, by their intimate contact with their congregations, and by their own needs for independence and free thought from all that might have fixed them in an attitude of empty solemnity. Calvinists at a time that the word meant rebels, they detached themselves not only from the old orthodoxy but also from the new when it became intolerant or pedestrian in its turn. We know that Joseph Emerson, minister at Malden, Massachusetts for more than half a century, was one of Whitefield's most enthusiastic supporters, and that he invited him to preach in his church when he visited New England in 1740.[22] Joseph's son William, the minister–soldier, was according to Moncure Conway the first Emerson to entertain religious ideas one might call genuinely liberal.[23] The citizens of Concord chose him as pastor in consequence of a controversy in which the Arminians (the majority) were opposed to the defenders of strict Calvinism. Here as elsewhere, then, Emerson's paternal ancestors remained

[21] Ibid.; the passage is also cited in G. W. Cooke, *Ralph Waldo Emerson: His Life, Writings and Philosophy* (Boston, 1881), p. 29.

[22] See Cabot, *Memoir*, 1.11.

[23] Conway, *Emerson*, p. 35.

within the limits of their ecclesiastical functions; but by using the margin of interpretation their faith allowed, they manifested that spirit of free investigation to which Emerson was to bring so devastating a consecration.

The biographers have for the most part been more reticent on the subject of Emerson's maternal ancestors; and we would be reduced to hypotheses if the filial piety of a certain Haskins (the maiden name of Emerson's mother) had not fortunately filled the gap.[24] Here the stock is less noble and less illustrious, to be sure, but it is not without character. The first Haskins needing mention is Emerson's great-grandfather. He arrived at Boston at the beginning of the eighteenth century and worked as a cooper. He died young, of the smallpox. We have more abundant information about his son John, which makes him out to be a vivid and even picaresque figure, full of a solid and appealing vitality. He learned the cooper's trade from his father, but longed to go to sea. He managed to set sail for the Antilles, was captured by the Spanish and then by the French, had the luck to be released by an American ship, and returned to Boston—healed, it seems, of his passion for the sea. He then accepted the offer of partnership made him by his mother's second husband, another cooper. Somewhat later he married a young woman from Malden (the officiating minister being none other than Joseph Emerson, Ralph Waldo's great-grandfather). Then, probably judging that coopering had no future, he became a distiller[25] and gradually assembled the means for a comfortable living. In 1765 he constructed a spacious house in Boston, in which his family continued to live after his death. He himself lived till 1814, but he remained, in manner (his descendant refers to a certain "military" straightness) and dress, faithful to the Boston of the colonial period. Let us add that this social ascent was accompanied by a change in religion: sometime between the ages of twenty and thirty, John Haskins left the Congregational Church for the Episcopalian. But he displayed a generous tolerance toward his family, permitting his wife the observances of strict Calvinism and allowing his thirteen children free choice in the matter when they came to the years of discretion. The result was that they split pretty much equally between the two churches. Emerson's mother Ruth chose the Episcopalian and held fast to it.[26]

[24] D. G. Haskins, *Ralph Waldo Emerson: His Maternal Ancestors* (Boston, 1887). Haskins was Emerson's first cousin. See also on this point a letter from Emerson to Nathaniel Frothingham, dated December 3, 1853 (L 4.407–408).

[25] There were people in abundance to denounce Emerson for this "taint" when he placed himself with his usual fervor on the side of the abolitionists.

[26] Haskins, *Emerson*, p. 105, partially reproduces the letter of a female relation who stayed

It is neither chance nor preconception that draws our attention so incessantly to matters of religion; it is the nature of things in that Boston of the turn of the eighteenth century. The dogmas had no doubt lost their edge, and people did not still have theological minds; one could, as John Haskins did, elevate enterprise and profit above the agonized meditation on the world to come. But all existence was nonetheless still bathed in a sort of providential twilight, and the idea of man's relations with God, however imprecise and vague, impressed itself on most minds as the fundamental component of human destiny. Thus Ruth Emerson decided at the age of twenty-seven to keep a journal. Like most Bostonian girls of good family, she had received a thorough religious education, though one without mystical excess or extreme fervor; and yet this is what she wrote as an introduction:

> I desire now in a better strength than my own to resolve that from this date—April 20 1795—I will, as God shall enable me, from time to time carefully notice all his providences towards my friends or myself, whether prosperous or adverse,—and conscientiously note down whatever appears to be for the glory of God, or the good of my own soul.[27]

One might see in this a dedication to the contemplative life, if the modest and prudent phrase "from time to time" did not offer an entry by which, at the opportune moment, the claims of the secular might assert themselves.

Offspring of a race of priests, son of a gently and deeply pious mother, Emerson was thus the heir of a spiritual capital that was always to appear to him more precious than the sum of worldly goods. His great-grandfather, the minister Joseph Emerson, seems to have prayed daily that none of his descendants would ever get rich.[28] Emerson had subtler notions on this point, but essentially he was in agreement with it. The meager circumstances in which he grew up are widely known, as is the way in which, when a student at Harvard, he had to perform certain poorly paid tasks to ease the family budget. This necessity never caused him any bitterness. The nephew of President Kirkland to whom he

---

with the Emersons in 1852–1853, shortly before Ruth's death: "during her sickness, she wished me to read a part of the Psalter every day, and frequently the lessons for the day. Occasionally, on a Sunday, she asked me to read the Communion Service, and requested that her grand-children should be present. The Prayer-Book used was her own, given her by her father, in January 1783."

[27] Cited in Haskins, *Emerson*, p. 43.

[28] The anecdote is given by Cabot, *Memoir* (1.9) as from the papers of Mary Moody Emerson.

gave lessons described him as "kind, easy, familiar, but self-sufficient, with a wall of reserve about him that no one could penetrate."[29] It is clear that his courtesy and his reticence proceeded from the same source; the young Emerson was unknowingly like Pascal. He did the expected homage to the powers that be and maintained a profound adherence to certain qualities of nature: honesty, that is, loyalty to oneself, and culture, understood in a spiritual sense as well as in a secular.

To the extent that conjecture is permitted in the absence of any journal prior to 1820,[30] it seems that the first years of Emerson's adolescence were characterized by intense religiosity. The poverty that touched the Emersons after the death of William in 1811 contributed to quickening Ralph Waldo's spiritual sense by the distinction it forcibly established between true riches and false; and even later, at a time at which Emerson could understand and justify the striving for material goods, he continued to think that poverty was the best of teachers[31] and that the man deprived of poverty, so to speak, had lost his best chance of attaining greatness. And the energies paradoxically liberated by the "iron band of poverty, of necessity, of austerity"[32] will be taken in charge by an exacting master, who will direct them toward the quest of a proud perfection.

It seems impossible to exaggerate the influence exercised on the young Emerson by his celebrated Aunt Mary. There are numerous descriptions, none more successful than Emerson's own, of this extraordinary woman,[33] whose life was a series of migrations at the inclination of her fancy from one end of New England to the other. At once capricious and ascetic, full of disdain for the baubles of this world, she had, she said, been created to rejoice in the virtue of others.[34] By that we should understand that she had a passion for souls. Did she happen to meet a young person she liked? She would immediately seek a conquest, and "by sympathy, by flattery, by raillery, by anecdotes, by wit,

[29] Rusk, *Life*, p. 69.

[30] We do possess a number of letters Emerson wrote to his brothers between 1814 and 1820; see L 1.5–80.

[31] See in particular "Domestic Life," W 7.120–121. The whole passage, with its strong autobiographical savor, is reproduced by Cabot, *Memoir*, 1.39. The original version occurs in the journal for November 25, 1837 (JMN 5.438–439).

[32] From the passage of "Domestic Life" referred to in the preceding note.

[33] See in particular Rosalie Feltenstein, "Mary Moody Emerson: The Gadfly of Concord," *American Quarterly* 5 (1953), pp. 231–246. For Emerson's own portrait of his aunt see W 10.399–453.

[34] "For the love of superior virtue is mine own gift from God" (W 10.405). Cabot, *Memoir*, 1.37, reproduces a disclosure by Aunt Mary that shows how that phrase is to be taken: she was, she said of herself, "never patient with the faults of the good."

by rebuke" she always "stormed the castle."[35] This is indeed what happened with her nephew Ralph Waldo, though with the difference that with him she had no resistance to overcome. In the portrait of her just mentioned, and also in a passage of the journal,[36] the mature Emerson removes himself from Mary Moody's personality and displays her on a historical background, distinguishing in her what derives from the past and what already hints at the future, making of her, as he says, a "representative" figure.[37] The child, one should note, was not so lucid. Aunt Mary was associated with the first awakening of his religious sensibility: she had written the prayers that were read together, morning and evening, in Emerson's home; and Ralph Waldo heard them echoing in his ears twenty-five years later, with their "prophetic & apocalyptic ejaculations."[38] Naturally enough, she became, by means of a correspondence beginning perhaps as early as 1810,[39] his spiritual director; and having recognized her nephew's extraordinary soul, she gave herself to the task with impetuous ardor.

The counsel she lavished upon him seems to us somewhat cold-bloodedly lofty, like the *sententiae* of the Stoics. But that impression is deceptive. Aunt Mary's religion was in its warmth and spontaneity the diametric opposite of Stoicism, even if it happened here and there to incorporate Stoicism's teachings. All his life Emerson felt the fascination of that thought, "always new, subtle, frolicsome, musical, unpredictable."[40] In addition to principles, it brought him the image of a complex and profound universe, in which the most abstract virtues had their ebb and flow, in which metaphysical concepts themselves were assembled from metaphors, as they are in Herbert or Browne.[41] The child was thus initiated early into the exercises of introspection; at the age usually given over to street games, he preferred solitude, lured by the mystery

[35] W 10.405.

[36] Cf. W 10.596. The editor places this text about 1837, but it shows up in the journal May 6, 1841 (JMN 7.445–447). It is used in much the same form in an unpublished lecture from 1843: "New England," part 1, "Origin" (H.199.1).

[37] Emerson uses the word at the very beginning of his portrait (W 10.399).

[38] JMN 5.323–324 (May 7, 1837).

[39] See Rusk, *Life*, p. 36.

[40] JMN 7.442 (May 4, 1841). A proper son of New England and eager to establish the family archives, Emerson kept his aunt Mary's letters. He reread them with pleasure and read them aloud to his friends. The intensity of the comments he devotes to them in his journal hardly diminishes even with age; as late as August 7, 1870, he records, "I find my readings of M. M. E. ever monitory & healthful as of old" (JMN 16.194).

[41] Or, one might add, in Melville. Emerson quotes (W 10.424) a fragment of his aunt's journal in which the relation Time : Fate : Freedom generates the same metaphor of the weaver as Ishmael makes in chap. 47: "The Mat-Maker," of *Moby Dick*.

of those continents of the interior[42] that the old Puritan religion had explored long ago. If later Emerson described the example offered in his youth by his aunt as an inestimable privilege,[43] it is because the revelation of the dramatic character of the moral life, coming to him at the moment at which his powers of imagination were newly awakened, committed him to an investigation of himself that proved astonishingly fertile in discoveries, even if certain stages of it bore the mark of an excruciating inward deficiency. There were hours in which he felt burdened by "The yoke of conscience masterful / Which galls me everywhere."[44] And his journal, above all before he turned thirty, resonates in many passages with the echo of his weaknesses, his inadequacies, his judgments passed against himself.[45]

One knows of course that he ended by achieving his own conquests, but his esteem for his ancestral religion was not thereby diminished. One has only to compare in this regard the "Historical Discourse at Concord" of 1835[46] with the portrait of Ezra Ripley six years later,[47] when Emerson had won renown if not fame. The "Historical Discourse at Concord" reveals, to be sure, a certain sympathy for the bold pioneers; but the author, wishing to be impartial, seeks to maintain a balance among the successive stages of the town's history—the text takes support from the past the better to engage the future, and the task is to forage among common memories for solid grounds of pride and for the will to carry on the predecessors' work in a manner worthy of them.

The portrait of Ezra Ripley is done with an altogether different pen; it is an elegy, in which is expressed Emerson's reverent affection for his grandfather and through him for the religion of which he was the incarnation. In it the austerity of the Puritan churches, with their grave and monotonous services, becomes their principal attraction: everything breathes rectitude and a simplicity that constantly sends us back to God. Like the other ministers of his generation, the venerable Dr. Ripley believed in the particular dispensations of Providence and shared

[42] "Be a Columbus to whole new continents and worlds within you" (Thoreau, *Walden* [New York, 1950], "Conclusion," p. 268).

[43] Cf. W 10.424.

[44] W 9.84, "The Park." Published in January 1842 in the *Dial*, the short poem expresses the author's nostalgia for the enjoyment of the world from which his education and temperament have cut him off.

[45] Thus the image of the mirror (second stanza of "The Park") and also that of the mental theater (cf. JMN 4.132 [1833]: "It is doubtless a vice to turn one's eyes inward too much, but I am my own comedy & tragedy"), with the idea of doubling they imply, are used by Emerson to suggest spiritual paralysis.

[46] W 11.29–56.

[47] W 10.381–395. On the personality of Ezra Ripley, cf. supra, and also L 5.145.

"the narrowness of King David and the Jews, who thought the universe existed only or mainly for their church and congregation."[48] It goes without saying that so naïve a faith has a certain picturesque quality, and Emerson does not forget to record some of the old pastor's quirks.[49] But the humor he permits himself here and there does not exclude reverence, any more than in the canvas of an Italian primitive the comic detail undercuts the piety. The humorous stroke works first by bringing the figure nearer, and second by distancing it in consequence of the space that soon establishes itself between the anecdotal and the spiritual. "He did not know when he was good in prayer or sermon, for he had no literature and no art; but he believed, and therefore spoke."[50] Despite his extraordinarily wide learning, Emerson conceived of his apostolic mission of affirmation in the same way; and one may wonder whether he did not judge that after all it was the old village pastor who had been the better servant of the truth.

The preceding remarks have digressed less far from the subject of Emerson's childhood than they may have seemed to; at the death of John Haskins in 1814, Ruth and her children came to live for six months under Dr. Ripley's Concord roof.[51] Once more, in our quest for spiritual sources, we have crossed back into the family circle. Between Mary Moody, irritable, difficult, and inspired, and the patriarch with the faith of a child there was a fundamental resemblance: both believed in the spiritual life; both recognized, though in different manners, the signs of its manifestation; and above all, both counted it incomparably more solid and more rich than the universe of the senses. The problem for those who brood over Emerson's youth is not to discover the origin of his idealism; it is rather to explain how, subjected to a spiritual pressure of several atmospheres' intensity, he managed not to be destroyed by it.

It is well known that the outcome was for a long time uncertain. Emerson's good luck was not to have to do battle alone. In his brothers

[48] W 10.384.

[49] Among them this one (W 10.386): during a severe drought, Ripley's assistant, the Reverend Goodwin, offered to conduct the prayers for rain in Ripley's place; but Ripley petulantly refused, with an air, Emerson says, that seemed to suggest, "This is no time for you young Cambridge men; the affair, sir, is getting serious; I will pray myself." The reader will note that Emerson gives a nice polish to the anecdote by providing words to make Ripley's gesture of refusal more explicit.

[50] W 10.394. It is significant that Emerson should have placed this phrase at the very end of the portrait—at the moment, that is, at which he undertook to extract a moral.

[51] In the portrait just mentioned, Emerson describes a carriage ride in Concord that he took when young at his grandfather's side.

William, Edward, and Charles[52] he had not only companions in fun (and in privation—the anecdote of the single coat the children wore by turns is piously retold by the early biographers) but also confidants, with whom he shared his curiosities, his ambitions, and his first anxieties. William, the eldest, was also the most robust and the most practical. Although he was destined early for the ministry and consulted Goethe himself when he felt his sense of vocation waver,[53] he had qualities of orderliness and good sense that were soon to make him a respected and prosperous lawyer. We know that he was not Ralph Waldo's favorite, a fact that the difference in their ages would suffice to explain; but if one must speak of sober affection rather than intimacy in characterizing their relationship, it would be unjust to see at the bottom of their feeling an indifference disguised by decorum. To compare William with Edward and Charles can only be misleading; both the latter died at the end of adolescence, thus leaving to their friends and family the pathetic memory of a destiny cut off, whereas William died comfortably, at the end of a long life and surrounded by his children.[54] What one rather remarks in going through the correspondence the two brothers exchanged in for more than fifty years is the solidity and tranquil consistency of their relations. Too unlike to share certain crucial experiences,[55] they know at least that they can count on each other in the details of daily life. The two families pay frequent visits, and the fruits of Staten Island are exchanged for those of Concord. Above all, William becomes Ralph Waldo's legal and financial adviser, and indeed his agent. And one remembers that it is also William who in 1843 invited Thoreau to come live with him and direct the education of his son.[56] None of this smacks of the heroic, to be sure; but the even tenor of William's existence, established against the background of tragedy in which Emerson's youth took place, becomes in its own way exemplary; one may suspect that the author of "Success" came to recognize its quality and value.

[52] There was a fifth son, Robert Bulkeley, but he was mentally retarded all his life, and his brothers had to contribute to his care.

[53] See Rusk, *Life*, pp. 105–108 and 113, and L 1.160–162.

[54] Emerson gives an account of his brother's death in a letter dated September 13, 1858 (L 6.33).

[55] For example: though written just after his celebrated Divinity School address, Emerson's letter to William on August 2, 1838 notes only that "at Cambridge some men hated my speech, some men said it was true" (L 2.151). A month later (September 2, 1838; L 2.157), he does mention the violent reaction of the Harvard theological authorities, but only so as to declare calmly, as if he were talking about somebody else's speech, that the theses being attacked will help "ascertain how men do think on a great question."

[56] Cf. the letter to William written on March 12 and 13, 1843 (L 3.157–159).

There are numerous descriptions of the fate of the two youngest brothers: more splendidly gifted, it seems, than Ralph Waldo himself but both carried off by tuberculosis before the age of thirty. And for the list of misfortunes to be complete one would have to add the episode of madness that led to Edward's temporary internment in 1828. The extraordinary character of these two lives, almost excessively perfect symbols of mortality,[57] ought not to efface what was heartening and joyful in their beginnings. Ralph Waldo's first letters to Edward, two years his junior, should be read as a sort of prologue to the journal.[58] The child presents himself there with the winning freedom of his fourteen years; remarks on the tiniest details of daily life alternate with literary impressions and first attempts at poetry. In a letter dated June 18, 1818,[59] he even reveals his literary ambitions, confessing a feeling of envy for the situation of the man of letters in England and regretting, with Freneau, that America does not know how to encourage its own poets. Nowhere in any case does one find that difficulty in communication that was the secret torment of the adult Emerson; on the contrary, the pleasures of the awakening mind (even if manifested only in puns and easy riddles) and the joys of sensibility are increased by his perfect freedom to confide them.

It quickly became clear, however, above all after the spell of insanity in 1828, that Edward would not long be able to resist the deep workings of the disease. That is why his death in 1834 hardly surprised his circle; it put the expected end to what Ralph Waldo was to call "a tragedy of poverty & sickness tearing genius."[60] But Charles remained, whose legal career promised great things, and who united great integrity of character with the energy and courage necessary for action.[61] All these promises were brought to nothing in a few days in May 1836; unknowingly ravaged by the same disease as his brother, he succumbed to it a few days after his arrival at William's house in New York, to which he had come in hope of a cure. This new sorrow was a catastrophe—

[57] Emerson himself contributed to making that image. See for example his poem in Edward's memory (W 9.261–265), one stanza of which begins: "Ah! brother of the brief but blazing star," and another of which ends: "All, all was given, and only health denied."

[58] The first, given by Rusk (L 1.17–19), is from October 1816.

[59] L 1.63.

[60] JMN 5.151.

[61] Rusk reproduces in a note (L 2.24) a passage of Harriet Martineau's autobiography paying tribute to the courage with which Charles Emerson had defended himself in 1835 before a hostile Boston crowd. The same year, Charles delivered a lecture on slavery that was remarkable not only for the precision and energy of its abolitionist arguments but also for the uncompromising frankness of its social analysis (printed in full in ESQ 16. [1959], pp. 12–22).

Emerson's journal[62] and letters[63] pathetically express the confusion he found himself thrown into. Not only did it seem to him that his moorings were broken and that he was drifting astray; he felt himself possessed by shame at the very idea of living (this confession of despair is in a letter to his second wife, Lidian). A few days later, in a letter to Abel Adams, an old family friend, he writes, "In [Charles] . . . I have lost all my society." For those familiar with Emerson's natural reticence, these cries of pain attest clearly to the depth of his wound. Even the death of his young wife Ellen Tucker did not affect him so cruelly; it would take the appalling death of his son Waldo in 1842 to shake his confidence in life more deeply.

Behind the expression of suffering it is possible to discern the spiritual bases of this remarkable friendship. Emerson hints at them himself in a letter to Harriet Martineau, written three weeks after the event, just as he was beginning to recover himself. "[Charles] was my philosopher, my poet, my hero, my Christian."[64] And ten months later, as if to give substance to that concise phrase, he undertook to build a memorial, copying into a notebook certain fragments of Charles's journal and letters.[65] In reading it, one notes certain affinities between Ralph Waldo and his brother that seem very much a product of will; but even with all these subtracted, the remaining similarities of interest and temperament are considerable. Like Ralph Waldo, Charles admires Burke and defends him against Goldsmith; he wants life to be heroic, that is, free of custom and tradition; and he preaches the doctrine of spiritual solitude (in a letter to his fiancée—the fact is significant) and compares the soul to an island.[66] If one recalls that in 1836 neither "Self-Reliance" nor "The American Scholar" had yet seen the light, one does in fact wonder whether Charles is not showing his elder brother the way. Certain of the transcribed pages even proclaim a distinctly later phase of Emerson's thought, as for example that in which an exacting sense of solidarity is allied to an acknowledgment of individual vocation:

> It is a miserable smallness of nature to be shut up within the circle of a few personal relations & to fret & fume whenever a claim is made on us from God's wide world without. It is the perversion of the friendly constitution of things & and an outlawry of ourselves

[62] See JMN 5.151–161.

[63] See L 2.19–25.

[64] Letter of May 30, 1836 (L 2.24–25).

[65] JMN 6.255–287.

[66] "The soul should sit island like a pure cool strait should keep the external world at its distance" (letter to Elizabeth Hoar, June 1834; "C. C. E.," JMN 6.267).

> from the commonwealth of Humanity. It is like nothing so much as those sulky giants in the old romances who lived all by themselves in their castles slaying whoever dared knock at their gates. If we are impatient of the dependence of man on man & grudge to take hold of hands in the ring the spirit in us is either evil or infirm. If to need least is nighest to God so also is it to impart most. We are to reflect on others that light we receive else the divine bounty only makes us niggards & the blessing we would hoard like manna putrifies & is lost to us. There is no soundness in any philosophy short of that of unlimited debt. As no man but is wholly made up of the contributions of God & the creatures of God so there is none who can reasonably deny himself to the calls which in the economy of the world he was provided with the means of satisfying. The true check of this principle is to be found in another general law that each is to serve his fellow men in that way he can best. The olive is not bound to leave yielding its fruit & and go reign over the trees. No more is the astronomer, the artist or the poet to quit his work to do the errands of Howard or to second the efforts of Wilberforce.[67]

No other human group was to give Emerson to the same degree as this small family circle the feeling of being at once understood and loved for what was best in him. Who can say whether the isolation he bewails in his journal and letters with an almost monotonous insistence does not in fact disguise a profound nostalgia? Or rather, circumstances need only cast his thoughts back a few years, and he himself will confess as much. Thus in 1841, he happens to reread some old letters from his aunt Mary, with whom his relations had for some time been, for reasons no doubt trivial enough, somewhat strained. He writes her at once, taking all the fault on himself and begging her to forget their quarrel in the name of what essentially united them: "our perception of one law . . . our adoration of the Moral Sentiment, and nearer earth . . . our cherished remembrance of those who made the hoop of our little broken circle: Ellen—Edward—Charles. . . ."[68] Two days later, he develops this thought in his journal: "I doubt if the interior & spiritual history of New England could be truelier told than through the exhibition of family history such as this, the picture of this group of M. M. E. & the boys, mainly Charles."[69]

[67] "C. C. E.," JMN 6.259. A philanthropist à la Wilberforce, John Howard (1726–1790) fought to improve English prison conditions.

[68] Letter dated May 4, 1841 (L 2.396–398). The metaphor used here—and many times throughout Emerson's work—is an allusion to *Antony and Cleopatra*, I.2. Emerson assigned himself the task of hunting down the reference as early as 1822 (JMN 1.138).

[69] JMN 7.446.

The same theme, albeit stripped of personal references, is taken up again in the first of a series of lectures on New England given in New York at the beginning of 1843.[70] Emerson notes the almost physical quality of his ancestral religion ("a religion in the blood"), then shows how the coherence of generations had fostered the development of a complex and intense spiritual life, affecting all the details of life: "The depth of the religious sentiment, as it may still be remembered in individuals imbuing all their genius, and derived to them from hoarded family traditions, from so many godly lives and godly deaths of sainted kindred, was itself an education. It raised every trivial incident to a celestial dignity."[71]

Whatever importance one attributes in the end to the role played by Puritanism in Emerson's adult thought,[72] it is at least sure that the image of the ancestral religion, refracted through the personality of Aunt Mary, constituted for Emerson a lasting ideal of excellence. Emerson's liberation has upon occasion been wrongly situated, and there has been too much said in connection with him of a fusion between the humanitarian and tolerant spirit of the eighteenth century and the more austere moral values of the seventeenth.[73] Where there is contradiction, Emerson would have said—he never understood very much of the Hegelian dialectic of progress—there cannot be fusion; and in fact the whole effort of his thought was to denounce the false premises of the philosophy of the Enlightenment. If he did not fall prey to dogmatism and arrogance, if he refused to impose the teachings of his conscience on others, it was because he supposed that others received the revelations they needed to conduct themselves well with equal authority. There is in any case a considerable distance between that intuitive faith and the abstract conviction expounded in the Declaration of Independence that certain truths are self-evident.

It goes without saying that this does not mean that Emerson considered the eighteenth century an unfortunate lapse to be forgotten as quickly as possible. The remainder of this study will, on the contrary, attempt to grasp the effects on his thought of the critical enterprise accomplished by the preceding generation. Convinced that the course of

[70] Cf. above, n. 36. The five lectures in the series are in the Houghton Library (H.199).

[71] "New England," part 1, "Origin" (H.199.1).

[72] See in particular Perry Miller, "Jonathan Edwards to Emerson," NEQ 13 (December, 1940), pp. 589–617. Miller situates Emerson's thought in a general resurgence of the intuitionist and mystical currents that rationalism and Unitarianism had for a time dried up.

[73] As Stephen Whicher notes, in a work that can justifiably be said to have transformed Emerson criticism—*Freedom and Fate*—p. 7, it is rather in Channing and the "orthodox" Unitarians of the preceding generation that this fusion is in fact accomplished.

history was irreversible, he was not tempted by the mirage of restoration; he knew that the old Puritan religion, glorious and poetical as it might seem to him, could not suit his contemporaries—or himself. But in a certain way he dedicated his life to discovering, in the midst of the nineteenth century, its qualitative equivalent. Along the way, under the influence of Coleridge and German Romanticism, and later of the thought of India, he was led to modify even the goal of his quest, with the result that his philosophy at its terminus can justifiably be considered a restored Calvinism. It is in any case true that the Emersonian revolution has its roots in the spiritual source of all conservatism: the striving to maintain or recover the greatness of the past. After reading the history of the beginnings of Plymouth colony, Charles felt the same admiration for the Pilgrim Fathers as had his brother and supplemented that admiration by the same emulative desire:

> The Puritans—what an Orion in the world's sky they were & are evermore. That they should have reproduced at that distant time an age & race so apostolic; simple as the babes whom Jesus blessed & sublime as John & Paul in their pious magnanimity does it not cheer us affirming the inextinguishable principle of Faith in man & how God waits for us in our long cold aphelion & draws us at last to himself.[74]

[74] JMN 6.286.

2

~ ~ ~ ~

HARVARD: AN APPRENTICESHIP IN SOLITUDE

EMERSON'S CRITICISMS of the Harvard of his youth are well known: the instruction was mediocre, the pedagogical methods absurd, the formation of personality systematically thwarted. Looking in 1837 for an example to illustrate the lamentable human propensity for leading a conventional existence, Emerson thinks first of his alma mater: "Is not life a puny unprofitable discipline whose direct advantage may be fairly represented by the direct education that is got at Harvard College? As is the real learning gained there, such is the proportion of the lesson in life."[1] A few years later, he concedes that a university is not necessarily harmful; he acknowledges in it at its best a sort of insipid innocuousness: "the college does not have more fine wits than the same population without a college, and it does not have less. It neither helps nor hinders."[2]

From these ungracious judgments to the conclusion that the young Emerson was immediately and irreducibly hostile to Harvard College the transition is easy and plausible; but it is also, as Rusk has clearly

[1] JMN 5.296 (April 11, 1837).

[2] "Education," the ninth lecture in the series "The Present Age" from the winter of 1839–1840; EL 3.294. Twenty years later he offers the same judgment in another lecture of the same title (H.205.3 [1860]).

shown, contrary to the evidence we possess.[3] We would like to think that Emerson was a rebel like Shelley, or at least that it was as a provocation that he adopted the reserved and withdrawn attitude mentioned by certain of his fellow students. The reality is both more complex and less lofty; between 1817, when he was admitted to Harvard, and 1821, when he received his diploma, he underwent an evolution that is unspectacular and, by reason of the paucity of documents bearing on it, difficult to retrace, but that was nonetheless decisive in bringing him to a sudden and intensely personal awareness of his resources and his weaknesses. One must remember that his four years of college coincide with the crucial period of his adolescence. Between the ages of fourteen and eighteen, Emerson was going through the most sensitive, the most receptively docile period of his life. But at the same time, the influences affecting him from the outside joined with a profound work of inner growth; and one can legitimately speak of a process of digestion, of the task by which diverse nutrients are transformed to the flesh and blood of a single organism.

His admission to Harvard College filled Emerson with pride. His first letters from Cambridge, particularly to his younger brother Edward, show him very much struck with his new dignity; in places he adopts a tone of forced banter that hardly disguises a certain self-importance and suggests the approach of the awkward age. He tries a little poetry, strings together a few rakish or mocking verses and adorns his family letters with them; [4] at other moments he advises the reading of Homer "by some melodious grove, pebbly brook or tall shadowy pinnacle."[5] If he was not the instigator of frolics, it was probably from good sense as much as from timidity; certainly he shows no prejudice against such collective activities. When at the end of 1818 his class got itself temporarily suspended for bad conduct, he did not desert it; and a few months later, he took great pleasure in his election to the Pythologian Club, composed of "the fifteen smartest fellows in each of the two classes Junior & Soph."[6] (The club aimed to develop in its members the art of "extemporaneous discussion.") Neither a leader nor a loner, Emerson in his first years at Harvard indulged with a good grace in social diversion and sought contact with those of his fellows whom he respected. His intellectual temperament, his tendency to reflection kept him of course from associating with the most tempestuous of them, but his dispositions for revolt or defiance were not yet in play; for this descendant of ministers,

[3] See in particular Rusk, *Life*, chapter 8: "Under the Tree of Knowledge."

[4] See for example the letter ca. December 20, 1817 (L 1.50–51).

[5] Letter of March 14 and 15, 1818 (L 1.58–60).

[6] Letter of June 20, 1819 (L 1.85).

the path of self-development still led in 1819 past the old establishment in Cambridge.

Emphasis has rightly been laid on the role played in the maturation of Emerson's thought by the philosophical reading—from Locke to Hutcheson, from Berkeley to Hume and Dugald Stewart—imposed by the Harvard College curriculum.[7] It is my intention not to repeat those arguments but to extend them, by showing that in his social or political interests also the young Emerson was the tributary of the attitudes and tendencies of his milieu. But we should not look for the thunderous gesture, the bold or violent declaration; in the Cambridge of 1820, heroism was not fashionable.

Boston had had its hour of glory, or at least of emotion, during the War of 1812. When the news of the taking of Washington by the English came in 1814 to the banks of the Charles, preparations to meet the expected invasion were made quickly. Volunteer militia flocked to Boston; merchants and shopkeepers took up pickaxes to erect earthen fortifications on the port's outposts. Forty-two years later, Emerson humorously recalled the part he had taken in this work of public safety:

> I have but one military recollection in all my life. In 1813 or 1814, all Boston, young & old, turned out to build the fortifications on Noddle's Island; and, the Schoolmaster at the Latin School announced to the boys, that, if we wished, we might all go on a certain day to work on the Island. I went with the rest in the ferry boat, & spent a summer day; but I cannot remember that I did any kind of work. I remember only the pains we took to get water in our tin pails, to relieve our intolerable thirst. I am afraid no valuable effect of my labor remains in the existing defences.[8]

On the whole, the war was regarded with extreme disfavor by the leading men, the merchants and lawyers, of New England. Not only did it seem to them fratricidal; it also threatened, by disrupting trade with England, to deal a fatal blow to the prosperity of the whole eastern seaboard, and in consequence to transfer political power to the adventurers of every stripe who were beginning to spread west of the Alleghenies. Daniel Webster, then a young New Hampshire lawyer, had even drawn up a motion explicitly threatening secession, should one part of the country come to exercise an abusive and illegal domination over the rest, and the Hartford Convention, convened on the initiative of the leg-

[7] See Whicher, *Freedom and Fate*, particularly chap. 1: "Discovery" and the notes in the appendix (pp. 175–181).

[8] JMN 14.90 (1856).

islators of Massachusetts, had apparently begun to put this threat into execution; but the news of the Treaty of Ghent arrived before any major decision could be made. America settled down in relief to peace, and relations with England quickly became cordial once again.

Despite the internal dissensions that marked these years of struggle, despite the tentative, not to say disastrous character of the military operations with which they were filled, a subtle political maturation had been achieved in the American mind. The "colonial complex" had been distinctly shaken off; America had shown to everyone that she was capable of holding her place among the great independent nations of the world, and that a bold system of political liberty did not entail any deficiency of power. Those born like Emerson at the turn of the century thus became the heirs of a sturdy confidence in their country's destiny; the decisive battles had been fought, and it remained for their generation to take the inventory of what had been won and to extend the benefits of victory without end—to resume, in short, with a reinforced optimism, the spreading of the gospel of light.

Emerson at Harvard shared in these views. To America, the promised land risen from the darkness, he opposes, so as to imbue himself more fully with the privilege of his birth, the barbarous countries still ruled by despotism and superstition. In one of his first journals he alludes to Russia, whom even her vast size has not saved from tyranny: "all the millions of population planted in this stretching territory & seemingly bound by no ties but the eternal bands of their common earth bow to the despotism of an individual like themselves."[9] Similarly, in his early poem "Indian Superstition"[10]—a derivative work, but ambitious and rich in literary allusions— he denounces the religion of India for its savage cult, its tainted gods, its systematic inequality. Kenneth W. Cameron's curiosity on this point led him to consult a number of contemporary periodicals; he found several articles establishing the interest Boston felt from the end of the eighteenth century for the civilizations of the Orient.[11] But this is not to say that to American eyes certain Eastern rites could seem other than scandalous; the custom of suttee, for example, according to which a widow would immolate her-

[9] JMN 1.16 (May 28, 1820).

[10] Published in Ralph Waldo Emerson, *Indian Superstition*, edited with *A Dissertation on Emerson's Orientalism at Harvard*, by Kenneth W. Cameron (Hanover, N.H., 1954). On the circumstances of the poem's composition see Rusk, *Life*, p. 83.

[11] See, besides the *Dissertation*, Cameron's "More Remarks on 'Indian Superstition' and Emerson's Oriental Sources while at Harvard," in *The Transcendentalists and Minerva*, 3 vols. (Hartford, Conn., 1958) 3.829–854, and "Articles of Possible Interest to Emerson and Thoreau in Concord Newspapers" (ESQ 12.3 [1958], pp. 48–49).

self upon the tomb of her dead husband, is made the object of numerous horrified descriptions, expressing the unqualified condemnation of this benighted practice by the most civilized country of the world. India would do well to study in the University of America: that in effect is the point of the exhortation at the end of Emerson's poem, when he displays to India the luminous vision of Columbia. It is ironic to note that Emerson was to exert himself twenty or thirty years later to suggest that the influence should perhaps go the other way.

As for the great European nations, America no longer fears comparison with them. France has been disgraced by the excesses of the Revolution, excesses so abundant as to call down punishment from heaven:"—To behead a king, to pillage a church . . . to blaspheme God—are crimes of the first dye and of deep condemnation. In the last stages of political degeneracy these enormities have become common and uphold a tremendous indication of coming retribution."[12] Thus disqualified by its recent history, France can no longer claim to lead mens' minds; its literature, the product of a rootless elite, does not reflect "the feelings, situation, circumstances, & character of the whole people which produced it."[13] Such at any rate was the teaching of George Ticknor, the young professor then occupying the recently created Harvard chair in modern languages; Emerson attended his lectures during his senior year. One may ask with Rusk whether Emerson's well-known prejudice against French culture does not go back to this experience of his youth; the criticisms he makes of the French in 1854—lack of depth, passion for effect, disdain for truth, and the like[14]—are more than hinted at in the account given by Ticknor in 1821.

As Germany had not at this time acquired entrance rights at Harvard (it was only in 1825 that a German liberal, Charles Follen, was charged with giving a course on the literature of his country), there was in the end only one nation with regard to which an American student might find difficulty in situating himself: England. But that one difficulty was immense; one may even consider that Emerson never felt it entirely vanquished, since he devoted the most original efforts of his political thinking, from "The American Scholar" to his lecture "The Fortune of the Republic"—which he was still giving in 1878, four years before his death—to defining in a context of race and tradition the particular situation of the American. At Harvard, however, the terms of the problem

[12] JMN 1.246 (1820).

[13] JMN 1.54 (May 2, 1821).

[14] In his unpublished lecture "France or Urbanity" (H.202–204), Emerson notes for example that the French in 1815 forgot the fact of their defeat in the brilliant spectacle of the enemy armies.

were still obscure. In a letter to his brother Edward, written in 1818, Emerson proposes an exercise in composition on the subject of "The Age of the American Scholar."[15] A striking anticipation of the lecture of 1837? The commentary by which the proposal is followed reveals that the prophecy is an involuntary one, and that Emerson has not yet gone at all beyond the perspective of the eighteenth century: "Imagine to yourself all the gratifications of taste and riches to form his library, philosophy room &c and take what is excellent out of Mr Gore, Mr Vaughan, Thos. Jefferson, and others of your distinguished country-men."[16] Little by little, however, the literary reveries are ballasted with reality—as in the debates set up among the sophomores in a certain club without a name,[17] in which attempts are made to determine whether savagery or civilization is more conducive to happiness, questions are raised concerning unrestricted immigration, and deliberations are undertaken as to whether American policy toward the Indians conforms to the principles of justice and humanity.[18] Although these discussions include a good bit of conventional rhetoric (the Rousseauist arguments in particular catch the attention from time to time), they also draw Emerson's attention to certain issues that later engaged his adult sense of responsibility, as in the Cherokee affair of 1838. To be an American is among other things to take note of the incessant threats to the common ideal.

But even at this time Emerson sensed the profound difference, the difference of kind, that separates America from all the other nations of the world. In one of the first volumes of his journal, full of reflections on the drama, he takes the corruption of the English stage as an occasion to exalt the virtue of his compatriots:

> Indeed I know not what of malignant crime, of dark enormity, or wide-spread wickedness would startle the public mind there. I am proud and thankful when I contrast this with the uncontaminated innocence of my own country and it is this comparative purity

[15] Letter of June 17, 1818 (L 1.64–65).

[16] According to Rusk, the reference here may be to the "Manlius Papers" of Christopher Gore (on whom see L 1.57, n. 14). Vaughan is probably Benjamin Vaughan, an English friend of Franklin's.

[17] In a long note (L 1.85, n. 41), Rusk explains the reasons that lead him to think that this is *not* the Pythologian Club. Kenneth Cameron makes the same distinction; cf. his *Emerson the Essayist*, 2 vols. (Raleigh, N.C., 1945), 1.437–440, for an enumeration of the anonymous club's members. The point is not in any case crucial.

[18] Cited by Rusk from an unpublished notebook of Emerson's (*Life*, p. 73; also L 1.85 for some information about the manuscript). See also Cameron, *Emerson the Essayist*, 1.441–458: "The Minutes and Financial Records of the Society Without a Name."

> joined to the energy of a youthful people still free from the complicated difficulties of an old government which constitutes the distinction and promise of this nation.[19]

And what is this but to say that the limitless confidence in human nature preached by the Unitarians of Boston applies to the American people but not to the whole of the species? This postulate is one of the guises worn by the myth of America during the whole nineteenth century. It impressed itself on Emerson very early; in 1822, just one year after leaving Harvard, he dedicated a volume of his journal to "The Spirit of America."[20] In the dedication, he describes the extraordinary perfections of the American people: that liberty does not degenerate into license; that education and intelligence keep house equably with morality; that property passes peacefully from one generation to another; that public offices are held by people remarkable no less for elegance than for integrity; in short, that the promise of humanity in the New World has been accomplished beyond the wildest dreams of the imagination: "If the Constitution of the United States outlives a century, it will be matter of deep congratulation to the human race; for the Utopian dreams which visionaries have pursued and sages exploded, will find their beautiful theories rivalled & outdone by the reality, which it has pleased God to bestow upon United America."[21] Experience, one suspects, will lose no time in soiling this exemplary image; but in a deeper sense it remains invulnerable. Faced with his countrymen's cowardice, or even simply with their mediocrity, Emerson will strive continually to see this image he has posited and the reality around him—however discouraging the latter may seem—as associated, and indeed as indistinguishable.[22]

To this description must be added an element that takes account of the role played in the formation of this image by Emerson's geographical situation, which determines what Emerson would doubtless have called his "angle of vision": because the ideal America is not being viewed from Sirius, or even from London or Paris, as Cooper was later to do; it is from Cambridge and Boston, *through* Cambridge and Boston, that the young Emerson directs his gaze. From this fact comes the

[19] JMN 1.287–288 (October 1821).

[20] The notebook ("Wide World 7," JMN 2.3–39) soon leaves its proclaimed subject behind—the episodic character of Emerson's thought is even by that time apparent.

[21] JMN 2.4–5 (July 11, 1822).

[22] See on this point the precise and richly documented study of Ernest E. Sandeen, *Emerson's Americanism*, University of Iowa Studies: Humanistic Studies 6.1 [Iowa City, 1942], pp. 63–118). Sandeen takes as the point of departure for his analysis the journal passage just cited.

hardly concealed paradox that the American is as innocent as the most thorough savage, yet possesses all the graces and talents of the man of the world. A good education, a sense of the proprieties, a reserve and a self-control, a certain instinct of dignity to be maintained in all situations, especially public situations—in a word, "manners," as Emerson will say later—are not in Boston simply ornamental virtues; they are the sign and the guarantee of a soul of quality, and thus the criterion by which social exclusions are decreed. When President Monroe came to Boston in 1817, Emerson wrote his brother Edward of the disappointment people felt, but refrained from giving the cause.[23] Another letter, written two years later, furnishes an indirect explanation: Dr. Kirkland, the president of Harvard College, paid a visit to the president of the United States, and Emerson diverts himself in imagining the meeting: "Should you not like to have been witness of the meeting of the two Presidents at Washington? People appear to think that our Prest will do himself as much honour as a man of the world as he will as a literary character. & that Mr Munroe in appearance is little more than a comfortable ploughman."[24] Light and bantering as it is, the tone has its self-assuredness and implies that a comparison between Boston and Washington can only be disadvantageous to the latter. And yet at other moments Emerson acts like a country boy eager to see the big city—as when he writes to Edward, then in Alexandria, Virginia, "Do hear the Missouri question if possible agitated debated or decided in the supreme Legislature of the United States. What an opportunity! I am very sorry you do not live 8 miles nearer then you might dwell in the Senate house. Give me some idea of the Capitol's external & internal appearance."[25] Then he adds, as if to comfort his pride: "Webster has gone to Washington to plead before the Supreme court I believe. Hear Hear."

Without giving these remarks more importance than the occasion and the correspondent justify, it is easy to hear in the words the somewhat forced tone that one in fact finds in most of the letters of this period. It is as if Emerson were deliberately assuming a personality of a certain detached elegance—ironic and studied, but given on principle to avoiding the difficult questions. What part in this stance is to be attributed to Emerson's desire not to reveal himself, indeed to wear a mask, and what to a sort of adolescent conformity it is difficult to specify. Describing the atmosphere of Harvard College after the War of

[23] See the letter to Edward Emerson of July 3, 1817 (L 1.38–40).

[24] Letter to William Emerson of February 14, 1819 (L 1.76–78).

[25] Letter to Edward Emerson of July 31, 1820 (L 1.89–91). The debates Emerson alludes to were to lead to the Compromise of 1820, fixing the northern limit of slave territory at latitude 36° 30′.

1812, Perry Miller portrays it as dominated by a feeling of indifference and lassitude, with a fair amount of affectation.[26] The sociological reasons for such a state of affairs seem obscure; but one may wonder whether it is not to a considerable extent the result—or the penalty—of the extraordinary luck with which the obstacles along the path of the young republic had been surmounted. Even the recent war with England, badly conducted as it had been, had ended well. In 1820 the "era of good feelings" had begun, with that expression's connotation of unexciting reasonableness. No large task presented itself on the Eastern seaboard, now restored to prosperity; bereft of application to the external world, the energies of bourgeois youth were reduced to inactivity or consumed, to adopt Miller's term, in a disillusioned "Prufrockism." A quietly happy, slightly tedious period, as Emerson himself wrote to a fellow student in 1822, on the eve of the Fourth of July:

> Indeed the only time when Government can be said to make itself seen & felt, is on festivals, when it bears the form of a kind of General Committee for popular amusements. In this merry time, & with real substantial happiness above any known nation, I think we Yankees have marched on since the Revolution, to strength, to honour, & at last to ennui.[27]

The banality of the age, with the air of routine and convention it maintained at Harvard College,[28] had the effect of throwing the young Emerson back on himself as his powers of reflection asserted themselves. But this withdrawal was never a violent rejection. Of the subjects he was taught—chemistry, history, mathematics, classical languages, philosophy, and so on—he retained what answered his needs. Thus the philosophy of the Scottish Realists, in particular Dugald Stewart, offered him an original conception of the moral sense with which he nourished his meditations for several years, and which he incorporated, altering it to his taste, into each of the phases of his thought.[29] What is striking in this young man of seventeen or eighteen is precisely the calm steadfastness with which he undertook to construct from the meager materials offered him, without falling either into con-

[26] See "Emersonian Genius and the American Democracy," NEQ 26 (March 1953), pp. 27–44, esp. 27–28.

[27] Letter to John Boynton Hill of July 3, 1822 (L 1.119–121) and Cabot, *Memoir*, 1.91.

[28] "Study at college was much the same as at the Latin School. Memorizing and reciting were the students' two serious occupations. But here there was less liberty, it seemed" (Rusk, *Life*, p. 67).

[29] On this subject see Whicher, *Freedom and Fate*, p. 14, and M. R. David, "Emerson's 'Reason' and the Scottish Philosophers," NEQ 17 (June 1944), pp. 209–228.

formity or into systematic rebellion, an interpretation of the world in accordance with his experience of the truth. From this perspective, the place he held in his class after four years of college—thirtieth of fifty-nine— becomes significant by its very mediocrity. Absorbed by his inward quest, Emerson found no time to practice the arts of success—or even the still more superficial arts of scandal.

One encounters here for the first time the split that runs through Emerson's personality and makes it so hard to define. Without in any way altering the face seen by the world around him (his last year at Harvard saw the production of "Indian Superstition" and a prize-winning essay on the present state of ethical philosophy), he formed the habit of descending deeper and deeper within himself, finding the tensions and conflicts that had taken refuge there, but also promises for the future. Solitude thus became the supreme means of cultivation; when in 1860 Emerson took a backward glance at the Harvard of his youth, he stressed a physical detail that in his eyes made up for all the imperfections of its pedagogy: he had a room of his own.[30] Sheltered from view and from distraction, he begins a fascinating dialogue with himself, which all his life would accompany the considerably less constant dialogue he carried on with others.

Emerson's decision to keep a journal allies him with one of the liveliest traditions of New England; but probably it was born specifically of the desire to stimulate and also to monitor his inward life. At the beginning of 1820, he was already reproaching himself with insufficient use of this device to "restore the sinking soul, to keep alive the fire of enthusiasm in literature & literary things, to be the register of desultory but valuable contemplations."[31] In the same spirit of what one might call spiritual economy, he began in 1819 to draw up catalogs of the works he had read or skimmed outside his course work.[32] Emerson's mental universe thus learned very early to reflect itself; we can, in consequence, follow its development with relative ease. It is true that no definite orientation can be discerned from the first list of readings, in which Cotton Mather's *Magnalia Christi Americana* is next to *Manfred* and *Don Juan*, and scholarly histories follow the "Ode to Melancholy"; in the journal, however, the entries tend to be organized around certain privileged themes. Not everything is equally significant, and a considerable part of

[30] See "Culture" in *Conduct of Life* (W 6.156). In 1823, writing to one of his former fellow students, William Withington, then studying at Andover Seminary, Emerson declares he has only one objection to make to his friend's "mode of study": that his room has to be shared (*Century Magazine* 26 [July 1883], p. 457).

[31] JMN 1.15 (April 30, 1820).

[32] See Rusk, *Life*, p. 85, and JMN 1.396–399.

the first volumes is given over to school essays and pure rhetorical exercises such as a description of Arabia.[33] But when Emerson touches on a personal subject it is not only the pronouns that change. His diction is free then of conventional cadences and takes on an unexpected energy—as in the passages concerning his friendship with a certain Martin Gay, a fellow student at Harvard.[34] We have only Emerson's version of this affair, so it is impossible to know exactly what happened; but everything, as Rusk suggests, inclines us to think that in it the principal if not the only agent was Emerson's imagination.

Gay's name appears in the journal for the first time on August 8, 1820. Himself a junior, Emerson notices among the new students a young man whose face suggests extraordinary character; he will, he says, attempt to make his acquaintance. A few weeks later, though he has not yet spoken with Gay, Emerson confesses his infatuation in a strikingly romantic passage:

> I begin to believe in the Indian doctrine of eye-fascination. The cold blue eye ______ [left blank in the manucript] has so intimately connected him with my thoughts & visions that a dozen times a day & as often by night I find myself wholly wrapped up in conjectures of his character & inclinations. We have had already two or three long profound stares at each other. Be it wise or weak or superstitious I must know him.[35]

When Gay makes his next appearance in the journal, on April 1, 1821, it is so that Emerson can express his disappointment and his resolution to break things off—still only in thought, of course. He has heard a discreditable story about Gay that shatters the lofty image he had constructed of him. He sketches by contrast the portrait of the ideal friend he had thought to find: "Before I ever saw him, I wished my *friend* to be different from any individual I had seen. I invested him with a solemn cast of mind, full of poetic feeling, & an idolater of friendship, & possessing a vein of rich sober thought."[36] A month later, the same journal records a genuine lovers' skirmish: Gay having made as if to accost Emerson, Emerson "most strangely" altered his path to avoid him.[37] The next day the roles are reversed; it is Emerson who goes to meet Gay and Gay who changes course.

[33] JMN 1.327–328.

[34] Rusk, *Life*, p. 85, sums up the episode in a paragraph on the basis of a note in J (1.28–29).

[35] JMN 1.39 (October 24, 1820).

[36] JMN 1.52–53.

[37] See JMN 1.54–55 (May 2, 1821).

Evidently that was all. It remained for Emerson to draw a moral from this aborted friendship, which he does in a long paragraph at the end of 1822.[38] The ardor of feeling is so far damped that he can hardly conceive how a being as cold as himself could ever have given it birth. He continues nonetheless to think that if Gay had not chosen that disappointing career,[39] their friendship might indeed have blossomed. But then, on the verge of real regret, Emerson recovers himself:

> But it were much better that our connexion should stop, and pass off, as it now will, than to have had it formed, and then broken by the late discovery of insurmountable barriers to friendship. From the first, I preferred to preserve the terms which kept alive so much sentiment rather than a more familiar intercourse which I feared would end in indifference.

In this little serial drama, the excesses and gaucheries of adolescence heighten almost to caricature Emerson's sensitiveness and vulnerability in the matter of human relations. An exchange of glances reveals infinite spiritual depths, and he thinks that upon this exchange he can construct a friendship by which two souls can be brought so near each other as to intermingle; then, when the inevitable disenchantment comes, he extricates himself with a disconcerting ease and justifies in principle the spiritual solitude into which he quickly resettles. Rid of its naïveté, the same schema later defines his relations with Margaret Fuller, with William Ellery Channing, and with Thoreau.

But however painful they may be, the disappointments of friendship do not occupy the foreground in these youthful journals. Another and still more painful subject recurs incessantly, a subject of two aspects according as Emerson finds himself galvanized or paralyzed by it: ambition. Stephen Whicher has rightly stressed the role played by that ambiguous quality in the Emerson family:[40] deadly for Edward and Charles, it found in Ralph Waldo a nature it could put to the test without breaking. Its activity was beginning as early as Emerson's time at Harvard; not as yet having any specific context, it was nourished by whatever flattered it. Thus during his junior year Emerson discovered in Edward Everett the tyrannical charms of oratory; he became so intoxicated by the cadences of a sermon that he undertook one day to reproduce the most memorable of them in a letter to his brother Ed-

[38] See JMN 2.59 (November 29, 1822).

[39] Probably the career of a soldier. Emerson describes Gay as "buried in his martial cares," and the editor of J informs us that Gay had shown considerable interest in the College Military Company (1.28–29). In the end he became a doctor.

[40] *Freedom and Fate*, p. 4.

ward.[41] Nor does he stop there; by imaginative sympathy, he creeps within the orator himself, to taste the orator's extraordinary dominion over his hearers: "let him come forth with dignity and all eyes will see him & him alone; the mind of all & every hearer will dilate & contract, will triumph & droop, as he shall desire."[42] Emerson played variations on this rhapsody on the power of the word till the end of his life.[43] One should note, moreover, that it is the student of sixteen—enthusiastic, receptive, and inexperienced—and not the pastor or the lecturer who discovers the theme: another example, after the remarks on the ideal America just preceding, of the fecundity of Emerson's years of adolescence, which were to nurture the thought of his maturity more richly than is commonly supposed.

Most often, however, his attention is occupied with the obstacles on the path to greatness. He examines them at length, as if by force of reflection he hoped to dissolve them. Sometimes he blames his laziness, which condemns him to mediocrity,[44] or his wandering mind, which makes him the slave of a "dinning throng of casual recollections."[45] If he falls sick, he suddenly judges that he has squandered his health.[46] Sometimes he takes exception to the popular argument that we have to reckon with others and, from a concern with the practical, to submit our conduct and thought to the judgment of the crowd:

> There is an apology which every man makes for himself when his independence is put to the test that by nature we are social beings & it is utterly against the order of things for a single man to presume to encounter all the prejudices & violence & power & war of the world, invidious & alone. With this plausible answer he stands his ground, worms himself into good opinion & patronage of men & secures himself present peace by the sacrifice of his high honour. But there are on earth great men who disdainful alike of the multitude's scorn & the multitude's applause elevate themselves by their own exertion to heights of human exaltation where the storm of varying opinion cannot hurt them & the levin-bolts of furious envy & disappointed passion will not reach or harm them. Every man of talents & application has it in his power to be one of these.[47]

[41] See the letter of January 31, 1820 (L 1.89–90).

[42] JMN 1.7 (1820).

[43] See in particular the two essays called "Eloquence," published in *Society and Solitude* and *Letters and Social Aims* (W 7.59–106 and 8.109–133).

[44] Cf. JMN 1.39 (October 25, 1820).

[45] JMN 1.41 (November 1, 1820).

[46] See, e.g., JMN 1.52 (March 25, 1821).

[47] JMN 1.7 (1820).

Though still blurred with rhetoric, the Emersonian stamp is unmistakable. By 1820, the young man had not only decided with all the force of his will to make something of himself and his life; he knew also that greatness is the fruit of solitary effort. In another passage of the journal, boldly granting the discrepancy between this doctrine and the virtue of charity, he cuts the knot without hesitation: "it is a very easy thing to dispense of the store with which heaven has lavishly supplied us. It is harder a thousand yea a thousand times harder to pull one plume from the mountain pinion of Ambition."[48] The spectacle of so much energy directed toward so vague a goal seems somewhat comic; and in fact, years were to pass before it found a worthy object. But even in the moments of Emerson's greatest depression, an obscure consciousness of his vocation, sustained by the feeling that his first obligations were to himself, would never abandon him.

[48] JMN 1.44 (December 4, 1820).

3

~ ~ ~ ~

THE SCHOOLTEACHER FEELS HIS WAY

In October 1821, less than two months after leaving Harvard, Emerson became his brother William's assistant and started teaching in the girls' school at the Emerson house. He seemed to be embarking on a typical New England career. His father had begun so, as had his grandfather William, the minister-soldier. Though poor in prestige, schoolteaching offered to this son of poverty the advantage of immediate remuneration, with which he could later resume and finish his studies as he chose. For the best men and women teaching was simply an interlude, which by force of will they made the occasion and means of their advancement; and Emerson as much as anyone would have been justified in considering his new state in that optimistic light. His students were the daughters of the most respectable Bostonian society, and his eighteen years were in consequence spared the humiliating experience of rowdiness and disorder; the salary was by his own avowal substantial and allowed him to help his mother and brothers, as he very much desired to do.[1] If he could only keep clearly in mind the goal to be attained once the test of patience thus imposed on him was past (and the numerous reaffirmations of his ambition in the journal seemed to guarantee that he could), he need not fear becoming the victim of routine.

In fact, however, he took up his new charge with an unconcealed bad grace. We have no journal for the second half of 1821, but a letter writ-

[1] See the letter to William Emerson of February 7, 1818 (L 1.57).

ten in November to his Aunt Mary already conveys the impression of a novice schoolteacher oppressed.[2] He had been far from idealizing Cambridge; but now a poetic halo seems to him to surround his old haunts there.[3] A few weeks later, meditating sadly on the change in his condition and contrasting the wretched schoolteacher with the romantic student still fresh in his memory, he admits to himself that for years he has lived in a dream. The pride of spirit, the poetical ambitions, the company of other youths equally disdainful of wealth and success, and above all the intoxicating and vague aspirations of adolescence had joined together to create an unreal world around him. Nine months sufficed to cast it down; in May 1822 he describes himself as "a disappointed spirit brooding over the fall of castles in the air."[4] He trod the path of the most insipid of routines, and his social obscurity was not even compensated for by appreciable growth in knowledge or mental resources.

This somber account is not all to be taken literally. The journal between 1820 and 1830 offers a good many other passages in which Emerson, under pretext of introspection, permits himself such apparently disillusioned disclosures. There is no doubt that his unstable health played a considerable part in the periodic return of these moments of depression; as Whicher has shown, a mute combat is going on in Emerson between the glimpses of greatness and the fluctuations in his vital energy, and the phases of that uncertain combat are registered in the journal.[5] But what is new in 1822 is the tone;[6] the conventional elaborations of the rhetoric class and the labored search for the witty remark hitherto so common in his letters gradually yield to a concern with expressing his inward debates simply and precisely. We come back in fact to Emerson's own self-diagnosis: the time of reveries is past, and the harsh rupture of his entry into William's school has occasioned a new grasp on reality.

But of what does that reality consist? With the mists of Harvard once dispelled, what is there to render fruitful, or even tolerable, the gray years that stretch out before him, evidently to eternity? According to Cabot, Emerson confided to Moncure Conway (who was between 1850 and 1860 one of his most fervent admirers) that his ambition on

[2] Letter to Mary Moody Emerson, November 8, 1821 (L 1.102–103).

[3] Cf. JMN 1.116 (February 1822).

[4] JMN 1.130 (May 7, 1822).

[5] Cf. Whicher, *Freedom and Fate*, pp. 3–4.

[6] In L 1.102, Rusk argues from the correspondence of Mary Moody Emerson that this maturation of thought and style appeared in Emerson toward the beginning of 1821. The paucity of letters and the scantiness of the journals from that time make any precision impossible. As if in compensation, the documents for 1822 are abundant.

leaving Harvard was to become a professor of rhetoric and elocution.[7] What has been said in the previous chapter of Emerson's admiration for the orator's art makes the anecdote plausible; but can this pious desire be distinguished from the fantasies he now had to leave behind him? In the first quarter of the nineteenth century, oratory, whether political or religious, was in New England the one living form of literature: the desire to shine in this area seems at least as much the reaction of Emerson's suppressed sensibility as the lucid evaluation of his gifts and opportunities. In truth, the letters and journals of Emerson's first year after leaving Harvard attest to a sort of mental paralysis. Not being able to put the resources of his will to the service of a well-defined goal, he stood by and watched them wither away, conscious only of the hiatus between what he could have been and what he had become.

But then, with a sudden surge of energy, he laid hold of anything and everything likely to offer sustenance in this period of prostration. Refusing to be wholly absorbed by his pedagogical tasks, he set aside several hours each day for reading and correspondence. He began to frequent the philosophers, Locke included, but gave little attention to theology, despite the immediate advantages its study might have entailed for his career. In a letter to William Withington—one of his fellow students at Harvard, then studying at the orthodox Calvinist seminary at Andover—Emerson alludes to the controversy between Unitarians and Calvinists in terms more reminiscent of Boileau than of Pascal:

> as many hard names are taken, and as much theological mischief is planned at Cambridge as at Andover. By the time this generation gets upon the stage, if the controversy will not have ceased, it will run such a tide that we shall hardly be able to speak to one another, and there will be Guelf and Ghibeline quarrel, which cannot tell where the differences lie.[8]

With its dry polemics and genius for abstraction, theology was no more attractive to him in 1822 then it was to be at the time of the Divinity School address. By now, an instinct was guiding him to works in which he could find not a blueprint but an image of the human condition; and he was prepared, if need be, to pay for the irreplaceable intuition of life by the malaise that the spectacle of life's contradictions evoked in the reflective mind.

Without setting out a fixed itinerary—which would have been con-

[7] Cabot, *Memoir*, 1.72.

[8] Letter to William Withington, Boston, July 7, 1822 (*The Century* 26 [July 1883], p. 454).

trary to his temperament—Emerson thus interested himself in a wide range of subjects and genres.[9] It is somewhat surprising that the first rank among them is occupied by novels and narrative histories. Never again was he to read so much imaginative literature. Irving, Cooper, and Scott—whom posterity, Emerson says, will not fail to rank directly after Shakespeare—[10]—have such a hold on him that in the privacy of his journals he ventures on a few novelistic attempts of his own. From history he expects other things: by its interpretive aid, he seeks to know and understand human nature, and behind that the order of providence. In particular, history permits him to nourish his reflections on the problem of evil, with its examples of corrupted and brutally ruined civilizations.[11] He quotes Montesquieu and Gibbon on the decadence of the Roman Empire, Sismondi on the Italian republics. Sismondi above all makes present to him the horror of those ignorant ages; he is disgusted with the manifestations of superstition in the Middle Ages, for example the processions of penitents going on pilgrimage to saints' tombs to expiate their sins and avert plagues and wars. But it is the church that receives the harshest blame, because it exploits such popular ignorance: "A consideration of the ecclesiastical & political history of the Middle ages will certainly establish the opinion that modern Europe boasts a state of society beyond comparison more composed, virtuous, & tranquil. The extravagant perpetrations of a church faction upon life & property went beyond all bounds, and often exceeded even savage ferocity."[12] In the recent past only the French Revolution has been guilty of comparable "devilish horrors."

Thus the philosophy of the Enlightenment asserted its claims, suggesting that if we are so shocked by Jacobin excesses it is by reason of the progress made since the time at which such practices would have passed unnoticed, drowned as they would have been in a flood of similar excesses. One has only to extend the ascending course of humanity a little farther to encounter America, with its promise of fulfillment in liberty, order, and peace. Emerson puts such confidence in his country's political system that he speculates that the existence of democratic institutions would probably have saved the ancient world from its decline

[9] Rusk, *Life*, pp. 92–93, gives a list of the works read or skimmed at this time.

[10] Cf. the letter to William Withington of July 7, 1822, p. 455.

[11] See in particular JMN 1.92–93. A long argument on providence and evil ends in a reference to history: "an enumeration of some of the most prominent evils in society will illustrate the variety & malignity of this disease."

[12] JMN 1.127 (May 1, 1822). Expanded, these reflections compose the substance of Emerson's first magazine article, "Thoughts on the Religion of the Middle Ages," *The Christian Disciple* (November–December 1822). See on this subject Rusk, *Life*, pp. 96–97.

and fall: "if the modern inventions of perfect representation had been tried in Rome it would have gone far to save the fortunes of the world."[13] And it is precisely on his compatriots' governmental "science" that he counts to release America from the tragic law—hitherto, by all appearances, universal—by which a nation's greatness and a nation's decadence are inextricably linked.

But it would be misrepresenting Emerson—even the incompletely formed Emerson at issue here—to reduce his vision of history to a grossly simplified vision of progress. As he recognizes, to the extent to which past events illustrate certain traits of the human condition,[14] they raise more questions than they help to resolve. Thus the prodigious edifice of the Assyrian Empire could not have been built without the collaboration of countless multitudes; and it endured only through a prudent managing of massed energies, furnished in generation after generation by an elite.[15] Does not this example bear against his discovery that the path of greatness goes by way of solitude? Extrapolating further, he next saw that it is always when at a distance from his fellow men that he himself has yielded to temptation: "Eve yielded in solitude to the tempter, and the sin was done in retired shades."[16] He must then have been wrong, and is obliged to recant, which he does obediently and without reservation: "Man was as evidently intended for society, as the eye for vision."[17] It hardly needs to be said that despite its categorical form this judgment does not express Emerson's definitive opinion any more than did the one it annuls. But it does permit one to catch at its very birth, so to speak, the natural movement of Emerson's thought: proceeding by contradictory affirmations, it brings ideas into confrontation both in the close combat of his meditations and in the more open battlefields of his experience. The debate between society and solitude echoes, sometimes mournfully, throughout the journal; and even after the Civil War it retains enough resonance for Emerson to take it as the title for a new volume of essays.[18] In this perspective, the journal entries from Emerson's eighteenth year offer important testimony: they reveal in him an almost obsessive anxiety concerning this problem, an anxiety that hints at formidable inward difficulties. One will not be surprised to

[13] JMN 1.70 (January 21, 1822).

[14] "We judge of the value of every portion of history by its usefulness in application to our own and other times" (JMN 1.82–83).

[15] Cf. JMN 1.96–97 (March 2, 1822).

[16] JMN 1.99.

[17] JMN 1.97.

[18] *Society and Solitude* (W 7), published for the first time in 1870.

encounter that anxiety in full prominence whenever important choices have to be made.

Having only just granted the necessity for human cooperation, Emerson next found himself grappling with another and still more serious difficulty: how is one to make possible a state in which the best can govern the many, can discipline the vulgar and lead them to work in the direction of the common good? The difficulty seemed insoluble. On the one hand, nothing guarantees that the most able men will desire to work for the city or the nation in the first place; and Emerson judges in fact that "the highest order of greatness, that which abandons earthly consanguinity, and allies itself to immortal minds, is that which exists in obscurity,"[19] since it has only disdain for the compensations of wealth, honors, and power by which society seeks to reward its services. The politician does not set his ambitions so high; he governs not by wisdom but by a mixture of intelligence and "cunning,"[20] by which self-interest is indulged even when a concern for the general welfare is retained. The chief obstacle is in any case elsewhere; it is a consequence of the perversity of the people, who refuse to be guided by the best precisely *because* they are the best. From China to Venice, human history has only confirmed this rule; and Emerson wonders whether it will ever change. "Will vulgar blood always rebel and rail and [sic] against honourable, virtuous, and opulent members of the same society? Will the good always be in peril from the misdeeds & menaces of the bad? . . . In the answer to these interrogations, truth leans reluctantly towards the affirmative."[21]

The acknowledgment was all the more bitter in that Emerson's own country, and indeed his own city, were in that same year the theater of a distressingly sordid political struggle. Emerson unburdens himself on the subject in a letter to his friend John Boynton Hill, which deserves to be read closely for what it tells us not only of Emerson's social ideas but also of his sympathies and instinctive aversions.[22] The population of Boston, Emerson explains, is divided like every other population into three great classes: the aristocracy of wealth and talent; the artisans and shopkeepers, and more generally all decent people willing to be governed and claiming no power of their own; and finally the lowest class, composed of day laborers and of the down and out of every sort—among them schoolteachers. Now after the election of Monroe as president,

[19] JMN 1.102 (March 1822).

[20] Cf. JMN 1.119 (April 1822).

[21] JMN 1.117–118 (April 16, 1822).

[22] Cf. L 1.110–114 (May 11, 1822). The letter is partially reproduced in Cabot, *Memoir*, 1.87–90.

Emerson continues, Boston went through an era of peace and tranquility that was not slow in some eyes to seem tedious; accordingly "a parcel of demagogues, ambitious . . . of being known, or hoping for places as *partisans* which they could never attain as citizens—set themselves down to devise mischief." Murmurs against the "aristocracy" were heard; a party was organized[23] and a town meeting was held. It was proposed there to print and distribute a sort of Domesday Book, listing according to the assessor's books, the amount of each Bostonian's wealth and the sums paid on it in taxes. A second motion was also adopted—a graver one in Emerson's eyes—asking the selectmen to solicit the legislature to repeal the law forbidding the construction of wooden houses within the city. When the rumor of all this reached the ears of certain eminent Bostonians, they lost no time in protesting, and the two proposals were officially rejected. But the demagogues did not think themselves beaten; they succeeded in interesting a great number of workers and other members of Emerson's second class in their projects, and addressed to the legislature of Massachusetts a petition bearing 2,600 signatures. At the same time they proposed a candidate for mayor; their opponent, the respectable Mr. Otis, "our first citizen," responded by withdrawing in favor of a third and blander man. This chain of events, Emerson writes, "promises little good to our civil welfare"; but he goes on to assure his correspondent that Bostonians are a sedate people, and that no violence is to be feared: "a *mob* is a thing which could hardly take place here."

Despite the ironic allusion to his present proletarian condition, Emerson avows his real allegiance freely. He takes from the Federalists not only their political theories (he speculates ingenuously that the tripartite class-division may be universal) but also their self-righteousness. It seems to him evident that political authority, both in the city and in the nation, belongs by right to the "respectable" members of the community, and he denounces the troublemakers who seek to describe "a very natural circumstance" as "a formal conspiracy to deprive them of their rights & to keep the power entirely in the hands of a few." The shift by which qualities of an essentially utilitarian order, such as thrift and method, come to be considered as the images of spiritual virtues and even as sure signs of divine election, has been the object of numerous analyses, which we need not restate here.[24] Emerson in 1822 has an ob-

[23] The party took the name of "Middling Interest" and could not, for reasons of propriety, have adopted a more plebeian title.

[24] The most famous is that of Max Weber, *Die Protestantische Ethik und der Geist des Kapitalismus* (1904–1905; English trans., *The Protestant Ethic and the Spirit of Capitalism*, 1930). See also R. H. Tawney, *Religion and the Rise of Capitalism* (Holland Memorial Lectures,

scure belief in that equation; he is persuaded that the class that possesses wealth has earned it by moral superiority and that political rivalries are less the expression of ideological discord than the outlet by which the base and veiled passions of the multitude seek satisfaction. By a curious transference, he attributes to this social elite all the privileges he himself admits, at least implicitly, having received from providence: a natural loftiness of vision, an intense striving for moral perfection, and even, in the end, an exemption from misfortune in its cruelest and most humiliating forms. This identification is all the more tenacious for Emerson's not being clearly conscious of it; and it will take the events of the decade before the Civil War for him to discover the magnitude of his misunderstanding.

But even in this frankly partisan letter, there is some independence of judgment. Emerson may censure the new party's demagoguery as he likes; he still cannot help but see the absurdity of the merchants when they panic at the thought of no longer being able to "conceal their coppers." No doubt there is a distinction of scale between the peccadilloes of the one party and the crimes of the other, but Emerson's glance takes in both; there is a source of further thought here, which circumstances will nourish. Indeed, in another letter to Hill written only two months later, Emerson professes himself alarmed to hear that in an obscure defamation case at the Boston Navy Yard, an unjust verdict was rendered by a court-martial in which the same person was both judge and accuser.[25] Can it be, asks Emerson, that "power may even in this country, triumph & trample over right"? Is "anticipation," that figure beloved of public orators, perhaps only a subterfuge to mask the grim realities of the present? Emerson was in no mood that day to pursue the matter, but the unanswered questions took root in his mind. In that citadel of virtue in which good fortune has decreed his birth, scandal is possible, as he knows—indeed he has proof that it exists. Affirming his faith in the exemplary destiny of his country is not enough; he risks Pharisaism if he cannot produce facts to justify it. He was thus led to sketch an analysis of the historical situation, to complete the account of the ideal America and furnish it with arguments that compel belief.

In the first rank of facts evident to every honest man Emerson puts the great movement to the west, begun the day Columbus first saw the shores of the New World and continued uninterruptedly ever since: in

---

1922; publ. New York, 1926). In a long note to the Mentor edition of his book (New York, 1947, pp. 261–263), Tawney explains his reservations regarding Weber's thesis; there is, according to him, no connection both necessary and sufficient between Protestantism and the development of capitalism.

[25] See L 1.119–122 (July 3 and 6, 1822).

North America, in South America, in the Caribbean; by the French, the Spanish, the English, and all the other nations of Europe. If the meaning of this movement was ever uncertain, the last doubts have now been resolved:

> And along the shores of the South Continent, to which the dregs & corruption of European society had been unfortunately transplanted, the fierceness of the present conflict for independence, will, no doubt, act, as a powerful remedy to the disease, by stirring up the slumbering spirits of those indolent zones to a consciousness of their power & destiny.[26]

The perspective is so intoxicating that Emerson's thought is borne off on the wings of rhetoric and lost in the clouds, but we can summarize it without great risk of error as follows: the two Americas are in the grip of a fermentation the strength of which Europe no longer possesses. As Crèvecoeur had remarked in crisper language at the end of the previous century, "Americans are the western pilgrims, who are carrying along with them that great mass of arts, sciences, vigour, and industry which began long since in the east; they will finish the great circle."[27]

But perceiving the direction and the movement of history is not enough; one has to understand how it works and by what means America has been able to acquire its decisive advantage over other countries. Describing in a journal passage the qualities of energy America displayed during the Revolution, Emerson attributes them to the "invigorating solitudes of her clime." The first man to break the ancient silence of the forests is not simply a common adventurer; when he takes his axe to the root of a tree, he commits not only himself but also his descendants and the whole of a people to an irrevocable future. The pioneer is "the representative of human nature, the father of the Country, and, in a great measure, the Arbiter of its future destinies."[28] Instead of lingering over the spectacle of unviolated nature, as had the impressionable eighteenth century, Emerson refocuses attention on man and on the conditions of human life in the new continent. Cut off from his friends, bereft of support from traditions and customs, the pioneer must find the answer to all the problems of life within himself. But this ne-

[26] JMN 2.72–73 (December 21, 1822).

[27] J. Hector St. John Crèvecoeur, *Letters from an American Farmer* (New York, 1957; orig. 1782), p. 39. The phrase is cited in a similar context by Sherman Paul, in the last chapter ("Prospects") of his suggestive but somewhat idiosyncratic *Emerson's Angle of Vision* (Cambridge, Mass., 1952), p. 225. I intend here to indicate that the phrase is also appropriate to the initial phase of Emerson's thought.

[28] JMN 1.146–147 (May 1822).

cessity is a source of progress; under the spur of need, human faculties shake off their lethargy and disclose unsuspected resources. "It was an early lesson of experience," Emerson notes, "that entire change of scene does very sensibly mature and develope the mind."[29] It is thus not at all utopian to expect from the pioneer an extraordinary contribution to the work of civilization; with unequaled energy, he will carry into the heart of the forest the latest acquisitions of humanity.

Emerson goes on to observe that American history is as a whole marked by change and rapidity. Within a few decades, it has traveled the same distance as Europe since the fall of the Roman Empire—or rather it juxtaposes in space the stages traversed by the Old World in time. In one of his notebooks, Emerson quotes Talleyrand's saying that "in a new country as N America to travel 1 or 2000 miles is as good as to go, in *time*, one or 2000 years."[30] This analogy, which Emerson found very striking—he alluded to it twenty years later[31]—is not without its anticipations of Turner's famous thesis. Emerson, however, focuses less on the inchoate character of the constantly moving frontier than on his compatriots' capacity for assimilation and invention. For China, by contrast, that model of stagnation which for three or four millennia has only perpetuated the most disgraceful traits of human nature, he has only contempt: "China, reverend dulness! hoary ideot!, all she can say at the convocation of nations must be—'I made the tea.' "[32] Indeed Asia as a whole must bear a share of this reproach, since it has not even managed, as has Africa with the wood of its forests, to aid in the development of other and more productive continents; its vast and wretched population has yielded nothing to the benefit of humankind.

America's spiritual and material successes are so numerous, Emerson feels, that no historian would have the stamina to draw up their catalog if he did not encounter along his way certain lofty figures who at once explain and symbolize all those successes together. The exemplar of this creative elite is Franklin. Emerson does him homage with surprising warmth: not only does he salute "the serene and powerful understanding which was so eminently practical and useful, which grasped the policy of the globe, and the form of a fly, with like felicity and ease"; he also celebrates a "transmigration of the Genius of Socrates—yet more useful,

[29] Ibid.

[30] Cf. JMN 2.232 (March 1824). Emerson indicates Edward Everett as the source of the remark.

[31] In the unpublished lecture "Origin" (H.199.1), from the series on New England given in New York in 1843.

[32] JMN 2.378–379 (April 6, 1824).

more moral, and more pure."[33] Even if one has difficulty following Emerson in this last step—though the kinship often pointed out between the Puritan virtues and the practical qualities of Poor Richard helps in understanding his enthusiasm—his characterization of Franklin as the architect of society is indisputable. Franklin was born in a nation that offered an unlimited field for the application of his talents. Although in Europe the era of the lawgivers is lost in the darkness of legend, in America one can still catch the transition from the man to the institution; Franklin won immortality as did Solon and Lycurgus, by a work in which his individuality was expanded and thereby, so to speak, abolished. He thus is a hero in the old sense of the term; but because he is not, as Solon and Lycurgus were, a personage of shadows and mystery, the superiority that distinguishes him from his compatriots can be appreciated more justly.

> The discovery of America & its settlement by civilized nations permitted these last ages to see in some measure repeated that part of the growth of kingdoms which was shrouded in the darkness of savage ignorance. It permitted men also to see their benefactors & to ascertain the true elevation of their characters by a just comparison of them with their contemporaries.[34]

Emerson is not, however, blind to the fact that all pioneers are not simply lesser Franklins. American simplicity has its coarseness, American energy its brutality. Returning from an excursion in the neighborhood of Boston, he regrets that the price for republican friendliness should so often be disconcertingly bad manners.[35] Yet this is Massachusetts, peopled by respectable, law-abiding farmers. Emerson knows also of the immense lands in the west, surging with a turbulent stream of immigrants; and that the elementary rules of good conduct were violated daily there was a fact that no one for some time had thought to deny—*Letters from an American Farmer*, in 1782, had already admitted as much in the otherwise radiant account it offered of the colonies on the eve of the Revolution.[36] Emerson does not underestimate the gravity of the problem. In a long meditation on the work that lies before the youth of America, he outlines the obstacles with sure strokes:

[33] J 1.375–376 (letter to Miss Emerson of April 30, 1824).

[34] JMN 2.223 (February 1824).

[35] See JMN 1.145–147 (June 9, 1822).

[36] Crèvecoeur, *Letters*, see particularly the third letter, "What is an American?" pp. 42–43. As a disciple of the physiocrats, Crèvecoeur argues for a connnection between moral degeneration and the abandonment of agriculture for hunting.

> The vast rapidity with which the desarts & forests of the interior of this country are peopled have led patriots to fear lest the nation grow *too fast* for its virtue & its peace. In the raw multitudes who lead the front of emigration men of respectability in mind & morals are rarely found—it is well known. The pioneers are commonly the offscouring of civilized society who have been led to embark in thise enterprizes by the consciousness of ruined fortunes or ruined character or perchance a desire for that greater license which belongs to a new unsettled community.[37]

He does not seek to conceal that the anarchy nurtured to the west threatens the national equilibrium politically, socially, and morally—communication with the frontier is uncertain, and government cannot reliably make its weight felt there. Thence the warning he pronounces in conclusion: if no means is found of imparting the language of reason to these ignorant and dissipated people, America will fail in its mission to reform the world.

The task thus defined is weighty and risky; but it is not accompanied by any moral dilemma. Upon the geographical division between East and West it is easy enough to superimpose a division between good and evil. On Emerson's side and Boston's are arrayed moderation, respect for property, and a taste for the life of the mind; in the other camp are theft, pillage, and general excess. To express the opposition in these terms, to juxtapose the Federalist bourgeoisie and the dregs of the frontier, is at the same time to determine the choice between them. But Emerson is not the sort of man to be satisfied with this sort of simplistic generalization. Without denying his solidarity with the ruling class, he intends to retain his freedom of judgment and to denounce the weaknesses even of his own friends.

In this same spirit of impartiality, a passage of the journal from 1823 undertakes to assess the benefits business confers on the life of the nation.[38] The careful arrangement of the arguments, their oratorical manipulation, the wealth of classical allusions give this text the air of a competent school-essay; but even here one can recognize certain constants of Emersonian thought. Business, Emerson admits, makes the world go round: "it is the Cause, the support & the object of all government"; without business, man would still be prowling in the desert, and society would not have been brought to the degree of refinement and courtesy we see it exhibit. Mandeville, Hume, and more recently Adam Smith had shown business to be based on self-interest, and thus ex-

[37] JMN 2.115 (April 8, 1823).

[38] JMN 2.137–140 (June 1, 1823).

plained its power. But Emerson is quick to distinguish himself from these philosophers and economists of the eighteenth century. Refusing to consider what is of most general benefit as being also of greatest benefit, he shows that the favor business enjoys rests on needs that all men hold in common. Through business, therefore, there is effected what one might call a reduction to the least common denominator; and the costs of this process are paid by art and literature: "the Scholar is quickly taught the unwelcome conviction, that, his studies are the later luxuries, which the world can easily forego; whilst it cannot spare its meat & its drink & the interests of *traffic*, which he holds in contempt." We see merchants amassing new riches far beyond their personal needs. At the beginning of their careers, they promise, once they have made their families safe from want, to serve the muses; but in the end, the game of business will not let them go. They are thus their own dupes, and they illustrate a grave imperfection of the human mind, the "universal misapprehension of the means for the end." Whole nations are guilty of the same fault; Phoenicia, Greece, and Rome established colonies with the sole end of extending their trade; and in general, with a few spectacular exceptions (among them the quest of the Pilgrims), history is marked by this moral failing from beginning to end. Emerson's judgment here is ambitious and absolute; but it already suggests forcefully the fundamental dualism that the distinction between understanding and reason, borrowed from Coleridge, will enable him to systematize and to establish at the center of his thought.

Perhaps it is in the same perspective—that of a debate between our ideal needs and the données of our experience—that one ought to read the pages Emerson devoted somewhat earlier to the question of slavery.[39] In an article carefully retracing the path he took before his public espousal of abolitionism, Marjory Moody minimizes the importance of these first reflections, in which she sees "a literary experiment more than a commentary upon a moral issue."[40] That Emerson chiefly intended to write elegant prose is undeniable; his account of slave hunting in the African forest was the product of an artificially stimulated imagination, and indignation (if there was any) was dissolved in the heat of rhetoric. Moreover, during the first quarter of the nineteenth century the problem generally did not seem so ominous. In the South, Virginia was to remain the politically preeminent state for some years, and it was widely remembered that Washington and Jefferson had both freed their

[39] See JMN 2.41–44, 48–49, 57–58 (November 1822). The question seems to have occupied Emerson's thought more or less continuously for about ten days.

[40] Marjory M. Moody, "The Evolution of Emerson as an Abolitionist," AL 17 (March 1945), p. 1.

slaves. Even in the Carolinas the institution was not as vital as it was to become later, as is clear from the fact that a federal law banning the importation of slaves was adopted in 1808 without serious opposition. In the North, there was little feeling of apprehension at the extension of a system opposed to northern political principles; the crisis provoked by the admission of Missouri to the Union had been managed without violence, and few men were clairvoyant enough to fear with Jefferson and John Quincy Adams that the settlement of the dispute provided by the Compromise of 1820 might not last.

The questions Emerson puts to himself and to his aunt Mary[41] in 1822 are metaphysical in nature; close by or at a distance they touch on providence and the question of evil. How can one reconcile the existence of slavery with the infinite goodness of God? What is one to think about the spiritual fate of these thousands of beings who live and die in brute ignorance? And above all, is man still, and always, and everywhere made in the image of his creator? Emerson lingers over this expression, which mechanical repetition has made habitual; he seeks "to aid our faith by freer speculation"[42] so as to see its implications more clearly. He observes that not only do historical period, family, country, and fortune establish a hierarchy among men; nature herself, making Europeans here, Tartars or Moors there, "has plainly assigned different degrees of intellect to these different races, and the barriers between are insurmountable."[43] She thus indicates her wish to see some command and others obey, just as she has ordained that the dog and the horse be subservient to man. At this point in his argument, Emerson must ask what are the distinctive qualities of human nature; but he finds that they all dissolve under analysis, beginning with that quality generally held fundamental, the faculty of reason:

> I saw ten, twenty, a hundred large lipped, lowbrowed black men in the streets who, except in the mere matter of language, did not exceed the sagacity of the elephant. Now is it true that these were created superior to this wise animal, and designed to controul it? And in comparison with the highest orders of men, the Africans will stand so low as to make the difference which subsists between themselves & the sagacious beasts inconsiderable.[44]

From there to considering them "an upper order of inferior animals," classified as human by "mere name & prejudice," there is only a small

[41] See the letter of October 16, 1823 (L 1.137–138).

[42] JMN 2.42 (November 8, 1822).

[43] JMN 2.43 (November 8, 1822).

[44] JMN 2.48.

step—and Emerson, grounded on his faith in his own individual experience, seems ready to take it.

But he does not. When he has pursued this "revolting" subject to its limits, when he has agreed that for many slaves happiness is obedience, he "knocks down the hydra" in a few sentences as if exorcising a nightmare: "No ingenious sophistry can ever reconcile the unperverted mind to the pardon of *Slavery*; nothing but tremendous familiarity, and the bias of private *interest*."[45] Raising the discussion to a more philosophical level, Emerson sets the advocate of slavery in a dilemma he believes insoluble: either God created us free, and it is monstrous that we should rob our fellows of their freedom; or he has submitted the United States to an arbitrary law, and it is not our part to make ouselves the accomplices of this "inhuman barbarity." But despite its air of logical precision, the argument is not entirely convincing: what is one to think of a Supreme Being that we are not in all circumstances to take as a perfect model? The violent jealousy of the Puritan God had implied in the zealous Puritan mind a sense of mystery, a humility before God's inscrutable ways, that Emerson's generation had lost. Behind the peremptory tone, then, there remains a pang of anxiety; the discontinuity thus revealed between metaphysical principle and lived experience is not to be terminated by syllogisms; one day the debate will have to be resumed and settled.

Moreover, had not Emerson learned long since, and at first hand, that inequality is an iron law to which all bend? At Harvard he had felt the fascination of his two southern classmates, and in particular that of the more gifted of the two, Robert Barnwell of Carolina, whom he praised in his journal for the loftiness of his oratorical imagery.[46] The dazzling impression made on him by these two young aristocrats survived the vicissitudes of his career. In April 1822, he wrote to one of them,[47] who had in the meantime returned to Charleston, to propose a correspondence. He is weary, he explains, of his condition; he needs to enlarge his horizons, and nothing would please him better than to know more of his correspondent's occupations and feelings:

> If it were necessary to say more, I might add that the peculiar & striking distinctions which we see at Cambridge separating our Northern & Southern Countrymen have always urged my curiosity to inquiries somewhat deeper and more general than common

[45] JMN 2.57 (November 14, 1822).

[46] JMN 1.38–39 (October 15, 1820).

[47] L 1.108–109. As Rusk's note explains, the identity of the addressee is not certain.

> conversation allows; and I should be glad of any hints upon your manner of education which may occur to you.

It is all very well for Emerson to affect at other moments an ironic posture toward southerners and to mock their bluster;[48] it is only too clear that he envies them. Have they not received at birth, as if from fairies, all the qualities that he lacks and despairs of ever acquiring, despite his stubborn efforts? His stay in Florida, four years later, confirmed his impression of natural elegance casually displayed; even the blacks clothed in rags greet one another in the street with the same "graduated advances of salutation" that one commonly sees in Boston at the meeting of well-bred strangers.[49]

Inevitably inferior in manners and lacking in presence—that is, in a certain felicity of carriage founded on innate physical qualities—Emerson nonetheless does not consign himself to mediocrity. Nature has made a hierarchy of races and, within races, of individuals, according to mysterious laws; and the world of minds is ordered in similar fashion, by a particular law of gravity that all men can acknowledge:

> Every man who enumerates the catalogue of his acquaintance is privately conscious, however reluctant to confess the superiority, of a certain number of minds which do outrun & command his own, in whose company, despite the laws of good breeding & the fences of affectation his own spirit bows like the brothers' sheaves to Joseph's sheaf. . . . He remembers also other some of his companions, over whom his own spirit exercises the same mastery.[50]

Here, inside that invisible universe, Emerson feels at home. It is not that the greatness he has dreamed of since his days at Harvard seems suddenly more accessible; his recent experiences rather persuade him of the contrary. But he knows there is only one path by which he can hope to find that greatness; and by the patient work of reflection and explo-

[48] For example, in a letter to his fellow student John Boynton Hill, like Emerson a native of New England but then residing in Baltimore, where he was teaching: "What kind of people are the Southerners in your vicinity? Have they legs & eyes? Do they walk and eat? You know our idea of an accomplished Southerner—to wit—as ignorant as a bear, as irascible & nettled as any porcupine, as polite as a troubadour, & a very John Randolph in character & address"(L 1.107 [March 12, 1822]).

[49] JMN 3.59 (December 1826). It is significant that Charles Emerson expressed a similar admiration for the blacks he saw in Puerto Rico: "They do not look poor & blasted as in our cold latitude but strut about the streets like the kings & queens of the land" (JMN 6.279). Charles jocularly announces his intention to introduce into the girls' schools of Boston a gymnastic exercise inspired by the sight of the island's poor: carrying a heavy weight on one's head, so as to learn to walk gracefully.

[50] JMN 2.68 (November 30, 1822).

ration of which his journals are the record, he closes off the paths that lead nowhere, then, divided between fear and enthusiasm, betakes himself to the one road still open.

He first attacks history, to strip it of a prestige he thinks it has usurped. The French Revolution, favorite target of his Federalist friends, serves his purposes best.[51] In the violence and pillage to which that revolution ultimately boiled down Emerson sees neither direction nor thought; rather the mob simply indulged its appetite for chaos, and some bold and brazen men exploited the situation afterward. But there is no meaning to be found in the work of chance: "the only connexion in these events was mere succession." It was the historians full of wise sayings who, when the fray was finally over, introduced order into chaos and went off to find the missing cause in the "profligate splendour of a king long dead." And all the world followed them, persuading itself that "with as imbecile a monarch & ill-advised a ministry Lord George Gordon's mob or Jack Cade's mob or Mr Cobbett's mobs might effect as bloody wonders in free & enlightened London."[52] Such naïveté conjoined to such skepticism provokes Emerson's amused irony: "but nevertheless the history is much farce." It is in the same commonsensical frame of mind that he refuses to attribute any magical value to the political system of a state, though the state be America and its charter the Constitution of 1787. Posing the problem of the relative influence of men and institutions,[53] he resolves it in favor of men. He is aware that if he gave preeminence to systems he would have to admit that they shape human character and accept the "repugnant consequences"—that is, the necessity of acknowledging unqualified determinism. Institutions are "but a paper fabric," and their principal merit is efficiency: they permit the transmission from one generation to another of certain "modes of feeling" and consolidate the lessons of experience. But their function is chiefly negative (they are conceived less to stimulate good than to obstruct evil); and in addition they are always in danger of being perverted—as was the case in France, where a government founded on notions of liberty and equality ended in notorious excesses.[54] What

[51] Cf. JMN 2.199–200 (January 1824).

[52] Ibid. The allusion is to the famous Gordon Riots, set off in 1780 by a statute that eased legal restrictions on Catholics. Jack Cade is the half-legendary figure who led a rebellion in County Kent in 1450. Cobbett had in 1802 founded *The Political Register*, which became the most vital organ of English radicalism.

[53] See JMN 2.209–210 (January–February 1824).

[54] "We must seek instructors therefore not only among the wise & fortunate legislators who settled N. England in 1620, but also among the bloody demagogues of the French Convention. For before the trial of their respective constitutions, the Scheme which completely failed

makes institutions function properly lies within each of us. Emerson notes in passing his distrust of those who proclaim their patriotism to the four winds; he is not sure that they always have hearts as pure or hands as clean as they would have one believe.[55] The best citizens do not abandon themselves to these showy demonstrations because their idea of what they owe their country is of a different nature: "I have sometimes thought the election an individual makes between right & wrong more important than his choice between rival statesmen," he notes ironically. Nor does this judgment err on the side of idealism; rather it is founded on the world as it is: "Your soul will last longer than the ship; & will value its just philosophical associations long after the memory has spurned all obtrusive & burdensome contents."

Thus by exercising that law of compensation the ubiquitous effects of which he has already described,[56] Emerson can find the obscurity of his condition useful in affirming his mental independence. The age has not spoiled him, and so he escapes its crazes. And as he does not see in the America of his time the realization here and now of the perfection of nationhood, neither does he accept a belief in the unlimited and inevitable progress of humanity. The young man of twenty observes the play of history with an absence of illusions worthy of Ecclesiastes. The preachers of his time, he remarks, repeat the exhortations of the ancient moralists with equal futility; suffering and sickness remain pretty much what they were; all the passions are still in flame; joy does not last.[57] The names that mark the course of the centuries illustrate, with a few variations due to transient circumstances, the unchanging substratum of human nature: "the history of nations is but the history of private Virtues & Vices collected in a more splendid field, a wider sky."[58] Indeed, he suggests, the student of psychological nuance will find more satisfaction in investigating the private life of a people than in following the vicissitudes of its public destiny—because the great political passions are the same everywhere, while private life, fashioned of diverse customs, offers a rich variety of feelings and beliefs.

One could hardly turn away from the ambition of making a great career more decisively;[59] but in Emerson the movement is not, indeed is

---

in France was infinitely the most alluring of the two to popular imagination" (JMN 2.215 [February 1824]).

55 JMN 2.302–303 (December 10, 1824).

56 See JMN 2.116–117 (1823).

57 See JMN 2.188 (December 14, 1823).

58 JMN 2.94 (1823). See also JMN 2.376–378 ("Priestcraft").

59 It is worth quoting a remark Emerson transcribed in his journal about this time; he does not name its author, but he found it striking and copied it twice: "Political distinction is like

far from being, a gesture of resignation. In March 1823, he reminds himself that the question of what place he is to occupy in the innumerable assembly of men cannot leave him indifferent.[60] Rather, haunted by his sense of the disparity of destinies, he attempts to make that disparity his opportunity and point of departure. He accepts the existence of aristocracy; indeed, with all due deference to those who judge otherwise,[61] he rejoices in it—but on the condition that every ambiguity inhering in the lofty word be removed, because for him it does not mean the retinue of the powerful. It refers to something less obtrusive and more lasting. He portray those who make up the aristocracy, and whose authority—whose spiritual authority, that is—extends far beyond their own lifetimes, as follows:

> Temperate unassuming men, they have conformed to the fashions of the times in which they fell, without effort or contempt. God, in their minds, removed the ancient landmarks of thought, or else gave them strength to overleap the boundary, so that they took in a mightier vision of the state of man than their fellows had done. In all this they did not see *differently* from them, but saw *beyond* the common limit. Accordingly it was no part of their pride to be at discord with men upon common matters of everyday's observation. Upon trifles of time & sense they all thought alike. Deeper thoughts & remote consequences, far beyond the ken of vulgar judgements and yet intimately connected with the progress & destinies of society were the points they fixed their eyes upon; and upon the distinctness with which they were able to detect these, they chiefly valued themselves.[62]

These lines are not only the homage of a pious mind. They outline a program, and those familiar with Emerson's work will hear in them a prophetic echo. Emerson does not, to be sure, think that greatness ought to be striven for in a spirit of provocation, but neither does he see it as nourished only on humility, achieved only, as his ancestral religion taught, in a paradoxical self-abasement. The moral universe he thinks about is not the universe of Christianity, defined and sustained by the

the pyramids where none can hope to reach the top but eagles or reptiles" (JMN 6.42 and 193).

[60] See JMN 2.111–113 (March 23, 1823).

[61] "Aristocracy is a good sign. Aristocracy has been the hue & cry in every community where there has been anything good, any society worth associating with, since men met in cities. It must be every where. 'Twere the greatest calamity to have it abolished" (JMN 2.202 [January 1824]).

[62] JMN 2.100 (March 12, 1823). The italics are Emerson's.

presence of the Christ. We are referred not so much to Jesus as to the ancient sages, to Prometheus and, indeed, to Lucifer. Ethical values closed in upon themselves do not interest him any more than does the jostling intimacy of relations with other men and women. He is enraptured with exploration, with mental discovery; he wants, with all the risks that this vocation entails (and all the glories), to be an adventurer of the mind. That is why he disdains the mass of men: not in virtue of distinctions of birth, but because the mass is incurably conformist:

> Thus a whole community go to church; acquiesce in the existence of a certain law, or in the government of a certain ruler while, if their hearts were all read, it might appear that these institutions had but a few strong favourers, & that, for the rest, each man leaned on his neighbor; nay, a critical inquiry should make it plain that the majority of opinions rebelled in secret against the custom complied with, but that doubts were too shadowy & unformed to venture to challenge an old established mode.[63]

Suppose, Emerson continues, one traces the political, religious, and philosophical ideas of a particular moment to their sources. Inevitably one will see that they are the product of three or four superior minds. From such minds others borrow the modes of thinking upon which, whether consciously or unconsciously, their actions later depend. The true masters of humanity are thus much less numerous and more powerful than the mass admits—"the kingdom of thought is a proud aristocracy," he notes in concluding, as if he himself were already sure of access.[64] And perhaps one needs to recapture something of the poet's exaltation to read without tedium, despite their conventional rhetoric and rigid prosody, the youthful verses in which Emerson proclaimed his loftiest pride:

> I wear no badge; no tinsel star
> Glitters upon my breast;
> Nor jewelled crown nor victor's car
> Rob me of my rest.
>
> I am not poor, but I am proud
> Of one inalienable right,
> Above the envy of the crowd—
> Thought's holy light.

[63] JMN 2.206 (1824).
[64] Ibid.

Better it is than gems or gold
And oh! it cannot die,
But thought will glow when the sun grows cold,
And mix with Deity.[65]

Unfortunately, just as was the case during his time at Harvard, Emerson's recognition of the desired end did not create the means of attaining it. Like novice mountaineers whom the sight of the peak they are to scale seems to rob of the use of their legs, Emerson has no sooner affirmed his ambition than he sees obstacles press about him, numerous and insurmountable. The most disturbing is his own laziness, "that slothful sensual indulgence" that cuts short every surge of energy.[66] At frequent intervals in the pages of his journal he rejects the convenient excuses—fate, the times—by which sometimes he seeks to veil his inactivity. He is irritated by the stargazing quality of his life, which he thinks is only a form of cowardice, born of the habit of defeat.[67] These charges seem so extreme that most critics from Cabot to Whicher have seen in them the indication of considerable mental disturbance. Refusing by temperament as much as by education to transfer the responsibility for his failures to some scapegoat, Emerson is led to make himself appear worse than he is. He calls himself weak, giddy, hedonistic; he claims to be incapable of answering the appeal of his better nature. But this frenzy of denigration deceives only Emerson. The very ardor he displays in accusing himself attests to qualities opposed to those he purports to describe; and in general we feel more compassion than disdain for the young man misled by his own loftiness of character.

We learn thus to interpret certain of the journal's confessions; and if here and there such flagellation seems dangerous to mental stability, the next page provides reassurance. As soon as Emerson is delivered from the torments of introspection, his boldness and confidence return at once, sturdier than ever. He must defend at all costs the integrity he has glimpsed against the encroachments of society; and the danger is great. Fear, "this palsied leprous principle"[68] that shares the domination of the world with love, is his sworn enemy; it is fear that maintains "the con-

[65] MS. H.136, "Poetry," reproduced with minor variations in JMN 2.196 (December 31, 1823).

[66] JMN 2.112 (March 23, 1823).

[67] See particularly JMN 2.153–155, 168, 244–246. Emerson's bad conscience is most freely expressed in a sentence of the journal written in September 1823: "We should be shocked at any formal resignation in words of our hopes of activity in life, while our abominable listlessness amounts to the same" (JMN 2.154–155).

[68] JMN 2.169–170 (December 1823).

ventions, as they are called, of civilized life, the artificial order & conversation of society." The critique being made here is far-reaching; it touches on all the powers by which the world is run, and in particular on the ruling class of Boston, more set on good manners than enraptured with truth. Emerson sees these implications, and tries to restore things to their proper perspective: "I would not be understood to cast imputation on good-breeding. In the human throng it is certainly a convenient, perhaps a necessary thing; and its absence could not be borne. But in the higher connexions of which I speak—it is to be treated *merely* as a convenient thing, and when it pretends to higher claims it is to be treated with contempt."[69] He establishes here an unconditionally distinct division between two orders, in Pascal's sense of the term. He intends henceforth to consolidate that division; he needs to establish his independence of mind, that token of all progress toward what he is already defining, in the same paragraph, as "the ripe excellence of . . . being."

Emerson's sense of his intrinsic dignity, founded on the direct relation between him and his creator, thus becomes the cornerstone of his philosophy. We can hold our head high before men even while avowing our ignorance and poverty because our intellectual and moral characteristics have been given to us by God: and it is from God also that we possess an immortal destiny, exempt in all circumstances from the will and authority of our fellows.[70] Conversely, when we diffuse smiles and praises, our faces set in admiration and our conscience ill at ease, we abase ourselves; we forget that the respect due to the creator forbids us these extreme marks of deference to any creature. Brooding over this inward greatness and the almost daily betrayals we inflict upon it, as if an irresistible force sought to strip us of our best selves, Emerson is possessed by a sort of holy anger and proclaims the splendor of his isolation with a fervor prophetic of "Self-Reliance":

> Who is he that shall controul me? Why may not I act & speak & write & think with entire freedom? What am I to the Universe, or, the Universe, what is it to me? Who hath forged the chains of Wrong & Right, of Opinion & Custom? And must I wear them? Is Society my anointed King? Or is there any mightier community or any man or more than man, whose slave I am? I am solitary in the vast society of beings; I consort with no species; I indulge no sympathies. I see the world, human, brute & inanimate nature; I am in the midst of them, but not *of* them; . . . I see cities & nations & wit-

[69] Ibid.; the italics are Emerson's.

[70] See JMN 2.192 (December 14, 1823).

> ness passions,—the roar of their laughter,—but I partake it not;—the yell of their grief,—it touches no chord in me.[71]

This purple passage has to be read as a manifesto, whose excesses are intended to throw a fierce light on certain principles often misunderstood by the author himself.[72] Emerson seeks to arrest the deadly movement by which we are all led away from ourselves, thrown into the social whirlwind, and in the end reduced to the state of onlookers. We behave like servants, he seems to be saying, though by inheritance we are masters. But at any moment we can take hold of ourselves, assert our rights, deny the obligations by which it was claimed we were bound. And once restored to ourselves by this act of independence, we can if we like turn our face again toward others, free to reclaim our freedom when circumstances seem to us to necessitate it.

The abundant comments on friendship in the journal of this period—though they do not always make clear whether the author is thinking of anyone in particular—offer an approximate echo of this argument. Emerson remains attracted by the thought of that mysterious current which passes between certain beings and which has been given the name of sympathy. He compares it with phenomena of polarity observed in the material universe; but the encounter of two minds, with the stimulus resulting from the almost spontaneous harmony of their modes of thought, seems to him still more fascinating.[73] Friendship is precisely the consolidation of that special experience. It introduces man into a new universe, in which his nature can bloom without constraint because it is sure of expressing the deep desire of the other. Through friendship we discover the paradoxical bond between liberty and solidarity because, to the degree that we give free rein to our inclinations and ignore the opinion of society, we are understood and loved. Neither does this noble feeling satisfy only our mental part; it is charged by delicious agitation, it changes tonality, it threatens to die and is then rekindled more brightly; in short, it lives like a passion. "Friendship," writes Emerson with adolescent intensity,

> is the sole romantic thing in life, that remains romantic. All childhood's poetry of hope & love, all youth's poetry of love fades after a brief bloom; but the delight of man's mind in man, the pleasing expectation & memory of his society as well as its present excitement,

[71] JMN 2.189–190 (December 21, 1823).

[72] At the bottom of the page Emerson afterward wrote the word "Pride," suggesting the extremity of the feeling expressed there. See the facsimile in JMN 2.352.

[73] See JMN 2.152–153 (September 6, 1823).

the ups & downs, the caprices of friendship do not fade, for aught I know ever.[74]

Who after reading this soaring bit of lyricism would not suppose that Emerson was repenting, that his desire for solitude was yielding to the powerful and insidious attacks of friendship? But this would be to leave out of account perhaps the most central trait of his character, which one might describe as reticence or modesty of soul. It is repugnant to him to show himself in undress to any other human being; not everything in us is noble, and no friendship can bear the revelation of our pettinesses: "He that loosely forgets himself here & lets his friend be privy to the words & acts which base desires extort from him has forfeited like a fool the love he prized. The waters of affection will soon dry up or disgust will flow in their place."[75] Behind a concern with decorum and inner dignity, Emerson reveals indirectly another feeling, and one not far from harshness; he expects no indulgence for his weaknesses and is not inclined to accord indulgence to the weaknesses of others. Friendship in certain respects is analogous to the knightly duel; if one of the partners reveals a weakness, the other may properly thrust at it: "your friend, if he has uprightly disdained to become the accomplice of your vileness, possesses a cruel advantage over you. . . . He may expose to the whisper & the scoff of society the secret guilt that lowers you in the scale of moral beings."[76] If friendship risks losing one "the richest treasure God imparts to intelligent creatures—[one's] own self-respect," then it is behavior of a higher order of virtue to preserve a perfect mastery of one's feelings, as Emerson invites one to do, and to temper "the indiscreet ardor of [one's] attachments."[77] Doing so will spare one "bitter lees."

But is it still friendship that is at issue here? Is it possible to found friendship upon reserve without distorting it, without perhaps even doing ourselves harm? Emerson was at this time reading Bacon's *Essays*[78] and had probably encountered the passage in which Bacon, citing Philippe de Comines, recalls the pernicious effect exercised on the powers of Charles the Bold, during the last years of his life, by his refusal to open himself to another being, to share his deepest apprehensions with either friends or counselors.[79] But all concern with mental

[74] JMN 2.198 (January 5, 1824).

[75] JMN 2.204 (January 1824).

[76] Ibid.

[77] JMN 2.227–228 (March 1, 1824).

[78] Cf. Rusk, *Life*, p. 99.

[79] See Essay 27, "Of Friendship" (London, 1909), pp. 82–83. The name of Philippe de Comines appears in a list of legenda Emerson made in 1825 (J 2.68).

health apart, Emerson's concept of human relations seems singularly dry and poor. He cannot imagine in another being that generosity which permits a feeling like love or friendship to survive clarity of perception. Saint-Exupéry's anguished question, "What shall I make of a friend who judges me?"[80] would have seemed to him not only indecorous in its self-complacency but also absurd and self-contradictory. For Emerson, friendship presupposes judgment, and he tells us that he could not bestow his friendship upon a grumbler, or a chatterer, or, a fortiori, upon a "plebeian," who would exhaust him with empty commonplaces.[81]

That so lofty a rigor is likely to make its possessor ill at ease, to create unrest and resistance in him and in others as well, seems confirmed by the journals and letters of the period. Emerson maintains his positions, not without courage, and reiterates on every occcasion the unaltered purity of his ideal; but would he have been compelled to such edgy repetition if he had touched, as he could and did on other occasions, the chords of sympathy in another human being? Even in this first debate the sincere elevation of the tone cannot mask a secret and essential coldness. The obsession with his obligations to himself shackles every spontaneous movement, every gesture of trust; it compels him to turn in upon himself, into a sort of inward empyrean, the boundaries of which are not to be crossed by any living breath. In the celebrated self-examination of 1824, Emerson confesses his awkwardness in the company of men and women; indeed he draws from it an argument for his unfitness to be a lawyer or doctor.[82] He might have vetoed all the other professions as well; he was calling into question, perhaps without wishing to, the whole principle of human association.

But while he waits, nature offers some amends to his frustrated and secretly wounded sensibility. In 1822, returning from the excursion that had revealed to him not only his compatriots' warmth but also their intolerable vulgarity, he notes that "upon a mountain-solitude a man instantly feels a sensible exaltation and a better claim to his rights in the universe."[83] The following year, his mother moved into Roxbury, then a rural suburb of Boston. The long shadows of the trees, the sunsets, the moonlit nights offered to Emerson's body and soul together a feeling of blissful tranquility and, as it were, of expansion: "there is an excellence in Nature which familiarity never blunts the sense of—a serene superiority to man & his art in the thought of which man dwindles to pigmy

[80] In *Lettre à un otage* (Paris, 1944), p. 69.

[81] JMN 2.199 (January 5, 1824).

[82] See JMN 2.237–242, and infra, chapter 4.

[83] JMN 1.138 (June 9, 1822).

proportions."[84] And it is precisely this same simple, almost silly pleasure that the knowing reader discerns behind the studied, Byronic cadences of "Good-Bye, proud world."[85] With all business put away, the young man stretches out beneath the pines and lives "in the warm day like corn and melons."[86]

There is a certain irony in concluding an examination of these four years, during which Emerson's deliberations on nature and on human destiny lack neither amplitude nor anxious intensity, with this image of the young teacher playing hooky. But looked at more closely, such a conclusion is no accident. The young Emerson submitted himself to relentless interrogation in answer to a sort of inward imperative; he had in his blood a voracious appetite for introspection. In addition, in the troubled confusion with which he was struggling—isolated from his peers and without a future, unreceptive to the prejudices of his class and doubtful of its doctrines—he needed, day after day and problem after problem, to test and experience the fundamental data of his condition. Thence comes this incessant confrontation with history, with the economic and political forces of his country, with slavery, "the special enigma of the time," as he was later to call it.[87] But the debate is carried on with a surprising independence of spirit, some evidently derivative passages notwithstanding. Emerson at this time was not under the spell of any one philosophy; he had as yet discovered neither Sampson Reed nor Coleridge; he did not know of de Gérando's valuable work on the history of philosophy; and even of Plato he had as yet read only scattered passages of the dialogues.[88] It is thus impossible without strained ingenuity to reduce the notes scattered through the journals and letters to two or three key notions. Indifferent to building a system, seeking only

[84] Letter to John Boynton Hill of June 19 and July 2, 1823 (L 1.133–134). With the passage of time, the affection nature inspires in Emerson will as if in compensation only be strengthened. In 1838, he writes in his journal that "trees look . . . like imperfect men. It is the same soul that makes me, which, by a feebler effort arrives at these graceful portraits of life. I think we all feel so. I think we all feel a certain pity in beholding a tree: rooted there, the would-be-Man is beautiful, but patient & helpless. His boughs & long leaves droop & weep his strait imprisonment" (JMN 7.42).

[85] Cf. W 9.3–4 and K. B. Taft, "The Byronic Background of Emerson's Good-bye," NEQ 27 (December 1954), pp. 525–526.

[86] *Nature*, W 1.59. One of Emerson's first critics, Francis Bowen, found the comparison shocking; cf. F. O. Matthiessen, *American Renaissance: Art and Expression in the Age of Emerson and Whitman* (1941, repr. New York, 1968), pp. 38–39.

[87] See his editorial in the *Massachusetts Quarterly Review*, December 1847 (W 11.390–391).

[88] Kenneth Cameron's already cited *Emerson the Essayist* is admirably full and thorough on the question of Emerson's reading during these formative years; my information on the subject has been derived from this source.

to know at each moment where truth is, Emerson inspects the evidence in his case with all the honesty and diligence he can muster.

That this inspection should with all its good intentions betray the preferences and, so to speak, the lines of force of Emerson's personality will astonish only the dogmatic. A complex being is gradually forming: curious, even anxious, proud of its intellectual quality, nobly ambitious, and yet also, despite a longing for friendship, uneasy among men and women, humble and yet lofty. It was this misfit who ran off to play hooky, one sulky day. But the time for the great escapade had not yet come; Emerson must first pass by way of the Divinity School.

4

~ ~ ~ ~

THE MINISTRY, OR, AN ATTEMPT AT THE SAFE MIDDLE WAY

ON FEBRUARY 11, 1825, Emerson registered at the Harvard Divinity School. Five days later, the theological faculty accepted him as a second-year student.[1] By this double ceremony Emerson's career among men seemed fixed, and fixed in the most docile and conservative manner possible. The young man was adding a link to the chain of ministers who in the past had given his name a more than common luster; and in choosing Harvard (he had for a time thought of the Andover Seminary, the new bastion of orthodox Calvinism), he indicated clearly that he was ready to go with the current in the Boston of Everett and Channing. Is one to see in that decision, as one of Emerson's biographers has suggested, the expression of an instinctive conformity, manifested whenever Emerson had to pass from theory to practice, that is, whenever there arose the problem of his integration into the world of men?[2] The journal reveals so much deliberation in Emerson's preparations for this step that we cannot accept the suggestion unreservedly; but the gap between thought and act is striking and deserves some examination.

[1] Rusk, *Life*, pp. 110–111.

[2] "It must be clearly realized that in questions of machinery, of the *modus operandi* of society and civilization, Emerson's temper was essentially conservative; his instinct was to grasp the approved tool, the existent mechanism" (Oscar W. Firkins, *Ralph Waldo Emerson* [Boston, 1915], p. 22).

If one follows as we have done the thread of Emerson's youthful meditations, it is impossible not to feel a growing respect for the audacity and independence they reveal. Emerson submits not only the past but also the present, not only his southern compatriots but also his Federalist friends, to an exacting and lucid critique. In particular, the language he applies to his friends is so vigorously incisive that we wonder how he can continue to be their agent. But of course he writes with such resolution because he writes for himself. His journal is a surrogate world in which he is able to forget a career of mediocrity; and soon, with habit reinforcing temperament, he comes to prefer this world of his books to any other because books bring him the joy of almost perfect intellectual communication, while the limits of human nature give to the intercourse of society a disagreeable and disappointing aftertaste.[3] But though attractive to so sensitive a mind, such an orientation entailed considerable risks; it cut Emerson gradually off from the land of the living, to whom, he knew, he was bound;[4] it led him to take refuge in himself for better but also for worse. At this stage his Yankee common sense comes into play; something within warns him of the danger and hints at a possible defense. During the whole trial of his time as schoolteacher, he had so dreamed of an elevated friendship as to condemn himself to perpetual solitude; but he had also longed to make himself a place in the world, and he was now convinced that the church offered him his best chance. Coming from so alert an intelligence, such a conclusion is troubling. Biographers have emphasized by contrast the attitude of Ralph Waldo's brother William, whom the ministry had tempted but who in his scruples had turned away from it.[5] Is one to suppose Ralph Waldo's conscience was more accommodating? An examination of the journals clears it of such suspicion, and at the same time illuminates the deep motives for his choice.

It was in April 1824, almost a year before his entry into the Divinity School, that he solemnly recorded his decision to dedicate his time, his talents, and his hopes to the church.[6] In the five pages that follow, with an often dramatic intensity, he undertakes to assess himself, to measure his chances for success. But his meditation is not exclusively introspec-

[3] Cf. JMN 2.399 (October 1824). Along the same line, Emerson later urges his brother Charles to distrust conversations, which "politeness ruins," and to seek the true image of the soul in the work of the pen (L 1.191 [February 23, 1827]).

[4] In a passage of the journal for 1825, Emerson expresses his impatience at hearing his aunt Mary's constant praise of their ancestors: "the dead sleep in their moonless night; my business is with the living" (JMN 2.316).

[5] For example, Firkins, *Emerson*, pp. 21–22.

[6] See JMN 2.237 (April 18, 1824).

tive; it reveals also what idea he has of the ministry, its nature and obligations. The obstacle one might have supposed most formidable, namely that resulting from Unitarianism's doctrinal vagueness, is disposed of at one stroke of the pen. In all times, Emerson supposes, theology has been vulnerable to controversy because men's minds are not to be won with syllogisms and subtle distinctions. Where the attributes of divinity are at issue, the highest form of reasoning is the fruit of a sort of "moral imagination," such as appears in the sermons of Channing. Now if Emerson is or holds himself to be a poor logician, in this other area he possesses considerable advantages; and thus he can hope to hold an honorable place among the ministers of New England.

But this skill is not yet the motivation of his choice. To discover it, one must recur to an ambition that burned in Emerson even at Harvard: to become a great orator, dominating and guiding the passions of the multitude. The relevance of this ambition to the ministry is clear. Within his parish (and indeed, thanks to the Unitarian habit of exchanging Sunday pulpits, often outside of it) he will have to awaken men's souls, reclaim erring consciences, arouse the just to action—subtly mixing the disinterested service of God and the pride of being his instrument. And as to his success here he is confident; the dignity of expression and manner inherited from his father, joined to the ardor of his convictions, will guarantee him success even where most men stumble and fall. "In Divinity," he says, curiously, "I hope to thrive."[7]

Besides preaching, Emerson admits an obligation of a social character (he calls it "private influence"): but he does not hide the fact that in this matter he is far more concerned with the spring than with the earth to be watered. Everything, he explains, depends on the "moral worth" of the minister, which determines both his behavior to others and the persuasive force of his speech. He must, therefore, put all his efforts into cultivating it, into learning to govern his instincts and to endure hunger and fatigue, in a word into training himself for virtue as assiduously as do the common run of men when they respond to the demands of their spiritual nature: "the coolest reason," he notes, "cannot censure my choice when I oblige myself *professionally* to a life which all wise men freely & advisedly adopt."[8]

Such a vocation is not essentially different from other vocations. If it admits a concern for charity, it is only secondarily and on the rebound. Emerson does not intend to get mixed up in sectarian debates; he does not imagine that dogmatic scruples will keep him from associating himself with some church, and still less that they will trouble the relations

[7] JMN 2.239. The sentence comes just before the discussion of oratory.

[8] JMN 2.240 (italics Emerson's).

between pastor and congregation. He believes he will serve those entrusted to him insofar as he is virtuous and insofar as his virtue inevitably expresses itself in actions and words. No apostolic mission here. The external world will doubtless perceive the dialogue between God and Emerson's soul, but it will not be urged to take part in it. As he straightforwardly writes at the end of this examination of conscience, he expects above all from the ministry that it will put an end to a disturbing spiritual drift, in which his ambitions and his hope for greatness are gradually being exhausted.[9]

Moreover, he arrived at the Divinity School ready to share, on most subjects, the Unitarian viewpoint. A long "letter to Plato," dating from 1824, shows him convinced of the unhealthy character of Calvinism and risen in revolt against the dogma of the fall.[10] In his eyes there is no rupture between human reason and revelation.[11] That is why in undertaking on occasion the defense of pagan thinkers, who were not all idolators,[12] he refuses to accord miracle and mystery a central place in the divine scheme. Christ did not come to disturb or scandalize but to rescue man from his blindness. Calvinism, he writes one day to his aunt Mary, "sounds like mysticism in the ear of understanding."[13] Still in agreement with the Unitarians, he thinks that the world has much advanced since those barbarous times in which heads were covered with ashes in expectation of Armageddon; but also like the Unitarians he regrets that a weakening or even a disappearance of the religious sentiment should have accompanied the march of progress: he criticizes the ingratitude of men led astray by success to forget what they owe to God.[14] He takes great pains, however, to uphold the principles underlying the society around him, which seem to him both an homage to providence and a guarantee of virtue: "It is . . . a blessed triumph in the eyes of the Christian to recognize that universal order in the doctrine of the Modern Political Economists that the moral character of a community is mended or relaxed with the greater or less security of property and that on the same security of property Civilization depends."[15]

[9] "My trust is that my profession shall be my regeneration of mind, manners, inward & outward estate" (JMN 2.242).

[10] See JMN 2.246–249, 250–251.

[11] "I hold Reason to be a prior revelation & that they do not contradict each other" (JMN 2.250).

[12] Cf. the letter to Mary Moody Emerson of March 1825 (J 2.63–66 and L 1.162).

[13] See the letter of December 17, 1824 (J 2.32–33).

[14] "I mourn at the scepticism of prosperity, the scepticism of knowledge, the darkness of light" (JMN 2.318–320 [January 1825]).

[15] JMN 2.288 (November 1824). In 1827 this passage is incorporated into a sermon for Thanksgiving Day (sermon 12, "Gratitude").

And is this not to issue America—or at least New England—a certificate of good conduct and good character? And what then were New England's ministers to do if not encourage the people to live still more honorably by exhortations judiciously compounded of the useful and the pleasant? Like the London of the previous century, the America of the nineteenth was ripe for the reading of a *Spectator*, in which fashionable faults might be severely censured and virtues persuasively praised.[16] Such a suggestion would clearly have been to the taste of Ralph Waldo's father William, whom the senators of Massachusetts had made their chaplain for his acute understanding of the spirit of the times.[17]

But discouragement was quick to succeed confidence. The steps of the evolution remain obscure because documents for 1825, both journals and letters, are rare. What is clear is that Emerson's return to Cambridge coincided with a sudden decline in his health. Like his brothers, he inherited a delicate constitution that predisposed him to tuberculosis; but his activities had never before been seriously hampered. In March 1825, however, he had to cease all mental work, even reading, under threat of blindness. He fought against his disease for more than a year, and at the same time had to become a schoolteacher once again to uphold his part of the family responsibilities. In the end he was cured; but other trials awaited him. Rheumatism in the hip made walking difficult, then his lungs were attacked; he was obliged to exile himself to the south, to Carolina and Florida, to avoid the rigors of a Boston winter. It was as Van Wyck Brooks says, the time of "the house of Pain";[18] and the melancholy ebb in Emerson's vital forces was accompanied by bitterness at the thought of what might have been but was not to be.

For several years, by an instinctive prudence, Emerson let himself be carried along by the world's current without attempting to control it.[19] As he writes to his aunt Mary in August 1826, he is a spectator of his own existence, accepting by inertia the direction he sees it taking: "In the fall, I propose to be *approbated*, to have the privelege, tho' not at present the purpose, of preaching but at intervals. I do not now find in me any objections to this step. —Tis a queer life, and the only humour

[16] Cf. JMN 2.278–279 (1824). Emerson playfully imagines himself as editor-in-chief.

[17] See Rusk, *Life*, p. 9.

[18] Cf. Van Wyck Brooks, *The Life of Emerson* (New York, 1932), p. 40. "The house of Pain" is Emerson's own phrase in a letter to his aunt Mary (J 2.180 [1827]).

[19] Emerson recognizes in a famous passage of the journal (JMN 3.136–137) that he owes his life to the considerable quantity of "silliness" mixed in with his intellectual nature. See also his letter to William of April 30, 1828: "Clear I am that he who would *act* must *lounge*" (L 1.233–235).

proper to it seems quiet astonishment. Others laugh, weep, sell, or proselyte. I admire."[20] Although he ponders the Old Testament and the Gospels when his health permits him, theology occupies him not at all. He senses certain of the dangers German historical criticism implies for the whole structure of Christianity, he fears that when all the forms have been abolished, decent people will find themselves "confronted with the ghastly reality of things"; but he has no energy to leap to the wall and span the gap, as he would like to do, no energy to defend his cause in battle.[21] In the passive role to which his wavering health had confined him, it seemed to him that individual problems were blurred, that the lines of his personality had lost their edge. For the first time in some years, Emerson ceased to be obsessed with himself and discovered, with a sincerity that may seem naïve, the social nature of man. In 1824, after reading Massillon, he had summed up in his journal the Catholic doctrine of charity: " 'tis no evil accident but an essential part of the system that there should be objects of Charity, —objects for the legitimate exercise of powers & feelings within others."[22] Now he became ready to accord much more to society, to credit it with a determining role, for better and for worse, in individual development: "He would do great injustice to the condition of man who should leave out of the account the immense force derived from his *social* relations by which he is drawn to virtue & to vice. The increased moral obligation which arises from the source of *Society* . . . is a subject of such weighty importance as to deserve our most anxious consideration."[23]

Such an evolution is not, of course, accomplished without resistance. Born, one might say, of Emerson's sickness, it receives from that sickness an equivocal character and provokes, at a level Emerson's consciousness is hardly aware of, a violent and troubled reaction. An interesting illustration of this biological shock is furnished by a letter of Emerson's to his aunt Mary from June 1826. The point of departure is a theory recently expounded by Edward Everett in a Phi Beta Kappa Society Oration.[24] Nurtured on the literature of European Romanti-

[20] Letter to Mary Moody Emerson of August 1, 1826 (L 1.169–171).

[21] Cf. another letter to Mary Moody Emerson (J 2.83–85, 1826). An unpublished and undated sermon ("The Freedom of Enquiry," H.387) explains in similar terms the formidable consequences recent German criticism entails. But fortunately, Emerson concludes, the testimony of the moral sense remains.

[22] JMN 2.401 (1824). The first chapter of R. H. Tawney's *Religion and the Rise of Capitalism* (New York, 1926) contains an excellent analysis of charity's role in medieval economy.

[23] JMN 3.82. The passage was probably written at the time Emerson was preparing the sermon "Setting a Good Example" (sermon 3, preached for the first time in June 1827).

[24] The fraternity was founded in 1776 at the College of William and Mary and subsequently

cism, Everett had argued that men of genius are only the spokesmen of their times, expressing the thoughts of all men with words that all men have forged. Qualified in certain respects, the idea later turned up at the heart of *Representative Men*; but Emerson in 1826 had not yet learned to recognize his own. Something in him was troubled at such a notion; is one not, in making such short work of originality and of individual responsibility, finally in danger of reinforcing the worst herd-instincts of the human race? But his distrust goes further. That generosity of nature which at every stage of creation has multiplied the forms of life in such abundance is felt by him as a personal threat; regretting that men cannot come into the world at long intervals like so many phoenixes, Emerson yields to a sort of intellectual Malthusianism:

> But this fulsome generation, this redundant prodigality of being, whereby they are cast out, clean and unclean, heroes and underlings, by millions, —begets a doubt whether the riches of eternity can be as prodigally spent, and whether such immense resources as each one feels his own capacities crave can be furnished from the storehouses of God to every one of the individuals of these inconceivable numbers of systems of life.[25]

Such a passage betrays not only outrage and indignation but also, and in at least as great a degree, the anguish of a creature attached to existence by the slenderest threads. Luckily, Emerson adds, the spirit can take refuge in its own heaven, in which bankruptcies made by imprudence or error are unknown.

Fatigued by his illness, betrayed by his physical forces, Emerson saw in universal dualism a source of solace. While waiting for that blessed dissolution which will liberate the spiritual principle from its bondage to the body, he contented himself with looking around him, analyzing the world's course calmly and lucidly—even discovering, now that he had renounced any hopes of playing a role in it, a good many new perspectives on it. History's vast procession, with its guides who boast themselves inspired and end by adoring idols, seemed to him of heartbreaking futility.[26] But a lesson emerged that transcends all men and reveals the government of providence: the eternal presence of a system of compensations. Nothing is won without being paid for, and plotters are their own dupes. "The history of retributions is a strange & awful

---

spread to many other colleges and universities; it was to the Cambridge chapter of Phi Beta Kappa that in 1837 Emerson delivered the "American Scholar" lecture.

[25] Letter to Mary Moody Emerson, June 15, 1826 (J 2.102).

[26] See the letter to Mary Moody Emerson of April 6, 1826 (L 1.167–168 and Cabot, *Memoir*, 1.112–114).

story," he notes at the beginning of a long discussion of the subject.[27] Already in 1824, Emerson was remarking that the revolution that liberates twenty thousand half-witted slaves also ruins a throng of decent and honorable masters.[28] Two years later he mused that the price paid for the American Constitution, the best thing in the world after the word of God, has been the gradual disappearance of the Indians, as if the "noble structure" of the Constitution could only be founded on another nation's annihilation.[29] The whole idea seemed to him so important that he dedicated one of his first sermons to it.[30]

But serene and detached as they seek to be, these speculations only contribute further to Emerson's distress. He had exiled himself from the world to escape intolerable pressure, and in exile discovered the still more implacable operations of universal law. The law of solidarity, for example, is written in the deepest depth of our nature; the man who denies it only lets fall on others the weight of his own insolence. There were even moments in which the thought of decisions yet to be taken filled Emerson with a paralyzing fear, because he did not know the meaning they would take on once caught up in the irreversible course of history:

> The best & surest advantages in the world are thought by large numbers of people & on very plausible grounds to be evils. The freedom of thought & action in this country often appears tending to the worst & most malignant results, chaos come again. The expediency of publishing truth is daily denied. The best manner of employing the mind whether in study or invention who will determine even for himself?[31]

But such skepticism is not the dominant note in this period, either in the journal or in the letters. At most it marks the limit of a new awareness. Emerson's mental horizon had been so far broadened that it took some time before he could recognize his former abode in the new pan-

[27] JMN 2.340–346 (1826).

[28] See JMN 2.277.

[29] "Great objects must be purchased by great sacrifices. . . . And it seems to be out of a sort of obedience & acknowledgement of this high and melancholy fate that America has yielded up her vast indigenous family tribe after tribe to the haughty Genius of Civilization who cannot found his noble structure on her shores but at this stern forfeiture of a national existence" (JMN 3.14).

[30] Sermon 4, "Wealth and the Law of Compensation," preached for the first time on June 17, 1827.

[31] JMN 3.102 (February 13, 1828). The date seems to indicate that the paragraph was written when Emerson was preparing the sermon "Improvement of Time" (sermon 15). If so, it seems that Emerson spared his audience the revelation of his inward hesitations.

orama. He had to locate it with respect to elements hitherto not in his field of vision. A letter to his younger brother Edward, probably written late in 1827, vividly suggests the new perspective in which he intended to set himself. The first part of the letter expounds with familiar impetuosity the theme of men's natural inequality: universal education is a delusion, Pericles became first citizen of Athens by "the inward craving of a great intellect," and the wretched day laborers who drag themselves about in the lower depths of society are the victims not of inadequate training but of mediocre talents. Still, Emerson hastens to add, men being after all creatures of reason, capable of foresight and progress, one has to be wary of oversimplification:

> I am no fanatic disciple of Mr Owen; I nourish no predilection for the exploded experiments of New Harmony—I do not adopt the cant of the *pupilage* of *circumstances* Yet I must venture on the repetition of an ancient truism that every man's character depends in great part upon the scope & occasions that have been afforded him for its development.[32]

If the call of the Revolution had not sounded in their neighborhood, would the farmers of Concord ever have suspected the military audacity they were capable of? Emerson grandiloquently concludes that Liberty herself was astonished at the multitude of her sons in arms.

The clearest result of this crisis was probably to prepare Emerson to accept the tasks of his future profession more receptively.[33] He had to assess the quantity of illusion attached to his concept of the ministry at the moment of his choosing it: even by the prestige of oratory, one cannot extricate oneself from the bonds that join us in mutual dependence. Rather it is a question of discovering the "safe middle path,"[34] distant equally from that categorical refusal which would deprive us of valuable advantages and that blind acceptance which is synonymous with capitulation and spiritual death. But if Emerson thus modified his position, he did not recant it. In Florida, Catholicism's puerile and gaudy pomp,

[32] L 1.219–221. The date is uncertain, but Rusk shows that it must fall between 1825 and 1828. New Harmony, Indiana was founded by Robert Owen in 1825, on land purchased from George Rapp's followers.

[33] It is difficult to date the beginning of Emerson's pastoral activity with any precision. In the winter of 1826–1827 he preached a few Sunday sermons in various places. In 1828 he was still refusing to commit himself to any one congregation, but gave a good part of his time to the Second Church of Boston. In 1829 the Second Church invited him to become its official assistant pastor, and thus consecrate an already existing situation. See also Rusk, *Life*, chapters 9 and 10.

[34] JMN 2.338 (1825). Emerson uses the expression "safe middle path" at the beginning of a discussion of solitude versus society.

associated with dubious forms of honesty, only aroused his disdain.[35] Somewhat later he noted disgustedly "the monstrous absurdities" of the North Carolina Methodists, who lowered themselves, under pretense of inspiration, to the level of a pack of howling dogs.[36] The superiority of the Unitarians, in his view, is precisely that they assign to the intelligence the right and indeed the duty of judging the impulses of the sensibility. There are problems in the "science of morals," thorny problems, and it would be gross error to suppose that the ignorant can resolve them by the faint light nature has given them; expert and experienced moral philosophers will clearly do better.[37] The minister is to be the enlightened guide of his sheep; he is to offer them a true doctrine sanctioned by rational theology:

> Understand now, morals do not change but the *science* of morals does advance; men discover truth & relations of which they were before ignorant; therefore, there are discoveries in morals. . . . It is obvious that an hour must arrive in the progress of society, when disputed truths in theology will cease to demand the whole life & genius of ministers in their elucidation but will be admitted on the same footing of acknowledged established facts as are the long contested doctrines of political science at the present day.[38]

Within this solidly orthodox frame, in the Unitarian sense of the term, the minister can be an innovator, because it is his province to adapt the observances of religion to the changing needs of society. Already in 1826 Emerson had confessed himself dissatisfied with public prayer. Men with little common concern would leave their work for a moment to hear a man having still less in common with them pray to God in their name. It is a ritual gesture, he says, respectable no doubt on account of the spiritual associations it conjures up, but bereft of all meaning: "the truth is public prayer is rather the offspring of our notions of what *ought* to be, than of what *is*."[39] Carrying on the debate thus begun, Emerson that same year devoted his first sermon to the theme of

[35] "I went yesterday to the Cathedral, full of great coarse toys, & heard this priest say mass, for his creditors have been indulgent & released him for the present" (JMN 3.116 [1827]).

[36] Cf. JMN 3.115 (March 1, 1827).

[37] See on this matter A. J. Kloeckner, "Intellect and the Moral Sentiment in Emerson's Opinions of 'the meaner kinds' of Men," AL 30 (November 1958), pp. 322–338. Emerson returns often in the sermons to the association between knowledge and virtue; and he urges all his hearers, without respect to distinctions of rank or talent, to cultivate their intelligence so as better to serve God. See in particular sermons 36, "Cultivating the Mind"; 83, "Spiritual Improvement Unlimitable"; and 84, "Acquiring True Knowledge."

[38] JMN 3.61–62 (December 16, 1826).

[39] JMN 3.22–23 (April 12, 1826). The italics are Emerson's.

prayer, and in it invites us all to descend deep within ourselves to find God.[40] For reasons of the same sort he made changes in the repertory of his congregation's hymns, judging some previously in use to be not spiritual enough; another sermon offered him an occasion for explaining these views.[41] But as always it is the preacher who occupies the center of the stage and receives, if need be, the severest criticism; thus in August 1827 some wretched minister, all clay when he ought to have been all "tuneable metal," obstinately hiding beneath conventional formulas the particles of originality that might have awakened his hearers' interest,[42] confirms the somber diagnosis that Emerson had made a few months earlier of the debility, not to say the degeneracy, of the New England clergy as a whole.[43]

In taking up his charge as assistant pastor of the Second Church of Boston on March 15, 1829, Emerson was careful to explain in detail (he devoted two sermons to the subject) his conception of the task before him.[44] He prudently kept silence on the reservations and hesitations explored in the journal. He asserted that the minister in prayer was the voice of his congregation, expressing aloud the requests each member had formulated in secret. He laid weight on his role as mediator in sacramental matters, and gave special treatment to communion, symbol of divine affection. He defined the almost familial relations uniting the minister with his faithful hearers, which attain their highest pitch of intimacy when at the hour of death he can "illuminate with glory the gloom of the chamber of death." And naturally he discussed preaching, which is, when it rises to eloquence, "like the breath of the Almighty moving on the deep." There Emerson was touching on cherished territory and also on the pastoral obligation most threatened by routine; so he noted forcefully his determination not to be bogged down in it: "I shall not be so much afraid of innovation as to scruple about introducing new forms of address, new modes of illustration, and varied allusions into the pulpit, when I believe they can be introduced with advantage." He even announced one of the principal themes of the "American Scholar"; he claimed the right to use in his sermons certain anecdotes of

[40] "Pray Without Ceasing," published in Arthur Cushman McGiffert, Jr., *Young Emerson Speaks* (Boston, 1938), pp. 1–12.

[41] See Rusk, *Life*, p. 140, and also sermon 131: "Hymn-Books," in McGiffert, *Young Emerson Speaks*, pp. 145–150.

[42] See the letter to Mary Moody Emerson of August 24, 1827 (J 2.214–215 and L 1.207).

[43] See J 2.202 (May 8, 1827). Channing, Emerson remarks, is the happy exception to this rule of universal decline.

[44] Sermons 28 and 29 ("The Christian Minister" 1 and 2), printed in McGiffert, *Young Emerson Speaks*, pp. 22–38.

daily life and assured his audience that Christ, if he were speaking to Americans, would speak to them of town planning, steam power, and the printing press.

All the extant records suggest that Emerson was an esteemed minister.[45] Stories were smilingly told of his misadventures, as when he went to visit several Boston families with no other claim on his interest than the accident of bearing the same names as certain of his parishioners; but people found the direct simplicity of his speech attractive. He succeeded very quickly in creating the sense of a direct relation between preacher and audience—an uncommon achievement in the Boston of his day—and he was able to give a sort of tangible reality to moral ideas. Pride and humility, slander and forgiveness (to mention the themes of some of his sermons) took on the solidity of physical objects. This success, won at the outset of his pastoral career, was some compensation, it seemed, for the years of frustration that had prepared him for it. At twenty-six he served one of the most prestigious congregations in Boston; and as the principal minister, who had been ill for some time, was thinking of leaving the church to occupy a chair at the Harvard Divinity School, Emerson could hope soon to replace him. He was in a fair way to become a renowned preacher, to add his name to the great Unitarian line reaching from Buckminster to Everett and Channing. Even earthly success was now his; 1829 was also the year of his marriage to Ellen Tucker, the frail girl he had met eighteen months earlier in New Hampshire. Was so great a sum of happiness not likely to provoke the gods' jealousy and call down nemesis?[46]

Ellen's death in February 1831 was fate's tragic answer. But in a deeper and more secret sense, Emerson's success was threatened by the seed of its destruction he bore within him. Whatever he may have wished, he was not of the same stuff as Everett. The respectful approval of his congregation would never take the place of his conscience; even when he strained to be like them, to find words of brotherly love to speak to them, his attention would remain directed inward, where he knew all judgments could be appealed. Moreover, despite—or perhaps because of—his sincerity, the program he outlines in taking over his

[45] See especially Rusk, *Life*, chapters 10 and 11; Cabot, *Memoir*, volume 1, chapter 4; and Elizabeth Peabody, "Emerson as a Preacher," in *The Genius and Character of Emerson*, ed. F. B. Sanborn (Boston, 1885).

[46] Cf. the letter to Mary Moody Emerson of January 6, 1829 (J 2.258–259 and Cabot, *Memoir*, 1.147–148). Emerson has just sketched an almost idyllic portrait of his condition—he has just become engaged, he is about to be ordained, and his brothers' health seems restored—but goes on to confess an almost superstitious fear for the future: "There's an apprehension of reverse always arising from success."

pastoral functions is charged with ambiguity. He promises his congregation to serve them according to Unitarian custom, but warns them he will not be encumbered with outworn forms; he declares his desire to come close to them so as to be at every moment their authentic interpreter, but he considers as still more important the obligation of fidelity to himself. Thence the impression of uncertainty and instability that a reading of the sermons gives, varying with the subjects and, one might say, with the day of the week.[47] Sometimes the preacher is absorbed in his milieu, conscientiously celebrating fasts and festivals, swelling with no apparent distaste the assembly of a satisfied people; sometimes, by contrast, he provokes, shocks, seduces—though thinking all this no heresy—to the point of eliciting courteous but firm warnings from his church's principal minister.[48]

Emerson's language itself is witness to this indecision. Most often it is honest and clear, unpretentious, expressing a concern with not being satisfied with fine words, with rendering thought in all its nuances, with making it precise wherever necessary by concrete illustrations. What is lacking is vitality. The structure is solid—more solid than it will ever be again—and is built of the proved forms, the traditional rhythms of religious eloquence; but there is no attempt to shape these forms and rhythms to an original impulse. The dominant trait is the will to communicate, which to better attain its end expresses itself in the voice of the people. If the sermons do, almost in spite of the author, bear his stamp, it is by the abrupt flash of a word, by an idea that breaks through, by a quick tremor, soon past but spreading its influence like an expanding wave. Emerson's first sermon, already cited, shows better than most the effect of this subtle reaction. Emerson is describing in passing the realm of human potential, and this beloved theme helps him to find words that reverberate: man, he says, "is no puny sufferer tottering, ill at ease, in the universe, but a being of giant energies, architect of his fortunes, master of his eternity."[49] Afterward Emerson undertakes

[47] The list of the approximately 175 sermons is to be found in McGiffert, *Young Emerson Speaks*, pp. 263–271, together with the date of the first and last occasion of each sermon's being preached and the total number of times it was given. McGiffert's selection is admirably representative, but does not give an entirely accurate idea of the sermons as a whole if only because it eliminates their monotony and tends to diminish the conventionality of their thought. For an account of the sermons' principal themes and sources see Kenneth Cameron, "History and Biography in Emerson's Unpublished Sermons," *Proceedings of the American Antiquarian Society* 66.2 (1956), pp. 103–108 (reprinted in ESQ 12.3 [1958], pp. 2–9).

[48] Cf. the letters to Henry Ware, Jr. of December 30, 1828 and July 1, 1829 (L 1.257–273). For the tenor of the letters Emerson received we have only the evidence to be deduced from the answers he made to them.

[49] "Pray Without Ceasing," in McGiffert, *Young Emerson Speaks*, p. 8.

to warn in strictly orthodox fashion that we must give an account in the next world of the use we have made of our abilities in this. But with the burst of brilliance so recent, the warning is neutralized—as the eye forgets the chrysalis when it sees the wing of the butterfly.

Much has been written on Emerson's political ideas; he has been seen with equal justice as a traditionalist conservative, as a democrat with inclinations to anarchism, and as a skeptic mistrusting all positions.[50] But whatever its later fluctuations may have been, no doubt is possible about his position at this time: he holds to the Federalist viewpoint with an absence of reservation that suggests an inactive social conscience. Effortlessly he falls in with the mood of his audience, uniting with the merchants in their national optimism and their professional prudence, paradoxically joining a confidence in human beings with a sense that very few of them are worthy of it. The terms of the 1822 letter to John Boynton Hill still hold.

Like most Americans since the Revolution, he celebrates the irresistible advance of enlightenment, not hesitating to introduce this theme even into a sermon on the Crucifixion: "Men are rejoicing in what they have lately learned and done. The philanthropist exults in the progress of public opinion. He is glad because the strongholds of error are broken down."[51] America represents both the most advanced point humanity has attained on the path of progress and the ideal goal itself, the exemplary nation, the heavenly Jerusalem come down to earth to receive within its walls all men of good will. Every Fourth of July, every Thanksgiving Day, he sketches the same diptych: we are rich with the rewards of providence; we enjoy a prosperity without equal in the course of history, and we ought if not ungrateful to give heaven unending thanks. But our thanksgiving must lead to a determination to act. The glorious image of our country entrusted to us by our ancestors, Puritans and Revolutionaries both, is a constant spur to emulation; contemplating the lessons of heroism, of sanctity, of independence they have bequeathed to us, we shall surely be able to preserve our country from corruption and shall make it what within our souls it already is, "a land enlightened by the Sun of Righteousness, where every useful and merciful act shall be done—where we shall resist temptation and take hold on life—where the race of glory shall be run and Jesus confessed

[50] For a concise account of the question, with references to the texts and articles most pertinent to it, see F. I. Carpenter, *Emerson Handbook* (New York, 1953), pp. 186–194. Despite its modest title, this book attempts in several places to elucidate certain aspects of Emerson's thought that have generally been ignored.

[51] Sermon 5, "We Preach Christ Crucified" (H.219). The sermon was preached twelve times between the beginning of 1827 and the end of 1828.

and God owned by the general mind of men and his will be done."[52] This and other such passages are the nadir of Emersonian eloquence; bombast is everywhere. The orator simply transcribes, and less well than others had, the clichés of national hagiography, somewhat retouched by Unitarian moralism.[53] Of real didactic intensity, of the desire to impart lessons based on immediate experience, there is little or nothing. Emerson's exhortation takes place in a vacuum; as he seeks to translate his terrestrial fatherland to heaven, he gets lost in a limbo of vagueness.

More significant because less platonic is the backing Emerson brings to the social principles of Federalism: the respect for property, the moral dignity of property owners, and consequently the distrust and even suspicion of everyone else. The liberal tradition has so rudely abused Federalism that even today, despite the vigorous rehabilitation undertaken by Viereck and Rossiter among others,[54] it is difficult to see in it anything but the ideological projection of class egoism. Does it need to be recalled that Washington himself, in the Farewell Address of 1796, associated religion, morality, and property? That the French Revolution had with its bloody violence aroused a horror not yet forgotten? That Burke, the most lucid enemy of that Revolution, enjoyed a lofty reputation in the well-bred circles of New England?[55] That Boston was not Birmingham or Manchester, and that the Industrial Revolution had in Boston not so vividly juxtaposed the extremes of wealth and destitution? The merchants and the shipowners were rich, to be sure, but they look like shopkeepers when compared with the tycoons of the second half of the century. Above all—and this is the important point for Emerson—they were no parasites. Their wealth had been won, if not with the sweat of their brow, at least by their own labor behind desks and counters. There was a visible connection between effort and success. The rich men of Boston brilliantly illustrated the grand law of compensation.

One of the most curious of these sermons touches on the problem of

[52] Sermon 80, "Patriotism" (H.293). The sermon was only given once. See also sermons 12, "Gratitude"; and 57, "Thanksgiving."

[53] See for example J. S. Buckminster, "The Peculiar Blessings of Our Social Condition as Americans," in *The Transcendentalists: An Anthology*, ed. Perry Miller (Cambridge, Mass., 1950), pp. 16–19.

[54] See on this point Cyrille Arnavon, "Les Nouveaux Conservateurs Américains," *Études Anglaises* 9.2 (April–June 1956), pp. 98–121.

[55] Emerson's "Blotting Book I" (JMN 6.11–57), a collection of striking passages encountered in his reading, contains numerous citations from Burke.

class from the unexpected perspective of "Sabbath Observance."[56] Having posited that the sabbath day ought for each person to be an occasion for intellectual and moral progress, Emerson observes that it is particularly beneficial for the working class, to whom it gives the one chance in the week of escaping the degradation of physical labor. But no sooner has he let slip this hint of sympathy for the underprivileged than he catches himself and gives the argument an altogether opposite orientation; without the peace of the sabbath, he says,

> They who had wealth and lettered leisure might still cultivate those arts and studies which are the glory of men, but the great bulk of the community would waste and corrupt in their bondage of ignorance. Their increasing moral inferiority in society would beget a dangerous malignity towards the other classes in the State. They would become
>
> "A savage horde among the civilized
> A servile band among the lordly free."[57]

But the argument does not reveal as hard a heart as one might think. There is a good deal of timidity in it, of perplexity in the face of the masses Emerson does not know, and in whom he always scents a sleeping beast. In all sincerity he desires that they be raised up and spiritually advanced; but as he has never thought about the circumstances of the problem, he falls back upon the only method of approach to it familiar to him, the one he himself practiced in the difficult times of his youth.

Moreover, if property is a right written in the nature of things, it is also a source of obligations. It does not imply uncontrolled enjoyment or the triumph of worldly appetites but rather an opportunity for moral action. In a sermon entitled "The Rights of Others," Emerson lists the obligations laid upon owners: he warns against deceit and perjury in fiscal matters, he discusses bankruptcy and the acknowledging of debts, he recommends that merchants observe a scrupulous honesty in all their transactions.[58] Thus property, which imposes on us a certain code of behavior toward our fellow men, contributes to our moral education. It is, says Emerson, a "discipline," thus using the term he will give as a title to the fifth chapter of *Nature*; it expresses the practical aspect of the evangelical message, which would have little value for us if it neglected our social condition.

[56] Sermon 7, "Sabbath Observance" (H.221). Between 1827 and 1829 the sermon was preached nine times.

[57] Ibid.

[58] Sermon 25, "The Rights of Others" (H.239). The sermon was preached six times, the last being in 1837.

Thus the long sequence of Sunday sermons gradually developed a morality of reasonableness, halfway between altruistic passion and egoism. Each historical period has its own tint in the palette of virtue. Faced with immense difficulties and often threatened by disaster, the Puritans laid stress on endurance, strictness, austerity. The nineteenth century, by contrast, fortunate enough to enjoy the Puritan heritage in peace, could dispense with "the sound of the trumpet" and by the example of the holy lamb cultivate gentleness and kindness.[59] The theme recurs periodically in Emerson's sermons, qualified by nuances and specifications that situate the author somewhere between the perceptive prudence of a Franklin and the fervor of a Channing.[60] The golden rule of morality is beneficence. God asks us first for works; faith is subordinate to that end and intended to render it easier and more pleasant. But the obligation to serve others is not, in spite of appearances, a constraint or disfigurement we impose on ourselves for the love of God; it is an efficient means of doing good to ourselves. Some may doubt the objective value of our acts of disinterestedness and judge that we are too weak to alter the sum of good and evil in the world; but it is nonetheless true that by doing good we have risen to a moral eminence that no superiority of intelligence would have permitted us to attain. At the end of the back-and-forth movement between individual and society, then, Emerson shows that the former is always the winner; who loses himself finds himself, not in the mystical sense of the seed that must die to spring up again but in the realm of practical experience. Taking over where the divine imperative leaves off, self-interest becomes the principal engine of mutual aid: "it was an early discovery of political economy that in no form could labor be exerted to less advantage than in an attempt to confine its fruits to the laborer."[61]

It remained to order social obligations in a hierarchy, and this task Emerson accomplished with good sense and moderation.[62] We belong, he says, to a series of groups that might be accurately represented by a series of concentric circles. The force of the bond that attaches us to each is in inverse proportion to its size. As a man with a family, Emerson un-

[59] Cf. sermon 33, "Gentleness" (H.247), preached twelve times between 1829 and 1835.

[60] See particularly sermons 8, "God to Be Loved"; 48, "Faith and Works"; 65, "Benevolence and Selfishness"; 77, "Christian Charity"; 79, "Doing Good." This concept of an essentially philanthropic religion had gradually won acceptance as the circumstances of daily life became less harsh—Cotton Mather had indeed already published his *Essays to Do Good* by 1710 (under the title *Bonifacius: An Essay upon the Good*).

[61] Sermon 65, "Benevolence and Selfishness" (H.278).

[62] See particularly sermons 10, "Showing Piety at Home"; 136, "The Occasion for Praise"; and 154, "Duty."

derstands that the family is to be served first; then come friends, between whom and family the distinction is tenuous. With regard to these two groups our obligations are strict, because they involve us alone and measure our real worth:

> He is a poor patriot who is a negligent father; . . . an unfaithful friend is not to be praised for his philanthropy, nor the ungrateful to say in his defence that he has visited the prisons and relieved the poor. For when was public virtue found where private was not? Can he love the whole, who loves no part? He be a nation's friend, who is in truth the friend of no man there? Certainly the place where each of us can accomplish the most good or evil is our own house, among our own kindred.[63]

To the extent that our spiritual emancipation is complete, however, we take cognizance of belonging to larger collectivities: we feel solidarity not only with our state but also with the Union, on which depends the good government of all; and a day will come when, acknowledging our universal vocation, we shall respond to the liberal institutions of France, the wisdom of Germany, the hope of all peoples who groan beneath tyranny, the dawn of a new civilization just rising upon Asia and the shores of Africa.[64]

Such was the comfortable and decent image of themselves that Emerson gave to the parishioners of the Second Church. It is also the image of a world all parts of which are in profound accord. An effort toward moral perfection is still asked of us; but at least conflicts of obligation, uncertainties, and collisions between common and particular interest have been eliminated. Providential order does not cease to bend reasonably self-interested conduct in the direction of the common good; and, correspondingly, acts of beneficence profit their authors above all. Hovering over this economic and moral universe is the blessed shade of Adam Smith, as is revealed in the frequent allusions to his theories and to those of his school.[65] Nonetheless, Emerson instinctively dissents

[63] Sermon 154, "Duty" (H.367).

[64] See in particular sermon 136, "The Occasion for Praise": "I would feel an interest and property in the kindred civilizations and arts and learning and laws and religion of England; in the liberal institutions of France; . . . in the wisdom of Germany; in the remembrances of Italy; in the patience of Spain; in the expectation of the children of freedom under every despotism; in all the virtue that fights with so much gross vice in Europe. I would feel an interest in the new dawn of commerce, and civilization, and so the hope of religion, in Asia, and the skirts of afflicted Africa."

[65] John G. Gerber, "Emerson and the Political Economists," NEQ 22 (September 1949), pp. 336–357, has pointed out the kinship between Emerson's ideas and the thought of Smith, particularly those aspects of Smith's thought set out in his *Theory of Moral Sentiments* (1759).

from such a theory. It is not that he was on the point of opposing to it a system of his own—his social thought was to crystallize only gradually, under the twofold influence of an inward revolution and the pressure of historical fact—but he was vaguely distrustful of so perfect a harmony, which appeared to him to make too short work of human experience. Even if one admits that for an observer without passions the world is like a marvelous and beneficent machine, utilizing everything and reconciling the gravest discords on the level of reason, one still has to make sense of what goes on within each individual consciousness. That there is an ultimate solution to the antagonism opposing individual and society does not permit us to dispense with explaining the tension all men feel between them. In other words—and though Emerson had not yet learned to pose the problem in these terms—the rationalism of the eighteenth century built its social philosophy on the ruins of individual autonomy.

Taken as a whole, the sermons reflect this inner contradiction.[66] They offer the disconcerting sight of a thesis officially maintained and progressively undermined by the same author. At first Emerson attempts a difficult balance of opposites, as is clear from two sermons less than a month apart, late in 1829.[67] In them Emerson makes an admirable effort to give society its due; it has, after all, been willed by God, and those who speak ill of it are the first to reap its benefits. He asks poets, for example, whether nature would be their mistress or muse if men had not lent her their language. But above all, the greatness of each individual depends on the particular social organism to which he belongs. Given equal talents, an English citizen has more chance than a Chinese or a Russian to attain the rank he deserves, because the structure of England favors the emergence of excellence. If a man is exceptionally gifted, he may even rise, no matter how low his beginnings, so high that he can shape the destiny of millions of men and women living at the other end of the world. Indeed, in all domains—in science, in art, in morality—society enlarges the range of our faculties' application; it is at once an invitation to do better and a rein upon our tendencies to evil:

It is striking, moreover, that as late as 1831 Smith's name turns up repeatedly in Emerson's lists in his journal of the works he has read in the course of the year.

[66] As McGiffert has noted in his introduction: "A well-developed philosophy of society controls all his remarks on the subject. It is curious, therefore, to observe that Emerson never explicitly applies his sociological theories to the church" (*Young Emerson Speaks*, p. xxx).

[67] Sermons 53, "Freedom and Dependence" (H.267), preached on October 24, 1829; and 55, "Society and Solitude" (H.269), on November 14, 1829. Both sermons were preached for the last time in 1837.

"no man can bear the execrations of other men; nor can any contemplate the sincere approbation of other men without desire."[68]

But Emerson's impartiality is not so perfect that one cannot say which side of the balance weighs more heavily for him. The particular situation of New England heightens the candor of his choice, because he reasons on the basis of the case most favorable to the cause he opposes: a community distinguished by its probity, by its desire to serve God in orderliness and freedom. If submissiveness to society ever deserves to be preached it is here, among a peaceable people with virtue as their motto. To this Emerson responds that there is no common measure between collective virtue and individual. The first is "poor and worthless tributary, obsequious . . . compared to the athletic virtue that grows up nursed by temptation, self existent, self consulting, a tower of strength equal to the shock of great emergencies."[69] To sweep up this latter in an anonymous flood would be to destroy it. Beware of imitation, Emerson challenges his audience, even the imitation of the good: "Be not satisfied to have your little bark towed by the great fleet of the State . . . because the waters are smooth and all are going the same way. . . . The paths of virtue and opportunity are many and infinite. To each his own course."[70]

The last word is always spoken in the solitude of the consciousness, face to face with God and aloof from others. Emerson comes back here to the cardinal affirmation of his youth, which is to sustain his philosophy till the last day of his life: that every man is "absolutely, imperially free";[71] every man occupies the center of the rainbow, the summit of the terrestrial globe. Only let society not make him forget his royal independence, not offer him its advantages and comforts as a pillow on which he may indolently rest his head. Unless a man can do without society, he is not ready to live in it.[72] Taken literally, such a formulation was the death knell of the compromise Emerson had attempted in his ministry. It is all very well for him to sketch in extremis a semblance of reconciliation, to declare that the human mind in full possession of itself profits from all of society's goods without letting itself be compromised by any of its vices; the balance simply will not return to equilibrium,

[68] Sermon 55, "Society and Solitude."

[69] Sermon 53, "Freedom and Dependence."

[70] Ibid.

[71] Sermon 55, "Society and Solitude."

[72] "It seems true that no man is fit for society who is not fit to stand alone" (ibid.). The same idea, expressed in almost identical words, is the basis of Emerson's political protest after 1850: "He only who is able to stand alone is qualified for society," he exclaims in his second speech on the Fugitive Slave Law (W 11.235).

because the argument has no weight and lacks the ballast of lived experience.

But it is only gradually that Emerson draws the consequences of his principle. At the beginning he cares chiefly to set his audience on guard against the social pressures capable of thwarting their vocation as "free and solitary Christians."[73] As occasions present themselves, he denounces the false proprieties that make us distort the truth when faced with a sick man or a coffin—as if sincerity were not the sole homage acceptable to pain.[74] He attacks the honor that, though capable of inspiring lofty actions, depends in the last analysis on the collective feeling of a changing elite and is thus vulnerable to that elite's caprices and may bear the mark of its imperfections.[75] He denounces the fear of being laughed at and the cult of fashion in a sermon whose title, "Trifles,"[76] sums up well what society is ready to offer us, namely, comfort and elegance in exchange for our integrity, worldly success at the price of a thousand petty compromises. We must once and for all reduce these knickknacks to their true value; otherwise they will reduce us.

Accordingly, without going as far as actually to take sides in the always latent conflict between urban and rural life, Emerson does let his sympathies in the matter be seen. Even if all citizens enjoyed decent housing—which in Boston is not, alas, the case[77]—the narrow, nauseating, dust-choked streets would still keep them from sharing in the splendor of nature's beauties, from following the perpetually changing course of the clouds in the sky.[78] The city kills that solitude without which, Emerson has no hesitation in repeating, there is no deep spiritual life.[79] The city replaces quality by quantity, and drowns all origi-

[73] See sermon 38, "The Christian Is Free and Solitary."

[74] See sermon 134, "Words Are Things" (H.347), delivered for the first time on November 6, 1831. The extraordinarily forceful tone seems to indicate the pain of personal affliction, and in reading a passage like the following one can hardly keep from thinking of Ellen Emerson's recent death: "What we mourn for is the loss of a friendship so near and intimate that it was wholly sincere. It had no need of the drapery of courtesy, and this hollow talk makes him feel the loss the more. It suggests to us the disapprobation which the departed would feel, or feels with us, and draws us nearer to the dead and farther from the living."

[75] See sermon 137, "The Choice of Theisms," in McGiffert, *Young Emerson Speaks*, pp. 151–161.

[76] Sermon 44, in McGiffert, *Young Emerson Speaks*, pp. 46–52.

[77] Cf. sermon 40, "Charity," H.254: "We live in a fair city. It is full of commodious and spacious mansions. But the eye that sees the morning sun shine on long streets of decorated dwellings is apt to forget how many obscure garrets, how many damp basements, are here and there found amid this magnificence." Kenneth Cameron reproduces the passage in the article on Emerson's sermons cited above.

[78] See sermon 39, "Summer," in McGiffert, *Young Emerson Speaks*, pp. 39–45.

[79] See sermon 112, "Peace and Solitude" (H.325): "Men need Solitude, that revealer of the

nality in an imposing but unedifying mass. One need not speak ill of it, but one ought not to sing its praises—so he writes one day to his brother William, whose declamatory praise of New York he finds irritating: "But after all it is nothing but a town & there are much greater & better things than streets or men considered *numerically*. e.g. the same things considered morally, intellectually, historically, & so on."[80]

By means of his critique of New York, model of the anonymous metropolis, Emerson was in fact venting his bile against all the forms of collective life. As McGiffert justly says, Emerson was by temperament incapable of cooperation;[81] uniting his efforts to someone else's for the accomplishment of a particular task always seemed to him less an augmentation of energy than a diminution, even a dissipation, of his own abilities. During the summer of 1829, he and Ellen visited the Shaker village at Canterbury, and what he saw there was hardly of a nature to modify that view.[82] The Shakers fervently urged the young couple to repent of their guilty intention to live as man and wife and in general made a poor enough impression:

> This society is divided into three families & own about 2000 acres of land, and excepting a shrewd handful of male & female oligarchs are a set of clean, well disposed, dull, & incapable animals. One man I have talked with was very well read in the bible & talked very logically from the Scriptures literally taken, but was strangely ignorant for a Yankee about every thing beyond his daily & weekly errands in the country round.

Such was Emerson's first contact with intentional communities; one may conjecture that the image of it was not entirely effaced when he had to decide, ten years later, whether to go to Brook Farm.

---

truth, Solitude the parent of Meditation, that hill that commands the wide prospect of life." The poem "Monadnoc," composed about 1845, amplifies this theme with a sometimes harsh irony toward city dwellers; cf. particularly W 9.71–72.

[80] Letter to William Emerson, May 27, 1830 (L 1.302–304).

[81] He speaks of Emerson's "temperamental disability to work effectively in an organization in constant and responsible connection with a group of people" (*Young Emerson Speaks*, p. xii).

[82] See the letter to Charles Emerson, August 7, 1829 (L 1.275–276). The Shakers—so named from the shaking of their limbs when the spirit of God attended them in their sacred dances—lived in "families" of thirty to ninety members, under the rule of ministers and elders. Celibacy was the rule; the two sexes, each of which was believed to reflect an aspect of the divine nature, were considered equal. In tribute to their chiliastic faith, they named themselves "The United Society of Believers in Christ's Second Appearing." ESQ 13.4 (1958), pp. 42–45, reproduces an article on the sect published in 1837 in the popular journal *Penny Magazine*.

For the moment, in any case, he was confirmed—if he needed confirmation—in his conviction that responsibility is necessarily individual, and that in submitting our attitudes and judgments to society's verdict we are literally yielding to a mirage.[83] This denial of man's social nature, presented sometimes as an ideal and sometimes as a fact of human experience, enables us to locate Emerson in the religious context of his time. The idea of covenant and its implications for earthly life,[84] even in the revivified form given it in the eighteenth century by a Jonathan Mayhew[85] and in the nineteenth by a Channing,[86] is deeply alien to him. He cannot assent to the church's engaging as a body in the conflicts of the moment, to its criticizing institutions and leading movements in order to reform them. This world does not deserve such zeal, he is saying as early as 1827: "it is really of trifling importance what events await America; for we are citizens of another country."[87] In referring his parishioners to the world unseen, which for him was neither a trope of rhetoric nor a submissive homage to his church's teachings, Emerson clasped hands over the years and centuries with all those among his compatriots whom the inward search for God had so fasci-

[83] ". . . the public is not to render up an account, but the individual must; not society, but each man is forming the character of heaven or hell" (sermon 53, "Freedom and Dependence"). In sermon 88, "The Oracle Within," Emerson posits that God can only be present in his church as inhabiting each of the individuals of which it is comprised.

[84] In the Second Church of Boston at Emerson's time there was a distinction between "Church" and "Congregation," the latter also being called "Parish" or "Society." The Congregation handled finances and chose the minister; the Church, a more restricted group including only certain of the members of the Congregation, handled disciplinary affairs and took communion. In sermon 50, "A Feast of Remembrance," Emerson criticizes this discrimination. Jesus, he says, desired the Lord's Supper to be a perpetual memorial, but assigned it neither a particular time nor a limited number of participants. Cf. McGiffert, *Young Emerson Speaks*, pp. 54–59 and (for the explanation given in this note) p. 224.

[85] Jonathan Mayhew was minister of the West Church of Boston from 1747 till his death in 1766; he distinguished himself both by his rationalist tendencies, in which he was a precursor of the Unitarians, and by the forcefulness of his stands during the Stamp Act crisis. He was an extreme liberal and a personal friend of John Adams.

[86] On the relations between Channing and Emerson, see Lenthiel H. Downs, "Emerson and Dr. Channing: Two Men from Boston," NEQ 20 (December 1947), pp. 516–534, and Elizabeth Peabody, *Reminiscences of Rev. William Ellery Channing* (Boston, 1880), pp. 365–373. The two men respected each other, but their personal shyness and their very different mental orientations—Emerson impatient with human weakness and Channing disposed to pardon it, Emerson in love with individual integrity and Channing attentive to the circumstances of human life—kept them from ever coming into real contact. The mixture of admiration and disappointment Emerson felt for Channing emerges clearly from a reflection of his, reported by Elizabeth Peabody: "in our wantonness we often flout Dr. Channing, and say he is getting old; but as soon as he is ill, we remember he is our Bishop."

[87] Sermon 12, "Gratitude," cited earlier. The phrase is quoted in McGiffert, *Young Emerson Speaks*, p. xxxi.

nated as to render them suspect to their communities: Jonathan Edwards, of whose banishment to Northampton the reasonable minister of the First Church of Boston, Charles Chauncy, had heard with considerable satisfaction; Ann Hutchinson and the Quakers, who had had to flee Massachusetts in the early days of the colony to escape the gallows. Certain others, like Edward Taylor, had succeeded in leading a double life, as one might call it, by hiding in their journals the excessively personal timbre of their meditations;[88] but the feeling of subjection to constraint was not thereby diminished.

In the Boston of 1830, circumstances were much different. Since the beginning of the century, the separation of church and state had put an end to ministers' civil functions and thus released them to give their entire attention to the spiritual needs of the faithful. In addition, the Unitarian church, now accepted by the whole of the enlightened bourgeoisie, was a model of liberalism, in which each minister, provided he proved himself sincere and open-minded, found pretty much unlimited room to maneuver and did not need to fear harsh summonses to order or official sanctions. Emerson's thought in the first years of his public life reflects this extraordinarily flexible and tolerant social situation. Contemplating the individual, he sees no obstacle capable of compromising or annulling his upright will. America, by the grace of God, has the most perfect government humanity has ever known, that is, the least oppressive. It guarantees its citizens liberty and does not bully them; it does not seek to meddle with their private lives; in short it realizes as nearly as possible the ideal of nonexistence.[89]

This concept of political power, with its well-known later consolidation in the work of Emerson's maturity,[90] has sometimes been compared with the doctrines of Jefferson—which is justified—and also presented as a recantation of Federalist principles—which is not.[91]

[88] Taylor, the minister of Westfield, Massachusetts toward the end of the seventeenth century, expressed in his will the desire that his poems never be published.

[89] "In a well constituted state, the government itself will be out of sight, will not be the prominent and exclusive object of attention whenever the country is considered. . . . The advantages of a government it is agreed must always be negative" (sermon 70, "The Individual and the State," in McGiffert, *Young Emerson Speaks*, p. 77).

[90] See for example the lecture "The Young American" (W 1.363–395), in which Emerson jubilantly announces the gradual atrophy of governmental organs, and the essay "Politics," in which he writes, "the less government we have the better, —the fewer laws, and the less confided power" (W 3.215).

[91] See particularly Vernon Louis Parrington, *Main Currents in American Thought*, 3 vols. (New York, 1927–1930), 2.390. Ernest E. Sandeen, in *Emerson's Americanism*, University of Iowa Studies: Humanistic Studies 6.1 (Iowa City, 1942), compares Emerson's views on

Jefferson was born a subject of the British crown, was a great admirer of the *philosophes*, and in addition was familiar with the Old World, its injustice and oppression; he saw in the disappearance of the machinery of state a good toward which one might properly strive but which one should never really hope to attain. If he defended individual independence and the goverment of oneself by oneself with such conviction, it was because he knew that ideal to be constantly threatened and in the end unrealizable. Hamilton said of him that his radicalism was more theoretical than practical, and his actions in the White House proved Hamilton right.[92] Emerson, by contrast, when he addressed his congregation from the pulpit of the Second Church, was politically innocent. Certain stains on the margin of national life—slavery, and perhaps the spiritual apathy engendered by trade—had, to be sure, troubled him from time to time, but never to the point of making him doubt the profound virtue of American institutions, as attested by the domestic tranquility they confer on American citizens. Jefferson, that is, looked toward an improbable future; Emerson invited his audience to sanction an existing political structure of which the Federalists were the kingpin. That power should belong to a few well-to-do or rich citizens did not bother him in the least, since order and liberty both benefit from the situation; the danger, which was just beginning, came rather from certain democratic turbulences—an uncontrolled press in the service of political parties, the disruptive pressure of selfish interests—that Washington had denounced as early as 1796.[93]

Insofar as Emerson allowed political issues to cross the threshold of his church, then, he showed himself a resolute conservative. But on his lips the conservative doctrines do not take on the prudent and defensive character we normally associate with them. To conserve is for him to preserve from degradation, and degradation is always moral. Hence the remedy—the panacea, one is tempted to say—that he offers on every occasion: since the congregation, the state of Massachusetts, the Union are in the end only you, reform yourself and the world is saved. Tire-

the ideal of government with the Jeffersonian tradition, but takes care to make clear that underlying these two very similar conceptions are quite different philosophical postulates.

[92] The chapter of Richard Hofstadter's *The American Political Tradition* (New York, 1948) devoted to Jefferson (called "Thomas Jefferson: The Aristocrat as Democrat"), admirably sums up modern historiographic judgment on Jefferson, which has shown the image of the militant and visionary democratic revolutionary to be untenable.

[93] It is in general in Fast Day sermons that Emerson recommends vigilance against these destructive forces. In addition to the sermon already mentioned called "The Individual and the State" (preached April 8, 1830), see particularly sermons 17, "The Duty of Penitence" (April 3, 1828); 113, "Fasting, Humiliation and Prayer" (April 7, 1831); and 150, "Fast Day" (April 5, 1832).

lessly he repeats the same injunction, climbing or descending the chain of being without ever stopping in the middle, bringing to his demonstration a mixture of fervor and logic that recalls Pascal, or the Edwards of "Sinners in the Hands of an Angry God." As Americans, he explains, we lament the misery of Ireland and Greece, we detest the Holy Alliance, we hope that Europe will one day for its own good be able to imitate us; if we consider ourselves not as citizens of the Union but as inhabitants of New England, we see in slavery a disease that subtly erodes the moral fiber of the southern states; if we restrict still further the social group in which we see ourselves reflected, we are soon shocked by the inadequacies of the system of public education, by the pedestrian dullness of the merchants and the narrowness and class prejudices of their churches; and so on, from larger to ever smaller units, until we encounter the fundamental element, at once the touchstone and rock of foundation, which can only be the judgment of our own conscience, astonished to find so much ignorance and disorder at its door.[94] Having reached the end of the chain, the argument bounces back, one might say, in the guise of a metaphor: "The independence of the State is the independence of individual men, and when that is gone, tho' the forms of a free government survive and hold sway over a degenerate race, it is but a reptile crept into the skeleton of a giant."[95] The public scandals we are sometimes so indignant about are the projection on a grand scale of our personal turpitudes, "like the insensible motion of the hand of a watch made sensible by being lengthened onto the dial of a clock."[96] There is strict continuity, even identity, from private attitude to professional conduct to national policy: "The political measures of this nation and of every nation may be regarded as an index whereon the average degree of private virtue is made known to the world."[97]

The consequences of this theory are formidable. Each of us is a new Atlas, on whom alone depends the continuation of the world. In vain does Emerson illustrate the positive side of the doctrine—every effort, every victory won over ourselves in the hiding places of the soul has its happy repercussion outside us—the fear remains that the responsibility

[94] Cf. JMN 3.103–104. This passage was written while Emerson was preparing the sermon "The Duty of Penitence." See also the peroration of "Fasting, Humiliation and Prayer": "It is not the State House nor the Capitol, that give their shape and character to the destinies of the nation, but it is the Exchange, the Tavern, the school-house, the parlor, the nursery, the church and the closet" (H.326).

[95] Sermon 42, "True Freedom" (H.256), delivered on the Fourth of July, 1829.

[96] "The Individual and the State," p. 79; and see also sermon 150, "Fast Day," in which the faults of a nation are described as the extension and realization of the faults of individuals.

[97] "The Individual and the State," p. 80.

is beyond our strength. As if to prevent that anxiety, Emerson elaborates at this time the concept of "character," with the double meaning, both inner and outer, that the word then bore.[98] The first time he lingers over the notion in the journal, he applies it equally to a geranium, a mineral, a horse, and a man.[99] The juxtapositions are illuminating, because they shift the word toward the sense of "nature," with the intimations of unconsciousness and stability that word necessarily conveys. It is precisely as nature that character acts on the world; it orients, influences, compels by its presence alone: "Ten good men would save Sodom & five or six good men are our examples, our evidences, and the pillars that we lean upon. . . . Consider the force of character; the impressiveness of the silence of a good man. I have known a pause in speech to do more than a harangue."[100] Emerson had discovered the spiritual cement in which he was to trust to the very end for the cohesiveness of society. But it was difficult for him, unless he were to resign himself to the spectator's powerlessness, not to brood over the question of this mysterious quality's foundations. And it is precisely this investigation, at once quest and inquest, that ends by absorbing him altogether and gives his sermons their chief interest.

Still, it was not always an easy investigation, nor was it regular in its progress. It seemed to hesitate between two directions. But as Whicher has shown, the perspective of time brings out an overall sureness in Emerson's course that makes it seem akin to biological tropisms, and unites necessity and vocation in an irresistible pressure.[101] The first episode—in 1826, before Emerson left for Florida—is surprising by the suddenness of its vigor. Probably influenced by Sampson Reed, the Swedenborgian pharmacist at Boston whose *Observations on the Growth of the Mind*[102] he had just read, Emerson rejoices that "bare reason, cold as cucumber," has transferred her authority to the hands of "her sister, blushing shining changing Sentiment," and that at last the

[98] With minor shifts of emphasis the concept of "Character" recurs in Emerson's work throughout his life. Two essays, published in 1844 (W 3.87–115) and 1866 (in the *North American Review*, reprinted W 10.89–122), use the word as their title.

[99] See JMN 3.190 (1830).

[100] JMN 3.132 (May 1828). These notes were probably written while Emerson was preparing a sermon on calumny (sermon 20, H.234), because they end in a denunciation of this failing, "the murderer of character." The sermon itself contains praise of character, "the muniment of virtue."

[101] In the first chapter, "Discovery," of his *Freedom and Fate*.

[102] See the letter to William Emerson of September 29, 1826 (L 1.176–177). Extracts from this important work are to be found in *The Transcendentalists*, ed. Miller, pp. 53–59, and Kenneth Cameron gives the whole text after the first edition (Boston, 1826) in his *Emerson the Essayist*, 2 vols. (Raleigh, N.C., 1945), 2.12–31.

barrier history sets up between God and man has fallen.[103] Emerson's first sermon—delivered in October 1826—avoids these terms, with their freight of theological controversy, but celebrates at its outset the incomparable superiority of that "inward estate" in which God is immediately present: "your reason is God, your virtue is God, and nothing but your liberty, can you call securely and absolutely your own."[104]

After this brief moment of illumination, there is a more indecisive phase, in which the work of spiritual growth goes on below ground, in the shelter of consciousness, lighted from time to time by glimmers of hope[105] but more often contained or thwarted by Emerson's fear of making a fool's bargain, of bartering his most vigorous and lucid thoughts for the uncertain and morbid indulgence of a feeling swathed in darkness.[106] Two encounters that symbolize the opposing attractions to which Emerson was susceptible took place during his travels in the South.[107] On the boat from Saint Augustine to Charleston, he became friends with Achille Murat, elder son of the king of Naples, who had settled as a planter near Tallahassee. Murat was a professed atheist and argued for his lack of belief—to the great astonishment of Emerson, who had thought such a thing impossible.[108] A conversation ensued between "this intrepid doubter" and himself, a conversation of great dignity in which each undertook to show that the other was in error. Each, of course, remained unconvinced, Emerson defending his faith in a God at once in the heavens and in us. But his adversary's sincerity at every occasion troubled him: "what matter if this Being be acknowledged or denied, if the faith cannot impose any more effective restraint on vice & passion, than morals unsupported by this foundation?"[109] The response came in part from a Quaker who was his traveling companion from Alexandria to Philadelphia and to whom Emerson makes frequent reference in the journal: "Stubler said the difference between brother Witherlee's preaching & his, was this: Brother W. said "If you do not become good you shall all be whipt" and himself said, 'If you will become good,

[103] Letter to Mary Moody Emerson of September 23, 1826 (L 1.174–175).

[104] Sermon 1, "Pray Without Ceasing," in McGiffert, *Young Emerson Speaks*, p. 4.

[105] Cf. letter to Mary Moody Emerson of August 17 and 22, 1827 (L 1.206–209): "I am curious to know what the Scriptures do in very deed say about that exalted person who died on Calvary, but I do think it at this distance of time & in the confusion of languages to be a work of weighing of phrases & hunting in dictionaries. A portion of truth bright & sublime lives in every moment to every mind. It is enough for safety tho' not for education."

[106] See J 2.222–223 (letter to Mary Moody Emerson of November 20, 1827).

[107] The comparison is implicitly made by Emerson himself, in a list in which he names five or six people as having "ministered to my highest wants" (JMN 5.160 [May 19, 1836]).

[108] See JMN 3.77 (April 6, 1827).

[109] JMN 3.78 (April 17, 1827).

you shall not be whipt.' "[110] Constraint, even logical constraint, must yield to the positive testimony of the conscience.

One can divide the sermons by the same dichotomy and distinguish those that invite us to the contemplation of God from those that call human energies to arms, or alternatively—to take over the terms of "Pray Without Ceasing"—between those that proclaim the divine nature of virtue and reason and those that make the good use of liberty the necessary condition and substance of every moral life. Until 1830, with some notable exceptions,[111] it is the second tendency that dominates. Each of us, says Emerson, is master of his destiny, little as he himself may wish to take charge of it; in a series of sermons all including the word "self" in their titles,[112] he exhorts his hearers to use their faculty of free determination to accomplish the conquest of themselves and thereby earn the respect of others: "Society seems to be severe on faults. It is merely a mirror reflecting back your own sentence on yourself. We wonder what shall befall us in one place or at a future time instead of deciding what we will have befall us i.e. what we will do."[113] Emerson will never go further in his defense of human initiative and his denial of Calvinism. The grace of God itself is impotent without the aid of our will—or such at any rate is the doctrine he expounds in the most Pelagian of his sermons, "Spiritual Influence Reciprocal."[114] With considerable deftness he finds the patent of nobility he needs in a text generally considered a model of submissiveness: the Lord's Prayer. When we ask God to forgive us our trespasses as we forgive the trespasses of others, it is, explains Emerson, as if our mercy had already constrained God to show himself merciful: "Draw nigh unto God and He will draw nigh unto you."[115]

But the law of Compensation, which governs all spiritual relations, makes God lose what man has won. From the instant that he *must* answer the appeals cast before him, his interventions become mechanical;

[110] JMN 4.96 (November 19, 1833). Cf. also JMN 3.185 (May 12, 1830) and 3.296 (June 29, 1831). The spread of these dates clearly indicates the persistence of the impression.

[111] For example, sermons 21, "Conscience, a Proof of God" (preached July 30, 1828) and 23, "Belief in God Innate" (September 24, 1828).

[112] Sermons 24, "Self-Direction and Self-Command" (preached October 12, 1828); 27, "Self-Knowledge and Self-Mastery" (December 14, 1828); and 47, "Self-Command" (August 30, 1829).

[113] JMN 3.143. These lines are dated November 1828 and were written while Emerson was preparing the sermon "Self-Knowledge and Self-Mastery."

[114] Sermon 118 (H.331), preached fifteen times between June 19, 1831 and November 1, 1835. The relative lateness of these dates suggests how imprudent it is to establish clearly demarcated stages in Emerson's intellectual growth.

[115] Ibid.

the universe is perhaps governed by laws, but it ceases to be guided by a personal intelligence. In the second part of his sermon, Emerson raises these objections himself and attempts to answer them: taking up one of the traditional proofs of God's existence, he maintains that our inward experience, in revealing our limits, is enough to persuade us that we are creatures. But the argument provokes a deeper confusion than the one it set out to resolve; God's omnipotence is perhaps restored, but is it still possible to speak of autonomy when we come up against impassable obstacles, inward as well as outward? Who shall guide our ship between the Charybdis of human freedom and the Scylla of divine prerogative?

It is in such a context that Emerson's discovery of Coleridge, at the end of 1829, takes on its full significance.[116] The English poet–metaphysician taught him to see behind apparent contradiction the fertile tension that rules the spiritual life; and once the distinction between Reason and Understanding has been accepted, matters become clearer.[117] By Reason, potentially perfect in each one of us, we have on the one hand access to the moral, intellectual, and aesthetic principles that are, as it were, the substance of God. Understanding, on the other, which varies in power from person to person, rules the domain of the contingent and the expedient; it discusses, calculates, compares, but never attains primary truth. Armed with this key, Emerson could take up again and resolve the problems that had hitherto resisted him.[118] Other reading also—in particular de Gérando's *Histoire comparée des systèmes de philosophie*, in which Emerson finds stimulating discussions of the pre-Socratics, Plato, and Plotinus[119]—also nourished his thought

[116] Emerson did not really "discover" Coleridge in 1829; he had read the *Biographia literaria* three years previously (see Cameron, *Emerson the Essayist*, 1.162–163). But it is James Marsh's 1829 edition of *Aids to Reflection*, with its ample notes and appendixes, that seems to have provoked the decisive shock in him. On December 10, 1829, he writes to his aunt Mary as follows: "I am reading Coleridge's *Friend* with great interest. . . . there are few or no books of pure literature so self-imprinting, that is so often remembered as Coleridge's" (J 2.277). On the proved and presumed relations between Coleridge's thought and Emerson's the reader will do well to consult the three chapters of *Emerson the Essayist* ("Emerson's Coleridge in Review," "Coleridge and the 'First Philosophy,' " and "Coleridge as the Key to Nature," 1.78–223), in which Cameron reproduces the material pertinent to the matter, stresses the most striking parallels, and cites numerous texts by both authors.

[117] For Emerson's own account of that distinction, see the letter to Edward Emerson of May 31, 1834 (L 1.412–414).

[118] The two terms occur for the first time in the journal for February 23, 1831 (JMN 3.235–236), but it is only gradually that Emerson grasps the implications of the Coleridgean idea, which is, as he writes, a philosophy in itself. See on this point Henry A. Pochmann, "The Emerson Canon," *University of Toronto Quarterly* 12, (July 1943), pp. 474–484.

[119] See JMN 3.360–370. Cameron, *Emerson the Essayist*, 1.17–56, gives ample extracts from and summaries of the work.

in this period of fermentation. The patient drifting of the formative years is over; a vigorous energy of curiosity and enthusiasm have succeeded it. In a few months, there emerges in the journals a new Emerson, in whom the general outlines of the mature Emerson can already be seen. By the judgment of his two most discerning intellectual biographers,[120] as of 1831 Emerson is in possession of the essential elements of his "First Philosophy."[121]

What this revolution was for Emerson himself is suggested by a remark in the journal for June 1830: "Conversion from a moral to a religious character is like day after twilight. The orb of the earth is lighted brighter & brighter as it turns until at last there is a particular moment when the eye sees the sun and so when the soul perceives God."[122] The immediate relation thus established between God and his creature makes sects of every sort not only useless but also pernicious, with their claims to dictate and judge our feelings. Where a direct dialogue exists, to look outward to orient it is to deprive it of all spontaneity, to substitute for the voice of God the pedantic glosses of his ministers.[123] That is why Calvinism and Unitarianism should both be dismissed; the first, which had its hour of truth, outlived itself in its pride and ignorance; the other, still more negative, exists only in opposition: "it is cold & cheerless the mere creature of the understanding, until controversy makes it warm with fire got from below."[124] If Emerson had been compelled to choose absolutely among the sects that struggle for our souls, his preference would no doubt have been for those that, in declining to impose human structures on the course of grace, invite man to an obedient, submissive harkening to God: Quakers first, Methodists next.[125] Even

[120] Cameron, *Emerson the Essayist*, 1.174–175, and Whicher, *Freedom and Fate*, pp. 23–25. Both scholars consider the poem "Gnothi Seauton" (J 2.395–399 [1831]) the most successful and complete formulation of Emerson's thought at this point.

[121] "By the First Philosophy, is meant the original laws of the mind. It is the Science of what *is*, in distinction from what *appears*. It is one mark of them that their enunciation awakens the feeling of the Moral sublime, and *great men* are they who believe in them" (JMN 5.270 [1835]).

[122] JMN 3.186 (June 7, 1830).

[123] Cf. JMN 3.259–260 (June 20, 1831): "A man may die by a fever as well as by consumption & religion is as effectually destroyed by bigotry as by indifference."

[124] JMN 3.301 (October 27, 1831).

[125] See sermon 133: "The Reality and Blessedness of Religion," preached October 30, 1831. In it Emerson praises the Methodist who goes through deserted streets to join his religious brethren in prayer and praise of God. It is significant that the critique of Calvinism and Unitarianism cited above occurs in the journal notes Emerson used in preparing this same sermon. In another sermon (98, "Perfect Love Casteth out Fear," preached December 5, 1830) Emerson invites all Christians to unite in a Universal Church founded on love.

when the sermons take up themes long familiar,[126] they do it in a new spirit, marked by an almost pietistic fervor. It is at this time that Emerson reads and recommends Thomas à Kempis, Scougal, Fénelon,[127] because these men, though so different from one another in development, have nonetheless known the same experience and have felt, beyond the particular forms of observance and concepts of theology, the radiant inwardness of a living principle.

From the heat of this divine presence is born a literally infinite spiritual energy, which lifts us up whole, and the world with us. Man has never touched the limits of his power; if he is not a demiurge, the fault is in his indolence: "You do not know what any man, your neighbor, your brother with whose thoughts you have been familiar for years can perform. You do not know what yourself can do. No one knows till he has tried how much he can accomplish—nor then, how much more if he had not ceased from trying."[128] The celebrated Emersonian idealism thus makes its entry as an impetuous dynamism. Something is within us, invisible, worth more than our actions because all our actions emanate from it,[129] eternally new and active because each of us exists for himself, independent of history and the past.[130] From the Coleridgean principle of identity (as distinguished from likeness) faith receives a divine substance and becomes the infallible instrument of spiritual perception;[131] the holy wrath resounding through the Old Testament symbolizes the sufferings born of our sin,[132] and in the same way it is in submitting our sensual inclinations to the soul's jurisdiction that in the theological sense of the term we do God's will.[133] The whole Christian

[126] Humility, for example, in sermon 82, "The Virtue of Humility," preached July 18, 1831; or God's presence in us, in sermons 88, "The Oracle Within" (September 11, 1830) and 93, "The Kingdom of Heaven Is Within" (October 31, 1830).

[127] See sermon 120, "Religious Books," preached July 3, 1831, and the letter to Miss Elisabeth Tucker of February 1, 1832 (J 2.458–459). Henry P. Scougal (1650–1678) was a minister in the church of Scotland and a professor at King's College, Aberdeen; he is best known for his *Life of God in the Soul of Man*, which profoundly influenced Whitefield.

[128] Second version, preached April 1831, of sermon 59, "Perseverance" (H.273).

[129] This is the thing Emerson calls "the tremendous idea of God," which men rack their brains to screen from their souls; see JMN 3.236–238 (March 13, 1831). The whole passage was written during the preparation of a sermon on the Holy Spirit (sermon 110).

[130] Cf. sermon 78, "Salvation Now" (H.291), preached June 12, 1830: "We are accustomed to speak of the past as having had some real existence to us, to speak as if we were not new men and women, but as if we took up the history of the world where our fathers left it; as if one individual were a part and not a whole; as if we wrought a few threads into the web of a common destiny."

[131] See sermon 121, "Spiritual Discernment," preached July 17, 1831.

[132] See sermon 89, "God's Wrath and Man's Sin," preached September 25, 1830.

[133] See sermon 96, "Doing the Will of God," preached November 28, 1830.

mythology, with its culmination in the person of Christ, is an illustration of the great law of universal purification by which the world is incessantly judged and condemned; Luther was the punishment inflicted on the church of Rome for its crime and deceit, "and now the progress of the same truth is reforming the Reformed Church."[134] Humanity is borne along in a vast process of purification, in which each of us is invited to participate.[135]

In the picture he sketched after the Civil War of the New England of his youth, Emerson refers with a mixture of tenderness and irony to the young men obsessed with change, born with "knives in their brain."[136] This, like so many other details of that reminiscence, is autobiographical in reference. As he was preparing the sermon just cited, his meditation on the conditions necessary for spiritual growth within each soul had revealed to him the central role played in the process by the faculty of analysis; it is to the extent to which we put asunder what habit has joined together that we attain a vision of things in conformity with the truth, and that, in consequence, we prepare the world's regeneration. The true benefactor of humanity is he who discerns principles. Because of the force with which at this time introspection and reform are bound together in Emerson's thought, it is worth citing the journal at length:

> whenever a man first perceives the supposed necessity of the Use of Ardent Spirits throughout the community to vanish in his own mind—when first he sees in his thought the custom of drinking separate itself from the idea of society, & feels for the first time satisfied that it is a thing wholly accidental & not necessary, then the empire of Intemperance receives a fatal blow. . . . And is not this the history of all advancement? We look at good & ill which grows together as indissolubly connected: if an improvement takes place in our own mind we get a glimpse of an almost imperceptible line that separates the nature of the thing from the evil admixture. By a more diligent inspection that division will farther appear, till it peels off like dead bark. This is the sense of Coleridge's urged distinction between the similar & the same.
>
> This is the merit of every reformer. One man talks of the abolition of Slavery with perfect coolness whilst all around him sneer or roar at his ludicrous benevolence. They with their sinful eyes can

[134] Sermon 95, "The Judgment of Christ" (H.308), preached November 13, 1830.

[135] And of course such participation may well take the form of an evasion or a betrayal—hence Emerson's exclamation apropos of Bentham and his disciples: "The stinking philosophy of the Utilitarian!" (JMN 3.323 [1832]).

[136] "Life and Letters in New England," W 10.329.

> not see society without slaves. He sees distinctly the difference, and knows that the crime is unnecessary. And this is the progress of every soul. What it joined before it now severs & sin & error are perpetually falling away from the eternal soul.[137]

Upon the harmonious and stable image of an organized society is thus superimposed, after a fashion, an atomistic vision of humanity. In the ideal world of this vision there is discontinuity, absolute rupture between ourselves and others; and that isolation, which is, as it were, the price of our union with God, cannot be broken except in passing by way of God, that is, by a supplementary effort, a bending back upon ourselves, which will permit us to recover his presence in us, token and source of comparable greatness in others. In a sermon preached early in 1831,[138] Emerson is thus led to reject as inadequate a theory he had thitherto made his own, that of the rationalist economists for whom beneficence proceeds in the last analysis from enlightened self-interest: "that the interest of the individual and society are one is most true and much more than this is true, and yet all together do not yet constitute the true motive of our social duty." The necessary supplement, weightier than all the rest together, is God himself, who has made even the humblest soul his chosen temple. The phrase of Luke 10, "Thou shalt love the Lord thy God with all thy heart, and thy neighbor as thyself,"[139] is a grandiose tautology. In the face of this blinding truth, social distinctions grow pale and faint. The most sordid beggar, the thief, the felon all have a right to our service because like us they partake of the divine nature. Emerson makes clear what it might cost a man of the world to bend to this law,[140] but the commandment is universal. Beneficence, which henceforth ascribes each of its acts to God, must put on the armor of charity.

But Emerson does not go very far in this direction. He recognizes the justice and the necessity of mutual aid, but he is much more occupied with the spiritual work of revealing souls to themselves (on one occasion indeed he warns his congregation against charitable institutions—they comfort only the body, he says, and often conceal great hardness of

[137] JMN 3.209 (November 10, 1830).

[138] Sermon 104, "Self and Others," preached January 12, 1831 (in McGiffert, *Young Emerson Speaks*, pp. 127–137). See also the preliminary notes to the sermon (JMN 3.222–225), in which Emerson engages, one might say, in a reconnaissance of the terrain.

[139] Cited by Emerson himself.

[140] He notes (p. 131) that those who most need our help are "commonly unlovely, uneducated, many of them stupid, often vicious, offensive frequently from the filth of their habitations, and sometimes much more so from loathsome diseases."

heart behind their generous facade[141]). That is why he gives a place of honor among altruistic activities to education—thus anticipating not only his own numerous speeches and essays devoted to this subject[142] but also the ideas of Bronson Alcott, who was, with the aid of Elizabeth Peabody, to open the boldly and even rashly innovative Temple School in September 1834.[143] Emerson focuses on the problem on two occasions, using first an anniversary and then an inauguration to draw people's attention to certain essential but misunderstood principles.[144] On both occasions he does homage to the inspiration he has drawn from Pestalozzi,[145] whose pedagogical theories, founded on the reason and goodness of men, had met with astonishing successes; but in discussing those theories Emerson holds fast to what they offer that is his own. He does not linger over the technical aspects of the system and passes by in silence the carefully calculated stages by which the child is to be led from observation to expression to writing and calculation; but he emphasizes with great force the distinctive quality of the method, the organizing principle of which had been brought out by Pestalozzi himself: " 'that the amelioration of outward circumstances will be the effect, but never can be the means of mental & moral improvement.' "[146] It was very fine grist, evidently, that the minister of the Second Church was securing for his mill; Pestalozzi illustrated, with the demonstrative force that success gives, an axiom of the Emersonian philosophy. Perhaps he did more; perhaps he procured certain late and vicarious satisfactions for the man who had proved himself so poor a schoolteacher.[147]

In any case, by 1831 Emerson had sufficiently reflected on the problem of education to discern the two principal demands to be made of it.

[141] In sermon 130, "Love Thy Neighbor," preached October 2, 1831.

[142] Throughout his public career, even during the Civil War, Emerson's attempts to attract his countrymen's attention to this crucial subject are indefatigable.

[143] Vide infra, chapter 8.

[144] In sermons 128, "The Objects of Education" (given September 23, 1831 on the occasion of the thirty-first anniversary of the foundation of a parish orphan-school), and 148, "Sunday Schools" (preached March 25, 1832 to celebrate the installation of the Sunday school in the church's new wing).

[145] Emerson had acquainted himself with Pestalozzi's theories through a book published in London in 1831 called *Heinrich Pestalozzi and His Plan of Education; Being an Account of His Life and Writings*. The author, a young German named Edward Biber, had taught at Yverdon in one of the schools using Pestalozzi's methods.

[146] JMN 3.286. Having copied the phrase, Emerson remarks that it expresses in a different form the content of the Gospel precept, " 'seek ye first the kingdom of God & his righteousness, & all these things shall be added unto you.' "

[147] Cf. sermon 148, "Sunday Schools": "It was something new in the world that a man of genius should be able to throw so much beauty and delight over an occupation oftener esteemed either irksome or mean" (H.361).

First, in conformity with its etymology, it must be a development of the potential qualities of the child; that is, it must seek to make of the child not a "useful satellite"[148] but a being capable of guiding himself and choosing his direction of progress. It must teach him to see with his own eyes, to guide himself by his own will, to judge by his own feelings. Care should, of course, be taken to protect him against certain dangers, but the limits of such care are strict; it is not by multiplying crutches that one learns to walk. Education is to be founded on experience and experiment, as Montaigne would have said; the child will be trained in a positive manner to put his faculties into play. The second principle seems the precondition of the first. The pedagogy in question, Emerson argues, will never bear fruit unless founded on trust, such a trust as presupposes genuine personal relations between teacher and pupil. On this point Emerson is categorical: collective processes are an aberration. In dealing with human beings everything has to be made by hand; "you must go and sit down with the child, and win its love as well as command its respect."[149] You will then discover qualities you did not suspect were there, because the child is lost, in every sense of the word, when dissolved in the mass. If in fact Sunday schools deserve praise, it is because they more than others, because of the small size of their classes, permit an intellectual exchange from person to person—from which, in the end, the teachers themselves benefit, since one cannot teach virtue without being, or becoming, virtuous.

In presenting education as a midwifery of the soul, Emerson was actually giving a new extension to a long-familiar concept, but one that the Coleridgean intuitions had immensely reinforced: the idea of individual vocation. From the time of his examination of conscience in 1824, and perhaps earlier, this idea had been working secretly, maintaining in him a sort of disgust for all that obliged him to strike a posture when the only true elegance was spontaneity. Gradually it took a more positive form, as in the sermon "Atheism and Ignorance," in which Emerson showed, almost in the manner of Fourier, that the human mind receives its unity and power from a ruling passion.[150] But the revelation of divine inwardness gave the idea the authority it had previously lacked; authenticated by this interior seal, it henceforth had the right to proclaim its originality before the world and the obligation not

[148] Sermon 128, "The Objects of Education" (H.341).

[149] Ibid.

[150] "The mind of a man is a chaos till it has some ruling passion. Every man needs some strong influence pushing his efforts in a single direction to give effect to his action. A man who has no profession, no particular calling, is apt to be a man of little efficiency" (sermon 51: "Atheism and Ignorance" [H.265], preached October 11, 1829).

to let itself be led astray. This proud certainty explains the triumphant tone of a sermon preached at the end of 1830 under the title of "Trust Yourself."[151] Emerson begins by saying that among God's intentions is that the universe be ruled by variety and that every being be fulfilled in a different way: "the elm is a bad oak," he had noted in his journal, "but a beautiful elm and the beauty of the walnut or the sycamore is not felt by comparing them with different species but with other individuals of their own."[152] But there is a tenacious superstition of uniformity. Each of us behaves as if he had been put into the world to play the role of a secondary creature. This, says Emerson, is not only a mistake but also a sin: "Let him fully trust his own share of God's goodness, that if used to the uttermost, it will lead him on to a perfection which has no type in the universe, save only in the Divine Mind."[153]

The reader of the essays will recognize, beneath the Unitarian cut of the outer garment, the principal theme and almost the tone of "Self-Reliance." But an immense difference separates the two texts when one situates them in the life of their author. The man who published "Self-Reliance" based his doctrine upon his experience; the preacher of "Trust Yourself" was proclaiming a bold thing but had yet to apply it. The period of nearly two years that separated the proclamation from the act of rupture with which it was pregnant indicates the extent of the obstacles Emerson had to overcome. Just as jurisprudence attempts through a thousand groping approximations to reconcile the principle of the law and the disconcerting complexity of fact, so Emerson had to invent the solution that would enable him to answer his true calling at the level of daily existence. The passage to that solution was laborious; all of Emerson's sincerity was engaged in it, but also all of his lucidity, so that in the end he never had to regret his final decision.

The first difficulty, he notes in 1830, has to do with our situation as free beings: "we do not grow up like a plant according to a conformation of a seed. On the contrary it is the privilege of our nature over that of flowers & brutes that we are our own law."[154] Society further complicates our task, because as it progresses it extends the range of possible choices; the day seems near when professions will be as numerous as individuals.[155] This reason alone compelled Emerson to consider whether

[151] Sermon 90, "Trust Yourself," preached December 1830 (McGiffert, *Young Emerson Speaks*, pp. 105–111). Again the preacher has softened certain phrases of the diarist; see in particular JMN 3.190–191 and 198–199 (July 20 and September 27, 1830).

[152] JMN 3.191.

[153] McGiffert, *Young Emerson Speaks*, p. 108, and J 2.310.

[154] JMN 3.191.

[155] See sermon 143: "Find Your Calling," preached February 5, 1832 (McGiffert, *Young Emerson Speaks*, pp. 163–169).

his proper place was in the bosom of the Unitarian church; but more immediate motives were quick to reinforce that doubt. An early sign of the crisis appears in the sermon he gave one year after having answered the Second Church's call;[156] the minister must preach to his congregation, but he must also comfort the sick and the discouraged. Although these two functions had been reconciled easily, as one remembers, in the self-examination of 1824, they had in practice proved incompatible. The progress of truth in the mind obeys capricious rules and is hard to adjust to the routine of observance; and when the minister can finally meditate in the solitude of his room, some parishioner turns up to seek advice. And many other obligations were added to these two; like his father, Emerson was named chaplain to the Senate and then was asked to sit on a committee for school inspection. In 1831, he spent considerable time investigating the pedagogic methods then in use, in consequence of a complaint made that certain teachers were guilty of brutality to students. Emerson acquitted himself of these various tasks honorably—but also, as one might guess, with weary resignation.[157]

But these were only trifles. An objection of infinitely greater gravity was gradually taking form in him against the profession of the ministry itself; he had the feeling that through fidelity and submissiveness toward his church he was suffocating God's voice in his conscience. Several sermons, dated late in 1831 and early in 1832, are built around the insurmountable opposition between the progress of the community and the progress of the individual.[158] Here one can see the point at which Emerson separates himself from the Unitarians—not in rejecting them but in passing them by, as becomes clear from the exordium of the sermon "Judging Right for Ourselves." He still shares the Unitarian optimism on the progress made by humanity as a whole: "the great body of the people have risen to the same degree of virtue that belonged to the most wise and pious individual of some former age."[159] But unlike the Unitarians, he is not complacent; he would like to see each man striving to surpass all others: "By the use of our moral and intellectual powers, we may outstrip the tardy progress of the race and anticipate future centuries in the short term of our mortal life. Hence arises the sacred duty of judging for ourselves."[160] As McGiffert judiciously suggests, behind

[156] See sermon 69: "The Ministry: A Year's Retrospect," delivered April 4, 1830 (McGiffert, *Young Emerson Speaks*, pp. 67–74).

[157] See Rusk, *Life*, chapters 10 and 11, in particular pp. 146 and 152–153.

[158] See particularly sermons 130, "Love Thy Neighbor," preached October 2, 1831; 145, "Judging Right for Ourselves," February 26, 1832; and 146, "The Education of the Soul," March 4, 1832.

[159] "Judging Right for Ourselves" (H.358).

[160] Ibid.

this opposition are two conceptions of the spiritual leader.[161] One only advances as far as those he has in charge can follow him; he slows his pace in difficult spots; he knows that the work of education is long and patient. The other defines his goals and explains his program, then sets off, eyes fixed on the objective, without caring whether others behind him are out of breath. He is a prophet and an orator. At the beginning of 1832 Emerson's choice between these two figures had already been made.

The decision to leave the ministry was nonetheless difficult. The journal bears here and there the trace of Emerson's inward debates, and the impassioned tone reveals that the conflict was strenuous: "It is the best part of the man, I sometimes think, that revolts most against his being the minister."[162] In any case, Emerson feels attached to his community by almost indivisible bonds; as we are spiritualized, he writes, our chains become subtler, but they do not fall off. Bodily passions yield to the fear of public opinion, of poverty, of death, then to the apprehension of offending or of being misunderstood; but we still defer to the judgment of others.[163] Finally, in a sermon preached early in February 1832, Emerson dealt with the problem directly.[164] Having drawn from his introductory evocation of certain powerful truths—God's particular care for each soul, the right to free investigation—the courage he needs to speak without hypocrisy or unnecessary provocation, he defines his position as follows: there is a way to meet our social obligations that is not degrading to our faculties, because our will can bend outward circumstances in the direction of our true vocation; it is of course our obligation to seek that solution; but if it is not to be found, and reconciliation seems impossible, if a collision seems inevitable, then the force of our inward feeling may then be its own justification, and must break what will not bend.[165] Applying this injunction to himself, Emerson all

[161] *Young Emerson Speaks*, p. xxxix.

[162] JMN 3.318 (January 10, 1832); see also JMN 4.27 (June 2, 1832). Cabot, *Memoir*, 1.167, cites a still more intemperate passage of the journal: "I hate goodies. I hate goodness that preaches. Goodness that preaches undoes itself. Goodies make us very bad. We will almost sin to spite them."

[163] See sermon 124: "Freedom," preached for the first time on August 14, 1831. The passage under discussion appears on a separate sheet, and may have been composed for a later occasion— the sermon was delivered eleven times between 1831 and 1835.

[164] Sermon 143, "Find Your Calling," already cited.

[165] A paragraph of the journal written while Emerson was thinking over this sermon indicates his readiness to draw the inevitable conclusions of his doctrine and to consider a change of profession: "Every man hath his use no doubt and every one makes ever the effort according to the energy of his character to suit his external condition to his inward constitution. If his

throughout the spring and summer attempts to find the point of equilibrium at which he and his congregation can meet and not reject each other. Hence the letter, now lost, that he wrote to acquaint his parishioners with the change in his feelings regarding communion and to propose certain changes in his administration of it. The sequence of events that Rusk details[166] is striking by its absence of commotion and even by its vagueness of contour; almost two months elapsed between the famous communion sermon and the vote taken by the proprietors of the Second Church to put an end to Emerson's pastoral charge, and in the interval Emerson simply continued to preach. Moreover, he was not looking for scandal; in the midst of the crisis he notes in his journal that "the most desperate scoundrels have been the over refiners" and that "without accomodation society is impracticable."[167] He distrusts all logical rigor and genuinely fears hurting the ignorant; he remembers that for centuries communion has been the channel of holiness. But at the same time he never loses sight of his guiding star. In a sermon preached in March 1832, he reaffirms the thesis of "Find Your Calling": if a righteous man engages in a course of action society condemns, he must on perceiving that condemnation reexamine the motives of his choice; "but if, at last, with the best light and in perfect simplicity, the man still approves his action, let him go and do it, though he go alone."[168]

To those who can envision Emerson's honest, persistent interrogation of his own soul, culminating in his retreat into the mountains of New Hampshire, his only companion the example of George Fox, the issue Emerson chooses as the ground of his final rupture will hardly seem surprising. Rusk is, of course, right to note that the administration of communion was preferable to a philosophical idea as being within the range of ordinary minds; he is also right to note that it was an old subject of debate,[169] which had cost Jonathan Edwards his Northampton pulpit before troubling the first generation of Unitarians. But if disputes on the matter had been carried on so heatedly, was it not because communion acted as a sort of diamond in which the fires of theological thought could be concentrated and the oppositions of systems and temperaments diffracted? Around the reasonable and deliberately restricted ar-

---

external condition does not admit of such accommodation he breaks the form of his life, & enters a new one which does" (JMN 3.324 [January 30, 1832]).

166 See Rusk, *Life*, pp. 160ff.

167 JMN 4.30 (July 15, 1832).

168 Sermon 146, "The Education of the Soul" (H.359).

169 Emerson's sermon (W 11.1–25) begins with a quick survey of the history of the sacrament till the time that the Quakers "denied the authority of the rite altogether, and gave good reasons for disusing it."

gument of the communion sermon is filigreed a whole philosophy; a number of contemporary texts help suggest what its outlines were.

In May and June of that same year, Emerson preached three sermons that when joined together constitute a formidably coherent atack against that scheme of redemption which was indispensable to the idea of communion.[170] The first, by its very title, proclaims communion pointless: "Thinking Well of Human Nature." Emerson has not entirely thrown off the notion of sin—but he reduces it to its proper size. Human nature, he affirms, deserves to be treated with reverence for its ample resources, its capacity for good, its as yet unsounded depths of meaning; "consciousness" stuns and dazzles him by its richness; all the universe can lodge in a thought. He invites his hearers to dive within themselves so as to recognize there, beneath vice and stupidity, the permanence of an essentially just nature. In the last part of the sermon, he gives the passwords he later makes so familiar: know yourself; respect yourself; be true to yourself.

The second sermon, given on the occasion of a solar eclipse, transfers the debate to the ground of the intellect. Anticipating Auguste Comte, who saw in the contemplation of the stars' ordered courses one of the most effective means of delivering the human mind from its theological prejudices, Emerson argues that the discovery of interstellar space has made null and void not only Calvinism but also all the other forms of anthropomorphic religion; Newton became a Unitarian and Laplace, living in a Catholic country, an unbeliever. God does, of course, exist, a God curiously defined as "an Infinite Mind, an awful, an adorable Being, yet as affectionate in his care as he is surpassing in wisdom"[171]—a description that would have prompted Comte to remark that New England was evidently still in the metaphysical stage—but this God evades all temporal systems, "St Paul's epistles, the Jewish Christianity" among them.[172] The third sermon extends and crowns the first two. Emerson begins by positing that divine unity subsists across time like

[170] Sermons 155, "Thinking Well of Human Nature," preached May 13, 1832; 157, "Astronomy" (in McGiffert, *Young Emerson Speaks*, pp. 170–179), May 27, 1832; and 158, "A Living Religion," June 11, 1832.

[171] McGiffert, *Young Emerson Speaks*, p. 176.

[172] Cf. JMN 4.26 (May 26, 1832): "Thus Astronomy proves theism but disproves dogmatic theology. The Sermon on the Mount must be true throughout all the space which the eye sees & the brain imagines but St Paul's epistles, the Jewish Christianity, would be unintelligible. It operates steadily to establish the moral laws, to disconcert & evaporate temporary systems." Such a judgment indicates how cautiously one needs to regard certain recent attempts to establish similarities between Emerson and Christian existentialism; see particularly Roland Francis Lee, "Emerson and Christian Existentialism," Ph.D diss., Ohio State University, 1952 (summarized in *Dissertation Abstracts* 18 [1958], pp. 2145–2146).

"one law, one nature, one truth, one goodness," and he draws from this concept an argument against the federal theology, worked out long ago by the Puritans and still implicitly accepted as dogma:

> It is a vulgar error and a great one that men group themselves together in their religious views. They think of God as speaking to the human race, or to the Jewish people, or to the Christian Church, and not as speaking to each individual man. And so the popular religious views represent Adam in terms as "the federal head" of his race, and that when he fell all his posterity sinned, and all rose in the second Adam.[173]

To replace this mummified cult, subject to the tyranny of history, Emerson imagines a religion of institutions and forms pulsing with life. But to realize this ideal man must learn again that he has God within him: "the human soul is so framed that when it is in healthful action, the thought of God appears in it as inevitably as a music box plays the tune for which it was constructed. The human soul is set to that anthem."[174] Eternity will then be seen for what it is, not sterile duration but original and unceasing creation, whose point of chief activity we represent at every moment. "Every man that is born is a new being in some respects different from any other. He needs a different worship. He cannot utter his feelings in the same words or forms that served the man of another education and a former age."[175]

Emerson's decision to abandon his pastoral cares is thus not only a liberation. It is an absolute departure, exalted and romantic, along a path still fresh with dew, or—to use one of Emerson's own metaphors—the beginning of an auspicious voyage over the infinite sea.[176] Before, man was like "a nest of Indian boxes . . . each a new puzzle," the last revealing only emptiness;[177] but people supinely accepted the deception. Now, however, we can quickly pass the "splendid barricade" erected around a man by his reputation, or the brilliance of his establishment, or the elegance of his manners, and arrive at the character that is his inward kernel. But here one really begins to explore unknown ter-

[173] Sermon 158, "A Living Religion" (H.371).

[174] Ibid.

[175] Ibid.

[176] See JMN 3.303 (November 1831). Emerson compares each mind to a room enclosed on three sides but open on the fourth to infinite space, then complicates the image by a nautical metaphor: "Let me embark in polit. economy, in repartee, in fiction, in verse, in practical counsels . . . & I am soon run aground; but let my bark head its own way toward the law of laws, toward the Compensation or action & reaction of the Moral Universe & I sweep serenely over God's depths in an infinite sea."

[177] JMN 4.51 (October 1832).

ritory. The potential of man has never been investigated; to the new generation accrues the mission of recognizing and mapping it. For the moment Emerson can only give certain vague indications of what this fulfilled and realized man will be, who has had no precedent in the past[178] and who will within himself harmonize contemplation and practicality, force and benevolence, eloquence and action.[179] Emerson then begins to seek new teachers and looks in particular to Goethe; the last sermon he preached before the break, on October 21, 1832, was at the same time an homage to Goethe and an extraordinarily urgent invitation to recognize the sacred character of every man's vocation.[180] Sincerity (today one might say authenticity) consists precisely in paying constant attention to our loftiest self, so as to construct and consolidate that "truth of character" which will set us in harmony with ourselves, justify our acts before the world, and in the end blend indistinguishably with the life of religion. The reversal is complete. We are asked not to love others for the sake of God but to love God through ourselves.

It was to take at least a decade for Emerson's thought to absorb the direct and indirect consequences of this revolutionary proposition. Along the way would arise a native form of romanticism, fed on the strongest sap of New England.[181] Springing up in this country that is at once very new and very old, to use Santayana's terms of analysis, a few rare volumes strangely compounded of intellectual subtlety and fervent inspiration were to be the answer to Sydney Smith's famous and insolent question, Who reads an American book? Seldom has the Zeitgeist been better served. At the same time, by a paradox that preserved his work's very human tone, Emerson in 1832 was keeping his eyes obstinately closed both to the direction and to the amplitude of the events taking place in his own country. Present at the rise of a great democratic wave, whose surge was to shape the nation's life till the slavery crisis, Emerson responded with virtuous indignation—just as John

[178] "When we look at the world of past men, we say, What a host of heroes but when we come to particularize, it is like counting the stars which we thought innumerable, but which prove few & rare. Bacon, Shakspear, Caesar, Scipio, Cicero, Burke, Chatham, Franklin, none of them will bear examination or furnish the type of a *Man*" (JMN 4.36 [August 1832]).

[179] "Unevenness of characters. Every man is one half of a man, either benevolent & weak or firm & unbenevolent, either a speaker & no doer, or a doer & no speaker, either contemplative or practical, & excellence in any one kind seems to speak defect in the others" (JMN 3.310 [December 10, 1831]).

[180] Sermon 164, "The Genuine Man," in McGiffert, *Young Emerson Speaks*, pp. 180–190. A paragraph of the journal dated August 18, 1832 (J 2.506–507) explicitly associates Goethe's name with the subject of sincerity, there understood as fidelity to oneself.

[181] Cf. Robert E. Spiller, "Critical Standards in the American Romantic Movement," *College English* 8 (April 1947), pp. 344–352.

Quincy Adams was some years later to stigmatize in his journal a certain young man named Emerson who, after having failed in the respectable professions of schoolteacher and minister, was now making himself the spokesman of a subversive doctrine offering all men a justification for their excesses.[182]

It was the mischievous irony of fortune that made Emerson's ministry in the Second Church coincide exactly with the first presidential term of Andrew Jackson. Jackson's election had been preceded by scheming, by pressures, indeed by violence, and all these phenomena had justifiably shocked New England consciences; nonetheless, a decisive turn had been taken in the nation's history. Universal suffrage provided a constantly growing throng of immigrants with the power to vote, and the march westward was reconstructing civilization from the bottom up, while steadily removing the national center of gravity from the original colonies, still oriented toward Europe. A great emancipation was being accomplished, and it was inevitable that the aristocratic states, notably Virginia and Massachusetts, should bear its costs. John Quincy Adams was the last president till Coolidge to come from New England. What Emerson did not understand in 1832 was precisely that the fits he saw agitating the people were not the expression of a fever stimulated by perverse physicians[183] but the elementary manifestation of an entirely new force, gropingly seeking its form and balance.

To explain this lack of discernment it might be enough to remark that Emerson was at once too provincial in temperament to understand the America in the making[184] and too universal in aspiration to take much of an interest in it. He is not, to be sure, unaware of the deterioration in the political climate, and a muffled note of uneasiness sounds in his sermons, above all in those from 1831 on;[185] but he continues to extol individual virtue as the sole bastion against these abuses—even if this means allowing, in desperate cases, a flight away from social commit-

[182] See Allan Nevins, ed., *The Diary of John Quincy Adams 1794–1845* (New York, 1929), p. 511.

[183] Cf. JMN 3.100: "It is said public opinion will not bear it. Really? Public opinion, I am sorry to say, will bear a great deal of nonsense. . . . It will bear Andrew Jackson for President."

[184] A passage of the journal from 1831 (JMN 3.276–279) gives an amusingly irreverent illustration of this limitation: a forceful diatribe against Jackson, puppet of the "Bad Party in the country," is followed shortly by the simple note, "Dined with President Adams yesterday at Dr Parkman's."

[185] See for example sermon 113, "Fasting, Humiliation and Prayer," previously cited. In it Emerson describes to his congregation the "evil signs" that the virtuous man discerns and that sadden his heart: the Indians are in danger of being expelled from the territory in which they have sought refuge; parties tear at one another's throats like beasts; power has become plunder for the unprincipled.

ments and a retreat within the self.[186] And this position is not only that of the minister, led by place and occasion to remain aloof from the world; it expresses the deep thought of the inward man. "I think respectfully enough of statesmen," he writes to his aunt Mary, "yet I have been reading Jefferson & can't but think that he & his great mates look little already, from this short distance where we stand, & he would be sorry to know my feelings about their ambition."[187]

In this respect at least, Emerson distinguished himself from his master Coleridge, who considered political action important and urgent enough to dedicate his *Statesman's Manual*, in which he undertook to show the great distance between the true statesman and the vulgar schemer, to the British aristocracy; and Coleridge was also aware, being the nineteenth-century European that he was, of the moral stake often hidden behind national rivalries and civil discords. Furthermore, in considering institutions he had always been careful to preserve the principle of their diversity; he was of the opinion that a government has to be judged by its effectiveness—which is to say that it was dependent on Understanding, and guided by Reason only in crucial choices.[188] These nuances of Coleridge's thought Emerson cannot see. In a sermon on envy,[189] oddly isolated amid the subversive triad, he emphatically denounces the projects of European revolutionaries: "At this moment, a new order of fanatics in the kingdom of France propose, under the name of religion and philanthropy, to destroy the machinery used in the arts, to take away the property from the hands that hold it, and distribute it anew according to their own better judgment."[190] The same hunger for possession exists in America, wrapped in the cloak of patriotism:

[186] Sermon 109, "God in the Soul," preached March 5, 1831, seems to indicate that the United States have in Emerson's eyes arrived at precisely such a state. Emerson's sketch of the disappointed and bitter statesman might well have been inspired by John Quincy Adams: "the secret cannot be concealed; it will out, louder and more unanimous every month, that it is no longer desirable, scarce creditable for one of good temper and good parts to mix in the conflicts of parties. Chagrin, odium, malevolence, and unfitness for peaceful and noble thoughts, follow the broken Statesman home to his unwilling retirement, and sour and disgrace his closing years" (H.322).

[187] Letter to Mary Moody Emerson of March 26 and April 1, 1830 (L 1.298–299).

[188] See *The Friend*, 3 vols. (London, 1844), "Section the First: On the Principles of Political Understanding," essays 3 and 4, pp. 238–278. In Coleridge's eyes, the theory of the general will advanced by Rousseau in *The Social Contract* precisely exemplifies the dangers to which one is exposed when entrusting the charge of shaping institutions to Reason alone.

[189] Sermon 156 (H.369), preached May 20, 1832.

[190] Ibid. It is probable that Emerson is thinking here of the disciples of Saint-Simon, who just after the revolution of July 1830 had published a proclamation demanding the sharing of wealth, the abolition of inheritance, and the emancipation of women.

> If any interest prospers, it is called a favored interest and denounced. If any institution, even of learning or of charity, is well-conducted and successful, somewhere a voice of accusation and menace is raised against it. If any district of the country thrives more than its neighbors, that is reason enough why its neighbors should combine against it.[191]

The Federalist habits of thought are too deeply rooted for him to think of evaluating them critically—of examining, for example, the difficult and controversial question of tariffs, not to speak of the right of property, the contingent character of which Coleridge for his part had clearly defined.[192]

The contrast between Emerson's unconscious conformity here and the immense effort of readjustment he had undertaken in other respects is so sharp as to make his personality seem almost incoherent. But what it lacks in harmony it gains in dramatic potential. The man simply does not correspond to the misleadingly pious description one customarily gives of him after having ceased to read his work. Before finding he had to seek; and his gaze, though enormously wide in range, does not grasp at once all the aspects of human experience; whole areas of it remain in the shadow, and he has no suspicion of their existence. To describe the progress of his thought is precisely to show how they emerge into the light one after the other. For reasons dependent both on his nature and on local circumstances, a political comprehension of his time was not easy for him. Too many other preoccupations led him away from it and too many secret discomforts. But he had broken with the church, he had chosen to be minister to the world, and nothing that touched his compatriots could now be alien to him. That is why, regardless of his digressions and his professions of indifference, he could not avoid returning to the matter once again, some time later.

[191] Ibid.

[192] "Now it is impossible to deduce the Right of Property from pure Reason. The utmost which Reason could give would be a property in the *forms* of things, as far as the forms were produced by individual power" (*The Friend*, "Section the First: On the Principles of Political Knowledge," essay 4, p. 275).

PART II

The Discovery and Glorification of the Self

5

~ ~ ~ ~

THE ROAD TO CONCORD

BY ONE of those brutal reversals that abound in the biography of his formative years, Emerson found in the abandonment of his ministry not the invigorating freedom he had imagined but the inexorable confirmation of his difficulties and doubts. After sustaining him at the decisive moments, the great image of Luther was now no longer useful, and grew faint.[1] No one now could take over Emerson's responsibility for his own destiny, or choose for him the elements of which it was to be made. Then, when he had need of all his mental resources, and perhaps more need still of an alertly obedient body, he was once again attacked by illness, this time in the form of a persistent diarrhea that left him "as white & thin as a ghost."[2] Long accustomed to cope with misfortunes of this sort, he chose to treat this latest trial by silence and irony, and transferred his hopes to the work to be accomplished when his health was restored. He writes to his brother William in November 1832:

> I have wiredrawn to an infinitesimal ductility all the sympathies of men women & children. for there is a limit beyond which peoples interest in other peoples bowels cannot go. Meantime the severing of our strained cord that bound me to the church is a mutual relief. It is sorrowful to me & to them in a measure for we were both

[1] Rusk (*Life*, pp. 164–165) shows that in October 1832 Emerson was encouraged by reading an unsigned article of Carlyle's on Luther in *Fraser's Magazine*; he transcribed Luther's speech to the Diet of Worms into his journal. Coleridge also (in *The Friend*, 1.169–177: "First Landing-Place," essay 1) had exalted the personality of the German "*son of Thunder*"; and two years later Emerson made Luther the subject of the third lecture in his series on biography.

[2] Rusk, *Life*, p. 166.

> suited & hoped to be mutually useful. But though it will occasion me perhaps some, (possibly, much) temporary embarrassment yet I walk firmly toward a peace & a freedom which I plainly see before me albeit afar. Shall I pester you with half the projects that sprout & bloom in my head, of action, literature, philosophy? Am I not to have a magazine—my ownty downty—scorning co-operation & taking success by storm. The vice of these undertakings in general is that they depend on many contributors who all speak an average sense & no one of them utters his own individuality. Yet that the soul of a man should speak out, & not the soul general of the town or town pump is essential to all eloquence, to originality. The objection to a paper conducted by one man is the limits of human strength The Goethe or Schiller that wd do it must have a constitution that does not belong to every lean lily-livered aspirant of these undigesting days. But give me time, give me strength & *co-operation*, *on* my *own terms*, *kai ten gen kineso*.[3]

Events were gradually to show that this reverie had a solid basis in reality; the invocation of the great German Romantics was the prelude to a more literary reorientation of Emerson's thought, and at the same time his somewhat extravagant journalistic ambitions[4] permit an early glimpse both of his courageous persistence and of his final failure as editor of the *Dial*. But the time was not yet ripe, and the present had its own grave threats. If Emerson himself concealed his own miserable condition, or made as if to forget it, his relatives did not. Thus Charles confesses his worry in a letter to Aunt Mary: "Waldo is sick. His spirits droop; he looks to the South, and thinks he should like to go away. I never saw him so disheartened. When a man would be a reformer, he wants to be strong. When a man has stepped out of the intrenchments of influence and station, he would fain feel his powers unimpaired and his hope firm."[5]

The dominant note is clearly anxiety; but one also hears, veiled but secretly insistent, the note of disapproval. Not everyone is a rebel who wants to be. An elementary prudence commands us to assess our forces before each undertaking and not to advance further than they can take

[3] Letter to William Emerson of November 19, 1832 (L 1.357–358). The italics are Emerson's. The last clause in Greek is evidently an allusion to Archimedes' famous remark, "Give me but one firm spot on which to stand, and I shall move the earth."

[4] Less extravagant, however, than they might seem today. Orestes Brownson published his own magazine for more than thirty years (1844–1875), calling it with no false modesty *Brownson's Quarterly Review*.

[5] Letter from Charles Emerson to Mary Moody Emerson of November 26, 1832 (Cabot, *Memoir*, 1.173).

us. Ralph Waldo, it appears, had forgotten this rule; he discovered too late that his challenge had not shaken up the indolence around him, but only plunged him deeper into his own uncertainty and discouragement. And the condemnation that Charles indulgently contents himself with suggesting is taken up soon by the more acerbic and categorical pen of their aunt Mary, who cannot forgive what she regards as her favorite nephew's apostasy: "you talk of his being a 'reformer & needing good health,' " she writes to Charles some weeks later, "A reformer—who on earth with his genius is less able to cope with opposition? Who with his good sense less *force* of mind—and while it invents new universes is lost in the surrounding halo."[6] Outside the family circle the news was greeted not with irritation or anger but with a vaguely disconcerted surprise. Certain of his Unitarian colleagues claimed to see in his decision the reflection of a certain Quakerish eccentricity; here and there whispers circulated, seconding the notion of an Emerson family taint. Emerson felt no need to reply to these reproaches and insinuations; he was too far advanced in the practice of self-trust to place a high value on a charge not acknowledged by his inward judgment. But whether he admitted it or not, Boston had for him become a prison, and he needed a change of air. It was not that anything irrevocable had happened—the warm and frank letter he sent to his congregation in late December was enough to show that they still enjoyed his esteem and he theirs;[7] furthermore, he continued to rely, despite the passing storm, on the fidelity of family affections. What was in question was a matter not of persons or ideas or feelings but of mental space. Like his new master Goethe's Wilhelm Meister, he was in search of such new experiences as would offer his soul richer and more savory nourishment. One chapter of his personal Bildungsroman is closed; the next one would need a larger frame.

That is why within a few days the project of a trip to Europe came into being, took form, and, all obstacles overcome, became reality. In vain had Emerson denounced in his journal some months before the illusion that makes us believe that human nature becomes suddenly clear when looked at from the other end of the world.[8] The "purpureal vision" of the Mediterranean shores had possessed itself of his imagination

[6] Letter from Mary Moody Emerson to Charles Emerson of January 8, 1833 (Rusk, *Life*, p. 167). The italics are the author's.

[7] Cabot (*Memoir*, 2.685–688) reproduces the letter in an appendix. In it Emerson defines among other things what he recognizes will be his vocation: "To me, as one disciple, is the ministry of truth, as far as I can discern and declare it, committed; and I desire to live nowhere and no longer than that grace of God is imparted to me, —the liberty to seek and the liberty to utter it."

[8] Cf. JMN 3.322 (January 1832).

and deadened his reflexes of mistrust.[9] His illness required sun and heat, of course, but considerations of climate played only a secondary role in this sudden enthusiasm—the prospect of a winter in Puerto Rico, even in the company of a beloved brother, had after all evoked in Emerson more resignation than real joy. Still more significant is that he was not thinking of visiting Germany, toward which so many affinities would have led him and in which, a few years earlier, he had at his brother William's urging thought of spending a considerable length of time.[10] He may have had Goethe in mind, or he may not; in any case he set sail in 1832 on an *Italienische Reise*, totally open to the freshness of new experience, expecting and desiring nothing else than an unpredictable disruption of his horizons.

The crossing on a small brig, with the discomforts, the uncertainties, and indeed the dangers such a crossing entailed, was for him the best possible school of disorientation. Awake early, alone in the shade of a sail before the infinities of heaven and sea, he saw at its source, beyond or before the works of man, the inexhaustible principle of creation—the gulls skimming the sea, "masterpieces of Eternal power strictly eternal because now active," seemed to mock by their perfection his imbecile desire to travel the world in search of contingent forms. "You get no nearer to the principle in Europe. It animates man. It is the America of America. It spans the ocean like a handbreadth. It smiles at Time & Space."[11] When this vision of *natura naturans* was denied him, he could still contemplate the hardly less impressive and certainly equally unfamiliar spectacle of the crew engaged in the thousand and one maneuvers of navigation on the high seas. Four times in his journal he praises the sailors,[12] and it is clear that his admiration for them has grown with his familiarity with their conditions of existence. He respects the calm courage, the unassuming boldness of these men who obey as quickly as soldiers and as submissively as children the orders on which their lives depend. But he knows their confidence is not misplaced; they have, in a long commerce with the elements, learned how to control them, sometimes by force or endurance, more often by cunning—as in the handling of the sails, through which human skill can in the end make the gusts of

[9] Cf. the letter to William Emerson of December 10, 1832: "I proposed to make a modest trip to the West Indies & spend the winter with Edward but in a few hours the dream changed into a purpureal vision of Naples & Italy" (L 1.359).

[10] One should note that Goethe had died that spring, and that in consequence, as Emerson noted, Germany had lost much of its fascination.

[11] JMN 4.104 (January 3, 1833).

[12] JMN 4.103 (January 2, 1833), 107 (January 7), 109–110 (January 14), and 114–115 (January 25).

wind blow the ship in any desired direction. One has only to supplement the practical qualities, the "ambidexterous invincibility" of the sailors with the intelligence of the navigator capable of steering by compass and sextant, and the image of a hero is quick to arise, realizing on the level of the Understanding the still-immaculate ideal of the fulfilled man. Standing somewhere between Christopher Columbus, archetype of the explorer—hailed during the crossing as an example of persistence and pluck—and the mythical figure of Ahab, invested by Melville with a mad longing for knowledge and control, the nameless and eternal sailor thus receives Emerson's homage. It is an homage in passing, to be sure, suggested in large part of course by Emerson's sense of his own deficiencies; but it is indisputably sincere, as witness the insistence with which he undertakes in later life to celebrate on every occasion the nobility, too often ignored or denied, of the sailor's trade.[13]

> Honour evermore aboard ship to the man of action, —to the brain in the hand. Here is our stout master worth a thousand philosophers—a man who can strike a porpoise, & make oil out of his blubber, & steak out of his meat; who can thump a mutineer into obedience in two minutes; who can bleed his sick sailor, & mend the box of his pump; who can ride out the roughest storm on the American coast, & more than all, with the sun & a three cornered bit of wood, & a chart, can find his way from Boston across 3000 miles of stormy water into a little gut of inland sea 9 miles wide with as much precision as if led by a clue.[14]

One remembers with some difficulty that the author of this hymn to force and to human ingenuity, this admirer of Ulysses and Achilles together, is also the patient and experienced theologian of the communion sermon. But precisely in this apparent incompatibility lies Emerson's distinguishing quality. Both tones are natural to him, evoke each other,

[13] Emerson reuses certain of the formulations recorded in the journal of the crossing in a lecture from January 1837 called "Trades and Professions," the eighth in the series "The Philosophy of History" (EL 2.113–129). He gives the sailor an honorable place again in 1843, in "Traits" or "Trade" (the first title is Emerson's, the second, perhaps more accurate, is Cabot's), the second lecture in the series "New England," again describing him with the aid of certain ably combined journal notes (H.199). Emerson also reviewed Dana's *Two Years Before the Mast* in the *Dial* (Dana was a former pupil of his); he praised the work's literary qualities, its novelistic charm à la Robinson Crusoe, then launched into a forceful plea on behalf of sailors: "it will open the eyes of many to the condition of the sailor . . . to the fearful waste of man, by which the luxuries of foreign climes are made to increase the amount of commercial wealth. . . . It will serve to hasten the day of reckoning between society and the sailor, which, though late, will not fail to come" (*Dial* 1.2 [October 1840], pp. 264–265).

[14] JMN 4.115 (January 25, 1833).

nourish each other. In 1831—that is, just at the beginning of the great Coleridge fever—Emerson in a letter to his aunt Mary sang the praises of Montaigne, "wild and savoury as sweet fern."[15] And from the passage just cited—forceful, yet somehow ingenuous—to the almost Nietzschean challenges of *The Conduct of Life*[16] a continuity exists, barely perceptible yet stubbornly present—like those secondary melodies an alert ear discerns beneath rich orchestration.

It is also true that this month-long voyage over a frequently rough sea distinctly improved Emerson's health. Flourishing in storms as if the descendant of one of those Vikings he was later to exalt,[17] he entrusts to his journal certain amusingly witty sketches—that for example of a passenger, "a much enduring man who bends under the load of his leisure. He fawns upon the Captain, reveres the mate, but his eye follows the Steward; scans accurately as symptomatic, all the motions of that respectable officer."[18] Elsewhere he describes in burlesque tone the encounter of the old world, all sickly and weary, with its young kinsmen from across the Atlantic.[19] All this is lively and bold, and attests to a considerable talent for seizing and exaggerating picturesque detail. One could wish that such passages—which are not as rare in Emerson's work as one might think[20]— appeared more often in anthologies. They might reconcile certain readers to the sage of Concord, so often described as bloodless or nebulous so as to justify the general indifference to him; and they would also aid us in understanding Emerson by revealing in him an alert playfulness, an elasticity of temperament and mind quite like Montaigne's. It is here more than anywhere else that Emerson gives proof of his fundamental health and sanity.

The first contact with Europe, or rather with its southern outpost the Isle of Malta, was marked by an incident Emerson might well have found disagreeable if his good mood had not permitted him to perceive its irony: the brig's passengers were quarantined for two weeks, and kept on board "for poor dear Europe's health lest it should suffer prejudice from the unclean sands & mountains of America."[21] This detention was, as one would suspect, the occasion for some surprising scenes;

[15] J 2.440–441 (December 25, 1831).

[16] See particularly the chapters entitled "Power" and "Considerations by the Way."

[17] In chapter 4, "Race," of *English Traits*.

[18] JMN 4.123.

[19] Cf. JMN 4.109 (January 14, 1833).

[20] See V. L. O. Chittick, "Emerson's 'Frolic Health,' " NEQ 30 (June 1957), pp. 208–234. Unfortunately Chittick has paid almost exclusive attention to Emerson's relations with the West and frontier humor, and thus limited and to some extent falsified his conclusions.

[21] JMN 4.115 (February 2, 1833).

thus hardly had the port officer ended his visit when a Maltese grocer approached the quarantined ship on a boat loaded with produce, and handed up his card at the end of a pole. Liberation came at last in mid-February, and Emerson was free to begin the long ramble that was to take him to Sicily, Italy, Switzerland, France, England, and Scotland before he embarked homeward from Liverpool in September 1833. The first months, spent beneath the Mediterranean sky in a strikingly exotic setting—yet one that because of its abundant classical associations was also profoundly familiar—were the most relaxed. Emerson surrendered to the experience with an abandonment as complete as his nature was capable of: "I bring myself to sea, to Malta, to Italy," he notes during his detention, "to find new affinities between me & my fellowmen, to observe narrowly the affections, weaknesses, surprises, hopes, doubts, which new sides of the panorama shall call forth in me."[22] And in contact with these gracious and spontaneous people something in Emerson did bloom that the proprieties of Boston had stubbornly thwarted. The crossing from La Vallette to Syracuse, on board a brigantine immodestly named *Il Santissimo Ecce Homo*, is the occasion for a delightful sketch in which Emerson's energy and mischief recall that other Anglo-Saxon minister Laurence Sterne.[23] At Florence Emerson meets a flower girl who comes every morning to the café where he has his breakfast and avenges herself on unwilling customers by haughtily giving them the bouquets they have refused to buy.[24] In a poor Sicilian inn, between Catania and Messina, he is feted and regaled by his lowly traveling companions, stupefied at the idea of having an American minister in their midst and greeting each of his attempts to express himself in Italian with a respectful and musical "Che bravo, Signore." Emerson responds cordially, almost fervently, to these marks of attention; in his journal he mentions his four hosts of one evening by name because, he says, "they were very kind to me."[25]

One would like to give further examples of such simplicity; but the student of the journal and letters needs little time to read them all. The linked habits of introspection and inhibition cannot be shaken off so easily. Emerson may strive as he pleases to coerce his inclinations, to force himself to go to the theater and the opera, even on occasion to the ballet so as to avoid the charge of narrowness made by Goethe against all those who would choose to remain ignorant of the irreducible originality of

[22] JMN 4.68 (February 10, 1833). The passage is also cited in Cabot, *Memoir*, 1.178–179.

[23] See JMN 4.121–122 (February 21, 1833).

[24] See JMN 4.175–176 (May 1833).

[25] JMN 4.132–133 (March 1833).

each form of art;[26] his self remains the same. The ballerinas seem "nearly ideotic"; at the Catania opera house he forgets the prima donna in concentrating on the mental theater within him;[27] and though some days later the memory of that evening recurs to him, it has by then been sublimated into a Carlylean meditation on the theme of appearance and reality.[28] Moreover, the Italians are not always as agreeable as his Sicilian traveling companions; often their simplicity becomes simply a gross absence of restraint; beggars, aggressive guides, with their wranglings and quarrels, threaten at every moment to discourage the traveler's good will, and to obscure the beauty of monuments and sites: "One must be thoroughly reinforced with the spirit of antiquity," he notes acidly at Naples—a city he finds a thoroughly disagreeable, swarming sort of place—

> to preserve his enthusiasm through all the annoyances that await the visitor of these ruins. Long ago when I dreamed at home of these things, I thought I should come suddenly in the midst of an open country upon broken columns & fallen friezes, & their solitude would be solemn & eloquent. Instead of this, they are carefully fenced round like orchards and the moment the unhappy traveller approaches one of them, this vermin of ciceroni & padroni fasten upon him.[29]

Several times he uses the word "Lilliput" to designate these "little men"—perfectly contemptible, but horribly irritating and encumbering.

In sum, then, after a brief moment of seduction, the Italy of 1833, with its wretched and idle crowds, its dizzying bustle and profound passivity, aroused in Emerson a repulsion not far from disgust. He had too much stoic rigor in him to appreciate as Cooper had the charms of a declining country, in which the harsh struggle for grandeur and power had yielded to the enjoyment of treasures acquired long since.[30] American artists were numerous even at this early date in Rome and Florence, and Emerson met the most famous of them; but even they are victims to the slackness of the environment: "so little enterprize is in the Artists who reside here," he writes his brother William, "that it is commonly

[26] See JMN 4.171 (May 11, 1833).

[27] See JMN 4.132 (March 1833): "it is doubtless a vice to turn one's eyes inward too much, but I am my own comedy and tragedy."

[28] See JMN 4.140 (March 16, 1833).

[29] JMN 4.143–144 (March 16, 1833).

[30] Cf. Van Wyck Brooks, *The World of Washington Irving* (New York, 1950), chapter 14: "Irving and Cooper Abroad," particularly pp. 340–341.

said that he who stays in Rome a fortnight, usually sees more than he who stays for months."[31] Little charmed by a population so deficient in dignity of manner, he was only seldom interested in the political and conditions of the life it led. The king of Naples, half tyrant and half buffoon, is dispatched in two lines of a letter.[32] After having spent several weeks in Florence, Emerson suddenly remembered as he left that his journal contained no commentary on the modes of Tuscan life, and he notes pell-mell within the same paragraph that the system of sharecropping is in force everywhere, that the introduction of the potato has considerably eased the lot of the peasants, that labor is ridiculously cheap, that taxes seem oppressive and badly allotted, and that every cow entering Florence has to pay eleven *francesconi* to the authorities.[33] With the best will in the world one could not cite these few remarks, in which anecdote mitigates after a fashion the absence of serious information, as evidence for decreeing their author an economist. For the moment that aspect of human activity did not touch him, and this fact explains his bringing out certain minor but striking details while missing the essential. In the same way, he was hardly troubled at the thought that Austria had oppressed Venice and Lombardy ever since the fall of Napoleon; it would seem to him pointless to choose between two tyrannies, and in addition he perceived so many atrocities in the history of Venice under the doges that the authority of the emperor seemed more annoying than truly cruel and gained a sort of indirect justification.[34] In 1871, Emerson was to send a letter of support to Theodore Roosevelt, then president of a committee for arranging a demonstration in honor of Italian unity at the Academy of Music in New York;[35] but that was far in the future. On the present visit, indeed, he reproved and condemned every sort of active participation in public life. That a scientist like Arago and a philosopher as eminent as Cousin should desert, the one his magnet and battery, the other his Plato, to join in the petty games of politics saddened Emerson profoundly.[36] Since the time that he warned his con-

[31] Letter to William Emerson of April 21, 1833 (L 1.379–381).

[32] "His majesty, I have not chanced to see though he rides much in the streets. His hobby is his troops who are ever parading the streets both horse & foot with all kinds of music" (Letter to William Emerson of March 23, 1833 [L 1.369–370]).

[33] See JMN 4.180 (May 28, in the morning).

[34] See JMN 4.85. This is an example—one of many—of how the memory of things read intervenes in Emerson between perception and interpretation, even to the point of emptying the former of its content for the sake of the latter. The process is much less common in Emerson the traveler of 1847–1848.

[35] The letter is dated January 11, 1871 (L 6.142).

[36] See the letter to Samuel Ripley and Sarah Bradford Ripley of June 9, 1833 (L 1.389–391).

gregation against the illusions and temptations of the forum, his beliefs in this area had only been reinforced.

If civil power evoked from Emerson only indifference or disdain, the Catholic church, though it also was supported by, and inseparable from, political institutions, fascinated him intensely. From the moment he landed at La Vallette it was there to greet him like a beautiful picture book, full of chanting monks, sculpted ceilings, silver doors, madonnas, and saints.[37] With a readiness surprising in a descendant of the Puritans he indulged joyously in the wealth of his sensations: the statues, the frescoes, the golden monuments in such lavish abundance made him deplore the tedious austerity of his own country; he liked the notion that the weary passerby can enter these sanctuaries day and night and find there, in the forms invented by art, the suggestion of a better world; he admired the elegance and exactness of the architectural designs, and grew indignant at the aesthetic absurdity Protestants commit in filling so pure a space with benches. Wherever he went he paid long visits to Christian monuments; he was delighted that at Syracuse Mass was said in the ruins of the temple of Minerva, because it was a way of doing homage to the ineffaceable presence of the "religious principle."[38] But it was Rome, where he arrived in time for the ceremonies of holy week, that revealed to him the ultimate splendors of the Catholic liturgy. He attended the pontifical blessing of palms amidst a retinue of cardinals. Three days later he heard the celebrated "Miserere" sung by the choir of the Sistine Chapel; on Maundy Thursday he saw Pope Gregory XVI, universally acknowledged a pious and learned man, wash the feet of thirteen pilgrims, one from Kentucky; finally, on Easter morning, he was present at St. Peter's Square as the leader of Christianity pronounced with a large and gracious gesture his benediction *urbi et orbi*.[39] These precisely ordered ceremonies impressed him more than he had expected, and the description he gives of them in his journal—slow, weighty, and full, almost like a page of Huysmans—retains something of his solemn emotion. Here also Italy revealed to Emerson a part of himself that he did not know and that he was to have little occasion to strengthen or develop; but circumstances were at long intervals to attest to its secret and obscurely nostalgic presence.[40]

[37] See JMN 4.84–85 (February 1833).

[38] JMN 4.124.

[39] See JMN 4.152–157.

[40] See for example the letter he writes from Baltimore to Margaret Fuller in January 1843: "This morning I went to the Cathedral to hear mass with much content. . . . The chanting priest, the pictured walls, the lighted altar, the surpliced boys the swinging censer every whiff of which I inhaled, brought all Rome again to mind. And Rome can smell so far! It is a dear

But the New England man in Emerson was not slow to discover, behind the blare of trumpets and the luster of priestly robes, certain of Catholicism's less glorious traits. He noted that the throngs of the faithful were composed principally of women and children.[41] Curious about the power of the religious orders, he discovered that the Benedictines of Catania lived richly amid the wretched people they made a pretense of aiding.[42] As for the Capuchins—if they deserved general respect, there was nonetheless something unwholesome in seeing them, themselves beggars, feed an army of beggars camped near their monastery. And what was one to think of their manner of burial, of their placing the dead erect in a small niche, so that the image of their fleshless bodies would be constantly present to the mind of the living?[43] Emerson felt no attraction to the macabre, and the practice seemed to him dubious. But all this was nothing in comparison to the scourge of superstition raging everywhere. At Naples he had been shown the blood of Saint January, which became liquid once a year; at Florence, he writes an old family friend, he had been witness to a real scene of "idolatry": "Two days ago I saw in the Duomo or Cathedral a priest carrying a silver bust of Saint Zenobio which he put on the head of each person in turn of the kneeling crowd around the altar. This ceremony is esteemed a preservative against the head-ache for a year, till Saint Zenobio's day comes round again."[44] As one might expect, he goes on to note that these forms of mindless devotion have engendered everywhere, by reaction, both unbelief and immorality. Here one sees, in the glaring light furnished by the extreme character of the example, Emerson's abiding charge against the Catholic church: that a religion founded on a fixed system of representations confuses the essential and the auxiliary and will be quick to fall into deceit. The critique he makes, when he has recovered himself, of the pomp of the Vatican (that it is "conventional," that it is based on customs and distinctions of no force for a mind not prejudiced in its favor[45]) anticipates the accusation he was later to make against Swedenborg when he denounced his "theologic determination" and his desire, in his disdain for the intuitions of the moral sense, to reestablish the principal elements of a Christian symbolic system.[46] This reluctance

old church, the Roman I mean, & today I detest the Unitarians and Martin Luther and all the parliament of Barebones" (L 3.115–117 and Cabot, *Memoir*, 2.470–472).

[41] See JMN 4.117 (February 16, 1833).

[42] See JMN 4.131.

[43] See JMN 4.138–139 (Palermo, March 7, 1833).

[44] Letter to Abel Adams, May 28, 1833 (L 1.383–385).

[45] JMN 4.153.

[46] Cf. "Swedenborg, or the Mystic" in *Representative Men* (W 4.134ff.). Emerson was al-

to fix life into forms, venerable and sumptuous as they may be, betrays one of Emerson's deepest tendencies; and it also explains why he was never seriously threatened by the undertow of the Transcendentalist wave, so to speak, which secured Orestes Brownson, Isaac Hecker, Sophia Ripley, and his old friend Anna Barker Ward for Catholicism.[47]

The effect of this political and religious rejection of Italy was to throw Emerson once again back upon himself and to transform his trip, intended as a diversion, into a solitary pilgrimage among shadows. As the tourist's euphoria dissipated and the Unitarian's sympathies were disappointed, the man of culture, familiar long since with this much-fabled country, pursued his quest for the past from site to site, purifying it of the blemishes in which the mediocre present might wish to envelop it. At Syracuse Emerson looked for the fountain of Arethusa, and with horror discovered it to be serving as a laundry for fifty or sixty townswomen.[48] At Baies—which as he explains to a woman correspondent in New England was the "Nahant" of imperial Rome[49]—he is outraged to see the temple of Venus, though excellently preserved, sheltering the tools of a cooper, and the nearby suites of Roman ladies transformed into goat stables.[50] Fortunately, the names of the heroes who once lived in these places, from Scipio to Ariosto, from Cicero to Petrarch, still hover intangible in the Italian air; and it is they far more than the size of the columns or the material of the temples that endow it with its powerful charm. At Florence, Emerson wandered about at length in the Church of Santa Croce and comes upon the tombs of a number of his heroes: "I passed with consideration the tomb of Nicholas Machiavelli but stopped long before that of Galileus Galileo, for I love & honor that man, except in the recantation, with my whole heart. But when I came to Michel Angelo Buonaroti my flesh crept as I read the inscription. I

ready expressing some reservations about the "descriptive theism" of Swedenborg's disciples in a letter to Carlyle from 1834 (CEC 109).

[47] For Emerson's violent reaction to the news of Mrs. Ward's conversion to Catholicism, see R. D. Birdsall, "Emerson and the Church of Rome," AL 31 (November 1959), pp. 273–281. Though excellent on the period it focuses on, approximately that between 1858 and 1863, the article pays no attention to the comments recorded in the journal for 1833. Precisely the reverse is true of R. C. Pollock's "The Single Vision," in *American Classics Reconsidered*, ed. H. C. Gardiner (New York, 1958), pp. 15–58, which, though justly emphasizing the kinship between Emerson's thought and certain philosophical principles the Catholic church has traditionally defended, errs in making too little of Emerson's instinctive and fundamental hostility to every discipline seeking to impose itself from outside.

[48] See JMN 4.124–125.

[49] See the letter to Susan Woodward Haven of March 22, 1833 (L 1.367–368). Nahant is a small town on the rocky peninsula northeast of Boston and was at the time a popular summer residence.

[50] See JMN 4.146.

had strange emotions."[51] The old dream of greatness thus took hold of him again, separating him from the living inhabitants of this decadent Italy and turning his meditations toward classical antiquity and the Renaissance. The second day of his visit to Rome, at once exhausted and triumphant, he composed a sort of hymn to solitude. The influence of *Childe Harold*, felt throughout Emerson's travels, is not entirely absent from it; but it contrasts with its model by a moral obsession evident from its first lines:

> Alone in Rome! why Rome is lonely too,
> Besides you need not be alone, the Soul
> Shall have society of its own rank,
> Be great, be true, and all the Scipios
> The Catos the wise patriots of Rome
> Shall flock to you & tarry by your side
> And comfort you with their high company.
> Virtue is company enough
> It keeps the key to all heroic hearts
> And opens you a welcome in them all.[52]

Yet into this invocation of the heroes, summoned as examples and sources of inspiration to supplement the mediocrity of the present, Emerson only puts one-half of himself. The other, as he writes to his aunt Mary, once again his confidante and oracle, persists in hoping:

> I never get used to men. They always awaken expectations in me which they always disappoint, and I am a poor asteroid in the great system subject to disturbances in my orbit not only from all the planets but from all their moons. The wise man—the true friend—the finished character—we seek everywhere & only find in fragments Yet I cannot persuade myself that all the beautiful souls are fled out of the planet or that always I shall be excluded from good company & yoked with green dull pitiful persons.

Then, with fervent prayers he invokes the figure of the instructor, the teacher, the "Master," full of truth, of heroic sentiment, and of unlimited benevolence.[53]

If one may use Emerson's metaphor to refute him, the longing ex-

[51] JMN 4.168.

[52] JMN 4.71 and W 9.396–397 ("Written in Rome").

[53] Letter to Mary Moody Emerson of April and May 1833 (L 1.375–377 and J 3.100–102). On this longing of Emerson's for the great man, or at least for the realized man, see also his letter to G.A. Sampson of March 23, 1833 (L 1.370–372) and that to Charles Emerson of April 16 and 21, 1833 (L 1.372–375).

pressed in these lines marks precisely the asteroid's return to its own orbit. From this point till the end of his long wandering, Emerson sought with more and more concentrated intensity this great man of his dreams. Landscapes, monuments, and crowds in his eyes ceased to exist. He made one more effort, in France, to extract some benefit from circumstance. He observed the Paris tradesmen;[54] he went to a gambling house and was surprised by its calm orderliness;[55] with an intimidating appetite for knowledge he attended all the literary, scientific, and philosophical lectures open to him;[56] and, still in Paris at the natural-history collection at the Jardin des Plantes, he had a sudden "intuition" of "occult" relations uniting man with the rest of creation.[57] But once Emerson crossed the English Channel, the tourist and curious traveler was dead; only once again did he come to life, to give us a detailed account of an excursion into the Scottish Highlands, boldly persisted in despite much rain and wind.[58] Any kind of political or social observation was, of course, out of the question. The journal's only judgment in this area (offered at the last moment, just before he sailed from Liverpool) is both vague and disagreeably complacent.[59] This indifference to things and people, this deliberate neglect of a country in the midst of economic transformation cannot be attributed, as certain of Emerson's remarks suggest, to a long familiarity with England acquired from books[60]—because how, then, would one explain that on his second trip to England, fifteen years later, when the country was still better known to Americans, Emerson should have found not only matter for comment in his journals but also the substance of a solid and deeply original book? The answer evidently derives from changes in the nature of the man himself: in 1833 it was not Manchester or Oxford or the *Times* offices that he wanted to see, but Coleridge, Wordsworth, and Carlyle.

Italy had given Emerson his first chance to meet with a remarkable individual in the person of Walter Savage Landor, with whom he lunched and dined in Landor's Fiesole villa.[61] To say that these two

[54] See JMN 4.197–198.

[55] See J 3.169–170.

[56] See Rusk, *Life*, p. 187.

[57] See JMN 4.198–200.

[58] See JMN 4.217–219.

[59] "The famous burden of English taxation is bearable. Men live & multiply under it, though I have heard a father in the higher rank of life speak with regret of the increase of his family" (JMN 4.81 [September 2, 1833]).

[60] "We know London so well in books & pictures & maps & traditions that I saw nothing surprizing in this passage up the Thames" (JMN 4.204 [July 20, 1833]).

[61] The first chapter of *English Traits* ("First Visit to England" [W 5.3–24]) reproduces al-

meetings disappointed Emerson would be excessive, but to claim that they provided what he expected would be no less so. Landor showed himself "noble and courteous" and spoke copiously, as his vast learning gave him right, on all subjects concerning art; but he introduced into his judgments a desire for originality at any price, a taste for whim and paradox that limited their range and import. It might be brilliant to disparage Socrates; but it was certainly unfortunate to sacrifice respect for moral truth to the superficial need for elegance, as Landor did in exalting Lord Chesterfield beyond reason.[62] So Emerson—a paragraph in the journal written at Paris attests as much[63]—transferred to England all the hopes neither Italy nor France could satisfy.

If for no other reason than the inhuman perfection he attributed to his idols, it was inevitable that Emerson should declare himself finally unsatisfied on one side of the Channel as on the other. The mature man who assembled his early journal entries to make the exordium of his book on England sees and defines well the nature of the mirage to whose temptation his younger self had yielded: "The young scholar fancies it happiness enough to live with people who can give an inside to the world; without reflecting that they are prisoners, too, of their own thought, and cannot apply themselves to yours."[64] He forgets only to note that the young traveler who came in search of light and counsel was himself strictly limited by his own concerns and had ears only for answers to the questions he would have wanted to ask.[65] But Emerson's disappointment of 1833 is not unqualified. Coleridge and Wordsworth, the two titans, the two illustrious vatic poets, seem to him almost caricatures of themselves: the first tactlessly obsessed with his own thoughts, a copious and impetuous talker;[66] the other simpler and more

---

most all of the journal accounts of Emerson's encounters with Landor, Coleridge, Carlyle, and Wordsworth.

[62] Cf. JMN 4.73 and 174.

[63] See JMN 4.76–77.

[64] W 5.4.

[65] It is striking that Wordsworth's and Carylyle's reflections on social problems—which *English Traits* carefully transcribes—draw no comment in the 1833 journal. Landor's passion for heroism and action, by contrast, and Wordsworth's appreciation of moral cultivation both evoke a more immediate response.

[66] This judgment on Coleridge is generally in accord with Carlyle's, after a visit to Highgate: "the conversation of the man is much as I anticipated—a forest of thoughts, some true, many false, more *part* dubious, all of them ingenious in some degree, often in a high degree. But there is no method in his talk: he wanders like a man sailing among many currents, whithersoever his lazy mind directs him; and what is more unpleassant, he preaches, or rather soliloquises. Hence I found him unprofitable, even tedious" (Froude, *Thomas Carlyle: A History of the First Forty Years of his Life*, quoted in Basil Willey, *Nineteenth Century Studies* [London, 1949], p. 109).

discreet, but no less limited in his interests, no less sealed off from the problems Emerson would have liked to discuss with him. In comparison with these two discouraging encounters, the day passed with Carlyle at Craigenputtock in an obscure corner of the Scottish coutryside was lit with radiant light. Emerson had before him there not an author but a man: generous, honest, overflowing with vitality and yet supremely in control of his talent when he directed it, to his visitor's great joy, toward anecdote and humor—a man capable like himself of doing homage to "the man that will manifest any truth to him."[67] There was immediate sympathy between the two men. Carlyle spoke of the "beautiful transparent soul" that had brightened the monotony of his retreat;[68] and twice in his journal Emerson noted how much he had been touched by the "amiableness" of his host—so unexpected and uncommon a compliment where Carlyle is concerned that the word seems to glow with extraordinary warmth.[69] And in fact the two men corresponded for nearly forty years, with a sincerity that though it disrupted their relations more than once was nonetheless recognized by both as each one's truest testimony of respect.

It was not until Emerson undertook to draw up an account of his experiences, on the eve of his departure for New York—in a sort of spiritual limbo between Europe and America—that the true stature of his four heroes became clear to him.[70] They all possessed the same quality, at once the sign and cause of their genius: sincerity. But all, even Carlyle, failed to correspond to the "*idealized* portrait" he had made of them. With all their learning, they lacked, though in varying degrees, religious intuition: "they have no idea of that species of moral truth which I call the first philosophy." Thus Emerson's trip to Europe represented for him the last step on his path toward intellectual maturity. A few months previously, when he had separated from his church, he had imagined that the road he was setting out on had been more or less clearly blazed by a band of inspired explorers, and that he could advance faster by following in their footsteps; now he judged great men "more justly, less timidly" and knew that Pestalozzi's "melancholy paradox," noted in the journal for 1832, that "no man is able or willing to help any other man," is strictly and unappealably true.[71] He was not disillusioned but undeceived.

The second and equally important lesson that his illustrious interloc-

[67] JMN 4.221.

[68] Rusk, *Life*, p. 195.

[69] See JMN 4.79 and 220.

[70] See JMN 4.78–80.

[71] JMN 4.19–20 (May 18, 1832).

utors taught him—by negative example—was the danger of fame. One talks to a Coleridge or to a Wordsworth as if to a child incapable of bearing the truth; one takes account of their prejudices, adapting what one knows to what they want to hear. Defended by a thick and probably lasting obscurity, Emerson did not himself feel menaced by this danger; but he found it so insidious that he warned himself against it once for all, so that he would never forget his own counsel:[72]

> I believe in my heart it is better to admire too rashly, as I do, than to be admired too rashly as the great men of this day are. They miss by their premature canonization a great deal of necessary knowledge. . . . I speak now in general and not of these individuals. God save a great man from a little circle of flatterers. I know it is sweet, very sweet, rats bane.[73]

The return voyage, most often in stormy weather, found Emerson so absorbed by his thoughts that he hardly noticed the other passengers. The great digression begun beneath the Mediterranean sun was over. He had without regret seen the shores of England disappear, and thought affectionately of the America waiting for him,

> Land without history lying all
> In the plain daylight of the temperate zone
> . . .
> Land where and 'tis in Europe counted a reproach
> Where man asks question [sic]—for which man was made.[74]

Such was the New World's mission: to discover the meaning of human existence. The frivolity and indifference he had found everywhere in Europe only made that mission more urgent. If he left for Europe perhaps too conscious of the wealth of culture it represented, he returned from it persuaded not only that at present it had no vital (that is, in Emerson's language, moral or religious) message for America, but also that America, now, was to take up the torch—indeed, that it had already done so, as a phrase of the journal, written with a tranquil sense that the supporting evidence is universally accepted, seems in fact to indicate: "I wrote above," he notes in a long paragraph written at sea, "my

[72] Emerson's intimates—and indeed a good number of people who met him only once—often noted that other people's problems and ideas found easy access to him. Moncure D. Conway, in *Emerson at Home and Abroad*, (Boston, 1882), pp. 6–7, tells how Emerson's answer to a letter he sent him as a youth of nineteen became his most cherished viaticum.

[73] JMN 4.79.

[74] From a poem Emerson wrote during the crossing (JMN 4.240–241). In it he celebrates—not without some bathos—his countrymen's proud simplicity and common sense.

conviction that the great men of England are singularly ignorant of religion. They should read Norton's Preface to his new book who has stated that fact well."[75]

But this newly acquired dignity, assumed by a small number of Americans, represents for each of them so difficult an obligation that Emerson is not far from thinking it a burden: "Ah me!" he writes the same day, "what hope of reform, what hope of communicating religious light to benighted Europe if they who have what they call the Light are so selfish & timid & cold & their faith so unpractical & in their judgment so unsuitable for the middling classes."[76] Without precisely distinguishing them—they are after all intimately connected—Emerson poses the two problems he must confront and resolve if he is not to add his name to the long and sad list of human failures. On the one hand he must stabilize his wavering faith, give it such strong nourishment that it need never again know uncertainty or decline; on the other hand, that faith must like the light upon the mountains attract, comfort, encourage, and perhaps convert all those within its range. Putting to good use the enforced leisure of the crossing, Emerson occupied himself with getting his bearings, with defining for himself—to the extent that the words of any definition are not themselves a betrayal—the fundamental truths that alone can sustain and satisfy us: that beauty is identical with goodness because it depends on the harmony inherent in the development of the moral law; that there is correspondence between the human soul and the whole of the creation; that man is his own law, and that he alone can help or harm himself; that consciousness is the means of access to the principles of nature; that the goal of action is to reveal us to ourselves; that there is no future life except insofar as we live in the present.[77] The first *Essays* only restate and amplify the affirmations here gathered together.

But there is an immense distance between defining a credo and living it, and an equal gulf between living it and helping others to live it. Stephen Whicher observes rightly that Emerson's interest is not at first in formulating an ethic; in this respect he is a docile pupil rather than an innovator or a teacher.[78] He says as much himself, in his own way, when

[75] JMN 4.80. The work in question is an attack on the doctrines of the Trinitarians by Andrews Norton, head of the Divinity School while Emerson was a student there, and best known for his denunciation of the Divinity School address in the speech called "The Latest Form of Infidelity." Clearly by 1833 the gulf between the two men had not yet opened.

[76] JMN 4.81 and 83.

[77] See JMN 4.84, the paragraph beginning, "But the men of Europe will say . . ."; these lines are doubtless the most succinct expression Emerson himself gave of his "theory."

[78] "His ethical teachings, though unquestionably edifying, and valuable in their aphoristic

in 1833 he confesses himself unable, or rather unwilling, to give precise delineations of moral truths: "Yesterday I was asked what I mean by Morals. I reply that I cannot define & care not to define. It is man's business to observe & the definition of Moral Nature must be the slow result of years, of lives, of states perhaps of being."[79] We must not be deceived by Emerson's diction here, or by our own habits of thought; for Emerson it is not morality but religion that seems a code externally imposed on the conscience and therefore condemned to a strictness, a rigidity that renders it unfit to be the conduit of universal laws.[80] In reality, after enunciating the ethical rules that he accepts as an inalienable legacy, that he does not, to be sure, renounce but that do not suffice to explain the fervor of his meditations on moral perfection,[81] Emerson seeks stubbornly and intensely to reach that spiritual state in which the fulfillment of the commandments would be neither the end nor the criterion of a nobly lived existence but rather would come of itself, without effort—elegantly, as he says in the journal[82]—and would be joined to the intuition of our spiritual nature as joy is joined to love.

But if this ambition is to express more than an ephemeral vision or the complacent pursuit of an inner dream, it must confront the problem of method. The traditional logical procedures, which were also those of the Unitarians and which continued to offer Transcendentalists like Theodore Parker and George Ripley a convenient framework for their writings, could hardly lend themselves to the evocation of a universe conceived precisely against them, conceived to restore what they neglected and reduce to their proper rank certain qualities they exalted to excess. So Emerson was led to develop a more flexible and more comprehensive strategy, the most effective instrument of which was (ide-

force, are on the whole neither original nor specific enough to command particular attention. What is interesting in his thought can usually be discussed without much reference to virtue and moral law; that fact is one reason why his thought is interesting" (Whicher, *Freedom and Fate*, p. 44).

[79] JMN 4.86.

[80] "The difference between religion and ethics. There is but one divine element feeding, vivifying all minds. Men, in the moment of its inspirations, are sensible of this unity. But in the off-hours, in this kingdom of custom in which they live, they distinguish between religion and ethics, as if ethics meant my own perception of right and wrong, —but religion always some other man's. My belief in eternal justice and the rule of right is ethics or morals; but Jesus' or Moses' belief is religion." This passage is cited by the editor of the Centenary Edition in connection with the essay "The Preacher" (W 10.555–556); the idea is developed at length in "The Sovereignty of Ethics" (W 10.181–214, esp. p. 212).

[81] See for example the famous rhapsody inspired by Emerson's reading of Milton's letter to Diodati (JMN 4.87–88).

[82] The remark is made in connection with the subject of temperance, which in a sermon so easily becomes "dowdy" (JMN 4.385).

ally, at least) poetical expression, and which borrowed its doctrines from Swedenborg's doctrine of correspondences, expanded *ad hoc* and purged of all rigidity. It is not our business here to follow the rich development of this technique, which belongs as a subject to literary aesthetics and which has been perceptively explored in the course of the past twenty years.[83] But it has been less often noticed that beyond this problem of form, though not entirely detachable from it, Emerson foresees another difficulty, before which he feels defenseless because he does not precisely understand its nature: the difficulty of communicating with other minds or souls that do not share his perceptions. "Men seem to be constitutionally believers & unbelievers," he notes on another of these fruitful days of the homeward trip:

> There is no bridge that can cross from a mind in one state to a mind in the other. All my opinions, affections, whimsies are tinged with belief, —incline to that side. All that is generous, elegant, rich, wise, looks that way. But I cannot give reasons to a person of a different persuasion that are at all adequate to the force of my conviction. Yet when I fail to find the reason, my faith is not less.[84]

Emerson grasps the problem with a penetration and a sense for sudden inversions and reversals that recall Pascal. He was to remain confronted with this contradiction for a long time, because he could not choose between two conclusions that appear to him equally irrefutable. It is true on the one hand, as is affirmed by those who believe in the power of teaching, that one can convert men, that it is enough to arouse them, to shake off the sluggishness in which ignorance and habit maintain them; but is is also true that "the most original sermon is adopted by each hearer's selflove as his old orthodox or unitarian or quaker preaching."[85] Only gradually would Emerson elaborate, under the pressure of a faith every day more certain and more blinding, his own distinctive rhetoric. The *Essays* were to reveal its sometimes disconcerting novelty, but also—as its effect on thousands of readers over several generations attests—its remarkable effectiveness.

But this is perhaps somewhat too audacious an anticipation, if not of the progress of Emerson's thought, affirmed in the journals of the pe-

[83] See particularly F. O. Matthiessen, *American Renaissance: Art and Expression in the Age of Emerson and Whitman* (1941, repr. New York, 1968); Vivian C. Hopkins, *Spires of Form* (Cambridge, Mass., 1951); and above all, because of the wide perspective in which it considers the problem, Charles Feidelson, Jr., *Symbolism and American Literature* (Chicago, 1953).

[84] JMN 4.88 (September 17, 1833).

[85] JMN 4.279. The two theses turn up in the journal at two days' distance—sufficient proof that the problem was central among Emerson's preoccupations.

riod with marvelous energy, then at least of the social role played by Emerson as he returned to his friends and family after an absence of nine months. To see him pick up his accustomed train of life so comfortably, preaching as invitations came and not declining to occupy, in October 1833, his former pulpit in the Second Church, one wonders whether the images of Sicily or Rome, the remembrance of the visit with Carlyle, the reflections and resolutions noted on the boat home have not been suddenly effaced, abolished, by the reality of New England scenes and New England people. The sermon Emerson gave to his former congregation on the relations between religion and society[86] introduces no innovation—indeed it suffers from the same incoherence as had Emerson's unfortunate attempts, between 1830 and 1832, to reconcile Coleridge with Unitarian orthodoxy. In it he develops eloquently, even grandiloquently, the theme of universal progress (defined here, to be sure, as "a history of growth"); he sings the praises of a good half-dozen philanthropic organizations by name; he extols the services of trade, "pacific and equitable Commerce"; then, without warning, he proclaims the greatest religious revolution of human history, which has already destroyed the myth of original sin and is preparing the advent of an era in which every human being will in the secret places of the individual soul be face to face with God. The restrained fervor of the last part shows clearly where the preacher's sympathies tend; but the hostages he feels obliged to give to the defenders of the Understanding reveal a still divided consciousness—whether by zeal or apprehension one hesitates to say.

In fact, the attractions of Boston society remained dangerously powerful for a half-emancipated soul like Emerson's. This was made evident when he agreed, some months later, to write a poem and to deliver it, as was the custom, before the Harvard chapter of Phi Beta Kappa. (The offer had been made to him once before, but he had declined on account of Ellen's recent death.) He acquitted himself of the task with care and, one must say, with considerable facility; but whether inspiration also came to his aid in the course of his effort is less certain. "Emerson's poem," notes Carl Strauch in an article on the subject, "strikes one as more interesting for what it does not say than for what it does say."[87] And it is true that instead of benefiting from the imaginative energy of his personal meditations, Emerson makes himself write this occasional

[86] Sermon 165, "Religion and Society," preached October 27, 1833 (in McGiffert, *Young Emerson Speaks*, pp. 191–202).

[87] "Emerson's Phi Beta Kappa Poem," NEQ 23 (March 1950), pp. 65–90. The article is in its rich documentation the source of my account of the circumstances of composition; Strauch was also the first person to publish the 290-line poem in its entirety.

poem in the most occasional way possible, with allusions to Imperial Spain, to haughty and disdainful England, to the generosity of America, and of course to La Fayette, who had been the chapter's guest in 1824, and news of whose death had just come from Paris. Again in accord with what the situation demanded, Emerson espouses the cause of the Federalists—whom henceforth one ought probably call Whigs, since it is under that name that the adversaries of Jackson and egalitarian democracy have come down to posterity. He further recalls the lofty moral mission of Boston, sentinel of justice and right on the shores of the New World; but he fears that this virtuous tradition, despite the courage of Webster and all those who continue to make it illustrious, will yield to the petty blows struck by Van Buren and the mediocrities of his administration: "The towers that generations did combine / To build and grace, a rat may undermine."[88] Moreover, the poem concludes with the same ambivalence as does the sermon just cited. Having first asserted his solidarity with the enlightened elite of New England, bearer of all American hope, Emerson makes a sudden about-face and declares that if the decline of the nation, already manifested in the corruption reigning at Washington, should become still more pronounced, there will remain the last recourse of an inward retreat to the "citadel" of the soul: "For the true man, as long as earth shall stand, / Is to himself a state, a law, a land."[89]

It would be disingenuous not to quote for comparison the disillusioned reflections Emerson was confiding to his journal while composing this very mediocre poem:

> We sit down with intent to write truly & end with making a book that contains no thought of ours but merely the tune of the time. Here am I writing a ΦBK poem free to say what I choose & it looks to me now as if it would scarce express thought of mine but be a sort of fata morgana reflecting the images of Byron, Shakespear, & the newspapers.
>
> We do what we can, & then make a theory to prove our performance the best.[90]

Strauch is probably justified in holding the form of the poem ("prose logic punctuated by grand bursts of rhetoric and rounded out with a statement of moral idealism") responsible for Emerson's dissatisfaction; but the content, as his own definition implies, cannot be isolated so eas-

[88] Ibid.

[89] Ibid.

[90] JMN 4.314–315 (August 19, 1834).

ily. Certainly one should note Emerson's inability to make original use of traditional poetic structures. His best poems—"Days" comes immediately to mind— are the result of a patient decanting of two or three prose sketches; and the prose's initial rhythms are still subtly dominant. When, instead, he ventures on the use of strict metrical forms and composes to order, the consequence is academicism. A striking illustration comes at the very end of his career, in the at once stilted and jerky poem (the choice of tetrameter exaggerates a certain inherent stiffness) that he dedicated to James Russell Lowell on the occasion of his fortieth birthday.[91] But explanation is no excuse. Even if we admit that the constraints of the heroic couplet rob Emerson of most of his resources and are responsible for the somewhat grotesque role of official poet to which we see him reduced here, one cannot blink the fact that he lent himself to this enterprise; and it is this "hypocrisy"—he uses the word twice[92]—that causes his discomfort.

In that sense, however, this literary experience was an important milestone on his spiritual itinerary. It suddenly revealed to him that the apparently familiar enemy was capable of disguise and could adroitly manipulate him into accepting certain compromises—and also that his misgivings had been lulled to sleep the first time they were put to the test. The lesson was learned well. Emerson took no second false step; and in addition, his determination to live by the only acceptable rule, that is, by a rule he himself had uttered, continued to affirm itself positively in certain gestures and perceptions that can now appropriately be examined.

Among the influences that contributed to this spiritual consolidation one has first to note that of the Quakers—though a whim of fortune made it result from a wholly fortuitous train of circumstances. Just after his return from Europe, Emerson was invited to occupy for an indefinite period the pulpit of an ailing relative, one Orville Dewey, then minister of the Unitarian church at New Bedford—the great whaling port that Melville made the scene of the first few chapters of *Moby-Dick*. From the time the Quakers had first been authorized to reside in Massachusetts, toward the end of the seventeenth century, they had lived in harmony as a prosperous New Bedford community. A major doctrinal dispute, however, had arisen between orthodox Quakers and a small

[91] "To Lowell, on his Fortieth Birthday," *The Century* 47 (November 1893), pp. 3–4. Even Charles Eliot Norton, who introduced the poem, admitted it was not very good.

[92] "Even the wit the sentiment that seasons the dinner is a sort of hypocrisy to hide the coarseness of appetite. The Child is sincere, and the man when he is alone, if he be not a writer, but on the entrance of the second person hypocrisy begins" (JMN 4.314).

group of Hicksite liberals,[93] and the community had succumbed to the strife; the liberal minority had joined the Unitarians. It thus happened that, without seeking to go beyond the framework of his prescribed tasks, Emerson found himself in contact with certain strong Quaker personalities whose faith had been anchored even more firmly by the crisis through which they had just passed. One woman in particular impressed him with her unshakable assurance, a certain Mary Rotch—"a sort of local Aunt Mary," as Rusk calls her.[94] In his journal Emerson transcribes some of her remarks, full of "sublime religion," and in all humility manifests his admiration for the confidence she reposes, without restriction or repentance, in the unexplained injunctions of a certain inward voice that resembles—Emerson makes the point himself—both Socrates' *daimon* and the "grand Unalterableness of Fichte's morality."[95] Moreover, the voice is in no way astonishing or miraculous; it indicates only "*a healthful state of the mind.*"[96] It is a first revelation of what the activity of our faculties will be when we have disencumbered them of their superstitions and healed them of their slavery to custom and sect.

Since George Bancroft, the parallel between the Quaker doctrine of the inner light and the intuitionist philosophy of Transcendentalism has been a commonplace in the history of ideas.[97] Emerson himself was, at the time of his full maturity, to emphasize the parallel and could perceive its historical significance through the detachment he retained amidst his most fervent impulses.[98] And it was also by deference toward a faith the solid simplicity of which he never ceased to esteem that he could answer, when he was asked one day to define his religious position: "I am more of a Quaker than anything else. I believe in the 'still,

[93] So named from their leader, Elias Hicks (1748–1830), a Long Island farmer and also a preacher; he exercised a striking influence within the Quaker communities in the East (Whitman's father was among the number of his admirers), though he belonged to no church and led the liberal splinter-group that seceded in 1827. See on this episode Frederick B. Tolles' thorough and precise "Emerson and Quakerism," AL 1. (May 1948), pp. 142–165.

[94] Rusk, *Life*, p. 199.

[95] JMN 4.263–264 (February 12, 1834).

[96] Ibid. The italics are Emerson's.

[97] See *The History of the United States*, 10 vols. (Boston, 1834–1874), volume 2, chapter 16, in which Bancroft puts Quakerism and Transcendentalism in the same camp and opposes them to the philosophy of Locke. For Emerson's mostly enthusiastic response to Bancroft's history, see JMN 5.83 (1837).

[98] See particularly a passage of the lecture on the Transcendentalist (W 1.338–339), in which Emerson interprets Puritanism and the Quaker teachings on the one hand, and nineteenth-century idealism on the other, as two manifestations of the same spirit of faith; he then goes on to suggest that the differences of tone and accent between them are due to historical context: Episcopal in the first case, Unitarian and mercantile in the second.

small voice,' and that voice is Christ within us."[99] But at that time Emerson had no further need of assurance; the benevolence with which he regarded all who like him cast themselves upon the inward sentiment was much more a benediction than an act of thanksgiving. In 1834, on the contrary, he was, so to speak, a beggar, and to see strong and just souls long since set out on the path he was promising himself to follow was an immense aid. One of his *Dial* articles, provoked by the letter of a reader who had on his own account compared the spiritual concerns of the Transcendentalists with those of the first Quakers, allows us to imagine the mixture of joyous exultation and surprise that had possessed him as he recognized this or that familiar thought and feeling where he had not at all expected them.[100] He had crossed the Atlantic in search of the Master and the Teacher, and illustrious writers had in spite of themselves revealed to him only a heartbreaking spiritual poverty; now in his own country he was discovering men and women indifferent to glory and deaf to all but the voice of God speaking to their consciousness: the guides, that is, that Europe had denied him. The paradox was worth contemplating.

And contemplate it he did, with all the seriousness the gravity of the issue demanded. Since the outward world was capable of corrupting even the best, it seemed one had to learn to do without it. Several times in 1834 the word "self-centered" flowed from Emerson's pen, as if he wished to make of it the goal of his efforts and ambition.[101] He resolves to reduce as far as possible the friction of the social machine—which is at bottom only a machine to inhibit living. In the face of formalities, of institutions, of account books, which without fail substitute themselves for even the loveliest of philanthropic ideas when one attempts to put such ideas into practice, Emerson asks whether all life is not like charity, a trade in which bustling activity covers only emptiness, in Pascal's sense a *divertissement.*

> We are always getting ready to live, but never living. We have many years of technical education; then, many years of earning a livelihood, & we get sick, & take journeys for our health, & com-

[99] The anecdote is recorded by D. G. Haskins in *Ralph Waldo Emerson: His Maternal Ancestors* (Boston, 1887), p. 118. Haskins tells another anecdote (p. 130) that reveals the limits of that acknowledgment; asked by Haskins in 1851 whether he believed in God, Emerson solemnly and unironically answered, "when I speak of God, I prefer to say: It—It."

[100] *Dial* 2 (January 1842), pp. 382–384: "Transcendentalism." The passage in question describes the effect on Emerson of reading Fox's journal and Sewel's *History of the Quakers.*

[101] Particularly in the praise of Webster included in the Phi Beta Kappa poem (W 9.399) and in his first letter to Carlyle (CEC 98). It is significant that in both cases Emerson uses the word about men he admires.

pass land & sea for improvement by travelling, but the work of self-improvement—always under their nose, —nearer than the nearest, is seldom seldom engaged in. A few few hours in the longest life.[102]

This appeal to immediate inward action,[103] with its intensely persuasive ring, might serve as frontispiece to the work of all the Transcendentalists—Alcott as well as Parker, Fuller no less plausibly than Thoreau. But Emerson—along with Thoreau, of course—is the one who assesses most accurately and most lucidly the consequences of that imperative for his social behavior. In 1834 he recognizes that he cannot undertake simultaneously others' education and his own:

every teacher acquires a cumulative inertia; the more forcible the more eloquent have been his innovating doctrines, the more eagerly his school have crowded around him, so much the more difficult is it for him to forfeit their love, to compromise his influence by advancing farther in the same track. Therefore the wise man must be wary of attaching followers. He must feel & teach that the best of wisdom cannot be communicated; must be acquired by every soul for itself.[104]

The discrepancy Emerson here foresees between a truly living soul's appetite for the new and the need for stability inherent in social groups increased as he continued to yield to his inspiration's guidance;[105] his strength was in not trying to reconcile the irreconcilable. Made confident by his conviction that each of us is ultimately the sole administrator of his destiny and that the influence of one person on another is always partial, indirect, "oblique,"[106] Emerson had no great difficulty in persuading himself that there was no grave failure of duty in his deciding to concern himself first and above all with himself. Indeed, as he gradually amplified his instinctive reservations and resistances toward the community, the community was itself turned into an absolute source of evil, at once a swamp and a snare, whose pernicious influence it became his duty to denounce from the rooftops.

The period between Emerson's return from Europe and the publi-

[102] JMN 4.276–277 (April 13, 1834).

[103] The epigraph for the journal for 1835 is, "To think is to act" (JMN 5.4).

[104] JMN 4.279 (April 23, 1834).

[105] Only a year later he notes in his journal, "The truest state of mind, rested in, becomes false. Thought is the manna which cannot be stored. . . . Not in his goals but in his transition man is great" (JMN 5.38 [May 13, 1835]).

[106] "[A man] cannot look to work directly on men but obliquely. Few men bring more than one or two points into contact with society at once, they must be content to influence it thereby" (JMN 5.26 [March 29, 1835]).

cation of *Nature* in September 1836 corresponds by and large to the first stage of this transition. Emerson extricated himself from every pressing obligation, not abruptly but with a deliberate and tranquil resolution. He did not provoke, or hurl anathemas; he dictated his conditions to the world, prepared to withdraw into his tent if they were not met. His New Bedford congregation was sympathetic to him and extraordinarily liberal; but he refused to become its official pastor, though Orville Dewey had wished him to, because the routine obligations this step would have entailed seemed incompatible with his need for independence. His preaching in Unitarian churches became less frequent, though it never entirely ceased;[107] he did after all need to make a living, and the constant movement from church to church, which spared him both administrative worries and the graver concerns of doctrinal harmony, was all in all the least burdensome way of doing so. But Emerson could not have so lightened his obligations and charges had he not been aided by certain favorable circumstances, the coincidence of which at this point of his destiny would almost suffice, as Whicher dryly suggests, to justify his trust in a providence full of loving-kindness.[108] On the one hand, the lawyers finally came to an agreement regarding the disposition of Ellen Tucker's legacy, and assigned Emerson an annual sum of two thousand dollars—which did not, to be sure, make for wealth or even for comfort—but which did insure him against destitution.[109] On the other hand, the rapid development in New England of institutions aimed at making new discoveries accessible to all (the lyceums are in this respect only an illustration, though the most familiar and the most vivid[110]) soon offered Emerson a whole gamut of secular forums, which were preferable to pulpits both in not exerting any pressure on his inward convictions and also in furnishing him with curious listeners: avid but unprejudiced and ready to share his discoveries, his enthusiasms, and indeed his dreams, in a way no congregation could

[107] The notebook in which Emerson recorded his Sunday preaching commitments (the dates are incorporated into McGiffert's chart of the sermons) indicates that he continued to preach regularly as late as 1838. One sermon from 1834, "The Miracle of our Being" (McGiffert, *Young Emerson Speaks*, pp. 204–212), was indeed given as late as January 1839—though one should add that in it Unitarian orthodoxy was roundly castigated and that its fervent and rhapsodic tone is much closer to *Nature* than to the moral exhortations of Emerson's early ministry.

[108] See Whicher, *Freedom and Fate*, p. 27.

[109] See Rusk, *Life*, p. 200.

[110] What distinguishes the lyceums from other institutions set up to educate people about science and art is their democratic character, which permitted them to reach even the outskirts of civilization, at first in the East and later in the West as it became more settled. See Carl Bode, *The American Lyceum: Town-Meeting of the Mind* (New York, 1956).

have done.[111] Emerson's public career was closely associated with the vitality of these institutions, and I shall have occasion to speak of them often.

But to reduce this gradual withdrawal to a simple exchange of platforms would be to distort its nature. Emerson's success as a lecturer, incontestable though modest,[112] did not at all tempt him astray. It had, after all, nothing in common with the almost organic shock the orator's activity should in theory evoke, and the ambition of an Emerson refused any lesser reward. Also, it would have been naïve for him to think himself ready for a public role. If, as he sensed each day with growing certainty, he was a bearer of that seed George Fox spoke of,[113] he must let it grow in darkness, in obscurity, so that it might rise in its full splendor before the eyes of the world when its time had come. A premature triumph would be ominous, as he writes to Carlyle regarding *Sartor Resartus*: "I feel like congratulating you upon the cold welcome which, you say, Teufelsdroch has met. As it is not earthly happy, it is marked of a high sacred sort."[114] And in the same letter he opposes to such noble unpopularity the adulation that followed Goethe everywhere, in which he sees the worst misfortune genius can experience.

As long, then, as the hidden life whose end is determined by God shall last, the only comforting sign is failure,[115] and the only reasonable philosophy a philosophy of waiting:

> The philosophy of *Waiting* needs sometimes to be unfolded. Thus he who is qualified to act upon the Public, if he does not act on many, may yet act intensely on a few; if he does not act much upon any but from insulated condition & unfit companions seems quite withdrawn into himself, still if he know & feel his obligations, he may be (unknown & unconsciously) hiving knowledge & concentrating powers to act well hereafter & a very remote hereafter.[116]

[111] See CEC 142–143 (April 8, 1836). In his attempt to persuade Carlyle to realize his plan of visiting the United States, one of Emerson's arguments is precisely the merits and benefits of the lyceums.

[112] For several years—indeed till the publication of the Divinity School address—Emerson's reputation hardly extended beyond the immediate vicinity of Boston.

[113] "Geo Fox's chosen expression for the God manifest in the mind is the Seed. He means that seed of which the Beauty of the world is the Flower & Goodness is the Fruit" (JMN 5.55 [June 29, 1835]).

[114] CEC 107 (November 20, 1834).

[115] It even seems that sometimes this paradoxical perspective leads Emerson to exaggerate his own blighted hopes—see for example the passage of the journal (JMN 4.315–316 [August 30, 1834]) in which, having shown that all his public activities have ended in failure, Emerson applies to himself a line of Mrs. Barbauld's, originally written of a brook: "And the more falls I get, move faster on."

[116] JMN 4.368 (December 22, 1834). It may be that here also one ought to see the tutelary

If generalized, of course, such a philosophy would risk opening the door to all capitulations; but Emerson in a way disarms that suspicion by his evidently robust and long-suffering faith—a faith unmistakably revealed, as the reader will note, even by the unconscious drift of the text. Thoreau's determined striving for achievement, with its keenness in seizing the passing moment, has in comparison something pathetic and forced about it.[117] Emerson, on the contrary, has *time*—not the parceled out and hurried time of men but that of the elements themselves. One would have to breathe life into the notion of eon to suggest Emerson's immense leisure. Lucretius was despite his unbelief of the same stock—in harmony with the slow pulse of things.

If after reading such passages one considers the spectacle of Emerson's America, with its factional rivalries, its uncontrolled egoism, its loud professions of patriotism, it is difficult not to share the disgust Emerson's journal so often reveals.[118] When he hears of Edward's death in the sunny exile of Puerto Rico, Emerson is not far from envying it. Edward will no longer have to suffer from "the tumults of the Natural World"; he will share the peace of George Washington, removed from earth by a special privilege with "the Hope of humanity not yet subjugated in him."[119] And even when Emerson attempts to overcome his repugnance and to look reasonably into the future, he finds that hope offers only tenuous reasons to cling to: "in the course of the last six years," he writes to Carlyle in May 1834,

> Government in the United States has been fast becoming a job, like great Charities. A most unfit person in the Presidency has been doing the worst things & the worse he grew the more popular. Now things seem to mend. Webster, a good man & as strong as if he were a sinner, begins to find himself the Centre of a great enlarging party & his eloquence incarnated & enacted by them. Yet men have not hope that the Majority shall be suddenly unseated.[120]

---

figure of Coleridge. Kenneth Cameron, in "Coleridge and the Genesis of Emerson's 'Uriel,' " *Philological Quarterly* 30 (April 1951), pp. 212–217, compares this passage of the journal to a passage of *The Friend* ("Introduction," 3.27) in which Coleridge describes the progress of humanity as like the course of a river, both in being slowed or blocked by a thousand obstacles and in being irresistible.

[117] This thesis is argued in particular by Perry Miller in his lengthy introduction to a volume of Thoreau's journal long thought lost: *Consciousness in Concord: The Text of Thoreau's Hitherto "Lost Journal," 1840-1841* (Boston, 1958).

[118] See particularly the reflections evoked by the caucus Emerson attends in New York in October 1834—a few days, that is, after his move to Concord (JMN 4.327–328). The bare memory of that day can still arouse him two months later (JMN 4.369).

[119] JMN 4.326 (October 27, 1834).

[120] CEC 1.16 (May 14, 1834).

Another letter, this one dated October 1835, shows Emerson still more discouraged: government is simply "trade"; politics attracts only the greedy; the rabble's law is dominant everywhere, even in the judicial system; society is near to sinking into absolute impiety.[121]

These comments, addressed to Carlyle who was hesitantly thinking of visiting America, reveal so much bitterness and confusion that they cannot be explained simply as a reaction of temperament. There are more solid and more impersonal reasons, and the two letters just cited suggest them clearly. There is first the fact that Emerson was present, and completely bewildered, at a political enterprise resembling nothing he knew either from experience or from history, which scattered to the winds the great national tradition Washington had inaugurated and which seemed to be leading America into an abyss of disorder and violence. The state had only recently been in the care of cultured men, chosen more or less by and from within a small ruling class, restricted but conscious of its responsibilities; now it was offered up to public auction, abandoned to the mob—which was debating in the marketplace, among shouts and howls, the problems on which depended the well-being and perhaps the survival of the Union. But above all, this carnival politics manifested the irresistible rise of a false principle, which decent citizens fight against at a disadvantage because there are some means they refuse to employ;[122] and it revealed in broad daylight the incomprehensible fascination evil can exercise on the human mind.

Emerson's optimism thus suffered a rude assault. He protected it as best he could by invoking the incipient regrouping of the Whigs, who would find in the depths of their humiliation the energy necessary for victory, or by affirming that the Good is indestructible by nature and will rise one day from the very forces that have flouted it.[123] But deeper still, at a level consciousness hardly illuminates, Emerson was almost in panic at the idea that these brute masses might set themselves free and suddenly transform into reality the somber visions of the future by which the best—whom later generations would sometimes call simply the more privileged—are sometimes assailed. "It is a great step from the

[121] See CEC 140–141 (October 7, 1835).

[122] See JMN 4.333 (November 5, 1834): "The children of this world are wiser than the children of light. The good cause is always on the defensive, the evil assailant. . . . The Whigs can put in their own votes. But the Tories can do this & put them in again in another ward or bring a gang of forsworn gallows birds to boot, to elect the officers that are to hunt, try, imprison, & execute them."

[123] See JMN 4.332 (November 5, 1834): "Should the Whig party fail, which God avert! the patriot will still have some confidence in the redeeming force of the latent i.e. deceived virtue that is contained within the tory party; and yet more in the remedial regenerative Nature of Man which ever reproduces a healthful moral sense even out of stupidity & corruption. Thus the children of the Convicts at Botany Bay are found to have sound moral sentiments."

thought to the expression of the thought in action," he broods one day in the secrecy of his journal:

> Without horror I contemplate the envy, hatred, & lust that occupy the hearts of smiling well dressed men & women but the simplest most natural expressions of the same thoughts in action astonish & dishearten me. If the wishes of the lowest class that suffer in these long streets should execute themselves, who can doubt that the city would topple in ruins.[124]

Such is the bundle of arguments, disappointments, and apprehensions one has to bear in mind to grasp the significance of Emerson's gesture in deciding, during this period of political disquiet, to move to Concord: the town in which his ancestors had lived, in which Ezra Ripley continued to exercise his ministry, and in which his brother Charles was preparing to take over a desk in the law office of Samuel Hoar, his fiancée's father.[125] It would, of course, be unjust to describe as an evasion in the face of imaginary responsibilities what was, in fact, the fulfillment of a perfectly respectable resolution, cherished for some time: to get closer to Nature, to be at each moment within reach of fields and trees so as to feel in them the pulsation of universal life and to decipher their language.[126] But that his move to Concord also eased him of a burden and procured him an intoxicating sensation of freedom is irresistibly suggested by a passage in the journal that Strauch has called Emerson's personal declaration of independence:

> Hail to the quiet fields of my fathers! Not wholly unattended by supernatural friendship & favor let me come hither. Bless my purposes as they are simple & virtuous. . . . Henceforth I design not to utter any speech, poem, or book that is not entirely peculiarly my work. I will say at Public Lectures & the like, those things which I have meditated for their own sake & not for the first time with a view to that occasion. If otherwise you select a new subject & labor to make a good appearance on the appointed day, it is so much lost time to you & lost time to your hearer.[127]

A first interpretation, superficial but surely correct, would explain this text in connection with the author's recent past. The betrayal he had committed in composing a poem without inspiration—that is,

[124] JMN 4.334–335 (November 1834).

[125] See Rusk, *Life*, pp. 208–209.

[126] He started talking about the book he was preparing about Nature in September 1833 (JMN 4.237). Two months later, he notes in his journal, "there is not a passion in the human soul, perhaps not a shade of thought but has its emblem in nature" (JMN 4.95).

[127] JMN 4.335 (November 15, 1834).

against his conscience—and in agreeing to read it because of social vanity, or at best because of a fear of disappointing or shocking others, continued to haunt his memory. A change of residence could be for him the opportunity for a new departure, just as the first of January is a convenient date for putting good resolutions in practice. But the quality of the language, that alloy of solemnity and fervor founded on inward analysis that authenticates it and keeps it from dissipating in grandiloquence, persuades us to look further. The return to Concord was a decision charged with significance for the future. Emerson arrived there with great things to do—with, in short, the ambition to reinterpret without external help the role and place of man in the creation. Is it then surprising that he should seek peace, avoid occasions of dissipation and distraction, and desire as much as possible to absent himself from the world's tumult?[128] The real question is rather to discover why he was right—right, that is, in thinking that he would find in Concord more than elsewhere the spiritual atmosphere he needed to carry out his work.

To reconstitute Concord as it must have appeared in the second quarter of the nineteenth century requires a considerable imaginative effort.[129] The town has first to be stripped of the museums and the products of the tourist industry that adorn it today, and indeed of whatever contributes to give it the air of Sleeping Beauty's palace, in which the visitor, confronted with Emerson's hat or walking stick, looks about vaguely for a Prince Charming to wake these objects from their slumber. But the real danger begins when Prince Charming has been found—in the abundant literature that has undertaken not only to describe Concord but also to resurrect it. As the century advanced, in fact, bringing to the America of Jefferson, of Webster, of Lincoln a series of shocks that altered even its sense of identity, a good many novelists and poets understood how deeply their own roots struck into the past; and whether out of weakness or out of fidelity, they directed a nostalgic gaze toward what they considered the Golden Age of New England.[130] Oliver Wendell Holmes's 1878 study of Emerson already pays homage

[128] Whicher notes perceptively (*Freedom and Fate*, pp. 48–49) that in Emerson the desire for purity and virtue is accompanied by an initially surprising acceptance of the existing social forms and structures.

[129] The township of Concord in 1830 had 2,020 inhabitants, the town itself only a fraction of that number.

[130] One thinks in particular of the writers usually grouped with the local-color school, among them Mary Wilkins Freeman and Sarah Orne Jewett, of whom one might say that they depicted a world mortally wounded but still tinged with the last flush of life. See Warner Berthoff, "The Art of Jewett's Pointed Firs," NEQ 32 (March 1959), pp. 31–53. Emily Dickinson escapes this classification by her capacity for inward retreat.

to a vanished world; the description he gives of Concord, nestled in green among her placid ponds, still resonant with the glory of her sons, carrying on in austere simplicity the example of the pioneers and the soldiers of the Revolution, belongs to the great tradition of national hagiography.[131] More recently, Townsend Scudder's work, though precisely documented and rich in historical insight, owed its great commercial success to similar causes; in giving density and substance to the image of Concord that all Americans had vaguely preserved from their schooldays, it aroused and justified their civic pride.[132]

But the exaggerations in the praise do not imply that it is entirely undeserved. To compare the accounts we have of Concord in 1830 or 1840—those of Emerson and Thoreau above all—with the composite portrait of the American small town as it emerges fifty or eighty years later in the works of Sarah Orne Jewett, Sherwood Anderson, Willa Cather, and Sinclair Lewis is rather to perceive the independence, the calm energy, and in a word the equilibrium of the earlier community. Concord shortly before mid-century seems at the summit of a curve graphing a complex system of coordinates. The difficult days of settlement and clearing were past; those of intensive industrialization, with its brutal migrations and class conflicts, were still in the future. The railroad was soon to put the libraries of Boston less than an hour away from the Old Manse, but the inhabitants of Concord continued to lead an existence the rhythms of which were patterned on those of the earth, and in which the practical wisdom of farmers and craftsmen set the tone for all conversation.[133] The population was stable and homogeneous, and was proud to include many descendants of families established on the banks of the Musketaquid in the middle of the seventeenth century;[134] but it was not closed to outsiders who honored it in choosing it for their residence. Thus Samuel Hoar, born in the neighboring village of Lincoln, respected as an upstanding lawyer, was designated in 1824 to wel-

[131] Holmes, *Emerson*, pp. 53–55.

[132] Townsend Scudder, *Concord: American Town* (Boston, 1947).

[133] Emerson is still contrasting the rural life of Concord to the false and pretentious world of the city as late as 1846: "in the city of Makebelieve is a great ostentation bolstered up on a great many small ostentations. I think we escape something by living in the villages. In Concord here, there is some milk of life, we are not so raving-distracted with wind & dyspepsia. The mania takes a milder form. People go a fishing & know the taste of their meat. They cut their own whippletree in the woodlot, they know something practically of the sun & the east wind, of the underpinning & the roofing of the house, of the pan & the mixture of the soils" (JMN 9.416). Perhaps one should note here that the two Concord papers were called the *Concord Freeman* and the *Yeoman's Gazette*.

[134] Emerson took the name of this small Concord river to mean "*Grassy Brook*" (W 11.32).

come La Fayette; and thus Emerson himself, in the second year of his residence there, was chosen to commemorate the town's bicentennial.

In any case, these qualities and auspicious circumstances made Concord at the moment of Emerson's moving there a worthy and happy community. It had not yet been left behind by the course of technical progress, nor agitated by serious political rivalries;[135] though it was susceptible, as was natural, to the aspirations of the period[136] and attended reasonably to its business with no qualms of conscience or misplaced ambition, chiefly concerned with providing all men and women with the peaceable existence to which they were entitled. All in all, as Emerson discovered in the municipal archives and the chronicles he examined when composing his oration, Concord had remained remarkably faithful to itself. "I find our annals marked with a uniform good sense," he notes toward the end of his speech;

> I find no ridiculous laws, no eavesdropping legislators, no hanging of witches, no ghosts, no whipping of Quakers, no unnatural crimes. The tone of the Records rises with the dignity of the event. These soiled and musty books are luminous and electric within. The old town clerks did not spell very correctly, but they contrive to make pretty intelligible the will of a free community.[137]

All of Emerson's respect and affection are explained in these last words—which account also for the extraordinary interest he took in deciphering so many crabbed and awkwardly written volumes. Following Concord's growth step by step from its foundation, he could grasp—as he could not have in the case of any of the old European countries—the necessary conditions of a political organization that had very early been able to resolve one of the thorniest political problems, namely that of the necessary adjustment between order and justice, between justice and liberty. The stroke of genius (or of necessity—the two words come more and more in Emerson's work to occupy the same territory) was the institution of town meetings,[138] which joined all the citizens of a city or village on a footing of equality and carried into effect the will of the

[135] Scudder reports that the inhabitants of Concord had been divided between Jeffersonians and Federalists but joined together against Jackson; in 1828, all but four voted for John Quincy Adams.

[136] See Rusk, *Life*, p. 227. Concord was, for example, just at this time first beginning to be affected by abolitionism and the temperance movement.

[137] "Historical Discourse at Concord" (W 11.83–84).

[138] In the French version of this book "town meeting" is translated by *assemblée communale*—the inspiration for that rendering being Tocqueville, who ordinarily and suggestively translates "township" by *commune*.—Trans.

majority after a frank and honest discussion. In his speech in 1835, Emerson sets the fundamental rectitude of the system in full view:

> In a town-meeting, the great secret of political science was uncovered, and the problem solved, how to give every individual his fair weight in the government, without any disorder from numbers. In a town-meeting, the roots of society were reached. Here the rich gave counsel, but the poor also; and moreover, the just and the unjust. He is ill informed who expects, on running down the Town Records for two hundred years, to find a church of saints, a metropolis of patriots, enacting wholesome and creditable laws. The constitution of the towns forbid it. In this open democracy, every opinion had utterance; every objection, every fact, every acre of land, every bushel of rye, its entire weight.[139]

The wonderful thing, Emerson feels, is that wickedness, despite the many opportunities offered it, has been so regularly suppressed and defeated. This triumph of the good cause on an open field of battle is the foundation for Emerson's optimism and confidence. A proof has been furnished—and a dazzling one—of man's capacity to govern himself.

These comforting conclusions, suggested by a close and earnest historical analysis, had the effect of sparing Emerson for several years the hesitations and regrets of a bad political conscience. He was intensely occupied with grave and lofty questions concerning human nature in the absolute; but he could, and with no sense of cowardice, consider the problem of man's life in society as resolved, practically as well as speculatively. That is why he accepted the various tasks his fellow citizens found it good to offer him, from the presidency of the school committee to the office (a mostly honorary one, as good luck would have it) of hog-reeve, which made him responsible for fining people who owned pigs and let them stray.[140] At the same time he was looking for a permanent residence and bought a large house located at one end of the developed section of town, in the middle of a lot that extended all the way to the river. He moved there in September 1835, some days after his marriage at Plymouth to Lydia Jackson: descendant of one of the oldest families of Massachusetts, daughter of a shipowner who had never concealed his hatred for Democrats, but on her own account a woman much subject to the spiritual fermentation of the period—to the point

[139] W 11.46–47.

[140] For more exhaustive information on Emerson's civic activities see Hubert H. Hoeltje, "Emerson, Citizen of Concord," AL 11 (January 1940), pp. 367–378. Hawthorne was also chosen hog-reeve, in 1844, and Dickens tells in *American Notes* of his surprise at seeing pigs wandering freely on the sidewalks of New York.

that a rumor went around that Emerson had married a mystical Swedenborgian.[141] This second marriage was in no way like Emerson's first and did not erase its memory. It was a soberly concluded alliance between persons of good common sense, a candid sharing of the joys and cares of each day; the very moderation of the feelings that were its basis (Emerson says as much in a letter to Lydia, with a frankness that to some might seem indiscreet[142]) was the surest sign that it would last.

After a few months, in any case, Emerson's life had fallen into the rhythm that it was to maintain for more than forty years—with the exception of the ever longer and more frequent absences his activity as a lecturer was to occasion. He divided his days between reading, writing, walking, and social or family obligations; he welcomed gladly those who joined him in sincerely seeking answers to the riddle of the human condition, but brusquely sent away the obstrusive. His overall attitude was thus distinctly different from Thoreau's; it was that of a prudent swimmer, letting himself be carried by the current so as to minimize his expenditures of energy. But as such a swimmer comes to love the wave that bears him up, to find pleasure in the sensations it offers him, so Emerson would in time become attached to Concord, to his neighbors, to his house, by feelings that in intensity and depth far exceeded the considerations of respect and advantage that had led him to leave Boston in the first place. Concord was for him not only a great window open to the spectacle of Nature, but the locus of his friendships (at least his American ones), the finished model of all civilized society, and, in consequence—and less paradoxically than it might seem—the obstacle that would for a long time keep him from understanding the nation being forged outside it.

[141] See Rusk, *Life*, p. 215. That the rumor was still alive in 1852 is attested by a letter of Arthur Hugh Clough (*Correspondence*, ed. F. Mulhauser, 2 vols. [Oxford, 1957], 2.334).

[142] Letter of February 1, 1835 (L 1.434–435).

6

~ ~ ~ ~

PROPHECIES AND EPIPHANY

ONE CANNOT expect from Emerson the striking gesture or challenge that would all at once impose him on the attention of his contemporaries and would justify an easy division of his biography into a period of obscurity and a period of renown. Just as his choice of the ministry had led him to assume a role of moral director considerably before he had found his own self, so he was to succeed in giving to each of his audacities, once he had reached his full intellectual growth, the appearance of a matter-of-fact truth accessible to any person willing to pay it a little attention. But this tranquil possession of self was itself the product of a long preparation; it presupposed a long and patient work of investigation, of reflection, of assimilation; it depended on a mind constantly on the lookout, rejecting the comforts of habit and modifying at every moment the map of the universe it bore within it; above all it attested to a spiritual destiny of exceptional good fortune—for other men have after all asked and not been answered, and who will ever make sense of the dichotomy? Emerson was aware of these imponderable factors, which orient us without our knowing toward success or failure:

> I will read & write. Why not? All the snow is shovelled away, all the corn planted & the children & the creatures on the planet taken care of without my help. But if I do not read nobody will. Yet am I not without my own fears. Capt Franklin after 6 weeks travelling to the N. Pole on the ice found himself 200 miles south of the spot he set out from; the ice had floated. And I sometimes start to think I am looking out the same vocables in the Dictionary, spelling out

> the same sentences, solving the same problems. —My ice may float also.[1]

But the intellectual history of the years between the trip to Europe and the publication of *Nature*, in September 1836, is rather that of a powerful and regular forward movement; it had its ebbings, of course, but rather in the manner of a tide that seeks in a temporary retreat the energy necessary for new and victorious surges.

Less than a month after his return to America, Emerson made his debut as a secular lecturer, speaking of "The Uses of Natural History" before an audience at Boston.[2] This rapid and unexpected metamorphosis demands an explanation. It seems at first glance that never before his departure for Europe had Emerson even thought of this sort of activity; to the very limited extent to which he envisaged a career outside the church, his preferences were for literary journalism[3]—though in the despondent state in which he had found himself at the time, even this project would seem rather to have served only a need for compensation. Moreover, the crossing and then the stay in Europe had made him forget it; and when he returned, he had no scruples in returning to his former pulpit. Others, however, who knew or guessed his capacities, were quickly at work to open new doors for him. Thus his brother Charles and a cousin named George Emerson (who with Daniel Webster and Josiah Holbrook had played an important role in establishing a Boston chapter of the Lyceum[4]) undertook all the work necessary to arrange a first lecture, to be given before the Natural History Society if the object of their scheme would only consent. Emerson agreed, and in the six months that followed, he spoke on three other occasions about scientific subjects, varying his audience for reasons of practicality.[5] This was the

[1] JMN 5.25 (March 27, 1835). Sir John Franklin was a British explorer who between 1819 and 1827 led two expeditions to northern Canada and Alaska to survey the shores of the Arctic Ocean. He later published an account of both voyages.

[2] The lecture was given on November 6, 1833 to the Natural History Society of Boston; it is reproduced with textual variants in EL 1.4–26 and 393–401.

[3] Vide supra, chapter 5.

[4] It was called the "Society for the Diffusion of Useful Knowledge." (See on this matter the introduction to EL volume 1, which is the source of the present account.) Josiah Holbrook (1788–1854), educator and reformer, founded the first American Lyceum at Millbury, Massachusetts in 1826, and at the same time published a grandiose plan envisaging the extension of the institution throughout the United States and indeed beyond it.

[5] The three lectures are entitled "On the Relation of Man to the Globe" (EL 1.27–49 and 401–404); "Water" (EL 1.50–68 and 404–411); and "The Naturalist" (EL 1.69–83 and 411–418). The last, like the first in the series, was given before the Natural History Society. The first was part of the Franklin Lectures, aimed at a less well-off audience. "Water" was delivered to the Boston Mechanic's Institution.

humble beginning of Emerson's long lecturing career, which was to take him beyond Boston, then later even beyond New England, and was to continue until fifteen years after the Civil War, into the presidency of Rutherford Hayes.

There remains the choice of subjects. With the exception of the sermon on astronomy discussed earlier, never before had Emerson touched on subjects pertaining to science. But the crisis that he had passed through in 1832 and that had led him to renounce his ministry had stimulated his interest in that area; the journals of the period make that clear, as do the directions of his reading, carefully traced by Kenneth Cameron. It is possible also that the vogue of popularization, a corollary of the lyceum movement, contributed to leading his mind toward scientific speculation—especially if one admits with J. W. Beach that literary men are more easily captivated by scientific accounts of the less precise sort.[6] But the massive borrowings to which he was driven when he had to discuss a particular matter at all closely ("Water" is the best example here) reveal clearly that his knowledge was hasty and vulnerable; from lack of time, and also from his constitutional impatience of detail, he wove together the known facts, the received interpretations, and his own personal comments into a hybrid fabric that illustrates perhaps more faithfully than one would imagine today the standard oratorical level of this sort of presentation. All the evidence suggests that Emerson was yielding to external pressure. The public seeks enlightenment, and in particular wants to be initiated into the mysteries of natural science, which are more accessible to the *profanum vulgus* than are those of mathematics or physics and have been since the previous century associated with philosophical rationalism.[7] But Emerson as lecturer would characteristically orient his subjects toward his personal concerns; and in doing so, he succeeded in making them serve his own instruction at least as much as his listeners' pleasure.

For all the labor involved, moreover, the task was to Emerson's taste.

[6] Cf. his "Emerson and Evolution," *University of Toronto Quarterly* 3 (July 1934), pp. 474–497, in which he formulates the idea that certain garbled but vivid versions of scientific data can catch a poet's attention and offer him inspiration where a rigorous account of the same facts or theories may well leave him cold.

[7] See the chapter in H. Schneider's *A History of American Philosophy* (New York, 1946) on "Natural Philosophy," pp. 72–76. In it the author describes the gradual transition from natural philosophy to the natural sciences and cites certain lecturers, among them Benjamin Rush of Philadelphia (1745–1813), who strove to show that the moral faculties were directly dependent on certain physical factors. In a passage written while he was preparing "The Naturalist," Emerson asserts that recent scientific discoveries have affected human relations in much the same way as did the colonization of America in the seventeenth century, or the sword of revolution in less distant times (EL 1.416–417).

In a period of political confusion it was comforting to be able to turn—and to turn others—toward a domain suffused with light, resonant and vibrant with astonishing wonders. A letter to his brother William, written just after his third lecture and at the end of a period of intensive reading, vividly reveals this feeling of profound reassurance:

> I am almost afraid to take up a newspaper I am so sure of being pained by what I shall read. Is it not a good symptom for society this decided & growing taste for natural science which has appeared though yet in its first gropings? What a refreshment from Antimasonry & Jacksonism & Bankism is in the phenomena of the Polar Regions or in the habits of the Oak or the geographical problem of the Niger.[8]

But there is more: the rigorous study of the visible world was to be a powerful aid in the battle Emerson must some day wage against the premier American vice: imitation. Following Channing, whose *Remarks on American Literature* (1830) had already expressed the American desire for intellectual independence, and before his own call to the American Scholar came thundering out, Emerson denounces his compatriots' passivity toward England, which continues its domination of American minds as if the Revolution had never taken place. The natural sciences constitute by far the most elegant means of shaking off this yoke: "Time will certainly cure us, probably through the prevalence of a bad party ignorant of all literature and of all but selfish, gross pursuits. But a better cure would be in the study of Natural History. Imitation is a servile copying of what is capricious as if it were permanent forms of Nature. The study of things leads back to Truth."[9] Already, it is clear, Emerson excels in locating what might appear to be intellectual investigations of the most specialized sort in a context in which the interests of man as a whole, and indeed those of the entire nation, are directly at stake.

With the possible exception of "Water" (in which Emerson's technical incompetence compels him to retreat too often behind his sources) the lectures are joined together by a sort of resistant Ariadne's thread, which gives them enough unity that the reader can at least partially ignore the discontinuity of their themes and the superficial rapidity of their exposition. This thread is the close and ubiquitous relation between man and the creation; and Emerson enumerates its modalities

[8] Letter to William Emerson of January 18, 1834 (L 1.404). Emerson expressed the same idea in his first lecture, comparing the effect of scientific studies to that of a great fresh wind, sweeping away the miasmas of a sickroom (EL 1.23).

[9] "The Naturalist" (EL 1.75).

inexhaustibly. Man on earth is at home. He is announced, expected, and welcomed by the objects he touches and no less by those deep in the bowels of the earth; and this providential adaptation (the words "fit" and "fitness" recur frequently) is the basis of his physical power and at the same time reassures him as to his eventual destiny. In this last point lies the incomparable value of science—for whether old Calvinism still practices its empire of terror and intimidation or has yielded, in breaking up, to such a chaos of brute passions as the political life of America in the 1830s poignantly illustrates, it is urgent that man be put in possession of his full inheritance. To study astronomy or chemistry, to learn about the water cycle, to investigate the sedimentation left by the withdrawal of oceans is not to turn one's back on the proper study of mankind; rather it is to nourish our faith in its privileged vocation with irrefutable arguments, to support the intuitions of consciousness upon positive certainties, and finally to dismantle a failing and obsolete theology and substitute for it the inexhaustible testimony of a world created as the basis of a universal ethic. Tirelessly in his scientific lectures Emerson confronts man with the universe that contains him, for the sake of his greater glory.

These lectures do not exhibit the sharp articulations that (at least outwardly) characterize *Nature*; but even here Emerson is already busy arranging hierarchically the teachings to be extracted from scientific practice, whether applied or theoretical. He points out the benefits to the body of a botanical expedition in the woods, or along the beach; he alludes to the economic advantages humanity has already drawn from its better understanding of nature and proclaims the certainty of their infinite continuation; but he is especially anxious to examine the record of spiritual victories, because it is chiefly at their level that he himself intends to make a contribution. Thus he accords considerable importance to the effort of inward discipline that is asked of us if we wish to subject the universe to our wishes. *Natura enim non imperatur nisi parendo*; the Baconian precept retains its validity in the mid-nineteenth century and accounts in particular for the superior character of country people, long used to reckoning with the harshness of the elements and thereby preserved from the irritating casualness too common in city dwellers.[10]

[10] In the only lecture he was subsequently to devote to the role of science in human life ("Humanity of Science," the second lecture in the 1836–1837 series "The Philosophy of History" [EL 2.22–40]), Emerson imagines the dismay of a Newton, a Cuvier, a Laplace entering a public meeting just as some "pert boy" is busy propagating as a law one or another of the foolish ideas thronging in his head, without the least care in the world whether it is compatible with the order of things or not. Happily, Emerson concludes, it is not given to every first-comer to change the course of human events.

And this exacting and sometimes bitter struggle gains a piquant savor from its very precariousness: man is always victorious, but only just. During his return voyage to America Emerson had already noted that the life of a sailor is composed of a thousand escaped shipwrecks.[11] In his second lecture, the most interesting because the most deliberately anthropocentric, he takes up this idea again and enriches it, showing that it conceals an essential element of the human condition: gigantic and terrifying as the animals around us may be, we can exempt ourselves from their law and even on many occasions impose our own, if we know how to take advantage of our resources. The whale swims faster than we do, but boats annul that superiority; man cannot pursue the eagle in the air, but he can launch an arrow into swifter flight than even the eagle is capable of. "The same balance is everywhere kept. A man is always in danger, and never. Let a man keep his presence of mind, and there is scarcely any danger so desperate from which he cannot deliver himself. For there is a very wide interval betwixt danger and destruction which men in peaceful pursuits seldom consider."[12] One need not press this text very far to find in it the expression of an almost barbaric primitivism—the opposite, say, of *Typee*'s. This would be something of a distortion, but the text does have a certain strong, almost acrid savor to it that one finds elsewhere in American literature also—in Thoreau, for example, in consequence of the same organic confidence in life, or in William James, whose optimism was similarly unaffected. At the same time it suggests an appetite for experience and a striving to push human faculties to their limit that when transposed to the mental level give Emerson's speculations their character of high adventure. Conversely, his philosophical audacities would have to depend on the sturdiness and, one might say, on the euphoria of an obedient organism, because the connection between health and inspiration—a recurrent theme with Emerson—is only an illustration of the strict law of reciprocity joining the two realms.

Of all the directions presenting themselves to the spirit of exploration, there is none more tempting than the history of the earth. Geologists and paleontologists have thrown an entirely new light on our species, and Emerson's voice betrays real exaltation in announcing as much: "By the study of the globe in very recent times we have become acquainted with a fact the most surprizing—I may say the most sublime, to wit, that Man who stands in the globe so proud and powerful is no upstart in the creation, but has been prophesied in nature for a thou-

[11] See JMN 4.236–237 (September 5, 1833).

[12] "The Relation of Man to the Globe" (EL 1.38).

sand thousand ages before he appeared."[13] Such in fact is the passionate game in which scientists indulge; magicians in reverse, diviners of the past, they seek to find the terms in which, along the sequence of ages, the creatures we are have been foretold. There was at first a mineral period, attested by the layers of granite uninterrupted by fossils; then plants came. They in their turn engendered the animal kingdom, but in a coarse and crude form, gigantic and unshaped, that the iguanodons reconstructed by Cuvier allow us to imagine. Then, finally, all was ready for the universe's favored child:

> Man is made; —the creature who seems a refinement on the form of all who went before him, and made perfect in the image of the Maker by the gift of moral nature; but his limbs are only a more exquisite organization, —say rather—the finish of the rudimental forms that have been already sweeping the sea and creeping in the mud; the brother of his hand is even now cleaving the Arctic Sea in the fin of the whale, and, innumerable ages since, was pawing the marsh in the flipper of the saurus.[14]

Despite the allusion to the successive transformations of a single organ through a sequence of species, Emerson's point of view here is not at all Darwinian. Rather it depends on the notion of a chain of being that is almost as old as humanity itself and that was accepted—with considerable variations of emphasis, of course—by a good many scientists and philosophers of the seventeenth and eighteenth centuries, from Leibniz to Lamarck, from Locke to Buffon and Goethe.[15] But Emerson, like Coleridge before him,[16] has no interest in the inert facts of a system of classification; rather he imagines behind the stable forms a spiritual movement from which they proceed, and he gives to that movement the traditional and familiar face of a God full of affection for his creatures: "Man is made; and really when you come to see the minuteness of the adaptation in him to the present earth, it suggests forcibly the familiar

[13] "The Relation of Man to the Globe" (EL 1.29).

[14] "The Relation of Man to the Globe" (EL 1.32). Emerson had just read Sir Charles Bell's treatise *The Hand: Its Mechanism and Vital Endowments as Evincing Design* (London, 1833).

[15] See on this subject H. F. Osborn, *From the Greeks to Darwin* (New York, 1894), particularly chapter 4: "The Evolutionists of the XVIIIth Century" (pp. 106–152), in which he distinguishes between "speculative evolutionists" (Diderot, Robinet, Oken, etc.) and "naturalists" (chiefly Linnaeus, Buffon, and Erasmus Darwin). The subject has been explored more recently by Arthur O. Lovejoy in his brilliant *The Great Chain of Being*.

[16] See on this point H. H. Clark, "Emerson and Science," *Philological Quarterly* 10 (July 1931), pp. 225–260 and Beach, "Emerson and Evolution." Beach reproduces a phrase of *Aids to Reflection* ("All things strive to ascend and ascend in their striving") that astonishingly anticipates the second epigraph of *Nature* (W 1.1).

fact of a father setting up his children at housekeeping, building them a house, laying out the grounds, curing the chimneys, and stocking the cellar."[17] Each element of the comparison refers to a specific aspect of human existence: the house is the shelter we derive from the materials accumulated by nature and also the air composed of oxygen and nitrogen in the only proportion suitable for our lungs; the well-furnished cellar symbolizes the coal lying in apparently inexhaustible reserves in the depths of the earth; the volcanoes finally are the safety valve, through which can flow inchoate matter that if blocked would cause a horrifying explosion. The tone and ideas vaguely smack of Bernardin de Saint-Pierre.

Science is thus for Emerson a springboard; it gives him a good leap up, and then he kicks it vigorously away. He is grateful to it, of course, for its supply of objective arguments for optimism; but having once identified them, he incorporates them into a teleological vision of the world, as if he could not wait to move beyond the inevitable tension between object and subject, means and end, discursive intelligence and moral consciousness, Understanding and Reason. At the same time he has no sense that he is preferring one set of terms to the other; rather he judges that he maintains an equal balance between them, or more precisely that he brings them together in such a way that each can impregnate the other (metaphors of sex and marriage are used several times[18]); and by this means can man discern the sublime ordering of all the parts of the universe: "I am not impressed by solitary marks of designing wisdom; I am thrilled with delight by the choral harmony of the whole. Design! It is all design. It is all beauty. It is all astonishment."[19]

The passage just quoted sounds the dominant note of these lectures, to which Emerson's enthusiasm adds its own overtones. It is difficult today for us to follow him through all the stages of his triumphal progress across creation; the idea of a point-by-point correspondence between natural laws and spiritual seems to us shockingly facile, perhaps because of the indifference it implies to the moral virtues (modesty, patience, and so on) that are the precondition of all serious scientific research.[20] Emerson would no doubt have been surprised to hear himself

[17] "The Relation of Man to the Globe" (EL 1.32).

[18] Cf. particularly JMN 4.310 and EL 1.79. The same metaphor appears again in *Nature* (W 1.28).

[19] Conclusion of "The Relation of Man to the Globe" (EL 1.49).

[20] That indifference suffices at any rate for some writers to argue that Emerson's thought is obsolete, even obscurantist. Thus H. B. Parkes can write in his penetrating criticism of Emerson that "this conception of science as a branch of ethics is scarcely nearer to the world of the

disparaged for irresponsible trifling; and yet the cheerfulness of his extrapolations as he slips irresistibly from a few observed facts to the Universal Idea, mimicking Goethe in his quest for the one primitive plant that would explain all the others,[21] amply justifies the charge. But this aspect of cosmic harmony is neither the only nor perhaps the most important to which he is sensitive; besides the structural laws his intelligence claims to grasp, he also perceives, through some special act of vision, the infallible architecture sustaining the most ordinary natural landscape: "Nothing strikes me more in Nature than the effect of Composition, the contrast between the simplicity of the means and the gorgeousness of the result."[22] To illustrate this idea he chooses the example of the shell that when gathered on the beach is iridescently radiant, dappled with the reflections of the sea and the sky, and yet seems mournful and plain a few hours later at the bottom of one's pocket. This image in fact seems to obsess him; used for the first time in a lecture, it turns up again in the journal and blossoms into the poem "Each and All," published in 1839 but probably composed late in 1834.[23] Perhaps its appeal lies in the fact that it suggests some mysterious complicity between the totality of things and the uniqueness of a man's angle of vision, thereby excluding the presence of others as such. It seems clear in any case that Emerson had by this time received from science all that it was capable of giving him; henceforth he seldom lingered over the modalities of phenomena, anxious as he was to pass beyond and arrive at their origin and meaning: "it seems the duty of the Naturalist . . . to make the Naturalist subordinate to the Man."[24] And that is in fact the overall lesson that he wishes to teach; his digression into collective and public knowledge ends by reinforcing the notion of man's solitude in the face of Nature. But it makes of it an "armed" solitude, in the sense in which Coleridge applies that expression to vision. Kepler, Laplace, Cuvier assure Emerson that the created world is permeable to man's mind; it is now incumbent on him to extend their work by new means, to decipher the final hieroglyphics, which are also those likely to be the richest of all in meaning.

When Emerson returned to an audience six months later, he offered for the first time a unified series of lectures, this one devoted to biogra-

modern physicist than primitive animism or the medieval search for theological symbols" (*The Pragmatic Test: Essays on the History of Ideas* [San Francisco, 1941], p. 50).

[21] See JMN 4.287–289 (May 3, 1834).

[22] "The Naturalist" (EL 1.73).

[23] Cf. JMN 4.291–292 (May 16, 1834) and W 9.5, lines 19–28.

[24] "The Naturalist" (EL 1.81).

phy.[25] It is possible that the general theme was pressed upon him by the organizers of the series—portraits of illustrious men were well liked in the lyceums—but Emerson retained the freedom to choose his examples and thereby found the occasion to pursue the great humanistic investigation he had begun by way of science on far more familiar terrain. His concern was to find in the past some brilliant signs of the greatness nature proclaimed, so as to show that his prophecies were not the dubious fruit of an imagination let loose without control, but rather—for those who could see—the universal promise of a state of being already realized, here and there, in human history. At the same time, Emerson undertook to recover by intellectual sympathy the state of consciousness from which the most striking thoughts and actions of his heroes had proceeded.[26] He used only sparingly the information furnished by their contemporaries; he preferred to plant himself at the very center of his subjects' souls, so as to observe the radiant beams that emanate from them and color the universe as they break upon its surface. Natural history, by the correspondence between its laws and ours, modifies our knowledge of ourselves; and in the same way a great man works powerfully on his milieu and ends by stamping his image on it.

We do not possess the manuscript of the first lecture in the cycle, entitled, according to Cabot, "Tests of Great Men."[27] The few notes bearing on it that have come down to us are too fragmentary and vague to be useful, except as regards Emerson's reasons for banishing Napoleon from this Pantheon.[28] But the journals between 1832 and 1835 contain numerous reflections on the subject, and it is probable that the lecture was to some extent constructed from them. Even before his departure for Europe Emerson was setting up distinctions among established reputations, asserting that the "vulgar great men" were to be recognized by two traits: they engage in action only with distrust and timidity because they are obsessed with the desire for a good meal or a comfortable bed;

[25] The six lectures were given before the Society for the Diffusion of Useful Knowledge between January 29 and March 5, 1835. After a general introduction Emerson discussed Michelangelo, Luther, Milton, Fox, and Burke. Cf. EL 1.93–201 and (for the textual variants) 424–466.

[26] A sentence of the journal shows that this procedure is deliberate: "I have not so near access to Luther's mind through his works as through my own mind when I meditate upon his historical position" (JMN 4.348 [December 2, 1834]).

[27] See Cabot, *Memoir*, 2.712.

[28] Emerson's notes on the matter are printed in EL 1. with the textual variants, pp. 424–425. The argument they give is essentially that Napoleon has the necessary stature but that he lacks a certain "worth": "He is great by armies, by kings, by physical power but by one generous sentiment never."

and "they lack faith in man's moral nature."[29] In fact the second point includes the first, and the names that occur to Emerson to illustrate the opposite type—Luther, More, Fox, Milton, Burke—have in common a determination, a stability of character based precisely on such a faith. The reader will have noted that four of the five examples offered are subjects of individual lectures in the series under discussion, More alone yielding his place to Michelangelo. This means that Emerson's criteria for greatness did not change appreciably in the intervening time; he continued to consider the moral sentiment, whether founded on written revelation or not, whether manifesting itself through art, religion, or even politics, as the only source of all that marks out a man for the admiration and respect of his fellows.

But during this same period, the conviction was taking root in Emerson that men reach this degree of eminence only when they escape from the snares of society. Nourished on Plutarch since his early adolescence, he had formed the habit of considering history as a tapestry with a grayish background serving as a foil for some subjects, or patterns, brilliantly executed in gold. That is why he does not share the pessimism of Carlyle, whose *Sartor Resartus* offered a virulent critique of contemporary England and more generally of a world given over to superstition and impiety.[30] It is true, Emerson concedes, that there are no more crusaders, no Puritans assembling in conventicles; but that does not at all mean that greatness has left the planet, because society has never been, and will never be, a proper measure or sign of it: "Societies, parties," he writes, remembering his early flirtation with natural science, "are only incipient stages, tadpole states of man as caterpillars are social but the butterfly not. The true & finished man is ever alone. Men cannot satisfy him; he needs God, & his intercourse with his brother is ever condescending, & in a degree hypocritical."[31]

Things are never simple, however—as Emerson himself admits at other points. Retaining his basic attitude of distrust toward society (he notes also that no one is safe from its bribes, that we seek its favors like beggars instead of being guided by the opinions of the just[32]), he rec-

[29] JMN 4.42–44 (September 17, 1832).

[30] See particularly book 3, chapter 10: "The Dandiacal Body." In the philosophy of clothing, the dandy marks the last stage of spiritual decay—in him appearance is its own reward.

[31] JMN 4.308 (August 9, 1834). Such a passage is enough to show how much Emerson's position differs from that of Victor Cousin, who in the tenth lecture of his 1828 *Cours de philosophie* described the great man as a synthesis of the individual and the general, that is, much more a herald than a prophet. Emerson owned this volume and praised its "*eclat*" in a letter to William from May 24, 1831 (L 1.322–323), but his admiration seems not to have met the test of time; cf. JMN 3.327, 4.58 (1832), and above all 5.455 and 458–459 (1838).

[32] See JMN 4.316–318 (September 13, 1834).

ognizes that great men have all made their place in it and even that in a certain sense they are its keystone; the world would be quick to collapse if there were not scattered at wide intervals through the thoughtless mob "real men . . . whose natural basis is broad enough to sustain these paper men in common times, as the carpenter puts one iron bar in his banister to five or six wooden ones."[33] There is thus no incompatibility but rather accord and harmony between the exceptional man and the society in which fate has placed him, in consequence of the spontaneous respect he feels for the qualities, at least the potential qualities, he discerns there. Such probably is the meaning of a rather bewildering passage of the journal, not at all illuminated by its context.[34] After all, had Emerson not reached similar conclusions long before, in pondering over the growth of human institutions in the context of the role played by Franklin in the establishment of American democracy?[35]

In spite of their common points, these scattered meditations fail to coalesce in the reader's mind into a coherent nexus. Working on living matter and bringing to its analysis the blend of sincerity and perspicacity characteristic of him, Emerson grapples with hydra-headed difficulties as his reflections develop and confront the fact that there is no universally valid solution possible in this area—only a series of partial answers given by men in function of their temperaments to questions posed them by circumstances. The lecturer's method is precisely adapted to this radical limitation. Not being able to seize the whole truth at once, he attempts to besiege it by successive approximations; not being able to give his listeners a Man, in the strong and full sense of the term, he opts for depicting several of the lofty moments of mankind, revealed, somewhat arbitrarily, in a Renaissance artist, a religious reformer, a writer of sacred poetry, another religious reformer, and a statesman. It would seem that Emerson expected two sorts of advantages from his spiritual intimacy with these considerably disparate personalities. There is first the effect of stimulation that results from the mere fact of their existence—an effect that the journals never tire of celebrating. We are at every moment just on the edge of greatness, but for

[33] JMN 4.310 (August 4, 1834).

[34] "We say every truth supposes or implies every other truth. Not less true is it that every great man does in all his nature point at & imply the existence & well being of all the institutions & orders of a state. He is full of reverence. He is by inclination (though far remote in position) the defender of the grammar school, the almshouse, the Christian Sabbath, the priest, the judge, the legislator, & the executive arm. Throughout his being is he loyal. Such was Luther, Milton, Burke; each might be called an aristocrat though by position the champion of the people" (JMN 4.376 [December 27, 1834]).

[35] Vide supra, chapter 3.

some reason we do not manage to pass over the threshold by which we are separated from it—just as worker bees, similar as they are to their queens, remain inexorably her inferiors.[36] Nothing is as helpful to us in surmounting this impotence as meditating on illustrious destinies, woven of the same thread as are the lives of the humblest men and women and thus suggesting the infinite potential dormant in us. It may even happen that to this general intuition is added the revelation of a "perfect sympathy," which across oceans and centuries puts us in touch with the sponsors we dreamed of to justify a feeling or a thought we could hardly confess to our dearest friends—and it is then as if we were, for a moment, free of mortality:

> Socrates, St Paul, Antoninus, Luther, Milton have lived for us as much as for their contemporaries. . . . We recognize with delight a strict likeness between their noblest impulses and our own. We are tried in their trial. By our cordial approval we conquer in their victory. We participate in their act by our thorough understanding of it.
>
> And thus we become acquainted with a fact which we could not have learned from our fellows, that the faintest sentiments which we have shunned to indulge from the fear of singularity are older than the oldest institutions, —are eternal in man.[37]

The comfort and exaltation born of this almost mystical communion are for Emerson "the great value of Biography." But his penetrating glance discerns another value, less lofty and more ambiguous, which has to do with the events, glorious or obscure, providing the frame in which it evolves. Every great life has to invent a solution to the problem posed by the world's relative imperviousness to the promptings of the moral sense. In the subtle conflict between Reason and Understanding, some—like Luther or Fox—have stubbornly taken the side of the first, while others—like Burke—have attempted not to denigrate or slight the second. The spectacle of their attempts to reconcile the two antagonists, or to subjugate the one to the other's authority, deserves in every way to be closely observed, because in it can be seen the operation of certain abiding rules of human activity that one can neither violate nor ignore with impunity. In surveying the five destinies he examines—and all, even Michelangelo's, contain moments of courageous choice—Emerson is in a sense conducting a reconnaissance. He who has never carried his audacity beyond a courteous abdication of his pastoral cares

[36] See JMN 4.310 (August 14, 1834).

[37] JMN 5.11 (January 13, 1835).

now accompanies his heroes into the center of the critical zone in which they once staked their place in history. And yet all the while, and perhaps unconsciously, it is himself he is measuring in their circumstances, enraptured and reassured when he discovers in himself auspices of a similar destiny.

The journal reveals the reasons that led Emerson to include Michelangelo in his portrait gallery: in Italy he had been made aware of his artistic greatness, and when he came back to Boston he had discovered, perhaps with even greater admiration, his aesthetic philosophy. Emerson sees in him the ultimate preacher of Beauty, excelling in all the high arts through hard and detailed work, and yet at the same time pursuing in each of his works the single idea capable of organizing its elements—*il piu nell'uno*, according to a formula Emerson had encountered in Coleridge's *Table-Talk*.[38] Emerson describes Michelangelo as a creator of forms near to divinity and yet considers the sculptor and painter inferior to the man. "The sublimity of his art is in his life." And Emerson recounts certain splendid incidents in support of this judgment—for example Michelangelo's refusal to clothe the nudes of the Last Judgment despite the urging of Paul IV, or his conditions for finishing St. Peter's Cathedral: that he be the only director of the work and that he receive neither salary nor recompense.[39] Emerson's portrait, though lofty and grand, misses the warmth and dramatic intensity of the Italian Renaissance; and are we not, today, tempted to smile at the author's simplicity in praising the artist's platonic love and interpreting his modesty as the sign of an absolute victory over his carnal nature?[40] However great Emerson's powers of empathy were, here they reached a boundary intrinsic to his nature; it is fortunate that for his second lecture he returned to a world more familiar to him.

With Luther, it is clear from the first lines of the portrait that direct, intimate, vital communication has been established. Emerson is aware of treating a subject relatively unknown to his audience; this awareness acts as a goad and makes his treatment of Luther take on life and warmth as the providential similarity between the career of the German reformer and his own forces itself upon him: "Luther's singular position in history is that of a scholar or spiritual man leading a great revolution, and from first to last faithful to his position. He achieved a spiritual revolution by spiritual arms alone."[41] Luther incarnates man's confidence in the simple, naked truth, and spectacularly manifests the effects of its

[38] See EL 1.101.

[39] See EL 1.110–111.

[40] Cf. EL 1.115.

[41] EL 1.127.

bursting into the world: before it, lies grow faint, imitations seem fragile, and its servant walks in a universe of enchantment. But there is also a historical Luther, curiously conditioned by his time and influenced by its superstitions, and to this Luther also Emerson pays intense attention. This is the Luther who attributes to the Bible the same literal truth as do his ignorant contemporaries and who sees in every event and creature the expression of the supernatural. "I am a bitter enemy to flies," one reads in his *Table-Talk*, "*quia sunt imago Diaboli et Hereticorum*."[42] This "gross and heathen theism"[43] disconcerts Emerson; he cannot reconcile it with the comforting image of the man who talked to the birds in his garden, the excellent husband, as susceptible to the charms of domestic affection as to the harsh joys of polemic. The portrait is rich to the point of contradiction; in closing, therefore, Emerson has a difficult task, and in the end he retains only the aggressively courageous Enthusiast, the disdainer of meek prudence, the simple and sincere man fighting for a cause in which all other causes are contained. The particular circumstances of his life dissolve before such prodigious spiritual energy: "By the force of private thoughts, (with an impulse that is yet far from being exhausted), he shook to the centre, not only the Ecclesiastical empire, but, as all religious Revolutions must, the whole fabric of tyranny in the world."[44] Luther the subversive, Luther the emancipator: the lesson would not be forgotten.

The third lecture, devoted to Milton, lacks the second's dramatic impetuosity. Milton belongs to that category of writers who evoke respect tinged with veneration, so much so that his efforts to descend to the level of controversy (as in his *Defense of the People of England*) seem unfortunate and even unbecoming.[45] But such dross is the least part of his work; through *Paradise Lost* and *Paradise Regained*, and still more through his treatises and letters, he has won lasting recognition and gratitude among English-speaking peoples because he possesses in a supreme degree the faculty of inspiration: "Virtue goes out of him into others."[46] He stands powerfully amidst his century, and by the same movement that makes him the interpreter of the moral sense and its laws to his wavering contemporaries, he delineates "a life of man, exhibiting such a composition of grace, of strength, and of virtue, as poet had

[42] Emerson quotes the phrase, EL 1.133.

[43] EL 1.134.

[44] The concluding sentence of the lecture; EL 1.143.

[45] It is striking that in the order of the lecture series aristocrats and plebeians regularly alternate. The aristocrats have the numerical preponderance, but the first name Emerson chose was that of Fox and the portrait he worked longest on was that of Luther.

[46] EL 1.148.

not described nor hero lived."[47] By him and in him humanity draws itself up proudly; he more than any other merits the epithet of "erect" that Emerson uses whenever he wishes to suggest an undominated and incorruptible character. Moreover, the nature of the historical situation made Milton stand out in a way that fascinates the imagination. Educated amid the refinements of art and knowledge, cast by destiny into a period of turbulence, he was the unfailing supporter of that Puritan cause which was hostile to all the graces he so cherished. That there was conflict between the aristocratic distinction of the poet and the vulgarity of the people at whose side his sense of obligation placed him Emerson does not attempt to conceal—indeed he emphasizes the contradiction, since the heroism of Milton's choice is thereby heightened. "Susceptible as Burke to the attractions of historical prescription, of royalty, of chivalry, of an ancient church illustrated by old martyrdoms and installed in cathedrals, —he threw himself, the flower of elegancy, on the side of the reeking conventicle, the side of humanity, but unlearned and unadorned."[48] Nor does Milton succumb to the intrigues and the basenesses of politics. He takes part in controversy without ever becoming a party man; he remains simply the apostle of the three cardinal liberties—domestic, political, and ecclesiastical—and this uncompromised adherence to a truly universal cause is enough, among the puppets of ambition that surround him, to make him the great Realist, that is, the Poet.[49] Is it not tempting to see in this portrait, which takes on animation as the historical circumstances take on flesh and blood, Emerson's own personal meditation and, God willing, his prefiguring of a similar destiny? America is not, to be sure, torn by civil war; but Emerson is aware of the split already separating an enlightened but anemic elite from a mass every day more resolved and more self-confident. Perhaps the moment would come for him also to choose; and how then could he not think of Milton, who could maintain in his political commitment the integrity of a soul equally inaccessible to self-interest and fear?

For Emerson to come from Milton to the extraordinary life of George Fox, the Leicester shoemaker who aroused enthusiasm and passion by the force of his religious feeling alone, is to take sides, as Milton had, for the Puritans, and at the same time to avoid the contradictions of a divided consciousness. The purity of the author of *Areopagitica* is of a secondary type, the product of an inward fire that consumes for its nourishment a profusion of worldly riches. Fox's is as simple as that of nature,

[47] EL 1.149.

[48] EL 1.159.

[49] In Emerson's working notes Milton finds himself compared with Burns and even with Béranger (EL 1.449). One can hardly be sorry that the passage was finally omitted.

the manifestation in its coarsest but most volcanic form of the divine principle that lives in every man. That is why Fox's career, despite the trials that marked it, offers an astonishingly harmonious and unified image. The passage from idea to action that is so formidable for a less thoroughly tempered soul never stops Fox at all. If he discovers that the clergy is failing in its vocation, that religious observances lead the faithful astray instead of enlightening them, he engages at once in combat against these deceitful symbols and founds a sect without clergy altogether. With disarming honesty and irresistible determination, he works to heal human nature of its deepest wounds: "His attitude from first to last is that of a consistent practical reformer. He exposes a falsehood but supplies a truth. He puts ever a thing for a hollow form."[50] And his disciples, who confronted whipping, stoning, and death itself with obedient heroism, are clear witnesses that Fox had aroused his passion for sincerity in them also.

But the implications of this simple doctrine, founded on the notion of an infallible guide in every man, only become clear in light of the progress made since Fox's death; and it is indeed this prophetic quality of Fox's that in Emerson's eyes constitutes his chief value. Emerson notes, for example, that in rejecting all dogmatic formulations potentially capable of defining and limiting it, Quaker faith comes close to certain more recent philosophies, notably Kant's and Fichte's: "the Reason of the philosopher is the Religion of the people," he wrote in one of his drafts.[51] The progress made since Luther is clear: in place of an eclectic and motley religion, encumbered with impurities and founded on a literal interpretation of the Bible, we now have the quintessence of religious feeling, analogous in its effects to the liberal education offered by philosophers in that there is no shorter or surer road to the truth than the enthusiasm it generates when possessed of so high a degree of concentration. With this, Emerson had reached a point he hardly ever passed; in the two speeches he gave after the Civil War in favor of the Free Religious Association he expresses the same desire for liberation from "technical" theologies and goes on to define education as an attempt to promote respect for the inner voice.[52] One might say that by now this voice, from which all transcendence has gradually withdrawn, has lost a good part of its vigor and edge; but other change there is none.

Further, in unconditionally and unrestrictedly situating the source of

[50] EL 1.174.

[51] EL 1.459.

[52] See "Remarks at the Meeting for Organizing the Free Religious Association, Boston, May 30, 1867" (W 11.475–481) and "Speech at the Second Annual Meeting of the Free Religious Association at Tremont Temple, May 28, 1869" (W 11.483–491).

all spiritual light within the consciousness, Fox and the Quakers were also preparing the way for an immense political revolution, of which the eighteenth century represents only the first phase, still obscured by considerable misunderstandings.

Certain chemical elements react upon one another when put in contact and produce something new; and in the same way it is enough to bring together and blend, as had Fox, the idea of the common man and the idea of infinity inherent in the doctrine of the divine presence to bring into being, inevitable, incalculable in its consequences, the principle of republicanism: "All religious movements in history and *perhaps all political revolutions founded on claims of Rights*, are only new examples of the deep emotion that can agitate a community of unthinking men, when a truth familiar in words, that "God is within us," is made for the time a conviction."[53] Fox fought against the established church because it had wandered into formalism; but the right of revolt against tyranny, which no American of Emerson's time would have dreamed of disputing, is based, Emerson argues, on an analogous foundation. It is the ultimate protest of spiritual integrity intolerably assaulted by worldly power. Reading the journal of 1834 and 1835 only confirms the existence in Emerson's mind of an organic connection between democracy and religious feeling in Fox's sense. One might further ask whether the development of this line of thought was not fostered or accelerated by Emerson's recent disgust at the demonstrations conducted by the followers of Jackson.[54] In the face of such a caricature, he had to reassure himself by defining the true democracy it travestied, and the necessary conditions of its proper functioning. At the same time he was fortifying himself in advance against the corresponding temptation of aristocracy, which had long been capable of stimulating in him a certain echo of complacence or envy.[55] Fox thus became, in a most unexpected

[53] EL 1.181. The italics are mine.

[54] It is in any case during the two months that follow this episode, and just after his move to Concord, that Emerson records in his journal the bulk of his observations on the political extensions of the inner light. See particularly JMN 4.342 (November 23, 1834): "The root & seed of democracy is the doctrine Judge for yourself. Reverence thyself. It is the inevitable effect of that doctrine where it has any effect (which is rare) to insulate the partizan, to make each man a state." In another and much longer passage Emerson explains that democracy exists only where men avail themselves of the Reason within them instead of profaning its name (JMN 4.356–357 [December 9, 1834]).

[55] A passage of the journal written in February 1834 acknowledges that force of character is often inseparable from the exercise of authority. Once again Emerson cites the example of the southerner, whose poise in society and self-assuredness both depend on a sense of his natural superiority. And he adds, almost nostalgically: "My manners & history would have been very different, if my parents had been rich, when I was a boy at school" (JMN 4.262–263).

manner, the spiritual godfather of a second America, meant to take the place of that inhabited by Jefferson and Thomas Paine.

One still has to explain Emerson's choice of Burke—a difficult choice, apparently not settled on until long after the others—and it is plausible to think of Emerson's attraction toward elegance and graciousness of manners as a cause. Burke is the author, Emerson recalls, of a "Theory of Taste"; his brilliance in conversation was unequaled, and among his friends were a number of celebrated painters. But Burke is also the French Revolution's most resolute enemy, and as such had won considerable esteem from American Federalists, who divided their admiration between the profundity of his arguments and the eloquence with which they were expressed. Emerson had known of Burke for some time, but probably more by reputation than by close first-hand reading;[56] certainly the 1835 lecture was for him the occasion of taking Burke's just measure and moreover of diverging, here and there, from received Boston opinion on the subject. In the portrait Emerson presents to the Society for the Diffusion of Useful Knowledge, Burke as the adversary of the French Revolution appears only incidentally. The accent is rather on the qualities of the philosopher, capable of rising above vain quarrels and party prejudices to grasp human affairs in their totality and discern their natural order. There was in Burke, as in few other politicians, a blending of intelligence and virtue. He had the penetration Marcus Aurelius lacked, Emerson says, but also the honesty deficient in Bacon, that if joined to his genius could have made him the greatest of all statesmen. Burke brought to the investigation and analysis of social issues the scrupulous diligence of the scientist and the scientist's power of unification. But he was no less remarkable for his disinterestedness, his loyalty, his love of liberty, and his inexhaustible generosity, attested by countless sublime and touching episodes. His public offices never destroyed in him the sensitivity of an extraordinarily responsive nature.

He would then clearly deserve to be counted among humanity's spiritual guides—if he were not also, and almost incomprehensibly, a conservative and a party man. Emerson admits that the incongruity is troubling. But the fact of Burke's attachment to tradition where one had the right to expect him to be an ardent reformer can be acknowledged with no damage to his integrity; indeed, Emerson suggests, it is precisely the strength and the exquisite sensitivity of Burke's affections that deter him from radical measures, because he never fails to see that for some

[56] The allusions to Burke in the journal before 1835 are for the most part hasty and general. A letter to Lydia Jackson from March 2, 1835 (L 1.439), moreover, indicates that the preparation of the lecture on Burke cost Emerson a considerable effort of reading and assimilation.

people at least their consequences would be grievous. "Solitary thinkers who avoid others and are avoided," Emerson writes, perhaps alluding discreetly to himself, "may come to reckon their opinions at so high a rate, as to think that society had better be disturbed than these not adopted."[57] The plea is interestingly and inversely subjective—one temperament defends its opposite—but after the fervent eulogy for Fox, it is singularly pallid, as if Emerson had borrowed the eighteenth century's blandest pastels for his portrait. When he undertook the partial rehabilitation of the conservative, in the second *Essays*, Emerson offered other and less sentimental arguments and also came much closer to the depths of Burke's thought. However, the other paradox—that the philosopher was also a party man—disconcerts Emerson even more. He cites in all loyalty the justification Burke himself offers, namely, that the good must unite to insure the triumph of their cause and checkmate the wicked always on the verge of conspiracy; but the absence of any amplificatory commentary on his own part reveals that he is not convinced. His old individualist instinct is reawakened; it cannot accept the picture of a statesman, even a virtuous statesman, buying his success and effectiveness in government at the cost of a portion of his independence. For his own part Emerson was always to be occupied with keeping his independence safe—a concern that gave a peculiar savor to each of his political commitments, but also multiplied his painful cases of conscience.

Whatever the reasons—intellectual honesty or aesthetic balance—which had urged Emerson to include the portrait of a statesman in his biographical gallery, the result was disappointing. Put at the end of the series, after the splendid surge culminating in the inspired commoner Fox, the lecture on Burke seems like a false window, satisfying a wholly external desire for symmetry. But apparently Emerson saw his error—ten years passed before he presented another image of the politician, and in the interval his philosophy had changed so perceptibly that his account of Napoleon, in *Representative Men*, assumes a very different and far richer meaning.

With the ten lectures on English literature presented in 1835–1836—as indeed earlier, in a speech given a few months before titled "On the Best Mode of Inspiring a Correct Taste in English Literature"[58]—Emerson could focus still more essentially on the ethical concerns that give his reflections on science or on famous men their essential fervor. He was now relieved of the obligation to transmit hard

[57] EL 1.191.

[58] The eleven lectures on literary subjects make up the second half of EL 1—pp. 203–385 and 466–536.

facts that Reason might have difficulty in absorbing, and one can measure the advantage this gave him by referring in contrast to the first page of the portrait of Burke, as monotonous and empty in its chronological account as an enumeration of stock prices for the uninitiated. The privilege of literature is to do away with all intermediaries, all barriers; there is no way of making Chaucer or Bacon appreciated except by quoting them, so as to bring two consciousnesses into immediate contact, thereby producing, if they are felicitously matched, a new miracle of transubstantiation: "A good book is like the Ancient Mariner who can tell his tale only to a few men destined to hear it. It passes by thousands and thousands but when it finds a true reader it enters into him as a new soul."[59] Now if one mind penetrates into the interior of another by the common and unreliable conduit of the printed page, despite the countless prejudices that would thwart the meeting, is there not in such communication a dazzling testimony to the power of ideas? Emerson's intention is undoubtedly to reveal the subtle or elaborate modulations ideas experience in a Shakespeare, a Herbert, a Coleridge; but his initial impetus is an intuition of their intrinsic authority and energy:

> A man thinks. He not only thinks, but he lives on thoughts; he is the prisoner of thoughts; ideas, which in words he rejects, tyrannize over him, and dictate or modify every word of his mouth, every act of his hand. There are no walls like the invisible ones of an idea.
>
> Such are the ideas of God, order, freedom, justice, love, time, space, self, matter. . . . He cannot exclude them from his mind. There they shine with their everlasting light upon him do what he will. He may wish them away, he may make mouths at them. But their reality is never the less. They intrude into his dreams, and, compared with their fixity and stability, his being is a dream and a shade.[60]

[59] "On the Best Mode of Inspiring a Correct Taste in English Literature" (EL 1.214).

[60] "English Literature—Introductory" (EL 1.218–219). Here also it is reasonable to trace the influence of Coleridge's thought, in which the concept of the idea plays an important normative role. It is interesting to compare this passage with a passage from the journal that was written while Emerson was preparing this series and that provides his thesis with a sort of demonstration a contrario—in the sense that he attributes the mediocrity of contemporary politicians to their inability to understand the function and value of ideas: "But it is the shame of our age that these are not times of thought, that the appeal is to empty names that tinkle well in people's ears or to some bugbear with which they have been used to be put to bed. Has Masonry or Antimasonry, or the Indian, or the African, or the Bank been argued up and down, or has mere noise—most of it interested noise—decided the fate of these things? The Newspaper goes up and down, and there is much speaking, but men get for their money that which is not bread. Let their reason be addressed, let them learn its grandeur so as to demand that it shall be" (JMN 12.49). It was, of course, the debate over the Bank that dominated

We have only to be imbued with the omnipotence of ideas, Emerson says, to perceive the means of avoiding the dissipation and the contradiction to which we seemed bound to yield. Only such a change in perspective was needed, Emerson argues, to reconstitute order among disjunct fragments. Even if, like Fabrice at Waterloo, we can never take the step back from the detail of the event that would endow it with a wholly satisfying meaning, we persist in believing, because the conviction is inherent in us, that the universe is guided by a "great and beautiful necessity" and that the designs of providence are "like enormous nets enclosing masses without restraining individuals."[61] It is as if the focal point were being removed to infinity before our eyes without ever weakening our certainty of an ultimate convergence. One has to keep both of these two laws firmly in mind—that which defines the unifying function of the idea and that which describes the modes of its action—to understand the importance Emerson accords to what one might call the liberty of disengagement. The greater the distance that separates us from the world, the clearer our vision of it; and the clearer our vision, the richer the image of the universe itself. Literature having as its goal precisely "to *give voice to the whole of spiritual nature* as events and ages unfold it,"[62] the writer must sacrifice to his universal vocation the temptation to act. The poet, who is also the philosopher, must take care lest anything cloud the purity of his vision, must resist the tendencies that would lead him to join the brawl of humanity, must assess troubling or low episodes as a "dumb show" played for the pleasure of a dispassionate spectator. And at the same time he must shake up old habits, bring to light truths long hidden; he will be like those Aztec priests who brought to each domestic hearth, after its annual extinction, a spark of the sacred fire kindled in the temple by the heat of the sun.[63]

It is hardly surprising that one consequence of this program of rigorous asceticism should be a reversal of the literary hierarchy received by the cultivated men and women of New England. Addison merits only a few lines; Johnson is given somewhat more generous treatment, and his monumental prejudices are pardoned in the name of his devotion to virtue. As for Byron—his easy acceptance of morbid or even de-

---

Jackson's second term; and without provoking quite such heated passions, the controversy over freemasonry had between 1830 and 1840 fueled certain polemics that had reached even Concord; see Rusk, *Life*, p. 227.

[61] "English Literature—Introductory" (EL 1.225). Under the cloak of metaphor Emerson here suggests a philosophical point of view destined for fame in William James's work under the name of "soft determinism."

[62] "English Literature—Introductory" (EL 1.226); italics are Emerson's.

[63] See "English Literature—Introductory" (EL 1.229).

cidedly immoral feelings wins him this stinging verdict: "how painful is it to feel on looking back at the writings of one who should have been a clear and beneficent genius to guide and cheer human nature the emotions which a gang of pirates and convicts suggest."[64] The metrical skill and insouciance of *Childe Harold* are acknowledged, but as surface qualities they cannot disguise the devastating sterility of its thought. Emerson is not reading for diversion or to provide himself with the malicious pleasures of critics; he reads to strengthen his perception of moral truths (his penultimate lecture—not, by the way, among the best—is called "Ethical Writers"), and he spends little time on authors who disappoint his expectations. The consequence is a strong didactic prejudice, but also an alert sensitivity to spiritual riches in every form.[65] If Emerson shows himself stiff and even sectarian when his sympathy is dormant, he also reveals an extraordinary generosity at even the slightest hint of promise; thus he can stress the mediocrity of medieval fables, so much less beautiful and insightful than the myths of Greece, and at the same time do sincere homage to the medieval fabulists, for the sake of the allegorical quality that they infuse into their work, which conveys, though perhaps not by their conscious intention, a dim presage of the power of the human mind.[66] As Emerson loved to repeat, only affirmation counts; let others if they like carry out the subtle and somewhat idle task of comparing lights and shadows. Emerson for his part turns away from these refinements, impatient to reach the kernel of universal truth, or—to employ an opposed metaphor, which nonetheless serves the purpose as well—avid to rediscover the broad spiritual horizons once contemplated by those possessed of a need for profundity and expansion comparable to his own.

Among the paths Emerson intends to open up, or rather clear of obstacles, the most productive is indisputably that of symbolism. The celebrated equations in the fourth chapter of *Nature*—that words are the signs of natural facts, that particular natural facts are the signs of particular spiritual facts, and so on—condense an argument made as early as the first lecture of the cycle of essays on literature. "All language," he stated there, "is a naming of invisible and spiritual things from visible things."[67] In the same way, Emerson's remarks on the concrete origins

[64] "Modern Aspects of Letters" (EL 1.374).

[65] Emerson does not, for example, commit the error of confusing moral value and propriety of sentiment. "If there be vigor of thoughts, the general influence is safe," he declares in the first lecture (EL 1.230), and as if to buttress the idea he asserts that in Cleopatra Shakespeare has for the first time made "even luxury sublime" (EL 1.311–312).

[66] See "The Age of Fable" (EL 1.260).

[67] "English Literature—Introductory" (EL 1.220).

of words later felt as abstractions figure in both texts in almost identical form. By restoring literature to its full range, by positing that it treated the whole life of the mind, from sensation to lofty intuition, Emerson was reclaiming its patent of nobility. He joined with Taliessin, the Celtic bard who pounded hard in his poems at the frivolity and parasitism of wandering minstrels;[68] with Shakespeare, whose imagination was so strictly subservient to his experience of reality that he seems to us today the "Secretary" of his age;[69] and with Herbert, in whom subtlety of analysis and felicity of metrical invention are always subordinate to intense piety.[70] "But when the French school came into English ground, when Dryden, Pope, and Swift and Gay, Darwin and many men of less genius were the popular writers with a frivolous style of thought, down went again the respect of the poet as a priest or divine man." [71]

The reason for Emerson's anger is plain enough: it is the current of empiricist thought, with its distrust of intuition, its falsely scientific cult of measurement and observation, in a word its underlying materialism, that has been the gravedigger of great poetry. It is significant, however, that the name at which blame is directed is not Locke's nor that of any philosopher in particular but "the French School" as a whole, as if its abrupt intrusion had brought about the ruin of traditional English virtues. It can, of course, be objected that this is going too fast, that it is at least imprudent to make so much of a single phrase isolated from its context. But similar implications occur elsewhere in Emerson's writings; a reading of the journals (especially of certain passages left out of the first edition) demonstrates that Emerson credits different races with different physical or moral qualities that are pretty much immutable, and also with varying capacities for progress.[72] And for an intelligence as infatuated with generalizations as was Emerson's, such beliefs offered a useful explanatory principle; in introducing a solid element of continuity across the centuries, the idea of national character took on a certain methodological value that legitimized it. It was in the realm of history comparable to such scientific theories as those of Copernicus or

[68] See "Traits of the National Genius" (EL 1.239–240).

[69] "But is not this the ordinary course of humanity that one man is made to take up into his genius whatsoever is excellent and worth preserving in his age? He becomes the Secretary for that Century or Nation" ("Shakespeare," EL 1.317).

[70] See "Ben Jonson, Herrick, Herbert, Wotton" (EL 1.349–353).

[71] "Chaucer" (EL 1.274). The reference is to Erasmus Darwin.

[72] Thus he writes on October 30, 1835—that is, while preparing the lecture series under discussion—"I suppose all the Saxon race at this day, Germans, English, Americans—all to a man—regard it as an unspeakable misfortune to be born in France" (JMN 5.106).

Linnaeus, like them a system assuring the mind a lasting dominion over reality.[73] One should, moreover, add that European Romanticism had lent considerable luster to whatever was of a nature to exalt the national spirit; that Niebuhr had revivified the history of Rome's first centuries by showing the role played in them by racial rivalries; that England had, since Henry VIII and the break with Rome, been pleased to emphasize its population's Germanic origin; and finally that quite recently Sir Walter Scott had given dramatic treatment to the opposition between Normans and Anglo-Saxons in the first chapter of *Ivanhoe*.[74]

This background was certainly present in Emerson's mind when he agreed to give a series of lectures on English literature;[75] but the texts he was led to read in seeking to sharpen his knowledge made it so much more vivid to him that he decided to devote a whole lecture—the second—to "Permanent Traits of the English National Genius."[76] His exposition of the subject borrows heavily from a work he had found particularly impressive, Sharon Turner's *History of the Anglo-Saxons*;[77] not only does he follow Turner in quoting abundantly from poems written before the Norman Conquest, he also, like Turner, paints the adventurous and unconquerable clans in a very flattering light, taking pains to contrast their portraits with those of other and less illustrious primitive tribes. Thus, having noted Tacitus' celebrated commentary on the German love of liberty and natural pride, he borrows from Turner two remarks of the minor Latin authors Vopiscus and Salvian regarding the duplicity of the Franks and their habit of perjury.[78] For a moment

[73] A passage omitted from the final version of the second lecture reads as follows: "I spoke in my last lecture of the value of Literature as it is the record of the rise power prevalence & succession of Ideas. . . . History is read carelessly as a Chronicle of unconnected events. . . . if we read actively . . . we may find its pages full of cheerful wisdom. Thus it is very remarkable how permanent are the features of national character" (EL 1.477).

[74] One of the notebooks Emerson was keeping in 1834 (JMN 6.317–401) contains abundant remarks on the Germans and the Saxons, and notably a phrase of Guizot's cited in translation in which the names of the two races are associated with the idea of individual liberty. The phrase seems to have been taken from *L'Histoire de la civilisation en France* (volumes 2–5 of the *Cours d'histoire moderne*, 6 vols. [Paris, 1829–1832]). Yet it seems probable that Emerson did not become acquainted with the work until after 1835; vide infra, chapter 13.

[75] In his 1834 Phi Beta Kappa poem (vide supra, chapter 5, at n. 87) he was already attributing a single genius to New and Old England alike, and defining it as follows: "That Genius is the Saxon love of Law / And Freedom, whence our daily peace we draw" (lines 233–234).

[76] EL 1.233–252 and 474–484; the title is Cabot's.

[77] Sharon Turner (1768–1847) was the first to explore the Anglo-Saxon manuscripts of the British Museum with a view to publication. He produced the four volumes of his *History of the Anglo-Saxons from Their First Appearance Above the Elbe to the Norman Conquest* between 1799 and 1805; they were greeted with considerable admiration.

[78] See EL 1.234–235.

Emerson even forgets the literary intention of his lectures altogether and offers a quick sketch of modern England in which the reader sees marshaled, not without surprise, certain of the major themes of *English Traits*: England, says Emerson, has more wealth than any other nation, but that wealth is the daily conquest over nature of intelligence and energy; England is the center of the world's nervous system, eminent among other peoples by the force of moral sentiment; it is the political model from which liberal Europe continues to draw inspiration. Nonetheless, Emerson agrees, there is a troubling contrast between the civilized courtesy of England at present and the violence of its remote ancestors, those "abominable savages" always eager for blood. Emerson's explanation is restricted to a brief reiteration of his optimism: "the order of things in this world always bends man to virtue."[79] Obviously the moment had not yet come for him to ponder the historical conditions necessary for human progress. On the contrary, he sees in the unifying role played through time by national character one of the means available for the American to understand himself.

In the last part of the lecture, accordingly, Emerson undertakes to bring out the seven fundamental Anglo-Saxon qualities, "which continue and reappear with some modifications from age to age and in whatever country they are planted."[80] The list is sound, and it anticipates even in its choice of examples the analyses of *English Traits*.[81] The first quality is a certain gravity sometimes passing into melancholy, the second a sense of humor to balance the first. Then come the love of home, the taste for the useful, the passion for justice and truth. The last two traits—respect for birth and for women—are the only ones not commented upon, even briefly, but the neglect is only apparent; in his lecture on Chaucer Emerson returns to them with such warmth as to leave no doubt of his according them a singular value. Indeed he sees in the consideration given women the supreme criterion of civilization, and judges Greece, Rome, and the countries of the Orient harshly for not having been capable of attaining so high a degree of delicacy and self-control: "A severe morality is essential to high civilization and to the moral education of man it needs that the relation between the sexes should be established on a purely virtuous footing."[82] One of Chaucer's

[79] EL 1.242.

[80] EL 1.249.

[81] The story of the Englishman who took his tea kettle with him to the top of Mount Etna is retold in chapter 7 of *English Traits*, "Truth" (W 5.124). The saying that it was an Englishman who had the idea to add a shirt to the ruffle invented by a Frenchman turns up in chapter 5, "Ability" (W 5.84).

[82] "Chaucer" (EL 1.280).

great merits, Emerson argues, is to have encouraged by such portraits as that of Patient Griselda a sense of profound veneration for the humility, the love, and the purity that distinguish woman's nature and endow it at certain moments with supernatural grace. This attitude of almost mystical reverence, strengthened no doubt by the memory of Ellen Tucker, was characteristic of Emerson throughout his life, and had its influence when he had to take a side on the question of women's emancipation.[83] Above all it revealed in him a spontaneous capacity for self-discipline that fortified him against sensual inclination. Whether this fortunate disposition was transmitted to him from a line of ancestors who had themselves fought for the victory of a strict morality, or Emerson received as his lot a temperament largely exempt from carnal temptation (he liked to allude to what he called his lack of animal spirits), one ought in any case to take cognizance of the prohibition thus proclaimed precisely at the moment he is announcing everyone's right to live by his own law. The repulsion evoked in him by the unbridled romanticism of a Byron suggests all too well the unconscious limits he himself set to the application of his theory.

The last typical English quality, the English respect for birth, is treated at still greater length than the others, beginning with a quotation from Coleridge: " 'Chaucer represents a very high and romantic style of society among the gentry.' "[84] But Emerson intends to go further; he is interested in the principle hidden behind that gracious appearance and defines it as "the idea of the gentleman." With his usual ease in sweeping through the world of concepts, and with the aid of Sir James Mackintosh, whose *History of England* he had read,[85] he undertakes to trace the development of the idea from the Higher Middle Ages onward. Aristocracy was at first hereditary because it was expected that the son would possess his father's virtues, an expectation that would compel him out of honor to follow the paternal path. Gradually the ranks of this elite based on birth were opened to men who had won renown by courage or intelligence, and a new aristocracy was formed. Finally America extended the institution to its natural limits by abolishing all outward marks of distinction, all costumes, coats of arms, and titles: "It is now on its true foundation. Neither birth, nor law, nor

[83] See his 1855 speech to the Boston Woman's Rights Convention (W 11.403–426).

[84] "Chaucer" (EL 1.276).

[85] Sir James Mackintosh (1765–1832) was a journalist and jurist rather than a historian; he had made a name for himself by answering Burke's *Reflections on the French Revolution* in a work called *Vindiciae Gallicae*: *Defence of the French Revolution* (Dublin, 1791). Late in his life he wrote for the Cabinet Cyclopaedia a three-volume *History of England from the Earliest Times to the Final Establishment of the Reformation* (1830–1832).

wealth, nor academick education can confer it. It is now to be obtained only by gentle behaviour."[86] One may doubt the validity of so cavalier an interpretation, but it offers Emerson the very substantial advantage of simplicity; it orders a long and complex series of human experiences into a pattern in which history and literature converge toward a single moral goal.[87] The idea of race is the indispensable bridge between them: the distinction of the Anglo-Saxons is to have conceived the moral vocation of our species so early, to have described and celebrated it in their poems and at the same time to have striven to conform to it in their institutions and customs.

Clearly it would be wrong to attach too much importance to a theory not touching on Emerson's essential concerns and showing clear signs of hasty construction.[88] The last lectures of the series lose sight of the theory altogether, while Pythagoras, Plato, Epictetus, Marcus Aurelius, and other authors as little Anglo-Saxon occupy the place of honor in the lecture "Ethical Writers."[89] But it remains a source of secret satisfaction. Stripped of its excesses, it suggests to Emerson that he shares in an exceptionally rich human capital and that his chances for spiritual progress are better, other things being equal, than those of a Frenchman, an Italian, a Slav. Even a superficial study of natural science had persuaded him that man's coming upon the globe had been long prepared. Perhaps his sense of belonging to the Anglo-Saxon race procured him a similar certainty: he has received at birth the benefit of his ancestors' virtues, and in consequence the most painful strayings have been spared him. Conscious of the advantage, his energy can gather itself for a victorious leap. That is why, no doubt, the series ends on a note of joy and triumph, even though his last comments on contemporary literature reveal some disappointment. Emerson takes the lead, alone, but sustained by the conviction that he recapitulates in himself the best part of human destiny:

[86] EL 1.277.

[87] In the same lecture Emerson cites another passage from Coleridge's *Table-Talk* that defends an analogous point of view but in which the order of terms is in a manner reversed: "Religion is in its essence the most gentlemanly thing in the world. It will alone gentilize if unmixed with cant, and I know nothing else that will alone. Certainly not the army which is thought to be the grand embellisher of manners" (EL 1.280).

[88] In 1848, in the course of his second trip to England, Emerson did compose a lecture on the theme of natural aristocracy; but the subject had in the intervening years become charged for him with personal resonances. The only evident connection with the lectures of 1835 is the epigraph, borrowed from Chaucer's Knight's Tale (see W 1.29–30).

[89] EL 1.358–359.

> The present moment against all time. Wherever is Man there as from its embryo point the Universe of light and love unfolds itself anew as it had never been. I believe in the riches of the Reason and not of Plato or Paul. "He that has been born has been a First Man." The stars and the celestial shell that overarch *our* spot of ground, are as brave and deep as those which Pindar or Petrarch saw, or those that shone on the faces of Ben Jonson and Shakspear, of Dryden and Milton, of Addison and Pope. Every rational creature has all nature for his dowry and estate. All nature, nothing less, is totally given to each new being.[90]

The short introductory chapter of *Nature* makes that small book seem the direct continuation of the paragraph just cited: "Our age is retrospective. It builds the sepulchres of the fathers. It writes biographies, histories, and criticism."[91] It has not been sufficiently remarked that the challenge is above all self-addressed; Emerson was after all among those who had sacrificed to the fashion denounced here. *Nature* is clearly intended as a decisive gesture of emancipation (though somewhat weakened by its anonymity): the time of oblique affirmations, of suggestions, of positions taken in the guise of a third person, is over. A language disencumbered of collective habits, straightforwardly articulated in the first person, will bear witness to Emerson's striving for originality. But precisely in that originality is the universal path. The author's movement back and forth between "I" and "He" does not drown his experience in a middling, colorless generality; rather it makes it exemplary. The mixture of shy modesty and free lyricism with which he speaks of the recent death of his brother Charles poignantly illustrates the manner in which he will henceforth seek to teach.[92]

The intensity and power of *Nature* are indisputable; but the meaning of the book as a whole, the relations between its different parts, and the philosophy that inspires it have all long been subject to controversy. Rusk makes a comment that nicely summarizes the hesitations and stumblings of even the best-intentioned reader: "In this first book Emerson approved mysticism, pantheism, idealism, in varying degrees, by turns. He was not satisfied with any of them, but he leaned most toward idealism. Mainly, though, his idealism was moderate."[93] Paradox-

[90] "Modern Aspects of Letters" (EL 1.384). The italics are Emerson's; the quotation has not been identified.

[91] W 1.3.

[92] See chapter 5, "Discipline" (W 1.46).

[93] Rusk, *Life*, p. 241.

ical as it may seem, among the causes of this confusion are Emerson's attempts at organization; the concatenation of the chapters with their multiple subdivisions (the lingering influence of Emerson the preacher) outlines a rather erratic course. The author sets us at the beginning in medias res by a sort of pantheistic rhapsody; then he steps some distance back, describes the material advantages Nature provides, observes her beauties with judicious and reflective pleasure, and holds her, so to speak, at arm's length before plunging into the rich diversity of her treasures by a series of remarks on language. Then comes another reversal, in "Discipline"; it is man now who bows before Nature so as better to understand her lessons, the most fertile of which are also the most rigorous. The two following chapters, "Idealism" and "Spirit," seem to interrupt this dialogue and to start a genuinely philosophical meditation. But the last, "Prospects," with its lyrical vigor and long personification, dissolves all conceptual relations once again and ends in a triumphant profession of faith, with the image of snows melting to let the grass spring up again reintroducing the crucial theme of youth repossessed.

One could imagine other reasons for perplexity in reading *Nature*, notably the startling and apparently uncontrolled succession of tones—they modulate from discursive exposition through invocation to aphorism. But it is important not to look in Emerson for the unifying principle where it cannot be found. If in the chapter on idealism he defends with conviction what he calls "the Ideal theory" against superficial and frivolous minds, he is also careful to avoid any speculative argument touching on the nature of nature itself. He refuses to indulge in the difficult analysis of the conditions of knowledge, both because he doubts the validity of such an operation and because it is enough for him to acknowledge the intuitions of Reason, which discerns beneath the surface of things a spiritual force active everywhere. He is, as he says in his journal, "the practical idealist,"[94] less concerned with offering explanations than with rendering an experience. That is why the Fichtean (or Carlylean) formula he employs in the introductory chapter in opposing the "me" and the "not-me" has to be read cautiously; instead of the effort of a mind disengaging itself from all that it is not, it suggests an intimately lived coexistence, a perpetual oscillation from identity to alterity, from separation to fusion.

The true unity of *Nature* lies in a balance of tension. At the beginning and the end, as if to intimate the fulfillment of a cycle, Emerson evokes a state in which all distinction between the "me" and the "not-me" is

[94] JMN 5.135 (March 5, 1836).

abolished; the memory of ecstasy in the woods corresponds precisely to the myth of the universal man elaborated by the orphic poet. But in the intervening pages, a productive exchange is established between subject and object, of which Emerson records the oscillations—thus Beauty is first "the simple perception of natural forms," then the backdrop Nature constructs around great human actions, then absolute order as contemplated by the mind: "The intellectual and the active powers seem to succeed each other, and the exclusive activity of the one generates the exclusive activity of the other. There is something unfriendly in each to the other, but they are like the alternate periods of feeding and working in animals."[95]

One of Emerson's goals in writing *Nature*, and the most practical if not the loftiest of them, was thus to consolidate man's authority in the universe by putting at his disposal the infinite resources the universe reveals. Much has been said of the mystical fervor animating certain pages of the book—and those its finest—without an adequate perception that on other pages Emerson seeks to cash in on that fervor to increase his own stature. A chapter like "Discipline" turns its back on ecstasy and the intoxications of sense to teach the reader how his will can be held taut, his intelligence grow in insight if he takes the suggestions Nature offers. There is no spiritual benefit without its counterpart on the level of Understanding; the poet who has grown up in the woods and fields, exposed to the soothing influence of seasons, will remember their message in the tumult of politics; further, in the hour of need it will be they who make him the orator capable of touching men's hearts and bending their wills: "At the call of a noble sentiment, again the woods wave, the pines murmur, the river rolls and shines, and the cattle low upon the mountains, as he saw and heard them in his infancy. And with these forms, the spells of persuasion, the keys of power are put into his hands."[96]

Through his "little azure-coloured *Nature*"[97] Emerson had killed two birds with one stone. In the first place he was taking up the challenge he had thrown down in his last lecture on English literature; he was cutting himself off from the sequence of human generations and turning on the world a gaze of such absolute freshness that he seemed himself that first man he had described. But his boldness had also won him access to a kingdom he had never ventured to dream of; the world around him, the plants, the animals, even the remote stars were suddenly confessing

[95] *Nature*, chapter 3, "Beauty" (W 1.22).

[96] *Nature*, chapter 4, "Language" (W 1.31–32).

[97] The expression is Carlyle's, in a letter to Emerson from February 13, 1837 (CEC 157).

him their friend, their master, almost their creator: "the Supreme Being does not build up nature around us, but puts it forth through us, as the life of the tree puts forth new branches and leaves through the pores of the old."[98] To this revelation he responded with a sense of sublime cosmic egotism: science had put man at the center of the world, but it had failed to notice that he was also the world's origin and pivot. Even Luther, even Fox, even Shakespeare had been ignorant of man's true measure: "Who can set bounds to the possibilities of man?"[99]

At this level any comment inspired by class or party interest is likely to seem absurd. Kicking himself free of the pull of gravitation, Emerson had soared above all that divides men in society, and it was with difficulty that one could imagine he would one day return there. Whatever definition one gives of *Nature*—philosophical essay, prose-poem, manual of spirituality—it was not a political treatise. But the contemporary periodicals that took notice of the anomalous work sought to judge it according to the various causes they served, and the result was a colorful spectrum of variegated attitudes.[100] The Swedenborgians were delighted by it, and ranked the author—whose identity they did not know—among their chief propagandists, till the day they discovered they had been duped by their own enthusiasm and rejected the poisoned gift with horror. The Unitarians were divided; some called it a work of genius, but the young professor of moral philosophy at Harvard, Francis Bowen, denounced in the *Christian Examiner* the obscurantist influence of German thought and vituperated Emerson's "arrogance and self-sufficiency." All in all it was the Jacksonian *Democratic Review* that showed the greatest discernment; it argued first that *Nature* brilliantly demonstrated the thriving vitality of the poetic spirit and second that the author had managed to address at the same time "the highest intellectual culture" and "the simplest instinctive innocence." There is no proof that Emerson noticed this article, the terms of which were pretty much based on his own vocabulary. But the "instinctive innocence" mentioned in it did not only reflect the faith of the Concord her-

[98] *Nature*, chapter 7, "Spirit" (W 1.64).

[99] Ibid.

[100] On the reception given *Nature* in the various American periodicals and newspapers, see G. W. Cooke, *Ralph Waldo Emerson: His Life, Writings and Philosophy* (Boston, 1881), p. 43; Rusk, *Life*, pp. 242–243; and above all Kenneth Cameron, who reproduces several contemporary articles at the end of the first volume of his *Emerson the Essayist* (Raleigh, N.C., 1945). The article in the *Democratic Review* appeared in February 1838; that in the *Christian Examiner* (January 1837) is partially reproduced in *The Transcendentalists: An Anthology*, ed. Perry Miller (Cambridge, Mass., 1950), pp. 173–176.

mit; it also defined the essential moral quality of America. It was the young nation's rallying cry, the comforting certainty offered to its people to encourage its ambitions. Had Emerson unconsciously spoken the language of his most turbulent compatriots? He was still too young to be able to measure the consequences of his glorious intoxication.

7

~ ~ ~ ~

ORGANIZING VICTORY

> A fact we said was the terminus of spirit. A man, I, am the remote circumference, the skirt, the thin suburb or frontier post of God but go inward & I find the ocean; I lose my individuality in its waves. God is Unity, but always works in variety. I go inward until I find Unity universal, that Is before the World was; I come outward to this body a point of variety.[1]

THIS PASSAGE of the journal, written while Emerson was working on his first book, expresses with singular concentration the central intuition of Emerson's thought. Two metaphors are symbolically mingled—that of the eccentric satellite and the emptiness of space, and that of the plenitude associated with the ocean—as if to suggest by their incompatibility the twofold character of human existence, which springs up from a rigidly bounded world and returns to it after having tasted divine abundance and fertility. Emerson thus places in vital opposition the single principle of all creation and the infinite variety of created forms; he recapitulates the ascent and descent of platonic thought, but grants man the liberty to choose his direction at every moment. "Go inward," "come outward"; by the almost insouciant ease of the verbs, Emerson distinguishes himself from the mystics who suffer the torments of spiritual aridity before knowing ecstasy, and also from the Stoics, for whom the peace of the soul is to be attained only in an amputation of the sensibility. Emerson renounces nothing; he neither abuses nor represses any of his faculties. Rather he indulges in their surprising elasticity, which permits them to turn with equal pleasure toward the infinity of

[1] JMN 5.177 (June 17, 1836).

the Spirit and the diversity of beings and objects. The particular mark of Emersonian optimism, its profoundly stimulating effect—attested by minds not at all suspect of complacency or facility[2]—is bound up with this extraordinary aptitude; the author of *Nature* and of the first series of *Essays* is fully and as it were playfully in control of the situation. From the strategic position constituted by his own consciousness, Emerson organizes the universe, time and space, the visible world and spiritual laws alike. He liberates objects from their perennial and oppressive heaviness; he joins the multitude of human generations in an eternal present and leads the facts most rebellious to thought in a sort of religious dance, in which whim vies with power for mastery.[3] But his art—as he knows—has to be nurtured with exercise; the minstrel's insolent readiness of wit is the fruit of persistent effort, and no more than the minstrel would Emerson be allowed to relax or to consider any of his successes or victories final. To recording the movements of the Spirit there is no end.

Consequently, the period after the publication of *Nature* appears at once a time of consolidation and a time of discovery. While it is reasonable to judge, with most critics, that the Emersonian Revolution is contained in its entirety, at least implicitly, in that slender volume, the modes of that Revolution's development are not without interest. Behind the even, eagerly lyrical self-assurance of the tone, there was in process a significant, if gradual, modulation of theme. The *Essays*, because of the eclectic methods of their composition, do not make this at all clear.[4] The journals would give a more accurate idea of that evolution if their quick passage from one of a hundred subjects to another did not render any overarching judgment risky at best. There remain, however, the talks and lectures; one forgets too often that they were until 1841 Emerson's only vehicle of public expression. Every winter for four years, Emerson offered his Boston audience a series of ten to twelve lectures, often linked only by the most elastic or flimsy of ties and joined together under titles so general that they permitted Emerson to discuss whatever he thought interesting.[5] Despite this slack structure—or per-

[2] André Gide, for example, writes in his journal in 1893, "Emerson, cette lecture du matin" (*Journal* 1889–1939 [Paris, 1948], p. 45).

[3] One thinks of the celebrated phrase of "Self-Reliance": "I would write on the lintels of the door-post, *Whim*" (W 2.51).

[4] The notes to the Centenary Edition give some information about the composition of the various essays. Certain of them are mostly juxtaposed lecture-passages, or even (as in the case of "Heroism") simply the transcription of a single lecture in its entirety. Others, instead, are the product of a thorough reworking.

[5] The four series are: "The Philosophy of History" (1836–1837), "Human Culture" (1837–1838), "Human Life" (1838–1839), and "The Present Age" (1839–1840). EL 2 re-

haps because of it—the lecture series are revelations of Emerson's thought. They boldly outline an ephemeral configuration that the journals would not enable one to imagine and of which the *Essays* retain only the firmest and most brilliant strokes. They alone, when juxtaposed to the great pieces on which Emerson's reputation rests ("The American Scholar," the Divinity School address), can restore for us the picture of a man in motion and struggling with his time, seeking in turn to understand it, to mark it with his stamp, and to resist it. They also suffice to rescue Emerson from the charge of "ventriloquism."[6]

Even if one might ignore Emerson's determination to be part of the world as revealed by the lecture, his daily conduct was an unmistakable sign, and one must acknowledge that like any good Yankee he had his feet on the ground. Season after season he tended his garden, planted trees, fattened pigs for household use, bought the bit of land adjoining his own. Urging Carlyle to come and stay with him in Concord, he notes—no doubt in the hope of overcoming Carlyle's last scruples—that he possesses besides his house a capital of 22,000 dollars bearing an average interest of 6 percent.[7] In his financial transactions he kept an astonishingly cool head: he refused, for example, to invest any considerable portion of his liquid assets in his brother William's legal practice because, as he bluntly explains, "in case of your death, I should not think it happy that I or my heirs should be drawing every thing that could be gotten from your wife and children."[8] But his prudence was neither petty nor selfish; in the same period he took over the American publication of Carlyle's history of the French Revolution and expended considerable energy to procure his friend some compensation for it, despite the absence of any copyright legislation. Alcott, Fuller, and Jones Very were his frequent guests; he "discovers" Thoreau in 1836 or 1837. Quite amenable to the merits of society on the condition that he choose it, he agreed to participate regularly in the debates of the Transcendental Club, which met for the first time on September 16, 1836—

---

produces the two former, EL 3 the two latter. There is an unreliable summary of them in Cabot, *Memoir*, 2.724–727. Emerson was aware of the vague—not to say arbitrary—character of his titles, but his modus operandi left him no other choice. Cf. the letter to Frederic Hedge of March 27, 1838 (L 2.121): "The notes I collect in the course of a year are so miscellaneous that when our people grow rabid for lectures as they do periodically about December, I huddle all my old almanacks together & look in the encyclopaedia for the amplest cloak of a name whose folds will reach unto & cover extreme & fantastic things."

[6] The reproach was made by Van Wyck Brooks in his youthful, wittily iconoclastic essay "Our Poets" (*America's Coming of Age* [New York, 1915], chapter 2; reproduced in *Literature in America*, ed. Philip Rahv [New York, 1957], pp. 118–135).

[7] See the letter of May 10, 1838 (CEC 160).

[8] Letter to William Emerson of July 10, 1837 (L 2.86).

one week exactly after the publication of *Nature*, that manifesto consecrated to the genius of solitude. If we further see Emerson as a father enraptured to have his biological succession secure (his first child, Waldo, was born in October 1836, and his birth was celebrated in the journal by a passage of unusual tenderness[9]), we have the portrait of a man wholly of this world, of keen intelligence and sincere and reasonable feelings, whom we can easily identify with the author of "Prudence" (or at least of that essay's first part). But what of the author of "Spiritual Laws" and the "The Oversoul"? The paradox is that we have first to free Emerson of a suspicion regarding his sincerity as an idealist.

Nor had it escaped Emerson himself that his financial comfort might cast a dubious light on his philosophy, might get him accused of dilettantism or at least, to use an expression of Bertrand Russell's, of "double thinking." In the journal he answers his hypothetical detractors by a characteristic affirmation of his belief in a lived hierarchy of values: "I please myself with the thought that my accidental freedom by means of a permanent income is nowise essential to my habits, that my tastes, my direction of thought is so strong that I should do the same things, — should contrive to spend the best of my time in the same way as now, rich or poor."[10] This passage touches on one of the axioms of Emerson's philosophy, the clearest expression of which is offered in the essay "Compensation." The iron rule Emerson has acknowledged and celebrated since his youth, the rule of exact proportion between action and reaction, in virtue of which no crime escapes punishment and all gain is acquired by effort, is not the whole of human experience. It is valid in a large domain, to be sure, the domain of "political economy,"[11] but there is an infinity beyond, access to which depends on us alone, in which all constraint vanishes and dissolves in the sense of pure spiritual existence. The last paragraph of the essay conjures up his own version of heaven, with the particular vibration his language exhibits when it passes through and beyond the realm of representations accessible to sense:

> There is a deeper fact in the soul than compensation, to wit, its own nature. The soul is not a compensation, but a life. The soul *is*. Under all this running sea of circumstance, whose waters ebb and flow with perfect balance, lies the aboriginal abyss of real Being. Es-

[9] See JMN 5.234–235. Emerson analyzes himself in his new role with a prepossessing blend of astonishment, irony, and joy.

[10] JMN 7.71 (September 15, 1838).

[11] It is under this title that Emerson explains in his journal the implacable law of compensation, and recalls how desire, fear, and danger are always the price of wealth (JMN 5.210 [September 28, 1836]). The passage is incorporated into "Politics," the fifth lecture in "The Philosophy of History."

sence, or God, is not a relation or a part, but the whole. Being is the vast affirmative, excluding negation, self-balanced, and swallowing up all relations, parts and times within itself. Nature, truth, virtue, are the influx from thence. Vice is the absence or departure of the same. Nothing, Falsehood, may indeed stand as the great Night or shade on which as a background the living universe paints itself forth, but no fact is begotten by it; it cannot work, for it is not. It cannot work any good; it cannot work any harm. It is harm inasmuch as it is worse not to be than to be.[12]

In dealing with this passage, in which it seems Emerson has striven to record an almost ineffable spiritual experience, one is hesitant to have recourse to the barbarous methods of the intellect; but the passage's very elevation aids us in discerning certain contours of the landscape around it more clearly. It illuminates, for example, a problem that has perplexed numerous critics, namely that of Emerson's attitude toward progress.[13] Strictly speaking, it seems, the only progress Emerson can conceive is that which leads us from the world subject to the law of compensation to the universe of spirit; it is less an evolution than a conversion, and it has no meaning except in reference to a particular person. Not that Emerson altogether denies the optimistic affirmations of his lectures on the natural sciences; rather he takes his ground on them, then asks us to liberate ourselves in a supreme effort from the limits of our created condition. All of Emerson's pedagogy oscillates between the glorification of instinct and the exaltation of will, but there also the conflict is for the most part only apparent; before tasting the blessedness of spiritual life we must open a passage for it in ourselves, make ourselves transparent to it, or rather "homogeneous" with it, as Emerson says in "Spiritual Laws." The belief in progress conceals behind its seductive facade the temptation of cheap intellectual comfort and betrayal, resulting in the abandonment of true autonomy—whence the gesture of irritation and disdain recorded in the journal for 1839: "Progress of the Species! Why the world is a treadmill."[14] It is no accident that at the same period Emerson is obsessed by the word "fall"—from his stand-

[12] "Compensation" (W 2.120–121).

[13] See particularly Mildred Silvers, "Emerson and the Idea of Progress," AL 12, (March 1940), pp. 1–19. The article is scrupulously documented and carefully avoids disputable generalizations, but one could wish its conclusions more solid; it is perhaps the author's refusal to treat the question chronologically that is responsible for the vagueness. The idea of progress was never at the center of Emerson's concerns, but because of its multiple implications—scientific, moral, and metaphysical—it was necessarily affected by the general evolution of his thought.

[14] JMN 7.220.

point *every* movement is a retreat, because the plenitude of the soul cannot be conveyed by images relating to space.

The other problem illuminated by the paragraph of "Compensation" under discussion has troubled Emerson's commentators still more: it is the problem of imperfection, of the existence of evil. It is true that Emerson seems to be offering critics sticks to beat him with; when he defines "Nothing" or "Falsehood" as mere elements of a background, he inevitably invites comparison with certain eighteenth-century theodicies that construed evil as the complement of good in much the way that in paintings light and shadow combine in harmony. This subjective and intellectual concept had been attacked by Voltaire and was to be the target of Melville's critique of Emerson himself.[15] But the objection is precisely valid only *outside* the Emersonian perspective; it considers illusory the reconciliation Emerson believes is effected at the moment that we leave the world of compensations behind us and attain the plenitude of the spiritual life. This vision depends on a faith difficult to analyze and more difficult still to communicate; indeed at times the peace of the soul coincides with the confusion of the intelligence. Emerson denies neither of these points.[16] He claims only to take note of a personal experience (an important part of which is the experience of death) in justifying the absoluteness of his optimism.

It is not surprising that at this point most of Emerson's readers abandon him, even if possessing the imaginative perception of a Melville. If Emerson's interpretation of the nature of evil be not the result and sign, as some writers have contended, of a profound aridity of heart (though Emerson's desire to communicate to others the serenity abiding inside him would suggest precisely the opposite), it is based on an intuition that to most men and women will always remain alien. Of the chief authors of the American Renaissance Emerson is the one who borrows

[15] In the margin of his copy of the *Essays*, opposite the passage of "Spiritual Laws" in which Emerson argued for the subjective nature of evil ("the good, compared to the evil which he sees, is as his own good to his own evil" [W 2.148]), Melville noted, "a perfectly good being, therefore, would see no evil. —But what did Christ see? —He saw what made him weep. . . . To annihilate all this nonsense read the Sermon on the Mount, and consider what it implies" (cited in William Braswell, "Melville as a Critic of Emerson," AL 9 [1937], p. 330).

[16] In "Individualism," the last lecture of "The Philosophy of History," Emerson in fact confronts the difficulty face to face: "We are confounded by the discord between our theory and the actual world. But when we apply it to ourselves, we feel no incongruity. . . . The hard knots which our philosophy cannot untie, the unexplained phenomena, the alleged inequality of human lot, the vicarious suffering and the like, are only embarrassing when an optimism is to be proved as now existing in the world. . . . A man may not be able to reconcile slavery, piracy, disease, which affect thousands, with the good of the whole, but in his own experience, however hard, he finds no stumbling-block" (EL 2.176).

most eclectically from far-ranging philosophies and cultures, and also the one whose work rests on the narrowest base—as if destiny had ironically chosen him as the example of an unfortunate confusion between idiosyncratic vision and universal data.

In any case, for those who wish to understand the meaning of Emerson's thought and its incessant debates (often disguised, to be sure, as contradictory affirmations) a continued attempt at sympathy with the extreme forms of his idealism is indispensable. "The Transcendant is Economy also," recalls a page of his journal.[17] For several years Emerson has no other motto; in his essays and lectures he argues that his doctrine is no hollow dream and that it is capable of overturning his listeners' lives at every moment—at work, at table, in company, and even during sleep. His ambition is unbounded because he is aiming at the total regeneration of man, with faith his only weapon. But his good fortune is to have as his audience the citizens of New England; it would be difficult to imagine in the first half of the nineteenth century another region of the world in which he could have encountered—outside a church, that is—an audience both so fervent and so respectful. The notorious thinness of American society, so persistently deplored by American writers from Cooper to James, was paradoxically Emerson's helper and ally. To the extent that "the experience of New England was an experience of two extremes—bare facts and metaphysics, the machinery of self-preservation and the mystery of life,"[18] Emerson's task was facilitated; he could resolutely play for high stakes without having to consider the attractions of middle-of-the-road humanism. Finally, Emerson had the example of Alcott, who had been his daily companion since the summer of 1836. With his vaguely sibylline aphorisms and his devastating lack of practical sense, his prophet's gravity and his bottomless simplicity, Alcott makes skeptics like ourselves smile; but it was for precisely those qualities that Emerson admired him. In a country like America, given over to greed, Alcott was a promise of redemption, and his inability to "succeed" strengthened the best men and women in their spiritual vocation and helped them to overcome the temptations of vulgar ambition.[19]

[17] JMN 7.259 (October 2, 1839).

[18] The phrase is taken from Brooks, "Our Poets," p. 130.

[19] Cabot, *Memoir*, 1.281, reproduces a passage of the journal that gives a vivid portrayal of Alcott's passion for spiritual integrity in all its picturesque extravagance: "We have seen an intellectual *torso*, without hands or feet, without any organ whereby to reproduce his thought in any form of art whatever, —no musical talent, no gift of eloquence, no plastic skill to paint or carve or build or write, . . . and only working by presence and supreme intelligence, as a test and standard of other minds. . . . Perhaps the office of these is highest of all in the great

Of the four lecture series given between 1836 and 1840, the first, "The Philosophy of History," is also the most harmoniously ordered. In the letter he wrote five years later to his English friend John Sterling to accompany a copy of the first *Essays*, Emerson speaks—already with a certain nostalgia—of the glowing freshness of ideas caught at their birth:

> I wish, but scarce dare hope, you may find in it any thing of the pristine sacredness of thought. All thoughts are holy when they come floating up to us in magical newness from the hidden Life, and 't is no wonder we are enamoured with these Muses and Graces, until, in our devotion to particular beauties and in our efforts at artificial disposition, we lose somewhat of our universal sense and the sovereign eye of Proportion.[20]

One could hardly evoke the spiritual quality of "The Philosophy of History" better: in it Emerson passes from literature to morals, from science to religion and professional activity without ever giving the impression—as he does in the following series—that he is choosing mutually opposed themes by design, so that the truth may spring up from the collision and establish itself somewhere in the middle. He directs his gaze toward the past and the future, and nonetheless manages to give the feeling of perfect contemporaneity. As the discussions proceed, it is indeed a philosophy of history (to use that term in its widest sense) that emerges from them and that recapitulates in an eternal present the entire experience of the race. I shall have occasion in the course of this chapter to refer to later lectures for the illustration of particular points, but the first series alone suggests a universe corresponding to the ancient notion of *kosmos*.

By his desire to "do away this wild, savage, and preposterous There or Then, and introduce in its place the Here and the Now,"[21] Emerson distinguished himself sharply from the New England historiographical school just then coming into being.[22] Since John Belknap's foundation of the Massachusetts Historical Society in 1791, there had been considerable interest among several groups in preserving and ordering the

---

society of souls. How often we lament the compensations of power when we see talent suck the substance of the man! How often we repeat the disappointment of inferring general ability from conspicuous particular ability! But the accumulation on one point has drained the trunk, and we say, Blessed are they who have no talent."

[20] Letter to John Sterling of March [?] 1841, cited in W 2.375.

[21] "History" (W 2.11).

[22] See particularly on this point Van Wyck Brooks, *The Flowering of New England* (New York, 1936), pp. 118–121.

documents of the colonial period and the Revolution, and also some attempt to assemble a stock of standard historical works; and from 1830 on, a good many young intellectuals, both clergy and laymen, turned to the study of history. Whether those decisions expressed a sense of personal vocation or, as has been suggested, only the force of circumstance (Boston libraries were poor in works from other disciplines) the result was the production in New England of a group of historians—Sparks, Prescott, Palfrey, and somewhat later Hildreth and Parkman—comparable in importance to Macaulay and Guizot.[23] But such detailed reverence for the past is not to Emerson's taste: "This is not History. This is its shell, from which the kernel is fallen. History is the portraiture in act of man, the most graceful, the most varied, the most fertile of actors."[24] If so many learned works peter out into dull narratives of battles and treaties, it is, Emerson believes, because their authors are incapable of judging and ranking men. To do that requires an accurate idea of human nature, one that would associate it with its eternal essence and purify it of the prejudices of temperament, family, and country: "than the individual nothing is less; than the universal, nothing is greater."[25] History must orbit around philosophy.

Emerson's almost dogmatic assurance should not, however, be allowed to conceal the rejection on which it is based. To reproach history with its excessive respect for particular events is at the same time to reject the solidarity binding men by means of their secular experience and to isolate them in the brief moment of their mortal existence. Emerson had first encountered the issue in its theological form, that is, as the question of "federal sin," and the way he met it has been discussed previously. But he continued to think about it long after he had left his church. In 1834 he expounds in his journal what he calls "the philosophy of the Wave":

> The wave moves onward but the Water of which it is composed does not. The same particle does not rise from the valley to the

[23] Bancroft's case is slightly different. He was a historian with a thesis, and also the only one of the group Emerson enjoyed reading: "he imports very good views into his book, & parades his facts by the brave light of his principles" (JMN 5.383 [October 2, 1837]).

[24] "The Philosophy of History," lecture 1, "Introductory" (EL 2.9). This judgment explains Emerson's sincere admiration for Carlyle's *French Revolution*, which he reviewed anonymously in the *Christian Examiner* 23 (January 1838), pp. 386–387. Citing Carlyle's formulation, "all history is poetry, were it rightly told," he comments that "the poetry consists in the historian's point of view. With the most accurate and lively delineation of the crowded actions of the revolution, there is the constant co-perception of the universal relations of each man."

[25] EL 2.11.

> ridge. Its unity is only phenomenal. So is it with men. There is a revolution in this country now, is there? Well I am glad of it. But it don't convert nor punish the Jackson men nor reward the others. The Jackson men have made their fortunes; grow old; die. It is the new comers who form this Undulation. The party we wish to convince/condemn loses its identity. Elect Webster President, —& find the Jackson party if you can. All gone, dead, scattered, Webstermen, Southerners, Masons, any & every thing. Judicial or even moral sentence seems no longer capable of being inflicted. France we say suffered & learned; but the red Revolutionists did not. France today is a new-born race that had no more to do with that regicide France than the Sandwich islanders.[26]

One may deplore this discontinuity or rejoice in it; one may see it, with Tocqueville, as the inevitable consequence of democracy, or as the manifestation of a universal law.[27] For Emerson it is a fact of experience to be absorbed before trying to construct any social philosophy. Strictly speaking, society does not exist; it is the product of an illusion preserved by our idleness alone. Other men properly serve only to represent; they are charged with illustrating the wealth of our own nature and with making public the secrets hidden deep within us.

It is as if Emerson had decided to play history, thus defined, against society; and the place he gives to this debate in the first *Essays*—"History" is the first piece in the collection—reveals the importance he accords it. Whereas society presses on us and hems us in, history nobly unfolds the traits of universal man, showing sometimes his power and sometimes his goodness much as the earth leans back and forth around its axis in its solar revolution. But these traits are our own, only magnified by distance. Emerson's argument is based in fact on a very simple syllogism: as human beings we participate in the Universal Spirit; history records the action of the Universal Spirit in the world; history, therefore, is our own biography. For the observant, we are surrounded by Caesars and Alexanders: "I have seen the first monks and anchorets,

[26] JMN 4.287 (May 1, 1834). The close of the paragraph is used with minor variations in "Individualism." The revolution Emerson refers to is the hope, entertained by many, that the Whigs would regain power under the leadership of Webster (this hope was ultimately defeated).

[27] In the celebrated chapter of *Democracy in America* in which he analyzes this new concept of individualism (volume 2, part 2, chapter 2), Tocqueville shows that the isolation of persons grows in proportion to the equalization of conditions. He then concludes that democracy, which makes every man forget his ancestors, his descendants, and even his contemporaries, "threatens in the end to confine him entirely within the solitude of his own heart" (*Democracy in America*, trans. Henry Reeve [New York, 1961], 2.120).

without crossing seas or centuries."[28] To all intents and purposes, Plutarch, whose lessons of greatness have so long kept company with Emerson's meditations, is made free of the city of Concord, as the pages of the journal list the famous names with astonishing familiarity; Archimedes, Plotinus, Beaumont and Fletcher, Goethe are for Emerson presences no less substantial and immediate than his honest farmer neighbors.

But history concerns us still more intimately because of the relation between the stages of our life and the successive periods of civilization. Basing his argument on such special events as political revolutions, in which the ideas of a few individuals can be clearly identified with collective circumstance, Emerson draws in bold strokes a theory of historical ages. The Greeks, who lived at the dawn of humanity, symbolize our first years, those in which our spiritual nature develops in profound harmony with our body; their dominant quality is an ingratiating unselfconsciousness, such as one still finds, albeit in a less elegant and less intense form, in the American Indian.[29] For the succeeding ages, the analysis becomes somewhat hazy, as if the theory failed to dovetail with reality; perhaps Emerson felt some difficulty in convincing even himself of the truth of his analogies. It is all very well for him to present Xenophon and his companions in the Retreat of the Ten Thousand as a "gang of great boys";[30] soldiers' truculence is for all time. But how can Emerson maintain that the Athens of Phidias and Sophocles knew neither luxury nor elegance, or ascribe simplicity to a people that produced Thucydides? The truth is that Emerson is thinking of a Greece lost in the Homeric mists, fertile in heroism and much closer to legend than to history. His natural inclination leads him to mythology, which by means of fable projects certain inexhaustibly significant fragments of human experience into a realm outside of time; Prometheus, Antaeus, Orpheus, Proteus, and most of all the sphinx have a density and suggestiveness in this essay that the historical figures lack.[31]

Behind this evident but adroitly managed conflict opposing society

[28] "History" (W 2.28). The journal is more circumstantial and gives names: Alcott is Simeon the Stylite, Jones Very, Saint John of Patmos (J 5.219–220 [June 12 and 16, 1839]).

[29] Cf. this passage of "Manners," the ninth lecture in "The Philosophy of History" (EL 2.136): "We believe that like the moose or the bison he hunts, he belongs to the great order of Nature. He is part of the morning and the evening, of the forest and the mountain, and he is remembered and provided for as the ravens are."

[30] "History" (W 2.25).

[31] See "History" (W 2.30–33). The figure of the sphinx is used in "Human Life," lecture 3, "The School," in connection with the facts we must incessantly decipher if we are not to become their victim; later the myth was to inspire one of Emerson's most difficult poems (W 9.20–25).

to history there soon takes form another and more fundamental antagonism. Emerson's essay deserves its title only by antiphrasis; despite the bridges implicitly constructed between periods by the theory of ages, the substance of history, and the color and warmth of its collective epic, are eliminated. Their place is taken by a universal force, impersonal and always equal to itself, that closely resembles Nature as conceived in ancient philosophy.[32] Such a modulation is the surest sign of a shift from a typically Christian mode of thought to a typically pagan one;[33] whatever the logical difficulties created by the introduction of a divine person into the framework of history, the incarnation is the rock on which all Christian philosophy must rest. Whoever denies Jesus' divine mediation without substituting for it some other agent of coherence (as Marxism does) robs humanity's destiny of its meaning; and it is this decisive step that Emerson had now taken, after long hesitation but without remorse.[34]) In one sense, perhaps, he was only pushing Protestantism to its ultimate conclusion. In a perceptive article contrasting the philosophies and careers of Emerson and Orestes Brownson, A. R. Caponigri shows that it is impossible to rectify history, as Luther, Melanchthon, and Calvin thought possible, without at the same time abolishing it.[35] Transcendentalism would then represent the second phase of Protestantism, the stage in the course of which all ambiguities pass away; it would ultimately consist in recognizing and proclaiming that man's spiritual life is intrinsically independent of history because it is inspired by spiritual principles that are themselves above and beyond it. One thinks in this connection of Oliver Wendell Holmes's witty definition of

[32] The change is noticeable even within the essay "History," which concludes by an assertion of our fundamental kinship with Nature: "I am ashamed to see what a shallow village tale our so-called History is. . . . What does Rome know of rat and lizard?" (W 2.40).

[33] Cf. Paul Tillich, *The Protestant Era* (Chicago, 1948), in particular the chapter "Historical and Nonhistorical Interpretations of History: A Comparison." Among the definitions of the nonhistorical, Tillich offers one that throws a vivid light on Emerson: "salvation is the salvation of individuals from time and history, not the salvation of a community through time and history" (p. 20).

[34] It is nonetheless striking that Emerson never attempted—as did Renan, for example—to compose a portrait of Jesus. Perhaps he did not feel sufficiently in sympathy with the teachings of the Sermon on the Mount; perhaps also he had not entirely shed a particular reverence for Jesus' person; cf. JMN 15.224 (1863).

[35] A. R. Caponigri, "Brownson and Emerson: Nature and History," NEQ 18 (September 1945), pp. 368–390. Brownson himself, after his conversion to Catholicism, vigorously attacked Transcendentalist philosophy in his *Brownson's Quarterly Review*; as late as 1869, in an article occasioned by the meeting of the Free Religious Association at Boston, he repeated his charge against Emerson: "he unchristianizes Christianity, makes it an element of human nature, confounds it with the natural laws of the physicists" (*Works*, ed. Henry F. Brownson, 20 vols. [Detroit, 1882], 3.414).

Emerson as "an iconoclast without a hammer, who took down our idols from their pedestals so tenderly that it seemed like an act of worship."[36] If Emerson's fervor, along with the persistence in his vocabulary at elevated moments of a fairly traditional phraseology, did in effect lead a good many of his contemporaries astray, there is also no denying that in his most serene remarks a formidable force is at work, subtly overturning familiar structures.

A short and apparently innocent passage in the journal provides an illuminating example of this stealthy revolution: "If Jesus came now into the world, he would say—You, YOU! He said to his age, I."[37] The affirmation of the potential divinity of each human being is less important here than the dramatic manner in which it is expressed, the gesture of Christ directing each of us to ourself as the only object worthy of wonder or love. The commandment of benevolence so dear to Channing dwindles and shrinks in contrast to another imperative that Emerson on numerous occasions calls "self-union." Menaced in our integrity by the incessant urgings of the world outside, subject to the erosion wrought by associations and crowds, we have no other recourse than that of a lofty and fiercely defended independence. The journals regularly reaffirm, sometimes calmly and sometimes with unrepressed annoyance,[38] our obligation to maintain about us at all costs a zone of silence and peace; in his most demanding moments Emerson goes as far as to rebel even against his correspondents, who snatch him away from himself and introduce "ugly brackets" into the course of his days.[39] One has to be alone, as Plotinus had said, to proceed toward the One. There is thus an apprenticeship in solitude, in the course of which the company of other men becomes more and more indifferent to us; and the man who truly possesses himself enjoys himself in proportion as his circumstances are wretched or sordid:

> When I stamp thro' the mud in dirty boots, I hug myself with the feeling of my immortality. I then reflect complacently on whatever of delicacy is in my taste, of amplitude in my memory. In a university I draw in my horns. On nothing does a wise man plume himself so much as on independence of circumstance that in a kitchen, or

[36] As recounted in Cabot, *Memoir*, 1.262.

[37] JMN 5.362 (August 14, 1837).

[38] On one occasion Emerson's irritation at these importunate visitors even results in a poem: "The Visit" (W 9.12–13).

[39] "I seldom write [letters] unless my belief in immortality is at the moment very strong and so indulges me in a free use of time; for unless one can live straight on through a letter it makes an ugly bracket in one's afternoon being neither study nor exercise" (letter to Margaret Fuller of May 4, 1838 [L 2.128–129]).

dirty street or sweltering stagecoach, he can separate himself from impure contact, & embosom himself in the sublime society of his recollections, of his hopes, & of his affections. Ambassador carries his country with him. So does the mind.[40]

It is significant, however, that these last citations are drawn from texts not intended for publication. In the ample landscape of Emerson's thought, there is no territory in which the bedrock of individual nature and temperament outcrops more clearly. The monistic concept of the universe rests in Emerson on a profound spiritual intuition; but the ethic he deduces from it, strictly dominated by the need for independence, has roots extending down into a much darker region of his being, that in which his reflexes take shape, and also his feelings—which Montaigne located at the juncture between body and soul. Reading through the journals from Emerson's adolescence onward, one is almost tempted to speak of an obsession—in the clinical sense of the term—when one is confronted with the problem for Emerson of his own life in the midst of other human lives. Whether he is affecting the Stoic sage's proud indifference or, as happens more often, is grieving over not finding in society the appropriate attitude, neither insolent nor servile, that would reconcile him with himself, he never succeeds in driving from his mind the idea that he is a misfit, almost an outlaw.[41] It is difficult to ascertain the degree to which his love of nature answers a need for compensation; but it is not at all in doubt, as was noted apropos "Good-bye, Proud World," that his joy at being alone amidst the woods is in part the consequence of resolved tension, of expansion after constraint. That is also why Emerson receives testimony tending to justify his aversion for social forms with such evident pleasure.[42] He is, perhaps without acknowledging it, in search of some decisive justification that will transform to

[40] JMS, H.140: "Art"; October 24, [1836?]. The passage appears in almost the same form in the journal for June 25, 1831 (JMN 3.261); but F. O. Matthiessen, who cites the first sentence (*American Renaissance: Art and Expression in the Age of Emerson and Whitman* [1941; repr. New York, 1968], p. 40), compares it with certain passages of *Nature*, and I would favor a distinctly later date than that proposed by the JMN editors, not only on the basis of the manuscript passage but also because of the firm tone and the racy and solidly aphoristic style of expression.

[41] It is perhaps this trait of character that is responsible for the mistaken notion that one source of Emerson's writings is the psychology of the pioneer (see particularly Lucy L. Hazard, *The Frontier in American Literature* [New York, 1927]). If one insists on finding a sponsor for Emerson, Rousseau is much more likely than Daniel Boone.

[42] He copies, for example, this sentence of Goethe's: " 'Our part in public occasions is, for the most part, Philisterei' " (JMN 5.190). As coming from a man whom Emerson had often reproached for his complacence toward worldly greatness, the remark had a particular significance.

strength what was once weakness; and it happens on occasion that a single word of his, endowed sometimes with positive value and sometimes with negative, allows one to seize in vivo the obscure process of spiritual rehabilitation that Emerson is undergoing.[43]

At the end of this metamorphosis, the hesitant, awkwardly self-conscious creature has yielded its place to the great man, drawing force and confidence from the universal spirit and filling out all by himself the immense gap yawning between God and the crowd of the ignorant. Neither Plotinus nor Montaigne, he must learn to be both at once: "He must draw from the infinite Reason on the one side, and he must penetrate into the heart and mind of the rabble on the other. From one, he must draw his strength; to the other he must owe his aim. The one yokes him to the real; the other to the apparent. At one pole is Reason, at the other common sense."[44] For the moment Emerson is not concerned to specify, to distinguish between the poet's role and that of the man of action. The illustrations he offers are literary, for the simple reason that, ideas being conducive to facts, poets must take precedence over heroes. But the superiority is, so to speak, only chronological; in Emerson's monistic universe, whatever has value derives from the same source. The problem posed to the poet and the man of action alike—their only problem, in fact—is how to maintain the channel by which they communicate with the Universal Soul clear of obstruction; to that end they must refuse compromises and reject the popularity they might easily win by speaking to the crowd in the language it most loves: "He comes with his word in his heart and fixes his eye on his countrymen, and the word takes its own fit form, as when the eye seeks the person in the remote corner of the house, the voice accommodates itself to the area to be filled."[45] Real distinction and elegance are the product of unfailing attention to the dictates of Reason;[46] through Reason the crudest man-

[43] Thus the word "porcupine" is first used in the journal about the great man protected against degrading familiarities by what one might call his spines (JMN 5.216–217 [September 30, 1836]); three years later, as Emerson is once again explaining the discomfort he feels in human intercourse, he speaks of his "porcupine impossibility of contact with men"; but the context makes clear that he appreciates the compensations his infirmity entails (JMN 7.301–302 [November 14, 1839]).

[44] "The Philosophy of History," lecture 4, "Literature" (EL 2.62). Borrowed and in a slightly different form from a paragraph of the journal (JMN 5.249), the passage occurs again at the end of "Literary Ethics" (W 1.182).

[45] EL 2.62.

[46] "The true gentleman seems to have no root whatever in the world, to owe nothing to any family, or party, or property, or nation, but to draw all his life from himself" ("The Philosophy of History," lecture 9, "Manners" [EL 2.140]).

ners lose their roughness, but our efforts to raise ourselves above vulgarity are idle when Reason is left out.

From whatever point Emerson's thought sets out, then, its terminus is the inspired activity of a superior being—in which it is easy to recognize the concept of genius inherited from the German Romantics by way of Coleridge. In the name of genius, tradition is rejected and the principle of authority undone, while an ethic of independence—or, as Orestes Brownson calls it, of "transcendental selfishness"[47]—is substituted for the ethic of the churches; even mores depend on it and borrow from it luster and dignity. In the lecture series he gave in 1838–1839 under the catch-all title "Human Life," Emerson set himself the task of defining the content of this key term. The essence of genius, he writes, is its spontaneity, its aptitude for seeing the truth instantaneously. But as truth is a living thing, it follows that genius never repeats itself; when it is faithful to itself it expresses itself in thoughts and deeds of absolute novelty. Indeed it is that novelty which exercises an irresistible appeal on us; genius never ceases to astonish us, yet we recognize each of its manifestations as expressive of ourselves, and as mysteriously fitted to our deepest being: "The men of genius are watchers set on the towers to report of their outlook to you and me. Do not describe him as detached and aloof. . . . Genius is the most communicative of all things."[48] By way of illustration, Emerson went on to refer his hearers to an experience that as Americans he might suppose they all had in common: the strange osmosis by which the orator's force and passion enter into us, suddenly enlarging and exalting us even as they subjugate us.[49]

But how is one to be certain that this irresistible power will always be exercised for good? How can good genius be distinguished from bad? Emerson's position is as simple as it is peremptory: to speak of bad genius is a contradiction in terms; moral purity belongs to genius by nature, since the authority of genius derives from infinitely good universal laws; if genius is not to be identified with the religious sentiment it is at least its ally. One would be tempted to accuse Emerson of naïveté here, or worse still of glibness, if one did not know that the theory he is proposing had long been pondered and confronted with fact. In the months preceding the composition of the lecture on genius, the journals record

[47] In a review of the Divinity School address in the *Boston Quarterly Review* 1, (October 1838), pp. 500–514.

[48] "Human Life," lecture 5, "Genius" (EL 3.81).

[49] There is no doubt that Emerson's conviction is based on personal experience; the argument advanced here takes its substance from a passage in the journal in which Emerson describes Webster's oratorical power in a transport of enthusiasm (JMN 5.428–429 [November 11, 1837]).

considerable reading about Napoleon.[50] Emerson is strongly impressed with Napoleon's perspicacity, his self-control at delicate moments, his inexhaustible activity till his exile; but these traits do not conceal a fundamental deficiency of his nature, a lack of generosity, of love. It seems that the author of the lecture, his mind still occupied with these criticisms, wanted to accentuate the comforting traits of authentic genius by contrast:

> Genius is always humane, affectionate, sportful. Always it is gentle. It has been observed that there is always somewhat feminine in the face of men of genius. Hence the perfect safety we feel whenever genius is entrusted with political or ecclesiastical power. There is no fanaticism as long as there is the Creative Muse. Genius is a charter of illimitable freedom.[51]

It is not enough to say that the genius has inherited Christ's mediating function in the realm of spirit; its jurisdiction extends to the realm of Caesar, which seems to have been silently annexed to the kingdom of God.

Emerson surely must have perceived the difficulties and dangers of this concept; it did, after all, unite in the same person unlimited power and extreme refinement, the leader's authority and the spouse's tenderness. Was describing such a *discordia concors* as the normal fulfillment of human nature not tantamount to encouraging an anarchy of the passions? Was it not in fact sinning by excess in a new form? The answer is contained in the distinction Emerson never failed to make between the universal and the individual. If we can discipline ourselves, if we can kill the fanatic in us,[52] the contradiction vanishes as if by magic. Among the numerous senses Emerson gives to the word "scholar," this strictly moral acceptation is one of the most important; among other things it inspires the third part of the speech given in 1838 to the students at Dartmouth: "Let him know that the world is his, but he must possess it by putting himself into harmony with the constitution of things. He

[50] See particularly JMN 5.472, 482–485, and 493–494.

[51] "Human Life," lecture 5, "Genius" (EL 3.80). In one of his notebooks, Emerson had copied in translation a text by Novalis affirming the absolute incompatibility of physical force and spiritual greatness: "The ideal of Morality has no more dangerous rival than the ideal of highest strength, of most powerful life. . . . It is the maximum of the Savage; and has in these times gained, precisely among the greatest weaklings, very many proselytes. By this Ideal, Man becomes a Beast-Spirit, a Mixture, whose brutal wit has for weaklings a brutal power and attraction" (JMN 6.319).

[52] "There is one mind. Inspiration is larger reception of it: fanaticism is predominance of the individual. The greater genius the more like all other men, therefore" (JMN 5.169 [June 4, 1836]).

must be a solitary, laborious, modest, and charitable soul."[53] Doubtless this injunction exploited certain atavistic impulses toward strictness and austerity, which may explain why contemporary audiences did not make much of it; one must bear in mind, however, that each summons to freedom was predicated, for Emerson, on a sense of stringent and deliberately accepted self-discipline.

At the same time, as a page of the journal for April 1838 candidly recognizes, the effort of self-discipline was apt to run into baffling obstacles:

> Last night, ill dreams. Dreams are true to nature & like monstrous formations (e.g. the horsehoof divided into toes) show the law. Their double consciousness, their sub- & ob-jectiveness is the wonder. I call the phantoms that rise the creation of my fancy but they act like volunteers & counteract my inclination. They make me feel that every act, every thought, every cause, is bipolar & in the act is contained the counteract. If I strike, I am struck. If I chase, I am pursued. If I push, I am resisted.[54]

It is far, of course, from this genuinely disquieting discovery to the serene and enigmatic philosophy of "Brahma,"[55] but the fundamental movement is the same, assigning limits to the exercise of our freedom precisely in proportion as we assert our power. Emerson's discomfort is that of the idealist obliged to consider his body, bound to endure its caprices without understanding them.[56] For those who truly think that "consciousness is God,"[57] sleep is difficult to accept; indeed it is a constraint that only a subtle manipulation of equivalences (the night of instinct is *also* God) manages to explain. But no casuistry has any hold over the absurd and independent world of dreams, which arise when

[53] "Literary Ethics" (W 1.173).

[54] JMN 5.475 (April 20, 1838). This is also the theme of *Moby-Dick*, Melville's beloved theme of the hunter hunted. Cf. on this point J. J. Mayoux, *Vivants piliers* (Paris, 1960), p. 31.

[55] W 9.195.

[56] An unpublished passage of the journal offers a striking mixture of disgust at the body and philosophical spiritualist indignation: "Malthus revolts us by treating man as an animal. When the wrong handle is grasped, the tresses of beauty remind us of a mane. It disgusts when genius is treated as a medical fact, an inflammation of the brain, and thought and poetry as evacuations. I heard once a loathsome lecture on precocity and the dissection of the brain and the distortion of the body and genius, etc . . . —a grim compost of blood and mud, that for a week I could scarce reflect without remembering my cerebral vessels. Blessed, thought I, were those who, lost in their pursuits, never knew that they had a body or a mind" (JMS, H.140: "Art").

[57] "To absolute mind, a person is but a fact, but consciousness is God" (JMN 5.466 [March 19, 1838]).

they please, distort objects and beings at will, and fade just as we prepare to grasp them. There Emerson was touching on a remote sector of the universe, which could indeed have properly been called maleficent—if, that is, qualities of that sort had found room in his philosophy in the first place.[58]

Now at the same period, all Boston was enraptured with the pseudosciences of hypnotism and animal magnetism.[59] People flocked to the lectures of Monsieur Poyen "of the University of Paris," who based his arguments on spectacular experiments. Nor was it only the common people who were interested in these wonders. Men of considerable seriousness confessed themselves troubled and were sometimes even won over; Emerson was piqued, and he resolved to devote a lecture in the series "Human Life" to "Demonology." He was conscious of the perplexity the term might cause a good number of his hearers, so he took care to define it at the outset. "The name Demonology," he explains, "covers dreams, omens, coincidences, luck, sortilege, magic and other experiences which shun rather than court inquiry, and deserve notice chiefly because every man has usually in a lifetime two or three hints in this kind which are specially impressive to him."[60]

The last part of the sentence shows that Emerson is not treating the problem as would a mocking skeptic; indeed there are good reasons for believing that he counted himself among that majority of men and women to whom, at wide intervals, strange revelations have been vouchsafed.[61] But taking cognizance of such phenomena is one thing; seeing in them a source of truth richer than the data of the consciousness

[58] Transcendentalist confessions of bewilderment at the world are rare, but there are some; R. W. B. Lewis, *The American Adam* (Chicago, 1955), p. 27, recalls the passage in which Thoreau describes the hooting of owls as "admirably suited to swamps and twilight woods which no day illustrates, suggesting a vast and undeveloped nature which men have not yet recognized" (*Walden*, "Sounds").

[59] "The gossip of the city is of Animal Magnetism. Three weeks ago I went to see the magnetic sleep. & saw the wonder" (letter to William Emerson of January 13, 1837 [L 2.55]). Rusk notes that a debate on the subject had been going on for several weeks in the columns of the *Boston Courier*.

[60] "Demonology" (W 10.3). The 1838–1839 lecture was published with important modifications in an issue of the *North American Review* from 1877. It appears in W 10 (*Lectures and Biographical Sketches*), pp. 1–28 and (for the notes) 511–519. The sense Emerson gives the word "demonology" here is based on the use Goethe had made of it in *Dichtung und Wahrheit*, in a passage Emerson cites on pp. 17–18.

[61] A passage of the journal from 1835 describes the mysterious communication that takes place from person to person by means of the "oeillade " (JMN 5.8). The following winter, Emerson described in a lecture the fascination "Natural Magic" had for Francis Bacon, and in particular that exercised by the eye; but he went on to warn his listeners against imprudent and excessive interpretations of such facts (EL 1.332–333).

is another, and with the latter view Emerson cannot agree: "however poetic these twilights of thought, I like daylight."[62] By sorting through and recording all the occult facts observed till now, he says, we might in the areas of medicine and physiology come by some scraps of knowledge; but we would not know better how to live—we would be like those dilettantes who dissect an animal's eye in the hope of improving their own sight.

Demonology is not, however, only "the shadow of Theology"[63]—that is, the more or less murky product of certain minds incapable of reconciling themselves to their times—it is also, far more seriously, a trespass upon the mind of another person. A brief paragraph from the journal of 1838 shows Emerson protesting with all his might against the methods of hypnotism, in which he sees not an indiscretion but a rape.[64] Five months later, the same idea recurs, this time presented impersonally but with undiminished vigor: "Phrenology & Animal Magnetism are studied a little in the spirit in which alchemy & witchcraft or the black art were, namely, for power. That vitiates & besmirches them & makes them black arts. All separation of the soul's things from the soul, is suicidal. So are phrenology & animal magnetism damned."[65] Finally, in February 1838, a new comment amplifies the disapproval by situating it in a wider context:

> Demonology seems to me to be the intensation of the individual nature, the extension of this beyond its due bounds & into the domain of the infinite & universal. . . .
>
> The divine will, or, *the eternal tendency to the good of the whole, active in every atom, every moment*, —is the only will that can be supposed predominant a single hairbreadth beyond the lines of individual action & influence.[66]

As usual with Emerson, whose thought is profoundly innocent of any dialectical construction, we seem to advance and then find ourselves back where we started: "than the individual nothing is less; than the universal nothing is greater." But the exploration has familiarized us with Emerson's peculiar approach to problems; it prepares us to grasp the unceasing oscillation from principles to facts, from facts to princi-

[62] "Demonology" (W 10.19).

[63] "Demonology" (W 10.28).

[64] See JMN 7.28 (June 21, 1838).

[65] JMN 7.162 (November 27, 1838). Hawthorne's conception of Chillingworth in *The Scarlet Letter*, who unites the medieval alchemist's hunger for knowledge with the morbid passion of the voyeur, seems to derive from an analogous feeling of outraged repulsion.

[66] JMN 7.167 (February 14, 1839); the italics are Emerson's.

ples, that characterizes the first stage of his social thought and makes of it less a system or a synthesis than a series of felicitous illustrations.

A few weeks before giving his twelve lectures on the philosophy of history at the Masonic Temple, Emerson noted in his journal the curious effect always produced on us by the description of a scene or an event in which we have taken part:

> That which we had *only* lived & not thought & not valued, is now seen to have the greatest beauty as picture; and as we value a Dutch painting of a kitchen or a frolic of blackguards or a beggar catching a flea when the scene itself we should avoid, so we see worth in things we had slighted these many years. A making it a subject of *thought*, the glance of the Intellect raises it.[67]

His analysis of social relations possesses the same power of transfiguration and is founded on the same remote and emblematic quality.[68] In it ideas have such brilliance that it is sometimes difficult to recognize in their intertwinings the society of New England around 1830, or indeed any other creatures of flesh and blood seeking with mixed success to combine conflicting interests. The patient efforts of generations take on in Emerson the luminous appearance of a general law gradually revealing itself; the dramas and antagonisms are emptied of their content by the great optimistic perspective into which they are fitted; the traditional organs of government, the assemblies, the legal structures are not so much criticized as reduced to their just proportions—for in these accidental phenomena an idea is being worked out, which affirms the infinite greatness of the individual and subordinates to it all the social forms in existence.

It is not until the seventh lecture, "Society," that one comes across a definition of the two complementary principles that underlie our social relations and make them fruitful. The first of them postulates the universal nature of man, in virtue of which we all construct for ourselves the same ideas of good and evil, justice and truth, regardless of climate or historical period. Here Emerson remains faithful to classical philosophy from Plato to Spinoza. The other principle, however, acknowledges the fact that each man is different from all others, has a particular vocation, and plays in the world an irreplaceable role. The social instinct (which Emerson does not deny) leads us gradually to discover

[67] JMN 5.212 (September 20, 1836). A similar idea occurs at the beginning of "The Philosophy of History," lecture 4, "Literature," in which the lawyer is described as "the dramatist of the common life" (EL 2.57).

[68] It was Emerson himself who said of Alcott that "his day-labor had a certain emblematic air, like the annual ploughing of the Emperor of China" (JMS, H.143c-ABA, p. 8).

this infinite mosaic of talents and at the same time reveals to us our real stature. Such is in fact, Emerson says, the law of our being: we must go by way of others to know ourselves. Society is the best means of our education;[69] it helps us to take up our inheritance, it stimulates us, it encourages our most tentative ambitions by showing them accomplished elsewhere. But it would exceed its rights if it claimed to do more; it has the obligation to respect the "sacred palisado"[70] that defends our integrity.

On the basis of this schema, Emerson examines the various possible modes of association—not without surprising us by the methodical spirit he deploys in doing so. He begins by discussing the elective affinities of marriage and friendship. He speaks of marriage rather than of love[71] because he is concerned with the stable cell of the couple and attaches no great importance to the first effusions of feeling; indeed he wants the mists of passion to break up as soon as possible, so that spouses may learn to know each other[72] and make character the cornerstone of their alliance. Friendship is distinguished from love, and a fortiori from marriage, in that it is of a wholly spiritual nature; it stimulates the ripening of what is best within us, but for precisely that reason it soon ceases to touch us—in the pure sphere of Spirit into which it leads us, the presence and the absence of the beloved are equivalent: "In those few moments which are the life of our life when we were in the state of clear vision, we were taught that God is here no respecter of persons, that into that communion with him which is absolute life . . . in that communion our dearest friends are strangers."[73] The images of love and friendship in the first *Essays* often seem solemn and frigid, though they are not entirely deprived of life (on occasion Emerson even has a little fun, as when he tells the story of the shop lad and his charming young customer). But in 1836, the two terms fence each other in with unmit-

[69] Appropriately enough, the theme is developed in the speech on education Emerson delivered at the Green Street School in Providence, Rhode Island on June 10, 1837 (EL 2.191–204).

[70] The expression is taken from "The Individual," the last lecture in the series (EL 2.186).

[71] The essay "Love" (W 2.167–189) was first a lecture in the series "Human Life," delivered in 1838–1839.

[72] A passage of the journal written some weeks after Emerson's second marriage suggests both the importance and the difficulties of such an apprenticeship: "People think that husbands and wives have no *present time*, that they have long already established their mutual connection, have nothing to learn of one another, and know beforehand each what the other will do. The wise man will discern the fact, viz. that they are chance-joined, little acquainted, and do observe each the other's carriage to the stranger as curiously as he doth" (JMN 5.108–109 [November 14, 1835]).

[73] JMN 5.170 (June 6, 1836).

igated severity. This quest of the self pursued through others, carried out persistently and almost callously, and this greedy strategy that intends to profit from the whims of nature[74] resemble a caricature of transcendental economy. One ought to remember, however, before settling on so harsh an estimate, the griefs Emerson had borne in almost unbroken succession: his first wife Ellen, his brothers Edward and Charles all dead within a few years. Emerson himself may have believed in the spiritual benefit of these lacerations; the reader, confronted with the aridity of certain pages influenced by them, retains the right to disagree and to find the price of this pact with death too high.

Emerson uses a less disembodied tone—perhaps because the subject does not evoke the shadow of personal memories—in discussing what matters less to him: philanthropic organizations, religious sects, and political parties. It is the philanthropists that he treats most roughly, on the ground of the distressing manner in which they confuse the goals of Reason with those of Understanding. They may think of themselves as missionaries, educators, pacifists, abolitionists, or prison reformers; they all worship at the altar of efficiency, which is to say that they have already succumbed to skepticism. Too often, Emerson notes, "in some proportion to the material growth is the spiritual decay."[75] He takes special aim at temperance societies, because they are guilty of a serious confusion in asking their members for a commitment in public: "They are using numbers, that is mobs and bodies, and disusing principles. They quit a spiritual for a material ally! If I yield to this force, I degrade myself, and have now exchanged one vice for another: self-indulgence for fear."[76] Emerson's use of the first person here is not dictated by its expressive value alone; it also reflects an inward debate, the echo of which is often heard in the journals, unfailingly ending in the same rejection.[77]

With respect to political parties, no such ambivalence is to be appre-

[74] "I see plainly the charm which belongs to Alienation or Otherism. . . . The very sentiment I expressed yesterday without heed, shall sound memorable to me tomorrow if I hear it from another. My own book I read with new eyes when a stranger has praised it" (JMN 5.254 [November 28, 1836]).

[75] "The Philosophy of History," lecture 7, "Society" (EL 2.107).

[76] Ibid.

[77] The first journal passage on the subject (JMN 5.126 [February 28, 1836]) defines Emerson's position with a handsome, majestic firmness:

> God manifest in the flesh of every man is a perfect rule of social life. Justify yourself to an infinite Being in the ostler, and dandy, and stranger, and you shall never repent.
>
> The same view might hinder me from signing a pledge. There is such an immense background to my nature that I must treat my fellow as Empire treats Empire, & God, God. My whole being is to be my pledge & declaration & not a signature of ink.

hended, and for a moment, as if comforted, Emerson indulges in irony: the party, he explains, is "an elegant incognito designed to save a man the trouble of thinking, whilst a few fatten on the madness of the rest."[78] Thus the father of William the Conqueror could be dubbed, as need or inclination demanded, either Robert the Magnificent or Robert the Devil! Imposture carried to this degree turns against itself and becomes harmless. But Emerson also concedes to parties, and in even larger proportions to religious sects, what he has more or less denied philanthropists; he admits they are necessary. Man being made so as never to see more than a fraction of the truth—the part that touches him directly—the play of parties and sects has the effect of continuously correcting their respective excesses or errors. Unitarians have clear minds and cold hearts, Universalists are moved by a powerful instinct for justice but are incapable of critical judgment; free traders consider it stupid and dangerous to interfere by laws with the natural course of business, while protectionists retort that abstaining from such interference is only depriving oneself of an efficient means of funding the expenses of government. Both are relatively right and absolutely wrong; Emerson, by a judicious proportioning of contrary positions, tries to be absolutely right. He prepares, once again, the triumph of the universal spirit—though with the reservation that here it has the faintly insipid taste of eclecticism.

Finally, below the sects, the parties, and the organizations of all sorts the author's gaze distinguishes only the anarchic and faceless crowd:[79] "The Mob is man voluntarily returning to the nature of the Beast. Its fit hour of activity is Night. Its actions are insane like its whole constitution. It persecutes a principle. It would whip a right. It would tar and feather justice by inflicting fire and outrage upon the houses and persons of those who have these."[80] In the somber passion of these lines, with their Carlylean thrust (the capital letters add as in Carlyle a certain odor of apocalypse), one has the impression of hearing a new voice, scandalized and horrified as if from beholding the spectacle of a world torn apart in Manichaean strife. Emerson has to muster his energies to confront this "blind mechanical force," which is tolerated by nature as nature tolerates "earthquakes and freshets and locusts"[81] but is refrac-

[78] "The Philosophy of History," lecture 7, "Society" (EL 2.108).

[79] Note that Emerson usually employs "mob" where the other Transcendentalists would employ "multitude."

[80] "The Philosophy of History," lecture 7, "Society" (EL 2.109). The passage is used again in "Compensation" (W 2.119).

[81] JMN 5.100 (October 21, 1835).

tory to Reason and rebellious against all its injunctions. It is as if the old Federalist dogmas on which Emerson's youth had been nourished finally received from his mouth their metaphysical consecration; at the heart of the new philosophy gradually taking form from lecture to lecture the same old axiom is still at work, dividing humanity between those who evoke and deserve our confidence and those who can only disappoint it. But a final surge defeats the monster—or rather, since Emerson's philosophy precludes the very notion of defeat—transfigures it, as in the story of Beauty and the Beast. The magician, in this case, is the orator, and the instrument of the miracle his eloquence, but on the condition that it go beyond superficial ornamentation and penetrate to the soul itself: "This knits into one all the discordant parts of that living mass, in a breathless silence or a thunder of acclamation. An assembly of men is searched by principles as an assembly of angels might be. A principle seems to swell to a sort of omnipotence so slender a creature as man."[82] Although this portrait of the orator is partly composed of historical allusions (the names of Demosthenes and Chatham occur repeatedly), how can one not see in it also—and more profoundly—the projection of an unacknowledged longing? The repulsion Emerson feels for the chaotic and brutal mob engenders in him an equally powerful desire to control it; if the occupations of minister and lecturer lent themselves better than any others in America to the highlighting of his oratorical gifts,[83] they were also circumscribed by strict boundaries—as Emerson found out for himself, in the aftermath of the Divinity School address.[84] The omnipotent orator Emerson dreams of in 1836 can only be a political orator, like his idol Webster. In this sense, scholars have not sufficiently emphasized the essential continuity between Emerson the Transcendentalist and Emerson the public man in the Civil War. The civic impulse to which he later so passionately yielded permitted a part of himself to blossom for the first time.

In the lecture series on the philosophy of history, Emerson gives a full description of the ideal state, which is at once the end result and the justification of the political organization the orator can cause to spring up spontaneously around him:

> There is something grand in the idea of a State. It is a melting of many interests in *one* interest, of many millions of men, as it were,

[82] "The Philosophy of History," lecture 7, "Society" (EL 2.110).

[83] As most of Emerson's lectures have not been published in their original form, critics have tended to ignore what one might call his public style. It is less forceful and epigrammatic than that of the *Essays*, but reveals a remarkable ear for the rhythms of speech and a surprisingly good sense for structure and sequence.

[84] Cf. chapter 8.

> into *one* man, and this for good ends purely, for better defence, for better husbandry, for better action. The common conscience of all the individuals becomes the law of the State and, invisible as conscience is, envelops like a net all the cities, villages, farms, over sea over land to the farthest island colony of the people.[85]

On closer scrutiny, this definition is not without ambiguity. The exemplary nation to which Emerson implicitly refers is by all appearances England, and a portrait of *civis Britannicus*, obedient to the law and defended by it wherever he finds himself, had already figured in one of Emerson's sermons;[86] but such dearly cherished English self-images as Burke, for example, would have to be drastically altered for England to recognize itself in that flawless block which for Emerson is the symbol of the perfect form of the state. In Emerson's mind, elements deriving from the English political tradition, which he continues to admire, have now been influenced by certain aspects of German Romanticism. Arthur Lovejoy was particularly interested in the history of the concept of totality, of *das Ganze*, which toward the end of the eighteenth century was gradually substituted for that of natural rights, and traced the evolution by which the new concept gradually took on political meaning even as Kant, in the *Critique of Judgment*, was still basing his discussion of organic unity on the model of the tree.[87] Fichte's celebrated *Reden an die deutsche Nation* (which Emerson appears not to have read) finally provided the notion with the consecration of history and set the emerging nineteenth century on the path of an imperious and eagerly mystical nationalism.

It would be an error to attribute to Emerson—whose social experience seems scanty in comparison with that of the German patriots—the profound ideas of a Fichte; but here and there the journal sketches a movement of thought somewhat analogous to them in its sweep and intensity: "At any time," Emerson notes in 1836,

> A great danger or a strong desire as a war of defence or an interprize of enthusiasm or even of gain will . . . knit a multitude into one man & whilst it lasts bring every individual into his exact place; one to watch, one to deliberate, one to act, one to speak, & one to record.

85 "The Philosophy of History," lecture 5, "Politics" (EL 2.69).

86 Sermon 55, "Society and Solitude" (H.269).

87 See in particular not only the last chapter of *The Great Chain of Being* but also "The Meaning of Romanticism for the Historian of Ideas," *Journal of the History of Ideas* 2 (June 1941), pp. 257–278. Lovejoy condenses the social and political theory of German Romanticism into three terms: *das Ganze*, *Streben*, and *Eigentuemlichkeit*.

> The generic soul in each individual is a giant overcome with sleep which locks up almost all his senses, & only leaves him a little superficial animation. Once in an age at hearing some deeper voice, he lifts his iron lids, & his eyes straight pierce through all appearances, & his tongue tells what shall be in the latest times: then is he obeyed like a God, but quickly the lids fall, & sleep returns.[88]

The very history of the union, the North's great awakening at the Civil War, the spontaneous distribution of tasks that for a while made Emerson into the herald he evokes here all give this paragraph a curiously prophetic resonance. The author seems to have foreseen every single event—even the somnolence into which he will sink, more quickly and more completely than others, when victory has been won.

Still, in the America of Jackson and Van Buren, fragmented by factions and torn by opposing ambitions, a state in conformity with Emerson's idealized description sadly resembled a bodiless utopia. But this, Emerson thinks, should not authorize his compatriots to turn their eyes away. Political errors are only corrected to the extent that it is possible to judge them by the yardstick of an "ideal commonwealth." Governments must strive to bring even the least of their acts into conformity with that standard; otherwise, and regardless of their popularity, they are in fact usurpers.[89] A corresponding obligation devolves upon the philosopher: he must not only define the ideal norms but also examine the political reality in all its complexity. With considerable prudence and a certain amount of perplexity, but also with real courage, Emerson accepts the challenge and undertakes an analysis of the American political system.

Once again the distinction between Reason and Understanding furnishes him with the lever he needs. Government must protect two sorts of realities, persons and goods. But as the same spirit abides (potentially, at least) in all men, the only system acceptable, if one is concerned only with persons, is democracy—a position that can be described as a mere restatement of the argument for self-respect made in the lecture on Fox. But the second task incumbent upon government, the protection of property, raises greater difficulties. The unequal distribution of wealth is a fact explained in varying degrees by individual expertise or

[88] JMN 5.161–162, "The One Mind" (May 19, 1836).

[89] In his irritation at the Jacksonians, Emerson sometimes—and very logically—is led to praise monarchy: "We republicans do libel the monarchist. The monarchist of Europe for so many ages has really been pervaded by an Idea. He intellectually & affectionately views the king as the State. And the monarch is pervaded by a correspondent idea & the worst of them has yet demeaned himself more or less faithfully as a State" (JMN 4.369 [December 22, 1834]).

prudence on the one hand and on the other by the laws governing inheritance. Emerson accepts without hesitation the operation of these three factors. He is in fact more timid on the question of inheritance than was Jefferson—who had envisioned a periodic recasting of the relevant laws—because he is afraid of upsetting the established order and introducing chaos into the state: "The law deciding on purely abstract grounds, not for the advantage of any one person, but looking to the advantage of the whole society, makes an ownership which will be valid in each man's view, according to his estimate of the public tranquillity."[90] As a consequence, Emerson is led to propose two sets of laws, one dealing with persons and the other with property. The mortal sin of slavery is precisely to ignore this distinction and to apply laws governing property to questions of persons. But there is a corresponding abuse, which is to argue from the political equality of persons to an equality of rights to wealth: this, Emerson says, is agrarianism. That Emerson uses the word in this pejorative sense clearly shows his disapproval of the theses advanced by extreme reformers;[91] but above all it invites us to measure the distance America had traveled since Jefferson. The agrarian tradition had, it seems, suffered the fate of all victorious causes and faltered under the burden of success. As early as 1836, Jefferson's ideal had to be defended against its own excesses.[92]

No sooner has Emerson posited the principle of a twofold system of laws than he recognizes that in practice laws governing persons and laws governing property constantly overlap: wars and acts of violence have as their cause the desire to appropriate other persons' wealth; the state punishes an offense against a person with a fine; government guarantees the defense of persons by levying taxes. Not to take account of

[90] "The Philosophy of History," lecture 5, "Politics" (EL 2.72). An abbreviated version of the sentence is incorporated into the essay "Politics" (W 3.203). The essay contains most of the ideas expounded in the 1837 lecture but fuses several layers of Emersonian thought—with some damage to its internal coherence.

[91] In 1829, Thomas Skidmore, one of the leaders of the Workingmen's movement, published a work entitled, somewhat subversively, *The Rights of Man to Property, Being a Proposition to Make It Equal Among the Adults of the Present Generation*; but he found only a wavering audience even among the movement's members. A few years later, G. H. Evans took up Skidmore's idea in a more practical form, arguing in the *Workingman's Advocate* that western land should be ceded free of charge to immigrants who lacked funds.

[92] On Emerson's agrarian sympathies, cf. D. C. Stenerson, "Emerson and the Agrarian Tradition," *Journal of the History of Ideas* 14, (January 1953), pp. 95–115. Stenerson is careful to emphasize that properly speaking Jefferson exercised no influence on Emerson (the lists of Emerson's reading included in the journals contain only two references to Jefferson's writings), but sees in the two men a common admiration for the farmer's simple and independent mode of life—which, one should recall, represented until the Civil War the standard American way of life.

this interference would be to philosophize in thin air—or to run away from the difficulty altogether. Compelled by a sense of his own obligations to define the most acceptable compromise, Emerson does not dodge the issue: "the rightful distinction demanded is that the proprietors of the nation should have more elective franchise than non-proprietors."[93] He sanctions, that is, the limitation of universal suffrage so as not to abandon the state to the ungoverned appetites of a new proletariat, and he remains loyal to the Whigs who have his instinctive trust.

But it would be a betrayal of Emerson's thought to accord excessive importance to this position, which is, after all, meaningless unless referred to its underlying principles and reflects a transient and local phase of their manifestation. The last and longest part of the lecture under discussion supplies an insight indispensable in this connection in describing the immense though slow movement by which the legislator gradually approaches the ideal code of laws universal consciousness demands. History is a long and tedious record of aberrations, but it also provides for the emergence of ideas, which become conscious of themselves through their own deformations: "The civil ethics of the Greek and the Roman were based on the principle that *the individual is to merge himself in the State*, which of course is only a version of the truth that the individual is to submit himself to the verdict of the Universal Man."[94] Turkish despotism, Venetian oligarchy, popular tyranny in the dark hours of the French Revolution are other examples of the same deviation. And for those who are shocked by the tardiness and uncertainty of progress, Emerson recalls that every generation is a sort of sealed enclosure and has to take up at the beginning all the problems already solved by the generation preceding.

Yet Emerson feels the need to qualify this view. His optimism is based in fact on a belief in what one might call the unequal viability of justice and error, excess and moderation, which is the projection of his belief in the goodness of universal law:

> The foolish party and the foolish heads die, and no more are heard of: the hot party words and measures fade out of memory, but the wise institution, the jury, the representative council, the judiciary severed from the executive and legislative, things that took no more time or concert to invent than the most fugitive scheme of frantic faction, these praise themselves to one generation after another, and go round the globe.[95]

[93] "The Philosophy of History," lecture 5, "Politics" (EL 2.72).

[94] Lecture 5, "Politics" (EL 2.73–74); the italics are Emerson's.

[95] Lecture 5, "Politics" (EL 2.74–75).

How then could one regard history's delaying action with anything but indifference? And will one not rather direct one's gaze toward the future, to salute the dawn of a universal reconciliation? Social classes are never so antagonistic to one another that in the end they do not recognize, when confronted with moral wrongdoing, the profound identity of their interests and feelings. Indeed, even the gulf between rich and poor, masters and servants, is being slowly bridged. "The progress of society tends to reconcile and to identify those two sovereign interests of persons and property, by destroying the class of paupers and slaves through making every man a proprietor. The growth of the propertied party destroys the war-party, and invites the Arts and embellishments of peace."[96] Spoken in 1837—a few months, that is, before the great depression that hit the American economy so hard—these sentences do not, as one might think, display the prophet's nearsightedness. Those whose business was government saw the coming storm no more than did Emerson; prosperity had prevailed pretty much without interruption for sixteen or seventeen years, and the two parties striving for power so fiercely nonetheless agreed that property was the cornerstone of the social edifice. While Emerson's robust optimism seemed neither excessive nor irresponsible, it owed more than he would have been ready to admit to an unstable concatenation of circumstances.

Emerson's serene confidence in the order of things is nowhere more evident than in the lecture "Trades and Professions" (also part of the 1836–1837 series, just after the lecture on society). Profitable activities are described there as so many episodes of a brilliant festival. It is the vision of William Morris in *News from Nowhere*, but with a more stimulating and cheerful quality, as if Emerson had substituted for the late spring sun caressing the fields of England the beams of a younger and brighter star, full of a sturdy expansiveness. The procession begins with the farmer in his earth-colored garments, his face grave and his walk slow; then comes the merchant, who remains in view somewhat longer. He is the "practical geographer," in his warehouses piled high with the products of the whole world; every day he risks his fortune on the seas, but his stout ships and bold crews transform every fresh challenge into a further gain. Finally there appears the "manufacturer," a term that for Emerson covers not only "the owner of 100,000 spindles" but also "the cottage dame who strings dried apples, makes straw braid or cuts fly curtains."[97] This bracketing together of widely different economic po-

[96] Lecture 5, "Politics" (EL 2.76).

[97] "The Philosophy of History," lecture 8, "Trades and Professions" (EL 2.117). One should note that at this time the farmer did not occupy in Emerson's eyes the high place on the scale of human activities that he was to be accorded later. Cf. JMN 5.301 (April 21, 1837):

sitions—made at a time in which Lowell, only a few miles from Concord, already had hundreds of operatives, while throughout the eastern part of Massachusetts the industrial revolution was beginning to impose oppressive servitude on a more and more considerable section of the population—this thorougly unexpected bracketing reveals Emerson's disarming indifference to the concrete conditions of existence. He yields so completely to the attractions of great ideas that the sufferings and dangers of countless human beings around the globe are in his work refined to the point of forming only a harmonious chain of solidarity—which he describes, moreover, with the imaginative force and the picturesque, racy amplitude that he so cherished in the authors of the seventeenth century:

> What more gratifying spectacle to the philanthropist, who considers that not a stroke can labor lay to without receiving therefore a new acquaintance with a natural fact, than the price-current of the newspaper, when he reflects on the industry, the address, the patience that conspired to that result; reflects how many hands gathered the salt, the opium, the camphor or the tea; how many hunters scoured the prairies, leaped the crags of the Alps of Cordilleras; swung in baskets on Orkney cliffs, or in Newcastle mines; sweltered by furnaces, or dived to the bed of the sea and rivers; trapped the elephant and raced with the whale; how many dug, fought, swum, watched, rode or ran to fill the columns of that weekly advertisement.[98]

I cite this lengthy passage because its learned disorderliness so nicely establishes Emerson's position. He does not care whether a man is an iron-master or a trapper, a harpooner or a coolie; all trades are noble[99] and none is unrewarding, because the law of compensations secures for every worker a literally immeasurable recompense in the form of an increased familiarity with the laws of the universe. Never did Emerson better bring out the essentially symbolic and ritual character of the activities of production than in this lecture—even though the subject seemed bound to take us to the very heart of the problems of the mo-

---

"It has been to me a sensible relief to learn that the destiny of New England is to be the manufacturing country of America. I no longer suffer in the cold out of morbid sympathy with the farmer. . . . I am gay as a canary bird with this new knowledge."

[98] "The Philosophy of History," lecture 8, "Trades and Professions" (EL 2.118). The desolate Orkney Islands supplied kelp for the shops of New England.

[99] In the same lecture Emerson cites an eighteenth-century German writer, Jean-Jacques Volckmann, who asserted in a series of letters on Italy published in 1770 that even among the *lazzaroni* of Naples idleness was unheard of!

ment. What we call our breadwinning wins us also the spiritual possession of ourselves and of the world—thence the expression of "virile innocence" that Emerson believes he sees on the blacksmith's face even as his muscles strain with effort. It would be necessary, Emerson intimates, to recover the spirit of the medieval guilds and reanimate their vocabulary to restore to labor its sacred ambivalence.

This exhortation, curiously anachronistic in Van Buren's America, is succeeded by a panegyric on trade and its benefits; the sequence illustrates once more the oscillations and the complex unity of Emerson's thought. It is only in appearance that he dreams; in reality, escape into the past is for him a means of taking the measure of his contemporaries more accurately. For years he had been saying that the earth belongs to the living, and the title of his penultimate lecture, "The Present Age," proclaims as much once again.[100] But his striving for rootedness in the present, as also his belief in the absolute plasticity of every moment, oblige him to keep free of illusion and indulgence, to denounce the faults of the age with the same fervor that other men of lesser faith would employ in praising it. If trade has hastened the course of democracy, has given substance to the idea of liberty by multiplying individual opportunities, has brought down the barriers between peoples and annihilated the prestige of arms, it has also dulled the values of our existence and made for a spiritual emptiness in us that we seek in vain to ignore. When we do not sink into madness or suicide,[101] we wrap ourselves about in a careful conformity, or substitute erudition for sincere feeling, or seek to bury every living principle under a laboriously erect mountain of facts. And what is most distressing in all this, Emerson goes on to note, is the sight of the young facing life with death in their souls:

> See the despondency of those who are just putting on the manly robe. At the age ludicrously called the age of discretion, each hopeful young man is shipwrecked. The burdensome possession of himself he cannot dispose of. Up to that hour, others have directed him—and he has gone triumphantly. Then he begins to direct him-

[100] Critics have not paid adequate attention to Emerson's attempts to analyze and understand his time. Yet even the titles he chooses are significant: for the 1839–1840 series he reuses the 1837 title of "The Present Age"; two years later, he gives a new series called "The Times"; finally, in 1843, contemporary America is dealt with in several of the lectures grouped under the title of "New England." Perhaps Sherman Paul (in *The Shores of America* ([Urbana, Ill., 1958], p. 176, n. 13) is right in suggesting that scholars have neglected the problem because so many of the texts remain unpublished.

[101] European travelers, and notably Tocqueville, were struck with the frequency of neurosis among the active classes of Americans; it seems that Arthur Miller's traveling salesman had a long ancestry.

> self, and all hope, wisdom and power sink flat down. Sleep creeps over him, and he sleeps down in the snow—And many a corpse and many a ruin we meet on the road to mark how sorely the conventions of society pressed on numbers, how vicious were the influences of the time, —and to some fatal.[102]

Among the most speculative minds, Emerson continues, the malaise has taken the form of an excessive penchant for analysis, for the unending dissection of ideas and beliefs. The simplicity of instinct without which no great thing is accomplished seems lost; introspection is triumphant everywhere, as if eyes had sprouted all over our bodies and led us astray as in a palace of mirrors. Philosophy is confined to criticism, incapable of the bold expeditions that once brought truth down to earth. The ghost of Gerontion, the old man one reads to while waiting for rain that will probably never fall, already haunts the thoughts of the young Americans of 1836.[103] But Emerson is of sufficient stature to fight it off and to exorcise it: "This despondency, this want of object in life, this nakedness are the temporary symptoms of the transition state, whilst the man sees the hollowness of the old and does not yet know the resources of the soul."[104] If we were sensible enough to lift up our eyes for a moment and look beyond ourselves, we would recognize that we were the victims of a psychological illusion: the dominion of ideas over us is forever absolute, but only slowly do we become aware of it; and when we finally attain a clear perception of that dominion, the idea whose authority we now confess has already ceased to guide us, and we follow another that we do not yet acknowledge. This produces a troubling discrepancy, but also a fertile one in that it keeps the world from growing rigid and us with it: "for my part," notes Emerson, "I am content there shall be a certain slight discord in the song of the morning stars, if that discord arise from my ear being opened to the undersong of spirits."[105]

Claiming to have found the core of a philosophy is always risky; but the subtle discord Emerson thus describes does seem to lead us a good distance toward comprehending his message. It illuminates the deep sources of an optimism that owes its resilience to its acceptance of ignorance, of error, and even—among the most lucid of its adherents—of contradiction immediately experienced. One day in his journal Emer-

[102] "The Philosophy of History," lecture 11, "The Present Age" (EL 2.170).

[103] Whicher, *Freedom and Fate*, p. 133, is also reminded of Eliot in reading certain statements by Emerson; and despite the antagonism between their philosophies, the two men are more similar in their spiritual experience than one would imagine.

[104] "The Philosophy of History," lecture 11, "The Present Age." See also "The American Scholar" (W 1.108–110).

[105] "The Philosophy of History," lecture 11, "The Present Age" (EL 2.171).

son observes that something seems to thwart all our efforts at system making. When we think we have found an explanation of the physical universe, animal magnetism comes along to refute it; when we have constructed our little cosmogony and set the nations of the world in it "like cherries into a tart," we notice that we have forgotten the blacks.[106] Ought one then to conclude that Emerson is lying to his hearers when in the fiery peroration of another lecture he proclaims the unity of the human race as beyond all differences of color and culture?[107] In fact, despite the irreducible contradiction, Emerson's sincerity is complete at both moments. Only the point of view has changed. If he admits in his journal the existence of obstacles that he like all of his contemporaries must encounter, he breathes not a word of it to his audience, because he has the inward assurance that the obstacles will be overcome, even though he does not yet know how. His particular task is to render audible to all ears the "undersong" with which his solitude is enchanted.

This programmatic optimism is nowhere manifested more forcefully than in the lecture on war that Emerson gave at Boston, under the auspices of the American Peace Society, in March 1838.[108] Set in its historical context, the subject almost seems too platonic: the last signs of the agitation provoked by the War of 1812 had long since been quieted, and the proclamation of the Monroe Doctrine, which closed off the American continent to the ambitions of European powers, had not aroused in those powers any very alarming responses. The only touchy issue was the Canadian border—it had not yet been defined precisely, and disputes arose from time to time about certain tracts of land, which Palmerston's stronghanded policy did not aid in settling—but from that to the thought of a general conflagration was a considerable distance. If the problem of war struck a profound chord in Americans conscious of their geographic privileges, it was for other reasons, more general and more noble. For Americans, it seemed that war, that "Master-evil" as Channing calls it in one of the three speeches he devoted to it,[109] sym-

[106] Cf. JMN 5.376 (September 19, 1837).

[107] "The American, the European finds to his surprise that the Patagonian, the Otaheitan, the Caraib is neither Centaur nor Satyr, has neither tail nor horns, is neither hoofed nor web-footed; but that his tattooed bosom beats with the same heart and his dark eye flashes with the self-same soul as his own" ("The Philosophy of History," lecture 7, "Society" [EL 2.112]).

[108] The lecture is printed in W 11, *Miscellanies*, 149–176. In 1815, at the end of the War of 1812, two peace groups were founded in New York and Boston. In the following years their number increased rapidly, and in 1828 William Ladd succeeded in joining them into a national organization called the American Peace Society. Cf. on this subject W. A. Huggard, "Emerson and the Problem of War and Peace," *University of Iowa Humanistic Studies* 10, (April 1938), pp. 1–76.

[109] The one delivered on July 25, 1835 (William Ellery Channing, *Works*, ed. William Henry Channing [Boston, 1896], p. 655).

bolized the prejudices, the errors, the misguided ambitions, in a word the obscurantism of past centuries; Napoleon's career was its splendid dying gasp, and since Napoleon the world had for the first time begun to live and hope. To observe the progress of the idea of peace was a great spiritual comfort, because it was to witness a change taking place in the soul itself. Hence, probably, Emerson's continued interest in that aspect of collective life despite his avowed mistrust of philanthropic organizations in general;[110] the field seemed to him so large and its perspectives so elevated that for once he need not fear the absurd claims of his fellow men to organize even the work of the Universal Spirit.

Predictably enough, the lecture barely mentions the project of a Congress of Nations, beginning just then to find a handful of advocates, and that mention is no endorsement of it but a refusal to pass judgment: "the mind, once prepared for the reign of principles, will easily find modes of expressing its will."[111] Abbé Saint-Pierre's plan for perpetual peace and the political writings of Rousseau detain Emerson at no greater length. In all such schemes what interests him is only "the rising of the general tide in the human soul,"[112] and it is a description of this powerful flow that he offers to his audience. His biographers have noted that Emerson originally intended to call the lecture "Peace" and only chose the opposite term at the last moment. That hesitation is itself significant, because it shows that he was less interested in celebrating peace or denouncing war than in tracing the metamorphoses of a principle. Whereas Channing, thinking the victory of the new spirit still precarious, had urged his fellow citizens to increase their efforts to consolidate it, Emerson took a stand outside the contingencies of history and passionately abandoned himself to the movement of an idea. That is also why he can concede to war what Channing adamantly refused it: war in Emerson's eyes has a positive value as the first avatar of an eternal principle, teaching us to rely on ourselves, to win our physical and mental independence. The peace-loving hero Emerson proposes as a model to his generation is to be no less courageous than his warrior ancestor; he has simply learned to recognize that the universal spirit dwells in every man and is to be honored and served. Emerson's position fails to take into account the pressure that events might suddenly exert on him—but

[110] In 1832, Emerson's journal records his satisfaction at a lecture of Channing's to the Peace Society (JMN 3.262–263). In 1835, he tells a member of the organization's governing committee that he will speak on "the circumstances which show a tendency toward War's abolition" (JMN 5.112 and L 1.458). In the event, the lecture was never given—unless the text now under discussion is the belated outcome of that project.

[111] W 11.175.

[112] W 11.160.

in 1838, the particular historical moment, which he affects to ignore, justifies his lofty confidence:

> as far as it respects individual action in difficult and extreme cases, I will say, such cases seldom or never occur to the good and just man; nor are we careful to say, or even to know, what in such crises is to be done. A wise man will never impawn his future being and action, and decide beforehand what he shall do in a given extreme event. Nature and God will instruct him in that hour.[113]

Emerson's sincerity and, indeed, the consistency of his views are unquestionable. Although it would be easy, with the knowledge hindsight gives us, to mock his tranquil assurance, perhaps it is best to take the lecture as the witness, and in its own way the very moving witness, of a faith blinded by its own light.

Emerson may have had an interest in the subject of war and peace; but his knowledge of it was in essence a purely literary one, as the anecdotes with which he ornaments his account clearly reveal.[114] No more than any other philosophy is idealism free of the need for support or correction from the data of experience. And that is why, conversely, "The American Scholar" (to which the final section of this chapter will be addressed) was able to electrify Emerson's contemporaries and send out shock waves even as far as our own time.[115] It was the admirably distilled expression of a program for life, which Emerson had elaborated point by point to fill the secret void left in him by the abandonment of his ministry.[116]

Once again it was Coleridge who played the role of initiator and model. In his late work "On the Constitution of Church and State," Coleridge defined the function of a national church: designed as a counterpoise to the other institutions of the state, it was to embody the "idea" of moral education, without which the life of the nation would be only a patchwork of violence, imposition, and rebellion. The national church was not to be identified with the established church, though it drew on

[113] W 11.169.

[114] For example, the remark of Fontenelle's that Emerson had cited in the lecture on Burke (EL 1.190) and now records again (W 11.156): "I hate war, for it spoils conversation." It is difficult not to feel that rhetoric is winning out here over sensibility and imagination.

[115] In 1932, the Phi Beta Kappa Society founded *The American Scholar*, so named in homage to Emerson's speech. The first issue began with an article by John Erskine arguing that Emerson's message still retained its interest and vivid freshness.

[116] The ensuing analysis is very much indebted to Henry Nash Smith, "Emerson's Problem of Vocation," NEQ 12, (March 1939), pp. 52–67. One of Smith's most insistently made points concerns the intense need Emerson felt to define his place in the social milieu that had borne him.

it. It was composed of all persons—clergymen, scientists, philosophers, professors—whose task it was to maintain and propagate the life of the mind. It was to form a "clerisy" and to establish the foundation of its influence and authority on the renunciation of all material ambition; but it was the business of the state, whose indispensable auxiliary it was, to guarantee the members of it a decent living and a regular salary.[117] Emerson read this "invaluable little book"[118] toward the end of 1834, and the journal recorded his enthusiastic praise of it.[119] Finally, in an address given in June 1837 to the students of a school in Providence—a sort of dress rehearsal for "The American Scholar"—Emerson publicly subscribed to Coleridge's views. Having noted the corrosive effects of material prosperity and deplored ministers' gradual withdrawal from the temple of truth, Emerson asserts that the body politic as a whole needs to be exposed to some new "redeeming influence": "For this reason, it is essential to Society that there should be a learned class, a clerisy, comprising that is the clergy, the literary men, the colleges, the teachers of youth, as the fosterers of the superior nature of man, and prompt to remind him of the mediate and symbolical character of things."[120] Where such spiritual perception is lacking, he continues, the people must perish, unknowing victims of their own appetites.

But for Emerson this program of a national statute for intellectuals only scratches the surface of the problem, or rather assumes it solved, because what is above all necessary is that men of the clerical vocation should learn to act without shame or timidity. At scattered intervals the journals show Emerson nurturing the message he will one day address to "scholars," and in almost all these passages the emphasis is on the need for courage.[121] That is in fact the dominant note, insistent and imperious but also powerfully exalting, in "The American Scholar":

> it becomes him to feel all confidence in himself, and to defer never to the popular cry. He and he only knows the world. . . . Let him not quit his belief that a popgun is a popgun, though the ancient and honorable of the earth affirm it to be the crack of doom. . . . if

[117] A good account of Coleridge's theses in this work is in Basil Willey, *Nineteenth Century Studies* (London, 1949), pp. 44–50.

[118] The phrase occurs in the lecture "Modern Aspects of Letters," given in January 1836 (EL 1.379).

[119] See JMN 4.369–372 (December 22, 1834).

[120] "Address on Education" (EL 2.202). Just after the Civil War Whitman was to defend a similar idea in *Democratic Vistas*.

[121] See for example JMN 5.164–165 (May 30, 1836): "in that Sermon to Literary Men which I propose to make, be sure to admonish them not to be ashamed of their gospel."

> the single man plant himself indomitably on his instincts, and there abide, the huge world will come round to him.[122]

The energy that had been slowly accumulating in him throughout his years of trial finds an outlet in a series of flashing aphorisms. Small wonder that logical minds confessed bewilderment at this zigzag progression, in which the exact concatenation of ideas is replaced by the intentionally iconoclastic authority of affirmation;[123] but the accounts of those who heard the orator,[124] as well as the success of the first printing of the address (five hundred copies were sold in less than a month) show clearly that Emerson had found his tone and voice. At last he yields unreservedly to the intuition that commands him to descend into himself to encounter others and to mock at proved formulas. The persuasive force of the piece grows precisely from this fusion of theme and method: Emerson preaches self-trust while oratorically illustrating it.

Indeed, unless the modern reader notes the extreme tension of the language and kindles for himself the sparks with which the words are charged, he is in danger of completely misapprehending the place and role of the address in American cultural history. It had been forty years since Freneau, in his "Literary Importations," had denounced the pernicious influence of Europe, and the theme had been restated frequently enough to become a commonplace of American literature throughout the first three decades of the nineteenth century.[125] In this sense Emerson's speech was nothing new; indeed it was, in comparison to certain contemporary discussions carefully enumerating the inherent advantages of the American writer's literary situation, something of a retreat.[126] But whereas most writers only wished for America's intellec-

[122] "The American Scholar" (W 1.102 and 115).

[123] See for example the notice in the *Boston Quarterly Review* 1 (January 1838), pp. 108–110, cited in Sherman Paul, *Emerson's Angle of Vision* (Cambridge, Mass., 1952), p. 235: "There are no developments of thought, there is no continuous flow in his writings. We gaze as through crevices on a stream of subterranean course, which sparkles here and there in the light, and then is lost." According to Theodore Parker, the notice was written by William Henry Channing; cf. on this point Clarence Gohdes, *The Periodicals of American Transcendentalism* (Durham, N.C., 1931), p. 74.

[124] Oliver Wendell Holmes, who was there, wrote that "the young men went out from it as if a prophet had been proclaiming to them 'Thus saith the Lord' " (*Ralph Waldo Emerson*, [Boston, 1884], p. 98).

[125] Noah and Daniel Webster, Buckminster, Channing, Bryant, Cooper, and Longfellow had all in various forms deplored the absence of an authentically national literature. Robert E. Spiller, "Critical Standards in the American Romantic Movement," *College English* 8 (April 1947), pp. 344–352, notes the numerous articles devoted to the theme in American periodicals between 1812 and 1825.

[126] See for example Channing, "Remarks on National Literature" (*Works*, pp. 124–138).

tual independence, Emerson declared it: "I embrace the common, I explore and sit at the feet of the familiar, the low. . . . What would we really know the meaning of? The meal in the firkin; the milk in the pan; the ballad in the street; the news of the boat; the glance of the eye; the form and the gait of the body."[127] This is Wordsworth's philosophy, with a rough and resolute quality betraying the keener air of the New World: "it has the stamp of the American who has leveled the forests with his axe and thinks the world of the intellect is to be assaulted in the same way."[128]

Despite or beyond its flippancy, the judgment strikes home. Emerson speaks in a country where work is honored, where the worst insult is the charge of indolence; he judges it prudent to devote a long passage to the role of action in the scholar's life, so that no one will be tempted to see scholars as effeminate phrasemakers: "Action is with the scholar subordinate, but it is essential. Without it he is not yet man. Without it thought can never ripen into truth. . . . The true scholar grudges every opportunity of action past by, as a loss of power."[129] To grow or even to stay alive, thought needs sustenance, and it is the vicissitudes of our life, our troubles, our needs, our fits of anger and our misfortunes that furnish it. Thought has vigor in proportion to the richness of our experience.[130] Emerson is of course careful to describe the process by which action becomes subsequently detached from life "like a ripe fruit" and dons the incorruptible garment of thought. It is nonetheless true that in the reader's mind, as perhaps in Emerson's own, the image of "Man Thinking" dissolves into that of the universal man, at once a hero of action and a priest of thought, a secular leader acclaimed by the crowd[131] no less than a contemplative philosopher. All the avenues of knowledge and power are open to him; to take up Stephen Whicher's metaphor,

---

Channing finds that the absence of paralyzing traditions, the equality of conditions, and the respect naturally accorded every human being should all favor the development of a national literature.

[127] "The American Scholar" (W 1.111).

[128] According to Carlyle, who quotes it in French in a letter to Emerson, this appraisal was offered by Madame Necker (CEC 260 [January 17, 1840]).

[129] "The American Scholar" (W 1.94 and 95).

[130] Matthiessen, *American Renaissance*, p. 21, n. 10, compares with this position the philosophy that underlies the novels of Malraux, notably *Man's Fate* and *Man's Hope*, the similarity being that both systems have the same sort of respect for the human mind and its aptitude for transforming event into experience.

[131] See on this subject the disturbingly enthusiastic passage of the speech in which Emerson describes the crowd's admiration for the great man and its desire to abandon itself to his power (W 1.106–107).

Emerson in "The American Scholar" is the new Moses, showing to the chosen people the pastures of Canaan spread out at his feet.[132]

In this refusal to choose, or rather in this cannily sustained ambiguity, there almost certainly resides the secret of the spell Emerson cast over his hearers and readers. Without ever escaping into the world of pure ideas, he maintains a position high enough above the world of the senses to avoid being constrained by any of its laws. The dissonance discussed earlier is resolved in the feeling of a potential both infinite and immediate: the universe of objects and beings lies within our grasp, open to our action, and we have the intoxicating sensation in the moment before we act that our power has no limits. We thus attain to the central meaning of the address for young America. The protest against the "courtly muses of Europe" is a preliminary maneuver—indispensable to be sure, since America in 1837 is still in the shadow of the Old World,[133] but clearly not sufficient. Just as the Declaration of Independence opened the path to a political reorganization without which it would have remained empty words, so "The American Scholar" supplements its rejections by a program embodying all the younger generation's positive aspirations. A few months earlier, Orestes Brownson had in his little book *New Views of Christianity, Society, and the Church* sketched a portrait of the American so close in its essential lines to Emerson's scholar that one has to acknowledge in both texts the imprint of a single Zeitgeist:

> In this country more than in any other is the man of thought united in the same person with the man of action. The people here have a strong tendency to profound and philosophical thought, as well as to skillful, energetic and persevering action. The time is not far distant when our whole population will be philosophers, and all our philosophers will be practical men. . . . Philosophers in other countries may think and construct important theories, but they can realize them only to a very limited extent. But here every idea may be at once put to a practical test, and if true will be realized. We have

[132] See Whicher, *Freedom and Fate*, p. 76.

[133] G. W. Cooke, in a lecture given before the Concord School of Philosophy and printed in *The Genius and Character of Emerson*, ed. F. B. Sanborn (Boston, 1885), pp. 320–321, cites a contemporary comment on the intellectual climate of the period: "it is but a few years . . . since we have dared to be American in even the details and accessories of our literary work; to make our allusions to natural objects real, not conventional; to ignore the nightingale and skylark, and look for the classic and romantic on our own soil. This change began mainly with Emerson. Some of us can recall the bewilderment with which his verses on the humble-bee, for instance, were received, when the choice of subject caused as much wonder as the treatment." The allusion is to the poem "The Humble-Bee" (W 9.38–40).

> the field, the liberty, the disposition and the faith to work with ideas. It is here then that must first be brought out and realized the true idea of the Atonement.[134]

It is a moment of glorious unity in which all seems easy in the dawn's early light, a first and exalted image of the American dream. But the profound differences of temperament we can discern between the styles of the two authors remind us that we are near to a watershed, and that the auspicious conjunction here may have no successor.

When Carlyle wrote Emerson to acknowledge the arrival of his address, he congratulated him warmly for the "*man's* voice" he heard there, but also warned him to be ready for great struggles: "may God grant you strength, for you have a *fearful* work to do! Fearful I call it; and yet it is great, and the greatest."[135] It is difficult to distinguish in this prophecy between spite and wisdom, between complacent misanthropy and a just appreciation of the adverse forces. But the motivation matters little. By linking the scholar's mental creativeness to his capacity for action, Emerson had well and truly cut himself off from his paradise of metaphysical reveries; almost against his will, he had bound himself to be, in Sherman Paul's felicitous expression, "our first herald of the liberal imagination."[136]

[134] Quoted in *The Transcendentalists: An Anthology*, ed. Perry Miller (Cambridge, Mass., 1950), pp. 122–123.

[135] CEC 173–174 (letter of December 8, 1837); the italics are Carlyle's.

[136] Reviewing F. I. Carpenter's *Emerson Handbook* in NEQ 26 (December 1953), pp. 546–548, Sherman Paul sketches a comparison between Emerson's position about 1840 and the role Lionel Trilling was attempting to play more than a century later (notably in the preface to *The Liberal Imagination* [New York, 1950]): "If it were not for Emerson's supposed aloofness from politics, he might well serve as our first herald of the liberal imagination; for the fundamental demand of this partisan of experience was the continuity of thought and action."

8

~ ~ ~ ~

FROM AFFIRMATION TO CHALLENGE

ONE CAN ARGUE, and not paradoxically, that one of the salient traits of "The American Scholar," despite its often pungent vigor, is a certain vagueness, an absence of precise and concrete directives. Not only does Emerson reserve his rather brief remarks on the America he lives in till the end; he refrains from anything that might look like a personal stand on any of the problems of his time. The economic crisis holding his countrymen by the throat is never mentioned, not even as background or by way of preterition. Emerson exhorts, rouses, sometimes scolds, but nowhere is he concerned with locating the scholar in the context of his own time. Yet if in the address he seems too angelic, too otherworldly, the journals reveal another Emerson, a man well acquainted with his country's financial troubles and eager to draw a moral lesson from them. The silences in the address are intentional; and it is legitimate to take account of them in offering a general interpretation of it, much as we have to include in our image of a play the developments occurring between the acts. By refusing to say certain words, to introduce certain references that would, he thought, weaken his message, Emerson implicitly offered a value judgment on that portion of our existence inscribed within the broad and yet accurately defined frame in which circumstances have placed us; he did not, it seems, regard it as substantial enough to deserve the least niche in the temple he intended to erect. The task at hand is to shed some light on that attitude and to observe its gradual modulation—for the pretense he makes of ignoring the social organism is surely in the America of 1840 a course of action difficult to sustain with honor. Such, at any rate, is the lesson that seems to emerge if one seeks to follow Emerson's evolution in the course of the three years that separate the serene, splendid audacity of "The American Scholar" from the proud challenges of "Self-Reliance."

But it is important to stress at the outset that this evolution owes nothing to the growth of a problem that considerably troubled many observers even then, namely the problem of slavery. It had not died out gradually, as certain liberal aristocrats from Virginia and the Carolinas had once hoped it would; indeed it had taken a new lease on life. The invention of the cotton gin at the end of the eighteenth century, the constantly increasing needs of the English textile industry, the settling of the fertile lands in the Southwest just in time to relieve the exhausted plantations of the South: all had gradually enriched and stabilized the southern economy,[1] but had also made it strictly dependent on black labor. From 1808 (when the international slave trade was outlawed) until 1840, the slave population increased by almost one million. At the same time, a social philosophy founded on the inequality of races, which invoked as precedents both the Bible and classical antiquity, was hardening the economic interests of the owning class into an ideology.[2] In the North, however, the abolitionists were gaining ground. On January 1, 1831, William Lloyd Garrison published in Boston the first issue of *The Liberator*, which was a call to immediate action. He rejected not only the idea of gradual abolition he had hitherto accepted but also, in the name of the principles he evoked, any accommodation or compromise whatever:

> On this subject, I do not wish to think, or speak, or write, with moderation. No! no! Tell a man whose house is on fire to give a moderate alarm; tell him to moderately rescue his wife from the hands of the ravisher; tell the mother to gradually extricate her babe from the fire into which it has fallen; —but urge me not to use

[1] Between 1805 and 1845, the annual southern production of cotton jumped from 60 million to 400 million pounds.

[2] Emerson transcribed without comment the following extract from a speech by George McDuffie, the governor of South Carolina, delivered to the legislature of that state on November 24, 1835 and printed November 27 in the *Charleston Courier*:

> So deep is my conviction on this subject that if I were doomed to die immediately after recording these sentiments, I could say in all sincerity, and under all the sanctions of Christianity and patriotism: "God forbid that my descendants in the remotest generation should live in any other than a community having the institution of domestic slavery, as it existed among the patriarchs of the primitive Church, and in all the free states of antiquity." (JMN 6.323–324)

> moderation in a cause like the present. I am in earnest—I will not equivocate—I will not excuse—I will not retreat a single inch—AND I WILL BE HEARD."[3]

Such resoluteness of course earned Garrison a good many enemies; he was at one point seized by an angry mob, in 1835, and saved only by the intervention of a husky carter. Indeed, abolitionism had become a sign of contradiction at the very heart of the old ruling class of New England: for one Wendell Phillips—brilliant graduate of Harvard, son of a rich Boston lawyer who had once been mayor—there were ten, even twenty businessmen eager to maintain cordial relations with the South at any cost, not only in deference to the letter of the law (legislation governing slavery was the prerogative of the individual states) but also because their factories needed Georgia and Carolina cotton.[4]

The problem, then, was serious and threatened to explode; these facts led Channing, ever active in matters concerning the community's moral health, to explain in a pamphlet titled *Slavery*, published in 1835, the reasons that compelled him not only to condemn slavery unreservedly but also to reject the plan for immediate emancipation called for by Garrison and those about him. This Fabian attitude does not, however, as one might think, reveal an ill-disguised partiality for the supporters of slavery; it rests on a clear-minded and highly generous argument. Channing feared the convulsions that would undoubtedly result throughout the South from so radical a measure as the sudden elimination of slavery; and he also sought to protect the blacks against the danger of being abandoned without preparation to the temptations of freedom. In any case his little book attracted Emerson's attention, who called it one of the "perfectly genuine works of the times"[5] and sent a copy to Carlyle. It may even, one may speculate, have contributed directly to the talk the former gave on the subject in November 1837.[6] Like Channing, Emerson exhorts his countrymen to reflect and deliberate, so that sound and enlightened northern opinion can gradually

[3] As quoted in *Great Issues in American History*, ed. Richard Hofstadter, 2 vols. (New York, 1958), 1.322. The capitals are Garrison's.

[4] In speaking of the unrest Garrison's activities provoked at Boston, Harriet Martineau—who was intensely sympathetic with the abolitionists—argued that Europe was wrong to see the disorder as caused by the lower classes: "the mobs of America are composed of high churchmen, (of whatever denomination,) merchants and planters, and lawyers" (*Society in America*, 3 vols. [London, 1837] 1.164). It was the mayor of Boston himself, she added, who permitted the destruction of the sign indicating the abolitionist organization's location.

[5] JMN 5.150 (May 4, 1836).

[6] The speech in question was never published, and the manuscript seems to have been lost; the journal notes used in its preparation are still extant (JMN 12.151–154).

gather strength: "Our great duty on this matter is to open our halls to the discussion of this question steadily day after day, year after year until no man dare wag his finger at us."[7] Again like Channing, he pays homage to the principles the abolitionists embody but rejects their external and superficial methods; and he concurs with Channing also in avoiding any censure of the slave owners and in carefully distinguishing the sin from the agent by whom it is committed: "Far be it from me to reproach the planter. I think his misfortune is greater than his sin."[8]

But despite these similarities in standpoint and attitude, the two treatments (to the extent that one can know Emerson's in the first place) leave profoundly different impressions. Channing suffers the pain of being unable to suggest an immediately applicable solution, because he imagines and as it were experiences the slave's degradation. Emerson cannot tolerate a confusion of principles, but he resigns himself fairly easily to the same impotence: "But when we have settled the right & wrong of this question I think we have done all we can. A man can only extend his active attention to a certain finite amount of claims. We have much nearer duties than to the poor black slaves of Carolina and the effect of the present excitement is to exaggerate that."[9] Unlike Channing, in fact, he is unwilling to account for the slave's moral inferiority solely on the basis of the appalling conditions of the slave's life. There must be another explanation; and it is furnished by Emerson's belief (already noted more than once[10]) in the essential inequality of races: "I think it cannot be maintained by any candid person that the African race have ever occupied or do promise ever to occupy any very high place in the human family. Their present condition is the strongest proof that they cannot."[11] The persistence of slavery as the basis of political organization thus shed its most disturbing traits, while Emerson's acknowledgment of a natural hierarchy inclined him to treat Garrison's disciples harshly, as potential martyrs compromising their cause by inopportune declarations and as egotists too often seeking the gratifications of pride under cover of self-abnegation.[12] Set against the majesty and power of

[7] JMN 12.152. Channing for his part wrote in his introductory chapter that "not a few dread all discussion of the subject, and, if not reconciled to the continuance of slavery, at least believe that they have no duty to perform, no testimony to bear, no influence to exert" (*Slavery*, in his *Works*, ed. William Henry Channing [Boston, 1896], p. 689).

[8] JMN 12.154. The moderation is surprising when compared with certain passages of the journal written precisely in November 1837, in which Emerson denounces the cruelties of slave owners and slave traders with considerable indignation (JMN 5.440).

[9] JMN 12.154.

[10] Vide supra, chapter 3, and chapter 6, pp. 171–172.

[11] JMN 12.152

[12] See particularly JMN 5.91, 505, and 507 (1838), and 6.71 (1838).

universal laws, such agitation seemed to him absurdly futile and confirmed him in his resolution to keep his distance.

Although the circumstances were in his eyes more immediately alarming, Emerson reacted in a similar manner to the economic crisis of 1837. He saw the signs clearly and did not seek to conceal their seriousness: financial institutions went bankrupt, prices collapsed, and factories closed, throwing tens of thousands of workers out of their jobs[13]—and jeopardizing domestic tranquility, since unemployment threatened to rouse the idle and resourceless mobs to riot. It is true that, though present at the cataclysm, Emerson did not himself suffer its consequences to any great degree. In the small town of Concord, still dominated by an essentially rural economy, physical violence was hardly to be feared; and the Boston banks (in which the majority of his assets were deposited) resisted the storm better than did those of New York, Philadelphia, and Baltimore.[14] But this relative immunity helped him to contemplate the disaster with a still more detached curiosity; in the collapse of fortunes, in the shower of bankruptcies, he read a terrifying lesson about the nature of the universe:

> The black times have a great scientific value. It is an epoch so critical a philosopher would not miss. . . . What was, ever since my memory, solid continent, now yawns apart and discloses its composition and genesis. I learn geology the morning after an earthquake. I learn fast on the ghastly diagrams of the cloven mountains & upheaved plain and the dry bottom of the Sea. The roots of orchards and the cellars of palaces and the cornerstones of cities are dragged into melancholy sunshine. I see the natural fracture of the stone. I see the tearing of the tree & learn its fibre & its rooting. The Artificial is rent from the eternal.[15]

The fact is that Emerson could measure the extent of the damage with such serenity because once again he was able to make use of the law of compensation on his own behalf; the very extremity of the catastrophe seemed a providential warning and persuaded him once and for

[13] See JMN 5.304 and 327 (April–May 1837). On the gravity and the political consequences of the crisis see Samuel Rezneck, "The Social History of an American Depression: 1837–1843," *American Historical Review* 40, (July 1935), pp. 662–687.

[14] William Charvat, "American Romanticism and the Depression of 1837," *Science and Society* 2, (Winter 1937), pp. 67–82, observes that on the whole Massachusetts suffered little from the depression; railroad construction, for example, was not at all hindered by it.

[15] JMN 5.332–333 (May 22, 1837). The same metaphor is developed in the speech on education Emerson gave at Providence on June 10, 1837.

all (as he thought) to turn his back on society.[16] The true remedy for social calamity, he notes in his journal, is sleep; and the nonchalant bumblebee he celebrates the same year in one of his poems applies this prudent advice by instinct: "Woe and Want thou canst outsleep. / Want and Woe which torture us / Thy sleep makes ridiculous."[17] But this somersault of Emerson's does not, a few days later, keep him from drawing up in due form a certificate of bankruptcy that acknowledges the end of one era and salutes the beginning of the next:

> Society has played out its last stake; it is checkmated. . . . Pride, and Thrift, & Expediency, who jeered and chirped and were so well pleased with themselves and made merry with the dream as they termed it of philosophy & love: Behold they are all flat and here is the Soul erect and Unconquered still. . . . Let me begin anew. Let me teach the finite to know its Master. Let me ascend above my fate and work down upon my world.[18]

Emerson had thus imperceptibly passed from speculative acceptance to spiritual action. In disillusioning him, the crisis of 1837 had thrown him still more completely than before on his own resources. The time of cosmic contemplation and universal harmony was past. The best service he could now render his contemporaries was to arouse and nurture the inward energy in virtue of which each of us can, regardless of social, economic, and material conditions, attain fullness and balance of life. We are back to "The American Scholar," which represents in its primal intensity precisely this same determination to awaken those who slumber. In not giving that text a carefully defined frame, Emerson intended to show that what counts is only the activity of the mind and the infinitely supple process of its growth. In just the same way, the lecture series he gave the following winter under the title of "Human Culture" situated itself unequivocally (but not belligerently) precisely at the community's edge: "I bear society no ill-will. I am willing that the powers that be and the shows that show should last as long as time, so they do not insist on my cooperation and good word. If they do, I draw my-

[16] This capacity for spiritual integration is the subject of Kenneth Burke's "Acceptance and Rejection," *Southern Review* 2 (Winter 1937), pp. 600–632; later included in Burke's *Attitudes Towards History* (New York, 1937). Burke writes that "as a transcendentalist, [Emerson] employs a variant of the same device that Hegel developed, and that Marx proposed to secularize. The pressure of good–evil conflicts on 'one' level brought forth the necessity for a solution, and this solution moved the issue to a 'higher' level."

[17] "The Humble-Bee" (W 9.40). The poem in fact seems the unexpected ricochet of the economic crisis. Cf. JMN 5.327 (May 14, 1837): "the humblebee & the pine warbler seem to me the proper objects of attention in these disastrous times."

[18] JMN 5.331–332 (May 21, 1837).

self into the shell of a deaf and dumb contumacy."[19] In so doing, Emerson could with good reason profess his civic loyalty; he was no Socrates endangering the laws of the city, rather he was helping democracy to realize the ennobled image it had formed of itself even before the Revolution.[20]

Stephen Whicher justly remarks that the concept of culture seems to fit better with the last phase of Emerson's thought, in which it encompasses the totality of influences contributing to humanize what in each individual is raw and aggressive.[21] In 1837 the word is used in an altogether different sense. It suggests the unfolding, the education of the faculties dormant within us, which we alone are responsible for awakening; it describes the new relation arising between us and the world when we have become aware of their power; it leads to the hydrostatic paradox (one of Emerson's favorite images), which metaphorically represents each individual's capacity to balance the rest of the universe. The whole of the series thus represents Emerson's most systematic attempt to illustrate the universality of human nature. *Homo sum, humani nihil a me alienum puto*—it is difficult not to be reminded of Terence's line when Emerson comes in the last part of his introductory lecture to sum up the means of culture that are offered us:

> *Proportion* certainly is a great end of Culture. . . . There are two ways of cultivating the Proportion of Character: 1. The Habit of attending to all sensations & putting ourselves in a way to receive a variety as by attending spectacles, visiting theatres, prisons, senates, factories, ships, museums, churches, & hells. . . . 2. The other mode of cultivating Gradation forming a just Scale is to compare the depth of thought to which different objects appeal.[22]

It would, of course, be silly to claim that Emerson treats the immense subject he has chosen satisfactorily—and uselessly silly, since the limits of our nature resist such treatment (as he himself recognizes, moreover, in a sentence omitted from the passage just quoted). He did, however,

[19] "Human Culture," lecture 6, "Being and Seeming" (EL 2.298).

[20] "The furious democracy which, in this country from the beginning of its history, has shown a wish, as the royal governors complained, to leave out men of mark and send illiterate and low persons as deputies, —a practice not unknown at this day—, is only a perverse or as yet obstructed operation of the same instinct, —a stammering and stuttering out of impatience to articulate the awful words: 'I am' " ("Human Culture," lecture 1, "Introduction" [EL 2.214]).

[21] See Whicher, *Freedom and Fate*, pp. 84–85. The best example is doubtless the chapter of *The Conduct of Life* called, in fact, "Culture."

[22] JMN 5.435–436 (November 24, 1837). The passage was included with only slight modifications in the first lecture of "Human Culture."

choose the expository method that best suited his design. Instead of drawing up a monotonous, yet inevitably incomplete list of the situations and circumstances that foster culture, he chose the more dramatic procedure of highlighting contrasted pairs: to the practical powers of the hand he opposed the contemplative tendencies of the eye and ear, to the intellect and its impersonal love of truth he juxtaposed the emotional needs of the heart, and as a pendant to the hero's boldness and pride he depicted the selfless humility of the saint.[23] And precisely because he did not even attempt to reconcile these reciprocally antagonistic virtues, he managed to give a dynamic image of the human condition and to suggest in depth the flexibility by which according to the dictates of the moment we can be either tender or violent, creative or receptive, distant or solicitous.[24] The secret of the cultured man as Emerson conceives of him at this period is to have no center of gravity—or rather to shift his center at every moment, in response to the play of forces that continually arrange themselves in him in new ways.[25] In the last analysis, the series can be viewed as a sequence of variations on the theme of Proteus.

For all his confidence in our ability to control circumstance, however, Emerson also and no less acutely recognizes that our lives pass through certain crises and that the most momentous of these is that of vocation; he devotes to this subject the substance of his second lecture, titled, rather inaccurately, "Doctrine of the Hands." While the disastrous effects of the recent depression are not explicitly discussed, one senses that their shadow still stretches over men's minds, and in particular over those of the young; and it is to the young that Emerson speaks first, like an elder whose struggle has not been easy but who for that reason has the right to express himself with authority. At the outset he situates the problem in the realm of morality and principle: nothing, he says, should be done for money that should not be done for its own sake, which is to say that the only work that does not degrade us is that which we choose

[23] A summary of the lectures composing this series is in Cabot, *Memoir*, 2.733–737. The titles have evidently been chosen within the dramatic perspective we are considering; but when Emerson selected only the seventh and eighth lectures ("Prudence" and "Heroism") for publication in the first series of his *Essays*, that perspective was considerably obscured.

[24] This seems to have escaped Henry David Gray in his otherwise penetrating and lucid *Emerson: A Statement of New-England Transcendentalism as Expressed in the Philosophy of Its Chief Exponent* (Stanford, Calif., 1917). Gray thinks that in the lecture series currently under discussion Emerson is trying in vain to find "the most impossible of compromises"; in fact he seems rather to be claiming not to explain but to describe the wonders of human nature from the viewpoint of a "believing man" (he applies the term to himself at the end of the first lecture).

[25] In this sense, the most perfect poetical expression of the ideal under discussion is the Whitman of *Song of Myself*.

freely, in accord with our particular aptitudes, and in which we take pleasure. When society seeks to intervene and to coerce our decision, it is our strict obligation to resist, whatever the price of that act of independence may be. Poverty, he reminds his hearers, is not necessarily a cause of affliction; the weak fear it, to be sure, but the strong make it the shield of their integrity.

Emerson thus gradually reaches a point at which he recommends a mode of life curiously prefiguring the experiment Thoreau was to try ten years later. And like Thoreau, Emerson is appalled at the spectacle of our joyless social conventions; the appeal he here makes to his young countrymen recalls the first chapter of *Walden*: "[The young American] is now to convert the warlike part of his nature, always the attractive, always the salient; the almighty part, and which lies in the lukewarm milky dog days of common village life quite stupid, & so leaves common life so unattractive." Let him accept a broken family with a light heart, let him see his protectors abandon him unsaddened; the new horizons of his liberty justify great sacrifices. "It is an immense gain if he reckon it well to have no longer false feelings & conventional appearances to consult. A few shillings a day will keep out cold & hunger & he will not need to study long how to get a few shillings a day honestly."[26] On the conditions and circumstances of this new life, Emerson, who has no patience with practical details, sees no need to dwell; it is of course to Thoreau's credit to have discovered through his interest in them their inexhaustible symbolic resources. But this first approximation of the theories developed in *Walden* is worth citing, because it already suggests the astonishing parallels between these two minds and raises the problem of their influence on each other. I shall return to it later in this chapter.

For the common run of men, however, Emerson is willing to speak a different language. He accepts the young American's ambition to succeed, provided it not be furthered by the dishonest aids of financial speculation. The factual lesson taught him by the recent depression stimulates him to a wholesale condemnation of the new economic practices developing around him and to a call for a return to the prudent moderation of earlier generations.[27] With perhaps one exception—that avail-

[26] JMN 5.420–421. The two passages were included in their entirety in "Doctrine of the Hands."

[27] In so doing Emerson seems much more a Jacksonian than a Whig. Marvin Meyers, *The Jacksonian Persuasion* (Stanford, Calif., 1957), throws light on the sentimental and nostalgic component of the Jacksonian program: to the Democrats every form of credit seems intrinsically bad because it makes the borrower a servant; they dream of restoring to human relations the nobility and simplicity they possessed before the iniquitous practice was invented.

able to those well-born young men who receive as their portion both wealth and an honored name—the only way open to youth is that of effort, perseverance, and, above all, patience:

> The true way of beginning is by austere humility and lowness. Leave far off the borrowed capital, and raise an estate from the seed. Begin with the hands, and earn one cent; then two; then a dollar; then stock a basket; then a barrow; then a booth; then a shop; then a warehouse, and not on this dangerous balloon of a credit make his first structure. Nor is this course merely theoretical. It has been done. Franklin, William Hutton and many of New England's merchant-princes are men of this merit.[28]

Emerson's recourse here to the example of eminent forebears betrays a certain weakness of thought. In the face of the formidable and irreversible operation of the economic forces now let loose, Emerson can only turn away with a feeling of embarrassment. Proud isolation and an imagined return to a golden age are only two manners, varying in difficulty but equal in futility, of denying the pressures of the external world. Emerson was led subsequently to recognize that those pressures were inescapable and even managed to incorporate them into his philosophy, as will be demonstrated in examining his attitude toward the reforming zeal soon to spread over New England. But (and his course here is more revealing of his instinctive attachments and sympathies than he would have liked to admit) he had first to consider the problem of his relations with society within the narrow and respectable context of the Boston intelligentsia. If that confrontation had its own considerable asperity, it was because it quickly became personal—as often happens when elites are in danger.

We have by a roundabout path returned to that need of Emerson's for active presence and visible witness which was mentioned at the end of the preceding chapter. To the extent that he identified himself with the persona of the American Scholar and took upon himself that persona's responsibilities and hopes, Emerson could not long hope to maintain toward society the position of somewhat sulky indifference that he claimed was most reasonable. In certain cases, peaceful coexistence seemed merely the product of wishful thinking, and the retreat within oneself an act of cowardice. So Emerson thought at any rate when he resolved early in 1837 to undertake the public defense of Bronson Alcott. The incident that provoked his intervention exhibits the odd mixture of courage and absurdity characteristic of Alcott and at the same

[28] "Human Culture," lecture 2, "Doctrine of the Hands" (EL 2.242).

time gives some idea of what Boston life was like during this period of Transcendentalist effervescence. Late in 1835, Alcott had begun in his Tremont Street school a study of the Gospels, following the method described by his assistant Elizabeth Peabody in a little book that came out a few months later, called *Record of a School Exemplifying the General Principles of Spiritual Culture*. Taking up from a new angle the experiment Plato describes in the *Meno*, Alcott attempted to lead his pupils to discover within themselves the divine concept of man as it is expressed in Jesus. Throughout the course, Peabody took notes, and Alcott decided to publish them. She urged him to suppress certain passages—on birth and circumcision—that might create scandal by their very innocence, but in vain. Alcott went further, in fact, and offered his fellow citizens the complete record of the course, under the programmatic title of *Record of the Conversations on the Gospels Held in Mr Alcott's School, Unfolding the Doctrine and Discipline of Human Culture*.[29] The Boston papers were quick to protest against this "visionary Pedagogue" who claimed to bring light to our dark world and corrupted youth while claiming to educate it.[30] Emerson, who had visited Alcott's school and approved of his methods, could not abandon his friend in such straits. The cause he was thus serving was moreover his own, since both men had taken on themselves the task of revealing to their contemporaries the abundant wealth of human nature (they used the expression "Human Culture" in the same sense). Accordingly, he decided to send the principal Boston dailies a letter, in which he vouched for the innocence and loftiness of Alcott's intentions, paid tribute to the originality of his pedagogy, and stood up against the unjust accusations aimed at Alcott even before his accusers had taken the time to frame a knowledgeable judgment of his enterprise.[31] Only the *Boston Courier* printed the letter, however; and the editor told his readers that his own condemnation of Alcott still stood.

Beyond the particular facts, which after all amount to very little, the interest of the episode is in its inward resonance. Considering the disingenuous attacks of the press, and knowing that he has done all one could legitimately ask of him, Emerson nonetheless reproaches himself

[29] *The Transcendentalists: An Anthology*, ed. Perry Miller (Cambridge, Mass., 1950), pp. 150–156, prints selections from the book; the childlike logic it manifests, unintentionally and with a fine poetical touch calling our adult concepts into question, abundantly justifies Peabody's fears.

[30] Rusk (L 2.61) quotes a few sentences from the article that the *Daily Centinel and Gazette* of March 22, 1837 devoted to Alcott under the ironic title of "A New System."

[31] Part of the letter is printed in G. W. Cooke, *Ralph Waldo Emerson: His Life, Writings and Philosophy* (Boston, 1881), p. 58.

in his journal for his paralysis in times of action: "the Newspapers persecute Alcott. I have never more regretted my inefficiency to practical ends. I was born a seeing eye not a helping hand."[32] The disturbance is further reflected, and very significantly so, in a letter he wrote to Alcott about the same time to express his sympathy. Not only did he reveal in it the choleric disdain aroused in him by Alcott's detractors; he also advised his friend not to consume himself in an empty struggle, and to direct his efforts rather to the more important territory of the written word:

> I hate to have all the little dogs barking at you, for you have something better to do than to attend to them: but every beast must do after its kind, & why not these? And you will hold by yourself & presently forget them. Whatever you do at school or concerning the school, pray let not the pen halt, for that must be your last & longest lever to lift the world withal.[33]

Not a little surprisingly, in view of his incorrigible love for grand abstractions, the gentle Alcott refused to follow Emerson here, and strongly reproached him (in his journal) for not having enough respect for persons, and loving only ideas.[34] But Emerson, as was his habit, stuck to his guns; returning in another letter to the question of a writer's primary obligation, he limited himself to explaining somewhat more clearly his personal reasons for not taking part in controversies.[35]

His conscience persisted, however, in getting in the way of the doctrine he preached. The Cherokee Indian affair, in the spring of 1838, caught him in the same contradiction and caused a still more acute discomfort; the matter was, to be sure, of intrinsically greater seriousness than was the half-heroic, half-farcical incident of Alcott's nonconform-

[32] JMN 5.298 (April 16, 1837).

[33] Letter to Alcott of March 24, 1837 (L 2.61–62).

[34] The passage deserves to be quoted; it shows convincingly that a mind can be both perceptive and dreamily speculative: "he holds men and things at a distance; pleases himself with using them for his own benefit, and as means of gathering material for his own work. He does not believe in the actual; his sympathies are all intellectual. He persuades me to leave the actual, devote myself to the speculative, and embody my thought in written works. Emerson idealizes all things. This idealized picture is the true and real one for him—all else is nought. Even persons are thus idealized, and his interest in them, and their influence over him exist no longer than this conformity appears in his imagination" (quoted in *The Genius and Character of Emerson*, ed. F. B. Sanborn [Boston, 1885], p. 53).

[35] In the letter to Alcott of May 10, 1837 (L 2.74–75), Emerson writes: "I should prefer some manual or quite mechanical labor . . . to any attempts to realize my idea in any existing forms called intellectual or spiritual, where, by defying every settled usage in society, I should be sure to sour my own temper."

ity. Since the previous decade, Georgia had laid claim to a portion of the Cherokees' land and had argued in particular that the federal government had exceeded its rights in drawing up a treaty guaranteeing the Cherokees the possession of the mountainous area into which they had fled at the end of the eighteenth century. Georgia's claim had at first met with Congressional opposition, and President Adams had dispatched federal troops for the Indians' protection. But when Jackson took office he recalled those troops—which amounted to leaving Georgia free to act at will. The Supreme Court, however, through the voice of John Marshall, decided in favor of the Cherokees. In an effort to remedy a rapidly deteriorating situation, in 1835 a delegate of the federal government and several representatives of the Cherokees settled on a dubious plan by which these latter agreed to leave the contested lands and move west of the Mississippi for a sum of five million dollars.

That a vast majority of the Indians had been scandalously mistreated and were indeed threatened with expulsion by violence escaped only the willfully blind; in Concord, where the policies of the Democrats had never been much esteemed, people organized a protest meeting, at which several speakers expressed their indignation and won approval for sending a petition to Congress. At this point a Mrs. Nathan Brooks, wife of a local banker and the first person to interest Emerson in the affair, pressed him to write to President Van Buren. Emerson hesitated, tried to withdraw, and finally and reluctantly yielded.[36] The letter was published by a Washington paper;[37] the wretched Indians were nonetheless forced to leave their Georgia land.

Parallel to this intrinsically consequential political crisis was Emerson's own personal drama, the drama of a divided conscience; and on two occasions the journal records his discouraged reflections on the matter:

> This tragic Cherokee business which we stirred at a meeting in the church yesterday will look to me degrading & injurious do what I can. It is like dead cats around one's neck. . . . I stir in it for the sad reason that no other mortal will move & if I do not, why it is left undone.

[36] These details are taken from Townsend Scudder, *Concord: American Town* (Boston, 1947), p. 157, and from Rusk's notes, L 2.126–127. Kenneth W. Cameron, *The Transcendentalists and Minerva*, 3 vols. (Hartford, 1958), 2.469, cites the following passage from the journal of a certain George Moore, dated May 20, 1838: "drank tea at Mrs. Emerson's. Mr. E., when we were expressing our joy that his letter to the President had been published, said that all that was put into his heart by the women, and that he was only *the pen in their fingers*" (italics Moore's).

[37] It is printed in Cabot, *Memoir*, 2.697–702 (appendix D) and in W 11.87–96.

> The amount of it, be sure, is merely a Scream but sometimes a scream is better than a thesis.[38]

Nonetheless, when the moment came to write the promised letter, Emerson found the proper tone; the letter as written seems neither an impulsive or angry gesture nor a banal supplication but the solemn protest of one citizen unobsequiously addressing another. It was Emerson's initial attempt in the genre, but with striking competence he took his place in the great democratic tradition of civic protest. Decent, simple people we were committed to protect have been cheated, he asserts;[39] if government does not redeem itself it is ruined, and we are ruined with it, because no principle can be flouted with impunity. "A man with your experience in affairs," Emerson concludes with a hint of irony, "must have seen cause to appreciate the futility of opposition to the moral sentiment."[40]

The firmness and elevation of the attitude Emerson adopts (though one might doubt his political savvy[41]) ought, it seems, to have consoled him; in his delicate situation had he not honored his civic obligations without compromising his personal integrity? In fact he felt no such thing: hardly had the letter been sent when his journal recorded not only a quantity of ill temper but also a resentment, only faintly disguised, toward those who had got him into this hornet's nest in the first place:

> Yesterday went the letter to Van Buren a letter hated of me. A deliverance that does not deliver the soul. . . . Yet I accept the Dartmouth college invitation to speak to the boys with great delight. I write my journal, I read my lecture with joy—but this stirring in the philanthropic mud, gives me no peace. I will let the republic alone until the republic comes to me.
>
> I fully sympathise, be sure, with the sentiment I write, but I accept it rather from my friends than dictate it. It is not my impulse

[38] JMN 5.477 (April 23, 1838); see also JMN 5.475 (April 19).

[39] Emerson considered Indians inferior to whites, but accorded them a capacity for advancement he denied blacks. Among the Emerson papers at the Houghton Library is the draft of a speech, apparently from this time, which lists the Indians' distinctive traits as force, courage, self-control, and a love of revenge coupled with a serene acceptance of adversity. Like Thoreau, Emerson felt considerable respect for the acuteness of the Indians' senses, for their practical skills, and for their intimacy with nature ("Sketch of Speech for the Indians," H.197.9).

[40] "Letter to President Van Buren" (W 11.95).

[41] Emerson barely disguises his disdain for the politicians of the Democratic administration and frankly denounces the degeneracy of political power, pp. 94–95.

> to say it & therefore my genius deserts me, no muse befriends, no music of thought or of word accompanies. Bah![42]

Thus under pressure of the event Emerson was led to define his position toward public power more unambiguously than he had ever done; his deep trust in the order of the universe and his skepticism regarding man's devices for improving it, the feeling that he betrayed himself whenever he left his own orbit, and, last but not least, the testimony of the artist in him protesting against the degradation of externally imposed tasks all joined in condemning any participation in matters of politics and indeed in every organized form of humanitarian action. The history of the next twelve years (till the sinister Fugitive Slave Law, which made his position untenable) consisted in great part of his efforts to remain faithful to the principle of abstention he here imposes on himself.

In many respects a simple inversion, point by point, of Emerson's grounds for inaction in politics would constitute a sufficient explanation of the intensity and influence of his Divinity School address.[43] On this occasion Emerson had as his subject not wretched and pale human artifices but the splendor of moral nature; and as he had long ago discovered, and as was confirmed daily by the fiery inspiration he felt within him, it was his mission to celebrate that nature's beauty and force and to communicate to all men its almost ineffable attraction. Here, with no forced effort on his part, his inward impulses and the demands of society were wonderfully in accord: "always the seer is a sayer."[44] But the very profundity of the fusion thus accomplished requires us to step back a little in explanation.

Despite its apparent tranquility, Emerson's break with the Unitarian church had stung a very sensitive part of him. Not in vain was he the inheritor of a long pastoral tradition; and doctrinal differences and heretical deviations could not keep him from feeling himself a preacher in the depth of his soul. His conscience forbade him to speak officially, so to speak, in God's name, but his need to testify only became more ardent in consequence, and his impatience at the mediocrity of the clergy more intense. During all this time he frequented the Unitarian Church of Concord; but the journals show that he often returned from services discouraged or angered. The luckless preacher decanted from his lofty pulpit a flood of words that flowed past the soul without touching it,

[42] JMN 5.479 (April 26, 1838).

[43] The full title is "An Address Delivered Before the Senior Class in Divinity College, Cambridge, Sunday Evening, July 15, 1838" (W 1.117–151).

[44] W 1.134.

because they had no relation to what the preacher was in himself, what he thought and felt and suffered.[45] Instead of offering his congregation an image of his inward struggles and triumphs, he detained them with inert doctrines contained in books—like the flowers that books are sometimes used to press and dry. Such ministers were of undeniably good will but were grotesquely entangled in a network of empty forms, and Emerson's attitude toward them wavered between pity and disdain:

> The men I have spoken of above—sincere persons who live in shams, are those who accept another man's consciousness for their own, & are in the state of a son who should always suck at his mother's teat. I think Swedenborg ought so to represent them or still more properly, as permanent embryos which received all their nourishment through the umbilical cord & never arrived at a conscious & independent existence.[46]

Emerson was in fact already contemplating the writing of an essay directed to the American clergy, intended to show them the grimness of their theology and, by contrast, the glory and sweetness of the moral nature, when the senior class of the Harvard Divinity School asked him to give the speech that traditionally preceded the young men's entering upon their pastoral duties. Emerson saw in the offer an occasion to make himself heard in the very citadel of Unitarianism and accepted it eagerly. His audience was small—space was limited—but profoundly attentive.

The speech's first phrases recall *Nature*; Emerson opens the door wide to the scents, the sounds, and the colors of the country and transforms them almost immediately by a sort of sensual meditation into spiritual symbols. The tone was thus given and the climate defined. Now, passing through the pronaos of the external world, he could attain to the supreme reality, the law of laws that is revealed to intuition alone and constitutes the very substance of the religious sentiment:

> This sentiment is divine and deifying. It is the beatitude of man. It makes him illimitable. Through it, the soul first knows itself. It

[45] Most often the erring preacher was the Reverend Barzillai Frost, who had become assistant minister at the Unitarian Church of Concord early in 1837, but occasionally Emerson's criticism referred to the chief minister himself—his venerable ancestor Ezra Ripley. Cf. Conrad Wright, "Emerson, Barzillai Frost, and the Divinity School Address," *Harvard Theological Review* 49 (January 1956), pp. 19–43.

[46] JMN 5.465 (March 18, 1838. The journal for 1837 and 1838 records numerous comments on the subject of the preacher, what he is and what he ought to be; see particularly JMN 5.324–325, 361, 463–464, and 500–502, and 7.20–22 and 31.

> corrects the capital mistake of the infant man, who seeks to be great by following the great, and hopes to derive advantages *from another*, —by showing the fountain of all good to be in himself, and that he, equally with every man, is an inlet into the deeps of Reason.[47]

From these words, as from a platform made fast to the center of the universe, Emerson sketches in broad, bright strokes the image of the new minister: he would, Emerson says, no longer aggrandize the person of Jesus to the point of superstition; he would learn to recognize in him the prophet of the human soul, the incarnation not of God but of the divine element in all men; finally, he would himself be capable of becoming for his flock the sign and living expression of Reason rather than its saddening parody. Then Emerson draws by contrast the portrait of the bad preacher, for which the journals provided the sketches, and, unequivocally holding the church responsible for that preacher's spiritual suffocation, in a long peroration he summons the uncertain and straying soul to seek in solitude—that is, in the intimacy of the divine presence—an ideal of excellence in comparison with which all rules and social virtues grow pale. Nothing, he says, could supply the place of inspiration; but where inspiration is, forms and rituals will as by a miracle begin to sing.

For those who follow the course of Emerson's thought step by step, the merit of this speech is in the resplendent passion of the language, the mixture of familiarity and elevation, of virile power and poetry, that raises it above its occasion and makes of it, as it were, the cathedral of Transcendentalism. But there is no corresponding merit in the novelty of its ideas. The ideal minister Emerson describes here is hardly more than a retouching of the American Scholar. Like the scholar, the minister is exhorted to cleanse his experience in the fire of his own thought,[48] to direct his trust to himself rather than to follow the opinion of the majority, to flee ossified forms and empty traditions. If there is a change, it is in the direction of subduing the verbal force and of a more marked insistence on the moral nature of things. Though careful not to dull it, Emerson gave his portrait something of the benevolent courtesy that in Channing's New England often seemed to keep company with the exercise of the ministry. Nor could one accuse him of having sought to settle an old score with the institution at which his theology had been learned; his intention was in no way personal. He sought only to shake off the torpor numbing the social organism and its natural guides.

[47] Divinity School address (W 1.125); the italics are Emerson's.

[48] "The true preacher can be known by this, that he deals out to the people his life, —life passed through the fire of thought" (W 1.138).

On those who heard it the address produced a very strong impression.[49] Here and there some criticisms were probably made, but of limited extent. A few days later, Emerson gave his promised speech on "Literary Ethics" to the students at Dartmouth without incident. What loosed the storm was rather the publication of the address, toward the end of the following month.[50] In a few weeks two camps had formed, while Emerson himself strove to remain aloof. The story of the debate, a sort of Hernani's battle of New England, has often been told.[51] Started by an article of unusual violence in the *Boston Daily Adviser* from the pen of the theologian Andrews Norton ("the old tyrant of the Cambridge Parnassus," as Emerson called him one day[52]) and prolonged by hostile responses from most of the literary and religious journals, the debate centered on the person of Jesus and culminated in the speech Norton gave a year later to the alumni of the Divinity School, under the still-celebrated title of "A Discourse on the Latest Form of Infidelity."[53] One result of the controversy was to deny Emerson access to Harvard till after the Civil War; but more immediately, it made of him the uncontested if involuntary leader of the new school. The venture of the *Dial* is a direct realization of the course set by the Divinity School address. A path had been blazed; there remained only to widen and level it to make it the new king's highway.

The violence and persistence of the agitation generated by this affair, moreover, threw an interesting light on what was held to be the enlight-

[49] We have in particular the testimony of Theodore Parker, who that evening noted in his journal, "in this [Emerson] surpassed himself as much as he surpasses others in a general way. I shall give no abstract, so beautiful, so just, so true, and terribly sublime, was his picture of the faults of the Church in its present position. My soul is roused; and this week I shall write the long-meditated sermons on the state of the Church and the duties of these times" (quoted in Octavius Brooks Frothingham, *The Life of Theodore Parker* [Boston, 1874], pp. 105–106).

[50] See on this subject D. Ellen Trueblood, "The Influence of Emerson's 'Divinity School Address,' " *Harvard Theological Review* 32 (January 1939), pp. 41–56. Trueblood argues from the delay that the young men who were Emerson's contemporaries were more responsive to the subversive force of the address than were the students to whom it was delivered—though it is true that of the latter there were only seven, and none of them ever made much of a reputation.

[51] See in particular Rusk, *Life*, pp. 269–273, and *The Transcendentalists*, ed. Miller, pp. 192–246. At the height of the commotion, Emerson wrote to Carlyle, "at this moment, I would not have you here, on any account. The publication of my "Address to the Divinity College," (copies of which I sent you) has been the occasion of an outcry in all our leading local newspapers against my 'infidelity,' 'pantheism,' & 'atheism.' The writers warn all & sundry against me, & against whatever is supposed to be related to my connexion of opinion, &c; against Transcendentalism, Goethe & *Carlyle*. I am heartily sorry to see this last aspect of the storm in our washbowl" (letter of October 17, 1838 [CEC 197]).

[52] JMN 7.63.

[53] Partially reprinted in *The Transcendentalists*, ed. Miller, pp. 210–213.

ened section of the population. The liberal tolerance freely boasted of among Unitarians had suddenly given way to an equal degree of explosion, rage, and indignation, and in the process laid bare the religious axioms on which the security of the group depended—much as the depression of 1837 had revealed the economic foundations of the nation. By attacking historical Christianity, Emerson came up against an unacknowledged tenet of orthodoxy, which because unacknowledged was all the more stubbornly held. True, Unitarianism had rid itself of certain cumbersome dogmas and reduced the number of its articles of faith; that did not, however, mean that it was prepared to jettison what remained—woe, rather, to the man who sought to lead it to this ultimate step! In the spring of 1840, assessing his latest lecture series, "The Present Age," Emerson confessed that he had stumbled once again over the same obstacle:

> In all my lectures, I have taught one doctrine, namely, the infinitude of the private man. This, the people accept readily enough, & even with loud commendation, as long as I call the lecture, Art; or Politics; or Literature; or the Household; but the moment I call it Religion, —they are shocked, though it be only the application of the same truth which they receive everywhere else, to a new class of facts.[54]

The awareness of this resistant element at the heart of a society he thought he knew thoroughly marked Emerson profoundly and inclined him to issue his appeals in a harsher tone. "The American Scholar" had still been in the optative mood; surrounded by sublime perspectives of universally appealing encouragement and promise, the theological assumptions had gone pretty much unnoticed. The reception of the Divinity School address was for Emerson "an angular intrusion of fact into the smooth world of his thoughts."[55] He could no longer deny that the religious heritage of New England was powerfully opposed to his work of spiritual liberation; he had not only to lift an inert mass but also to conquer an active and solidly entrenched force of resistance, and in the light of that fact even his methods seemed dubious. To show the development of the new orientation that was Emerson's response to this situation will be the aim of the last section of this chapter.

To begin with, the aloof reserve Emerson managed to maintain under the surge of criticism ought not to be taken at its face value. He succeeded in comforting himself only with considerable difficulty. (In read-

[54] JMN 7.342 (April 7, 1840).

[55] The phrase is Whicher's, in *Freedom and Fate*, p. 73.

ing the alternately tranquil and agitated paragraphs of the journal, one has the impression of watching the needle of a fine-tuned seismograph.) After the appearance of Norton's article in the *Boston Daily Advertiser*, Emerson proclaimed himself unmoved because the whole universe supported his cause. He was not, he said, pursuing any selfish or vulgar ambition; he was too fond of his "melons & his woods" to think of founding a sect; he was only an "observer," a "dispassionate reporter," singing out of his love for music and therefore invulnerable.[56] As the debate grew hotter, however, and Emerson found himself publicly exposed both to praise and to blame, a pervasive sense of discomfort took hold of him; in particular the fact that he was overwhelmed with compliments no less than with opprobrium disturbed his equanimity, and gave him the impression that he was being delivered defenseless to his enemies' vengeance.[57] He regretted not knowing how to fish or hunt or farm, should he be ostracized from other activities.[58] He needed to feel about him the calming, almost motherly presence of his wife Lidian; and the tribute of trust he paid her in these difficult days reveals in him an unexpected and touching human fragility.[59]

But in a few weeks the man of faith was himself again. Let him only experience the peace of a starry night, and the wounds of his pride were reduced to their true worth; the vanity of arguments and controversies was clear to a mind bathed in the infinite.[60] Such is the state of mind evident in the celebrated letter Emerson wrote to Henry Ware, his former colleague at the Second Church and now professor of theology at the Divinity School.[61] In it Emerson denies having sought to conduct a polemic against the champions of Unitarianism and protests his incapacity for devising arguments in his defense—it is the credo of Rousseau's Vicar of Savoy all over again, even down to the same calculated innocence: "I will not argue with you, nor even try to win you over; I only want to show you what I believe in the simplicity of my own heart. As I speak, consult yours, and you have done all that I ask."[62] For dialogue, for the exchange of incomplete truths, for reciprocal judgment Emerson substitutes the inward method of illumination; and if illumi-

[56] JMN 7.60 (August 31, 1838).

[57] Cf. JMN 7.65 (September 8, 1838) and 95 ("Censure and Praise"; September 29, 1838).

[58] See JMN 7.96 (September 30, 1838).

[59] Cf. ibid. (September 29, 1838) and 112 (October 20, 1838).

[60] See JMN 7.98 ("Compensation"; October 5, 1838).

[61] Dated October 8, 1838 (L 2.166–167). Cabot also prints the text, and with it the communication from Ware it answers (*Memoir*, 2.691–694 [Appendix B]).

[62] From Rousseau's *Émile*, book 4 (*Oeuvres complètes* [Paris, 1882], 2.236–237).

nation is both uncontrollable and evasive, that is a price he is willing to pay for the cherished certainties with which it provides him.

This sort of priesthood—for it is as a priesthood that Emerson in the letter quoted above conceives of the testimony offered by intuition—had the advantage of simplicity; but at root it was more difficult and demanding than any other, because it cast him implacably upon his own resources and at the same time constrained him to mix with the crowd, for which he was to be the burning coal rekindling the embers. At certain moments Emerson would remember Catholic cathedrals or the beauties of the Anglican liturgy, and a feeling of nostalgia would steal over him; yet he refused with all his heart and soul to be a preacher or a minister. This was a troubling dilemma, and the deep cause of it escaped him: "something is wrong, I see not what."[63] A poem he wrote in November 1839, appropriately called "The Problem," was organized around the same contradiction, stated in the first six lines:

> I like a church; I like a cowl;
> I like a prophet of the soul;
> And on my heart monastic aisles
> Fall like sweet strains, or pensive smiles;
> Yet not for all his faith can see
> Would I that cowled churchman be.[64]

The remainder of the poem sheds light on the riddle: Chrysostom, Augustine, Jeremy Taylor ("the Shakespeare of theologians") served God no better than did Michelangelo working on the ceiling of St. Peter's, or the swallow fashioning her nest. It is necessary, Emerson implies, to extend the idea of priesthood to include all creation; the same "fiery Pentecost" burns in the heart of every living thing.

At a still deeper level, the controversy over the Divinity School address necessitated Emerson's acknowledgment of another problem, namely that of communicating truth. Emerson had spoken in entire sincerity, had uttered words of life; and by a movement of mind incomprehensible to him his contemporaries had closed their ears. A page of the journal written as Emerson was regaining confidence denounces in a sort of sacred frenzy his contemporaries' batlike fear of the light of day, their cowardly attachment to lies and illusions; but, he prophesies, the force of thought is not a force one can resist, and light will spring up

[63] JMN 7.60 (August 28, 1838); see also 7.174, 194, and 196–197 (1839).

[64] W 9.6. On the poem's philosophical underpinnings and its sources in Emerson's reading, see Kenneth W. Cameron, "Early Background for Emerson's 'The Problem,' " ESQ 27.2 (1962), pp. 37–46.

upon the ruins of banks and cities.[65] Still, an obscure feeling of failure remained deep in Emerson's mind; it is crystallized, as Stephen Whicher has shown, in the ironic allegory "Uriel."[66] Uriel (the name given in Milton's *Paradise Lost* to the archangel of the sun) brings the inhabitants of heaven the revelation of the supreme law; but this revelation disturbs their image of the universe ("the balance-beam of Fate [is] bent"), so that Uriel's words are received with hostility and the archangel is forced to retreat, stripped of his rank and bereft of his power;

> Whether doomed to long gyration
> In the sea of generation,
> Or by knowledge grown too bright
> To hit the nerve of feebler sight.[67]

In "Uriel" and "The Problem" one can see clearly the particular significance of Emerson's poems in the context of his work as a whole. Not only do they illustrate ideas or situations and elevate them by the play of images to a loftier dignity; they also humanize them. They correct the excessive abstraction that constantly threatens Emerson's idealism by showing us how that idealism takes on resonance and color within his own consciousness. They are like pearls, the brilliant encrustations formed around the impurities of existence;[68] the best of them (one thinks of Matthiessen's penetrating analysis of "Days"[69]) succeed precisely in bringing together and fusing within a single spiritual experience the act of faith and the reality's denial of it. Conversely, the author of the lectures strives to communicate a belief in the absolute coincidence of principles and facts, inundates the least corner of shadow with a flood of light, and leads his hearers in an irresistible advance; it is this latter aspect of Emerson that is brought forward now in considering the

[65] See JMN 7.126–127 (October 30, 1838).

[66] See W 9.13–15. The editor's notes (408–410) contain a rough sketch of the present analysis, but it was Whicher who gave it its full development, first in his unpublished thesis "The Lapse of Uriel" (Harvard University, 1942), then in *Freedom and Fate*, pp. 72–76. See also Kenneth W. Cameron's "Coleridge and the Genesis of Emerson's 'Uriel,' " *Philological Quarterly* 30 (April 1951), pp. 212–217.

[67] W 9.14.

[68] In this sense Emerson's poetry would offer an excellent illustration of the theory developed in Robert Penn Warren's "Pure and Impure Poetry," *Kenyon Review* (Spring 1943), reprinted in *Criticism: The Foundations of Modern Literary Judgment*, ed. Mark Schorer et al. (New York, 1948), pp. 366–378.

[69] *American Renaissance: Art and Expression in the Age of Emerson and Whitman* (1941, repr. New York, 1968), pp. 55–64.

lecture series of 1838–1839 and 1839–1840, both distinguished by a success that Emerson himself found surprising.

In naming the earlier of these series "Human Life,"[70] Emerson committed himself to nothing in particular; moreover, to judge from the titles of the ten lectures composing it, they did not seem to have much in common: what, one wonders, can join "Home" and "Comedy," "Demonology" and "Love" and "The Protest"? In fact, however, the unity of the series is real and profound—if one is willing to see in it an illustration of the "Doctrine of the Soul" that Emerson chose as the title of the introductory lecture. "The Philosophy of History" was given under the banner of harmony and contemplation; "Human Culture" was presented as a dynamic exploration of the human condition; "Human Life" rather describes its ultimate goal and traces the ascent by which we approach the Oversoul.[71] As if to answer the skeptics scandalized by the Divinity School address, Emerson lingers over his description of the irresistible work of Reason in us; he shows how it gradually detaches us from our wealth, our friends, our habits, how it teaches us to live as strangers in the bosom of our own families, how above all it allows us to pierce through the veil of appearances so as to accomplish our spiritual destiny. The first section of the series is wholly concerned with this powerful though somewhat chilly current of thought, in which one is tempted to see Emerson's native element. "Home" becomes a stubborn flight from the fixed and the particular, a striving for the infinite, a sort of pilgrimage into the essence of things. "The School" keeps the soul company in its self-discovery through the data of experience; "Love" transcends attachment to particular persons to lose itself in the "society of all true and pure souls."[72] Only with the fifth lecture, "Genius" (analyzed in the previous chapter) does Emerson permit himself the exultation of contemplating Reason's consummate work. But the end of the series disrupts that harmony, long sought and only briefly achieved; in "Tragedy," "Comedy," and "Demonology," Emerson examines the mingling of the universal and the individual in our daily life, and thus circles back to where he began.

I have thus far intentionally ignored the sixth lecture in the series, "The Protest," not only because it touches more closely on the subject of this book but also because of the dramatic quality of the theme it discusses. Whicher draws twice on this lecture in *Freedom and Fate*, in the

[70] EL 3.1–171; summary in Cabot, *Memoir*, 2.737–741.

[71] The essay that bears this famous title (W 1.265–297) is much indebted to the series "Human Life," particularly to lectures 1 and 3 ("Doctrine of the Soul" and "The School").

[72] W 2.182. The essay "Love" in the first series of *Essays* (W 2.167–188) is almost an exact transcription of the lecture "Love" in "Human Life."

course of an argument that recognizes its unusual interest;[73] but the idealist perspective in which he locates it prevents him from assessing the full extent of its significance, which is at once and indissolubly autobiographical, social, and intellectual. From the simultaneous presence of these three aspects derive both the intensity of the lecture's argument and the aphoristic vigor of its style.

Insofar as Emerson thought of the life of Reason as a ceaseless, unwearied movement, distancing us ever more from the world of facts and continually revealing new horizons, he was vulnerable to the brutal refutations of experience; we are not, after all, pure spirits. The first sentences of the essay "The Oversoul" say as much and recognize that inspiration comes to us by fits and starts, in brief and isolated moments, whereas our imperfections and vices have the dubious advantage of long duration. It is only by establishing a qualitative difference within the sequence of moments that Emerson, anticipating Bergson, can circumvent the obstacle; "some thoughts," he writes, always find us young, and keep us so."[74] But there is another ebb against which we are completely helpless, that is, our growing old: the further we advance in life, the less frequent the mind's illuminations.[75] It is perhaps because the scandal over the Divinity School address had imperceptibly sapped Emerson's mental energies that the journal for September 1838 records for the first time an avowal of fatigue and, as it were, of inner attrition: "After thirty a man is too sensible of the strait limitations which his physical constitution sets to his activity. The stream feels its banks, which it had forgotten in the run & overflow of the first meadows."[76]

"The Protest" deals with this bitter premonition of decline but extends it to the whole human race, thus introducing into "Human Life" its one authentically tragic element:

> The Fall of Man is the first word of History and the last fact of experience. In the written annals, or in the older tradition of every nation, this dark legend is told of the depravation of a once pure and happy society. And in the experience of every individual, somewhat analogous is recognized. . . . What is the account to be given of this persuasion that has taken such deep root in all minds? What but this that it is an universal fact that man is always in his actual life lapsing from the Commandments of the Soul? . . . There is

[73] Whicher, *Freedom and Fate*, pp. 100–103 and 126–127.

[74] "The Oversoul" (W 2.272).

[75] Here one can only refer the reader to Whicher's remarkable analysis of this decline in chapters 5–7 of *Freedom and Fate*.

[76] JMN 7.71. The paragraph is included with some modifications in "The Protest."

> somewhat infirm and retreating in every action, a pause of self-praise; a second thought. He has done well and he says: I have done well, and lo! this is the beginning of ill. . . . This old age, this ossification of the heart; this fat in the brain, this degeneracy is the Fall of Man.[77]

Emerson admits his inability to understand the psychological mechanism at work here but cannot deny its universality: the soldier harks back to his old victories, the scholar catalogs and indexes his opinions—even the saint, once past sixty, cares only to maintain his reputation and prepares to write his memoirs. The whole art of society is to make this horrible stagnation tolerable and even pleasant: "it pillows itself in usages and forms until the man is killed with kindness. Its tediousness is torture to a masculine and advancing temper."[78]

The new element in this critique is that on its rebound it strikes Emerson himself. The compromising and toadying of which society makes its daily bread are bound by an unbroken chain to the decay he is beginning to experience. Despite his efforts, his age connects him with the errors he condemns and disqualifies him in advance for his role of rebellious leader. The necessary protest, the "Redemption" after the "Fall,"[79] can only come from youth; youth alone has the passion and the freedom that had already been the weapons of the American Scholar: "He is of no party, but is the patron of every just cause, of every liberal opinion. . . . He is solicitous only to be whole and true and fair himself, and strangely negligent of producing anything."[80] Nonetheless, as it is in the nature of ideas to be organized into institutions, into laws, into social systems, the young man encounters on his path the ponderous obstacle of established forms, and the drama at once comes to a head. One might imagine that Emerson chose this indirect presentation of the conflict for tactical reasons and that the protagonist is only a projection of himself, charged with life and presence by what one might, following a line of thought suggested by Henry Nash Smith, call Emerson's faculty of personification.[81] In fact this is not the case. One can easily see behind

[77] "Human Life," lecture 6, "The Protest" (EL 3.86–89).

[78] Ibid. The allusion is evidently to Thomas Heywood's *A Woman Killed with Kindness*.

[79] This reinterpretation of the Christian myth ought to have been dealt with in Frederic Carpenter's "The American Myth: Paradise (to Be) Regained," PMLA 74 (December 1959), pp. 599–606, as a companion piece to the classic analysis in which Carpenter shows that the Transcendentalist position is based on a postulate of absolute innocence.

[80] "The Protest" (EL 3.92).

[81] In "Emerson's Problem of Vocation," NEQ 12 (March 1939), pp. 52–67, Smith argues that the scholar, the genius, the visionary, the poet are all representations of the same heroic

the stubbornness Emerson ascribes to youth specific conversations and comments, heard or overheard, that he was at the time scrupulously transcribing.

He had, for example, been struck by the spiritual quality of the "No!" his friend Caroline Sturgis had the courage to hurl in society's face, and in the lecture he amplifies her refusal to the point of making it youth's distinguishing trait.[82] Jones Very also had on several occasions furnished Emerson with examples of resistance to social pressures.[83] It was Thoreau, however, who by the rigor of his principles seems to have impressed him most strongly. The journal of November 10, 1838 records a conversation the two men had during a walk. Thoreau had attacked the idea of property, which for him was an intolerable deprivation of certain natural pleasures and, because he had never given his consent to existing laws, constituted a permanent violation of his person. Emerson had defended the rights of society as best he could and had advised Thoreau to transform his bile into poems. One recalls that Emerson had previously made a similar suggestion to Alcott; but Thoreau was a keener antagonist and offered Emerson a devastating argument:

> He replied, that he feared that that was not the best way; that in doing justice to the thought, the man did not always do justice to himself: the poem ought to sing itself: if the man took too much pains with the expression he was not any longer the Idea himself. I acceded & confessed that this was the tragedy of Art that the Artist was at the expense of the Man. . . . And truly Bolts & Bars do not seem to me the most exalted or exalting of our institutions.[84]

Thoreau was fully taking up the ideal of "Man Thinking" and refusing any fragmentation of its integrity even in the name of art—an embarrassing reminder, since the ideas Emerson was condemned by were his own.

"The Protest" records the lesson submissively. For the first time Emerson is publicly condemning (though by the intermediation of the young man as his surrogate) certain excessive claims of property and

---

type; and their force, he adds, is in their capacity not for logical demonstration but for dramatic revelation and illustration.

[82] JMN 7.23 (June 18, 1838), and "The Protest" (EL 3.90).

[83] "Jones Very came hither two days since & gave occasion to many thoughts on his peculiar state of mind & his relation to society. His position accuses society as much as society names it false & morbid. & much of his discourse concerning society, the church, & the college was perfectly just" (JMN 7.116–117 [October 26, 1838]). See also JMN 7.122–123 (October 28).

[84] JMN 7.143–144. The journal for February 11, 1838 had recorded an earlier encomium of Thoreau's independence and firm principles (JMN 5.452).

also calling into question the dogma according to which a government of laws offers everyone what he deserves to possess. Whether he admits it or not, he already had one foot outside the Federalist fold, and the discomforts of that position would in time compel the other foot to move as well. But the moment had not yet come; in the remainder of his talk, Emerson contents himself with offering a new sketch of that simple, unencumbered life, resolutely centered around Nature, which seems to him the surest means of safeguarding the soul. He thus gave Thoreau as much as he borrowed from him; he took from him the rebellious impulses the extreme courtesy of his nature could not provide,[85] and offered him in recompense the image of a new hero. We cannot here recapture in detail the daily history of their friendship; but we can easily intuit the fertile exchange that was bound to ensue between two men so similar in ideals and so different in temperament.

The weakness of "The Protest" lies in its conclusion and has to do with Emerson's optimism; in the tranquility of his faith he places his trust in purely verbal solutions. After tracing a deeply alarming portrait of the forces bent on our destruction and then raising up against them, like some splendid Achilles, every young man entering the world, he abruptly slackens the dramatic tension and evokes the state of harmony that will succeed the necessary but transient phase of rebellion: "Quite naturally his own path opens before him. His object appears; his aim becomes simple and losing his dread of society which kept him dumb and paralytic he begins to work according to his faculty. He has done protesting: Now he begins to affirm."[86] It is all very well for Emerson to appeal to Michelangelo, to Luther, to Columbus in showing how genius always overcomes its difficulties; the demonstration is not convincing because it substitutes the solved problems of the past for the necessarily unsettled enigmas of the present. Emerson is perhaps the unconscious dupe of the spokesman he has chosen; the young man remains foreign to him, external to him, and it is rather toward the young man's enemy that Emerson is unwittingly but irresistibly drawn. He has yet to make the effort that will portray him to his age in his own person; and it is the result of that effort that Emerson offers his audiences the following winter, in a series of lectures entitled (for once appositely) "The Present Age."

[85] A few days before this walk with Thoreau, Emerson's journal further laments his trepidation in the face of action, the stiff dignity of manner by which the creations of his imagination are kept from blossoming into deeds and positions (JMN 7.131–132).

[86] "The Protest" (EL 3.100). The two paragraphs that conclude the lecture (EL 3.102) are in pencil in the manuscript; as the tone seems less forthright and militant, one wonders whether they might not belong to a later phase of Emerson's thought.

The months that preceded his work on the new series were for Emerson a time of stress, even of crisis. No doubt his inward faith remained intact;[87] but he was saddened to see the distance between promise and act, between ideal perfection and its fulfillment. As in 1832, he went off to the New Hampshire mountains in search of the physical and mental solace he needed;[88] on his return, still divided between ardor and despondency, he decided to mount the platform once again and show how the man of Reason could be entirely present to his age without denying his soul. The demonstration was addressed to himself as much as to others—as he half-confessed in a magnificent letter he wrote at the time to Margaret Fuller:

> I see movement, I hear aspirations, but I see not how the great God prepares to satisfy the heart in a new order of things. No church no state will form itself to the eye of desire & hope. Even when we have extricated ourselves from all the embarrassments of the social problem it does not please the oracle to emit any light on the *mode* of individual life. A thousand negatives it utters clear & strong on all sides, but the sacred affirmative it hides in the deepest abyss. . . . It looks as if there was much doubt, much waiting, to be endured by the best, —the heavy hours. —Perhaps there must be austere elections & determinations before any clear vision of the way is given. Yet eternal joy & a light heart dwell with the Muse forever & ever and the austerity of her true lovers can never be harsh moping & low. Today is ours & today's action; why should I cumber myself with these morrows, these optical illusions, these cobwebs of time? —I hoped not to read lectures again, at least not in the old way but I am about determining to do that chore once more.[89]

Emerson had begun the enterprise in inward apathy; he went on to engage in it all his resources and intellectual energies. None of the previous series had been to this extent the product of his will. Positing proudly that "never was anything gained by admitting the omnipotence of limitations,"[90] he raised the banner of the free and insatiable soul against a closed society, in which every generous intention, every idea sprung of Reason slowly died for lack of air. The series is distinguished

[87] See for example the letter written August 11, 1839 to H. G. O. Blake, a former student at the Divinity School; Emerson encourages Blake to trust in his own thought—which *is* the community, both civic and ecclesiastical, when it obeys eternal truth (L 2.212–213).

[88] See particularly the letter to Margaret Fuller of September 3, 1839 (L 2.220).

[89] Letter of September 6, 1839 (L 2.221–222).

[90] JMN 7.290 (November 6, 1839). The passage is included in "Reforms," the sixth lecture in the series.

from its predecessors not so much by its ideas as by its tone. In it Emerson speaks with the authority of a prophet whom the wonders and allurements of his period leave untouched, and indeed reinforce in his inward conviction. At the same time, he knows that he is making his way as if on a tightrope; seeking to confront the ephemeral traits of the age with the demands of the soul, he is in danger of sacrificing the thrust of inspiration to the minute precision of analysis—or the reverse. He has to sympathize without succumbing, understand and yet not forgive.[91] "The Present Age" owes a good part of its packed intensity to the antagonistic effects of these two inclinations.

In the first lecture, Emerson goes right to the heart of the matter and offers his audience an interpretation of the age. As in every age, he explains, two parties are struggling for the minds of men: the party of the past, or the establishment, and the party of the future, or of movement. The first, though entrenched firmly in positions called property, law, and custom, is doomed to defeat by the very nature of things. In vain have certain eminent men—Burke, Coleridge—attempted to win for conservatism the fresh force of youth; they were going against Reason itself and striving to wither its inexhaustible fecundity. The success of the opposing party has never been more certain, as witness those uneducated philanthropists who reason or plead like anointed orators because justice speaks in their mouths and sharpens their talents. But, Emerson continues, though a break with numbing tradition is indeed characteristic of contemporary America, the soul has been cheated of its victory by a usurper; the modern age is the age of the Understanding made king, the age of analysis, the age of trade. As early as 1823, the journal recorded a critique of mercantile activity;[92] but that critique seems a timid warning next to the thundering malediction Emerson now hurls down:

> Commerce realizes this autocracy to the senses. Analysis, like the Devil, promised the world to the man if he would sell his soul, and Commerce is the fulfilment of the bargain. Commerce which looks at every fact only in one aspect: its gainfulness, which turns its penny amidst sublime scenery, and on the worst calamities: on a

[91] While brooding over the series, Emerson recorded in his journal an account of the delicate position he had attempted to maintain in the form of a parable: "*Character* PLUS *Sensibility*. They were self centred: Willow was not. He went to them more than was due. He would be poised, & they should pass & repass. Yet was this mobility of his only superficial & in manners. The flintiest brow in the hall did not surmount a purpose as fast as his to its natural objects, or one as impatient of a false position. He was a rocking stone always tilting but never overthrown" (JMN 7.337 [February 3, 1840]).

[92] Vide supra, chapter 3.

> revolution, a famine, a fire, a war, a plague, sees everything partially.[93]

The desire to get rich is an epidemic; it subordinates government to economic interests, degrades education, uses religion itself to goad the appetite for profit: "There is nothing more important in the culture of man than to resist the dangers of Commerce. An admirable servant, it has become the hard master."[94]

At the end of the first lecture it is clear that Emerson is breaking away from the party of the future (in the sense given that term by most of his contemporaries) no less than from the party of the past. The following lectures seek to trace, amidst the thickets of the age, the lonely, glorious path of the truly living soul.[95] Thus in "Politics," his fourth lecture, the title of which must in some eyes have seemed an impertinent irony, Emerson—under the pretext of revealing the foundations of political reality—sketches a doctrine marked unmistakably by the traits of anarchism. "The Wise Man is the State"; "Character is the True Theocracy";[96] these brutally simple aphorisms are now the distillation of the law and the prophets. All governments are not only useless but also pernicious, because their existence requires that we surrender to them a portion of our autonomy. The body politic is condemned before its birth. Conversely, if some philanthropic itch drives us to take responsibility for our fellow men, we have to remember that the highest virtue always looks inward: "When, moved by love, a man . . . does at an immense personal sacrifice . . . somewhat public and self-immolating, like the fight of Leonidas, or the hemlock of Socrates, or the cross of Christ, it is not done for others, but to fulfil a high necessity of this proper character; the benefit to others is merely contingent, is not contemplated by the doer."[97] Strictly speaking, we can be said to live side by side like so many omnipotent monads; but for the government of the world to attain perfection we would need only to give unfailing obedience to the profound law of our being.

The same exasperated passion for independence and integrity inspires the sixth and seventh lectures, "Reforms" and "Religion," which one can properly discuss together because at root they deal with the same subject. Considering the attempts at reform his century has thus

[93] "The Present Age," lecture 1, "Introduction" (EL 3.454).

[94] Lecture 1, "Introduction" (EL 3.190).

[95] Cabot gives a copious and characteristically uneven summary, *Memoir*, 2.741–747.

[96] "The Present Age," lecture 4, "Politics" (EL 3.243 and 479). The maxims turn up in slightly modified form in the journal (JMN 7.331 and 334) and in the essay "Politics" (W 3.215–216), the eclectic composition of which I have already noted.

[97] EL 3.247.

far witnessed, Emerson is chiefly concerned with protecting the creative spontaneity of individuals, lest character be assaulted or degraded to the level of a mere expedient: "Accept the reform, but be then thyself sacred, intact, inviolable, one whom leaders, one whom multitudes cannot drag from thy central seat. If you take the reform as the reformer brings it to you, he transforms you into an instrument."[98] All true reform, Emerson thinks, is in the direction of simplification and purification; it leads us to abandon the outward positions to which in ignorance and habit we cling, and returns us to the citadel of the soul. Denouncing the useless and sometimes genuinely harmful appurtenances with which we so love to be surrounded, Emerson makes a particularly forceful attack on money. Perhaps the theories of Edward Palmer, the visionary editor of the *Herald of Holiness*, which their author had discussed with Emerson during his visits to him in Concord, had touched Emerson more deeply than he wished to admit;[99] but the condemnation is also based on an argument Emerson had long cherished (he had employed it in his denunciation of the methods of the temperance organizations). "The system of money," he explains,

> is a system of pledges. You will not take my word that I have labored honestly and added to the amount of value and happiness in the world, but demand a certificate in the shape of a piece of silver or paper. By this exchange, we are both degraded. We have exchanged the broad brow of honor for the wrinkles of suspicion and the insinuation of a threat.[100]

But money spreads its destruction still further. The development of trade brings about a situation in which the pledges are held by a small number of hands, so that certain people acquire power and authority well beyond what they might have claimed by their own labor; any notion of a just reward disappears, and what remains is the exploitation of a privilege unfairly and immorally won. Emerson does not discuss the principle of inheritance by name, but clearly it is liable to the same strictures—the passing on of property does inevitably alter the natural relations embodied in labor that connect men to the universe.[101]

[98] "The Present Age," lecture 6, "Reforms" (EL 3.260).

[99] See Rusk, *Life*, p. 259; Emerson's journal comments on Palmer as follows: "a gentle, faithful, sensible, well-balanced man for an enthusiast. He has renounced since a year ago last April the use of money. When he travels he stops at night at a house & asks if it would give them any satisfaction to lodge a traveller without money or price? If they do not give him a hospitable answer he goes on but generally finds the country people free & willing. When he goes away he gives them his papers or tracts" (JMN 7.108 [October 16, 1838]).

[100] "Reforms" (EL 3.486).

[101] One interesting but only approximately datable passage of the journal portrays the heir's

The most remarkable and consistent trait of this critique is Emerson's stubborn persistence in remaining on the "poetic" level, that is, in refusing to address himself to the social or material consequences of the abuses he denounces and considering only their effect on the soul. If reforms are simply humanity's crutches, helping it only to drag its misery farther along, it is better to throw them away. Emerson is aiming at a regeneration of living cells. The reproaches he directs at the various religious sects (Swedenborgianism alone excepted, though according to Emerson even the Swedenborgians err by an excess of reverence for their founder's writings) all proceed from the same dissatisfaction with their built-in invalidism. That a belief in miracles, for example, should have become the sole criterion of faith strikes Emerson as the height of decay and superstition: "a material miracle to abut a spiritual law! The thing is intrinsically absurd and impossible."[102] As they are purified, in fact, reform and religion tend to coalesce, transforming our daily existence and garbing it in a sort of heroic simplicity. The house and fireside will take the place of sanctuaries. The farm, if we can make of it more than an opportunity for profit, will be a scene in which our noblest faculties can bloom.[103] But we must be ready for struggle, Emerson goes on, because despite its innocence such an ideal will provoke the world's hostility: "I do not think this peaceful reform is to be effected by cowards. [The new hero] is to front a corrupt society & speak rude truth & emergences may easily be where collision & suffering must ensue."[104]

Emerson's refusal to accept anything from the world that he has not previously judged to be in conformity with his inward law, along with his persistent quest for a perfection based on the relinquishing of encumbrances (which was to be Thoreau's central aim also), ends up

---

distress at the crushing abundance of his inheritance: "a man who supplies his own with one of these as for instance with a boat to go a fishing finds it quite easy to caulk it or put in a pin or mend the rudder but a man whose father had successively surrounded himself with all these things & who has orchard, bridge, cattle, hardware, wooden ware, a great house, carpets, cloths, provisions, books, money, to look after & made none of them himself has his hands full to look after these things or means; they will no longer be the means but masters" (JMN 12.470–471). Emerson expands and refines the passage for his 1841 lecture "Man the Reformer"; see W 1.238–240.

[102] "The Present Age," lecture 7, "Religion" (EL 3.278). Even alone this remark suggests the heightening of tone since the Divinity School address.

[103] See for example JMN 7.238 (September 14, 1839). What Emerson later calls "the doctrine of the Farm" differs radically from other reforms; it is, so to speak, Emerson's *Walden*. It is not vitiated by any dependence on mechanical means; it educates by the continued contact it entails with the realities of nature; and for those who put it sincerely into practice, it strengthens their independence and heightens their moral purity.

[104] JMN 7.219–220 (June 27, 1839). The whole paragraph, being in fact a summary of this new religion, is included in the lecture "Religion."

making of him an unclassifiable loner. On hearing the first lecture one might still have hesitated. Theodore Parker, who was captivated by it, described it as "*democratic-loco-foco* throughout";[105] were commerce and banking not after all pilloried in it? Was the apathy of the educated class not thoroughly castigated? Above all, was Emerson not allying himself explicitly with the "Movement Party" of which Orestes Brownson had just written that it was, in an America long threatened by atheism, finally reconciling the instinct of man with the instinct of God?[106] Any doubt, however, was soon dissipated, and by the fourth lecture, "Politics," Parker confessed his disappointment. True, Emerson made common cause with the Democrats in attacking the conformity of the rich, and in this sense the reputation he had rapidly acquired of being a dangerous extremist was well deserved. But Parker's error was in refusing to see further: that Emerson sharply denounced the moral and political mediocrity of the Whigs did not mean, as A. I. Ladu has rightly shown, that he had gone bag and baggage into the camp of their opponents.[107] Unlike Brownson, Emerson persistently refused to ignore the weaknesses and the vices of the Democratic Party in the name of the universal ideal of which it might be the vehicle.[108] Behind the word "movement" he for one saw a pure spiritual reality that could never become one with the political strategies of the moment, even those of the left; and it was that perception which allowed him in the last lecture, "Tendencies," to dismiss both the advocates of credit and the defenders

[105] Quoted by Rusk, *Life*, p. 259. The Locofocos were the most radical segment of the Democratic party; for an account of the theories of William Leggett, one of their chief leaders, see Meyers, *The Jacksonian Persuasion*, pp. 141–156 (chapter 9, "A Free Trade Version").

[106] In "Democracy and Reform," *Boston Quarterly Review* 2 (October 1839), pp. 478–517. Brownson first notes that the early reformers (Robert Owen and his son, Frances Wright, etc.) were unbelievers and hoped for the defeat of religion in the victory of democracy; he therefore joyfully greets the coming of a new spirit in America, the reformer as Christian. But, he goes on, one step remains to be taken: the Christian reformer is to rejoin the Democratic Party, which as being the party of patriotism, liberty, and progress deserves in fact to be called the party of Christianity.

[107] In his "Emerson, Whig or Democrat," NEQ 13 (September 1940), pp. 419–441. In support of his thesis Ladu cites a passage from the journal from October 1839 (JMN 7.99–100) in which Emerson denounces "Van Burenism" and its sordid cult of numbers and the mob.

[108] That is in fact the point that according to Brownson should force sensitive souls to overcome their scruples: "the democratic party embraces the majority of the people of the United States. To complain of the party as these men do is but saying that the majority of the people of the United States are unworthy to be the party associates of a man of respectability. This is not very complimentary, and we suspect they who say so still retain a considerable portion of the leaven of the Pharisees, of which they would do well to get rid as soon as possible" ("Democracy and Reform," p. 484).

of hard currency, the "foolish Whigs" and the partisans of a "profligate government." Their common fault was to lose sight of the fundamental distinction between ends and means: "there is never salvation but in life."[109]

A modest and even commonplace conclusion, one would be tempted to say—not, however, if one takes it as seriously as did Emerson, and so can see in it the nonconformity, the contempt for public opinion, the joyous acceptance of the soul's spontaneity and surface inconsistencies, in a word the very substance of "Self-Reliance."[110] There was at that moment no lesson, no example that the Boston audiences, and beyond them the American nation as a whole, needed more urgently. All the European travelers who visited America between 1825 and 1850, from Frances Trollope through Harriet Martineau and Tocqueville to Dickens, reported sadly or angrily on the distressing conformity of individual people, their entire and apparently unprotesting submission to the law of the majority; everywhere "the worship of opinion"[111] was triumphant: "If great writers have not at present existed in America, the reason is very simply given in these facts; there can be no literary genius without freedom of opinion, and freedom of opinion does not exist in America."[112] Thus, by a paradox that only gradually yielded its meaning, it was only in turning away from his contemporaries and their immediate desires, in stubbornly going it alone, in deliberately disappointing Theodore Parker and the other "social" Transcendentalists that Emerson rendered real and lasting service to the American democracy. For several generations, as the nation gradually transformed itself into a gigantic machine geared to production—and sometimes to destruction—Emerson's thought was a salutary leavening. John Jay Chapman[113] and Edgar Lee Masters[114] confessed their debt to him in

[109] "The Present Age," lecture 10, "Tendencies" (EL 3.309 and 306).

[110] Stephen Whicher's very interesting anthology, *Selections from Ralph Waldo Emerson* (Boston, 1957), contains on pp. 481–483 a table showing the sources of "Self-Reliance" paragraph by paragraph, and sometimes sentence by sentence. One column indicates the borrowings from the lectures, another those from the journal. "Tendencies" is a particularly rich source and contributes some of the most challenging passages, particularly that on nonconformism and the "hobgoblin of little minds" (W 2.55–58). Whicher does not indicate that this last phrase actually originates in a passage of the journal in which Emerson attacks the abolitionists for having given their vote not to a man but to a motto: "Consistency! Nonsense with your wooden walls . . ." (JMN 7.223 [July 3, 1839]).

[111] The expression is Harriet Martineau's, who saw in this capitulation of the individual the most striking trait of American civilization—more powerful, she specifies, than the lust for profit (*Society in America* 3.7).

[112] Tocqueville, *Democracy in America*, trans. Henry Reeve (New York, 1961), 1.312.

[113] In his lively and, for its time, astonishingly frank "Emerson Sixty Years Later," *Atlantic*

tones of surprising intensity. He was the emblem of the noble rebellion kindled in the heart of every adolescent when he dares to compare the world as it is with the world as it ought to be. The philosophical assumptions, the belief in the Oversoul took second place or even were entirely forgotten. But the image of a new Adam seeking to rename all the beasts of the field and the gods of heaven[115]—and, by force of passion, succeeding in the attempt—remained alive for a long time in the American mind. One has only to think of Whitman.

Monthly (January–February 1897), reprinted in *The Shock of Recognition*, ed. Edmund Wilson, 2d ed. (New York, 1955), pp. 595–658.

[114] In his preface to *The Living Thoughts of R. W. Emerson* (New York, 1940), p. 2, in which he explains the crucial role played by the *Essays* and more particularly by "Self-Reliance" in his own intellectual emancipation: "out in middle Illinois, when I was in high school, we eager young found ourselves stifled by the parochial orthodoxy that surrounded us—the unsmoked sky was above us, the fields and woods were around us, yet we needed air. We could not be free without knowing what we were, and what we possibly could do. We could not think, speculate, examine the evidence of things without being emancipated from the bandages that tied us in. We were bound to crawl on as crayfish in the mud if we were not told that there were hills of pure air to which we could ascend. We needed some one to say that we had possibilities. . . . Emerson did this for two or three of us in the school . . . as he told an old theologian that he must go his way, and if he were a child of the devil, it had to be so, we too could stand forth as children of the devil, if that was our role in life. We did this very thing, and were happy and strong as we did it."

[115] See JMN 7.271–272, "Lectures" (October 18, 1839). Written at a moment of proud exaltation, the passage sketches the ideal image Emerson was concurrently attempting to evoke in "The Present Age."

PART III

From Ideal Democracy to Natural Aristocracy

9

~ ~ ~ ~

MALAISE

EMERSON had no sooner bidden farewell to the approximately four hundred persons who had attended his lectures on "The Present Age" than he drew up in his journal an inexorable account of his failure:

> These lectures give me little pleasure. I have not done what I hoped when I said, I will try it once more. I have not once transcended the coldest selfpossession. I said I will agitate others, being agitated myself. I dared to hope for extacy & eloquence. A new theatre, a new art, I said, is mine. Let us see if philosophy, if ethics, if chiromancy, if the discovery of the divine in the house & the barn, in all works & all plays, cannot make the cheek blush, the lip quiver, & the tear start. I will not waste myself. On the strength of Things I will be borne, and try if Folly, Custom, Convention, & Phlegm cannot be made to hear our sharp artillery. Alas! alas! I have not the recollection of one strong moment. A cold mechanical preparation for a delivery as decorous, —fine things, pretty things, wise things, —but no arrows, no axes, no nectar, no growling, no transpiercing, no loving, no enchantment. —
>
> And why?
>
> I seem to lack constitutional vigor to attempt each topic as I ought. I ought to seek to lay myself out utterly, —large, enormous, prodigal, upon the subject of the week. But a hateful experience has taught me that I can only expend, say, twenty one hours on each lecture, if I would also be ready & able for the next. Of course, I spend myself prudently; I economize; I cheapen: whereof nothing

> grand ever grew. Could I spend sixty hours on each, or what is better, had I such energy that I could rally the lights & mights of sixty hours into twenty, I should hate myself less, I should help my friend.[1]

It would be unjust, and, all things considered, naïve, to take this confession as a statement of fact. We have in refutation of it the testimony of contemporaries like Parker, on whom Emerson's oratory had a considerable effect; and in addition we recognize in Emerson's passion for self-flagellation one of the most abiding traits of his personality—the descendant of the Puritans could never entirely divest himself of a feeling that in a different theological context would have amounted to a sense of certain damnation. But the passage in question does more than exhibit Emerson's dissatisfaction with himself; it also conceals the intuition of a far more radical deficiency, as if, in the very heart of reality, a mysterious anemia were consuming the forces of life, preventing them from projecting and expanding in universal harmony. A few weeks earlier, Emerson had sounded a paean to the glory of human abilities and their "irrevocable elasticity";[2] now he was the first to denounce it as a lie. There is a sad irony here in seeing him first define the very qualities in which he had clothed the exemplary man of his last lectures and then deny that he himself possesses them.[3]

It is true that in 1838 the reception offered the Divinity School address had given him the experience of spiritual failure; but that failure was due to the inertia of the social organism, and thus in his own eyes had subtly increased his stature. It is not enough to say that he had been reconciled to the general bewilderment the address evoked; he had indeed striven for it, cultivated it, and provoked it, finding in the confusion or censure of the crowd the surest mark of his own integrity. Borne along henceforth by the living flow of all things, he refused every possible port for fear it might harbor a Circe. In January 1840 he agreed to speak in celebration of a church's completion in East Lexington; but the use he made of the occasion was precisely to exhort his hearers not to yield to the justifiable and yet deadly sense of accomplishment: "Life is a song of degrees. . . . Round every thought of ours, is already dwelling a greater thought, into which after some time we enter, and find it in

[1] JMN 7.338–339 (February 19, 1840).

[2] "Prospects," EL 3.372.

[3] Similarly, the chart he offers of the human condition in the seventh stanza of "The Sphinx"—probably also composed in 1840—seems an ironic variation on the theme, and almost on the terms, of "Self-Reliance." Cf. W 9.22.

turn circumscribed by a higher truth."[4] He seeks with all his passion to dissolve every form, to reintegrate it with the diffused and surging abundance of the universe. But at that point this incomprehensible drama comes to a head; something in Emerson is exhausted, or is giving way, as the world around him is suddenly frozen, shatters into tiny pieces, gapes with cracks irrevocably separating one person from another, one object from another, even the signs from the things signified: "Ah! that I could reach with my words the force of that rhetoric of things in which the Divine Mind is conveyed to me day by day in what I call my life. A loaf of bread, an errand to the town, a temperate man, an industrious man."[5] It is not the least consequence of this inward cataclysm that it ruins the great Adamic dream of giving a new name to everything in the world—a dream that Emerson had feverishly nurtured the preceding autumn while preparing to return to the platform.

The discovery of this insurmountable weakness—or rather this confirmation of the profoundly troubling experience recorded as early as "The Protest"—deeply and lastingly altered the orientation of Emerson's thought. Without ever ceasing to assert the absolute prerogatives of the Oversoul, Emerson found himself constrained to acknowledge those realities of fact which seemed at every instant to contradict them. That the process of reconciliation was arduous and delicate, that it was attended by tormenting uncertainties, and that it ended by producing a new solution to most of the unresolved problems at issue are all truths forcefully demonstrated by Stephen Whicher's *Freedom and Fate*, which is built specifically around this long crisis.[6] It is not necessary to repeat here the substance of Whicher's analysis, though on occasion I may draw inspiration from it; rather I will extend it along the particular line of this study.

Of all of Emerson's essays, "Experience"[7]—which he thought of dedicating to "The Lords of Life"—seems the most richly autobiographical. Reading it, one can grasp the author's daily struggle to decipher the enigma of the world and to maintain his spiritual identity despite the snares continually set in his way by enemies full of cunning. Yet the last word is one of confidence and hope: "Never mind the ridicule, never mind the defeat; up again, old heart! . . . there is victory yet for all justice."[8] The image of the battered but victorious warrior evoked by this

[4] "Address to the People of East Lexington on the Dedication of their Church" (H.198.7). The reader will recognize the basic theme of "Circles," published in the first series of *Essays*.

[5] JMN 7.488 (February 21, 1840).

[6] See particularly chapters 5 ("Circles"), 6 ("Skepticism"), and 7 ("Acquiescence").

[7] Published in the second series of *Essays* (W 3.43–86).

[8] W 3.85–86.

apostrophe admirably defines the personage with which Emerson wished the public to identify him. He still thought and wished himself the teacher of optimism—so much so that posterity, for once too docile, has never forgiven him for that pose and has seen in it a certain narrowness of nature. Several critics, however, have sought to clear up the misunderstanding by showing that if Emerson himself obstinately denied the dark side of human life, his work—when read closely—offers a sad testimony to its presence and extent.[9] But this is not going far enough. Along with the man tradition presents, the unshakably serene and satisfied sage of Concord, there is another, plagued with doubts, oppressed with a sense of powerlessness, concealing in his private journal the avowal of his rebellions.[10] This second man, less consistent than the first and terribly jealous of his anonymity (one should recall here the harsh judgments registered by the early journals on Byron)—this double of Emerson passed easily unnoticed except by a few discerning contemporaries.[11] But a close reading of the journals between 1840 and 1842 cannot help but reveal him. Since the abandonment of his ministry and his trip to Europe, never had Emerson felt less sure in his philosophy; and never had that unity of vision which was his obsession but also his essential vocation seemed more in jeopardy.[12]

[9] See particularly Whicher, "Emerson's Tragic Sense," *The American Scholar* 22 (Summer 1953), pp. 285–292 and Newton Arvin, "The House of Pain," *Hudson Review* 12, (Spring 1959), pp. 37–53.

[10] Characteristically Emerson cast his protests and confessions of discouragement in the mold of verse; the most striking example is the sixty-line "The Skeptic," written in 1842 but published for the first time in 1957 with an important commentary by Carl Strauch ("The Importance of Emerson's Skeptical Mood," *Harvard Library Bulletin* 11, pp. 117–141).

[11] See particularly Brownson's review of Emerson's poems in *Brownson's Quarterly Review* for April 1847: "His volume of poems is the saddest book we ever read. The author tries to cheer up, tries to smile, but the smile is cold and transitory in the talks of music and flowers, and would fain persuade us that he is weaving garlands of joy; but beneath them is always to be seen the ghastly and grinning skeleton of death. There is an appearance of calm, of quiet, of repose, and at first sight one may half fancy his soul is as placid, as peaceful, as the unruffled lake sleeping sweetly beneath the Summer moonbeams; but it is the calm, the quiet, the repose of despair. Down below are the troubled waters. The world is no joyous world for him. It is void and without form, and darkness broods over it. True, he bears up against it; but because he is too proud to complain, and because he believes his lot is that of all men and inevitable" (*Works*, ed. Henry F. Brownson, 20 vols. [Detroit 1882], 19.189–202). Clearly one should not neglect the personal factor in this assessment; Brownson had converted to Catholicism three years earlier and condemns in Emerson's stoic resignation a spiritual state very like those he had recently experienced. His criticism is that of a proselyte and almost of a catechumen.

[12] Henry A. Pochmann, in *German Culture in America* (Madison, Wisc., 1957), pp. 602–603, notes that the distinction between Reason and Understanding on which Emerson's militant idealism was based is made for the last time in the journal for November 3, 1839; the years that follow witness the development of a new set of coordinates.

Logically enough, he retreated inward, declining all public engagements for many months. The preparation of the first series of *Essays* occupied him for most of 1840; not content with piecing together passages from lectures and journals, he made almost every essay the occasion of a personal stock-taking. In two cases, that of "Circles" and to a lesser extent that of "Friendship," he deliberately diverged from earlier versions and thus confessed the nature of his new concerns. "Circles" takes up the doctrine of compensations, here symbolized by the perfection of the circle closed upon itself; but it also decisively corrects that doctrine, by subordinating it to a law of infinite growth. It is as if Emerson, though now painfully conscious both of his individual limits and of the general poverty of human energy, had resolved to ignore both phenomena, or better still to annihilate them, by removing himself from the condition of mortality. He defines this literally transcendental angle of vision in a letter written in May 1840, during the work on "Circles":

> I have never been able to announce my faith with fulness, and perhaps never shall be; but are we not continually, as our eyes open, shamed out of the limitations we have conceded? . . . The hope of man resides in the private heart, and what it can achieve by translating that into sense. And this hope, in our reasonable moments, is always immense, and refuses to be diminished by any deduction of experience, inasmuch as our experience is always dishonest, unequal whilst the idea is always total, accusing and inexorable to our excuses.[13]

By a supreme effort of purification, spiritual existence came to be defined by a repeated denial of each moment in which it claimed to be embodied.

The sense of the other essay composed during that same year, "Friendship," is to some extent clarified by the preceding arguments; but both the nature of its subject and its connections with Emerson's life require more extended treatment. If "Circles" in a sense eludes the judgment of experience because of its superhuman perspective, "Friendship" does not. Here we are once again at human level; biography and philosophy blend indissolubly,[14] and give the essay a delicacy of perception for which it is seldom given credit.

The subject of friendship had always fascinated Emerson (one has only to look at the journals of his adolescence), because he saw in it a

[13] Letter to Richard Monckton-Milnes of May 30, 1840 (in T. Wemyss Reid, *The Life, Letters and Friendships of Richard Monckton-Milnes*, 2 vols. [London, 1890], 1.241–242).

[14] The autobiographical basis of the essay is discussed in John McNulty, "Emerson's Friends and the Essay on Friendship," NEQ 19 (September 1946), 390–394.

manifestation of certain of nature's irreducible contradictions. One's friend is both the man who is like one and the man who resists one, the man one needs when despondent and the man who will, if one is not careful, destroy one's integrity.[15] But such ambiguities provoke the liveliest resources of the mind, and Emerson for his part did not hide the pleasure he took in disentangling these knots.[16] The essay's first pages, full of gentle passion and crowded with personal reminiscence, tell of Emerson's admiration for the ways of providence. He has not, he says, courted friendship, yet in his despondence friends have come to him from all directions: after Fuller, Thoreau, and Very have come Caroline Sturgis, Samuel Gray Ward, and Anna Barker; after Carlyle, John Sterling, drawn toward Concord, which he was never to see, by a sort of inexorable gravitation.[17] But then comes the movement of withdrawal, the expression with a barely contained violence of Emerson's instinct for spiritual self-preservation: the friend does not exist, is only an illusion of the heart, fatal to those who abandon themselves to it. The second and considerably longer part of the essay sets out to illustrate this severe truth, and draws up the chart of authentic friendship, directed beyond the veil of persons to Being, Truth, and Justice.[18] These pages breathe a curiously rarefied atmosphere; they somehow provoke uneasiness and prevent the reader from appreciating the agility with which Emerson links together principles, precepts, warnings, and disguised confessions.

More specifically, the essay should not be reduced to a metaphysical discussion of friendship. From his fundamental postulate, according to which the most secret part of ourselves is also the most universal, or, as Emerson likes to call it, the most "public," Emerson deduces rules of conduct valid in daily life. The first is to avoid promiscuity and to make sure that feeling cannot be diverted from its spiritual goals by the resistant denseness of a physical presence: "Why insist on rash personal relations with your friend? Why go to his house, or know his mother and

[15] The paradox is already at the heart of "Étienne de la Boéce [sic]," a poem probably written in 1833 (W 9.82). Sheltered by a name celebrated in the annals of friendship, Emerson defends that inflexible independence which in his eyes is the only way for a friend to do his friend true service.

[16] See the letter to Samuel Gray Ward of June 22, 1840 (in *Letters from Ralph Waldo Emerson to a Friend*, ed. Charles Eliot Norton [Boston, 1899], p. 21).

[17] Most of these friendships are reflected in Rusk's edition of the letters; Emerson's correspondences with Carlyle, Sterling, and Ward are published separately.

[18] "I cannot deny it, O friend, that the vast shadow of the Phenomenal includes thee also in its pied and painted immensity, —thee also, compared with whom all else is shadow. Thou art not Being, as Truth is, as Justice is, —thou art not my soul, but a picture and effigy of that" ("Friendship," W 2.197).

brother and sisters? Why be visited by him at your own? Are these things material to our covenant? Leave this touching and clawing. Let him be to me a spirit."[19] One gathers from this that letters or conversations on a topic of morality are one's only means of true connection with a friend. One will learn, Emerson goes on, to make more of a letter from a friend than of a costly gift that profanes the giver and receiver alike. And friendship needs not only space but also time to develop; all precipitateness is fatal to it, because it blossoms with the solemn deliberateness of natural things: "I am a worshipper of Friendship," Emerson writes in his first letter to Sterling, "and cannot find any other good equal to it. As soon as any man pronounces the words which approve him fit for that great office, I make no haste: he is holy; let me be holy also; our relations are eternal; why should we count days and weeks?"[20] Finally, though friendship is for each of us a providential means of progress, it ought not to divert us from our first obligation, which commits us to fidelity to ourselves even if this requires that certain other affections be denied. It is justifiable and even desirable for us to pass through several circles of friendship in our lives, just as according to Plato the soul assumes a succession of bodies in the course of its earthly pilgrimage. Consequently one has to have the ruthless courage to reject a friend who clings to one when his time is past: "Who are you? Unhand me: I will be dependent no more."[21] One may perhaps think with Montaigne that whoever thus takes back his word destroys friendship's essence[22] and that a feeling in which one progresses cautiously and warily does not summon up what is best in us. But that is not the issue; and the sincerity with which Emerson continually strove to shape his life by the gospel he preached earns at least our respect.

That respect, moreover, is soon accompanied by curiosity and sympathy if one retraces the course of Emerson's lived friendships as recorded in the writings—notably the letters—not intended for publication. Reviewing Cabot's *Memoir* of Emerson, which was published shortly after Emerson's death, Henry James regretted that Cabot had chosen to depict only the life of his subject and not in addition the milieu that had fostered it, with its traditions, its conscious and unconscious beliefs, its inhibitions, and its imperatives.[23] One cannot contend that

[19] "Friendship," W 2.210.

[20] Letter of May 29, 1840 (in *A Correspondence Between John Sterling and Ralph Waldo Emerson*, ed. Edward Waldo Emerson [Boston, 1897], p. 28).

[21] "Friendship," W 2.214.

[22] "De l'amitié" (*Essais* 1, no. 28).

[23] "Emerson," in *The American Essays of Henry James* (New York, 1956), particularly pp. 52–54.

the letters reveal or betray the constitutive elements of a *mentalité*; a sociologist's hunger would in no way be appeased by them. But a novelist expert in seeing through the disguises of the heart—a James, for example—might well find in them material to stimulate his imagination. It is after all Emerson himself who confessed to his brother William, in October 1840, at the height of his epistolary passion, that the polishing of the *Essays* seemed to him mechanical and unrewarding in comparison with the composition of these marvelous "romances of letters" with which he had filled the "idle happy summer" just then ending.[24]

The history of Emerson's actual friendships does not at all evince the arid monotony one would have expected from "Friendship" and is, in fact, made up of sharply contrasted sorts of experience. In general, one has to agree that he succeeded in maintaining the demanding austerity the essay defines, aided sometimes by geographical separation (what would have happened to his friendship with Carlyle if the two men had lived as neighbors is vividly suggested by the friction evident in Emerson's 1848 visit to London) and sometimes by the choice of a confidant no less watchful of his independence than Emerson himself ("as for taking Thoreau's arm, I should as soon take the arm of an elm tree," he wrote one day—vaguely disappointed, it seems[25]). There were even moments of poignant grandeur when in dialogue with a soul as lofty as his own he gave himself up to inward and intimate meditations under the guise of philosophizing.[26] But on at least two occasions—his relations with Anna Barker and Margaret Fuller—he departed from his usual equanimity, and the resulting disturbance, however modest, reveals a new facet in his personality and invites us to reflect on certain gaps in his psychology.

John Jay Chapman observes in a famous sentence of his essay on

[24] Letter to William Emerson of October 19, 1840 (L 2.348). Cited by Sherman Paul, *Emerson's Angle of Vision* (Cambridge, Mass., 1952), p. 182, in a penetrating though excessively compressed account of Emerson's relations with his various friends.

[25] JMN 10.343 (1848).

[26] See the letter Emerson wrote to Sterling in July 1844, when Sterling had hardly two months left to live. Alluding to his own hopes for the development of their friendship, Emerson writes, "this must now be renounced, and the grand words I hear and sometimes use must be verified, and I must think of that which you represent, and not of the representative beloved. Happy is it whilst the Blessed Power keeps unbroken the harmony of the inward and the outward, and yields us the perfect expression of good in a friend! But if it will disunite the power and the form, the power is yet to be infinitely trusted, and we must try, unwilling, the harsh grandeurs of the spiritual nature. Each of us more readily faces the issue alone than on the account of his friend. We find something dishonest in learning to live without friends: whilst death wears a sublime aspect to each of us" (*Correspondence Between Sterling and Emerson*, p. 92).

Emerson that "if an inhabitant of another planet should visit the earth, he would receive, on the whole, a truer notion of human life by attending an Italian opera than he would by reading Emerson's volumes," because the opera would at least teach him that there are two sexes, which one could hardly guess from reading Emerson's essay on love.[27] Chapman was thus the first, it seems, to venture to compare Emerson's "natural asceticism" to a "functional weakness," which he also found manifested in the bloodless, bodiless impoverishment of Emerson's judgments on art. But Chapman's reproach contains a good amount of irritation and disappointment; he admired Emerson too much to pardon him this dangerously unworldly trait[28] and is unjust in putting Emerson's temperament on trial without consideration of its nuances.[29] The times of confusion Emerson experienced in his friendships come rather when nature—often Emerson's own nature, in fact—irrefutably denies what one really has to call Emerson's romantic or pseudo-mystical theory of women.

It seems clear that the image of his child bride Ellen, taken from him after a few months of married life, remained imprinted deep in his sensibility and never ceased to influence his behavior toward other women. It certainly guided him in his readings, though of this he was not entirely aware; how else can one explain his passion for Elizabeth Brentano, Goethe's "Bettina"?[30] It led him to transcribe certain other writers' praises of women into his journal.[31] It may even have overcome his instinctive prejudices against France; Emerson always exempted the institution of the salon from his criticism and saw in it the most refined expression of womanly grace and intelligence as well as an edifying example of the civilizing influence women exercise when they are allowed to shape the social code rather than merely having to endure it. And one

[27] "Emerson," in *The Shock of Recognition*, ed. Edmund Wilson, 2d ed. (New York, 1955), p. 644.

[28] As is well known, Chapman as a young man deliberately burned his hand in an uncontrollable fit apparently caused by a romantic disappointment; the experience marked him for the rest of his life.

[29] Less, however, than certain modern critics who, infatuated with D. H. Lawrence's eulogies of sex, carried their dislike for Emerson to the point of coarse vituperation, such as Holbrook Johnson, *Dreamer of Dreams* (London, 1948), particularly pp. 188–189.

[30] "What can be richer and nobler than that woman's nature. What life more pure and poetic amid the prose and derision of our own time. . . . If I went to Germany I should only desire to see her. . . . It seems to me she is the only formidable test that was applied to Goethe's genius" (letter to Margaret Fuller, date uncertain [L 2.210]). Goethe's "correspondence" with Bettina was published in 1835.

[31] For example, a passage of Jean Paul Richter claiming that women embody each age's Zeitgeist (JMN 8.267).

should add that the small world of Concord, which constituted the frame and bulwark of Emerson's own existence, might well have justified such respect. He had been from his earliest years in contact with a number of remarkable women capable of reconciling a passion for books with a taste for the household, and he must have considered that happy balance, the difficulties of which we can now fully assess, as something altogether natural. The tradition of simplicity and culture that easily joined the housewife's broom and the dialogues of Plato is, moreover, one of the misunderstood legacies of Puritanism to the beginnings of the nineteenth century.

In any case, it is between 1840 and 1844 that the pages of the journal express this almost religious reverence toward woman with the greatest intensity.[32] Woman's proper vocation, Emerson writes, is to be a vessel of the Universal Spirit; every finite task degrades and disfigures her; and it is an unspeakable misfortune that our society, blind to its true interests, should persist in treating her as an instrument. Woman is made to be our lodestar, our infallible and silent guide in the maze of daily choices:

> Always men, if they have talent, though they be tolerably simple, have a little lawyer in them who argues & suspects & provides, & would construct bridges for the Impassable, & is no match for the Oracle in Woman, wh. convoys her without hands & without stairs to the heights of sentiment. Now I will identify you with the Ideal Friend, & live with you on imperial terms. Present, you shall be present only as an angel might be, & absent you shall not be absent from me.[33]

One senses that Emerson has deliberately silenced in himself all that could remind him of women's physical characteristics; true chastity in his eyes is entirely "poetic."[34] He does touch on the subject of virginity—but only by way of allegory, to illustrate the attitude of respect by which authentic friendship is distinguished.[35] The subject of marriage, by contrast, gives birth to a curious dream, a good subject for a psy-

[32] See particularly JMN 8.149–150, 307–308, 380–381; 9.103. It was also at this time that Emerson translated Dante's *Vita nuova*. (J. Chesley Mathews prints the text of the translation, previously unpublished, in *Harvard Library Bulletin* 11 [1957], pp. 208–244 and 346–362.)

[33] Letter to Caroline Sturgis of September 13, 1840 (L 2.333–334). It seems there was some difficulty in making Emerson's relations with Sturgis—whom he called his "sister of fate"—correspond to this program: see particularly L 2.324–327.

[34] JMN 7.256 (October 1839).

[35] See JMN 7.371 (June 1840).

choanalyst,[36] or on other days incites him to reflect sadly on the inconstancy of men—which last word is used for once in its distinctive rather than its inclusive sense.[37] It is clear what risk is being run; whether by unconscious conformity or by temperament, Emerson is ignorant of the natural rules governing the dialogue between the sexes. He insists extravagantly on woman's spiritual qualities, but tries to forget that incarnation is a universal law, and that in discrediting our rationality he is abandoning himself to the forces of instinct—and not only other persons' instinct but also his own. It was on this unstable ground that the "romance" of the two friendships mentioned above took place; it is now appropriate to trace its course as the letters and journals reveal it.

Anna Barker appeared on Emerson's horizon late in 1839. She was originally from New Orleans and displayed a richly emotional nature. At first she disconcerted Emerson, who did not see in her the intellectual solidity of a daughter of the Puritans and yet was attracted by her "instinctive elegance."[38] It did not take him long to yield to the new delights of intensely personal communication: "Anna's miracle," he writes in a fragment of a letter rediscovered by Rusk,

> next to the *amount* of her life, seems to be the intimacy of her approach to us. The moment she fastens her eyes on you, her unique gentleness unbars all doors, and with such easy and frolic sway she advances & advances & advances on you, with that one look, that no brother or sister or father or mother of life-long acquaintance ever seemed to arrive quite so near as this now first seen maiden. It is almost incredible to me, when I spoke with her the other night—that I have never seen this child but three times, or four, is it? I should think I had lived with her in the houses of eternity——[39]

Barker responded to this intense sense of intimacy with a profound trust, an abandonment of soul. Margaret Fuller was aware of the young woman's feelings, and one day accused Emerson of abusing them—in an acrid tone in which there seems to be something of personal resent-

[36] See JMN 7.544 (December 1840).

[37] "In a right state the love of one, which each man carried in his heart, should protect all women from his eyes as by an impenetrable veil of indifferency. The love of one should make him indifferent to all others, or rather their protector & saintly friend, as if for her sake. But now there is in the eyes of all men a certain evil light, a vague desire which attaches them to the forms of many women, whilst their affections fasten on some one. Their natural eye is not fixed into coincidence with their spiritual eye" (JMN 8.95 [1841]).

[38] See JMN 7.259–260 (October 7, 1839). Emerson speaks several times in his letters of Barker as an American Récamier.

[39] L 2.333, n. 364; the passage is probably from a letter written to Caroline Sturgis in September 1840.

ment.[40] By imperceptible degrees the relation grew deeper, and when in the course of the summer of 1840 Emerson heard the news of Barker's marriage (to Samuel Gray Ward, the "friend" of *Letters to a Friend*), he admitted it was a considerable blow for him: "what shall I say to you," he writes to Margaret Fuller,

> of this my sudden dejection from the sunlit heights of my felicity to which I had been as suddenly uplifted. Was I not raised out of the society of mere mortals by being chosen the friend of the holiest nun? began instantly to dream of pure confidences & "prayers of preserved maids in bodies delicate," when a flash of lightning shivers my castle in the air. . . . the fragment of confidence that a wife can give to an old friend is not worth picking up after this invitation to Elysian tables. . . . Ward I shall not lose. My joy for him is very great.[41]

It would be impossible—for Emerson, at least—to confess more explicitly that spiritual friendship is sometimes as selfish as love. The selfishness speaking here is of a peculiar nature. It expresses neither a need for possession nor an imperious will. It is rather the avowal of a deficiency, almost a cry for help, and one wonders whether it does not reveal more true humanity than all the aphorisms of "Friendship" and "Love." Anna Barker was for Emerson a sort of April sun; in the gentle warmth of her rays he felt his coat of ice crack and split.[42] But spring was hardly begun, and the healthful thaw just started; was he now bound to return to his inward winter? A few days before his friends' marriage, he wrote them to thank them for remaining loyal to him; his letter is not only an acknowledgment but also a supplication:

> There are many degrees of sincerity, & persons like us three who know the elegance of truth may yet be far without their own highest mark of simple intercourse. . . . What benefactors then like those who by their celestial sincerity can speak to this high prisoner, can give me for the first time to hear my own voice & to feel the health of my own motion? Your frank love suggests to me the hope that I shall yet speak & yet hear.[43]

[40] See L 2.309–310, n. 266, and 2.313.

[41] Letter to Margaret Fuller of August 29, 1840 (L 2.327–328). The phrase Emerson quotes is, according to Rusk, a much distorted passage from *Measure for Measure*; Emerson's being reminded by this marriage of the Shakespeare play most powerfully obsessed with the sullied flesh clearly reinforces the present interpretation.

[42] Paul, *Emerson's Angle of Vision*, p. 253, n. 10, observes that Emerson often uses the metaphor of ice in regretting his unfitness for friendship.

[43] Letter to Samuel Gray Ward and Anna Barker of September 1840 (L 2.338–339).

But the intimacy he evokes here he essentially knows has been condemned without appeal; and that is why in the same letter he prepares in spirit to return to the familiar territory of his solitude. Only the frequent allusions to Barker in his correspondence indicate the interest he continued to feel in her; her conversion to Catholicism in 1857 or 1858 was a great affliction to him.[44] She was, as he notes in the journal, a "Helen grown up unawares in these trivial New Yorks & New Orleanses of ours,"[45] and he could never entirely console himself for Paris's having stolen her away.

But one ought not exaggerate either the incident's extent or its repercussions. It touched to the quick a sensibility that did not know itself to be so vulnerable, and it took on a sort of elegiac charm as the years passed;[46] but it did not stir Emerson up in the sense in which one says a sudden storm stirs up a river. With Margaret Fuller the case was altogether different; and the story of her relations with Emerson, which has been told numerous times already,[47] has as good a claim to the subtitle of "the ambiguities" as does Melville's *Pierre*. Fuller was seven years younger than Emerson and passionately desired to meet him, because she expected of him the spiritual direction she had sought from other teachers, notably Harriet Martineau, in vain. When Lidian Emerson invited her for a stay of three weeks, and she finally crossed the threshold of Emerson's house, "a sense of triumph" filled her being. Her host was far from sharing her euphoria, and was to reveal as much fifteen years later in describing that first meeting: "She was then, as always, carefully and becomingly dressed, and of ladylike self-possession. For the rest, her appearance had nothing preposessing. Her extreme plainness, —a trick of incessantly opening and shutting her eyelids, —the nasal tone

[44] "I grieve that she has flung herself into the Church of Rome, suddenly. She was *born* for social grace, and that faith makes such carnage of social relations" (from Emerson's letter to Clough of May 17, 1858, in H. F. Lowry and Ralph L. Rusk, eds., *The Emerson-Clough Letters* [Cleveland, 1934], p. 31).

[45] JMN 8.176 (June 15, 1842).

[46] Anna Barker-Ward figures under her initials in "Gulistan," an unpublished noteboook containing Emerson's remarks and judgments on various friends; there Emerson dedicates to her Propertius' line "Est tibi forma potens, sunt certae Palladis artes" (JMS H.108 [1848], p. 32).

[47] See McNulty, "Emerson's Friends," and also H. R. Warfel, "Margaret Fuller and Ralph Waldo Emerson," PMLA 50 (1935), pp. 575–594, which retraces the drama's multiple episodes in detail, and Perry Miller, "I Find no Intellect Comparable to My Own," *American Heritage* (February 1957), pp. 22–25 and 96–99, a briefer but brisk and often perceptive account. For the present perspective the fundamental text remains that multiply authored homage to Fuller's memory, *Memoirs of Margaret Fuller Ossoli*, 2 vols. (Boston, 1852); Emerson wrote the fourth and fifth parts of the first volume (pp. 199–351).

of her voice, —all repelled; and I said to myself, we shall never get far."[48] To this instinct of aversion was soon added an irritated impatience at Fuller's frivolity and her manifest desire to allure and entice:

> I remember that she made me laugh more than I liked; for I was, at that time, an eager scholar of ethics, and had tasted the sweets of solitude and stoicism, and I found something profane in the hours of amusing gossip into which she drew me. . . . Margaret, who had stuffed me out as a philosopher, in her own fancy, was too intent on establishing a good footing between us, to omit any art of winning. She studied my tastes, piqued and amused me, challenged frankness by frankness, and did not conceal the good opinion of me she brought with her, nor her wish to please. She was curious to know my opinions and experiences. Of course, it was impossible long to hold out against such urgent assault.[49]

The military metaphor that closes this vivid paragraph gives the key to the coming difficulties by locating them in the proper area: an irreducible opposition of temperaments. Emerson is the low-keyed valetudinarian, compelled to deploy his impoverished energies prudently and thriftily; Fuller represents vitality and the generous outpouring of natural force. Emerson is forever regretting that a fragile constitution keeps him from enacting the goal he has set for himself.[50] Fuller has to beware of "superabundant animal spirits" ready to dissipate themselves in pointless or harmful agitation.[51] The contrast is so strong that Emerson is not far from thinking himself in the presence of a being of a different species:

> In the first days of our acquaintance, I felt her to be a foreigner, —that, with her, one would always be sensible of some barrier, as if in making up a friendship with a cultivated Spaniard or Turk. . . .
>
> When I found she lived at a rate so much faster than mine, and which was violent compared with mine, I foreboded rash and painful crises, and had a feeling as if a voice cried, *Stand from under*! —as if, a little further on, this destiny was threatened with jars and reverses, which no friendship could avert or console. This feeling partly wore off, on better acquaintance, but remained latent; and I had always an impression that her energy was too much a force of blood.[52]

[48] *Memoirs of Margaret Fuller Ossoli*, 1.202.

[49] *Memoirs of Margaret Fuller Ossoli*, 1.202–203.

[50] See for example JMN 5.344 (July 19, 1837).

[51] *Memoirs of Margaret Fuller Ossoli*, 1.203.

[52] *Memoirs of Margaret Fuller Ossoli*, 1.227–228.

As coming from Emerson such reservations amount to a condemnation—one has only to refer to the argument of his lecture on demonology.[53] He was wary of occult phenomena because the half-light they flourish in lends itself to a thousand fearsome distortions. He knew that self-control is the cost of the conquest of the universal, and that the nexus of our feelings and instincts is a subtle obstacle in that process. Fuller, however, thrived in these equivocal realms; her chosen homeland was not Attica but Thessaly, the land of sorcerers,[54] because she preferred the fantastic play of the imagination, the iridescent sparks of her own mythology, to the sober light of the intellect. It was this "sentimentalism" that alarmed Emerson; to what purpose are the love of truth and the desire for personal integrity if we treat the extravagances of our sensibility with such indulgence? He feared lest in following his friend he transport himself to a land still unknown, in which every false step might tumble him from a cliff. His stiffening was a defensive reaction; had he felt the threat of certain obscure inner powers less vividly, he would have taken less care to combat their spells in others.

In fact the drama of Margaret Fuller was the drama of a frustrated personality; and it was bound up, as Emerson later perceived clearly, with circumstances of time and place.[55] Hawthorne, who did not appreciate her, caricatured Fuller as Zenobia in *The Blithedale Romance*; but she rather makes one think of Hester Prynne.[56] Like Hester, she has the mettle of an impassioned lover, and like her also she must repress her burning hunger for life. Hawthorne draws the reader's attention to his character's "rich, voluptuous, Oriental" soul and shows how the severity of her costume, the humble routine of her domestic activities, and even the cottage she inhabits at the end of the village are transfigured by it. In a notebook dedicated to Fuller's memory, Emerson suggests a similar metamorphosis:

> So I should say of this repeated account of sumptuousness of dress, I think *that*, like her beauty seen by some persons, was simply an effect of general impression of magnificence made by her & mistakenly attributed to some external elegance for I have been told by one of her most intimate friends who knew every particular re-

[53] Vide supra, chapter 7.

[54] See *Memoirs of Margaret Fuller Ossoli*, 1.230.

[55] "I think most of her friends will remember to have felt, at one time or another, some uneasiness, as if this athletic soul craved a larger atmosphere than it found; as if she were ill-timed and mis-mated. . . . Beethoven's Symphony was the only right thing the city of the Puritans had for her" (*Memoirs of Margaret Fuller Ossoli*, 1.231–232).

[56] The comparison is made in F. I. Carpenter, *Emerson Handbook*, (New York, 1953), p. 33.

> specting her at that very time, & learn that there was nothing of special expense of splendour in her toilette.[57]

It took the extraordinary episode of Fuller's Italian marriage, her courage as a nurse to the wounded, and finally her death in a shipwreck—which gave Emerson his access to her journal—for the scales to fall from Emerson's eyes.[58] If there seems at first a note of insensitiveness bordering on cruelty in certain of his letters, the excuse is his innocence.

As one might expect, the instinctive repulsion Emerson felt on his first interview with Fuller was not conquered in a few days. McNulty has pointed out the significant alteration in the salutations of Emerson's letters, which proceed from "dear Miss Fuller" (1837) to "my dear Margaret" (August–September 1840), by way of "my dear friend" and "excellent friend." It is perhaps because Fuller was in the autumn of 1839 recovering from a difficult passage of her life and was gradually learning a less agressive self-assurance that during that time the tone of Emerson's letters becomes more personal and more direct. One seems to hear in them a cautious invitation to a not entirely cerebral sort of sympathy—as when Emerson humorously alludes to "his honorable prison—my quarantine of temperament wherefrom I deal courteously with all comers, but through cold water."[59] He seems ready to try the experience of a friendship that, instead of forever seeking to inquire into itself, would willingly obey the flow and ebb of emotions.[60] Emerson and Fuller also exchanged books and lent each other portfolios of drawings and engravings, as was the custom throughout the period. But what brought them closer than anything else was the *Dial*.[61] Fuller assumed the official direction of the magazine, and Emerson helped her as best he could, discussing with extreme care the merits of this article and the weaknesses of that, and sometimes problems of payment or scheduling. This ardent collaboration, uncomplicated and free of ulterior motives, toppled the last barriers of reserve—or at least certain concrete signs, like the charming domestic scene he sketches in one of his letters,[62] made it seem so. In reality, the rapprochement between them had

[57] JMN 11.190.

[58] "The unlooked for trait in all these journals to me is the Woman, poor woman: they are all hysterical. She is bewailing her virginity and languishing for a husband" (JMN 11.500).

[59] Letter to Margaret Fuller of November 27, 1839 (L 2.238–240).

[60] "I . . . startled my mother & my wife when I went into the dining room with the declaration that I wished to live a little while with people who love & hate, who have Muses & Furies, and in a twelvemonth I should write tragedies & romance" (letter to Margaret Fuller of December 23, 1839 [L 2.245–247]).

[61] On the reasons for Emerson's interest in the magazine vide infra.

[62] "If you wish to know what you ask so gaily yet so affectionately know then that my moth-

not cleared up any of the fundamental causes of their mutual incomprehension; but it did make possible a debate that for the first time really got to the bottom of things. The letters Fuller and Emerson exchanged from August to October of 1840 (some of which have unfortunately not come down to us) constitute a sort of dramatic supplement to the essay on friendship. To say that reading that correspondence is easy and pleasant would be to ignore the philosophical verbosity the age so cherished; but the intensity of the personal problems is such that they retain every contour of their shape despite the fog of words surrounding them. There is surely no moment in Emerson's work in which one feels so distinctly the need of one soul conscious of being exceptional to explain itself to another.

It all began, apparently, in a conversation during which Fuller reproached Emerson with his "inhospitality of soul."[63] Speaking for Caroline Sturgis as well as for herself, she complained that their friendships were making no progress because Emerson could only weigh and count when they expected from him the comfort of a shared feeling: "they feel wronged in such relation, & do not wish to be catechised & criticised." A few days later, Emerson wrote Sturgis a long letter, less to exculpate himself than to explain in terms resembling those of the essay the apparently selfish but in fact universal character of a friendship lived in accordance with the universal spirit.[64] With Fuller his tone is less official; he promises to quit his voluntary exile and "deserve [his] friends."[65] But his honesty could not let him stop there. At the end of September, he himself rekindled the quarrel, determined this time to settle it: in vain, he said, did they persuade each other that they were united in a profound affinity, in vain did they claim to share in the same vocation:

---

er's benignity is unbroken that Lidian is for these two days past petrified to a water dropping stone by the novel of Deerbrook: yea this day had it in her lap at the dinner table; that Waldo the Less draws praiseworthy *ps* on the slate and asks—(yesterday) why there is no "telling" on the frame of my microscope? by which I learn that he means, —why no maker's name & place told. Unfortunately for him in the hot weather his mother thinks his hair so "seraphical," that I cannot engage her to cut it. Ellen is quite past my praise; she celebrates every step she takes with a song sweeter than Bob o Lincoln's. The dog, thank you, is hearty. Not possibly can I get rid of him. The two kittens grow like my cucumbers. The black one will stay; the grey one will go to Mrs Hoar's. —The old gentleman in the study wastes, it must be owned, good time: dips a pen in ink, affects to write a little from upper dictation, but presently falls to copying old musty papers, —then to reading a little in Plato, a little in the Vedas, then picks his pea vines a little, or waters his melons, or thins his carrots; walks a little, talks a little, and the marvellous Day has fled forevermore" (letter to Margaret Fuller of July 27 and 28, 1840 [L 2.319–320]).

[63] See JMN 7.509–510 (August 16, 1840).

[64] L 2.324–327. The two dates Rusk gives (August 16 and 20) are both problematical.

[65] Letter of September 13, 1840 (L 2.332–333).

> I on the contrary do constantly aver that you & I are not inhabitants of one thought of the Divine Mind, but of two thoughts, that we meet & treat like foreign states, one maritime, one inland, whose trade & laws are essentially unlike. I find or fancy in your theory a certain wilfulness and not pure acquiescence which seems to me the only authentic mode. Our friend is part of our fate; those who dwell in the same truth are friends; those who are exercised on different thoughts are not, & must puzzle each other, for the time.[66]

But, he hastens to add, the separation is temporary: eternity, which dissolves all barriers, will prevail.

Fuller's response came back at once, betraying the wounded animal: "I felt that you did not for me the highest office of friendship, by offering me the clue of the labyrinth of my own being. . . . did not you ask for a 'foe' in your friend? Did not you ask for a 'large formidable nature'?" She hesitates to pursue her thoughts to their conclusion, to charge the man who had been her idol not only with harshness but with pettiness of soul; "when my soul . . . stretched out its arms to you as a father," she asks, "did you then say, 'I know not what this means; perhaps this will trouble me'?"[67] To this message, in which disappointed trust seems ready to turn to hatred, Emerson responded with a curious compunction—sincere, tactful, yet distant and somehow unconcerned. He accepts all the charges and no doubt has incurred more of them, but denies any culpable intention: "tis imbecility not contumacy, tho' perhaps somewhat more odious."[68] Their conversation would clarify nothing, he says, were it to continue till the end of time. Fuller demands an acknowledgment of *her* truth, while for Emerson there is one truth only, in which all individual truths participate and which we discover to the extent that our life forces permit. One speaks of sympathy and the other of power; but Emerson's drama is not the less compelling, and Fuller's reproaches do lead him, though by a detour, to the gnawing paradox of the human condition: "strange disproportion betwixt our apprehension & our power to embody & affirm!" Although it had started in the mode of contrition, the letter gradually changed into an almost Nietzschean proclamation: "as soon as we are more catholicly instructed we shall be helped by all vices & shall see what indispensable elements of character men of pride libertinism & violence conceal."

As Emerson announced to Fuller a few weeks later, the debate on

[66] Letter of September 25, 1840 (L 2.336–337).

[67] Rusk reprints this almost indecently pathetic letter in a note (L 2.340–341).

[68] Letter of October 2, 1840 (L 2.342–343). The date is conjectural.

friendship was practically closed.[69] Since, he says in essence, the discussion leads nowhere and threatens to destroy what it touches, let us be friends as brothers can be friends and maintain a perfect silence on the matter: "I see very dimly in writing on this topic. It will not prosper with me. Perhaps all my words are wrong. Do not expect it of me again for a very long time." It is not the least curious trait of the affair that he could not keep his word. Just as his letters were recovering their former informality, not to say their abandon,[70] he brought up the preceding autumn's dispute all over again, the memory of which seems to have continued to trouble him: "Among other things I have discovered that the cause of that barrier some time talked of between us two, is that I have no barrier, but am all boundless conceding & willowy."[71] It needed all of Emerson's ingenuousness—or, perhaps, his extreme inhumanity—to keep him from seeing that his efforts at explanation were not helping his friend but rather were placing her in a still more uncomfortable situation. If in fact he wanted to be treated as a substance without shape or distinct qualities, how could she comfortably endure his presence? The sequel to this bizarre imbroglio is in the message she composed a few weeks later during a visit to the Emerson house, on which Emerson later wrote "letter written at Concord from room to room":

> I like to be in your library when you are out of it. It seems a sacred place. I came here to find a book, that I might feel more life and be worthy to sleep, but there is so much soul here I do not need a book. When I come to yourself, I cannot receive you, and you cannot give yourself; it does not profit. But when I cannot find you the beauty and permanence of your life come to me.[72]

In the same period—as an echo, one might say, of Fuller's words—Emerson wrote agitatedly in his journal of their relationship's disconcerting ambivalence:

> I would that I could, I know afar off that I cannot give the lights & shades, the hopes & outlooks that come to me in these strange,

[69] Letter of October 24, 1840 (L 2.352–353). The letter was partially reprinted in Cabot, *Memoir*, 1.367–369, and was commented on by Henry James in his review of that work; but James's ignorance of the other facts in the case led him to underestimate the force and depth of the feelings involved in it (*American Essays of Henry James*, pp. 63–64).

[70] "But in sunshine & in frost yes even in my native glaciers, am I ever yours affectionately" (letter of June 23, 1841 [L 2.410]); "Dear Margaret, ever to me a friendly angel with a cornucopia of gifts" (letter of July 31, 1841 [L 2.437]).

[71] Letter to Margaret Fuller of July 31 and August 2, 1841 (L 2.437–439).

[72] L 2.455. The letter's exact date is not known, but a note in Emerson's hand places it in October 1841.

> cold-warm, attractive-repelling conversations with Margaret, whom I always admire, most revere when I nearest see, and sometimes love, yet whom I freeze, & who freezes me to silence, when we seem to promise to come nearest.[73]

One can imagine the light a Freudian might cast on these texts. As one recent critic has suggested, the protagonists of this "curious Yankee melodrama . . . were toying with temptations they were both too virginal to recognize."[74] The introduction into Emerson's traditional Puritanism of the scarcely controlled forces of European Romanticism is here displayed with extraordinary vividness, while the opposition of the temperaments involved—the one embodying Romanticism still suffused with Puritanism, the other Puritanism rekindled by the Romantic ambiance—gives the dialogue an unexpected tension barely revealing the play of hidden feelings. Impatience, perplexity, the desire for a rupture—or for a withdrawal—regret tinged by remorse cumulatively convey the intensity of the shock Emerson had sustained, till finally he seized upon the occasion offered by his participation in a posthumous homage to Fuller to revive, and thereby to comprehend, the strange history of their relationship. The striking trait of his portion of the *Memoirs of Margaret Fuller Ossoli* is the absence of conventional elements, the almost brutal sincerity with which he sketches Fuller's image. Nothing of what had given their relations their often bitter savor is sacrificed. Rather, the antagonisms manifested all along the way occupy the foreground, testifying to Emerson's fidelity but also to his desire to contemplate sub specie aeternitatis a part of the natural order long obscured by the intrusion of subjectivity. One recalls Montaigne, who in introducing the *Essais* notes that he has sought to serve neither the reader nor his own glory. Whatever force the sense of piety or obligation may have had initially, it is clear that in tracing his frank and bold portrait of Fuller Emerson was effectuating a long delayed catharsis.

Never again, in any case, in the course of the forty years remaining to him was Emerson to have an experience of this sort. Friendship became for him what he had always wanted it to be, namely, an intellectual confrontation rigorously defended against the intrusions of feeling. But the memory of the maelstrom he had only barely escaped intensified his suspicions, and subsequently he was quick to guard himself against the danger no matter how far off he sensed it. He writes to Elizabeth Hoar in 1847:

[73] JMN 8.109 (October 12, 1841).

[74] Miller, "I Find no Intellect Comparable," p. 25.

> I sometimes think how glad I should be if I had a friend to whom I could tell things. Alas & alas, I have not health or constitution enough to bear so dear demanding a relation. So do not soar another pitch in your bounty, & say, you will be my abbess, & hear my shrift. I have not music enough to modulate the egotism which would grate intolerably without music, and I must mope awhile longer.[75]

And it was all too true that Emerson was condemned to tread a difficult path between the imperious and devouring modes of friendship, against which he protested with the whole force of his being, and the ideal solitude he still dreamed of but knew to be only intermittently possible. From 1839 on, he was to admit the necessity of external stimulation in keeping the soul at its highest level of intellectual activity,[76] and he would repeat till the end of his life that if " 't is hard to mesmerize ourselves, to whip our own top," it is also true that "through sympathy we are capable of energy and endurance."[77] Society, it seems, will no longer exhibit the hyena's rapacity he had so often denounced.

It is appropriate to record briefly the successive steps this evolution took. Emerson's temperament so strongly inclined him to solitude that at first he could only visualize a very rudimentary sort of social life, attended by weighty guarantees of personal independence. For example, he would have liked to have had New England imitate Addison's London and offer its writers agreeable places to meet, in which minds might polish and sharpen one another.[78] But the project he cherished most urgently and persistently concerned a sort of purely geographical community, a locus in which most of his friends might simply reside, Car-

[75] Letter to Elizabeth Hoar of December 28, 1847 (L 3.459). Hoar was Charles Emerson's fiancée; and after his brother's death Emerson continued to treat her as a member of his inner family.

[76] Cf. this passage from the journal for October 26, 1839: "Perhaps the true solution of this problem of spending a day well, is to be found for me and such as me in that social activity which I forbear. If I should, (or say, *could*) set myself to the unhesitating mission of inviting all persons from house to house to come up into my way of thinking & seeing, —boldly & lovingly affirming the peace which I find in my detached position & perfect reliance on the Universal Order, & demonstrating the contentment & new life & enlarged resources which society would find in the reception of the same, that would be occupation, excitement & the prolific occasion, no doubt, of antagonisms, of rencontres, & friendships & aversions public and private, —coincidences & collisions with the laws & the law-makers, that would elicit deep traits of character in myself & in my fellows" (JMN 7.280).

[77] "Society and Solitude" (W 7.11). This is the title essay of the 1870 collection, which was the last prepared by Emerson himself.

[78] JMN 7.430 (April 19, 1841). The same wish was expressed at the end of a lecture given in 1835 (EL 1.216).

lyle and Sterling among them.[79] It was to this end that he kept Thoreau under his own roof, sought a lodging for the impoverished Alcott, and gave a glittering account—in a letter to Fuller—of the benefits and charms of the Transcendentalist university likely to be born from this gathering:

> I did not tell you of our University which Mr A. & I built out of straws the other day until it looked very goodly. We two are quite ready & perhaps Parker Ripley Hedge Bradford & others may be soon to undertake, say in this town of Concord, to give lectures or conversations to classes of young persons on those subjects which we study. . . . The *terms* of the courses shall rest in the ability & discretion of the student. Is he poor—he shall not pay; is he not instructed—he shall not pay: is he rich & is he benefitted—he shall pay what he thinks fit. . . . Now do you not wish to come here & join in such a work. What society shall we not have! What Sundays shall we not have![80]

Nothing practical emerged from these splendid musings, and the community free both of obligations and of sanctions never saw the light of day. But Sherman Paul is right to observe that a good part of the urgency of the project disappeared at the completion in June 1844 of the Concord–Boston railway;[81] henceforth Emerson could satisfy his social needs by a brief trip, and as often as the mood took him he could trade the forest paths of Concord for the bookshop of Elizabeth Peabody, or later for the pleasant amenities of the Saturday Club.[82]

The only tangible result of these utopian impulses was the creation of

[79] See the letter to Sterling of May 29, 1840: "there are three or four persons in this country whom I could heartily wish to show to three or four persons in yours, and when I shall arrange any such interviews under my own roof I shall be proud and happy" (*Correspondence Between Sterling and Emerson*, p. 31). Three months later Emerson expressed the same desire in a letter to Carlyle (August 30, 1840 [CEC 277]).

[80] Letter to Margaret Fuller of August 16, 1840 (L 2.323–324; a version of this letter, containing numerous important variants, is printed in Cabot, *Memoir*, 2.409–410). Emerson's journal for the day records this passage: "how joyfully would I form permanent relations with the three or four wise & beautiful whom I hold so dear, and dwell under the same roof or in strict neighborhood. That would at once ennoble life. And it is practicable. It is easier than things which others do. It is easier than to go to Europe, or to subdue a forest farm in Illinois" (JMN 7.510).

[81] The chapter "Friendship" in *Emerson's Angle of Vision* contains what is probably the best analysis we have of the ideal community Emerson so stubbornly desired and sought. See particularly pp. 183–193.

[82] In 1840, Elizabeth Peabody opened a bookstore in Boston that very quickly became the Transcendentalist rendezvous. On the Saturday Club, founded in 1858, vide infra, chapter 13, n. 125.

the *Dial*, the most famous of the Transcendentalist periodicals;[83] and it is significant that Emerson did not at first ally himself with the idea of such a publication.[84] But his position was soon abruptly reversed, a change probably hastened by the defection of Frederic Hedge.[85] As long as he was not responsible for the enterprise[86] he was glad to take part in it, because it seemed to come at an opportune moment and to answer an immense and silent prayer ascending from the nation itself:

> There seem to me so few ready to speak what multitudes are plainly waiting to hear, & wondering that they do not hear, that I feel at times a certain urgency to write some deliberate words on the great questions which we all silently revolve. Wherever I go I meet many persons who if you will address them as human beings and not as camp-followers or appendages to this Grand Caravan of Society will eagerly own the salute as an honor & a great obligation.[87]

The *Dial*'s first editorial, prepared by Emerson and Fuller jointly,[88] is nothing but this intention consummated; it was for the authors a question of aiding men of goodwill, however dispersed amidst the American immensity and isolated by social position or profession, to become aware of one another and to believe that other minds quite nearby were struggling with equal heroic and ignored passion for the triumph of the new spirit. Despite a certain rhetorical complacency, which is after all

[83] The best introduction to this subject is the two volumes by G. W. Cooke, published in 1902 when the the *Dial* was reprinted by the Rowfant Club; Cooke's work permits Clarence Gohdes, in *The Periodicals of American Transcendentalism* (Durham, N.C., 1931), to restrict his own account of the *Dial* to ten pages (pp. 27–37).

[84] At any rate, that is what seems to emerge from a rather disgruntled passage of the journal in which, in discussing a meeting of the Transcendentalist Club, Emerson does not even mention that publishing a periodical might be in the offing—whereas Alcott's journal for the same day indicates that such a venture was the chief subject of discussion (JMN 7.242 [September 18, 1839] and, for the Alcott citation, J 5.256).

[85] Cf. Rusk, *Life*, pp. 275–276, and the letter to Margaret Fuller of March 30, 1840 (L 2.271).

[86] He returns to this stipulation on several occasions in his letters to Fuller; see particularly L 2.225, 242–243, and 270.

[87] Letter of April 13, 1840 to W. H. Furness (in Furness, *Records of a Lifelong Friendship, 1807–1882* [Boston, 1910], p. 9). Furness was Emerson's childhood friend; later he lived in Philadelphia and corresponded with Emerson, not at any great length but with remarkable regularity.

[88] Emerson's part in the composition of this manifesto seems to have been the preponderant one, at least for certain passages recorded in draft in the journal and letters. *The Transcendentalists: An Anthology*, ed. Perry Miller, (Cambridge, Mass., 1950), pp. 247–251, reprints the editorial in full.

the mark of the whole period, the appeal has retained its freshness. A generous spirit breathes in it, evoking the people of New England at this moment of their history, ministers and day laborers, schoolmasters and housewives, rich and poor, young women and old maids: one is reminded of Bancroft, with an extra touch of evangelicism.

But the eloquence was barely sufficient to make up for a severe paucity of content. Once past the swell of words, there remained, aside from the pressing invitation to a sort of *denuo nasci*, little but negative promises, refusals of commitment and definition. Everyone must find his own path of growth, and the *Dial*, submissive to this principle, will go where the spirit of the age takes it: "It cannot foretell in orderly propositions what it shall attempt. All criticism should be poetic; unpredictable; superseding, as every new thought does, all foregone thoughts, and making a new light on the whole world."[89] Before taking this text to the printer Emerson should have read his own remarks on the weakness of superlatives;[90] a good many of the *Dial*'s insipidities derive from the text's mixture of the sublime and the hazy. For Emerson, whom his lucidity accompanied even in visions of apotheosis, and on whom the demands of form never released their hold, the danger was not fatal; even a derivative article like "The Senses and the Soul," published in the *Dial*'s second issue, harbors several penetrating observations couched in handsome language.[91] But with the run-of-the-mill writer of the small Transcendentalist world it was different; the authors were prolific but satisfied only themselves. For some, the *Dial* erred by excessive generality; for others—like Alcott—it was not spiritual enough. For the most reasonable—Brownson, Parker, Carlyle—it lacked weight.[92] In

[89] *The Transcendentalists*, ed. Miller, p. 250.

[90] See "The Superlative," W 10.161–179, in which Emerson attacks those who abuse that grammatical form, "not perceiving that superlatives are diminutives, and weaken; that the positive is the sinew of speech, the superlative the fat" (p. 164).

[91] See for example the passage in which Emerson denounces the universal deceitfulness of the senses: "in trade, the momentary state of the markets betrays continually the experienced and long-sighted. In politics, and in our opinion of the prospects of society, we are in like manner the slaves of the hour. Meet one or two malignant declaimers, and we are weary of life, and distrust the permanence of good institutions. A single man in a ragged coat looks revolutionary. But ride in a stage-coach with one or two benevolent persons in good spirits, and the Republic seems to us safe" (*Dial* 2, [January 1842], p. 378).

[92] Brownson's criticism is particularly interesting because it employs the terminology made popular by Carlyle to construct a vivid comparison between the French Revolution and the America of 1840: "it may be regarded, we suppose, as the organ of the Transcendentalists, or exquisites of the movement party, —radicals indeed, of a most ultra stamp, but nevertheless radicals, who would *radicalize* in kid gloves and satin slippers. The Diallists belong to the genre *cullotic*, and have no fellowship with your vulgar 'sans-cullottes' [sic]" (*Boston Quarterly Review* 4 [January 1841], pp. 131–132; "Literary Notices: *The Dial*").

1852, Emerson cast a retrospective glance on the enterprise—which had, he agreed, had a certain nobility and had indeed nourished a good many hopes—and tried to discover why in the end it had failed:

> the agitation had perhaps the fault of being too secondary or bookish in its origin, or caught not from primary instincts, but from English, and still more from German books. . . . But the workmen of sufficient culture for a poetical and philosophical magazine were too few. . . . Its scattered writers had not digested their theories into a distinct dogma, still less into a practical measure which the public could grasp.[93]

Against such handicaps, it was remarkable that the *Dial* lasted four years—as long, Emerson observed one day, as a presidency.[94]

That the sobered Transcendentalist of 1852 should reproach the *Dial* with insufficient attention to concrete situations will surprise no one. It is more striking to note that as early as 1840—that is, just after the publication of the first issue—Emerson was already avowing that his ideas had changed and was circumstantially describing in what direction he would take the magazine if the responsibility for it were his alone:

> I would not have it too purely literary. I wish we might make a Journal so broad & great in its survey that it should lead the opinion of this generation on every great interest & read the law on property, government, education, as well as on art, letters, & religion. . . . So I wish we might court some of the good fanatics and publish chapters on every head in the whole Art of Living. . . . I know the dangers of such latitude of plan in any but the best conducted Journal. It becomes friendly to special modes of reform partisan bigoted. perhaps whimsical; not universal & poetic. But our round table is not, I fancy, in imminent peril of party & bigotry, & we shall bruise each the other's whims by the collision.[95]

Emerson's proposition has value chiefly in what it reveals to us of its author's state of mind. Good sense and a certain sort of integrity join to-

[93] *Memoirs of Margaret Fuller Ossoli* 1.322. The judgment Emerson offers in "Life and Letters in New England" (W 10.343–344) is considerably more succinct.

[94] In a letter to Furness announcing the *Dial*'s imminent demise: "its last number is printed; & having lived four years, which is a Presidential term in America, it may respectably end. I have continued it for some time against my own judgment to please other people, and though it has now some standing & increasing favour in England, it makes a very slow gain at home, and it is for home that it is designed" (April 4, 1844; Furness, *Records*, p. 33).

[95] Letter to Margaret Fuller of August 4, 1840 (L 2.322–323). See also a passage of the journal, JMN 7.388 (July 31, 1840), listing the areas of life to be touched by the *Dial*'s voice: "Government, Temperance, Abolition, Trade, & Domestic Life."

gether against excessive abstraction.[96] It is not enough, after all, to proclaim the preeminence of the Spirit and its eternal springtide; one has to go into the matter a little more closely to see how that force can undertake to reknead the world's ancient dough. The shift of accent is noticeable; without denying the content of his faith, Emerson was now asking more precisely what practical sanctions it was to receive. To an exclusive desire for the deeply inward life was added at this time, in order to authenticate and on occasion to rectify that life, the examination of individual behavior with regard to the realities of society.

Once before, in 1837, Emerson had declared himself in solidarity with all reformers, abolitionists and supporters of temperance and utopian socialists alike: "I have strict relations to them all. None of these causes are foreigners to me."[97] That was the period during which, in the context of a series of lectures on human culture, he had sought to render appropriate homage to the power of the human heart.[98] But he had also warned his listeners against "a certain excess of the social principle" that ended by weakening personal vocations through urging them in many directions at once—no one, he said, citing a Spanish proverb, can balance three watermelons on one arm. Since then the reform movement had advanced in seven-league boots; stimulated by the depression of 1837, nurtured by such men of undeniable magnanimity as Horace Mann and William Lloyd Garrison, it had both diversified and intensified, and now touched on all the aspects of social life.[99] This surge of goodwill had in the end shaken even Emerson's reserve; in a letter to John Sterling dated May 1840, he declares that "the problems of reform are losing their local and sectarian character, and becoming generous, profound, and poetic."[100] Of the three epithets it is the last that is by far the most significant; it indicates that in Emerson's mind the division he had deplored between the inward burst of inspiration and the works that claim to express it was near to being abolished. The overall unity of man is being shaped anew, but the means of access is precisely the opposite of that proposed in "The American Scholar." No longer

[96] It would be unjust, however, to ignore the social and concrete character of certain articles in the *Dial*, and in particular those of Theodore Parker. They emerge here and there from the flood of Transcendentalist rhapsodies like reefs of a reassuring firmness.

[97] JMN 5.437 (November 24, 1837).

[98] In "Human Culture," lecture 5, "The Heart," given in the winter of 1837–1838. Vide supra, chapter 8.

[99] "I suppose the number of reforms preached to this age exceeds the usual measure, and indicates the depth & universality of the movement which betrays itself by such variety of symptom: Anti-money, anti-war, anti-slavery, anti-government, anti-Christianity, anti-College; and, the rights of Woman" (JMN 7.207 [June 6, 1839]).

[100] Letter of May 29, 1840 (*Correspondence Between Sterling and Emerson*, p. 31).

does thought take nourishment and support from action; rather the transformation of the world testifies to the activity of thought.

In all candor, Emerson sought to extend the practical reforms demanded by this vision of integrity regained to his own domestic kingdom: "See this wide society of laboring men and women. We allow ourselves to be served by them, we live apart from them, and meet them without a salute in the streets. . . . Thus we enact the part of the selfish noble and king from the foundation of the world."[101] He asked the cook and the maid to sit at the family table, so as to proclaim here and now the doctrine of universal equality; but the cook refused to leave her pots and the maid declined the invitation by way of maintaining ancillary solidarity. Evidently the reformation of the world was not going to take place unopposed even by those who had the most to gain by it. Emerson did not insist, and the project was abandoned. A little later he was attracted by vegetarianism; he had in this area considerable prejudices of his own to overcome,[102] but his reading of Porphyry's *De abstinentia* had almost convinced him: "Pirates do not live on nuts & herbs. The use of animal food marks the extremely narrow limits of our ideas of justice. We confine our justice to man alone; according to Porphyry's remark. Certainly our whole life ought to be a benefit and the heliotrope & sweetbriar & thyme should not smell sweeter."[103] Unlike Alcott, however, who was also familiar with Porphyry and who had attempted to apply his teachings at Fruitlands,[104] Emerson was never seriously concerned with exploring the regenerative possibilities of such a course; other, considerably more immediate and central concerns were pressing.

As the reform movement gained in power, the issues involved in it became clearer; thus clarified, they implied obligations for every honest and sincere citizen:

> The questions which have slept uneasily a long time are coming up to decision at last. Men will not be long occupied with the Christian question, for all the babes are born infidels; they will not care for your abstinences of diet, or your objections to domestic hired service; they will find something convenient & amiable in these.

[101] "Man the Reformer," W 1.252. The passage was originally formulated in the journal for April 1840 (JMN 7.207).

[102] As late as June 1840 he writes in his journal that "it is a superstition to insist on vegetable or animal or any special diet. All is made up at last of the same chemical atoms. . . . All the religion, all the reason in the new diet is that animal food costs too much" (JMN 7.369–370).

[103] JMN 7.433 ("Animals"; April 21, 1841).

[104] Vide infra, chapter 10.

> But the question of Property will divide us into odious parties. And all of us must face it & take our part.[105]

Emerson was thus led to a perception of the moral issue hidden behind political quarrels. If a young man without fortune has to begin by "selling himself" for ten years as a weaver, a farmhand, or a sailor to win the independence that is his right, society is inflicting a spiritual injury on him, because "the present hour is as sacred & inviolable as any future hour." And who does not see that the social edifice rests on a criminal injustice to which we all lend our aid?

> Of course, whilst another man has no land, my title to mine is at once vitiated. The state then must come to some new division of lands and all voices must speak for it. Every child that is born must have a chance for his bread. Inextricable seem to be the twinings & tendrils of this evil and we have all involved ourselves the more in it by wives & children & debts.[106]

It is important to realize that these lines reveal a new tone in Emerson's work. In his discussion of the relations that bind property and government three years earlier, he had distinguished between laws governing persons and laws governing property so that he could assign greater electoral power to the wealthy, on the ground of their particular interest in having the public domain well regulated.[107] As late as the previous winter, though his distrust of material goods had grown, his condemnation of excessive wealth had been situated on the ground of individualism; he had, that is, described great wealth not as a sign of iniquity but as a threat to the moral health of the person possessing it.[108] But now he was discovering that every human society is a community de facto, because in it individuals inosculate in a thousand open and concealed ways. The only difference was perhaps that sometimes, as in Europe, the bonds were evident, and at other times, as in America, they remained agreeably—or hypocritically—invisible. This is the new context in which to consider the problem posed by Brook Farm:[109] could

[105] JMN 7.513 (September 16, 1840). See also the letter to William Emerson of September 24, 1840 (L 2.334–335).

[106] Ibid.; these passages all turn up in "Man the Reformer" (W 1.234).

[107] Vide supra, chapter 7.

[108] Vide supra, chapter 8.

[109] Brook Farm—also known as the West Roxbury Community—has been the subject of numerous studies, of which the most recent is Katherine Burton, *Paradise Planters: The Story of Brook Farm* (New York, 1939); a bibliography is in Lawrence S. Hall, *Hawthorne, Critic of Society* (New Haven, 1944), pp. 191–193. But it is the contemporary accounts that best help one to grasp the spirit of the community and so to understand the problem that confronted

Emerson, ought Emerson to join the community that George Ripley—who like Emerson had resigned his ministry, apparently for the same reasons—was proposing to found?

In mid-September 1840 the first allusion to the project occurred in Emerson's correspondence.[110] His reaction, soon amplified in the journal,[111] was skepticism tinged with irritation; it is madness, he thinks, to expect salvation from a period more "social-minded" than those preceding it; the reformers ought to disperse and vanish into the crowd, elevating it as leaven raises dough. But the journal of that autumn makes clear that the debate was not over; in fact it lacerated him, and more painfully as the necessity of answering yes or no crystallized the natural tendencies of his temperament and opposed them to the advantages his friends hoped to draw from their communal experience.[112] The conflict thus joined found its solution—its provisional solution—in a passage that, though often cited, deserves repetition for its terse, proud beauty:

> Yesterday George & Sophia Ripley, Margaret Fuller & Alcott discussed here the new social plans. I wished to be convinced, to be thawed, to be made nobly mad by the kindlings before my eye of a new dawn of human piety. But this scheme was arithmetic & comfort; this was a hint borrowed from the Tremont House and U.S. Hotel; a rage in our poverty & politics to live rich & gentlemanlike, an anchor to leeward against a change of weather; a prudent forecast on the probable issue of the great questions of pauperism & property. And not once could I be inflamed, —but sat aloof & thoughtless, my voice faltered & fell. It was not the cave of persecution which is the palace of spiritual power, but only a room in the Astor House hired for the Transcendentalists. I do not wish to remove from my present prison to a prison a little larger. I wish to

Emerson. See particularly Elizabeth Peabody, "Plan of the West Roxbury Community," *Dial* 2 (January 1842), pp. 361–372; reprinted with a substantial introduction in *The Transcendentalists*, ed. Miller, pp. 464–469.

[110] See the letter to Elizabeth Hoar of September 12, 1840 (L 2.330–331).

[111] See JMN 7.401 (September 26, 1840).

[112] A letter of Ripley's to Emerson (quoted in *The Transcendentalists*, ed. Miller, p. 464) defines these advantages with engaging precision: "Our objects, as you know, are to insure a more natural union between intellectual and manual labor than now exists; to combine the thinker and the worker, as far as possible, in the same individual; to guarantee the highest mental freedom, by providing all with labor, adapted to their tastes and talents, and securing to them the fruits of their industry; to do away with the necessity of menial services, by opening the benefits of education and the profits of labor to all; and thus to prepare a society of liberal, intelligent, and cultivated persons, whose relations with each other would permit a more simple and wholesome life, than can be led amidst the pressure of our competitive institutions."

> break all prisons. I have not yet conquered my own house. It irks & repents me. Shall I raise the siege of this hencoop & march baffled away to a pretended siege of Babylon? It seems to me that so to do were to dodge the problem I am set to solve, & hide my impotency in the thick of a crowd. I can see too afar that I should not find myself more than now, —no, not so much, in that select, but not by me selected, fraternity. Moreover to join this body would be to traverse all my long trumpeted theory, and the instinct which spoke from it, that one man is a counterpoise to a city, —that a man is stronger than a city, that his solitude is more prevalent & beneficent than the concert of crowds.[113]

But the letter of refusal remained to be written, and two months passed in hesitation and delay. Ripley counted on Emerson's authority to give the enterprise an auspicious impetus at its beginning, and that fact troubled Emerson;[114] rarely had he had to measure the effects of his own behavior on someone else so precisely. Moreover, the project had its temptations; not only did it connect with his desire to give a greater place in his life to physical labor, it also promised to offer him the guidance and the models he needed in that area. Above all there was the school, which Ripley and his friends intended to set up within the community itself to be both a testing ground for the new pedagogy inspired by Pestalozzi and a philosophical club, in which the diverse inclinations of the teachers might confront one another in complete and friendly mutual respect. Finally, Ripley's sincere liberalism assured Emerson that Brook Farm would avoid the snare of regimentation; it would be up to each member to determine the level of socialism he wished his own life to incorporate—meals, for example, would be eaten communally only by those who wished to do so. All these arguments march through the letters from these two months in 1840; on one occasion Emerson even describes himself (in a letter to Lidian) as a "dangerous husband" who might suddenly sell house and garden.[115] Finally, however, he said no (a decision for which Ripley never entirely forgave him), insisting on the "personal" character of his reasons—not denying, that is, that some people might well live more fully and more authentically in a community removed from the pressures of the world, but knowing surely that he was not one of them. Neither Concord nor his place in society was responsible for his failure, and it would be as unjust on his part to blame

[113] JMN 7.407–408 (October 17, 1840). Tremont House and the Astor House were hotels in Boston and in New York, respectively. See also the letter to Caroline Sturgis of October 21, 1840 (L 2.350); date conjectural.

[114] See the letter to Margaret Fuller of December 1, 1840 (L 2.362–364); date conjectural.

[115] Letter to Lidian Emerson of November 15, 1840 (L 2.360).

them for it as it would be cowardly to entrust Brook Farm with the burden of his emancipation.[116]

The last word had thus been said, and Emerson's fidelity to himself had prevailed. The debate that preceded the final decision had revealed, like a sort of geological core-sampling, the thickness of the sedimentations he would now have to traverse to reach the unchanged substratum. That is the point worth attending to. The fact that in the same weeks Emerson was both conducting a close investigation into friendship and seriously weighing the merits of a utopian community indicates clearly that the gospel of "Self-Reliance" was in need of some adjustment. The final extension of this large movement in the direction of other people, at once its culmination and its conclusion, is the lecture Emerson gave in January 1841, the title of which alone—"Man the Reformer"—indicates by its abstraction that in it Emerson speaks unveiled.[117]

Emerson accepts all of Ripley's criticisms of contemporary society. Gainful activities are ruled by selfishness, which never recoils from oppression; and as daily existence would be impossible without Cuban sugar and Carolinian cotton, every consumer and every American bears the responsibility for a global injustice. Also like Ripley, and in truth in the same spirit, Emerson wishes to protest against this universal degradation; but he judges the communal method cumbersome and complicated and prefers to it the solitary effort by which each one of us, wherever he may be, exerts himself to preserve his own integrity.

While Ripley calls for a collective retreat by men of goodwill, Emerson advocates a discrete series of limited severances—such, clearly, is the meaning of what he calls (amplifying a suggestion made earlier in the series "The Present Age") the "Doctrine of the Farm." Ideally every human being is capable of self-government; failing that, working the land will put people in an elemental relation with nature, and from this contact they will draw force and confidence: "I confess I should not be pained at a change which threatened a loss of some of the luxuries or conveniences of society, if it proceeded from a preference of the agricultural life out of the belief that our primary duties as men could be better discharged in that calling."[118]

[116] Letter to Ripley of December 15, 1840 (L 2.368–371). Cabot, *Memoir*, 2.436–438, prints what seems to be the passage of the journal constituting Emerson's sketch of his answer; the tone is more direct there and indicates Emerson's determination not to take part in the undertaking still more forcefully.

[117] The lecture was given January 25, 1841 at the Mechanics' Apprentices' Library Association in Boston (W 1.225–256).

[118] "Man the Reformer," W 1.235. See also the letter to William Emerson of December 21, 1840 (L 2.371–372).

The emergence of this militant variety of Jeffersonianism in Emerson's thought marks the confluence of two distinct currents. On the one hand, manual labor is considered to be a healthful exercise, the necessity of which presses on the philosopher in proportion as his reflections or his indoor conversations have previously lowered his spirits.[119] Whether for good or ill, the mind is lodged in a body, and mysterious exchanges take place between the two partners. If the one is enervated, the other grows anemic; thus our muscles serve more than a material interest when they thrust a spade into the earth. "We must have a basis for our higher accomplishments, our delicate entertainments of poetry and philosophy, in the work of our hands. We must have an antagonism in the tough world for all the variety of our spiritual faculties, or they will not be born."[120] But Emerson is aware of a possible objection. In using the same word for physical relaxation and gainful labor had he not avoided the real problem, namely that of finding out whether beyond a certain point the laborer's activity will not turn against that of the philosopher and poet? And can the philosopher or poet who is responsible for a family always make sure that the point has not been exceeded? Emerson does not dismiss the difficulty; but he recalls firmly, though calmly, that "no separation from labor can be without some loss of power and of truth to the seer himself."[121] Here we come upon the second of the currents mentioned above. Because manual labor—and above all farmer's labor—submits to Nature even as it shapes it, it makes us both creators and disciples. We learn by the very gesture that asserts our authority over things, and our possession of the world introduces us to its laws. The theme is not new even in Emerson—it inspired the lecture on trades in 1837, and in the following year that on the "Doctrine of the Hands." But here it has been freighted with a more concrete substance, as it were succeeding to the glorious but unfulfilled prophecies of "The American Scholar." Emerson has renounced, it seems, the ideal

[119] "I know no means of calming the fret & perturbation into which too much sitting, too much talking brings me so perfect as labor. . . . my good hoe as it bites the ground revenges my wrongs & I have less lust to bite my enemies. I confess I work at first with a little venom, lay to a little unnecessary strength. But by smoothing the rough hillocks, I smooth my temper; by extracting the long roots of the piper grass, I draw out my own splinters" (JMN 7.211 [June 12, 1839]).

[120] "Man the Reformer," W 1.236, and, slightly modified, JMN 7.495 (May 1840). It is notable that this aesthetic justification of labor—one thinks of Valéry and his theories about the necessary intractability of poetic material—is discussed in a review of Emerson's early writings by Monckton-Milnes (*Westminster Review* 33 [March 1840], pp. 345–372). Emerson knew the article, and certain similarities in vocabulary show that its influence was still with him.

[121] "Man the Reformer," W 1.242.

of action he then painted so brilliantly, and his hopes have been transferred to the daily tussle with Nature.[122] Henceforth what is to be honored in Cincinnatus is not the general but the farmer.

After this long justification of personal choice, in which the concern for other people is manifested only as it shows through the exemplary quality of the author himself, Emerson oddly concludes the lecture by an appeal to brotherly love. He is saddened by the existence of prisons, condemns masters' harshness to servants, regrets that the nation is divided between rich and poor, when our "affection," in being directed to the most disadvantaged, "would operate in a day the greatest of all revolutions."[123] He celebrates the humble and prudent force of love with a fervor reminiscent less of Whitman than of Francis of Assisi:

> Have you not seen in the woods, in a late autumn morning, a poor fungus or mushroom, —a plant without any solidity, nay, that seemed nothing but a soft mush or jelly, —by its constant, total, and inconceivably gentle pushing, manage to break its way up through the frosty ground, and actually to lift a hard crust on its head? It is the symbol of the power of kindness.[124]

And he extends the image by the luminous evocation of a world in which all men might love one another and misfortune would dissolve under a universal sun.

The contrast between the body of the lecture in its severe analysis and the conclusion in its almost Lamartinian humanitarianism[125] is so striking that one doubts Emerson's sincerity; might he not, one wonders, have yielded in extremis to a need to please and affect? But the journal forbids such an interpretation; on September 20, 1840 it records a long account, and one perfectly Emersonian in theme, in which Love is saluted as "the unknown & inexhaustible continent."[126] Thus under the influence of the Zeitgeist the meaning of the word "love" has been al-

[122] In one of his "Orphic Sayings," Alcott offers—with his characteristic rhetorical inflation—a similar praise of labor: "Man discourses sublimely with the divinities over the plough, the spade, the sickle, marrying the soul and the soil by the rites of labor. Sloth is the tempter that beguiles him of innocence, and exiles him from Paradise" (*Dial* 1.354).

[123] "Man the Reformer" (W 1.253).

[124] "Man the Reformer" (W 1.254). E. G. Berry, *Emerson's Plutarch* (Cambridge, Mass., 1961), pp. 224–225, suggests that Emerson owes this image to a passage in Plutarch's *Moralia*.

[125] Emerson never met Lamartine, but was in the Chambre des Députés when Lamartine gave his great speech on Poland in June 1848. The mildly amused comments Emerson records in a letter (L 4.77) make clear that he was not very much impressed—though one should note that he did not understand French very well.

[126] JMN 7.396–398.

tered; without losing any of its spiritual quality, it has incorporated a certain fervor that makes the need for human brotherhood more pressing. But—and here the *sequence* of the steps is essential—Emerson can conceive of this opening up toward another person only as the continuation of an inward reform, which will have begun by restoring us to the bosom of universal order: "Nature is the mercury of our progress," he notes in the journal,[127] one week before giving the lecture just discussed.

Perhaps one ought to talk not of insincerity but of the unequal pressures to which the two sections of the lecture respond. Whatever he may strive to make others—and himself—believe, Emerson is still interested only in the relations between Nature and the individual man; his critique of society is general and remote; he seeks to leave it altogether out of the crucial issues that engage his mind. He prefers the farmer's life because cities—a collective creation par excellence—degrade and diminish us.

> I always seem to suffer from loss of faith on entering cities. They are great conspiracies; the parties are all masquers who have taken mutual oaths of silence, not to betray each others secret, & each to keep the others madness in countenance. You can scarce drive any craft here that does not seem a subornation of the treason. I believe in the spade and an acre of good ground. Whoso cuts a straight path to his own bread, by the help of God in the sun & rain & sprouting of the grain, seems to me an *universal* workman. He solves the problem of life not for one but for all men of sound body.[128]

This spontaneous hostility to the city, coming just when New York—to take only the most striking example—was growing at a breathtaking rate,[129] seems symptomatic on more than one count. It shows that however little Emerson was prepared for the actual activity of farming, his "agrarianism," as he called it, was more than an amateur's passing fancy; more important still it hints at a serious misunderstanding of his country's political and economic situation. By way of conclusion to this chapter, a few historical references will help us to fix the limits of Emerson's perception more precisely.

[127] JMN 7.412 (January 17, 1841).

[128] Letter to Carlyle of March 18, 1840 (CEC 260–262). Many Transcendentalists shared this horror of the city; cf. particularly Elizabeth Peabody's article on Brook Farm, in which she defines the development of cities as the history of human hatred.

[129] Emerson himself gives figures in the letter just cited, saying that between 1800 and 1840 New York grew from 20,000 to 350,000; in fact by 1800 its population was already 60,000.

It would probably be possible to reuse here the terms employed earlier in defining the scope of Emerson's interests[130]—a fact that bespeaks a curious immobility in a mind so committed to progress as Emerson's. Obsessed with each individual's obligation to secure his own independence, receptive at the same time to the sense of a destiny affecting the whole of humanity, Emerson was almost blind to the intermediate horizons of collective life—which are, for all their dullness and confusion, an inevitable stage in a progress toward the universal. His almost total indifference to the presid ntial election of 1840 is the most illuminating proof of this blindness, because of the historical perspective in which we can now situate it. Since the depression of 1837 and the Whigs' gaining control of Congress in 1838, Van Buren's political fate had been sealed; and at the end of a campaign in which the discussion of issues was even more contemptible than usual, General William Henry Harrison, the one-time scourge of Indians from Tecumseh to Tippecanoe, was elected president by a comfortable margin. But the interest lies elsewhere; the election of 1840 is remembered in history as a particularly glaring illustration of the political mechanisms that the American democracy of the time had learned to use extensively. Around Harrison's colorless though respectable personality was fabricated a whole popular mythology; he was portrayed as an easygoing Davy Crockett, content with a barrel of cider and a log cabin, and the succinct slogans and jingles in celebration of "Old Tip" multiplied abundantly. Jacksonianism had founded a school, and even its adversaries admitted that only with its own methods could they defeat it.

James Fenimore Cooper, whose loyalties had all along been torn between republicanism and aristocracy, was stunned at such demagoguery; he turned his back on the present and took refuge in the conviction that the Americans of the previous generation would never have abased themselves so thoroughly.[131] At the other end of the ill-defined spectrum of the Democratic Party, Orestes Brownson received the news of the Whig victory with dismay. He had based his social philosophy on the emancipation of the masses because he thought them capable of political good sense, and Harrison's election suddenly showed

[130] Cf. chapter 4.

[131] See Vernon Louis Parrington, *Main Currents in American Thought*, 3 vols. (New York, 1927–1930), 2.226–228 (chapter 4). Parrington's remarkable chapter on Cooper may be considered the beginning of a very fruitful analysis of Cooper's political thought that has been pursued both by historians (for example Marvin Meyers, *The Jacksonian Persuasion* (Stanford, Calif., 1957), chapter 4, "The Great Descent") and by literary critics (for example Marius Bewley, *The Eccentric Design* [New York and London, 1959], chapter 3, "Fenimore Cooper and the Economic Age").

him the colossal error of judgment he had committed.[132] But all this agitation touched Emerson not at all; he rejoiced in Van Buren's defeat in terms that make one doubt his political maturity.[133] Further, the grotesque imagination exercised in the Whig campaign actually attracted him; he confesses in his journal having enjoyed watching his countrymen push along the great ball that the Baltimore Convention had made its emblem:

> The most imposing part of this Harrison celebration of the Fourth of July in Concord as in Baltimore was this ball 12 or 13 feet in diameter which as it mounts the little heights & descends the little slopes of the road draws all eyes with a certain sublime movement especially as the imagination is incessantly addressed with its political significancy. So the Log Cabin is a lucky watchword.[134]

A more exact understanding of the political circumstances would doubtless have spared him the absurdity of this lofty interpretation.

Amusing though it may be, however, Emerson's commentary also reveals the incorrigibly "poetical" character of his thought—in the sense used by Plato, who defined the poet as a being endowed with irresponsible lightness. "We doubt," wrote Fuller, "this friend raised himself too early to the perpendicular and did not lie along the ground long enough to hear the secret whispers of our parent life."[135] Another episode from the same period illustrates the same odd insensibility still more strikingly. When Brownson understood that the Whigs were prepared to do anything for the sake of victory, he resolved to anticipate them and strike a great blow against their cause. Taking as his occasion the recent

[132] Arthur Schlesinger, Jr., in *Orestes Brownson: A Pilgrim's Progress* (Boston, 1939), pp. 110–113, sees in this disillusionment a shock of crucial importance for Brownson's later development—which, one will recall, led to his conversion to Catholicism in 1844.

[133] "I am an indifferent Whig & do not care for Mr Harrison but since the election of J. Q. Adams I do not remember any national event that has given me so much content as this general uprising to unseat Mr Van Buren & his government. Would that his successors could carry into Washington one impulse of patriotism one aspiration for a pure legislation!" (letter to William Emerson of November 9, 1840 [L 2.357]). Emerson does, however, foresee the scramble for spoils that the change in political responsibility was to occasion.

[134] JMN 7.378–379 (July 4 or 5, 1840). The symbolism of the ball rolled along by the crowd so struck Emerson's imagination that he was still alluding to it in his 1844 essay "The Poet" (W 3.16).

[135] Quoted by Paul, *Emerson's Angle of Vision*, p. 237, n. 40. In reviewing the second *Essays* for the *New York Tribune*, Margaret Fuller compared Emerson to the poet–legislators of early Greece, who taught both how to labor and how to avoid evil; she likened Emerson's lectures to theogonies adorned at solemn moments with odes and at casual ones with eclogues (Fuller, *Life Without and Life Within* [Boston and New York, 1859], pp. 191–198; reprinted in *The Writings of Margaret Fuller*, ed. Mason Wade [New York, 1941]).

publication of *Chartism*, the first work of Carlyle's to be focused on the misery of the working class, he undertook to put his own country on trial, and in his subversive violence left Carlyle's suggested remedies far behind. Considering the constant worsening of their daily circumstances, he argued that the "proletarians" (the word is his) had the right to rebel, and he made the abolition of inherited property a crucial tenet of the new social order.[136] His analysis was impaired by excess and vagueness, and the theories of French revolutionaries like Saint-Simon played too conspicuous a role in it; the Democrats themselves noticed as much and were quick to disavow it. But if the conclusions were disputable, the point of departure was not. Under the increasing and linked pressures of industrialization and capitalism, a not inconsiderable portion of the population had seen its opportunities for attaining economic independence diminish and sometimes entirely disappear; but at the same time, agrarianism was not the panacea that some liked to think it. "Few, comparatively speaking, of the proletaries in any of the old states can ever become land-owners. Land there is already too high for that. The new lands are rapidly receding to the West, and can even now be reached only by those who have some little capital in advance."[137] Theodore Parker was sufficiently impressed by Brownson's indictment to publish two articles in the *Dial*—one on the organization of society and the other on labor[138]—that with the exception of the notion of bloody class struggles took up Brownson's ideas pretty much untouched.

Emerson's reaction was very different. He did not, as Channing did,[139] apocalyptically fret and fume, but retained toward Brownson's argument the detachment of the sage: "I began Bancroft's 3d Volume & read a part of Brownson's Laboring Classes. The last hero wields a sturdy pen which I am very glad to see. I had judged him from some old things & did not know he was such a Cobbett of a scribe. Let him wash himself & he shall write for the immortal Dial."[140] Such is his derisive

[136] See "The Laboring Classes," *Boston Quarterly Review* 3 (July 1840), pp. 358–395 and (October 1840), pp. 420–512. *The Transcendentalists*, ed. Miller, pp. 436–446, partially reprints the two articles.

[137] "The Laboring Classes," p. 473.

[138] "A Lesson for the Day, or the Christianity of Christ, of the Church, and of Society," *Dial* 1 (October 1840), pp. 196–216, and "Thoughts on Labor," *Dial* 1 (April 1841), pp. 497–519.

[139] In a letter to Elizabeth Peabody cited in Peabody's *Reminiscences of Rev. William Ellery Channing* (Boston, 1880), pp. 414–416. The letter argues that the lot of young doctors and lawyers is in general harder than that of servants and laborers.

[140] Letter to Margaret Fuller of December 21, 1840 (L 2.372–373). It seems that *Chartism* interested Emerson less than Carlyle's other works. When he received a copy, he sent his com-

praise for the new American Samson. We can understand that he should have found Brownson's solution both utopian and monstrous; it concerns a question he had posed himself in pondering the basis of property rights. But the complacent tranquility of his response,[141] coming from a man otherwise quick to strip off masks wherever he finds them, is surprising and disconcerting: "he was constitutionally averse to interference with the existing economic order, much as he tampered with superannuated creeds and traditions."[142]

If one were to look among the Transcendentalists for another exponent of this attitude of distant indifference to the situation of the working class, one would have to choose Alcott; it is he who shares Emerson's unlimited and sometimes ungentle faith in the supremacy of the spirit:

> In the theocracy of the soul, majorities do not rule. God and the saints; against them, the rabble of sinners, with clamorous voices and uplifted hands, striving to silence the oracle of the private heart. Beelzebub marshals majorities. Prophets and reformers are always special enemies of his and his minions. Multitudes ever lie. Every age is a Judas, and betrays its Messiahs into the hands of the multitude. The voice of the private, not popular heart, is alone authentic.[143]

These are ominous words, if a temporal leader were to avail himself of them in formulating a program of action. But Alcott is an honest man writing in an almost empty continent, in which the most strident calls fade into silence. It is here that the particular situation of America in 1840 comes into play. Whatever Brownson may say, the socioeconomic situation is not such as to jeopardize the nation's equilibrium in any foreseeable future; given America's spatial configuration, there remains

---

pliments to the author (letter of April 21, 1840 [CEC 266–267]), but they are vague and conventional, and barely disguise his dissatisfaction.

[141] Compare by contrast the generous and grandiloquent indignation of a Parker: "Where shall we find a savage nation in the wide world that has, on the whole, been blessed by its intercourse with Christians? . . . Let this question be put to the nations we defraud of their spices and their furs, leaving them in return our Religion and our Sin; let it be asked of the Redman, whose bones we have broken to fragments, and trodden into bloody mire on the very spot where his mother bore him; let it be asked of the Black man, torn by our cupidity from his native soil, whose sweat, exacted by Christian stripes, fattens our fields of cotton and corn, and brims the wine-cup of national wealth" ("The Christianity of Christ, of the Church and of Society," *Dial* 1 [October 1840], p. 210).

[142] This is John Flanagan's conclusion in "Emerson and Communism," NEQ 10 (June 1937), pp. 243–261.

[143] "Theocracy," in "Orphic Sayings," *Dial* 1 (July 1840), p. 89.

considerable room to maneuver and, among other things, to defuse incendiary manifestoes at their inception.

The long process of trial and error in which we have seen Emerson engaged has at least revealed to us not only his often troubled considerations about friendship, communal life, and property rights, but also the strict limits of his sympathy. Even when he assented to the diagnoses the reformers offer, he would not or could not bring himself to unite his efforts with theirs in concerted action. The more aware he became of the world's imperfections, the more he struggled against collective obligations and the more rigid he grew within himself. In the course of the next stage of his thought he was to seek to work out a philosophy that would lastingly reconcile him with reality, men and women as well as things; once again, however, the path he chose owed nothing to the philanthropists.

10

~ ~ ~ ~

EXPLORING THE PROBLEMS

DESPITE the continuity of intention and attitude brought out in the previous chapter, this account of Emerson's thought can make no further use of the terms appropriate for discussing "Compensation" or "The American Scholar." Something new has come into being, and the reader is aware of it even when he does not choose to analyze it. Not that Emerson's fundamental doctrines have changed—one could hardly claim that after 1840 he became less idealistic or optimistic. But the equilibrium of his philosophy was subtly modified by the introduction of new elements; and what is perceived in the bare reading as a suggestive displacement of accent, a significantly different distribution of light and shadow, can on more attentive reflection be interpreted more precisely.

> Emerson's growth was a complicated ascent in a series of recapitulations and affirmations. As Emerson reached a new level on the ascending spiral, he brought with him as a subtly compacted essence all the reading that, on a lower level five years earlier, is readily distinguishable as "sources;" and this creative process may be seen renewing itself in continuously ascending projections of the Emersonian cosmos.[1]

It is, of course, important not to neglect the role of experience and temperament in this gradual ascent. Emerson, who expected above all of his

[1] Carl Strauch, "Emerson and the American Continuity," ESQ 6 (1957), pp. 1–5.

reading that it should help in setting off his thought,[2] would have demurred at the image of slow distillation Strauch evokes—or rather would have asked, with a hint of mischief, why certain ingredients, for example utilitarianism and empiricism, resisted distillation so well.

The reorientation of Emerson's thought beginning in 1840 is, as we have seen, the consequence of a fundamental intuition at once psychological and metaphysical. The certainty of a destiny without limits is now juxtaposed in his mind to a lived sense that such a destiny cannot be realized. Time, which he had thought under his dominion, reveals itself his invincible enemy;[3] it has already destroyed the best part of him in ruining his early hopes, and if he does not learn to make his peace with it, it will soon take him altogether into oblivion. Prometheus is once again chained to the rock and has need of patience and sagacity: to endure the vulture's attacks without flinching, but also—and this by a strategy in which human intelligence is seen at its best—to domesticate it, to make it his servant. Such is the new Emerson constructing himself piece by piece before our eyes. Instructed by his recent failure, he was henceforth to refrain from the direct confrontation of man with society, mind with matter; but this renunciation was no capitulation. If the Romantic was dead, the optimist had survived him and was ready to make a virtue of necessity. Instead of tormenting himself, therefore, as does Hawthorne, with the present's ghostly thinness; instead of yielding, as does Melville, to the vertigo of evil, Emerson would now work simply to *think better*; his ambition would be to fling out a new bridge—less ethereal, less harmonious perhaps, but tougher—between the One and the Many. Beating back the temptation to resist and the subtler temptation to escape, he was to take it upon himself to be the champion of the acknowledged facts, honored in their richness and diversity. His meditations come to draw more sustenance from Carlyle, for whom "the actual well-seen *is* the ideal";[4] indeed, considered from a certain point of view, he was to pursue the speculation still farther than did Carlyle himself, because he was not subjugated to Carlyle's hates and obsessions. It is the various stages of this slow but powerful reaction that I shall now attempt to discern—bearing in mind all the while, however, that the es-

[2] See the often cited passage from "Nominalist and Realist": "I read for the lustres, as if one should use a fine picture in a chromatic experiment, for its rich colors" (W 3.233).

[3] See JMN 7.421 (February 12, 1841; "There is no Time"). This revelatory passage is partially quoted in Whicher, *Freedom and Fate*, chapter 5, "Circles."

[4] In one of his letters to Emerson (CEC 287; December 9, 1840), Carlyle contests his friend's description of Goethe as "*actual*, not *ideal*." "At bottom," he observes, "is not the whole truth rather this: The actual well-seen *is* the ideal? The *actual*, what really is and exists: the past, the present, the future no less, do all lie there!" (Carlyle's italics).

sential task is still to grasp the consequences of this adjustment for Emerson's social thought.

Nearly a year elapsed before Emerson actually began this new exploration—a period that he put to profitable use in reconstituting his reserves of energy. At the beginning of February 1841, the journal registers a state of extreme prostration: "But lately it is a sort of general winter with me. I am not sick that I know of, yet the names & projects of my friends sound far off & faint & unaffecting to my ear, as do, when I am sick, the voices of persons & the sounds of labor which I overhear in my solitary bed."[5] It was not the first time depression had lain in wait for Emerson, but it is legitimate to postulate a connection between this particular sudden fit of dejection and the intense interrogation to which he had subjected himself in the course of the preceding months. Once again the instinct for survival came into play: since the strikingly social year of 1840 had wounded him so deeply, he would make 1841 a year of regeneration under the aegis of Nature. When summer came, he withdrew for fifteen days to Nantasket, on the ocean—which he had never, except during his trip to Europe, had occasion to contemplate so closely and at such length. Its charm worked on him with calm power. In addition to the pleasures of physical exercise and the play of his own imagination (he dreamed of Malta, of Sicily, above all of Greece "lying in the arms of that sunny sea"[6]), he experienced the spell of the "satiating expanse,"[7] with its delicate azure sparkling toward infinity to the unwearied beating of the waves on the shore. Even men and women, when by chance they engaged his attention, soon dissolved into the elemental temporality of all things.

> Every hour of the day has a certain serenity and amplitude from the always visible blue sea line over which the little white columnar sail flee into the invisible like the pretty trifles we call men & women with each his own poise, compass, & errand; now & then comes by a more imposing pilgrim, as yesterday the English steamer coming in, & a few hours afterward the English steamer going out, or a man of war, (for, yesterday fruitful in ships the hundred gun ship Ohio went by,) like some burlier individual a noisy Webster or Napoleon or Luther ploughing along our Main of Time gazed after by all eyes & all spyglasses from all the other craft, but these pass too, all are fugitive, nothing but the broad blue line endures, night & morning in shade & shine, ever & aye.[8]

[5] JMN 7.419 (February 4, 1841).

[6] Letter to Margaret Fuller of July 13, 1841 (L 2.422–423).

[7] Letter to Caroline Sturgis of July 13, 1841 (L 2.423).

[8] Letter to Elizabeth Hoar of July 18, 1841 (L 2.428–430).

Emerson abandoned himself so freely to "this metaphysical flux which threatens every enterprise, every thought, and every thinker" that he feared he would find himself, before the end of the day, a "Turk & fatalist."[9]

These texts mark the extreme point reached by the pendulum in its return motion, following that curious "law of double frenzy" described by Henri Bergson.[10] One can trace its progression in the correspondence and the journals[11] and discern the gradual movement by which Emerson opened himself more and more to Eastern influences: first Plotinus, next Zoroaster, then India and the Vedas. Although he continued to call himself an idealist, he had ceased to be one in Kant's sense or even in Coleridge's.[12] The universe comes gradually to resemble that "old Two-Face, creator-creature, mind-matter, right-wrong" which he was to evoke in "Nominalist and Realist,"[13] and of which the sea, by its hypnotic presence, is in some sense the realization.[14] A lecture Emerson gave the same summer, on "The Method of Nature,"[15] was already so immersed in the pantheistic flux that his listeners confessed to understanding very little of it; the word "ecstasy" recurs in it like a leitmotif, applied now to Nature and now to human beings and thus compounding the confusion. At the same time Emerson shows himself incapable of completely recanting anthropocentrism; in developing his central theme of the indeterminateness of things, he makes a sudden turn and extends the theme in a way that nullifies it:

> Who would value any number of miles of Atlantic brine bounded by lines of latitude and longitude? Confine it by granite rocks, let it wash a shore where wise men dwell, and it is filled with expression;

[9] Letter to Samuel Gray Ward of July 1841 (*Letters from Ralph Waldo Emerson to a Friend*, ed. Charles Eliot Norton [Boston, 1899], pp. 35–36).

[10] In the last chapter of his *Les Deux Sources de la morale et de la religion* (Paris, 1932).

[11] See in particular the letter to Margaret Fuller of March 14, 1841 (L 2.384–385), where Emerson, recalling the revelation brought to him by his early reading of Berkeley, describes himself as the Idealist before whom objects "oscillate a little & threaten to dance."

[12] In a note in his *Selections from Ralph Waldo Emerson* (Boston, 1957), p. 487, Stephen Whicher presents Emerson's idealism as a synthesis of four distinct influences: Berkeley and Hume, the post-Kantians, Plato, and India. A careful study of Emerson's use of the term would show much about how these four currents succeed and interpenetrate one another.

[13] W 3.245.

[14] The soothing influence the sea exerted on Emerson's imagination is genuinely remarkable. The poem "Seashore," written in 1857 after a two-week seaside stay, is one of the few works of Emerson's maturity in which the choice of pentameter as metric form seems natural and inevitable—one is tempted to say that the ample, regular rhythm of the waves had for once triumphed over Emerson's beloved jerky brevity (W 9.242–243).

[15] The full title is "The Method of Nature, an Oration delivered before the Society of the Adelphi, in Waterville College, Maine, August 11 1841" (W 1.189–224).

> and the point of greatest interest is where the land and water meet. So must we admire in man, the form of the formless, the concentration, the house of reason, the cave of memory.[16]

As Whicher has noted, "The Method of Nature" incorporates two irreconcilable perspectives and suffers from a profound incoherence.[17] The two perspectives can coexist in Emerson's mind, however, and their intersection potentially defines what in a certain critical vocabulary is called the ironic point of view.[18] If that expression seems inappropriate or exaggerated when applied to Emerson, the problem is with the *form* of his work; fragmented into journal paragraphs, or letters, or essays, which are themselves patchworks of fragments, the form hardly allows that juxtaposition of opposites which is irony's prerequisite. That such diffuseness is unfortunate no one would deny; but it seems to me that it can be partially overcome if attention is directed to the various lecture series, which are better organized and more solidly articulated than is generally admitted. The eight talks given in the winter of 1841–1842 under the title of "The Times," for example, when once set in order (and despite considerable gaps in the manuscripts[19]), offer all the symptoms of a philosophy striving for balance, or at least of a reflection seeking its center of gravity with considerable tentativeness. One may deplore the author's centrifugal disposition of mind, which keeps him from transforming the profoundly contradictory impulses within him into dialectical movement; but that incapacity has its compensations, insofar as the diverse facets of his thought are each thrown into relief and become the matrix of an interesting gallery of characters.

A few weeks before returning to his audience in the familiar setting of Boston's Masonic Temple, Emerson wrote a few lines in his journal describing the movement of History as it appeared to him from the position he then occupied—halfway, one might say, between the contentions of the public arena and the limitless peace of the Infinite.

> On rolls the old world and these fugitive colors of political opinion like dove's neck lustres chase each other over the wide encampments of mankind, whig, tory; pro- & anti-slavery; Catholic, Prot-

[16] W 1.205.

[17] In *Freedom and Fate*, p. 147.

[18] Notably in R. W. B. Lewis's *The American Adam* (Chicago, 1955), which distinguishes in American cultural history not only the two antagonistic parties of Memory and Hope but also a third party of Irony. Lewis presents Emerson as one of the leaders of the party of Hope; but his desire to sharpen the contrasts has regrettably led him to minimize the often hidden conflicts that mark the progress of Emerson's thought.

[19] EL 3.335–382.

> estant; the clamor lasts for some time, but the persons who make it, change; the mob remains, the persons who compose it change every moment. The world hears what both parties say & swear, accepts both statements, & takes the line of conduct recommended by neither, but a diagonal line of advance which partakes of both courses.[20]

If certain of these expressions still evoke what Emerson had once called the Philosophy of the Wave,[21] the temporal dimension formally acknowledged in the last sentence alters their meaning profoundly. Emerson continues to believe in the absolute value of the present—what Browning calls "the infinite moment"—but he has rejected the illusion of a universe in perpetual revolution, borne on by an inexhaustible fecundity. As he acknowledges in the exordium of his introductory lecture, a compromise has been struck between time and eternity. "The Times are the masquerade of the eternities; trivial to the dull, tokens of noble and majestic agents to the wise, the receptacle in which the Past leaves its history; the quarry out of which the genius of to-day is building up the Future."[22] The myth of the first man—articulated, as I have noted, even before *Nature*—evaporates and is replaced by the time-honored concept of tradition. This is why in his second lecture Emerson can draw the portrait of the conservative with such firm strokes and why he can admit that from a certain point of view the conservative's position is unassailable. What exists, what the conservative spends such energy defending, is also the work of God. The reformer may indeed set himself up against the established order; but he must know that the universe will refuse to justify him until he has conquered: "nothing but God will expel God."[23]

As Emerson must still maintain the prerogatives of the Idea, which remains for him the primary reality, he is led to distinguish quite pragmatically between the desirable and the possible: "although the commands of the Conscience are *essentially* absolute, they are *historically* limitary. Wisdom does not seek a literal rectitude, but an useful, that is, a conditioned one, such a one as the faculties of man and the constitution of things will warrant."[24] Only let a different interlocutor be imagined, only let the destructive rationalism of Tom Paine and the Jacobins be substituted for the irritating but hardly dangerous reveries of the radical

[20] JMN 8.86 (September 1841).

[21] Vide supra, chapter 7.

[22] W 1.259.

[23] W 1.304.

[24] W 1.302.

reformers of America, and the commonsensical position Emerson defends here echoes that of Burke's *Reflections on the Revolution in France*. Emerson does not of course have Burke's penetration or range in describing the complex functioning and honorable antiquity of institutions, nor does he understand the paradox by which the exercise of liberty implies a previous renunciation of autonomy; but now he can join Burke in appreciating the salutary role the conservative plays in the economy of a nation.

> These continent, persisting, immoveable persons who are scattered up & down for the blessing of the world—howsoever named Osiris or Washington or Samuel Hoar, have in this phlegm or gravity of their nature a quality which answers to the fly-wheel in a mill which distributes the motion equably over all the wheels & hinders it from falling unequally & suddenly in destructive shocks.[25]

Viewed from so judicious a perspective, even the Established Church deserves some respect; for the many it is "the accredited symbol of the religious idea," and he who would abolish it absolutely would deprive the farmer of his best chance of bettering himself and condemn him to the exclusive company of his apples, his hay, and his animals.[26] The reformer's error is precisely to forget that without the collective achievement of civilization upon which he stands he could not be a reformer in the first place. "The past has baked your loaf," Emerson writes wittily, "and in the strength of its bread you would break up the oven."[27]

But the conservative, though invulnerable when he takes refuge behind a fact with a place in the universal order, concludes that because the world is solid it has grown old; and he looks about him morosely, as if the sole hope now permitted were that of somewhat alleviating an essentially desperate situation: "The conservative assumes sickness as a necessary fact, and his social frame is a hospital, his total legislation is for the present distress, a universe in slippers and flannels, a bib and papspoon, swallowing pills and herb-tea."[28] There is his error, and thence arises his mischief. Having failed to see that if the fact is indeed the accomplishment of the act, the act, even as a potentiality, has nonetheless its own authentic existence in that it is sustained by the creative power diffused throughout the universe, the conservative ends up altogether denying our spiritual nature and, by the most scandalous and

[25] JMN 7.411.

[26] See JMN 8.15 (July 1841).

[27] W 1.305.

[28] W 1.319. The passage also appears in JMN 8.87, where it is offered as a critique of the Whigs and particularly of the politics of Tyler.

hypocritical of misappropriations, exalting the service of things above the moral sentiment itself.

> The contractors who were building a road out of Baltimore, some years ago, found the Irish laborers quarrelsome and refractory to a degree that embarrassed the agents, and seriously interrupted the progress of the work. The corporation were advised to call off the police and build a Catholic chapel; which they did; the priest presently restored order, and the work went on prosperously. Such hints, be sure, are too valuable to be lost. If you do not value the Sabbath, or other religious institutions, give yourself no concern about maintaining them. They have already acquired a market value as conservators of property.[29]

So understood, religion—as elsewhere justice, or education—is only a sordid simulacrum, a sort of chloroform to numb resentment and prevent revolt.

Looking at this passage in all its bitterness, how is one not to think of Marx and his analysis of bourgeois superstructures? But the proximity is transient and the similarity tangential;[30] just as for Descartes physics would be incomprehensible without metaphysics to ground it, so for Emerson the small spiritual flame burning at the center of every individual consciousness is the radiant center from which polities are developed and organized. The problem is not, as it is for Marx, simply to throw down false pretenses; it is to show the way in which, between the Spiritual Fact and the resistant nature of things, a continuity can exist that is neither dream nor betrayal. At the end of the lecture, in a fable rather than in a demonstration, Emerson introduces the "hero" through whom this difficult connection is achieved; but it is a little too much like a deus ex machina to be convincing, except perhaps to its author.[31] To

[29] W 1.320–321. One might adduce here the comment on Transcendentalism made by Dickens: "Transcendentalism has its occasional vagaries (what school has not?), but it has good healthful qualities in spite of them, not least among the number a hearty disgust of Cant, and an aptitude to detect her in all the million varieties of her everlasting wardrobe. And therefore if I were a Bostonian, I think I would be a Transcendentalist" (*American Notes* [London, 1893], p. 34).

[30] In all of Emerson's works the name of Karl Marx is mentioned only once (JMN 13.127). The Communist Manifesto dates from 1848, so there is clearly no Marxist influence on the passage just quoted.

[31] Commenting on this conclusion, Henry Nash Smith writes in "Emerson's Problem of Vocation," NEQ 12 (1939), p. 65 that "here the Transcendental merging of a divine *logos* with an apotheosized humanity is not so much affirmed as casually taken for granted; the idea seems to come straight from the subconscious."

devise a more workable solution Emerson would have to undertake a more attentive analysis of the data of human life.

The fourth lecture in the series is "The Transcendentalist," and to the extent that it depicts a type of human being radically opposed to the conservative and yet distinct from Emerson himself, it constitutes a first step in that analysis: "Please observe that in the Transcendental Lecture," he writes later to his aunt Mary, "I only write biographically,—describing a class of young persons whom I have seen—I hope it is not confession and that, past all hope, I am confounded with my compassionated heroes and heroines."[32] That Emerson judges it appropriate to remove the misunderstanding is nonetheless testimony to its plausibility; and one of the lecture's considerable attractions is precisely the delicate balance he strives to maintain in it between a personal belief ready to burst in at every moment and the attitude of a detached observer, almost of a chronicler, that he sought to adopt at the beginning.

For the ignorant American of 1840, the very word Transcendentalist was clothed in charm and mystery, and very strange stories were told of the creature.[33] Emerson had first to sweep away these cock-and-bull stories before restoring the phenomenon to its historical reality: "what is popularly called Transcendentalism among us, is Idealism; Idealism as it appears in 1842."[34] Transcendentalism is a Fact, and therefore one can neither ignore it nor keep it from existing.[35] But when Emerson undertakes as objectively as he can to define for his audience the nature and the content of this revived idealism, it is evident that the substance of his account is being drawn from his own experience or belief: the inconsistency of materialism, the symbolic value of work and property, the praise of solitude, and the justification of antinomianism for fear of the letter that kills are all themes that he has defended on his own ac-

[32] Letter to Mary Moody Emerson of June 20 and 22, 1842 (L 3.65).

[33] At which Emerson was the first to be diverted. From Providence, where he was giving a series of lectures, he wrote his mother in March 1840, "you must know I am reckoned here a Transcendentalist, and what that beast is, all persons in Providence have a great appetite to know: So I am carried duly about from house to house, and all the young persons ask me, when the Lecture is coming upon the Great Subject? In vain I disclaim all knowledge of that sect of Lidian's, —it is still expected I shall break out with the New Light in the next discourse. I have read here my essay on the Age, the one on Home, one on Love, & one of Politics, —These seem all to be regarded as mere screens subterfuges while this dread Transcendentalism is still kept back. They have various definitions of the word current here. One man, of whom I have been told, in good earnest defined it as 'Operations on the Teeth'; A young man named Rodman, answered an inquiry by saying 'It was a nickname which those who stayed behind, gave to those who went ahead.' Meantime, all the people come to lecture, and I am told the Lyceum makes money by me" (L 2.266–268).

[34] "The Transcendentalist" (W 1.329)

[35] See JMN 8.133 (October 23, 1841).

count as his thought became aware of itself. Even when he calls Transcendentalism "the Saturnalia or excess of Faith" he is not, as he might seem to be, standing at a distance from it, because he adds at once that it is "the presentiment of a faith proper to man in his integrity, excessive only when his imperfect obedience hinders the satisfaction of his wish."[36] The mode of utterance, moreover, often shifts from description to the greater strength of aphorism—as if, in consideration of the size of the stake, Emerson had decided to cast his own authority into the balance.

It is not until the second part of the lecture, a description of the Transcendentalist attitude to society, that one feels a real cooling in Emerson's relation to his subject. No doubt a basic sympathy remains: "the view taken of Transcendentalism in State Street," he remarks mischievously on an approximately contemporary page of the journal, "is that it threatens to invalidate contracts."[37] And he has too often warned his friends and listeners against a certain charlatanism inherent in action not to approve of the Transcendentalist distrust of charitable organizations and a fortiori of political factions. But the ideal of human integrity deep within him obliges him to a certain lucidity, and to judge as impotence, or at least as a limitation, what the Transcendentalists in their enthusiasm often proposed as their purest glory. He does not accuse them of duplicity, as he had the conservative; their fault, if that is what it is, is rather that they behave like "children," like "novices," not yet capable of judging the world. What they proclaim is true; but their science is limited and their experience laughably incomplete because it ignores that "double consciousness" which is the torment of maturity:

> the two lives, of the understanding and of the soul, which we lead, really show very little relation to each other; never meet and measure each other: one prevails now, all buzz and din; and the other prevails then, all infinitude and paradise; and, with the progress of life, the two discover no greater disposition to reconcile themselves.[38]

A prisoner except during those moments of what he calls an "Iceland of negations," Emerson would be the first to rejoice in the victorious innocence of his friends if he did not detect an illusion in their triumph: "There is an instinct about this too. It is in vain that you gild gold & whiten snow in your preaching if when I see you, I do not look through

[36] "The Transcendentalist" (W 1.338–339).

[37] JMN 8.108 (October 1841).

[38] "The Transcendentalist" (W 1.353–354).

your pure eye into a society of angels & angelic thoughts within."[39] The more time passed, the more he became tempted to blame them for what in the lecture he describes as their reproach to the world in general: "their quarrel with every man they meet is not with his kind, but with his degree. There is not enough of him, —that is the only fault."[40] They thus go about proclaiming themselves the legislators of the world; but when the scepter is offered them they are incapable of grasping it. Prophecy is their refuge; celebrators of their time—and they have at least expressed its beauty—they are like the minstrels of some golden kingdom of courtly love.[41]

If the subtly nostalgic delicacy of the analysis shows that all ties have not been broken between Emerson and the unreconstructed Transcendentalists, it shows also that he has resolved to advance beyond this adolescent passion. He was no longer able, and would become less and less so, to cherish seriously the hope of a universe in which idea might of its own impetus become fact and inspiration victory. A gulf has been fixed between action and contemplation, as he emphasized even in the very first lecture in the series;[42] the members of the party of Hope are either reformers or philosophers, but nowhere, as Henry Nash Smith notes, has there emerged that Priest-King by which the world might be reconciled with itself.[43] Attracted by two almost incompatible modes, Emerson tested both at length in search of a difficult synthesis. The debate was finally to be settled by the second series of *Essays*; and one may see a symbolic intention in the order Emerson gave that book, reserving the first place for the poet and banishing to the end, almost as if to an appendix, the lecture given in March 1844 under the title of "New England Reformers."

In any case, the man who engaged in this inquiry no longer much resembled the idealist at bay who had refused to settle at Brook Farm. One does notice an undercurrent of disquiet rising to the surface at widely scattered intervals—notably in "Experience"—but what emerges from reading the letters and journals of this period is a growing impression of force and serenity. Doubtless Emerson's now secure reputation counts for something in this change; when he learns from Car-

[39] JMN 8.73 (October 1841; "Antitranscendentalists").

[40] "The Transcendentalist" (W 1.344).

[41] JMN 8.370 (March, 1843). The judgment was provoked by a remark of Alcott's on the audience the *Dial* should find but had not.

[42] Emerson distinguishes between the "actors," who constitute the visible church of the present generation, and the "students" or "speculators," enraptured with solitude and perfection ("Lecture on the Times" [W 1.268–269 and 285–286]).

[43] In his "Emerson's Problem of Vocation," p. 66.

lyle that the first set of *Essays* has made a deep impression in England[44] or that the radicals of Lancashire have seen fit to reprint "Man the Reformer,"[45] when he is invited to lecture not only in Boston, not only in New England, but also in New York,[46] in Philadelphia, and in Washington, how could he not see in such consecrations the justification of the methods and principles he had been defending incessantly since "The American Scholar"? His assurance grew; he feared contact with crowds less and less and came to acknowledge the special value of their messages.[47] He became an exact and informed observer of the problems of his time, and his gaze, passing over and beyond the small world of Concord and Boston, confronted the entirety of the forces engaged in shaping contemporary America. On occasion he could act, as when in the spring of 1842 he took on himself the responsibility of publishing the *Dial*, lest it fall into hands unworthy of it;[48] and he even accepted the role of spiritual director if accident brought him into the presence of an ardent admirer, as was the case with Giles Waldo, to whom a common relative introduced him in the course of his stay in Washington.[49] What one does not find any longer is the wavering attitude qualified by impulses of generosity that had marked the year 1840.[50] Henceforth Emerson was to present to the world a countenance of tranquil assurance—though crossed surprisingly often by a gleam of mockery, partic-

[44] See Carlyle's letter to Emerson of November 19, 1841 (CEC 312).

[45] See Carlyle's letter to Emerson of November 17, 1842 (CEC 334).

[46] After his lecture tour outside New England, Emerson expressed his satisfaction at this expansion of his sphere of influence in a letter to Carlyle: "I have read at New York six out of eight lectures *on the Times* which I read this winter in Boston. I found a very intelligent & friendly audience . . . many persons came & talked with me, and I felt when I came away that New York is open to me henceforward whenever my Boston parish is not large enough" (March 31, 1842 [CEC 398–399]).

[47] As he wrote to Margaret Fuller from Philadelphia, early in 1843, "I *accept* this travelling, & I suppose it does me as much good as exercise taken against one's will. It is always instructive to see people in heaps or groups, or, shall I say more properly, *in streams*, —they are so pictorial, & illustrate laws better" (January 31 and February 2, 1843 [L 3.137–138]; the italics are Emerson's). See also the letter to Samuel Gray Ward of January 26, 1843 (*Letters to a Friend*, pp. 51–52).

[48] See JMN 8.203 (March 20, 1842).

[49] See the letters to Lidian Emerson of January 12 and January 20, 1843 (L 3.119–121 and 128–130). The bulk of Emerson's correspondence with Waldo is lost, and little is known of the "fiery friendship" that Emerson describes as "much the most romantic incident" of his Washington stay.

[50] Particularly significant is Emerson's judgment on John L. O'Sullivan, the young editor of the *United States Magazine and Democratic Review*, a man known for his populist inclinations and high-pitched nationalism: "Today I dined with Mr O'Sullivan . . . but the man is politico-literary and has too close an eye to immediate objects" (letter to Fuller of February 12, 1843 [L 3.146–147]).

ularly when he dealt with those reformers whose trail the traveler at that time could not help but cross.

Thus in February and March 1843 he made the acquaintance of Albert Brisbane, an American disciple of Fourier who tried gamely to make Emerson another. Brisbane had published in 1840 an account of Fourierism called *Social Destiny of Man: Or, Association and Reorganization of Industry*, which Emerson had reviewed in the *Dial*.[51] He was only moderately impressed; but Horace Greeley, the energetic and active chief editor of the *New York Tribune*, had contracted a great admiration for the Fourierist notions and in the first upsurge of his enthusiasm had made Brisbane and his friends free of his newspaper. After so spectacular a conquest Brisbane could hardly doubt that the prince of Transcendentalism would succumb in his turn as well—or so much at least emerges from Emerson's letters, in which he humorously describes the assault he had to endure from Brisbane,[52] who was too absorbed in his speculations to discover that his interlocutor was "a poet and of no more use in their New York than a rainbow or a firefly." Luckily the poet received unexpected reinforcement from a visitor he did not know, the elder Henry James, who undertook to answer Brisbane and "told him the truth a good deal better than I should probably have done."[53]

Despite these implicit reservations, Fourier receives in Emerson's work an attentiveness other social theorists are denied. The appearance in the *Dial* of an article by Brisbane called "Means of Effecting a Final Reconciliation Between Religion and Science" was one occasion for Emerson as chief editor to weigh the system's merits and flaws;[54] he returned to the subject in the course of a lecture given in 1844[55] and

[51] *Dial* 1 (October 1840), pp. 265–266. Emerson begins by warning the reader that the text is characteristically French and thus necessitates a careful distinction between principles and applications; but he goes on to laud Fourier for having raised the serious question of the connection between capital and labor and for having given a scientific analysis of the theory of cooperation.

[52] Three letters are important here: two to Lidian Emerson, of March 1 and March 3, 1842 (L 3.17–18 and 20–22), and one to Fuller of March 1, 1842 (L 3.19–20). A letter to Thoreau with a vivid account of Brisbane seems also to belong to this period, though its editor places it in February 1843 ("The Emerson–Thoreau Correspondence," *Atlantic Monthly* 69 [May 1892], pp. 580–581).

[53] Letter to Lidian Emerson of March 5, 1842 (L 3.22–24). It was in fact during this stay in New York that Emerson first met the elder James, and a friendship sprang up almost immediately. Their correspondence is printed in Ralph Barton Perry, *The Thought and Character of William James*, 2 vols. (Boston, 1935), 1.39–96.

[54] "Fourierism and the Socialists," *Dial* 3 (July 1842), pp. 83–96. The central pages of the article are included in "Historic Notes of Life and Letters in New England" (W 10.348–353).

[55] See "The Young American" (W 1.380–384).

touched on it again in the last paragraph of "Napoleon."[56] The reasons for this lasting interest seem both general and personal. Between 1840 and 1850, Fourierism enjoyed considerable favor in America; phalansteries grew up everywhere, spreading from New Jersey to Massachusetts under the impulse of more or less visionary reformers. They flourished, then scraped along for a while before disappearing amidst popular indifference. An article by Elizabeth Peabody, published in the *Dial* for April 1844, discusses a meeting held at Boston three months previously, in the course of which the principles and the operating conditions of Fourier's theories had been presented at length by self-appointed popularizers of them;[57] and Peabody reveals more clearly than had Emerson the attraction exercised on an undisciplined intelligence by such a mixture of rigor and daydream, dogmatic precision and cosmic maundering. Peabody's America was astonishingly free of restraints, whatever the discontented might say; and Fourierism offered a program tailored to the ambitions and hopes of a new race. Surely no less intoxicating promise would have succeeded in inciting as contemplative a man as George Ripley to make a phalanstery of Brook Farm.[58]

Emerson was of course sensitive to the system's breadth of vision, and he admired an audacity capable of pushing the mechanistic theory of the world so far as to attain the realm of mind without any evident break in continuity. Its central postulate excepted, Fourierism seemed an optimism similar to his own in the confidence of its approach. Its correspondences here and there with certain doctrines of Swedenborg[59] gave it a poetic dimension; and its vindication of manual labor, which was the focus of Fourier's last works and the chief factor in Brisbane's conversion, matched and perhaps extended the "Doctrine of the Farm" that Emerson had recently preached. As Fourier had, moreover, unlike Saint-Simon and most European Socialist theoreticians, shown a great tolerance to private property, it was impossible in good conscience to consider him a descendant of the Jacobins; and this moderation consti-

[56] W 4.258. The journal records numerous judgments and reflections on Fourierism throughout 1845, and the question remained of interest to Emerson as late as 1847 (cf. JMN 10.154).

[57] "Fourierism," *Dial* 4 (April 1844), pp. 473–483.

[58] One ought not to underestimate the role played in this evolution by personal contact. Brook Farm's conversion to Fourierism was preceded by several visits from Brisbane and Greeley, and the two men were received sympathetically and warmly. See Lindsay Swift, *Brook Farm: Its Members, Scholars, and Visitors* (New York, 1900), pp. 273–281.

[59] The comparison between Fourier and Swedenborg is made also by Elizabeth Peabody, "Plan of the West Roxbury Community," *Dial* 2 (January 1842), pp. 361–372; see further Sherman Paul, *Emerson's Angle of Vision* (Cambridge, Mass., 1952), pp. 194–195.

tuted a useful passport, even in the Boston of 1840 and for Emerson and the Transcendentalists.

But despite these positive elements, in the end the balance was decidedly in the negative. With the summary quickness he could sometimes command, Emerson reproached Fourier with being French and therefore immoral, with misunderstanding the true nature of woman and thus flouting her profound chastity: "The Stoic said, Forbear, Fourier said, Indulge. Fourier was of the opinion of Saint-Evremond; abstinence from pleasure appeared to him a great sin. . . . The Fourier marriage was a calculation how to secure the greatest amount of kissing that the infirmity of human constitution admitted."[60] Fortunately "the thin veil of the French language" concealed these shameful notions, and Fourier's American disciples had quickly made the necessary adjustments in transmitting his doctrines. It was on other grounds that on behalf of his countrymen Emerson attacked Fourierism—or rather ridiculed it. Far from presenting it as a school of cynicism and debauchery, he mocked its naïveté, its pretentions, its callow belief in the millennium.

> Then know you one and all, that Constantinople is the natural capital of the globe. There, in the Golden Horn, will the Arch-Phalanx be established; there will the Omniarch reside. . . . Poverty shall be abolished; deformity, stupidity and crime shall be no more. Genius, grace, art, shall abound, and it is not to be doubted but that in the reign of "Attractive Industry" all men will speak in blank verse.[61]

As for the organization of the phalansteries and the distribution of workers in series and groups, both processes are too much at odds with common sense to last: "London, New York, Boston, are phalanxes ready made where you shall find concerts, books, balls, medical lectures, prayers, or Punch & Judy according to your fancy on any night or day."[62] Fourier thinks he can lead the world to perfection through a massive use of numbers, and in fact is offering it only a wretched quackery nostrum.[63]

[60] "Life and Letters in New England" (W 10.354). Emerson's distaste is more virulently expressed in the journal, in which Fourier is described as "one of those salacious old men . . . in their head, it is the universal rutting season" (JMN 9.191). Emerson's verdict is a little off; it is chiefly in the first of Fourier's works, the *Théorie des quatre mouvements et des destinées générales*, published when he was thirty-six, that sexual freedom is defended. Later the emphasis is rather on the practical conditions for social organization.

[61] "Life and Letters in New England" (W 10. 351). The caricature owes much to Emerson's recent conversation with Brisbane; cf. L 3.21.

[62] JMN 8.249 (November 26, 1842).

[63] "Fourier our Paracelsus," Emerson adds (JMN 8.305), after having defined Browning's Paracelsus as the thinker who "at last finds himself arrived at being a quack" (JMN 7.303).

In sum, then, Emerson's objection was that all the ingenuity, all the complexity of Fourier's system cannot keep it from being precisely a *system*, that is, an artificial construction, proposing to substitute itself for nature and striving without success to imitate its processes. Fourier is thus not essentially different from the less ambitious reformers in which the age abounded; he was obsessed with the realization of order, but like the others forgot that order detached from creative flux is nothing:

> He treats man as a plastic thing, something that may be put up or down, ripened or retarded, moulded, polished, made into solid or fluid or gas, at the will of the leader . . . but skips the faculty of life, which spawns and scorns system and system-makers; which eludes all conditions; which makes or supplants a thousand phalanxes and New Harmonies with each pulsation.[64]

It is this belief in a life force that gives passion and vividness to Emerson's criticism. In vain does he assert a few lines further on that our devotion to justice makes us the center of a "holy and beneficent republic," thereby paying his respects to the old spiritualist philosophy; in fact the two attitudes of thought do not match as exactly as he would like us to imagine. An awareness of that ambiguity gradually insinuated itself into his mind and nurtured the fresh attempt at unification that will be examined in the next chapter.

Fourier does not, however, occupy the whole spectrum of reform. There are other reformers; and one is somewhat surprised to note Emerson's persistent attention to them, since by all appearances he did not hope to find in them any of the guiding principles of his own life. But the experimenter in him kept an open eye; unstable and grotesque as the reformers' efforts often seemed, they nonetheless were facts and constituted lines of force on the neutral background of the period. That is why in October 1842 Emerson could offer the readers of the *Dial* an astonishingly detailed account of the reform movement in England.[65] It goes without saying that considered as literature the article is mediocre; but it gives a good idea of its author's curiosity and power of attention. It was through Alcott, whom his admirers had invited to stay in a school named after him,[66] that Emerson had received from England a copious assortment of newspapers and journals; and he then set himself the task of examining them, blanching neither at the pedantic or empty theories

[64] "Life and Letters in New England" (W 10.352). New Harmony was the Indiana community that Robert Owen founded in 1825.

[65] "English Reformers," *Dial* 3 (October 1842), pp. 227–247.

[66] The Alcott School attempted to apply the methods devised earlier at the Temple School in Boston (vide supra); it was at Ham, in Surrey.

nor at the bad prose. Two tendencies emerge from the long enumeration of forgotten names;[67] they are of unequal importance, but both are represented by one vivid and distinct character. The first, toward which Emerson was avowedly drawn by argument and temperament alike, was that of the reformers of "a more universal tendency," whom we would call utopians; and the central figure here was James Pierrepont Greaves, a devotee of Transcendentalism and a vegetarian, who in Switzerland had been a student of Pestalozzi's before devoting himself to the establishment of nursery schools founded on the principles to which his teacher had paid tribute.[68] He died just before the *Dial* article appeared, but his papers were brought to the United States by Charles Lane and Henry Wright, and Emerson read them with admiration.[69]

Now these lovers of the absolute, concerned with regeneration far more than with reform, were nonetheless attracted by Socialism. The phenomenon may owe something to Greaves, who toward the end of his life saw an authentically spiritual community as the only remedy for the ills of the world; or it may proceed from an analysis indicting idealism for its tendency to restrict itself to "the history of the private mind." Emerson was not sure which explanation was valid, but he could not decline to discuss a second class of reformers, "humbler, but far larger" than the first. The representative here was "a sort of Camille Desmoulins of British Revolution," Goodwyn Barnby, a young radical dreaming of brotherly love, chief editor of a penny magazine called *The Promethean or Communitarian Apostle*, which described itself as "the paper the most devoted of any to the cause of the people; consecrated to Pantheism in Religion and Communism in Politics." Emerson smilingly notes the writer's syntactical awkwardness, but pays homage to his message's sincerity and still more to its moderation. The spokesman

[67] Notable among them are Heraud, Coleridge's disciple and editor of the *London Monthly Magazine*; J. Westland Marston, drawn at once to literature, to Toryism, and to reform; Francis Barham, dramatist and journalist, and author of a pamphlet on American literature of which he sent Emerson a copy; Charles Lane and Henry Wright, whom Alcott brought to America with him; and Doherty, editor of the *London Phalanx* and Fourier's personal friend. Emerson also praises the generosity and moderation of a book called *Chartism: A New Organization of the People* (1841), written by William Lovett and John Collins during their term in Warwick prison.

[68] Lane published two articles on Greaves in *Dial* 3 (October 1842), pp. 247–255 and (January 1843), pp. 281–296); he indicates that it was Harriet Martineau who was the link between Alcott and the small group of English reformers, Greaves among them, who set up the school at Ham.

[69] "Greaves is a great man. I have a book full of his sentences on my table which is like some Menu transmigrated into Burton Street, London" (letter to Fuller, November 16, 1842 [L 3.97]).

of the most oppressed of the working class, Barnby restrained the hatred one would have expected and instead preached temperance, nonviolence, and marriage based on love:

> In a time of distress among the manufacturing classes, severe beyond any precedent, when, according to the statements vouched by Lord Brougham in the House of Peers, and Mr. O'Connell and others in the Commons, wages are reduced in some of the manufacturing villages to six pence a week, so that men are forced to sustain themselves and their families at less than a penny a day; when the most revolting expedients are resorted to for food; when families attempt by a recumbent posture to diminish the pangs of hunger; in the midst of this exasperation the voice of the people is temperate and wise beyond all former example. They are intent on personal as well as on national reforms.[70]

Nowhere perhaps did Emerson come closer in a text destined for publication[71] to assenting to the position of reformers who held faults in social organization responsible for the masses' spiritual suffocation, or to admitting that beyond a certain threshold of poverty and misery the moral sense itself can die. But England was far away, and in the America of 1840 it was still possible to preserve an elementary dignity at a cost something less than that of superhuman heroism. When in *Past and Present*[72] Carlyle records with terrifying humor the story of the Irish widow left penniless with three children, who when dead demonstrated by infecting the whole neighborhood with her diseases the reality of those human bonds that had been denied while she was alive, he was appealing to an experience that Emerson in Concord could neither imagine nor comprehend.[73]

The incursion into the domain of the English reformers had no sequel; the journal and the letters for 1842 and 1843 do, however, attest to a lively curiosity regarding the experiments going on in America. In March 1842, Emerson participated in a rather odd conference at Boston on the validity of Scripture. Having aroused little public interest, it

[70] "English Reformers," p. 240.

[71] By contrast, Emerson's letters during his second stay in England are full of a mournful sadness at the misery the great industrial cities reveal; see particularly the letter to Lidian Emerson of December 1 and 2, 1847 (L 3.442–445).

[72] Book 3, chapter 2, "Gospel of Mammonism."

[73] This is clear from Emerson's review of *Past and Present* in the *Dial* for July 1843 (printed in W 12.379–391). The "lurid stormlights" that light up the work seem to Emerson dependent on its author's personality. Had Carlyle been more skeptical of his own whims, Emerson claims, he would have seen that all the scenes of history are bathed in the same "calm daylight." See also the letter to Carlyle of April 29, 1843 (CEC 342).

adjourned indefinitely at the end of the first session; but though still-born, it had value, Emerson thought, as a sign:

> As a historian of the Times one would certainly wish to be there. These Chardon Street conventions to which this was the sequel have been full of all the Protest of Protest; all the fanaticism of all shades & forms: three men with long beards have attended them; Mormons came & spoke. The Bible Society had its agent with tracts at the door; mad men & mad women were there, & madly did behave.[74]

Other signs were offered by the communities Emerson was visiting at the time. On an autumn day in 1842 he and Hawthorne went to visit the small town of Harvard and its company of Shakers. He found the spectacle of these decent farmers no more edifying than he had in 1829;[75] but he notes that the sect had become more interesting because the present period gave the theories of Socialism so particular a luster.[76] In much the same way, he followed very closely the evolution of Brook Farm; he was not immune to a certain respect tinged with sympathy for the members of that community, but he feared the effect on the most delicate of them of a life too exclusively and deliberately spiritual. A counterbalance was needed, and in its absence the resources of character were put to a harsh test: "the young people who have been faithful to this their testimony, have lived a great deal in a short time, but have come forth with shattered constitutions."[77] Hawthorne, for one, who had stayed some months at Brook Farm during 1841, speaks of his experience as a deviation that might have been fatal to his inner life, though for other reasons.[78] One is sorry not to know the remarks on the subject the two men must surely have exchanged.

[74] Letter to William Emerson of April 2, 1842 (L 3.41). In the *Dial* for July 1842, Emerson gives a humorous account of the three meetings he alludes to; the article is printed as "The Chardon Street Conventions" in W 10.371–377.

[75] Vide supra, chapter 4.

[76] See JMN 8.274.

[77] JMN 7.377; cf. JMN 7.392–393 (May 1843). "Life and Letters in New England" contains a lengthy evocation of Brook Farm based on notes made at the time in the journal; but the portrait that emerges from it is softened and vaguely hazy in its outlines, as if with the passage of time what had stuck in Emerson's memory was the Arcadian aspect of the venture (W 10.359–370).

[78] He writes as follows in his notebooks on September 3, 1841: "really I should judge it to be twenty years since I left Brook Farm; and I take this to be one proof that my life there was an unnatural and unsuitable, and therefore an unreal one. . . . there had been a spectral Appearance there, sounding the horn at daybreak, and milking the cows, and hoeing the potatoes, and raking hay, toiling in the sun, and doing me the honor to assume my name. But this

It was, however, Emerson's lot to witness much more closely the germination, the brief flowering, and the final failure of a communal project of still more radical principles. Alcott returned from Europe accompanied by two English reformers, Charles Lane and Henry Wright (whom Emerson had warned in vain against the hazards of such a voyage) and undertook to found a community dedicated to observing the universal law of Love as strictly as possible. No money would be used, food would consist only of fruits and vegetables, and only clothing made originally from vegetable products would be worn. The products of slave labor—cotton, sugar, and rice, for example—would be excluded. Emerson had condemned the unworldliness of such an enterprise in advance, so to speak.[79] He nonetheless lent an attentive ear to his friend's arguments but was impatient at seeing him caught in self-contradiction from the outset by his pleas to have a generous person furnish him with the funds for buying the necessary land. Either, Emerson somewhat petulantly argued, one is driven by an irresistible movement of the soul to change the mode of one's existence, and refrains from counting on other people, and invents the necessary forms of action; or one recognizes that one cannot do without money, and refrains from mystifying others and oneself. Like poets, reformers are born and not made.[80] For good or for ill, however, the community was born. In July 1842, Alcott, his family, and some of his disciples settled at Fruitlands, in Harvard, as a community committed to the spirit of Socialism. Emerson's first impressions during a visit were favorable, but he prudently decided to postpone his final judgment until December.[81] Events confirmed the wisdom of his decision; the winter was unusually harsh, and Alcott, sick at heart, had to give up the game. But his failure was at least distinguished by a size and scope he had hitherto lacked:

---

spectre was not myself" (quoted in Octavius Brooks Frothingham, *Transcendentalism in New England* [New York, 1876], p. 174).

[79] In a paragraph of the journal ironically titled "Optimates":

> Sir, said Heavenborn, the amount of labor you have spent on that piece is disgraceful. For me, not even my industry shall violate my sentiment. I will sit down in that corner & perish, unless I am commanded by the universe to rise & work.
>
> And what became of Heavenborn?
>
> What a pragmatical question! Nothing to tell of: —yet I suppose the new spirit that animates this crop of young philosophers, and perhaps the fine weather at this very hour, this thoughtful autumnal air, may be some of his work, since he is now, as we say, dead." (JMN 8.50 [September 12, 1841])

[80] See JMN 7.255 (November 1842); the central portion of the passage is printed in Cabot, *Memoir*, 2.439–442.

[81] See JMN 8.433 (July 8, 1843).

> Very sad indeed it was to see this halfgod driven to the wall, reproaching men, & hesitating whether he should not reproach the gods. The world was not, on trial, a possible element for him to live in. A lover of law had tried whether law could be kept in this world, & all things answered, NO. . . . I was quite ashamed to have just revised & printed last week the old paper denying the existence of tragedy, when this modern Prometheus was in the heat of his quarrel with the gods.[82]

Emerson's lecture "New England Reformers"[83] was delivered less than two months after the disbanding of Fruitlands, and in the circumstances became something of an assessment of it. But the ferment around him had troubled Emerson more than once, and the lecture also became an occasion for clarifying his own responses to it—thence the layering, so to speak, of the argument. Beginning with a concrete analysis of the period and its traits, it gradually ascends, striving to put the problems that the controversies of the moment deform rather than illuminate into their proper perspective. As good-natured or stinging satire yields to a profession of faith, the familiar Emersonian themes (the universal presence of the Spirit, the hydrostatic paradox applied to the balance of individual and society) appear once more, but are somehow inaccessible to immediate experience, less an illumination than a fleeting and sometimes distorted truth that we must strive to regain in its purity. Read from this angle the lecture supplements the lecture on the Transcendentalist given two years previously. Like the reformer, the Transcendentalist oversimplifies reality, through a deficiency of both his intelligence and his faculty of intuition. Moreover, the two errors echo each other and correspond—a fact that was to encourage Emerson to try to define a third attitude that would be valid for himself, if not for mankind at large.

Such is the central argument of "New England Reformers"; but of course to reduce Emerson's thought to so abstract a pattern is to misrepresent it. The problem of how to respond to the reform movement had not by the end of 1843 been provided with a solution to which Emerson could serenely subscribe.[84] How, moreover, could one offer a

[82] JMN 9.86 (March 1843). "The Tragic," an adaptation of the seventh lecture of the series "Human Life," from 1838–1839, appeared in the *Dial* for April 1844, and is reprinted in W 12.405–417.

[83] The full title is "New England Reformers, a Lecture Read Before the Society in Amory Hall, on Sunday, March 30 1844" (W 3.249–285).

[84] "I am nominally a believer: yet I hold on to property: I eat my bread with unbelief. I approve every wild action of the experimenters. I say what they say concerning celibacy or money or community of goods and my only apology for not doing their work is preoccupation of

single answer to ten distinct questions? The reforms seemed alike only to the most superficial observer; if some were external, others in fact prepared the flowering of the soul—those, for example, concerning education. In this area Emerson was a committed opponent of the status quo; Pestalozzi's methods had attracted him as early as the time of his ministry, and he continued to denounce the ills of a system that mocked life and turned its back on common sense.[85] As early as 1844, saluting Horace Mann's efforts as head of the Massachusetts Department of Education to get instruction out of its rut and train competent teachers, he specified the reforms he would like to see introduced: he wanted experience to supplement book-learning; he did not want the dead languages and mathematics to constitute the kernel of all education; he wanted children to learn to make their bodies responsive and flexible instruments. When one remembers Emerson's classical education and the width of his reading, one appreciates all the more the esteem he accorded to the "self-made men"[86] who had forced an access to the conservative circles of Boston and New York.

Besides education there was another theme often disputed by the reformers that found a particular resonance in Emerson—though he did not, for reasons of modesty and prudence mixed together, dare to push it as far as honesty would require: "The more intelligent are growing uneasy on the subject of Marriage. They wish to see the character represented also in that covenant. There shall be nothing brutal in it, but it shall honor the man and the woman, as much as the most diffusive and universal action."[87] These brief lines are Emerson's frankest statement of position, and the edition of the journals prepared by his son at the beginning of the century observes considerable discretion in this area.[88] But the debate ought not be made the subject of vulgar interpretations, because it revolves around this question: is it fitting that in our progress toward the universal we should be slowed or hampered by the necessity of advancing at an equal rate with someone with whom we are no longer in communion? Milton and Shelley did not think so, and Emerson gave

---

mind. . . . My Genius loudly calls me to stay where I am, even with the degradation of owning bankstock and seeing poor men suffer whilst the Universal Genius apprises me of this disgrace & beckons me to the martyr's & redeemer's office" (JMN 9.62 [December 1843]).

[85] He was still giving lectures on education in 1861 and 1864; cf. C. Cestre, "La pédagogie d'Emerson," *Annales de l'Université de Paris* (July–August 1929), pp. 302–318, and Hazen Carpenter, "Emerson, Eliot and the Elective System," NEQ 24 (March 1951), pp. 13–34.

[86] Emerson uses the term in "New England Reformers" (W 3.260).

[87] "Lecture on the Times" (W 1.274–275).

[88] But Whicher, *Selections*, p. 480, notes that discussions of marital relations nonetheless occur frequently in J for 1841 and 1842, e.g., J 6.72–73, 209, and 243 (JMN 8.95 and 173–174 and 7.467).

them credit for having risked unpopularity rather than deny themselves. But from another point of view, how can a man who has thus regained his liberty be certain he has not yielded to impulses of sensuality, like those voluptuaries Emerson condemned in the system of Fourier?

The two aspects of the problem are dealt with in turn in a journal passage Emerson's son did not publish, which finally does confirm marriage's claims to existence.[89] But if the distressing interferences between mind and body kept Emerson from preaching free love, he was not slow in compensation to recall that the idea, and only the idea, is the true measure of all human union.[90] At the most exalted level of contemplation, marriage has no meaning or substance: "I have experiences that are above all civil or nuptial or commercial relations: and I wish to vow myself to those. If you ask how the world is to get on, &C. &c. I have no answer. I do not care for such cattle of consequences. It is not my question, it is your own; answer it who will."[91] The mystic's imperiousness is here Emerson's defense against his own intelligence, which has come up against an evidently insoluble problem.

In "New England Reformers," however, he refrains from revealing such inward thoughts, because he is convinced that they would trouble his audiences without aiding them: "do you complain of our Marriage? Our marriage is no worse than our education, our diet, our trade, our social customs."[92] It is the familiar argument that reform is one and indivisible, and it has here an acerbic energy in which one recognizes the impatience of a man of good sense at the impositions of all fanatics:

> I cannot afford to be irritable and captious, nor to waste all my time in attacks. If I should go out of church whenever I hear a false sentiment I could never stay there five minutes. But why come out? the street is as false as the church. . . . When we see an eager assailant of one of these wrongs, a special reformer, we feel like asking

[89] "Plainly marriage should be a temporary relation, it should have its natural birth, climax & decay without violence of any kind, —violence to bind or violence to rend. When each of two souls had exhausted the other of that good which each held for the other, they should part in the same peace in which they met, not parting from each other, but drawn to new society. The new love is the balm to prevent a wound from forming where the old love was detached. But now we could not trust even saints & sages with a boundless liberty. For the romance of new love is so delicious that their unfixed fancies would betray them, and they would allow themselves to confound a whim with an instinct, the pleasure of the fancy with the dictates of the character" (JMN 8.95 [1841]).

[90] Cf. "Swedenborg," W 4.128–129, and the poem "Initial, Daemonic and Celestial Love" (W 9.103–118).

[91] JMN 9.63 (1843). See also "Experience" (W 3.77).

[92] "New England Reformers" (W 3.262).

> him, What right have you, sir, to your one virtue? Is virtue piecemeal?[93]

Emerson's second complaint against the reformers concerned their confidence in methods based on collectivities. The theme was again not new, but now the formulas attained a lapidary precision they would never display again.[94] It is more interesting, however, to note that the two criticisms proceeded from the same fundamental intuition, and both aimed at recovering for man an integrity beyond the fragments and conglomerates accepted by the reformers in the name of morality itself. Emerson argued, that is, that the activity of reform is possible only by a renunciation of the inner life; reform turns away in fact from the riches of life, which always lie within, and seeks an illusory satisfaction in agitation, excess, and sham solidarity.

A poem Emerson wrote in the summer of 1843 opens with this abrupt declaration: "Give me truths; / For I am weary of surfaces / And die of inanition."[95] In modern editions the poem is called "Blight"; when it appeared in the *Dial*, in January 1844, it was called "The Times."[96] The detail is important; it gives the hunger for depth and unity expressed throughout the poem a set of precise temporal coordinates. The modern world is devitalized, and the reformers' worst error is to further impoverish its substance in the attempt to purify it. Such is the reproach Emerson directs in his journal against Garrison, a defender of good causes if there ever was one:

> We want to be expressed, yet you take from us War, that great opportunity which allowed the accumulations of electricity to stream off from both poles, the positive & the negative. —Well, now you take from us our cup of alcohol as before you took our cup of wrath. We had become canting moths of peace, our helm was a skillet, & now we must become temperance watersops. You take away, but what do you give me? . . . If we can get no full demonstration of our heart & mind we feel wronged & incarcerated: the philosophers & divines we shall hate most, as the upper turnkeys.[97]

[93] "New England Reformers" (W 3.262–263). The journal records a good many occasions of such exasperation at the aggressive narrowness of such "monotones"; see for example JMN 8.29.

[94] "No society can ever be so large as one man. . . . There can be no concert in two, where there is no concert in one. . . . The union is only perfect when all the uniters are isolated" (W 3.265–267).

[95] W 9.139.

[96] As is noted in W 9.450.

[97] JMN 8.116–117 (October 1841).

This note of warning is surprising when one considers that it comes from the man who only a few weeks earlier had abandoned himself to the pantheism of the "Method of Nature"; but both texts manifest the same appetite for plenitude and the same rejection of reasonable moderation.

In any case, several recent studies of the development of Emerson's thought have stressed his capacity to descend within himself—even when what he finds there profoundly disorients him.[98] In 1842, Emerson gives a detailed description of a dream he had in which he unhesitatingly acknowledged the work of sorcery, the expression of a "devilish will" that had borrowed the voice and the breath of the wind.[99] It is in the same sense, it seems, that one ought to interpret certain enigmatic reflections he records after his son's death. The death was appallingly sudden; even today one can hardly read unmoved the series of notes, generally restrained but then, suddenly, almost embarrassingly candid, in which he tells the tragic news to his friends and family.[100] A month after the event, however, he was regretting that grief had passed over him without touching him: "I chiefly grieve that I cannot grieve; that this fact takes no more deep hold than other facts, is as dreamlike as they; a lambent flame that will not burn playing on the surface of my river. Must every experience—those that promised to be dearest & most penetrative, —only kiss my cheek like the wind & pass away?"[101] What is in question here is neither the existence nor even the intensity of the moral hurt; it is its meaning. Emerson's drama lies in his receiving no illumination from his suffering; in vain does he wait for that divine depth of sorrow about which Carlyle, following Goethe, had spoken. A fine film is stretched out between him and the universe, and its deceptive transparency only heightens his unhappiness.

Some individuals at least have tried to remove such a curse by violence; and Emerson, who had only sarcasm for the fanaticism of reformers, warmly salutes the boldness and the passion of noble natures thus gone astray:

[98] One thinks chiefly of Whicher and Strauch, particularly of the latter's "The Importance of Emerson's Skeptical Mood," *Harvard Library Bulletin* 11 (1957), pp. 117–141. Even Melville admired Emerson as a man who dived deep; see J. J. Mayoux, *Melville par lui-même* (Paris, 1958), p. 73.

[99] JMN 8.215–216.

[100] See L 3.6–9.

[101] Letter to Caroline Sturgis of February 4, 1842 (L 3.9–10). The idea is expressed in a similar form in "Experience" (W 3.48–50). Here Emerson speaks a language that our own century has often echoed; cf. the remark of Camus's Caligula, that "people think a man suffers because the person he loves dies in a day. But his real suffering is less trivial: it is seeing that the sorrow doesn't last either. Even pain doesn't mean anything" (*Caligula*, IV.13).

> We crave a sense of reality, though it comes in strokes of pain. I explain so, —by this manlike love of truth, —those excesses and errors into which souls of great vigor, but not equal insight, often fall. They feel the poverty at the bottom of all the seeming affluence of the world. They know the speed with which they come straight through the thin masquerade, and conceive a disgust at the indigence of nature: Rousseau, Mirabeau, Charles Fox, Napoleon, Byron, —and I could easily add names nearer home, of raging riders, who drive their steeds so hard, in the violence of living to forget its illusion: they would know the worst, and tread the floors of hell.[102]

The Faustian fascination with knowledge becomes an appetite for experience, a boldly asserted desire to bring man into contact with the extreme boundaries of his fate, beyond good and evil. Taking his start from Goethe but already looking toward Nietzsche, Emerson would resemble the latter more closely still if he did not have the faculty of vision denied to the heroes he is here evoking. Hence also his idea of the poet as a person passing beyond all appearances and breaking through all surfaces because his inalienable function is to represent, to reconcile, and to liberate.

When the new edition of all Emerson's poems is at last published,[103] it will become clear that this vocation did not, however profound and natural its source, easily come to fruition. A lengthy fragment called "The Discontented Poet: A Masque"[104] reveals the sadness and discouragement of this "cripple of God," in whom the Promethean spark is powerless to set the universe on fire. But whether unpromising or not, the path was marked out. Fate had created Emerson to *portray*;[105] and happiness, if he were ever to have it, would come as recompense for unfailing fidelity to this mission—as is suggested in the poem "Saadi," whose title means "fortunate."[106] In this context, the essay on the poet that opens the second series of the *Essays*[107] becomes both and inextricably a profession of faith and a program, an acknowledgment of an inner law and an appeal to kindred souls.

It is true that in this essay Emerson takes up a good number of themes from *Nature*, "The American Scholar," and numerous lectures; but he

[102] "New England Reformers" (W 3.273–274).

[103] Carl Strauch has been working on it for some time. See *Eight American Authors: A Review of Research and Criticism*, ed. Floyd Stovall (New York, 1956), p. 51.

[104] JMS H.136-P, pp. 153–156. A later version of this poem, from which, as the editor himself admits, the most "morbid" lines have been excluded, is printed in W 9.309–320.

[105] See JMN 9.49 (October–November 1843).

[106] See W 9.129–135.

[107] W 3.1–42.

orchestrates them in a manner strikingly new—he is above all more precise, sacrificing less to the demon of abstraction and seeking to resituate the poet within the community. The poet is the figure of integral man, temporarily isolated by his faculty of intuition, but at a deeper level linked to all those who participate in the mystery of life:

> Who loves nature? Who does not? Is it only poets, and men of leisure and cultivation, who live with her? No; but also hunters, farmers, grooms and butchers, though they express their affection in their choice of life and not in their choice of words. The writer wonders what the coachman or the hunter values in riding, in horses and dogs. It is not superficial qualities. When you talk with him he holds these at as slight a rate as you. His worship is sympathetic; he has no definitions, but he is commanded in nature by the living power which he feels to be there present.[108]

There, irrefutably established, is the poet's right to men's esteem and respect; all others seek—often unconsciously—what he alone has found. To give names to things, to use words rooted in a primal language is a work more essential and more beneficent than the laborer's plowing the furrow to plant seed. My work, Thoreau was to say, is writing.

From this particular grace proceed both the poet's function and his power. Because the streams of life pass freely through him, the poet is the great reconciler, or, to paraphrase Emerson's penetrating intuition, the natural link between power and form. But the definition gains its full meaning only when referred to the American intellectual climate of the period, and to the pale neoclassicism that at the time stood for art in the few circles with an understanding and a taste for the life of the mind. Emerson topples philistines and aesthetes with a single gesture, showing the first their vulgarity and asserting to the second that "what would be base, or even obscene, to the obscene, becomes illustrious, spoken in a new connection of thought."[109] In illustration of this maxim, he goes on to celebrate the development of the railways—notoriously the despair of the Romantic soul—because they too have their place in the universal order and draw from that organic relation a beauty in no way inferior to that of the stars.[110] The true poet knows only one subject: the presence of Life, abundant, various, continually transformed and never decaying.

[108] W 3.15.

[109] W 3.17.

[110] W 3.19. The journal for the period contains at least two passages glorifying the railroads (JMN 8.281 and 482); the second is a sort of prose hymn, snorting like the engine it sings of and celebrating the economic revolution of which the train is the instrument.

But the essay seeks to go further and to grasp the process by which the poet can communicate the truth revealed to him. At one time it was oratory that Emerson considered the most effective form of expression, the one form that permitted feeling to be conveyed in full fidelity and power. Now it seems to him that the orator is only a preparatory sketch of the poet—and a coarse one at that, given the means the orator uses.[111] The poet, on the contrary, refuses to hunt down the truth as a hunter hunts down his game. Rather he plays upon the correspondences of which the universe is woven and sends out his words obliquely, thus making them say more than the intelligence can grasp.

> The use of symbols has a certain power of emancipation and exhilaration for all men. We seem to be touched by a wand which makes us dance and run about happily, like children. We are like persons who come out of cave or cellar into the open air. This is the effect on us of tropes, fables, oracles and all poetic forms. Poets are thus liberating gods.[112]

This formula recurs twice in the essay and is at the heart of Emerson's thought. It is pregnant with so many promises, defines so lofty a mission, meets so burning a need of human nature that the last nostalgia for action in the more ordinary sense evaporates entirely.[113] If the poet wishes to fulfill his office properly, he must accept obscurity, perhaps even scorn, as Emerson reminds him at the end with that tone of authority which Henry James saw as his hallmark:

> God wills also that thou abdicate a manifold and duplex life, and that thou be content that others speak for thee. Others shall be thy gentlemen and shall represent all courtesy and worldly life for thee; others shall do the great and resounding actions also. Thou shalt lie close hid with nature, and canst not be afforded to the Capitol or the Exchange. The world is full of renunciations and apprentice-

[111] In the 1841 lecture "The Poet" (number 3 of the series "The Times" [EL 3.347–365]), Emerson writes of oratory as of an art form not to be praised unreservedly, and opposes it to poetry, which always elevates those it touches.

[112] "The Poet" (W 3.30). F. O. Matthiessen, *American Renaissance: Art and Expression in the Age of Emerson and Whitman* (1941; repr. New York, 1968), pp . 55–58, has an analysis of this poetical technique, which Emerson—like Whitman—calls "indirection." On the general problem of aesthetic communication in Emerson's work see Vivian C. Hopkins, *Spires of Form* (Cambridge, Mass., 1951), particularly pp. 148–161.

[113] The fact is that even as he was proclaiming the scholar's need for action, Emerson was revealing a personal preference for solitude and contemplation; and Brownson rebukes him for it as early as 1839, in reviewing "Literary Ethics" in *Boston Quarterly Review* 2 (1839), pp. 1–27; partially reprinted in *The Transcendentalists: An Anthology*, ed. Perry Miller (Cambridge, Mass., 1950), pp. 431–434.

> ships, and this is thine; thou must pass for a fool and a churl for a long season.[114]

One could hardly imagine a more intimate fusion between the Romanticism of Europe and the intellectual tradition based on self-discipline and austerity that had characterized the culture of New England since its beginnings.

Clearly it is inappropriate to identify this portrait of the ideal poet in its original state with the personality of its author. The decade between 1840 and 1850 found Emerson less and less in rebellion against his environment; and at the same time a public of growing size and increasing sophistication was reading his books and flocking to his lectures. No American could have imagined portraying the man who embarked for England in 1847 as a "fool and a churl." But at a deeper level, the position of the historical Emerson was in fact in conformity with the rule of abstinence the essay propounds. He came up against the city, success, and popularity, and was not led astray. He sensed that he did not belong to anyone because the particular bonds of sympathy or hate were incompatible with the universal character of his mission. To the extent that he sought to be a poet—that is, an observer and, at least indirectly, a legislator—he needed to depersonalize himself; and his judgment strove to work on the scale of the realities that do not change.

The essay "Politics" is, as noted, the fruit of long reflection;[115] and although it necessitates particular judiciousness in the reading, one can in the end see clearly what the final version adds to the lectures of 1837 and 1840. That an evolution had taken place in Emerson's mind is explicit in the text itself, which rejects the 1837 distinction between laws governing persons and laws governing things. Beyond human intention, the government of the world belongs to Nature, which watches and will continue to watch to insure the triumph of its order:

> Things have their laws, as well as men; and things refuse to be trifled with. Property will be protected. Corn will not grow unless it is planted and manured; but the farmer will not plant or hoe it unless the chances are a hundred to one that he will cut and harvest it. Under any forms, persons and property must and will have their just sway. They exert their power, as steadily as matter its attraction.[116]

[114] "The Poet" (W 3.41).

[115] Vide supra, chapter 7, n. 90. Whicher, *Selections*, pp. 490–491, gives useful details on how Emerson kept revising the text till its publication as "Politics" in the second series of *Essays* (W 3.197–221).

[116] "Politics" (W 3.205).

Emerson's attachment to the doctrine of free trade and indeed to economic liberalism in its most extreme form finds here its source and justification.[117] When in 1848 he expresses his admiration for Cobden and his struggle against the Corn Laws,[118] when in *The Conduct of Life* he affirms that political economy has no other rule than the rule of supply and demand,[119] and when after the Civil War he protests in his journal against the taxation of oranges and pineapples from Cuba,[120] he obeys on each occasion the feeling that our best shield against the selfishness of our fellow men is the operation of natural law. The argument is invincible if one accepts the postulate that the order of things, in this case defined negatively, coincides with the order of justice. But the problem is being looked at from too high up, and the data are being dangerously simplified: "every man owns something, if it is only a cow, or a wheelbarrow, or his arms, and so has that property to dispose of."[121] Marxism inserts a wedge between the second and third terms of the list and shows that the worker who possesses only his hands becomes the slave not only of the owner of the wheelbarrow but also of the wheelbarrow itself. Of this disquieting inversion Emerson had, of course, no intimation.

Here again Emerson's economic thought proves weak and flawed; but the distance he keeps from his subject fosters a historical understanding that hitherto his analyses had not exhibited. At the same time that they incorporate America into a temporal continuity, they admit a modicum of relativism. The political structures of past centuries—that is, feudalism and monarchy—were, Emerson argues, the best possible then, and could claim to be founded in morality with no less justification

[117] In the lecture "The Young American," given in 1844, Emerson firmly opposes all forms of public aid: "we concoct eleemosynary systems, and it turns out that our charity increases pauperism" (W 1.374). He also thinks that the postal services will gradually depart from federal control and be taken over by private companies, more efficient and less wasteful (W 1.385). It is ironic to note that these theories are shared by the Locofocos and stated in some of William Leggett's articles; see Marvin Meyers, *The Jacksonian Persuasion* (Stanford, Calif., 1957), pp. 141–156.

[118] Emerson had just heard Cobden lecture at Manchester; he was impressed by Cobden's force and calm, and the man himself, as he wrote Thoreau, seemed to him "above all, educated by his dogma of Free Trade, led on by it to new lights and correlative liberalities, as our abolitionists have been, by their principle, to so many reforms. . . . It was quite beautiful, even sublime, last night, to notice the moral radiations which this Free Trade dogma seemed to throw out, all unlooked for, to the great audience, who instantly and delightedly adopted them" (January 28, 1848; *Atlantic Monthly* 69 [June 1892], p. 746).

[119] See "Wealth" (W 6.105–107).

[120] See JMN 16.85–86 (1868). The professions of faith in free trade are particularly frequent during Reconstruction; see for example JMN 16.47 and 175.

[121] "Politics" (W 3.207).

than can democracy today;[122] conversely, the government of the United States in 1844 is far from having reached the perfection attributed to it by national arrogance. This argument is followed by the passage on parties, too often remembered only for a single phrase: "one has the best cause, and the other contains the best men."[123] The commentary that follows—and still more the reflections scattered in the journal—demolish both parties with equal disdain. The Whigs have better people, Emerson admits, but by their timid and selfish behavior and by their distrust of good causes they are like so many wretched Joshuas, seeking to stop the sun. Only those entirely ignorant of the universe and its inexhaustible vitality could imagine that it could be confined within the straitjacket of Whiggish rules.[124] As for the Democrats—their mediocrity is heightened, not mitigated, by the cause they claim to defend. They are Whigs *manqués*, whose strength is consumed with envy and who, in consequence, add to the baseness of ambition the sin of duplicity: "In our parties there is no great difference: the democratic party is not more humane than the whig. I think the leaders, in my little experience, to be worse men than the whig leaders. I think their democracy no more principled than the conservatism; that it is only a little worse whiggism."[125] The liberty that the Democratic party makes its flag leads to nothing—unless one counts as a goal the brute desire to overturn and destroy.[126]

[122] The journal offers the argument in an abrupter version: "we are . . . democrats, and are nowise qualified to judge of monarchy, which to our fathers living and thinking in the monarchical idea was just as exclusively right" (JMN 1.xxxii).

[123] "Politics" (W 3.209); the phrase is recorded in the journal for November 1842 (JMN 8.314).

[124] It is difficult to know whether Emerson's definition of Whig included the type of industrialist then so rapidly multiplying in New England. Carl Strauch has recently published (*Harvard Library Bulletin* 10 [Spring 1956], pp. 245–253) a poem called "New England Capitalist," probably composed in 1843, and in commenting on it notes the contradictions that this first sketch of the tycoon contains. On the one hand the capitalist is the modern man; his machines testify that the universe is accessible to the human mind and prophesy new conquests not only in science but also in economy and the organization of society. He thus prepares the final triumph of the arts of peace. At the same time, his success depends on a monstrous narrowing of his abilities, and his enterprises are built on misery—he "eats up the poor"—and violence—from New Hampshire to Carolina, the citizens "must help to drag the coach of the acquisitive New England capitalist." Emerson's perplexity becomes clear in the disappointing weakness of the last line: "Now let him make a harp!"

[125] JMN 8.287–288 (October 1842). Cf. also JMN 8.76 and "The Young American" (W 1.388). A passage of the journal for 1842 (JMN 8.264) describes the rich and the poor as two panels of a diptych; they are ruled over by the same idea, and each group exists only in terms of the other.

[126] See "Politics" (W 3.210) and JMN 8.341–342. A. I. Ladu, "Emerson, Whig or Democrat," NEQ 13 (September 1940), pp. 419–441, has aptly shown the shift by which Emer-

On reading this gloomy account, one thinks inevitably of Carlyle; on both sides of the Atlantic alike there is the same bottomless depth of vulgarity, the same despairing absence of direction and inspiration. The Gospel of Mammon has corrupted every heart. But what differentiates Emerson and Carlyle is their divergent ideas about a solution. Carlyle awaits and summons the hero, who will take hold of the tiller of government, subject the crew to his law, and show that a people's best use of its liberty is to yield it into the hands of a leader. For Emerson, by contrast, the evil comes precisely from personality in excess; he establishes a curious distinction between true parties, those founded on the basis of deep instincts, as natural as the ice and the east wind, and parties that degenerate into personalities because they have been diverted from their true goals by leaders either petty or selfish. One may as well admit that Emerson is performing a little sleight-of-hand here; he refuses the name of party to an entity that has always been defined by it and transfers it to a series of groups that in ordinary discourse have no claim to it: religious sects, and also movements favoring free trade, universal suffrage, and the abolition of slavery or of capital punishment. But by his verbal play he has, from his own point of view, won a decisive advantage: he has lifted the debate from the area of persons—in which, in fact, all sorts of corruptions are likely—to the area of principles, perpetually pure in their ideal substance.

It is at this level, it seems, that one should oppose Emerson's democratic faith to Carlyle's sympathies for authoritarianism. A republic is like a raft, said Fisher Ames; you always have your feet in the water but you never sink. Borrowing Ames's Federalist comparison, Emerson seeks to justify it by arguments at which Ames himself could only have been astonished: "No forms can have any dangerous importance whilst we are befriended by the laws of things. . . . The fact of two poles, of two forces, centripetal and centrifugal, is universal, and each force by its own activity develops the other. Wild liberty develops iron conscience."[127] Emerson's thought here maintains a delicate balance. It continues to claim absolute autonomy for every citizen—the anarchist picture of 1840 is still vivid—but at the same time it includes a general view of things in which a beneficent and ubiquitously active necessity orders and harmonizes the multiplicity of individual behaviors. Now what precisely coincides with this double vision is democracy. Democracy is the absence of mediation between the individual and the whole;

son comes to denounce not only the leaders but also the doctrine of the Democratic Party, in which he finds only the same materialism as that of the Whigs.

[127] "Politics" (W 3.211–212).

it liberates individual energies for which other political systems cautiously seek narrow channels,[128] but at the same time it incorporates those energies into the great scheme of law. America's originality is exactly to have permitted the experiment for once to be tried.

Tried—but not yet achieved. At this point Emerson is led by several converging lines of thought to reflect on his country's destiny, now dramatically arrived at a point at which History may either suddenly reveal the direction toward which it has been tending or simply lose itself in an acceleration without meaning;[129] and he turns the possibilities about repeatedly, at first not seeing them very clearly. In April 1841, while deciding what to say to the students of Waterville College, he feels himself encompassed on all sides by agitation and cowardice:

> We are a puny & fickle folk. Hesitation & following are our diseases. The rapid wealth which hundreds in the community acquire in trade or by the incessant expansions of our population & arts, enchants the eyes of all the rest, the luck of one is the hope of thousands, & the whole generation is discontented with the tardy rate of growth which contents every European community. America is therefore the country of small adventures, of short plans, of daring risks, not of patience, not of great combinations, not of long, persistent, close woven schemes, demanding the utmost fortitude, temper, faith, & poverty.[130]

This severe diagnosis reflects and amplifies Tocqueville's judgment in the second volume of *Democracy in America*[131]—the book was pub-

[128] Ernest E. Sandeen, *Emerson's Americanism*, University of Iowa Studies: Humanistic Studies 6.1 (Iowa City, 1942), observes that democracy as Emerson conceives of it is only the political extension of the principle of free trade.

[129] See for example the letter to Fuller of May 6, 1841 (L 2.398–399). Himself yielding to the irresistible force of time, Emerson wonders whether the same law does not also apply to the nation as a whole and condemns it to sterility: "do you not hate these racing Days? I must think they charge us Americans foolishly with our national hurry It is Time, it is this foolish world & fantastic constitution of things we live in, that spends with this immoderate celerity & lights both ends of its candle." But in "Prospects," the last lecture of the series "The Times" (given in the winter of 1841–1842; [EL 3.366–382]), Emerson beseeches his audience not to rush either into action or into the writing of literature; he proposes that they rather adopt the motto: "patience and truth."

[130] JMN 7.431–432 (April 20, 1841). Only a few sentences of this passage were used in the introduction of "The Method of Nature" (W 1.191–192).

[131] See particularly part 3, chapters 17, "How Society in the United States Is at Once Turbulent and Monotonous," and 19, "Why in the United States One Finds so Many Ambitious Men and so Few Large Ambitions." Meyers, *The Jacksonian Persuasion*, pp. 24–41 (chapter 3, "Virtuous Conservative: Tocqueville's Image of the Democrat"), gives an excellent account of Tocqueville's analysis.

lished in 1840, and it seems Emerson got to know it very quickly.[132] Even Tocqueville, steeped in tradition as he was—indeed perhaps because of the special sensibility tradition confers—had seen how great America's destiny was likely to be. Emerson transcribes Tocqueville's majestic evocation of the pioneers' unwearied progress westward, and goes on to comment, "America & not Europe is the rich man."[133] Finding the same opinion expressed in a letter of about the same date, one wonders whether it was not paradoxically the European aristocrat who reanimated in Emerson an interest in the West he had hardly expressed since his days at Harvard.[134] In any case, once revived the interest remained lively. When two years later Margaret Fuller traveled at length in the region of the Great Lakes, Emerson wrote to her from Concord: "I envy you this large dose of America. . . . We have all been East too long. Now for the West."[135]

At the same time, and as it were correspondingly, Emerson was directing an unprecedented intensity of attention toward the New England of his ancestors. Only two weeks of the journal separate the passage on the West from a long and passionate meditation on that subject. For reasons he did not go into, Emerson had immersed himself in family papers, and among them a prominent place was occupied by the letters of his aunt Mary. Through them he had felt the peace of the Sabbath that once stretched out over the country rise like the half-forgotten scent of incense, and the depth of his rootedness in that past suddenly flashed into his mind.[136] Nor was the emotional shock experienced on that occasion ephemeral. A few months later, his grandfather, Ezra Ripley, died; the very beginning of this study discussed the exquisite sensitive-

[132] In the introduction of "Prospects," Emerson quotes (in English) a remark from Tocqueville's second volume on the characteristic American melancholy: "a cloud always hangs on an American's brow" (EL 3.367).

[133] JMN 7.433 (April 21, 1841). The passage Emerson transcribes is the following: " 'this gradual and continuous progress of the European race towards the Rocky Mountains has the solemnity of a providential event; it is like a deluge of men rising unabatedly & daily driven onward by the hand of God.' "

[134] "If I had a pocketfull of money, I think I should go down the Ohio & up & down the Mississippi by way of antidote to what small remains of the Orientalism—(so endemic in these parts)—there may still be in me. . . . We must presently learn that the rich man is not Europe but America; and our reverence for Cambridge which is only a part of our reverence for London must be transferred across the Allegany ridge" (letter to Fuller of April 22, 1841 [L 2: 394–395]).

[135] Letter to Fuller of June 7, 1843 (L 3.180). Fuller used her visits to Chicago and the lake states as material for *Summer on the Lakes*, published in 1844; Emerson read the book with pleasure (see letter to William Emerson of June 7, 1844 [L 3.255]).

[136] See JMN 7.442–447 (May 4–6, 1841), particularly the paragraph entitled "New England Theology."

ness of Emerson's account of him.[137] Emerson remained a firm believer in the necessity for everyone to take upon himself the responsibility for his own historical moment; the difference lay in the way he felt that *his* historical moment had, almost without his being aware of it, been enriched in complex and delicate ways. Special ingredients, so to speak, go into the making of an American moment, and are not to be found in its British equivalent;[138] like a refined essence, history henceforth imbues all the scenes of the order of the universe.

One can measure the strength of this inward patriotism by the irritation Emerson felt on reading Dickens' *American Notes*, published in 1842. He reproaches Dickens with his unkind partiality and for not having been able to discern central American traits beneath the fashions and the mannerisms of the moment—which, Emerson says, are themselves perhaps not so widespread as Dickens suggests. The whole book—its accounts of behavior, the conversations and linguistic peculiarities it records—seems to him false because it does not put things in proportion. In the fabrication of romantic fiction, he writes petulantly, wild exaggeration is a secret at all men's disposal.[139] But what Emerson detests in Dickens still more than his facile manipulation of the picturesque is his facile vulgarity of feeling, which leads him to stress America's most evident evils and maintain a good conscience at little cost: "He is a gourmand & a great lover of wines & brandies, & for his entertainment has a cockney taste for certain charities. He sentimentalizes on every prison & orphan asylum, until dinner time. But science, art, Nature, & charity itself all fade before us at the great hour of Dinner."[140] One is somewhat bewildered at the uncharacteristic malice of these lines. Dickens was, to be sure, little concerned with balance and moderation; he liked to accentuate the dark corners and set them near the center of his portrait, rather as Simone de Beauvoir has done more re-

[137] See chapter 1. On January 31, 1844, Emerson wrote to John Sterling, "sometimes I dream of writing the only historical thing I know, —the influence of old Calvinism, now almost obsolete, upon the education of the existing generation in New England. I am quite sure, if it could be truly done, it would be new to your people, and a valuable memorandum to ours" (*A Correspondence Between John Sterling and Ralph Waldo Emerson*, ed. Edward Waldo Emerson [Boston, 1897], p. 81).

[138] The journal for the period records a number of remarks tending to distinguish America from England with respect not only to external matters like institutions but also to inward and intrinsic traits: "there is a certain hard finish about the Englishman which contrasts with this plain simple boundless Jonathan" (JMN 8.278). Two months later, Emerson contrasted his compatriots' good health and innocence with Europe's devastating hereditary diseases; see JMN 8.320–321.

[139] See JMN 8.222–223 (November 25, 1842).

[140] Ibid.

cently in *L'Amérique au jour le jour*. But only a thorough misunderstanding of him could see him as a model of Victorian hypocrisy, and only a mind strangely prejudiced could deny to the author of *Oliver Twist* any capacity for deep emotion at the sight of a mistreated child.[141] One prefers, therefore, to interpret Emerson's judgment as an outburst of temper, composed at least in part of his familiar exasperation at the jeremiads and indignant cries of the reformers. Significantly, Emerson himself soon undertook to reorder the perspectives on this subject, in a series of five lectures given at the beginning of 1843, under the modestly geographical title of "New England"; in that series the temporal and spatial coordinates of the American adventure are recognized clearly for the first time.[142]

The title of the lecture gives a wrong idea of its contents. Emerson restates in a lengthy exordium the theme of national character he had developed previously;[143] but then personal memories begin to emerge, and they soon crowd in to the point of almost transforming the exposition into an elegy. The noble tutelary figure of Aunt Mary is the subtle inspiration for Emerson's sketch of a New England imbued since its founding with religious idealism, then gradually invaded by doubt, but paradoxically retaining all its fervor and developing a lofty tradition of culture that makes the region the nation's educator.

The second lecture, strikingly vigorous in contrast to the first, evokes an industrious people of farmers, sailors, and shopkeepers untroubled by any concern with the world beyond. Emerson is troubled, however, by the beginnings of an exodus to the cities; it is the best who depart, tempted by the thought of less primitive conditions, and they make room for a "semi-barbarous legion" of Irish immigrants.[144] One senses that Emerson's sympathies are with an America already condemned, the America of yeoman farmers of irreverent independence, living con-

[141] And it seems Emerson's was; everything is surface and "*flash*" in the book, he writes; "it begins & ends without a poetic ray & so perishes in the reading" (JMN 7.244–245 [1839]).

[142] The comparison between *American Notes* and Emerson's "New England" is at least suggested in his letter to his brother William of November 25, 1842 (L 3.100). The five lectures (H.199) are titled "Origin—Genius of the Anglo-Saxon Race," "Traits" (which Cabot wrongly reads as "Trade"), "Manners," "Literature and Spiritual Influences," and "Results." A part of the manuscript is missing, and the last lecture in particular is fragmentary. A letter of Emerson's (L 3.233) implies that the series was reworked in January 1844.

[143] In "Permanent Traits of the English Genius" (EL 1.233–259). Vide supra, chapter 6.

[144] The construction of the railways had drawn a good many Irish laborers toward the interior; and when the work was finished they were often disinclined to leave. The Concord farmers told Emerson of the worries this influx of competition was causing them. On Emerson's feelings about the Irish—turbulent, unruly, yet hardworking and cheerful—see the beginning of "The Young American" (W 1.453–455).

tent with little, obliging, honest, and ever ready to celebrate public holidays with joyous parades.[145] Emerson was to hold onto the illusion that capitalist enterprises would break up on the rock of such men's integrity until the Civil War. His reaction to the shopkeeper is less spontaneously enthusiastic, but he conceals his qualms[146] and does homage—as he has often done—to the shopkeeper's sense of concrete reality, to his boldness, and to his inexhaustible activity. Boston's prosperity and the new advantages the city could reasonably expect from the construction of the railways do, moreover, justify to some extent Emerson's solid optimism. Let Europe sneer at our instability all it likes, is Emerson's somewhat chauvinistic challenge; that instability bears witness to the wide field of our resources and to our expertise in making use of them.

With the third lecture, the arithmetical though not the real center of the series, the argument begins to be qualified, as shadows mingle with light, portraying a nation in active combat with the wholesome contradictions of life. Probably because he is thinking about the next round of lectures, which will take him as far as Baltimore and Washington, Emerson begins by juxtaposing brief portraits of the northerner and the southerner; and the diptych exhibits both balance and perceptiveness:

> The Southerner lives for the moment; relies on himself and conquers by personal address. He is wholly there in that thing which is now to be done. The Northerner lives for the year, and does not rely on himself, but on the whole apparatus of means he is wont to employ; he is only half present when he comes in person; he has a great reserved force which is coming up. The result corresponds. The Southerner is haughty, wilful, generous, unscrupulous; will have his way and has it. The Northerner must think the thing over, and his conscience and his common sense throw a thousand obstacles between himself and his wishes, which perplex his decision and unsettle his behavior. The Northerner always has the advantage at the end of ten years, and the Southerner always has the advantage to-day.[147]

[145] The lecture gives a vivid description of "Cornwallis Day," an annual celebration of the English general's 1781 surrender at Yorktown.

[146] Thus he notes in the journal for February 1841 that "in the Feejee islands, it appears, cannibalism is now familiar. They eat their own wives and children. We only devour widows' houses, & great merchants outwit & absorb the substance of small ones and every man feeds on his neighbor's labor if he can. It is a milder form of cannibalism; a varioloid" (JMN 7.421–422). Emerson restates the idea in the 1843 lecture, but more cautiously, saying that *some people* contend that business is only a milder form of cannibalism.

[147] "New England," lecture 3, "Manners" (H.199.3); cited by Cabot, *Memoir*, 2.594–595. The page attests to Emerson's desire to be fair-minded even toward the slavery advocates, and

Later, when with the initial frame of the series considerably widened Emerson comes to examine the behavior and character of contemporary America, he is overwhelmingly critical. He admires only the lyceums, because they seek to do the work of the churches and join in an atmosphere of beneficent liberty the love of eloquence and the desire for knowledge. For the rest, the nation is given over body and soul to the demon of superficiality; phrenology, hypnotism, the rage for novelty are all manifestations of the same lamentable absence of wisdom and solid foundation. One recognizes here an expression of Emerson's principal preoccupation in this period of reevaluation and readjustment; it had been on no other ground, after all, that he had rejected the methods of the reformers. But now it is America in its entirety that he subjects to the heat of his criticism, and his sentences crackle like a fire of green wood:

> Our countrymen love intoxication of some sort. . . . All foreigners and we ourselves observe the sort of hunger, the voracity for excitement which haunts us . . . one is drunk with rum, and one with politics, and one with barter and one with impossible projects. Our trade is wild and incalculable. Our people are wide travellers. Our steamboats explode; our ships are known at sea by the quantity of canvas they carry; our people eat fast; our houses tumble; our enterprizes are rash; our legislation fluctuating. The cases of insanity in this country are said greatly to outnumber the patients in Europe. The last President could not stand the excitement of seventeen millions of people but died of the Presidency in one month.[148]

In this atmosphere of mad hurry and bustle, men have lost all sense of value; and Emerson vigorously and mischievously satirizes the irresponsible predictions that newspapers pandering to the cult of progress have made popular:

> The men and women shall be galvanically conveyed, or may be put in large quills and propelled across the Atlantic by the pressure of the atmosphere; or dressed in diving-suits manufactured (no 6 Tremont Street, Boston) by the Roxbury Company, and conveyed by submarine siphons and come up near Liverpool in fountains spouting men and women, or a tunnel may run under the sea, and

at least partially clears him of charges regional resentment has inspired; see for example Jay Hubbell, *The South in American Literature* (Durham, N.C., 1954), pp. 375–385.

[148] "Manners." The allusion in the last sentence is of course to President Harrison, who just had time to choose his cabinet before dying. Tocqueville's influence is clear throughout the paragraph.

> they may go dryshod. In order to avoid the danger of submarine volcanoes, strenuous measures are to be adopted by the countries abutting on the two ends of the canal. It is disgraceful that every two years an earthquake should be allowed, from mere want of proper ventilation, to swallow a town like a custard. It only needs timely and vigorous attention, from the Congress of Nations . . . It may hereafter be found best when the structure of the human body is better understood, and the science of anatomy is perfect, to take passengers to pieces and transport them in the air or under the sea in parts chemically packed, to be put together by the Transportation Company on the other side at the Depot, and the greatest care given to keep the packages identical.[149]

If we have given this passage an emphasis its literary merits probably do not justify (though its mordant irony redeems to some extent its stylistic looseness), it is because it firmly resituates Emerson within his time and sets him against the fads and fashions of his contemporaries with a virulence that the more philosophical *Essays* hardly permit one to imagine. Nothing in Emerson's eyes is inconsequential; the phantasmagorias the crowd indulges in may very well end as nightmares in a world deprived of soul, in which men would be slaves to their own creations or mechanically jointed like common puppets. It is not Wells in his innocent utopias but Huxley that Emerson resembles here. But one need not look so far ahead; these Americans who depend more each day on their own machines and new technologies are precisely those who doubt and succumb to dejection and to the obsession of failure. As Emerson solemnly declares, "we shall never have heroes until we have learned that it is impossible to fail."[150]

To this prostration Emerson characteristically opposes the resources of character; but for the first time he also suggests that the problem may have a solution in geography: "In the brave West, I rejoice to see symptoms of a more man-like sentiment. . . . The frank Kentuckian has a way of thinking concerning his reception by his friend that makes him whole: 'Here I am, if you do not appreciate me, the worse for you.' "[151] In the following lecture, devoted to literature, the West is again presented as the living element of the nation, that which has given birth to the only authentically American works that Europe has deigned to acknowledge.[152] The theme of the West seems (the manuscript is too frag-

[149] Ibid.

[150] Ibid.

[151] Ibid.

[152] With slight modifications, this passage is used in the first part of an article published in *Dial* 3 (April 1843), pp. 511–521, under the title "Europe and European Books." The key

mentary for certainty) not to have been pursued in the last lecture; but it appears with still greater force in the lecture given in February 1844 on "The Young American".[153]

"The Young American" is borne up by its unusual imaginative force; like the optimistic panoramas of the eighteenth century, but with greater boldness, it describes the progress of the human spirit thus far achieved or imminent on this new continent that has a right to describe itself as "the home of man."[154] The oration is among Emerson's best. The sincere passion of the tone, the flexibility and range of the diction, and the calm assurance of a mind clearly at ease in such broad perspectives make these pages a worthy companion to "The American Scholar." But the resemblance goes no further. The oration of 1837 burned with a fire hot enough to fuse in a single flow the arguments carefully separated by the artifices of typography. The text of 1844 has no real unity, and its *vis rhetorica* cannot hide the weaknesses, indeed the incoherences, of its structure. What role, for example, is in the America of tomorrow to be assigned to trade? Will it be abolished by the development of agriculture? Will it perhaps take the place of institutions controlled by the government and extend its influence through all levels of society? One has the feeling that the author is pushing several distinct lines of thought to their conclusions but that an ultimate effort of synthesis remains to be made. This is in fact the perennial defect in Emerson's political and economic notions—though it is also the good fortune of his critics, who in consequence can find in his work material to justify several contradicting interpretations with equal plausibility. But the critic attempting to discern the order in which the controlling themes arise and, so to speak, are superimposed in a meaningful pattern, finds himself richy rewarded; "The Young American" restates a good many familiar ideas, but never before has Emerson attributed such importance to the intertwined subjects of the West and the American land.

In the little world of Concord an important event had taken place be-

---

sentences are quoted in W 1.416: "our eyes will be turned westward and a new and stronger tone of literature will result. The Kentucky stump-oratory, the exploits of Boone and David Crockett, the journals of western pioneers, agriculturalists, and socialists, and the letters of Jack Downing, are genuine growths which are sought with avidity in Europe, where our European-like books are of no value." The letters published over the signature of Jack Downing were the work of the Maine journalist Seba Smith, who began publishing them in the *Portland Courier* in 1830; they were so successful and so widely imitated that in 1833 he collected them in *The Life and Writings of Major Jack Downing of Downingville*. See Constance Rourke, *American Humor* (New York, 1931), pp. 29–32.

[153] The full title is "The Young American, a Lecture Read Before the Mercantile Library Association—Boston—February 7, 1844" (W 1.361–395).

[154] "The Young American" (W 1.391).

tween 1840 and 1844, the social consequences of which Thoreau himself was later to assess: a railway line had been built, and the resulting ease of movement was already affecting the rhythm of Concord life.[155] Emerson was quick to generalize this experience and to apply it to the nation at large. Gradually covered by a steadily expanding network of rails that extended and completed the facilities provided by the steamship, the nation was entering a new phase of its destiny. The conquest of hitherto virgin land was to continue at an accelerated rate; the resources of the land, no matter how far from the sea, would be methodically assessed and exploited: "railroad iron is a magician's rod, in its power to evoke the sleeping energies of land and water."[156] But at the same time, the dangers of dislocation posed by the country's nearly limitless size, which Tocqueville among others had stressed, were on the point of vanishing altogether: "an hourly assimilation goes forward, and there is no danger that local peculiarities and hostilities should be preserved."[157] Emerson had with a sure instinct grasped the continuity of the American venture in the very heart of the ongoing revolution.

But the nation's future had yet to be given imaginative content; and here Emerson shows more fervor than sagacity. He presses his countrymen to break Europe's spell over them, but dreams only of Florentine gardens and English parks. He admires and celebrates the independence of the American farmer, but shares Carlyle's nostalgia for the days of sharecroppers under the protection of benevolent masters: "These rising grounds which command the champaign below, seem to ask for lords, true lords, *land*lords, who understand the land and its uses and the applicabilities of men, and whose government would be what it should, namely mediation between want and supply."[158] But there are graver problems as well. When Emerson imagines the happiness of western farmers, free in their self-sufficiency of the curse of economic fluctuation, he completely fails to see—as do many of his contemporaries, by the way[159]—that the new economy is inextricably agricul-

[155] "Have not men improved somewhat in punctuality since the railroad was invented? Do they not talk and think faster in the depot than they did in the stage-office? There is something electrifying in the atmosphere of the former place. I have been astonished at the miracles it has wrought; that some of my neighbors, who, I should have prophesied, once for all, would never get to Boston by so prompt a conveyance, are on hand when the bell rings. To do things 'railroad fashion' is now the byword" (*Walden* [New York, 1950], p. 97; chapter 4, "Sounds").

[156] "The Young American" (W 1.364).

[157] Ibid. "Railroads make the country transparent," Emerson notes elsewhere in the journal (JMN 9.78 [1844]).

[158] "The Young American" (W 1.384). There seems to be some influence here from *Past and Present* and its energetic and righteous Abbot Samson .

[159] Henry Nash Smith, *Virgin Land* (Cambridge, Mass., 1950), chapter 14, "The New

tural, commercial, and industrial at once. He forgets that farmers have to lay out a portion of their crop to clothe and educate their children, and that in proportion as they produce more the rise and fall of the market has more of an effect on them. And yet Emerson knew—the journal attests as much, and "The Young American" echoes it[160]—that the life of his farmer neighbors was a long sequence of unprofitable efforts, that they had no time for reading and self-cultivation, and that in the end they too were subject to financial difficulties. One day a Boston merchant told him that the future belonged to conglomerates, and that small proprietors would have to band together to survive;[161] the idea had stuck, and one discovers its expression in "The Young American."[162] But the components of a workable solution are neither coordinated nor ordered in a hierarchy; too often a pious hope is made to do for an answer.[163]

This amounts to saying that even in this supremely concrete domain Emerson behaves like a poet. Land is for him a spiritual reality, and there is more Wordsworth than Quesnay in the list he compiles of the land's virtues:

> The land is the appointed remedy for whatever is false and fantastic in our culture. The continent we inhabit is to be physic and food for our mind, as well as our body. The land, with its tranquillizing, sanative influences, is to repair the errors of a scholastic and traditional education, and bring us into just relations with men and things.[164]

The West thus becomes not so much a promise of success and democratic equality as an invitation to self-discovery issued to the American too long an exile on his own territory:

> The land was ours before we were the land's.
> She was our land more than a hundred years
> Before we were her people. She was ours
> In Massachusetts, in Virginia;
> But we were England's, still colonials,

Calculus of Western Energies," has convincingly demonstrated the persistence of the yeoman ideal in the West even as it was denied and fatally assaulted by daily experience.

[160] See JMN 8.405–406 (May 20, 1843) and "The Young American" (W 1.381).

[161] See letter to William Emerson of April 2, 1842 (L 3.40–42).

[162] W 1.382–383.

[163] As, for example, when a contrast between traditional and modern methods of culture lamely concludes with "if any means could be found to bring these two together!" ("The Young American" [W 1.381–382]).

[164] "The Young American" (W 1.365–366).

Possessing what we were still unpossessed by,
Possessed by what we now no more possessed.[165]

To escape from Europe and the anonymity of cities, to ally with the strong simplicity of trees, rivers, and deserts is thus in the purest sense to be Americanized. Patriotism maintains a vital relation with the inviolate lands of the West that neither merchants nor plain citizens perceive but that the poet when arisen will celebrate as the fountain at which he drinks.[166]

Thus the first and strikingly unexpected result of Emerson's conversion to the world of facts was to reveal to him the strength of his national attachments. If the United States had been a country like Spain, France, or even England, committed by a long history to a fixed destiny, he would no doubt have been antagonized by these conditioning circumstances. But in 1844, as the continent's physiognomy changed from year to year—and indeed from month to month—under the pressure of westward movement, it was no very extravagant intellectual gesture to compare the young American to the new Adam. Patriotic obligation and moral obligation thus coalesced, as Emerson emphasizes in a *Dial* editorial published in October 1843 in response to the sickly misgivings of certain of his correspondents.[167] When about the same time the elder Henry James announced his imminent departure for Europe, Emerson indicates his displeasure courteously but firmly. The trip, he declares, "will not do that which you will ever hold before you to be done, but that will remain to be achieved afterward as now."[168] Till the Civil War America would, with its grandiose promises and the disappointments it inflicts, foster Emerson's impatience, his anger, and his trust. But it would never be far from the center of his thought.

165 "The Gift Outright," lines 1–7, in *The Poems of Robert Frost* (New York, 1946), p. 399. In a speech published later as "On Emerson," *Daedalus* 88 (Autumn 1959), pp. 712–718, Frost himself, in paying tribute to Emerson as one of the four greatest Americans (Washington, Jefferson, and Lincoln are the others) acknowledges that between his own work and that of the author of "Monadnoc" the kinship is deep.

166 See "The Young American" (W 1.369–370. Whitman, whom this part of the lecture seems to herald, and who sang of the American land with such fervor, wrote most of his poems about the West before ever having really seen it; for him as for Emerson the subject's value is essentially an imaginative one. Cf. Roger Asselineau, *L'évolution de Walt Whitman* (Paris, 1954), pp. 413–416.

167 Reprinted in W 12.392–404.

168 Letter to Henry James of July 21, 1843 (in Perry, *William James* 1.50); see also the letter to Elizabeth Hoar of August 31, 1843 (L 3.203–204). The journal's condemnation of such dilettante travelers is far harsher: "All America seems on the point of embarking for Europe. Every post brings me a letter from some worthy person who has just arrived at the execution, he tells me, of a long cherished design of sailing for Europe. This rottenness is like the cholera in the potato" (JMS, H.122-Salvage, p. 228).

11

~ ~ ~ ~

EQUILIBRIUM REGAINED

If one seeks in Emerson's work only the dialogue of an individual soul with the world's soul, and, in the name of the impersonal idealism Emerson had by this time come to profess, if one considers the uncertainties and disturbances of history as negligible, it is legitimate to situate the final stabilization of his thought around 1844:

> My faith in the Writers as an organic class, increases daily, and in the possibility to a faithful man of arriving at statements for which he shall not feel responsible, but which shall be parallel with nature. Yet without any effort I fancy I make progress also in the doctrine of Indifferency, and am certain content that the truth can very well spare me, & have itself spoken by another without leaving it or me the worse.[1]

Stephen Whicher saw in this almost voluptuous renunciation of the use of liberty a resurgence of Emerson's ancestral Calvinism, the one thing that was finally capable of offering balm to the always throbbing wound of his powerlessness.[2]

Still, one ought not to push the equation too far. What is entirely extinguished in Emerson is the proud trust in his own resources, the conviction that the individual can become like the God in whose image he is made; and that change does indeed, as Whicher shows, offer a solution to an inward conflict. The title Whicher gives to one of his later

[1] Letter to Carlyle of February 29, 1844 (CEC 358).

[2] See *Freedom and Fate*, pp. 139–140. The judgment is based on a passage of "The Young American" (W 1.371–372).

chapters, "Acquiescence," felicitously suggests the passage from moral to contemplative reflection: the hateful part of the self having finally been overcome, the remaining task is simply that of celebration. But here a new difficulty begins. Though accepting his limits, though rejoicing that a "sublime and friendly destiny" (as he calls it in "The Young American") leads individuals toward a goal that transcends them, Emerson has not abandoned his ethical requirements nor learned to accept in self-effacement the decrees of a supreme and eternally inscrutable will. He has agreed, that is, to give up his role as the creator of values ("the only right is what is after my constitution; the only wrong what is against it," he had written in "Self-Reliance"[3])—but on the condition that he be free to discern the moral sense that operates at every level of the universal order like an entelechy, saving the whole of existence from the taint of dishonesty and deceit. A bold extension of his angle of vision, making it possible for him to comprehend the entirety of things and beings in a single and ordered process of development, becomes the means by which he can answer—at least theoretically—this fundamental need of his nature.[4] In a sense he was to retrace the steps he took ten years earlier, when the lectures on science served as prelude to the rhapsodies of *Nature*.

But there is a considerable difference—the poisoned fruit of maturity, so to speak. The universe has lost its radiant coherence forever. Depending on whether one chooses to turn on it a shortsighted or a farsighted gaze, whether one adopts a cosmic perspective or seeks for evidence of human greatness in the passing moment, one offers opposed judgments, one wavers between optimism and pessimism, between doubt and admiration. This ambiguity, or rather doubleness, is ubiquitous; but nowhere is it manifested more clearly than in the field of politics, which one might define as the jousting ground of human destiny, with order and anarchy locked in combat, and persons rising up against the majesty of universal laws. The word "America" covers this doubleness admirably: it connotes both a continent only partly cultivated, for which speculators and swindlers are struggling, and a promise of expansion and growth for humanity as a whole. Emerson has long reflected on this twofold sense of the word, and he can in consequence

[3] W 2.50.

[4] This new concept appears most distinctly in "Nature," in the second series of *Essays* (W 3.167–196). Whicher cites the most striking paragraph, and observes rightly (*Freedom and Fate*, p. 145) that evolution and the origin of species are in the end much less important in Emerson's thought than is this almost infinite extension of the world's history—hence the importance to be accorded to Emerson's lifelong reading in geology. It is certain, for example, that Lyell's *Principles of Geology*, which he read about 1836, influenced him profoundly.

take an interest in political events—however disappointing—without playing false to his vocation of poet-philosopher.[5] But on occasion the spectacle disturbs him deeply; the observer in him always has considerable difficulty in severing itself from the moralist and the citizen.

But let us return to the year 1844, rich in stocktakings ("New England Reformers") and promises ("The Young American"). As he explained to Carlyle in the letter cited earlier, Emerson's ambition was currently to become the pure transcriber of the natural order, above any consideration of person or place. In the course of the Concord summer, a rather cerebral, platonic celebration of the tenth anniversary of British West Indian emancipation offered him an opportunity to trace firmly and at length nature's line of progress in a singularly perplexing domain.[6] It was the first time since 1837 that Emerson had taken a public position on slavery; and, so as to preclude any polemical interpretation of his speech, he chose as his occasion this anniversary of an episode entirely foreign to the history of his own country. Oratory was for him a way to project poetry onto the level of action; if it encouraged action, it did so obliquely and indirectly, through an illustration charged with the value of a universal symbol.[7]

Emerson's speech on slavery will never have many admirers. Too many passages in the first part of it are too evidently derivative, and the somewhat conventional rhetoric that pervades them reminds one of Theodore Parker's manner, though they lack Parker's homely touch. One would be glad to encounter the Emersonian stamp more often, to find other passages equal in quality to that in which the slave owner is gracefully and ruthlessly compared to a spoiled child on the ground that both find all their pleasure in tormenting others. But the last third of the speech rewards the perseverant reader; the thought suddenly expands, and the narrative, hitherto submissively faithful to the order of events, blossoms into a sort of cosmic poem. It is no longer a question of knowing how England abolished slavery, or even why; the real issues now are

[5] One regrets that F. I. Carpenter's *Emerson Handbook* (New York, 1953) separates the section on Emerson's political ideas from that on his sense of the American dream. As Emerson grows older, the American dream becomes the explicit or implicit point of reference for all his political ideas.

[6] "Address Delivered in Concord on the Anniversary of the Emancipation of the Negroes in the British West Indies, August 1 1844" (W 11.97–147).

[7] A few weeks after this speech was given, Emerson refused to take part in an abolitionist meeting despite an urgent invitation from John Greenleaf Whittier. As it happened, what kept him at Concord was pressing work; but, he explained in all sincerity, he would have refused even if it had not, because he simply was not made for the active role people seemed to expect him to play (letter to Whittier of September 13, 1844 [L 3.260–261]). See also the letter to Carlyle of December 31, 1844 (CEC 373).

the destiny of the blacks and the modalities of the law of progress on a universal scale—a juxtaposition sufficiently new in Emerson's work to justify an examination of its genesis.

Among the reasons that dissuaded Emerson in 1837 from supporting militant abolitionism was, as I have noted, his belief in the natural inequality of races, which justified in his eyes the de facto supremacy then held by whites.[8] As late as 1840 his conviction was unchanged:

> Strange history this of *abolition*. The negro must be very old & belongs, one would say, to the fossil formations. What right has he to be intruding into the late & civil daylight of this dynasty of the Caucasians & Saxons? It is plain that so inferior a race must perish shortly like the poor Indians. Sarah Clarke said, "the Indians perish because there is no place for them". That is the very fact of their inferiority. There is always place for the superior.[9]

But the reading Emerson did in preparing the speech now under discussion had revealed new and unsuspected horizons. The British functionaries were unanimous in stressing the beneficent influence of emancipation on the blacks' intellectual and moral development. The violence some had feared had not taken place. The economy of the islands had not been disrupted; indeed, once emerged from the ancestral sloth in which slavery had maintained them, the former slaves had become mechanics, architects, journalists, lawyers, and doctors. And had not the British abolitionist Clarke been gathering a collection of African art since the beginning of the century?[10] The weight of these remarkably convergent accounts led Emerson to repudiate his past errors—though without excessive compunction: "it now appears," he writes blandly enough, "that the negro race is, more than any other, susceptible of rapid civilization."[11]

But this passive statement is not enough. England's gesture in freeing its slaves would have remained futile if the slaves themselves had not been equal to taking effective advantage of it; and there is the new and crucial element. After centuries, indeed millennia of degradation, the blacks emerge into the daylight; they come to take their place in the procession of intelligent beings, following an order willed and defined

[8] Vide supra, chapter 8.

[9] JMN 7.393 (September 10, 1840). A year later, another passage of the journal asserts that the blacks alone are responsible for their own degradation, and that abolitionists' efforts to free them from their misery are in vain, or more exactly benefit only the abolitionists themselves (JMN 8.119 [October 1841]).

[10] See "West India Emancipation" (W 11.140–141).

[11] Ibid.

since the beginning of the world. This almost geological aspect of Emerson's thought has been discussed previously; but the particular fusion accomplished here between scientific data and idealist faith is so bold as to justify citing this unjustly ignored passage in its entirety:

> Our planet, before the age of written history, had its races of savages, like the generations of sour paste, or the animalcules that wiggle and bite in a drop of putrid water. Who cares for these or for their wars? We do not wish a world of bugs or of birds; neither afterward of Scythians, Caraibs or Feejees. The grand style of Nature, her great periods, is all we observe in them. Who cares for oppressing whites, or oppressed blacks, twenty centuries ago, more than for bad dreams? Eaters and food are in the harmony of Nature; and there too is the germ forever protected, unfolding gigantic leaf after leaf, a newer flower, a richer fruit, in every period, yet its next product is never to be guessed. It will only save what is worth saving; and it saves not by compassion, but by power. It appoints no police to guard the lion but his teeth and claws; no fort or city for the bird but his wings; no rescue for flies and mites but their spawning numbers, which no ravages can overcome. It deals with men after the same manner. If they are rude and foolish, down they must go. When at last in a race a new principle appears, an idea,— *that* conserves it; ideas only save races. If the black man is feeble and not important to the existing races, not on a parity with the best race, the black man must serve, and be exterminated. But if the black man carries in his bosom an indispensable element of a new and coming civilization; for the sake of that element, no wrong nor strength nor circumstance can hurt him: he will survive and play his part. So now, the arrival in the world of such men as Toussaint, and the Haytian heroes, or of the leaders of their race in Barbadoes and Jamaica, outweighs in good omen all the English and American humanity. The anti-slavery of the whole world is dust in the balance before this, —is a poor squeamishness and nervousness: the might and the hight are here: here is the anti-slave: here is man: and if you have man, black or white is an insignificance.[12]

Natural violence is so cheerfully stressed in this passage that in commenting on it the editor of the Centenary Edition alludes with a certain

[12] (W 11.143–144). In the journal entry containing a good part of this argument (JMN 9.124–126), the name of Toussaint-Louverture is supplemented by that of Frederick Douglass—a further proof that in his public speech Emerson meant to maintain the attitude of a dispassionate observer.

embarrassment to the doctrine of the survival of the fittest.[13] But there is no need to have recourse to Darwin here, and in 1844 Emerson had most likely never even heard the name. On several occasions previous chapters have stressed the yearning for power that tormented him and that never found real gratification, unless perhaps (and only transiently) in "The American Scholar." Gradually Emerson had given up courting heroism for its own sake; in compensation he had come to affirm the high dignity of the poet. It is only too clear that the vision he presents here of a progressive ascent of races is essentially the vision of a poet—as is confirmed by the ease with which the world of ideas is substituted for the world of brute force, or rather is superimposed on it to crown and consummate it. It is, moreover, Emerson himself who introduces very near the end of the speech the suggestive image of an orchestral score, fitted out with precise indications of the entry points of the various instruments and their dynamic level at every moment of performance. The feeling of power that fills Emerson at the sight of universal becoming is fundamentally similar to the exaltation produced on a sensitive listener by Beethoven's Ninth Symphony.

No more need be said about the speech—if it were not for a few pages toward the middle of it that jar curiously with the rest. The nobility that English statesmen have shown in decreeing abolition leads Emerson to meditate on his own compatriots' slack cowardice. In the ports of South Carolina, Georgia, and Louisiana, black cooks or sailors were often seized on board the ships that employed them, even though they were often citizens of another state; Massachusetts blacks were put in southern prisons and sometimes even sold as slaves. In considering this scandal, by which all the citizens of Boston ought to have felt sullied, Emerson abruptly quits his role of chronicler and finds a more penetrating, almost a shriller version of the tone he had once used in his letter to Van Buren:

> If such a damnable outrage can be committed on the person of a citizen with impunity, let the Governor break the broad seal of the State; he bears the sword in vain. The Governor of Massachusetts is a trifler; the State-House in Boston is a playhouse; the General Court is a dishonored body, if they make laws which they cannot execute. The great-hearted Puritans have left no posterity.[14]

[13] Cf. W 11.577. Rather one should think of certain doctrines of early nineteenth-century philosophical idealism. Philip Nicoloff, *Emerson on Race and History* (New York, 1961), pp. 74–77, demonstrates a striking resemblance between such passages in Emerson and Victor Cousin's theories on the ideal meaning of the different nations and the law governing their growth and decline.

[14] "West India Emancipation" (W 11.131).

This time Emerson had been pressed to take a position by no one; the feverish quality of his words is the more striking in consequence. He vituperates the timidity of New England men and announces—in 1844—that the Union no longer exists, because certain states have decreed themselves the jailers of others. Finally he calls for vigorous governmental intervention—just as if he had not expressed the desire some months previously that government be gradually abolished![15] In any case he was caught in a vise; he had, it seems, attained contemplative serenity only to find that his country and state were the accomplices of a repulsively reactionary crime. Could he for long celebrate the progress of persons and races if he found himself linked as a citizen with a work of darkness? The debate echoes and reechoes sadly in him before it finds—for a brief moment—an acceptable solution.

Moreover, the political situation was beginning to tighten considerably. After the rivalries and conflicts under Jackson and Van Buren, Tyler's presidency had seemed a sort of pale interlude. But the slaveholding plantation owners of the South were not inactive during his term; and now, relying on the Democratic rank and file, they affirmed an insolent self-assurance, seeking, as Emerson's speech recalls, to impose the principle of racial superiority even by acts of violence. On several occasions the Supreme Court of Massachusetts had denounced such actions, but in vain. Finally, in December 1844, it resolved to send to South Carolina a representative entrusted with the task of investigating the circumstances in which certain citizens of Massachusetts had been arrested and illegally detained. The man chosen for this mission was the Concord lawyer Samuel Hoar, who has already been mentioned on several occasions and who in Emerson's eyes embodied the traditional virtues of New England. Hoar reached Charleston; but a few days after his arrival a hostile crowd gathered outside his window as a delegation informed him that the local authorities were determined to use force, if necessary, to bring about his departure. The lawyer bowed and returned to Boston.[16] Emerson felt the insult inflicted on his compatriot so deeply that he resolved to denounce the iniquity of the South in public. It is unlikely that his speech on the subject was ever delivered;[17] but Cabot found the notes used in its preparation, and by cross-checking

[15] Cf. "Politics," in the second series of *Essays*, notably W 3.215.

[16] In this connection see Emerson's article on the occasion of Hoar's death (W 10.437–444); the editor supplies interesting details about the historical context (602–603). See also the letters of December 17 and 31, 1844 (L 3.272–275).

[17] The letters for the period make no mention of it, and the letter to Carlyle of December 31 (CEC 372–373) only reaffirms Emerson's intention to remain outside of the public fray.

with the journal one can reconstruct a rough sketch of the argument:[18] that Massachusetts will not stoop to the *lex talionis*, that citizens of South Carolina visiting Boston will neither be watched nor inhibited in their movement, that the liberty thus accorded them will be a condemnation of their intolerance. They will discover that in New England every citizen thinks for himself and is not asked to refer to some local Calhoun before offering an opinion. It is clear that Emerson is hesitant to call for physical confrontation; he would prefer to base his case on the moral qualities of Massachusetts—his true country—in the hope of a more decisive victory.

But the danger was growing with every passing year, and the problem of slavery was more and more strictly linked to the expansionist pressure toward the West. The annexation of Texas, which was the central issue of the 1844 campaign, revealed to Emerson and to other independent minds the gravity of this connection, as well as the ferocity of the interests involved. Since 1835, when the American immigrants in Texas had rebelled against Mexico and formed an independent republic, a good number of their countrymen had followed Calhoun in campaigning to get the vast territory joined to the Union. But the Texas constitution permitted slavery, and the abolitionists were quick to assess the danger.[19] Channing himself in 1837 sent Henry Clay an open letter describing the proposed annexation as madness compounded by crime.[20] For reasons less pure than Channing's, the Congress rejected a resolution proposing annexation, and for some years afterward the problem had lain dormant. But now the southern states feared that Texas would abolish slavery in return for certain guarantees England was prepared to offer it, and the problem became acute once again. In 1843, Webster's successor as secretary of state, a Virginian named Upshur, began negotiations with Texas regarding its joining the Union. Once again, however, the Senate rejected the treaty of annexation.

Such was the situation when the campaign to elect Tyler's successor began. The Democrats had the wit to construct a platform that left the issue of slavery in the background and situated the question of Texas in

[18] See Cabot, *Memoir*, 2.751–752, and JMN 9.173–175 (1845).

[19] A pamphlet called "The War in Texas," published in 1836 by the veteran abolitionist Benjamin Lundy, made a considerable stir. Lundy had tried to found an antislavery colony in Texas, but in vain; and, returning bitterly to New England, he wrote his book in an attempt to discredit the lawless and deceitful adventurers by whom, he wrote, Texas was governed, and to argue that the revolt against Mexico was the result of a plot to open new slave markets and provide the more ambitious cotton planters with virgin land.

[20] "A Letter to the Hon. Henry Clay. On the Annexation of Texas to the United States" (*Works*, ed. William Henry Channing [Boston, 1896], pp. 752–781).

the glorious context of patriotism. "Reoccupation of Oregon, re-annexation of Texas" was the slogan, chosen as if to keep a balance between southerners and northwestern frontiersmen. The tactic succeeded and obtained the presidency for James Polk of Tennessee, an obscure man entirely committed to what since that period has been called the doctrine of manifest destiny[21] and determined to carry that doctrine into the realm of fact. An ambitious task, though less arduous than it might seem; for Polk only needed to yield to the people's inclination to accomplish it:

> The "manifest destiny" of the United States to expand westward and southward, and prove the democratic principle on a scale hitherto undreamed, became the theme of countless newspaper articles, Fourth of July orations, and political speeches. Much talk there was, too, of Anglo-Saxon genius in colonization and self-government. Parson Wilbur of the Biglow Papers might preach that "all this big talk of our destinies is half on it ignorance, an' t' other half rum," but no good Democrat or Westerner believed him. . . . Jeffersonian simplicity was dead, and the new note of emancipation was silenced by the war-whoops of strutting democracy.[22]

From this point on, the conquest of the continent was to proceed inexorably, through war and through peace, until within less than ten years the Union had almost reached its present borders. The annexation of Texas was easily approved by Congress in February 1845. In January 1846, Polk ordered federal troops into Mexican territory. The news that hostilities had begun was received with enthusiasm through the whole Mississippi River valley; volunteers came by the thousands, eager not only for heroic exploits but also for booty. Elsewhere in the country, to be sure, the enthusiasm was less; Calhoun himself feared a victory that by further expanding the Union's territory could only unsettle the precarious balance of forces between slave states and free. In the Northeast, opposition to the war was proclaimed officially; the legislature of Massachusetts called it a war of aggression, undertaken to please slave owners and thus contrary to the Constitution. Here and

[21] The expression had been coined, or at least popularized, by John O'Sullivan, editor of the *United States Magazine and Democratic Review*, who used it in an article in August 1845. Cf. John Q. Anderson, "Emerson and Manifest Destiny," *Boston Public Library Quarterly* 7 (January 1955), pp. 23–33.

[22] Samuel Eliot Morison and Henry Steele Commager, *The Growth of the American Republic*, 2 vols. (New York, 1940), 1.482–483. The first series of the *Biglow Papers* was published in 1848; in it Lowell brilliantly attacked the deceptively generous enterprises of the party in power, reserving his keenest strokes for the Mexican War.

there individual acts gave witness to outraged consciences. Thoreau, as is well known, refused to pay his tax and spent a night in the Concord jail; what was more important was that he drew from his experience the matter of his essay on civil disobedience, which Gandhi said influenced him at the time that he was working out his own political doctrine—a magnificent example of Emersonian compensation.

It seems necessary to have this background in view because in this troubled period of American history Emerson's journals, lectures, and even poems respond to contemporary events more often than one would imagine. It is not that there exists a rigorous and demonstrable connection between a particular political episode and a particular inflection of Emerson's thought. But the times left a profound mark on an activity of speculation that wished and claimed to be independent—another illustration of Goethe's dictum that a living work is always to some degree the product of specific circumstances.

If one seeks to assess the tension gradually insinuating itself into Emerson's thought, one may take as a benchmark two paragraphs of the journal written early in 1844. Solidly ensconced in his poetical empyrean, Emerson looks on at the juncture and fusion of the world of the geologist and the world of Plotinus, of the world governed by the physical law of evolution and the world still mindful of the Being from which it emanated: "The question whether the trilobites or whether the gods are our grandfathers; and whether the actual existing men are an amelioration or a degradation, arises from the contingence whether we look from the material or from the poetic side."[23] About the same time, he directs an equally broad and serene attention to the apparent contradictions of History:

> The question of the annexation of Texas is one of those which look very differently to the centuries and to the years. It is very certain that the strong British race which have now overrun so much of this continent, must also overrun that tract, & Mexico & Oregon also, and it will in the course of ages be of small import by what particular occasions & methods it was done. It is a secular question. It is quite necessary & true to our New England character that we should consider the question in its local & temporary bearings, and resist the annexation with tooth & nail.[24]

[23] JMN 9.77, "The Two Histories." Carl Strauch, "Emerson as Literary Middleman," ESQ 19.2 (1960), pp. 2–9, gives a good analysis of the quality of imagination by which Emerson can give simultaneous allegiance to two apparently irreconcilable interpretations of the universe.

[24] JMN 9.74. In another entry, Emerson declares that "the greatness of the centuries is

Emerson does not, however, seem to have noticed that in leaving the domain of speculation he is giving the problem a new meaning. That meaning, as it happened, was to be revealed by his efforts to bring together within himself the witness and the man of action—at the cost of an unceasing oscillation between them.

When in August 1844 Emerson asserted that the blacks have reached maturity, he discovered also that abolitionism was not the craze of a few sensitive souls but very concretely represented a vital principle of progress in the United States: "Abolition the Scotland of our politics immeasureably higher than Whiggism."[25] At the same time the leaders of the antislavery movement assumed in his eyes an importance and dignity he had hitherto denied them. In December 1844, he praised Garrison, whom he had visited "in his dingy office";[26] a month later he got Wendell Phillips an invitation to speak at the Concord Lyceum, so persuaded was he that the "iniquity of slavery"[27] must be denounced unwearyingly and unsparingly. He himself in November 1845 declined an invitation from the lyceum at New Bedford because it did not admit blacks on the same footing as whites.[28] That same year he again agreed to speak at a public ceremony in Waltham held in further commemoration of British West Indian emancipation.[29] Once again he stands up against the superstition that blacks are intrinsically inferior to whites; but he deprecates the use of violence in securing their freedom. Rather educate their masters, he advises, and you will see them renounce their indecent privileges of their own accord. Trust was still the hallmark of Emerson's public attitude: reparation for injustice is written in the nature of things, so that one needs only forbearance, or, in his own phrase, "sublime patience."

But for the reader of the journal things look very different. To pass from the speeches to the private comments contemporary with them is

made out of the paltriness of the days & hours," and adds, "See with what motives & by what means the railroad gets built, and Texas annexed or rejected" (JMN 9.67).

[25] JMN 9.272 (1845). As printed in JMN, the phrase ends with "if" and a dash; for "if" I read "is," which though it does not finish the assertion at least does not make it conditional.

[26] JMN 9.134.

[27] JMN 9.102 (January 30, 1845). A few weeks earlier, Emerson's journal recorded a comparison between the oratory of a Webster or an Everett and that of Phillips that is entirely to the credit of the latter. Phillips's art, he writes, rests on the most reliable of all facts: moral facts (JMN 9.136–137).

[28] See L 3.312 and 323, n. 4. Rusk notes that Emerson's letter of refusal was published in Garrison's *Liberator*.

[29] The text of this speech has not been preserved, but we do have detailed contemporary reviews of it. See Louis Ruchames, "Emerson's Second West India Emancipation Address," NEQ 28 (September 1956), pp. 383–388.

to discover the existence of a twofold record, so marked in its contrasts that one comes to suspect Emerson of seeking in his public appearances quite simply to save face. He loudly rejoices in being a citizen of Massachusetts, in which the antislavery movement has such deep roots and individual liberty refuses to yield to intimidation; but in secret he is ashamed of his state's servile policies and harbors no illusions about the abolitionists' moral character:

> It is not possible that these purists accept the accommodations of hotels, or even of private families, on the existing profane arrangements? If they do, of course, not conscience, but mere prudence & propriety will seal their mouths on the inconsistences of churchmen. Two tables in every house! Abolitionists at one & *servants* at the other![30]

Emerson underlines the word "servants" in irritation—perhaps remembering his own unsuccessful experiment, which had left a bitter aftertaste.

As for the Whigs, with whom he would dearly love to find himself in sympathy—they being after all the inheritors of the great Federalist party and representing the class, or at least the milieu, from which he has emerged—they exhibit in his eyes a passivity verging on complete apathy:

> A despair has crept over the Whig party in this country. They the active, enterprizing, intelligent, well meaning, & wealthy part of the people, the real bone & strength of the American people, find themselves paralysed & defeated everywhere by the hordes of ignorant & deceivable natives & the armies of foreign voters who fill Pennsylvania, N. Y., & New Orleans, and by those unscrupulous editors & orators who have assumed to lead these masses. The creators of wealth and conscientious, rational, & responsible persons, those whose names are given in as fit for jurors, for referees, for offices of trust, those whose opinion is public opinion, find themselves degraded into observers, & violently turned out of all share in the action & counsels of the nation.[31]

Sometimes during walks in Boston Emerson felt as if he were living a nightmare, meeting not other men but "decapitated trunks."[32] Although Concord, with the solid probity of its farmers protected in their

[30] JMN 9.122 (1844).

[31] JMN 9.160–161.

[32] "I stood methought in a city of beheaded men, where the decapitated trunks continued to walk" (JMN 9.195 [1845]).

isolation, had not been deeply affected,[33] the malaise had not left the country untouched. The mountaineer, once a friend of liberty, had become the accomplice of the slave owner; betraying the "vicegerency" he received from God, the countryman left his fields for the tavern.[34] All of New England seemed to Emerson to harbor a degenerate race.

But the most odious trait of the period for him was a certain flat staleness of individual souls, what Revelations refers to as water neither hot nor cold, to be spewed out of the mouth. Whether by weakness or by design, the whole world was cheating and playing with marked cards. It was not enough that the Whigs were willing to compromise with the nation's rabble; even honest men, who believed in certain principles and continued to invoke them, looked on supinely as those principles were mocked and flouted because their supreme attachment was to their comfort. At such slackness—or hypocrisy—Emerson's indignation would take on extraordinary fervor; even during the controversy over the Divinity School address, while lashing at the latest sermon or preacher in the pages of his journal, he had never attained such solemn virulence:

> Ah thou evil two-faced half & half! how can I forgive thee? Evil, evil hast thou done. Thou it is that confoundest all distinctions. If thou didst not receive the truth at all, thou couldst do the cause of virtue no harm. But now the men of selfishness say to the absolutist, Behold this man, he has all thy truth, yet lo! he is with us & ours. —Ah thou damnable Half-and-half! choose, I pray you, between God & the whig party, and do not longer strew sugar on this bottled spider.[35]

To the small extent to which dispelling lies and clearing the air of fumes was his responsibility, he owed it to himself to meet it. And that, no doubt, is why the Fourth of July speech he gave at Dedham in 1846 bore so little resemblance to the panegyrics usually pronounced on such

[33] See JMN 9.132–133 (October 1844). In this long passage Emerson analyzes the process by which the Boston merchant becomes the friend and accomplice of the Carolina planter, whereas the villager—especially the village farmer—escapes that temptation.

[34] As was characteristic of him in periods of tension or crisis, Emerson's disappointment—perhaps "disgust" would be a better word—at this degradation of the villager is expressed in verse; see particularly "Monadnoc" (W 9.62 and 64), and the fourth and fifth stanzas of the Ode to Channing (W 9.76–77). The bitterly critical though transient note reveals how deep a discouragement is beginning to overcome him.

[35] JMN 9.317–318 (1845). The use of "thou" accentuates the maledictory quality of the passage.

occasions.[36] Hope was not entirely absent from it, but it shone only dimly, and in every direction clouds were piling up: the Boston merchants, aware of their own interests, were smiling upon the cotton planters of the South;[37] the belligerent faction common to all countries was hunting with hound and horn for blood and adventure; if there was a third category of citizens, it was paralyzed by fear of the law—human law, that is, as was clear from the governor of Massachusetts' sacrificing the moral integrity of his state rather than refuse troops to the Washington firebrands. Like a gradually expanding patch of oil, the pessimism of the diarist had now suffused the words of the public orator. And even the final profession of faith, the appeal to the nation to ally itself with abolitionists, was a little forced—like the encouragements offered an army in stampede.

There was, in fact, a gap between the speech—as reported at any rate in the local press—and the journal fragments used in constructing it.[38] Gradually and against his natural inclination Emerson had come to see the Whigs and their eminent supporters as dummies, capable no doubt of deception and smooth manners but empty of substance, hollow inside, like the figures who stimulated one of Eliot's gloomiest poems. The Whigs' opponents were shocking in their vulgarity and in the brute energy of their ambitions; but at least they were alive and had that rude nobility which always accompanies the use of force. "Our relations to fine people," writes Emerson late in 1844, "are whipped cream & not necessary bread."[39] And then, by contrast, two pages further on: "there is a certain pleasure in getting on to the lowest ground of politics; because there is plain dealing & no cant."[40] One might easily cite a good number of such passages, both those in which Emerson anticipates Philip Rahv's famous distinction and prays for a sturdier race to end the dominion of the palefaces[41] and those in which with still greater brutality he salutes the Mexican War as the triumph of a fiercely sustained will

[36] The speech was printed in its entirety by the *National Antislavery Standard.* See Louis Ruchames, "Two Forgotten Addresses by Ralph Waldo Emerson," AL 28 (January 1957), pp. 425–433. Garrison presided at the meeting, and Phillips and William Henry Channing were among the speakers.

[37] "They are old traders, and make it a rule rarely to shoot their customers, and never until the bill is paid" (Ruchames, "Two Forgotten Addresses," p. 427).

[38] One thinks particularly of several unpublished entries from 1846: JMN 9.415, 424–425, 427, 430–431.

[39] JMN 9.129.

[40] JMN 9.131.

[41] See JMN 9.388. Rahv's essay "Paleface and Redskin" is the first piece in his collection *Image and Idea* (Norfolk, Conn., 1949).

adroit enough to use its enemies' weaknesses.[42] Emerson strives in his remarks for a hard-won lucidity; but they also betray the attraction he feels toward every form of power. Once again we encounter that nostalgia for the effective act which had haunted him since his youth.

Thus shaken by a sequence of events the consequences of which he both appreciated and feared, thus torn between two worlds that are for varying reasons equally repugnant to him, Emerson took refuge in reading. It was at this time that he studied the theology of the Vishnu Purana and the Bhagavad-Gita[43] and that he attempted, though feebly enough, to penetrate the technical armor encasing the philosophy of Schelling;[44] simultaneously he renewed his respect for geology, familiarizing himself with the theories explained by Chambers in the book one might loosely call the anteroom of Darwinism, *Vestiges of the Natural History of Creation* (1844). Carl Strauch has shown in a remarkable essay how Emerson managed to establish connections between the teachings of science and the myths to which the great philosophies have always resorted in seeking to communicate certain eternal truths.[45] At this level of pure speculation, Emerson must have experienced the serenity that attaining to an intuition of the unity of things inevitably procured him.[46] But there was a part of himself, a deep and obscure part, that this reconciliation did not touch; and as after the Divinity School address, this gnawing dissatisfaction sought in poetry the outlet that other forms of expression did not seem to permit.

It is for the most part impossible to date the composition of the individual poems at all accurately; but we know from several sources that the years 1845 and 1846 were unusually fertile in them,[47] and it is no chronological superstition that inclines one to see in the works dating

[42] See JMN 9.445 (1846). At moments, however, Emerson does get indignant at the "indirections" by which the Democrats' success was obtained; cf. JMN 9.422.

[43] See L 3.290, 293, and 298–299 (May-August 1845). The role played in Emerson's intellectual development by Indian thought does not, of course, come within the scope of this study and has been often discussed elsewhere, notably in F. I. Carpenter, *Emerson and Asia* (Cambridge, 1930) and in A. E. Christy, *The Orient in American Transcendentalism* (New York, 1932).

[44] See L 3.299 (September 1845). Estimates of Schelling's influence on Emerson vary; what is certain is that Emerson came to Schelling late and read him chiefly at second hand. See Henry A. Pochmann, *German Culture in America* (Madison, Wisc., 1957), pp. 202–203.

[45] Carl Strauch, "Emerson's Sacred Science," PMLA 73 (June 1958), pp. 237–250. This is a groundbreaking article for the study of Emerson's thought subsequent to the *Essays*.

[46] See JMN 9.241–242 (cited by Strauch).

[47] The editor of W gives most of the necessary references, though he errs (and Rusk corrects him, L 3.341) in dating the composition of "Alphonso of Castile" in 1847; the poem was written in 1846, at the same time as "Mithridates" and "Merlin." As early as June 1845 a letter of Emerson's mentions the "rhyming mania" in which his correspondent has left him (L 3.290).

from those years a common manner and a common inspiration. All of them—"Bacchus," "Mithridates," "Monadnoc," "Alphonso of Castile," and most notably the Ode to Channing[48]—are distinguished by the same harshness of tone, and all suggest the same need to press beyond the effete graces of civilization and find the original force slumbering in the heart of things. Thus, for example, the wine of Bacchus draws its intoxicating power from the depths in which it is brewed:

Let its grapes the morn salute
From a nocturnal root,
Which feels the acrid juice
Of Styx and Erebus;
And turns the woe of Night,
By its own craft, to a more rich delight.[49]

That force to be sure is not separable from excess and violence—but, says Emerson, don't let that stop you! Alphonso of Castile, the philosopher-king dreaming of what the world would have been if God had only consulted with him, would have exterminated the weak rather than resign himself to the impotence and debility he sees everywhere around him:

Earth, crowded, cries, "Too many men!"
My counsel is, kill nine in ten,
And bestow the shares of all
On the remnant decimal.
Add their nine lives to this cat;
Stuff their nine brains in one hat.[50]

Then—and only then—can there appear "a man of the sphere," toward whom the universe unconsciously tends.

In all these pieces Emerson's sincerity seems indisputable, and the almost obsessional character of the subjects chosen bears witness to their affinity with a fundamental trait of his personality; but one should also note the masterfulness of an art arrived at full maturity. Emerson excels in displacing his feelings, in drawing on the resources inherent in symbolic treatment—less, however, to conceal what a personal confession would inevitably offer in the way of raw emotion than to give greater

[48] All these poems are printed in W 9 and were part of Emerson's first collection, published in 1847.

[49] "Bacchus" (W 9.125). The theme of Night as original source of energy appears frequently in the journal for this period and may owe something to Schelling; cf. JMS, H.12-Salvage, p. 164.

[50] "Alphonso of Castile" (W 9.27).

extension and resonance to an individual experience.[51] The consequence is that in general the creation of the later poems is wrapped in a deeper mystery.[52] Yet, though it would be irresponsible to claim to discern all the links of the chain, from the first emotional stimulus to the finished product, the centrality of certain themes invites one to speak of causes rather than of mere coincidences. The image Emerson develops in "Alphonso of Castile," for example, of an exhausted and languid world may very well have been suggested to him by the spectacle of his own country. At any rate, so much is suggested by this remark in his journal: "But in America I grieve to miss the strong black blood of the English race: ours is a pale diluted stream. . . . Irving thin, & Channing thin, & Bryant & Dana, Prescott & Bancroft. There is Webster, but he cannot do what he would; he cannot do Webster."[53] In this broader context, the poem becomes—among other things— the protest of a disappointed citizen and the imaginative compensation he permits himself out of despair.

But the Whigs were not the whole of America. Outside of New England, at any rate, were resolute men who believed in their star and exploited the advantages of unscrupulousness. The Mexican War was the work of such men, and Emerson detested it, but he was also compelled to see in it the sign of irresistible energy. Here also the poems and the journal illuminate each other. In the spring of 1846, when hostilities were about to begin, the journal records these disingenuously untroubled statements: "The United States will conquer Mexico, but it will be as the man swallows the arsenic, which brings him down in turn. Mexico will poison us."[54] A few months later, Emerson composed Mithridates' boastful monologue, and made the barbarian king the ambiguous symbol of his desire for power. The theme of poison—"Hemlock for my sherbet cull me"[55]—is naturally at the poem's center, and one can see from the preceding quotation how it is connected with Emerson's more general reflection on American destiny. But the poem marks a shift in thought, which is stressed and clarified by the use of myth. Mithridates is obsessed by an enormous and insatiable appetite for life. What interested Emerson in him was less his capacity for resistance to misfortune

[51] See J. R. Reaver, *Emerson as Mythmaker* (Gainesville, Fla., 1954), particularly chapter 4, "The Shaping Intuition."

[52] But not without exception: some of the earlier poems, notably "Uriel" and to some extent "The Humble-Bee," also remain obscure in many respects.

[53] JMN 9.83 (1844). Early in 1846 Emerson was still deploring in his journal the absence of "the male principle" in America (JMN 9.444–445).

[54] JMN 9.430–431.

[55] W 9.29.

than his mad frenzy for experience.[56] Emerson had by imagination freed himself as completely as he could from the shackles of temperament and education; he had by a sort of empathy identified himself with the anarchic natures of the men of the American West, who went far beyond the ideal of self-reliance he had once conceived. But the harsh tone of the poem also indicates an immense nostalgia, which is perhaps that of a man seeking forgetfulness of mediocrity in tragic adventure (the brief concessive clause with which the poem concludes opens onto death). "Mithridates" has already something of the desperate finality of Rimbaud.[57]

The "Ode Inscribed to William Henry Channing" is more explicit and aphoristic;[58] it lacks the troubled resonance of "Mithridates," but offers what one might call a map of Emerson's soul in this period of ordeal. The poem falls into two halves, which threaten to break apart. Even earlier, in "The World-Soul" (definitely an earlier composition), Emerson's inspiration had been subject to considerable tension, but the increasing surge of mental energy ended by giving the first strophes in their dark and mournful tone the character of a purely rhetorical point of contrast. In the Ode, the drama is deeper because its scene is personal morality. Emerson compares his conduct with that of Channing, "the evil time's sole patriot,"[59] and tries to justify his own inaction by invoking what William James called "a fidelity to the limits of his genius."[60] But the role of observer to which he condemns himself by vocation only deepens his pessimism. He sees violence, cowardice, and hypocrisy reigning over the world unchecked. The short and labored verses, the abundance of animal imagery (from the animals evoked in the poem one could put together a substantial bestiary) emphasize man's miserable condition, enslaved to the law of things and uncrowned by his own victories. Then, rather suddenly, like a diver who must touch the bottom of the sea before he can ascend back toward the sun, in the relaxed atti-

[56] This trait appears more distinctly in a manuscript version of the poem, in which line 25 is more forcefully worded as "Dark powers, and mad, and merry" (JMS, H.132-X, p. 222).

[57] Yvor Winters, *In Defence of Reason* (New York, 1947), p . 586, in particular compares "Mithridates" with Rimbaud's "Fêtes de la faim."

[58] As Whicher notes (*Selections from Ralph Waldo Emerson* [Boston, 1957], p. 505), Irving Babbit and the neohumanists were fond of citing these three lines: "There are two laws discrete, / Not reconciled, — / Law for men and law for things."

[59] W 9.76. William Henry Channing was William Ellery Channing's nephew; a reformer by vocation, soon committed to a program of social regeneration, he had, just after the Divinity School address, charged that Emerson was blind to man's collective instincts. Emerson heard him preach in New York during one of his trips and described him in a letter to Fuller as "a princely person" (February 25, 1843 [L 3.149]).

[60] In his *Memories and Studies* (New York, 1911), p. 23.

tude of a man who knows that the water is his ally, Emerson regains the universe familiar to him:

> Let man serve law for man;
> Live for friendship, live for love,
> For truth's and harmony's behoof;
> The state may follow how it can,
> As Olympus follows Jove.[61]

But this optimism abruptly won back is founded on no illusion. The world is no hunting ground for poets; the wicked and the stupid will continue their muddling till their death. Confidence shines out in the last two stanzas, but it is because men and women have been surreptitiously removed from the scene. The principle of creation is intrinsically good and patiently draws good from evil:

> The over-god
> Who marries Right to Might,
> Who peoples, unpeoples, —
> He who exterminates
> Races by stronger races,
> Black by white faces, —
> Knows to bring honey
> Out of the lion;
> Grafts
> gentle scion
> On pirate and Turk.[62]

Emerson has thus managed to escape the torments of evil and impotence by shedding his particular self (Mithridates was by contrast a distillation of selfishness), diving like Empedocles into the furnace and becoming flame amidst flame—a poetical transmutation if ever there was one, and profoundly appropriate to Emerson's genius.

The reason for lingering so long over poems that despite their energy retain a certain cerebrally schematic quality, and that painfully reveal Emerson's limited metrical inventiveness, is that they help in situating and understanding *Representative Men*, the only major work Emerson wrote between 1844 and 1850. To say that is not to forget that the seven lectures grouped under this title were given for the first time in the course of the winter of 1845-1846 or that the poems just discussed come after them. But the book itself was not published until 1850, and

[61] "Ode Inscribed to William Henry Channing" (W 9.79).
[62] Ibid.

Emerson kept tinkering with the manuscript till the very end (the first chapter, "Uses of Great Men," makes use of notions recorded in the journal in 1849); and both the book and the poems exhibit the same quality of inspiration linked to a particular historical situation. The poems reveal a more secret side of Emerson's personality, and so deserve to be discussed first—they have over the lectures the right of aesthetic priority, so to speak, somewhat as the sketches of certain painters reveal labored geometric patterns that the final canvases then tone down or disguise, while still structured around them.

It has been traditional since the nineteenth century for those assessing *Representative Men* to compare it with Carlyle and in particular with *Heroes and Hero-Worship*. A hundred times scholars have pointed out the two writers' common veneration for exceptional men, and a hundred times have distinguished Emerson's democratic ideals from Carlyle's aristocratic ones. Though a commonplace, the comparison is not simply an exercise in rhetoric, since there was unmistakably influence and then reaction between the two men: in 1841, Carlyle sent Emerson a copy of *Heroes and Hero-Worship*, and one can trace astonishingly close echoes of it in the lecture series Emerson gave the next winter.[63] In addition, Emerson adopted certain key terms of Carlyle's thought—as is clearly established by the last part of the Ode to Channing, which is organized around the words "right" and "might." Emerson would not have denied the debt; he would, however, have protested against seeing too close an assimilation. In Carlyle, the attention is fixed intently on beings of flesh, endowed with particular charisma, fulfilling in themselves by implicit commission the destiny of a whole historical era. There is in this respect a perceptible kinship between Carlyle's heroes and the subjects of the six biographical lectures Emerson gave in 1835—the portrait of Luther, for example, has in both authors the same earthy density, due to the interpenetration of perishable and transient qualities with more widely, almost timeless human traits. But in *Representative Men* the movement of thought is in some sense reversed; instead of following the progress of spiritual energy into the elite soul, in which it is concentrated as are the sun's rays in a magnifying glass, Emerson progresses from the particular to the universal and requires of the exceptional man a quality whose absence from Carlyle's work he deplores: transparence. Such is the deeper meaning of the book's title—as Emerson himself takes care to establish on a page of the journal:

[63] The most distinct are in the last lecture of the series, "The Times." Vide supra, chapter 10, n. 19.

> Swedenborg & Behmen saw that things were representative. They did not sufficiently see that men were. But we cannot, as we say, be in two places at once. . . . Work in thy place with might & health, & thy secretion to the spiritual body is made, I in mine will do the like. Thus imperceptibly & most happily, genially & triumphantly doing that we delight in, behold we are communists, brothers, members one of another.[64]

The six characters (I intentionally avoid the word "hero") thus presented to us are the partial and mutually complementary elements of a whole, accessible only to the imagination. Despairing of finding the great man for whom he has been hunting for fifteen years, Emerson undertakes to construct him—facet by facet, by a process of rotation suggested by Nature itself.[65] But it would be wrong to view this construction as a perfect hexagon, or to seek in the order of the chapters for the key to their composition. If Plato, who comes first, is also the book's culmination, we know from the journal and letters that the first portrait Emerson worked on was that of Napoleon.[66] The detail is significant in a number of respects. The fact that Napoleon was judged worthy of such an honor suggests that by 1845 Emerson had finally overcome his Federalist prejudices. As a comparison with the earlier, somewhat callow lecture on Burke will make clear, the choice of Napoleon was also the indication of a more mature interest in political issues. Finally, by confronting Napoleon's disquietingly ambiguous personage Emerson was asserting once again his determination to be rigorously lucid. Napoleon symbolized a reality that in Emerson's America was terribly urgent, a reality either to be endured or to be commanded through a special effort of the mind. Of all the lectures in the series, moreover, it is the one on Napoleon that had the greatest success, notably in England;[67] is that not due to the fact that people saw in it, beneath the tight weave of anecdote and analysis, the philosopher's endeavor to incorporate into his universe an element hitherto refractory to it?[68]

[64] JMN 9.342 (1845). Emerson may owe the phrase "representative men" to Cousin; see Nicoloff, *Emerson on Race and History*, pp. 71–72.

[65] See "Uses of Great Men" (W 4.19).

[66] The journal for the first few months of 1845 contains numerous notes on reading about Napoleon; see also a letter of September 29, 1845, in which Emerson writes of the Napoleon essay that "it was the first written, though it should be last in the course" (L 3.305). As it turned out, the final ordering of *Representative Men* had "Napoleon" followed by "Goethe."

[67] See Townsend Scudder, "Emerson's British Lecture-Tour," AL 7 (May 1935), p. 175.

[68] This interpretation is considerably indebted to Perry Miller's remarkable "Emersonian Genius and the American Democracy," NEQ 26 (March 1953), pp. 27–44. Miller believes

But Emerson's fascination with Napoleon was not the fortuitous result of a novel political situation. In 1815, at the age of twelve, Emerson gave the French leader a place next to Xerxes and Philip in a "Poetical Essay" on the crimes of ambition.[69] Napoleon's name appears twenty-two times in the journal between 1820 and 1834, most often to illustrate some moral observation.[70] But in 1835 Emerson eliminated him from his list of great men, on the ground that he possessed neither the elevation of thought nor the generosity prerequisite to that status.[71] He was thus restating in condensed form the verdict of William Ellery Channing, who some years earlier had published a long essay on the subject in the *Christian Examiner*.[72] Then, in 1837, there arrived in Concord a copy of Carlyle's *The French Revolution*, in which Napoleon was presented not as a selfish monarch bent on conquest but as an organizing force delivering democracy from the anarchy that was its endemic disease. This new interpretation touched Emerson's imagination; the journal for 1838 records numerous comments on Napoleon revealing a fresh surge of curiosity on the subject and its practical implications.[73] Napoleon's image is so present to him that he introduces a long paragraph in his honor into "Literary Ethics"—the lecture in which he most urgently commends the renunciation of earthly greatness.[74] Still, all things considered, the traits that Emerson deemed essential were lacking. Napoleon was a beast of fine mettle, powerful and lithe and of magnificent carriage, but a beast all the same; and in a page

that *Representative Men* is intended to teach neither heroism nor the cult of the hero; rather it shows us "how an intelligent and sensitive man lives, or must learn to live, in a democratic society and era" (p. 41).

[69] See L 6.330–332. The poem is in heroic couplets and is a good example of the poetic diction then taught in New England schools.

[70] There is an excellent edition of "Napoleon or the Man of the World" with an introduction and notes by Frank Davidson (Indiana University Publications, Humanities Series 16, [Bloomington, 1947]. Davidson has searched through the journal with great care and has also identified most of the numerous quotations—Emerson said he had absorbed a veritable library of memoirs on the subject—incorporated into the text without attribution; his erudition is the source of many of my remarks.

[71] Vide supra, chapter 6.

[72] Channing's essay, entitled "Remarks on the Life and Character of Napoleon Bonaparte," was in two separate parts, published in 1827 and 1828 (*Works*, pp. 522–559); it was intended to temper the excessive reverence of Sir Walter Scott's *Life of Napoleon Bonaparte*. Calmly, but with principled forcefulness, Channing explained the reasons for which he could never admire a despoiler and a tyrant. A passage of "Life and Letters in New England" (W 10.339) establishes Emerson's high opinion of the essay.

[73] Some particularly interesting ones are JMN 5.472, 482, 487, 493–494, and 507–508. In particular Emerson had read Las Cases' *Mémorial de Sainte Hélène* and O'Meara's two-volume *Napoleon in Exile, or A Voice from Saint-Helena*.

[74] W 1.178–180.

of the journal written in November 1839, Emerson sends him once and for all (or so it seems) back to his natal jungle:

> As we admire in Napoleon the obedience to animal instincts, the self command, the objectiveness, the combination, the immense executive faculty, & so cannot read his life without feeling that here was honor done to faculties of mine which have nowhere been so great & yet as we turn from a crocodile or a tiger which we have gazed upon with wonder in a menagerie, if an illustrious Man goes by in the street, so on the approach of spiritual greatness we turn away with pity from a man who was incapable of apprehending the loftier instincts of his Nature.[75]

Three or four years passed, in the course of which Napoleon remained, without being completely forgotten, at a subordinate level among Emerson's concerns. Then, in 1844, his interest reawoke, and his reading on the subject recommenced. But this time it was not only Napoleon's size and stature that impressed Emerson; now his political genius (which in the meantime Carlyle had celebrated once again[76]) seemed the response to the problem posed by his compatriots' appalling incompetence: "I read Napoleon's memoirs lately," he wrote during the last days of Tyler's administration, "& could not help grudging to Europe that grand executive faculty which in this vast empty Eden of ours with so many fine theories & so many white-robed candidates, might consolidate, organize, put in action, so much."[77] As he wrote in a notebook one day, "the true romance [is] the transformation of genius into practical power."[78]

The result of these meditations was to give the lecture in its final form a distinctly Carlylean tone, though without Emerson's having had on that account to deny himself. By contrast with the feeble leaders of the second half of the eighteenth century, Napoleon is "a working king,"[79] and in this respect he is revolutionary and modern, as Carlyle had powerfully shown. He represents "the class of business men in America, in England, in France and throughout Europe; the class of industry and skill."[80] Emerson has a considerable investment in this idea; it is ex-

75 JMN 7.288–289.

76 In the last lecture of *Heroes and Hero-Worship*, devoted to Cromwell and Napoleon.

77 Letter to Samuel Gray Ward of December 2, 1844 (L 3.267–268).

78 JMN 12.578.

79 In the same notebook (JMN 12.532), Emerson applies the expression to Napoleon and boldly underlines it; one remembers that he had chosen it for the motto of "The Young American" (W 1.386).

80 "Napoleon" (W 4.224). Daniel Aaron's analysis of Emerson's deeply ambivalent attitude

pressed at the beginning and returns toward the end, when Napoleon appears as "the liberal, the radical, the inventor of means, the opener of doors and markets, the subverter of monopoly of abuse"—in a word, as "the giant of the middle class."[81] It is not that Emerson has suddenly begun to worship what he would formerly have burned; he bluntly chastizes "the boundless liar," the "impostor," and the "rogue." It is rather that these attacks are directed toward a side of Napoleon different from that which attracts his praises. He is severe to the man himself, whom in the last analysis he reproaches with not being a "gentleman"; but he passes lightly over the excesses of the sovereign, the violence of the oppressor and the tyrant. One senses that liberty, which was so dear to Channing's generation, has lost a part of its attractiveness, that it can now be enlisted in the service of other values, to which in certain circumstances it must yield precedence.[82] But this lukewarm estimate is not indifference, and still less a kind of despair as in Carlyle. Rather, it proceeds from a faith that has never been so pure—that is, so dehumanized. One day, weary of nourishing this "exorbitant egotist," Europe cries out "*Assez de Bonaparte*,"[83] and the page is turned; but the universal laws remain.

From this point the transposition to the American scene is easy, and Emerson himself at intervals establishes the correspondence: Napoleon is "the incarnate Democrat;"[84] thanks to him "the old, iron-bound, feudal France was changed into a young Ohio or New York."[85] This was pretty clearly to undertake the defense of the "rabble party," as he had once called it, and to recognize that its turbulence was the consequence of its healthy vigor. The Whigs lack frivolousness but otherwise resemble the nobility of the Ancien Régime; they belong to a respectable past and continue to cling to it, but their grip slackens as the life forces withdraw from their limbs.[86] The Democrats, by contrast, have the approval of Nature, who does not seek her favorite children among Sunday-

toward Napoleon in *Men of Good Hope* (New York, 1951), pp. 8–13, brings out the significance of that attitude in its American context. Aaron recalls the fascination exercised by Napoleon on the great captains of industry at the end of the nineteenth century and shows that from a certain standpoint one can regard Emerson as their advocate—on condition, of course, of ignoring a whole part of Emerson's work.

[81] "Napoleon" (W 4.252–253).

[82] "Freedom is frivolous beside the tyranny of genius," Emerson comments in a notebook from about 1845 (JMN 10.376).

[83] W 4.258.

[84] W 4.224.

[85] W 4.242.

[86] The journal records several phrases associating the Whigs with images of corpses and petrifaction; see particularly JMN 9.269 and 381.

school students and closes her eyes when they disobey the Commandments.[87] Emerson had not yielded to this truth of his own experience without resistance, and the closer it pressed him the more hurtful it seemed. But in meditating on Napoleon, he had found the perspective necessary to make it acceptable. By a characteristic maneuver of Emerson's thought, Jackson's incorporation into American history followed what in another mind would have been simply an extravagance of imagination.

The step thus taken was considerable. The dilemma evident as early as "Politics" (that is, the dilemma of how to choose between the best men and the best cause) here found its solution in an interpretation, no longer purely theoretical but rather concrete and profound, of the natural forces embodied in the Democratic Party. Perry Miller has on this point opposed Emerson's elastic optimism to the discouragement and rigidity that took hold of Cooper when he came into conflict with the America of *Home as Found*.[88] Emerson, he explains, is capable of conceiving a new form of democracy, one that will add a stage to the history of Western societies. Nothing is truer—on the condition that this optimism is interpreted correctly; Emerson is no Pangloss. "Bonaparte represents the Business Men's Party against the Morgue," he writes in his journal, and finishes the sentence as follows: "but the Morgue is only the Business Men's Party gone to seed."[89] Thus the two factions that divide the world are inexorably united by a law of senescence. Napoleon ended by creating a nobility even more artificial than the Ancien Régime's, so deeply did he resemble his antagonists in his inability to live on the level of eternal truth. His place on the ladder of exceptional achievement and quality is not very high.

The next step is represented by Goethe, whom Emerson—doubtless remembering the celebrated meeting with Napoleon at Erfurt—sees as embodying the other half of the nineteenth century.[90] Over the years, Emerson had at Carlyle's insistent urging learned to admire in Goethe not only the novelist of *Wilhelm Meister* but also a master thinker,[91] and

[87] Cf. "Experience," (W 3.64).

[88] See Miller's "Emersonian Genius." In the narrative of *Home as Found*, Cooper bitterly satirizes his Cooperstown neighbors as hypocritical demagogues. This brought him furious attacks, and at least a dozen of his maligners were sued by him for slander or forced to recant.

[89] JMN 9.192 (1845).

[90] "I described Bonaparte as a representative of the popular external life and aims of the nineteenth century. Its other half, its poet, is Goethe, a man quite domesticated in the century, breathing its air, enjoying its fruits, impossible at any earlier time." (W 4.270).

[91] See John McCormick's "Emerson's Theory of Human Greatness," NEQ 26 (September 1953), pp. 290–314, which carefully traces the stages of the evolution; "the record of Emer-

this gradual acceptance reminds one to some extent of the process by which Napoleon also had worn down Emerson's inward resistance. The journal, moreover, admits freely, by a charmingly indirect implication,[92] that there was an affinity of temperament between Weimar's sage and Concord's, that the two men shared a desire to remain unperturbed in all circumstances. One might, therefore, have expected the portrait of Goethe at least to equal Napoleon's in force and penetration. Unfortunately this is not the case. Emerson cannot warm up to his subject; even the praises he accords him (which Goethe would certainly have appreciated, since in them the man of science is honored no less than the man of letters) one notices a persistent reserve, which is explained at the very end of the essay when Emerson charges Goethe with a lack of abandon. There was, to be sure, in Napoleon an egotism still greater than Goethe's; but as a man of action he called forth, in an intellectual like Emerson, a bewilderment tinged with envy that mitigated his less attractive traits. Goethe in himself was neither the perfect mystic nor the conquering hero; and Emerson unconsciously resented so hybrid a nature.

It was fated, apparently, that poets should not inspire Emerson in writing *Representative Men*, for the portrait of Shakespeare, the fourth in the series, is another of the book's less successful ventures. In vain does one seek in it the joyous thrill of wonder, the subtlety of perception, the desire to snatch away a few at least of the artist's secrets that constituted the charm of the two lectures in 1835. Emerson spends considerable time defining genius—not, in the late phase of Romanticism, a very original thing to do—and when he undertakes to apply the idea to Shakespeare he is only following a trail already blazed by Jones Very.[93] More interesting is the effort at aesthetic and sociological analysis by which Emerson describes the poet both in the continuity of his tradition and in the context of his contemporaries. He can now write that "the poet needs a ground in popular tradition on which he may work, and which, again, may restrain his art within the due temperance."[94] And in the same way, somewhat further on, when he speaks of

son's reactions to Goethe," McCormick writes, "is the record of his evolution of the theory of the hero" (p. 293).

[92] That is, in a chart in which opposite each of the representative men Emerson put the name of an inhabitant of Concord. His own is set opposite Goethe's, and Thoreau's opposite Napoleon's (JMN 11.173 [1849]).

[93] See Sherman Paul, *Emerson's Angle of Vision* (Cambridge, Mass., 1952), p. 252, n. 39. Emerson had read Very's essay on Shakespeare in manuscript, and had judged it "a noble production." *The Transcendentalists: An Anthology*, ed. Perry Miller (Cambridge, Mass., 1950), pp. 346–353, gives substantial extracts from it.

[94] "Shakespeare, or the Poet" (W 4.194).

the "wide social labor" that always accompanies the creations of genius, when in the wake of Schlegel and many others he insists on the collective character of masterpieces, is he not at last vindicating Orestes Brownson, who reproached him with dissociating the thinker from the rest of the nation and enclosing him in infertile solitude?[95] F. O. Matthiessen has acutely identified here the rudiments of a new type of criticism, one less arrogantly iconoclastic, more inclined to accord tradition a constructive role, and more eager to recognize the limits of individual invention.[96] It seems that Emerson is now prepared to go quite some distance along the bridge his notion of genius as representative has constructed between the Romantic universe and the classical one, as the traits and essential qualities of the latter are defined, say, by the thought of a T. S. Eliot. But, Matthiessen adds, Emerson was by temperament unfitted to carry his analysis in this area to the conclusions his premises imply;[97] the sketch ends infelicitously on a note of moralization, with Emerson regretting that Shakespeare has in his stupendous frivolity contented himself with being "master of the revels to mankind."[98]

Thus the portrait of Shakespeare suffers from a certain coldness, Emerson not having succeeded in giving his subject the orientation necessary to awaken his own spontaneous response. The case is altogether different in the third portrait, that of Montaigne. Emerson had savored Montaigne's strong simplicity very early and had always read him with delight and excitement; these experiences protected him from his own natural austerity. Some of the pages he devotes to him, direct, pungent, and boldly original, are among the best he ever wrote and certainly among those that touch our own century most acutely.[99] But readers who expect from the title of "Montaigne or the Skeptic" that Emerson is setting out on a predictable course are likely to experience a feeling of frustration on discovering that he rather circles around his

[95] See Brownson's review of "Literary Ethics" cited earlier. Miller, in *The Transcendentalists*, p. 436, sees in that review the line of demarcation between Emersonian mystical Transcendentalism and social Transcendentalism as understood and practiced by such men as Brownson, Ripley, and William Henry Channing.

[96] See *American Renaissance: Art and Expression in the Age of Emerson and Whitman* (1941, repr. New York, 1968), pp. 634–635.

[97] Emerson did gradually temper his peremptory calls for absolute literary originality. Like Gide, celebrating the virtues of imitation and influence after *Les Nourritures terrestres* had fully illustrated his rebelliousness, Emerson when past fifty wrote the moderate and calmly self-assured "Quotation and Originality" (W 8.175–204).

[98] W 4.217, and a favorite quotation ever after.

[99] One hears without surprise that Emerson's passage on Montaigne's language found a particularly sympathetic response in the young Robert Frost; see his "On Emerson," *Daedalus* 88 (Autumn 1959), p. 713.

subject than really takes hold of it. Whether by omission or deliberate exclusion, the "Apology for Raimond Sebond"—in which, after all, Montaigne launches his most formidable attacks on the claims of reason, and which was to inspire a whole section of Pascal's apologetics—is never mentioned.[100] The fact is—and here the reader is referred to Whicher's insightful analysis, which demonstrates the continuity between "Montaigne" and "Experience" but also the shift of perspective between the two essays[101]—Montaigne was for Emerson not so much a teacher of philosophy as the unashamed herald of the human condition, its faithful and lucid witness, the sworn enemy to Sartre's *mauvaise foi*, which plagues all times and countries. The only homage agreeable to fidelity is the practice of fidelity itself. Emerson has more restraint and self-control than his model, but not, to judge from the parallel passages of the journal, less sincerity; and his essay is a revelation of himself à la Montaigne, an exorcising of the idealist's temptations as he casts them forth from his own mind. These fumes and mists once dispelled, Emerson finds himself naked and poor in the presence of the only truth to which experience, when honestly accepted, can lead: that a gulf is fixed between what we feel ourselves called to accomplish and what mean-handed providence allows us to achieve. This is the tragedy of impotence, Emerson's obsession since "The Protest."

It is at this point that the Te Deum of the peroration thunders out, altogether unexpected and owing nothing to Montaigne at all:

> Things seem to say one thing, and say the reverse. The appearance is immoral; the result is moral. Things seem to tend downward, to justify despondency, to promote rogues, to defeat the just; and by knaves as by martyrs the just cause is carried forward. . . . We see, now, events forced on which seem to retard or retrograde the civility of ages. But the world-spirit is a good swimmer, and storms and waves cannot drown him. He snaps his finger at laws: and so, throughout history, heaven seems to affect low and poor means.[102]

Whicher, who cites the passage,[103] separates his discussion of it from the rest of the previous chapter and presents it as the point of departure for a new one, so as better to emphasize the reversal it brings; but the perspective in which his analysis is framed does not allow him to bring out the specific historical context of the passage. Behind the general for-

[100] See chapter 2 of C. L. Young, *Emerson's Montaigne* (New York, 1941).

[101] See *Freedom and Fate*, pp. 112–122 (chapter 6, "Skepticism").

[102] "Montaigne or the Skeptic" (W 4.185).

[103] *Freedom and Fate*, pp. 123–124 (chapter 7, "Acquiescence").

mulas there was a particular political situation,[104] which for some time had been in Emerson's eyes a source of outrage and perplexity. Set in this context, Montaigne and the skepticism he teaches are only a metaphor for the situation of contemporary America. In the inner world of feeling and belief, they play a role like that of the democratic pressure within the nation, uncovering certain disagreeable realities stubbornly hidden under a bushel; they dislodge masks and oblige people to think without complacency about the structure of the world. But in proportion as illusions are revealed as such, optimism is strengthened. It is precisely in this paradox that the particular nature of Emersonian faith resides; it is constructed of successive triumphs over pretensions incessantly reborn, in one form or another, from the individual self.

Nothing is more illuminating in this respect than the portrait of Swedenborg, called "The Mystic." The epithet chosen is the counterpart of that applied to Montaigne and is opposed to it at every point. The author of the *Essais* abandons himself with delight to the undulating diversity of the world; the author of *Oeconomia regni animalis* (which Emerson had just read in Wilkinson's edition) is one of those "missouriums and mastodons of literature" who have embraced everything and seek to unite and to weld everything together. Montaigne's mind is perpetually on guard, fearing to be tricked not only by the evidence of its senses but also by that of reason; Swedenborg abandons himself to the blinding light of intuition without a suspicion of the risks he runs. By temperament Emerson is closer to Swedenborg, because he shares the Swedish philosopher's spontaneous—one is tempted to say visceral—faith. But the portrait he offers of him is startling for the density of its shadows. Swedenborg is in his way like a man of the Old Testament, athletic like Michelangelo's Moses but stiff and literal-minded, incapable of imagining that the universe might exceed in richness the image of itself it deposits in a human mind. Pushing his analysis still further, Emerson attributes this narrowness to an excess of moral self-consciousness (as sharply distinguished from moral sentiment); Swedenborg "makes war on his mind . . . on all occasions, traduces and blasphemes it,"[105] but he expiates this blasphemous mistrust by an obsession with evil and hell: "There is an air of infinite grief and the sound of wailing all over and through this lurid universe. A vampyre sits in the seat of the prophet and turns with gloomy appetite to the images of pain."[106] In sum, then, and despite his towering mental capacity, Swedenborg

[104] The phrase "the world-spirit is a good swimmer" has its origin in a journal entry occasioned by the long-feared and now imminent annexation of Texas (JMN 9.180 [1845]).

[105] "Swedenborg or the Mystic" (W 4.130–131).

[106] Ibid.

embodies morbid genius, unbalanced genius, which elevates its whims and limitations to the level of universal qualities. Emerson's criticism goes so far and suggests so deep a repulsion that one wonders why he chose to include Swedenborg at all. One probable answer is: in fidelity to himself, since Swedenborg had played an important role in his intellectual emancipation.[107] But also and chiefly Emerson was motivated by a more general desire to take stock, a need to draw up an account at the end of an evolution he now viewed as complete. By a law the journals frequently register, Swedenborg's stature continued to decrease as Emerson's own originality and independence of thought were being asserted.

It is not enough to say that the place vacated by the northern star in the philosophical firmament is for Emerson now occupied by Plato, "a sound, sincere and catholic man, able to honor, at the same time, the ideal, or laws of the mind, and fate, or the order of nature."[108] Rather Plato in himself, Emerson says, is philosophy in toto, that of the East no less than that of the West. Several critics have pointed out that this is untrue;[109] what concerns us here, however, is only its significance for Emerson. Plato illustrates the receptive capacity of the human mind; he represents an almost perfect victory over the resistances and insubordinations of the individual person. He is diametrically opposite to Swedenborg, whom his "introverted faculties" kept prisoner; and that is why the theme of balance recurs throughout the portrait like a leitmotif. Plato is the quintessential reconciler of the One and the Many; he can rise to a contemplation of the totality of things without losing sight of the order governing their diversity. But this felicitous capacity of perception reveals in its turn a privileged historical situation—not all periods, Emerson argues, are equally generative of such harmony:

> There is a moment in the history of every nation, when, proceeding out of this brute youth, the perceptive powers reach their ripeness and have not yet become microscopic: so that man, at that instant, extends across the entire scale, and, with his feet still planted on the immense forces of night, converses by his eyes and brain with solar

[107] Vide supra, chapter 8.

[108] "Plato or the Philosopher" (W 4.45). S. G. Brown, "Emerson's Platonism," NEQ 18, (September 1945), pp. 325–345 has shown that after 1840 the dialogues subsequent to the *Republic*, particularly the *Timaeus* with its figure of a demiurge who orders the world but has not created it, exercise a profound influence on Emerson's thought.

[109] See particularly J. S. Harrison, *The Teachers of Emerson* (New York, 1910), who explains the distortions brought about by Thomas Taylor, the translator and unreliable commentator of both Plato and Plotinus. See also Carpenter, *Emerson Handbook*, pp. 213–215.

> and stellar creation. That is the moment of adult health, the culmination of power.[110]

As is his habit, Emerson picks and chooses from among Plato's works so as to bring the outward image into accord with the ideal image he bears within. One could hardly guess from the essay that the first books of the *Republic* contain the definition of a political philosophy far removed from Emerson's American egalitarianism; nor is those books' fundamental role in the economy of Plato's thought anywhere acknowledged. But although the figure Emerson draws is incomplete, it is alive; it is even, for the America of the nineteenth century—itself emerging from primitive obscurity and arrived, or almost arrived, at the gates of maturity—a fraternal and comradely figure:

> He is a great average man; one who, to the best thinking, adds a proportion and equality in his faculties, so that men see in him their own dreams and glimpses made available and made to pass for what they are. . . . He has reason, as all the philosophic and poetic class have: but he has also what they have not, —this strong solving sense to reconcile his poetry with the appearances of the world, and build a bridge from the streets of cities to the Atlantis. He omits never this graduation, but slopes his thought, however picturesque the precipice on one side, to an access from the plain.[111]

Thus, as Emerson recalls in one of those long lists of opposed terms he was so fond of,[112] democracy is connected to the spiritual pole of the universe. Plato, the loftiest and most admirable of the representative men, is, with Montaigne, the one Emerson treats most naturally and as if on an equal footing.[113] "All men are at last of a size,"[114] he proclaims in the introductory lecture, and this unselfconscious familiarity is in its manner a proof of that notion.

It is also clearly what distinguishes most sharply between Carlyle's philosophy and Emerson's in their definitions of human greatness. The

[110] "Plato" (W 4.46–47). This is the epigraph to Matthiessen's *American Renaissance*.

[111] "Plato" (W 4.61). Plato recounts the myth of Atlantis in the first pages of the *Timaeus*.

[112] "Plato" (W 4.51).

[113] A letter to Elizabeth Hoar from 1841, when Emerson had just been reading the *Phaedrus*, the *Meno*, and the *Symposium*, already reveals this sense of affinity: "what a great uniform gentleman is Plato! Nothing is more characteristic of him than his good-breeding. Never pedantic, never wire-drawn, or too fine, never obtuse or saturnine; but so accomplished, so good humored, so perceptive, so uniting wisdom & poetry, acuteness & humanity into such a golden average, that one understands how he should enjoy his long augustan empire in literature" (July 18, 1841 [L 2.429–430]).

[114] "Uses of Great Men" (W 4.31).

Carlylean hero cannot be conceived without the cloud that separates him from the rest of humanity and maintains between the one and the other an impassable barrier; the hero is with men without being of them. Emerson, on the contrary, thinks that the function of representative men is to comfort and reassure; and so instead of addressing his audience in the arrogant tone of a prophet, he invites them to remember the royal blood that runs in their veins, feebly perhaps but unmistakably: "The truth seems to be, there are no common people, no populace, but only juniors & seniors; the mob is made up of kings that shall be; the lords have all in their time taken place in the mob."[115] Such is the only honorable acceptation of the word "democracy"; an equalization, if one likes, but an equalization at the top. If America has abolished noble titles it is in order to remind free citizens that each of them is potentially a king, and that any less glorious title is an insult.

In thus proclaiming his trust, in offering his country the stimulus of a few exemplary destinies, Emerson is nonetheless aware of the immense difficulties still to be overcome. Though freed two generations ago from the shackles under which Europe still labors, America now delights in a new sort of bondage, more insidious, more tyrannical, and more degrading than the old: "Majorities," notes Emerson in 1846 in an outburst of his old irritation, are "the argument of fools, the strength of the weak."[116] In the introductory lecture, "Uses of Great Men," his old disgust at the crowd, the unorganized and anonymous mass, breaks out with irresistible force: "enormous populations, if they be beggars, are disgusting, like moving cheese, like hills of ants or of fleas, —the more, the worse."[117] Till the day of universal apotheosis, meditating on the lives of great men will remain the most efficacious remedy for such nausea: "the search after the great man is the dream of youth and the most serious occupation of manhood."[118] The tone is indisputably sincere. Unlike Carlyle, who waited to canonize heroes till they were dead, Emerson insisted on seeking the inconspicuous signs of an exceptional destiny in his own vicinity. He says frankly that he has sometimes felt dizzy at the very idea of encountering a new person, so great was his need to believe that greatness was there, within earshot, and might cross his path. Every man prefers the company of his superiors to that of his equals, he had asserted in "New England Reformers,"[119] because the natural movement of the soul leads it to look upward. Much as we

[115] JMN 9.246 (1845).

[116] JMN 9.324.

[117] W 4.4.

[118] W 4.3.

[119] W 3.274–275.

may call ourselves democrats, and be so by profound conviction, by instinct we behave like aristocrats.

As if to give form to this inward dialectic, during his second visit to England Emerson wrote a lecture he called "Aristocracy."[120] Before being published in 1883 it was considerably reworked, so much so that one can with Perry Miller see in it "Emerson's most mature, though most inconclusive, discussion of the confrontation of Self and society, Genius and the democracy."[121] Although the adjectives used here faithfully measure the distance Emerson had come since "Self-Reliance," to elucidate them more fully it will be necessary to take a step backward.

Since the period of his ministry, and during all the time that his thought was engaged in a process of rapid evolution, Emerson had felt a need to discover within himself an element of continuity resistant to the assaults of systems; and he had named that stabilizing force "character."[122] The term denotes, beyond the permanence of an original nexus of inclinations, a capacity to assimilate into the self the intellectual or emotional shocks experience has in store for it. It did not take long, certainly, in the America of democracy which was also the America of conformity, for Emerson to come to identify character with aristocracy. Just as Nature has scattered here and there an infinitesimal quantity of a substance chemically identical to coal but as precious as coal is common, so there are men who are like diamonds, few in number, incorruptible and invincible in virtue of an inward disposition received at birth. There, precisely, is the mystery; character is at once "a natural power, like light and heat" and the "moral order seen through the medium of an individual nature";[123] it is situated at the juncture between the material and the spiritual, a sort of hub of the universe, in which the soul's energy is transformed into action, but also in which simple physical presence refers to something infinitely beyond it. And it is this second aspect that fascinates Emerson, oddly enough; like Whitman later, but with a feeling of unease that reveals his hereditary restraint, he salutes the "magnetic" man who needs only to appear to bring about miracles: "The coldest precisian cannot go abroad without encountering inexplicable influences. One man fastens an eye on him and the graves of the memory render up their dead; the secrets that make him wretched either to keep or to betray must be yielded; —another, and he cannot

[120] Printed in W 10.29–66. To avoid any misunderstanding, Emerson offered the lecture to his British audiences under the title of "Natural Aristocracy."

[121] *The American Transcendentalists: Their Prose and Poetry*, ed. Perry Miller (New York, 1957), p. 287.

[122] Vide supra, chapter 4.

[123] "Character," W 3.95–96.

speak, and the bones of his body seem to lose their cartilages."[124] One hesitates to say which feeling is dominant, admiration or fear. As in his essay on demonology, Emerson touches here on the boundaries of the unconscious—though he does not venture to cross them, one senses he is not eager to leave them behind. Emerson's worship of strong personalities and his respect for the work of a writer like Landor[125] depend in the last analysis on certain troubling experiences that he could accept only by idealizing them.

But there were also certain forms of "magnetism" that rebelled against the control of the mind, and they expressed themselves with particular insolence on the political scene of Emerson's America, in which the fragility of governmental and administrative structures left them almost unlimited room to maneuver: "the Best are never demoniacal or magnetic," writes Emerson in a self-justifying passage of the journal for 1840, "but all brutes are. The Democratic party in this country is more magnetic than the Whig. Andrew Jackson is an eminent example of it. Van Buren is not, —but his masters are who placed him in his house."[126]

In awarding this certificate of purity to "the Best," however, Emerson was in no way alleviating the formidable and insidious threat that the others constituted to the spiritual integrity of all. Conscious of the difficulty but incapable of attacking them on their own territory, he strove to organize his own defenses and to raise against their encroachments a sort of inward bulwark that he called "manners"—that is, good manners. In the second series of *Essays* he undertook to grasp the content of this elusive concept;[127] but he did not succeed very well, because his analysis swings rather engagingly between the two poles of sociability and reserve before finally settling toward the latter. Perry Miller was wittily right to say that one could easily collect from the journals the elements of a "manual of Bostonian snobbism,"[128] and the essay in question would add some very pretty ornaments to it. Although Emerson refrains from doing homage to custom and situates fashion sometimes

[124] "Character" (W 3.110). On the subject of personal magnetism see also p. 90, and "Nominalist and Realist" (W 3.228–229).

[125] In an article published in the *Dial* for October 1841 (reprinted in W 12.337–349), Emerson praises Landor for his capacity to appreciate "character" beneath all its disguises and gives the term this definition: "a moral force, yet wholly unmindful of creed and catechism, intellectual, but scornful of books, it works directly and without means, and though it may be resisted at any time, yet resistance to it is a suicide" (p. 345).

[126] JMN 7.376. The house in question is evidently the White House.

[127] "Manners" (W 3.117–155).

[128] In "Emersonian Genius," p. 29.

on this side of character and sometimes on that,[129] one senses that he is more than tolerant of the refinements of good society. Is it not piquant to find him writing the praises of Fox?—not George Fox, this time, but Charles, George III's cabinet minister, famous for his love of gambling and pleasure.[130] And one is no less surprised to discover his indulgence for "creole natures, and sleepy languishing manners,"[131] unless what is intended is a discrete tribute to his one-time friend, the graceful Anna Barker Ward. This unexpected side of Emerson is at least refreshingly human, and one could wish to see him taking an interest in "grotesque sculpture about the gates and offices of temples"[132] more often. But such a charming conception of social relations is really in Emerson nothing but a dream indulged. In reality his austere and priestly temperament[133] is shocked at the coarseness and frivolity of those he is led to keep company with, and his reaction (spontaneous first, strategic only later) is to look for a break with them. Several images, among them that of an island[134] and that of a surrounding atmosphere,[135] thus express, as the lectures and essays go by, his need to maintain an unbridgeable distance between other men and himself. Now "manners" are the most effective instrument we possess to that end. They are the product of constant discipline; they protect us against the betrayals of the body and repress such awkward explosions of feelings as tears—and, above all, laughter. Life in society would be intolerable for Emerson if a certain ritual of reserve and calculated coldness were not there to govern it. Despite appearances, the compliments people pay one another are means of keeping them apart.

Between these two conceptions of manners, which are differentiated rather than assimilated by their common label, Emerson did nonetheless see a possible reconciliation. On several occasions he refers to the invisible community that exceptional men always form and toys with the idea of a sort of secret society, accessible to all men whose qualities exalted them above the mass. When, for example, he defines—not very clearly—the subject of *Wilhelm Meister* as being "the passage of a dem-

[129] "Fashion is founded on Character, yet Character is *not yet admitted*" (JMN 12.502); in "Manners" he defines it as "virtue gone to seed" (W 3.128).

[130] See "Manners" (W 3.141–142).

[131] "Manners" (W 3.140).

[132] "Manners" (W 3.145).

[133] Paul, *Emerson's Angle of Vision*, p. 177, shows clearly how in Emerson's temperament the preacher and the minister concerned with the proprieties coexist nicely with the poet drunk on the wine of Bacchus.

[134] See "Manners" (W 3.137).

[135] See "Aristocracy" (W 10.55–56).

ocrat to the aristocracy,"[136] he is probably referring to the secret society that receives the hero in the last part of the novel and helps him to discover himself. A more explicit variation on the same theme appears in "Aristocracy":

> The Golden Table never lacks members; all its seats are kept full; but with this strange provision, that the members are carefully withdrawn into deep niches, so that no one of them can see any other of them, and each believes himself alone. In the presence of the Chapter it is easy for each member to carry himself royally and well; but in the absence of his colleagues and in the presence of mean people he is tempted to accept the low customs of towns. The honor of a member consists in an indifferency to the persons and practices about him, and in the pursuing undisturbed the career of a Brother, as if always in their presence, and as if no other existed.[137]

The metaphor used here translates one of Emerson's fundamental needs; it fortifies him against the dangers inherent in democracy and justifies his desire for isolation, but does not wholly cut him off from the human community. As he writes in his journal during the same period, "in our best moments society seems not to claim equality, but requires to be treated like a child, to whom we administer camomile & magnesia, on our own judgment, without consultation."[138] This does not imply that the child on coming of age will not have to decide by himself what suits him best. But until that time it would be mad and criminal to depend on him. After the romantic and adolescent rebellion of "Self-Reliance," "Aristocracy" can be read as the adult expression of a self-control considerably strengthened over the course of time. Emerson is as jealous of his independence as ever, but he no longer feels the need to defend it aggressively. The state itself, he now concedes, is "a poor good beast who means the best."[139] His disdain is qualified by pity; he seems ready to attend with the solicitousness of an elder to the miseries of the unenlightened.

To this inward consolidation there corresponds on the level of spec-

[136] "Goethe or the Writer" (W 4.279). Emerson does not distinguish between the *Lehrjahre* and the *Wanderjahre*, probably because Carlyle, who translated both, presented them as a single unit.

[137] "Aristocracy" (W 10.60–61).

[138] JMN 10.372 (1847).

[139] JMN 9.446 (1846). In this long passage, Emerson indicts extremists like Alcott who rage against the state, charging it with all the sins of the world, when all the while their "true quarrel is with the state of Man."

ulation an acceptance of the methods of Nature that was no longer merely resigned or even simply serene, but joyous and cheerful. The obstacle cast on his path by a disturbing political experience was overcome, and he found himself stronger, because more unified, than before. The materiality of things, their physical components, whether in himself and or in others, ceased to distress him. As early as "Nature," in the second series of *Essays*, he had developed the idea that we are each created to accomplish some particular task and that our bodies respond with appropriate gestures to the design providence has for us.[140] This law applies most cogently to those whom Nature intends for command: "She moulds a large brain, and joins to it a great trunk to supply it; as if a fine alembic were fed with liquor for its distillations from broad full vats in the vaults of the laboratory."[141] Thus aristocracy begins with the germinal cells of the embryo; it is in the strictest sense of the term organic, and Emerson, borne away by his own enthusiasm, is ready to claim that it is only that: "Genius is health and Beauty is health and Virtue is health."[142] Set against the hierarchy intended by fate, the democracy devised by men makes a poor figure; and neither newspapers, nor parties, nor the Congress, nor even the guillotine, has the power to abolish "the offence of superiority in persons."[143]

By an inevitable linkage of ideas, Emerson draws from the concept of natural inequality some very significant political conclusions; but even in America the theory is less heretical than it seems. In a mitigated form it is at the very center of the Federalist philosophy; and Jefferson himself, as is clear from a letter to his old friend and antagonist John Adams, agreed to its fundamental principle: "For I agree . . . that there is a natural aristocracy among men. The grounds of this are virtue and talents . . . the natural aristocracy I consider as the most precious gift of nature, for the instruction, the trusts, and government of society."[144] But in the meantime the country had experienced Jacksonianism, and Jefferson's measured language and Rousseauesque belief in virtue seemed to give off a scent of days gone by. "Aristocracy" seeks to adapt a theory as old as humanity to new times marked by the twofold sign of egalitarianism and violence. Emerson proposes that a sort of tacit pact be made between the leaders and the body of the nation. The leader is to gain recognition and authority through his character, without which neither

[140] See W 3.184–187.

[141] "Aristocracy" (W 10.43).

[142] Ibid.

[143] W 10.35.

[144] Quoted by Eric Bentley, *A Century of Hero-Worship* (Boston, 1957), pp. 9–10. The letter was written in 1813, after the end of Jefferson's second term.

honorable intentions nor even ordinary competence can have any effect. The true questions the voter ought to raise with regard to the candidate seeking election are these: Does he have a real will? Can he make his opinions prevail? Because, Emerson adds, for the benefit of the ambitious politicians America teems with:

> It is not sufficient that your work follows your genius, or is organic, to give you the magnetic power over men. More than taste and talent must go to the Will. That must also be a gift of Nature. It is in some; it is not in others. But I should say, if it is not in you, you had better not put yourself in places where not to have it is to be a public enemy.[145]

But this Will must conquer particular oppositions in the interest of a common cause, with which it will come to be fused. In other words: the destiny that lifts the leader above the crowd must be justified morally. Rank is a reward only in decaying and dying societies; elsewhere it simply means service, and the obligation devolving upon a president, a cabinet minister, a representative to *accomplish* something sums up all that he will be asked to answer for. The populace does not expect saintly virtues; it will pardon a leader's choleric temper, his love of luxury, his passion for money or gambling. It will not pardon his indolence or his idleness. But if he is so ill-advised as to treat power as a sinecure, the populace, aware of the outrage, will make him pay dearly for his transgression; in the end, he will have brought about his own ostracism. "To live without duties is obscene," writes Emerson, as a proper conclusion to this new social contract.[146]

Such a notion, with the underlying brutality it frankly posits in the relation between the two partners, is radically different from the anarchic reveries of "Self-Reliance." Addressing Bostonians ten years earlier, Emerson preached the doctrine of insubordination—in order to wake them from the lethargy into which they had drifted, but also because he knew he could count on their being subject to certain inward restraints that would come into play before anything very drastic could happen. Now, since the delivery of "The American Scholar," his human horizons had considerably expanded. He had discovered that his western and southern countrymen shared neither the virtues nor the deficiencies of New Englanders, and that urging them to rebellion was en-

[145] "Aristocracy" (W 10.50–51).

[146] "Aristocracy" (W 10.51–52). The editor notes that a certain English aristocrat was disturbed to hear this defense of violence spoken while the threat of revolution was in the air and asked Emerson to omit the passage if he repeated the lecture. Emerson of course did nothing of the kind.

couraging fearsome appetites indeed. He had thus come gradually to grasp the law by which even the most violent excesses, extortions, and miscarriages of justice promoted the general good. One is hardly surprised to note that the religious sentiment as he had so long exalted it, the intuition of divine presence at the level of the individual consciousness, had ceased to occupy the nerve center of his thought.[147] As is suggested by a sentence in the journal under the rubric of "The Age," what had taken its place was a reflection on the human significance of Science understood in its widest sense: "the moral of Science is the transference of that trust felt in nature's admired arrangements to social and moral order."[148] Emerson strove to accomplish this transference till the end of his life, just as it had been one of the aims—and one of the consolations—of his years of maturation.[149] During his second trip to England he discovered no star in the literary firmament not already visible in America; but he drew supplementary support for his optimism from the lectures of Richard Owen and Michael Faraday.[150] As the universe took form and order in the eyes of science, it revealed to his marveling spirit the processes of a providence prematurely reviled.

At the same time, and in obedience to a profound law of his nature, Emerson was withdrawing from the political tumult still agitating the nation. In the editorial he wrote in 1847 for the first issue of the *Massachusetts Quarterly Review*,[151] he was still virulently denouncing the

[147] In an unpublished speech given in May 1847 to the members of the Unitarian Church at Nantucket ("Discourse at Nantucket," H.199.11), Emerson confessed that though his belief in the primacy of the moral sentiment remained intact, it had ceased to occupy the center of his attention.

[148] JMS, H.107-Index 11 (September 1847), p. 16. Probably Emerson was very much subject in this area to the influence of Agassiz, the Swiss naturalist resident in Cambridge of whom "Aristocracy" offers an anonymous portrait (W 10.53–54).

[149] Indeed the preceding quotation is only the slightly condensed version of a sentence from "Humanity of Science," the second lecture in the series "The Philosophy of History," delivered in the winter of 1836–1837 (EL 2.39).

[150] See letter to Fuller of April 15, 1848 (L 4.63). The memory of these scientific lectures inspires a passage in the essay "Powers and Laws of Thought," based on a lecture Emerson gave in London in 1848: "On listening to Richard Owen's masterly enumeration of the parts and laws of the human body, or Michael Faraday's explanation of magnetic powers, or the botanist's descriptions, one could not help admiring the irresponsible security and happiness of the attitude of the naturalist; sure of admiration for his facts, sure of their sufficiency; sure too of their immense relations and of the grandeur of their tendency, and yet himself deriving an honest dignity from the nobility of his studies, they lend him a certain severe charm" (W 12.3 and 425).

[151] See W 11.381–393. In the absence of a much-desired Anglo-American review, a new periodical was launched in 1847 under the direction of Theodore Parker. Emerson refused any responsibility for the venture; but when asked to introduce it to the public, he had to yield.

political methods employed by unscrupulous opportunists; but he was also inviting the reader to rise above the fray, to turn away from party quarrels and transfer his attention to subjects worthier of it: "history," he writes in his journal in 1848,

> is the group of the types or representative men of any age at only the distance of convenient vision. We can see the arrangement of masses, & distinguish the forms of the leaders. Mythology is the same group at another remove, now at a pictorial distance; the perspective of history. The forms & faces can no longer be read, but only the direction of the march, & the result; so that the names of the leaders are now mixed with the ends for which they strove. Distance is essential. Therefore we cannot say what is *our* mythology.[152]

Thus the thinker independent of the contingent phenomena seeking to limit him asserted his rights once again.[153] The talks and lectures Emerson gave on his return from Europe illustrate the same attitude of mind, the same need to conquer the shortsightedness of the present, and show him striving to find some elbow room to maneuver with reference to daily events. In the speech he gave in 1849 on the occasion of the fifteenth anniversary of British West Indian emancipation, he portrays the slave-owning planters as primitive creatures, still afflicted with a wholly animal nature but bound despite themselves to a nobler destiny—we can, he said, rejoice in the impotence of human will.[154] The same faith animates a lecture given in January 1850, which we know chiefly from newspaper accounts of it, called "The Spirit of the Age";[155] in it, after a casual survey of human history, Emerson situates its latest episode, the California gold rush, in the context of an irresistible upward surge of

---

On the history and stance of the *Massachusetts Quarterly Review*, see Clarence Gohdes, *The Periodicals of American Transcendentalism* (Durham, N.C., 1931), pp. 157–193.

[152] JMN 10.289–290.

[153] At the end of 1848, with America experiencing once again the excesses and inflated promises of a presidential campaign, Emerson notes in the journal that "it is plain that some men may be spared from politics. The salvation of America & of the human race depends on the next Election, if we believe the newspapers. But so it was last year, & so it was the year before. . . . The whole action of the scholar is mediate & to remote ends, and voting is not for him. His poem is good because it is not written to any person or moment, but to life generalised & perspectived" (JMN 11.7).

[154] The manuscript of the speech has disappeared; but Ruchames, "Two Forgotten Addresses," has reprinted the review—regrettably scanty—published in the *Liberator*.

[155] See Jeanne Kronman, "Three Unpublished Lectures of Ralph Waldo Emerson," NEQ 19 (March 1946), pp. 98–110; the review used is that printed in the *New York Times*. But in this case the manuscript of the lecture has been preserved, and it seems that Emerson took from it the first paragraphs of "Life and Letters in New England" (W 10.325).

civilization: "The right men rushed in at the proper time. Such a promising, true-bred, well-appointed colony was never known, —every colonist trained in the principles and details of politics in this country, being a walking American Constitution among the placers of Sacramento."[156] There is doubtless not the least insincerity in Emerson's enthusiasm, but one cannot but be uneasy at noting that it is nourished with arguments that have always, whether equipped with metaphysical considerations or not, served to salve the consciences of advocates of belligerent nationalism.

As soothing as this panoramic view of things may have been, it nonetheless ended by emptying the present moment of all its moral substance; history, now deprived of the drama of individual choice and commitment and reduced to the revelation of some unspecified design traced since the beginning of the world in invisible ink, is simply the locus of the human determinisms in which the liberty of each individual must learn to be engulfed, as the Stoics once learned to walk calmly to their own voluntary deaths. It is at such a philosophy, depressing in its very optimism, and at the dangers it entails for our inward dignity that Melville takes aim in one of the characters of *The Confidence Man*, Mark Winsome, "the mystic." A contemporary scholar[157] has judiciously compared the sentence of *Representative Men* in which the image of the rattlesnake is invoked to illustrate natural order[158] with the page of Melville's book in which the same image is used to show what absurd conclusions that notion leads to:

> When charmed by the beauty of that viper, did it never occur to you to change personalities with him? to feel what it was to be a snake? to glide unsuspected in grass? to sting, to kill at a touch; your whole beautiful body one iridescent scabbard of death? In short, did the wish never occur to you to feel yourself exempt from knowledge, and conscience, and revel for a while in the care-free, joyous life of a perfectly instinctive, unscrupulous, and irresponsible creature?[159]

It remained for our own century to resume the attack, and no one did so more vigorously than did Yvor Winters, in an essay nominally devoted

[156] Kronman, "Three Unpublished Lectures," p. 107.

[157] E. S. Foster, in her introduction to a recent edition of *The Confidence Man* (New York, 1954), in which she adroitly clarifies Melville's satiric intentions; see especially pp. lxxiii–lxxxii.

[158] "We like to see every thing do its office after its kind, whether it be a milch-cow or a rattlesnake" ("Napoleon" [W 4.235]).

[159] *The Confidence Man*, p. 213 (chapter 36, "In Which the Cosmopolitan Is Accosted by a Mystic, Whereupon Ensues Pretty Much Such Talk As Might Be Expected").

to Hart Crane,[160] but in which the fire is directed principally at what Winters calls Emerson's doctrine of "social beatitude." Crane was nourished on Whitman, who himself got his matter from Emerson; and Crane committed suicide at the age of thirty-three. This in Winters' eyes is proof that the doctrine of the Concord sage contained behind its agreeable and innocuous exterior a lethal poison. Criminal violence or disintegration of personality: such is the somber dilemma toward which, if we believe those whom his position of optimism unqualified alarms, Emerson irresistibly presses us.

But the error—and it is an excusable one—of this criticism consists in seeing only Emerson's optimism. Emerson himself was so intensely aware of the difficulties intrinsic to the practical conduct of life that he chose that phrase as the title of one of his last books. Even after his most irritating evasions, the hour would come for him to look reality in the face, and his beloved equanimity would have to go. One of the last pages of "Aristocracy" furnishes a convincing illustration of this process. The revolutions of 1848 had caught Emerson in the middle of his second European trip. He had seen Paris in the hands of the republicans; and even in England there was much agitation, and the wretchedness of the working classes suggested what excesses their rebellion might entail. If "the two nations," to use Disraeli's phrase,[161] were to collide, where would Emerson's place be? On which side would he take his stand? It is to this heavily charged question, which is after all a personal question, that he finds it necessary to address himself publicly:

> The man of honor is a man of taste and humanity. By tendency, like all magnanimous men, he is a democrat. But the revolution comes, and does he join the standard of Chartist and outlaw? No, for these have been dragged in their ignorance by furious chiefs to the Red Revolution; they are full of murder, and the student recoils, —and joins the rich. If he cannot vote with the poor, he should stay by himself. Let him accept the position of armed neutrality, abhorring the crimes of the Chartist, abhorring the selfishness of the rich, and say, "The time will come when these poor *enfans perdus* of revolution will have instructed their party, if only by their fate, and wiser counsels will prevail. . . ." Meantime shame to the fop of learning and philosophy who suffers a vulgarity of speech and habit to blind him to the grosser vulgarity of pitiless selfishness . . . who

[160] "The Significance of *The Bridge*, by Hart Crane, or What Are We to Think of Professor X?" *In Defence of Reason*, pp. 577–603. Winters' argument, as he himself acknowledges (p. 268, n. 6), owes much to H. B. Parkes' remarkable *The Pragmatic Test* (San Francisco, 1941).

[161] *The Two Nations* is the subtitle of Disraeli's *Sybil* (1845).

> abandons his right position of being priest and poet of these impious and unpoetic doers of God's work.[162]

One can fault the position thus defined for its impracticality, if one does not share its author's optimism; one can consider it excessively subtle, and to that extent difficult to communicate, because it is the attitude of a man at home in his study, disconcerting to and disconcerted by the crowd. But one cannot with Winters accuse Emerson of writing as if the cost of independence were a deliberate and carefully nurtured obliviousness of other human beings. Emerson's effort here to reconcile the brutal shocks of life with a faith almost consubstantial with him is touching in its very awkwardness. Emerson was not the man of a system, or at least not yet. As long as he remained vulnerable to experience, and with tenacious humility strove to strengthen the edifice of his thought at its weakest points, he would have something to say that would merit even today something more and better than a condescending attention.

[162] "Aristocracy" (W 10.63–64).

PART IV

Individual *and* Citizen

12

~ ~ ~ ~

THE THORN IN THE FLESH

ALMOST all critics concerned with the development of Emerson's thought have argued that after a period of intense fermentation it gradually stabilized in the decade between 1840 and 1850.[1] There is, to be sure, a good quantity of scribbling after that decade, but it is for the most part lectures Emerson is composing or recomposing at need from passages in his notebooks. The two works he published before the Civil War, *English Traits* and *The Conduct of Life*, do attract one by the rugged firmness of their style, their sound and often penetrating judgments, and by a certain form of humanism that suggests that Emerson has at last made his peace with the world and its rules. They have the serenity of an Indian summer, while their energy reminds one that in America that season is accompanied by a last surge of growth in plants and trees. But they lack the impetuosity, the sparkle, the boldness that won the younger and more rebellious Emerson friends and foes of equal fervor. As the stream dug its bed it grew calmer; it flowed now in an ordered course, without waterfalls or unexpected rises, just at the level of a man living on the flatlands.

As often happens when one generalizes, however, this description is something of a distortion. It fits the philosopher better than the man struggling with his times or than the writer who partakes of both. For although he repeatedly reaffirmed his vocation as observer and poet,

[1] The most notable exception is Henry A. Pochmann, who sees a new phase of Emerson's thought beginning about 1850 under the influences of Hegel and Darwin. See *German Culture in America* (Madison, Wisc., 1957), p. 198–207.

Emerson never excluded the possibility that a day might come for him to defend his dignity as a moral creature tooth and nail:

> Whilst the man keeps himself thus sacred and aloof from the common vices of the partisan let him only bide his time and not hold himself excused from any sacrifice when he finds a clear case on which he is called to stand his trial. . . . Be sweet and courtly and merry these many long summers and autumns yet and husband your strength so that when an authentic, inevitable crisis comes and you are driven to the wall, cornered up in your Utica, you may then at last turn fairly round on the baying dogs all steel with all Heaven in your eye and die for love with all heroes and angels to friend.[2]

Despite his professed yielding to beneficent necessity, despite even the obstinate effort to minimize the importance of individual action in the shaping of a common destiny, he continued—perhaps unknowingly—to harbor the feeling that a part of himself remained irreducibly autonomous and that it could, if need be, stand up against the course of things alone. The attitude was illogical and irrational; but it linked Emerson to his Calvinist ancestors, who when they sought to justify their election by earthly works knew perfectly well that the inscrutable will of the Almighty had destined them to hell or heaven since the beginning of time.

In 1850, the "authentic, inevitable crisis" finally came. It was set off by the passage of the Fugitive Slave Law, which allowed the federal authorities to hunt escaped slaves throughout the union without recourse to individual state jurisdictions. Emerson was, of course, not the only man to feel this measure as an intolerable insult; Whittier, Dana, Parker, and even Whitman all denounced it with equal vigor. But Emerson's indignation was the greater for the event's having taken him by surprise. He compared it to "a sheet of lightning at midnight,"[3] because it affected him with lightning's suddenness and revelatory force. At one blow the veil was rent that had for so long masked what he called "the slightness and unreliableness of our social fabric."[4] He discovered with horror the extent of an evil that had worked its way into the body of the

[2] "The Present Age," lecture 6, "Reforms" (EL 3.268). The conclusion of this paragraph, minus the ellipsis, is copied from a passage of the journal for 1838 (JMN 5.407) in which Emerson warns himself against the reformers' superficial enthusiasms. The same point of view had already been expressed in 1832 (JMN 3.321), and had not much changed by 1846 (cf. JMN 9.446–447).

[3] In his first speech on the Fugitive Slave Law, given at Concord on May 3, 1851 (W 11.182).

[4] Ibid.

nation while he had been discoursing on the modalities of universal progress. It was the hour of truth—or rather of reality, with all that word's connotations of brutality and inevitability. Without having been consulted he had been made the legal accomplice of the slave owners. The government he had thought he could mock had avenged itself for his sarcasms with devastating irony: it had taken away his own liberty by forcing him to restrict that of others. Unlike the other problems of life in society, slavery could not be resolved by a judicious combination of energy and disdain. In fact, it had violated even the sanctum of his own consciousness and compelled him to do battle if he were not to deny his own self. It is somewhat perplexing that the psychological, philosophical, and indeed the literary consequences of this political crisis should have occupied critics so little. Unless one imagined that by 1850 Emerson was tranquilly prepared to accept unconditionally whatever might happen, one would assume that the pressure of such circumstances would inevitably give birth to a new man—which is in fact what happened. This study is concerned with the relations between a body of work and its time, and it has accordingly seemed necessary to begin this chapter by defining the climate that brought about, with such startling suddenness, the birth of this new man.

If Emerson had preserved his optimism in the fit that shook the nation's constitution in 1845 and 1846, it was not without having to draw considerably on his inner resources of energy. Once the alarm was over, the law of alternation we have noted several times before came into play, and he found himself weakened and languid. Here and there the journal for the period reveals a sort of shrinking fear of the crowd: "The question recurs whether we should descend into the ring. My own very small experience instructs me that the people are to be taken in very small doses. Vestry meetings & primary assemblies do not edify me. And I caution philosophers & scholars to use lenses & media."[5] A little later Emerson complains more openly of his inherent apathy: "We have experience, reading, relatednes enough, o yes, & every other weapon, if only we had constitution enough. But, as the doctor said in my boyhood,—'You have no *stamina*.' "[6] When he directs his gaze outward, he seems to see in America as a whole, if not an equal lassitude, then at least the same incapacity to use the energy it harbors, to create by dint of application and discipline the object or form that will affirm the triumph of the spirit. The nation is richer in promise than any other, and yet it "runs to leaves, to suckers, to tendrils," as if some evil spell had loaded

[5] JMN 10.31–32.

[6] JMN 10.110 (1847).

the air of the New World with "poppy, with imbecility, with dispersion, & sloth."[7] This feeling of Emerson's, this distress at the spectacle of sterile and inhuman profusion heralds Emily Dickinson's unease at the inscrutability of natural forces, and perhaps also Thoreau's deep perturbation when face to face with the bare rocks of Maine. America is not yet humanized; and the abyss Emerson discovers between its sublime geography and the mediocrity of its inhabitants leads him, almost against his will, to look more closely at the homeland of his ancestors.

Thus, in setting sail for Liverpool in October 1847[8] Emerson was not simply gratifying a writer's ambition—though the honors done him might reasonably have flattered his pride as an American citizen—nor was he only giving himself the change of air that entries in the journal for the period just preceding indicate he genuinely needed. He was also setting out to discover a great people, calm in its supremacy, rich in developed personalities, just as fifteen years earlier he had searched across the sea for the great man who could help him discover himself. He hoped to meet powerful minds, active and perfectly adapted, and his expectations were not disappointed: "The only girth or belt that can enable one to face these Patagonians of beef & beer, is an absorbing work of your own. Otherwise with their excessive life they hustle you out of their world.[9] If in the American land of extremes men measure their petty sickliness against nature's opulence, the English have learned to domesticate nature and assimilate at least a part of its energy. They are the descendants of Bacon, and they have anthropomorphized the universe by obeying its laws.

Curiously enough, a sort of osmosis took place between the traveler and his new milieu: one has only to read the correspondence of the period to realize that, as the months passed, Emerson became more and more partial to everything England represented. He may talk as he likes of lassitude, and declare that he is eager to return to Concord and America's robust egalitarianism; he yields nonetheless, and without great resistance, to the blandishments of his hosts. His letters recount a series of receptions, dinners, strolls through a countryside strewn with manors: not a *very* democratic way of passing the time. Doubtless he observed what offered itself to his gaze with keen attention, but his attitude was not controlled by the detachment for which he gave himself credit. In-

[7] JMN 10.79 (1847). See also pp. 29–31 and 95–96.

[8] On the circumstances and notable events of Emerson's second European trip see Townsend Scudder, *The Lonely Wayfaring Man: Emerson and Some Englishmen* (New York, 1936); Rusk, *Life*, also has an excellent account of the subject (pp. 350–359; chapter 19, "Not a World to Hide Virtues In").

[9] JMN 10.181.

vited to dine with the Duchess of Sutherland, led by her through the splendors of her palace, "the best house in the kingdom, the Queen's not excepted," he shudders to think that the "iron hand" of revolution might one day sweep down on Stafford House and its inhabitants.[10] Under the English skies the Whig he had always remained at heart was reinvigorated, and it was that Whig to whom Arthur Hugh Clough bade farewell in July of 1848, aboard the ship that was to take him back to America: "he is very Yankee to look at," Clough commented soon afterward,

> lank and sallow and not quite without the twang; but his look and voice are pleasing nevertheless and give you the impression of perfect intellectual cultivation as completely as would any great scientific man in England—Faraday, or Owen for instance, more in their way perhaps than in that of Wordsworth or Carlyle. . . . One thing that struck everybody is that he is much less Emersonian than his Essays. There is no dogmatism or arbitrariness or positiveness about him.[11]

On his return to America Emerson remembered his lessons in the art of conviviality; and it is from this visit to Europe that one can date the unexpected sociability that marked the second half of his career. At London, as a letter to his wife announces with somewhat embarrassed satisfaction, he had been voted an honorary member of the Atheneum.[12] Hoping perhaps to secure some of the advantages the Atheneum offered, he took part early in 1849 in the organization of an informal society intended to facilitate literary, scientific, and even philanthropic intercourse between city men and country men like himself. It quickly became clear, however, that the Town and Country Club lacked specific goals. Certain of its members proposed to strengthen it by admitting women; Emerson was firmly opposed to such a suggestion, and foresaw in it the institution's death sentence.[13] But the patient was fatally ill, and not even this spurt of misogyny could prevent its final demise.

Still, the concerns one can discern behind this half-beguiling, half-forbidding facade were those of a thinker wrapped in his meditations.

[10] See letter to Elizabeth Hoar of June 21, 1848 (L 4.88–90).

[11] Letter to Tom Arnold of July 16, 1848 (*Correspondence of Arthur Hugh Clough*, ed. F. Mulhauser, 2 vols. [Oxford, 1957], 1.215–216).

[12] See letter to Lidian Emerson of March 23 and 24, 1848 (L 4.42).

[13] See Kenneth Cameron, "Emerson, Thoreau and the Town-and-Contry Club," ESQ 8 (1957), p. 2. The article contains Emerson's letter of protest. See also the letter to William Emerson of May 23, 1849 (L 4.146).

Emerson had begun to read again, and with all his former appetite was expanding or renewing his old interests. It was this period in which through reading Quetelet he was initiated into "the new science of Statistics," that ancestor of sociology,[14] and in which Stallo helped him to understand contemporary German thought better and to elaborate his own epistemology.[15] But there is little or no real sense of immediate problems. During the summer of 1849, he asked the elder Henry James to give a lecture at the Town and Country Club; when James answered that he would like to talk about Socialism, Emerson received the proposal with benevolent tolerance: "socialism," he observes, "is as good a topic as a brave man who likes it can choose. We all have a leaning towards it from the 'anxious benches,' an expectation of being convicted and converted, on account of a certain geometry that is in it, notwithstanding that we are born hermits."[16] Yet Emerson had been in Paris when Barbès and his followers almost toppled the official government.[17] How can one be surprised at his not sensing the growing dangers in America?

Yet a good many symptomatic and distressing facts had been indicating the course of future events for ten years or so. A first Fugitive Slave Law had been passed in 1793; and though it had fallen into disuse, no measure had been taken to secure its repeal. Visiting the United States during Jackson's second term, when the slavery issue was relatively dormant, Harriet Martineau had nonetheless accurately measured its dangers:

> I know that slavery is only recognised by the constitution as a matter of fact . . . but the fact remains that a man who abhors slavery is compellable by the law which his fathers made, to deliver up to the owner a slave whose act of absconding he approves. It is impossible to estimate the evils which have proceeded from, and which will yet arise out of this guilty but "necessary" compromise.[18]

[14] W 6.17; see also JMN 11.68: "Quetelet's problem is to write the biography of the average man."

[15] Cf. Pochmann, *German Culture in America*, p. 194. Johann Bernhard Stallo, a lawyer and journalist of German origin, published in 1848 *General Principles of the Philosophy of Nature*; Emerson's journal contains numerous quotations from it.

[16] Letter to Henry James of September 7, 1849 (Ralph Barton Perry, *The Thought and Character of William James*, 2 vols. [Boston, 1935], 1.59).

[17] See the letter to Lidian Emerson of May 17, 1848 (L 4.72–75). Emerson was not unmoved by the insurrection; the tone and still more the suppressed excitement of his account of it show as much. But at the end of his letter all that he has just written seems to be taken back when he asks, "is there not one of your doctors who treats all diseases as diseases of the skin?"

[18] Martineau, *Society in America*, 3 vols. (London, 1837), 1.52. Emerson was not to use comparable terms till 1854; cf. JMN 13.333–334.

The history of the United States from 1845 till the Civil War was to give tragic substance to that prophecy. Even today it is difficult to understand how both North and South could experience such extraordinary violence and hatred. But each camp believed itself vitally menaced; and so positions hardened, demands grew more peremptory, and ideology took hold of the debate, transforming adversaries into enemies. It was clear even before 1850, to those who could see, that the nation was rushing into an abyss of disaster.

The compromise proposed by Henry Clay, which included among its provisions a strengthening of the Fugitive Slave Law, was intended to halt that fatal movement. The election of 1848 had left a bitter aftertaste in all men's mouths, Emerson's included;[19] but it had settled nothing. A break threatened to occur at every moment, and when California, which had just constituted itself as a free state, asked to join the Union, it seemed that the crisis had come. In presenting his proposals, Clay did not claim to have devised a definitive solution. He wanted simply to avoid the worst, to make the two parties agree on a de facto truce from which they might go on to work out some statute acceptable to everyone. And that is why Webster, in his famous speech of March 7, 1850, pledged him his support. Like Clay, Webster was in the twilight of his career and was intensely committed to the preservation of the Union for which he had fought his roughest battles. He was, moreover, persuaded that any secession would be accompanied by bloodshed, and to the defense of the compromise he applied all his energy, talent, and sincerity. "No speech more patriotic or evincing a higher degree of moral courage had ever been made in Congress," writes Allan Nevins; "for once Webster rose to the highest level of statesmanship."[20] But Webster's speech was greeted in New England—and not only among abolitionist circles—as an act of treason. Whittier's poem is well known, in which he bemoans "A bright soul driven, / Fiend-goaded, down the endless dark."[21] The darkness was that of wholesale recantation, by which Webster annulled in an instant a whole life of rectitude and honor. The extreme violence of the northern reaction is indeed perplexing. Was the situation so chaotically jumbled that the only choice was between ignoble submission and open war? And why had it taken so long to assess the danger's extent? Why such fanaticism after such patience? I shall at-

[19] On the eve of the balloting, he notes that "here has passed an Election, I think, the most dismal ever known in this country. Three great parties voting for three candidates whom they disliked" (JMN 11.47). The third party was that of the Free-Soilers, who had separated from the Democrats to combat the establishment of slavery in the newly annexed territories.

[20] Allan Nevins, *Ordeal of the Union*, 2 vols. (New York, 1947),1.290.

[21] "Ichabod," lines 14–15 (*Works*, 4 vols. [Boston, 1893] 4.62).

tempt to answer these questions—but indirectly, by investigating Emerson's writings during the period.

One should begin by saying that the meaning and the magnitude of the slavery issue took considerable time to become clear to Emerson—as it did to most of his contemporaries. (Parker himself was no exception.) For a number of years he classed abolition among the desirable reforms that would someday be achieved because the principle governing the world was intrinsically good, but the importance of which should not be exaggerated. In this respect, like Carlyle, he distrusted "geographical virtue,"[22] in which he saw a convenient subterfuge for avoiding more immediate or more difficult obligations. Even after the 1844 speech on British West Indian emancipation, Emerson's position on the issue remained loftily abstract; what he valued in abolitionism was the affirmation of a moral principle, and he was little troubled with the situation of the slaves themselves. To the extent that he admitted that blacks had given proof of their intellectual capacity, he found that white guilt in the perpetuation of slavery was in fact mitigated. Had a new Fugitive Slave Law not been passed, had Emerson not in consequence been in a sense personally involved in the issue,[23] it is quite likely that he would have continued to refrain from militant action for an indeterminate period of time. The slavery issue had to take on a truly political coloring to force itself on his notice and suddenly introduce into his world a dimension he had persistently denied. But it would be unjust to reproach him for a blindness most of his countrymen shared. Emerson was in the years 1850 and 1851 a more representative man than at any other moment of his life; and the awareness growing in him portrays with uncharacteristic exactness a whole moment of New England history.

I have laid considerable emphasis on the meaning of Emerson's move to Concord, after the period of his ministry.[24] By that move he deliberately narrowed his political horizon to a community of small landowners, in which a sense of independence and a respect for other persons' freedom had been firmly anchored throughout the town's history. Boston, by contrast, not infrequently left him ill at ease; faced with the big city, he needed to know of the counterpoise of the towns and to count on them to keep the state on the path of faithfulness. By "the state" he

[22] "Lecture on the Times" (W 1.280).

[23] "I have lived all my life in this state," he states at the beginning of the first Fugitive Slave Law speech, "and never had any experience of personal inconvenience from the laws, until now" (W 11.179).

[24] Vide supra, chapter 5.

meant of course Massachusetts, the only political entity he could in any strict sense feel part of.[25] The Union was rather a federation, a defense league, a mutual-aid society, a Zollverein harmonizing complementary interests; it was not and had never been a *patria*. Calhoun was not alone in brandishing the threat of secession; Garrison's abolitionists were quick to learn to use the threat themselves. And when the Mexican War broke out, seeming to subjugate the North to the law of the West and the South, Lowell expressed the angry shame of a good number of his New England compatriots in writing,

> Massachusetts, God forgive her,
> She's akneelin' with the rest,
> She, that ough' to ha' clung ferever
> In her grand old eagle-nest.[26]

At the same time—and the crisis of 1850 set the paradox in a fierce light—Emerson firmly believed in an American vocation independent of the boundaries of Massachusetts. If the word could be washed clean of the dirt obscuring its brilliance, he was willing to be called a patriot. In the editorial he wrote in 1847 for the first issue of the *Massachusetts Quarterly Review*, he had already explained his position on the matter:

> We hesitate to employ a word so much abused as *patriotism*, whose true sense is almost the reverse of its popular sense. We have no sympathy with that boyish egotism, hoarse with cheering for one side, for one state, for one town: the right patriotism consists in the delight which springs from contributing our peculiar and legitimate advantages to the benefit of humanity. . . . Certainly then this country does not lie here in the sun causeless; and though it may not be easy to define its influence, men feel already its emancipating quality in the careless self-reliance of the manners, in the freedom of thought, in the direct roads by which grievances are reached and redressed, and even in the reckless and sinister politics, not less than in purer expressions. Bad as it is, this freedom leads onward and upward, —to a Columbia of thought and art, which is the last and endless end of Columbus's adventure.[27]

[25] Similarly, when Thoreau in "Civil Disobedience" invites his countrymen to rise up against the authority of the state if it attempts to enforce unjust laws, it is not to the Union but to Massachusetts that he refers. Addressing those who advocate secession, he invites them to practice it themselves: "do not they stand in the same relation to the State that the State does to the Union?" (Thoreau, *Works*, 20 vols. [Boston, 1906], 4.366).

[26] The *Biglow Papers*, first series, in *Works* (Boston, 1894), 8.49.

[27] "Editors' Address" (W 11.386–387).

It would be easy here to add other names—to show, for example, how Parker at this time was exalting the young nation's destiny in precisely the same fashion.[28] Whether as sublimation or excuse, the American dream had gained strength from the popular fervor evoked by enterprises of national expansion. People wanted to forget the gap between present and future, or at least were persuaded that it would gradually but inexorably disappear. With the passage of the Fugitive Slave Law, however, it became impossible to use the word "emancipation" without feeling the sting of irony in its double meaning. The sky had suddenly grown dark and the shadows were thickening, threatening to spread as far as the eye could see.

Few passages of the journal suggest this dismay, this overwhelming oppressiveness as much as do those written during the spring and summer of 1850. In Congress, in the course of a long debate that had mustered men, rather than arguments, for a decisive fight, the representatives of New England had shamefully capitulated.[29] What was worse was that Boston, a city designated by its whole history as a citadel of resistance to such oppression, had approved of their conduct; among its inhabitants were eight hundred reprobates who thought fit to send Webster a letter of congratulation: "this was a day of petticoats, a day of imbecilities, the day of the old women," notes an Emerson even more dismayed than he was outraged. "Many of the names very properly belong there, —they are the names of aged & infirm people, who have outlived everything but their night cap & their tea & toast. But I observe some names of men under forty!"[30] It is fairly clear, however, that a part at least of Emerson's condemnation fell on his own head. At the crucial moment, when he ought to have shown resolution and independence, his energies had betrayed him. He discovered bitterly that in persuading himself of the effectiveness of his vocation he had played the fool: "it is the scholar's misfortune that his virtues are all on paper, & when the time comes to use them, he rubs his eyes & tries to remember what is it that he should do."[31] For the first time since his earliest youth, his discouragement was so deep that he sometimes doubted the value of life itself: "the badness of the times is making death attractive," he confides

[28] See the speech he gave several times in 1848 under the title of "The Political Destination of America and the Signs of the Times" (partially reprinted in *The American Transcendentalists: An Anthology*, ed. Perry Miller [Cambridge, Mass., 1950], pp. 348–366). Parker's analysis, incidentally, is more comprehensive and more balanced than Emerson's.

[29] See JMN 11.233 and 244 (1850).

[30] JMN 11.249 (1850).

[31] JMN 11.255. A passage contemporary with this confesses the oppression Emerson feels in hotels at his companions' "excessive virility" (JMN 11.248).

to his journal,[32] and it was probably at the same time that he sketched the first draft of a half-elegiac, half-stoical poem in which he prepares himself for the great retreat.[33]

One has to keep these confessions in mind and appreciate the distress they express to understand Emerson's disturbance at Webster's defection. Not that Emerson, as certain commentators have wrongly claimed,[34] ever accorded Webster an entirely uncritical admiration. He had first noted Webster's weaknesses in 1843, and the journal lists them unsparingly: the mediocrity of ambition that prompted Webster to seek the honors of this world so intensely; the partisan obligingness toward certain unworthy "friends"; and above all the inability to rise to the level of true religion, to go beyond the universe of the Understanding.[35] But Emerson tolerated these imperfections because of a quality that put them all in the shade: a striking physical and moral energy, a calm power bespeaking a man in harmony with himself and in consequence endowed with irresistible radiance, in short a rocky solidity of character—in Emerson's sense—unique in America. In many respects Webster was Emerson's complement, as self-assured in action as Emerson could be timid and hesitant. Webster was for Emerson the guarantor and surety he needed in moments of doubt. As Emerson was thought, or consciousness, with the vacillation that inevitably accompanies consciousness, so Webster was instinct or nature;[36] and the coexistence of the two men was in a way a pledge of their fusion in generations to come.

[32] JMN 11.250.

[33] See Carl Strauch, "The Date of Emerson's 'Terminus' " PMLA 65, (June 1950), pp. 360–370. Strauch has shown from a close examination of the manuscript sources that the first version of the poem probably goes back to 1850 or 1851; and whereas the final version (W 11.251–252) is about the approach of old age, this earlier version reveals a weariness so profound that the thought of death seems a refuge. Cf. for example the beginning four lines: "As the bird trims herself to the gale / So I trim myself to the Tempest of Time, / And I shall find something pleasant in my / Last throb that I am getting out of mean politics."

[34] Particularly Arthur Schlesinger, Jr., who speaks of a "mirage" by which Emerson alone among the literary men and women of his time was beguiled; see *The Age of Jackson* (Boston, 1945), chapter 5 ("Jacksonian Democracy and Literature"; reprinted in *The Transcendentalist Revolt Against Materialism*, ed. George Whicher [Boston, 1949]).

[35] See particularly JMN 7.357–359 and 382–383, and 9.42. Webster had occasion in 1843 to plead in Concord court—hence the number and extent of Emerson's comments on him. The portrait of Webster in the second speech on the Fugitive Slave Law (W 11.220–223) is mostly drawn from these entries.

[36] A passage of the journal for 1843 (JMN 7.362–363) compares Webster to some powerful animal, some tiger or leopard— one will recall that a similar set of images, based on memories of a visit to a menagerie, possessed Emerson's mind some years later in connection with Napoleon. Vide supra, chapter 11.

It is because of this unexpressed but intimately lived bond that the March 7 speech evoked from Emerson so astonishing a response. The political motives analyzed above did not seem to him acceptable, nor could they excuse the fact that a tacit but hallowed alliance between Webster and himself had been shamefully broken. The situation has illuminating literary analogues in the fiction of Henry James, for whom the theme of betrayal, or rather the becoming aware of betrayal, gives the novel one of its fundamental motifs; and one remembers that in James the lucidity thus achieved is bought at an appalling price—so much so that to sweep away illusion is often tantamount to overthrowing the edifice of a whole life. It would, of course, be absurd to compare Emerson with Isabel Archer or Milly Theale; but in Emerson's exaggeratedly cerebral domain, Webster's recantation had the same sort of disastrous consequences, and in the same all-encompassing and all-illuminating way called certain fundamental postulates of his thought into question. At the same time one ought not to overdo this resemblance to James and his complex mirror-games. Emerson believed in the simplicity of the world; he believed that behind appearances, though they are often misleading, the truth subsists and in the end is manifested. That is why on reflection Webster's speech seemed to him less like a betrayal than like a long-delayed revelation, a sort of epiphany of evil whose bitter lesson he must strive to assimilate: "the little fact comes out more plainly," he writes early in 1851,

> that you cannot rely on any man for the defence of truth who is not constitutionally of that side. Wolf, however long his nails have been pared, however neatly he has been shaved, & tailored, & taught & tuned to say "Virtue" and "religion," cannot be relied on when it comes to a pinch, he will forget his morality, & say morality means sucking blood.[37]

But what comfort could this late discovery offer? If Hobbes was right, if the world was in effect peopled with wolves disguised as shepherds, what chance did lambs have? A harsh test, this, for a faith that had stripped itself of subjective illusions with great difficulty and had thought to establish itself once and for all by affirming its solidarity with the process of history.

Quickly enough, however, Emerson took hold of himself and went on the attack, revealing resources of temperament he perhaps did not know he possessed. "The exhibition of Emerson as a fighting animal is

[37] JMN 11.347. The substance of the passage was used in the first Fugitive Slave Law speech, W 11.183.

magnificent," remarks one of the few critics interested in this aspect of his personality, "No other nature but Webster's ever so moved him; but it was time to be moved, and Webster was a man of his size. Had these two great men of New England been matched in training as they were matched in endowment, and had they then faced each other in debate, they would not have been found to differ so greatly in power."[38] This passage from prostration to combat, from something very like despair to the hard-won but stubborn affirmation of an unaltered faith, reveals as perhaps no previous episode has done the extreme boundaries of a nature far greater in range than one often imagines it.

In the first and most painful, most troubling stage, it appeared to Emerson that the moral law no longer lived in his countrymen's hearts: "the worst symptom I have noticed in our politics lately," he notes in April 1850, "is the attempt to make a gibe out of Seward's appeal to a higher law than the Constitution, & Webster has taken part in it. I have seen him snubbed as "*Higher-law-Seward*."[39] That in his eyes was the supreme fall, and certain passages of the journal show him overwhelmed with disgust and haunted by images of decay and a corruption whose symbol is gold:

> Every glance at society—pale withered people with gold-filled teeth, with scalps tied on, ghastly, & with minds in the same dilapidated condition, drugged with books for want of wisdom, —suggests at once the German thought of the Progressive God, who has got thus far with his experiment, but will get out yet a triumphant & faultless race.[40]

Interestingly, however the survival instinct was once again in play. The dance of death evoked here is no procession of the damned; there remains the distant hope of a universal apotheosis. As if to buttress this renascent optimism, Emerson now undertook to find and assemble the opinions of famous jurists from Bacon and Grotius to Blackstone regarding the validity of laws.[41] The idea was not new even to Emerson; when tracing the history of abolition in the address on West Indian

[38] John Jay Chapman, in "Emerson" (*Shock of Recognition*, ed. Edmund Wilson, 2d ed. [New York, 1955] p. 627). A more recent analysis of Emerson as public man is Stuart Gerry Brown's "Emerson 1803–1953," *Ethics* 64 (April 1954), pp. 217–225.

[39] JMN 11.248. Seward was a senator from New York and one of the Conscience Whigs; he answered Webster on March 11, 1850, speaking of a higher law than the Constitution, immovable and implying certain immutable obligations on all legislators.

[40] JMN 11.263 (1850).

[41] The journal for the period contains a whole juristic anthology (JMN 11.280–282), the substance of which passed into the first Fugitive Slave Law speech (W 11.190–192).

emancipation, he had become interested in the judicial decisions that constituted its milestones, notably a judgment by which Lord Mansfield in 1772 had refused to return a slave to his legal owner.[42] But the change of atmosphere in New England made the progressivist perspective of the 1844 speech seem anachronistic. In the pressure of battle, he had to find allies even at the cost of violating his inmost nature;[43] and this recourse to external guarantors (among whom some, Blackstone for example, were disciples of Locke) shows Emerson with his back to the wall. The proud solitude of "Self-Reliance" could no longer be nurtured by the sense of its own invulnerability.

Still, it was not until it became clear what results the Fugitive Slave Law would have that Emerson's protest attained the intensity Chapman describes. As the months passed, he had gradually ensconced himself in a sort of half-confident, half-resigned patience that seemed to him the most reasonable attitude one could take toward human mediocrity, as it spared him the dissipation of vain efforts to save men despite themselves. Congratulating Carlyle in August 1850 on the "sturdy tone" of his latest book, the *Latter-Day Pamphlets*, he had nevertheless also cast doubt on the effectiveness of his "crusade against the Times," because, he explained, "we are beleaguered with contradictions, and the moment we preach, though we were archangels, things turn on their heel and leave us to fret alone."[44] But early in 1851 the full force of the new law fell on two slaves who had sought refuge in Boston. The first, named Shadrach, was freed from his captors, and a sympathetic crowd aided his escape and helped him to get to Canada. The second, named Thomas Sims, had worse luck; the governor of Massachusetts determined that jurisdiction in his case belonged by right to a tribunal in his state of origin and had him brought to the harbor by night and under escort, to be put on a brig leaving for Georgia.[45]

[42] See "West Indian Emancipation" (W 11.105–107).

[43] The journal for the period shows Emerson sometimes balking at the effort and protesting the uselessness of his chosen task: "The persons to whom I speak need no quotation from Blackstone to convince them that all immoral laws are void. I shall not encumber my pages with authorities which, adding nothing to my own conviction, can add none to any others'. For I do not argue, but simply say what appears true, and if it does not appear true to you, it will not for much speaking" (JMS, H.127-EF, p. 41). The reader may note that this is precisely the point Emerson makes in his letters to Henry Ware after the Divinity School address; see L 2.146–150 and 166–167.

[44] Letter to Carlyle of August 5, 1850 (L 4.223). Four months later, Emerson wrote to Samuel Gray Ward returning from Europe that at home all was calm: "only political mice have cheeped" (December 3, 1850 [L 4.237]).

[45] On these two episodes and the reaction they aroused in abolitionist circles, see Harold Schwartz, "Fugitive Slave Days in Boston," NEQ 27 (June 1954), pp. 191–212. See also

For Emerson the infamy was now consummated. During the period of the Mexican War he had not wanted to distinguish between idea and act;[46] but the enforcement of the Fugitive Slave Law seemed to him a degradation distinct from its enactment.[47] He could no longer hold his head up; the sun's light had lost its radiance; he felt guilty in the sight of his own children.[48] But an unsuspected streak of polemical invective took its rise from the very depth of this humiliation, and nothing is more striking than the contrast between these first helpless comments in the journal and what soon followed them: a good ten pages of furious imprecation, of refusals to obey or bend, of contemptuous criticisms of eminent men without principles. The raging indignation that possessed him brought into play all the language of hate and disgust. Webster evoked the image of the prostitute,[49] the New England clergy that of putrefaction.[50] Slavery became a shameful illness, a leprosy or a tumor that spared no one, covering bodies with purulent encrustations and driving minds mad.[51] Reading such passages one wonders that the legend of an Emerson so sweet and benign as to seem bland and insipid could ever have come into being; even Thoreau, though also scandalized at his compatriots' cowardice, is more moderate in his invective and retains more of his sense of irony.[52]

This intensity of feeling is that of the great satirists, from Persius to Pascal and Swift, and it invites one to ask why Emerson could not like them direct his indignation toward the making of some major work. He

---

Charles Francis Adams, *Richard Henry Dana: A Biography*, 2 vols. (Boston, 1891), esp. 1.178–201 (chapter 10, "The Fugitive Slave Cases of 1851").

[46] See JMN 9.430: "the people are no worse since they invaded Mexico, than they were before, only they have given their will a deed."

[47] See JMN 11.343ff. Certain friends of Emerson's followed his reasoning and remarked that the problem was no worse than before, only it had now become visible; but Emerson responded, "well I think *that* worse. It shows the access of so much courage in the bad, so much check of virtue, terror of virtue, withdrawn."

[48] Ibid.

[49] "The word *liberty* in the mouth of Mr Webster sounds like the word *love* in the mouth of a courtezan" (JMN 11.346).

[50] "As for the Andover & Boston preachers, Dr Dewey & Dr Sharpe who deduce kidnapping from their Bible, tell the poor dear doctor if this be Christianity, it is a religion of dead dogs" (JMN 11.351).

[51] See JMN 11.361.

[52] See *The Journal of Henry David Thoreau*, ed. Bradford Torrey and Francis Allen, 14 vols. (Boston, 1949), 1.174–180. Thoreau feigns to feel "a slight degree of pride" in noting that the preacher who prayed as Thomas Sims embarked on the boat to Georgia was from Concord. Thus, he ironically explains, are the revolutionary traditions of the village maintained; he then complicates the irony, saying that his second feeling "was one of doubt and shame, because the *men* of Concord in recent times have done nothing to entitle them to the honor of having their town names in such a connection."

was not less troubled by the Fugitive Slave Law than was Pascal by the casuistic morality of the Jesuits. He believed no less than did the Swift of *The Tale of a Tub* in the essential dignity of human nature, and suffered no less to see that dignity flouted by the most "enlightened" of his contemporaries. Powerfully agitated by the circumstances around him, he recalls Swift even in the quality of his imagination—indeed one wonders, reading such a mixture of horrified response and lapidary precision, whether he may not be simply imitating him.[53] But here as elsewhere Emerson had not sufficiently reflected on the presuppositions and laws of literary creation; he had not understood that anger does not beget anger, and that the secret of true power lies in artistically exploited detachment. The decline in his creative activity is revealed precisely by this inability to conceive personae, to project himself dramatically into this new situation as he had done in "The American Scholar."[54]

But Emerson's nobility in these dark times was to give precedence not only to the man before the author but also to the citizen before the man. In April 1851, he sent his copy of the *Bhagavad-Gita* to a woman friend he had met the previous year during a lecture tour. He urges his correspondent to read the book very slowly, calls it "one of the bibles of the world," then admits his inability to give himself up to meditation: "at this moment, in the cruelty & the ignominy of the laws, & the shocking degradation of Massachusetts, I have had no heart to look at books, or to think of anything else than how to retrieve this crime."[55] Henry Nash Smith once criticized the conception of the role of action in the life of the American Scholar as somewhat *fin de siècle*.[56] Let us venture to

[53] Thus, for example, a passage of the journal in which Emerson extrapolates the consequences of northern deference to the point of atrocity seems an exact transposition of Swift's strategy in "A Modest Proposal": "and if the Southern states should find it necessary to enact the further law in view of the too great increase of blacks, that every fifth manchild should be boiled in hot water, —& obtain a majority in Congress with a speech by Mr Webster to add an article to the Fugitive Slave Bill, —that any fifth child so and so selected, having escaped into Boston should be seethed in water at 212, will not the mayor and alderman boil him?" (JMN 11.360).

[54] The journal does, however, contain a richly ironic passage in which Emerson imagines himself in conversation with Everett, who had become a heated advocate of union at any price: Pascal's technique in the *Provincial Letters* is brilliantly recaptured, but is soon let go. A somewhat later passage in a different mood implies that Webster's destiny contains the germ of a modern tragedy (JMN 13.64 [1852]).

[55] Letter to Emily Mervin Drury of April 14, 1851, *Modern Language Notes* 55 (June 1940), p. 427.

[56] Henry Nash Smith, "Emerson's Problem of Vocation," NEQ 12 (March 1939), pp. 52–67, takes Emerson's statement that "if it were only for a vocabulary, the scholar would be covetous of action" (W 1.97–98) as evidence both for doubting the value of such a subordination

say that in 1851 Emerson would have agreed with him. Professional scholars, he argued, have been destroyed by such refinement; they think they love liberty with the passion of Demosthenes when in fact they savor only the cadences of his oratory. The populace is right in considering them dilettantes; it tolerates them because they remain shut up in their libraries and only emerge on election day to vote for the party of slavery.[57]

Thus Emerson discovered that insofar as America was turning away from its true vocation, seeking only to follow in the footsteps of Europe, liberty was at best a fragile acquisition and at worst a painful dream not to be profaned with words:

> Once I wished I might rehearse
> Freedom's paean in my verse,
> That the slave who caught the strain
> Should throb until he snapped his chain.
> But the Spirit said, Not so;
> Speak it not, or speak it low;
> Name not lightly to be said,
> Gift too precious to be prayed,
> Passion not to be expressed
> But by heaving of the breast.[58]

This fervent tone, condemned to restraint by its very intensity (one thinks by contrast of Eluard's poem on the subject), is infrequent in Emerson's poetry, which by and large is keyed to a mood of celebration. Literary expression here reaches one of its limits. Liberty is not a word or even an idea; it is experienced and embodied, and that is why Emerson's admiration goes first to men fitted by temperament for action: "my warmest thanks for the Fast-Day Sermon," he writes to Theodore Parker soon after the capture of Sims, "which, I believe, stands the foremost consolation to me in the bad times. It half exculpates the State, that the protest of the minority is so amply & admirably uttered in the very place & hour of the crime. We all love & honour you here, & have come to

---

of art to action and for showing how confused Emerson was at the time about the real relations between his aesthetics and his practical philosophy.

[57] These "ornamental scholars" are attacked with particular energy in a journal passage from 1851 (JMN 11.380).

[58] "Freedom" (W 9.98). The poem seems to have been composed in 1853. As early as 1851, the journal has a paragraph called "History of Liberty" (JMN 11.365). The editor of W mentions a manuscript notebook in which Emerson copied a number of remarks and anecdotes on the subject; see W 6.332–333. (The original has disappeared, but there is a copy at the Houghton Library; see JMN 1.412, n. 10.)

think every drop of your blood & every moment of your life of a national value."[59]

In fact, behind this strikingly humble gratitude one senses anguished doubt: will liberty find enough of the able servants it needs? Will all those who have been allotted the qualities of a leader and in whom resoluteness of soul culminates in boldness and energy of action hear and answer the call? It is quite likely that in the awareness of his own incompetence Emerson looked around him for possible guides and deplored the unconcern that Thoreau seemed to him to wave like a flag. In "Civil Disobedience" Thoreau had told the story of his spending a night in prison for refusing to pay the poll tax; then, irreverent to the end, he had concluded as follows: "When I was let out the next morning, I proceeded to finish my errand, and, having put on my mended shoe, joined a huckleberry party, who were impatient to put themselves under my conduct."[60] Emerson saw the symbolic nature of the episode clearly, and it is perhaps not pure accident that he extracts its meaning in a paragraph of the journal for this dark year of 1851: "Thoreau wants a little ambition in his mixture. Fault of this, instead of being the head of American Engineers, he is captain of a huckleberry party."[61] Like the Goethe of the *Wilhelm Meister* he admired, Emerson was now making service to others the crown of individual virtue.

The evidence we have suggests that he strove to suit his practice to his preaching and protested against this legal infamy wherever his protest seemed likely to have weight.[62] He gave his talk on the Fugitive Slave Law several times. Once, at Cambridge, he was interrupted by hostile listeners—whether southern students or hooligans is still not clear—and the description of his response that one of his admirers has left us is worth quoting:

> It was curious to watch him, as at each point he made he paused to let the storm of hisses subside. The noise was something he had never heard before; there was a queer, quizzical, squirrel-like or bird-like expression in his eye as he calmly looked round to see

[59] Letter of April 18, 1851 (L 4.249–250). Rusk prints Parker's answer in a note; it was a tribute to a former teacher: "much of the little I do now is the result of seed of your own sowing."

[60] "Civil Disobedience," Thoreau, *Works*, 4.380. The essay was published in 1849.

[61] JMN 11.400. The passage was expanded for use in the essay "Thoreau" (W 10.480).

[62] An unpublished letter of Charles Sumner to John Gorham Palfrey, probably written in May 1851—that is, a few days after the first Fugitive Slave Law speech—accords Emerson's political role at the period real importance: "His voice will reach many corners not easily penetrated by our cry. . . . No speech from a politician could have given me the peculiar delight I have in this effort" (Palfrey Papers, Houghton Library; the letter was brought to my attention by the courtesy of M. F. O. Gattell).

> what strange human animals were present to make such sounds; and when he proceeded to utter another indisputable truth, and it was responded to by another chorus of hisses, he seemed absolutely to enjoy the new sensation he experienced. . . . The experience was novel; still there was not the slightest tremor in his voice, not even a trace of the passionate resentment which a speaker under such circumstances and impediments usually feels. . . . During the whole evening he never uttered a word which was not written down in the manuscript from which he read.[63]

This chapter will conclude by examining briefly the text of this explosive piece of oratory.

It is regrettable that the editor of the Centenary Edition thought fit to print not the original conclusion but that of a speech Emerson gave later, when his position on slavery had been consolidated and clarified.[64] In 1851, the practical preconditions of a solution acceptable to both sides were not among his chief concerns. He cared above all to expose the monstrous character of the new law, to stimulate his countrymen's courage, and to nourish their readiness for struggle by demonstrating that the whole universe was protesting in his words. Seldom was Emerson so successful in joining argument to profession of faith, in reinforcing aphorisms now by irony and now by the cadences of a strikingly rhythmic rhetoric. The speech thus exhibits considerable tonal fluctuation—but at the cost of some damage to its inner balance, because the logician is not on a par with the metaphysician or even the polemicist. Why, for example, did Emerson put the arguments in numbered paragraphs when from one paragraph to the next they are almost identical?[65] The middle pages, moreover, despite their frequently felicitous expression, do not stand up very well to critical examination, especially if one compares them with the writings of such adroit dialecticians and expert manipulators of political ideas as Jefferson and Paine. But in the beginning and the end, the intensity of feeling gives every sentence the passionate and broad intensity that is manifested whenever the preservation of a moral principle is at issue. One touches here on what is probably the deepest source of Emerson's eloquence: he has to be able to say "I" in the most direct, avowed manner possible; but he must also

[63] E. P. Whipple, *Recollections of Eminent Men* (Boston, 1886), pp. 140–141. Cabot finds the portrait at odds with Emerson's peaceable nature, and doubts its veracity; see *Memoir*, 2.585–586.

[64] The speech in question has not been published; it was given January 26, 1855, under the title of "American Slavery." Vide infra, chapter 13.

[65] Thus the moral sense's role as monitor in the area of legislation is affirmed in the first and third paragraphs alike (pp. 188–191 and 194–195).

shed his particular self and so be open to the radiance of unchanging truth.

Now the truth for him was always a source of optimism, because it seemed to him endowed with inexhaustible freshness. Webster's error is his inability to discern the universe's power of recovery:

> He has no faith in the power of self-government; none whatever in extemporizing a government. Not the smallest municipal provision, if it were new, would receive his sanction. In Massachusetts, in 1776, he would, beyond all question, have been a refugee. He praises Adams and Jefferson, but it is a past Adams and Jefferson that his mind can entertain. A present Adams and Jefferson he would denounce.[66]

Sustained by this intuition, Emerson overturns insubstantial obstacles; the dilemma by which some are obsessed—Union with slavery or secession and war—does not exist for him, because it proceeds from a logical fallacy founded on an erroneous moral perception: "One thing appears certain to me, that, as soon as the constitution ordains an immoral law, it ordains disunion. The law is suicidal, and cannot be obeyed. The Union is at an end as soon as an immoral law is enacted."[67] Here his logic is for once rigorous, and leads him to transfer to Massachusetts alone the hopes and obligations the Union has proved incapable of bearing: "one thing is plain," he writes with the same sturdy assurance, "we cannot answer for the Union, but we must keep Massachusetts true."[68]

Such is the steadfast and proud conclusion to a speech begun by a confession of shame. The movement accurately reproduces Emerson's own evolution. The despairing reflections in the journal amount after all to no more than a modest island. Confidence was soon to be reborn, and with it courage. Indeed, certain of the arguments Emerson would untiringly present to his fellow citizens in the coming decade were first formulated in the sadness of 1851: "America is the idea of emancipation. Abolish kingcraft, Slavery, feudalism, blackletter monopoly, pull down gallows, explode priestcraft, tariff, open the doors of the sea to all emigrants."[69] As the idea of a crusade against the forces of evil takes root in men's minds and it becomes necessary to justify the brutal form that crusade takes, the theme of the ideal America gains in precision and richness; but it is probable that it would not have aroused in Emerson so ardent a sympathy had it not initially sprung up as a defensive reflex of his intellectual being against a threat to its life.

[66] "The Fugitive Slave Law" (W 11.204).

[67] W 11.206.

[68] W 11.210.

[69] JMN 11.406. The same passage occurs with very minor variations in J 10.195.

13

~ ~ ~ ~

A SURROGATE OPTIMISM

IN THE LAST PART of Emerson's career there is a striking disparity between the abundance of biographical fact and the paucity of critical interest.[1] Rusk fills three of six fat volumes with letters written after 1847; Whicher sees that date as the end of Emerson's creative period, the beginning of the time of reaping and garnering. But the productivity of this last phase demands further reflection. Are so voluminous a correspondence, so copious a flow of speeches, simply the compensations Emerson consciously or unconsciously permits himself for the onset of profound sterility? Or can one perhaps see in them an urgent need for communication, stimulated by new social and political conditions? It seems unlikely that the charm of fame was entirely or even initially responsible for the emergence of the public personage with whom, from 1851 on, Emerson was more and more often confounded. He did indeed enjoy his trips away from Concord more than he had previously, and one suspects he had difficulty in recovering the intoxicating richness of solitude; but he was also led in this direction by what he viewed as his civic obligation, in the exact and exacting sense of the word: "when the ship is in a storm," he explains one day to some Cambridge students visiting him, "the passengers must lend a hand, and even

[1] Philip Nicoloff's *Emerson on Race and History* (New York, 1961) reached me just as the present chapter was being written. As its subtitle—*An Examination of "English Traits"*—indicates, it is focused on Emerson's later work; it fills a large gap and opens the way to a juster and better informed understanding of Emerson's thought. The frequent references to it in the following pages reveal how much I have benefited from its aid.

women tug at the ropes."[2] And until the fateful attack on Fort Sumter, indeed until the Union's final victory, he continued to remind his countrymen—sometimes directly, sometimes by way of historical or philosophical reflection—of the obligations incumbent on them and the reasons for which they ought not to despair.

One should not, then, imagine in Emerson on the basis of other people's accounts of him a transformation of social behavior so profound as to resemble a conversion. There could be no second road to Damascus for the author of *Nature*—as he himself admits, almost reluctantly, in a celebrated passage of the journal for 1852:

> I waked at night, & bemoaned myself, because I had not thrown myself into this deplorable question of Slavery, which seems to want nothing so much as a few assured voices. But then, in hours of sanity, I recover myself, & say, God must govern his own world, & knows his way out of this pit, without my desertion of my post which has none to guard it but me. I have quite other slaves to free than those negroes, to wit, imprisoned spirits, imprisoned thoughts, far back in the brain of man,—far retired in the heaven of invention, & which, important to the republic of Man, have no watchman, or lover, or defender, but I.[3]

Even when Emerson engaged in political struggle with characteristic passion, his journals and letters reveal the distrust tinged with irritation that forms of collective action continued to evoke in him even when they seemed clearly necessary.[4] The essence of his nature remained unchanged; at most there was a reversal of proportion between the part of his work occupied with communal obligations and that reserved for the celebration of autonomy and the praise of individual virtues. Here the journal is a faithful mirror, giving an exactly inverted image of things, and confirms this diagnosis; instead of registering as it once had the reservations suggested to Emerson by the very extravagance of his anar-

[2] Retold in Moncure D. Conway, *Emerson at Home and Abroad* (Boston, 1882), p. 309.

[3] JMN 13.80.

[4] In 1853, Emerson expressed his skepticism at Garrison and Phillips' abolitionist activities as follows: "Very dangerous is this thoroughly social & related life, whether antagonistic or *co*-operative. In a lonely world, or a world with half a dozen inhabitants, these would find nothing to do" (JMN 13.281). Conversely, just as he was about to make a further statement on the slavery question, his sense of his unfitness for the role assigned to him led him to compare himself with Hamlet (see the letter to William Emerson of January 17, 1855 [L 4.484–485]). And a few months later, when his friend W. H. Furness pressed him to speak out before the citizens of Philadelphia, he refused and alleged his powerlessness: "Ah if you knew how puny & unproductive I am!" (October 10, 1855; *Records of a Lifelong Friendship, 1807–1882* [Boston, 1910], p. 109).

chic tendencies, it now records his protests against an organization of human energies he knew to be indispensable to the nation's safety.

After the tragic episode of Sims's capture and return, tension in Boston gradually decreased, and the city had no further crisis till the Burns affair in 1854.[5] In the rest of the country also, the tendency was to prudence and appeasement. The publication of *Uncle Tom's Cabin* in 1854 aroused enormous interest; but that same year the Democratic candidate Franklin Pierce, a personality equally devoid of energy and of distinction, was elected to the presidency by an overwhelming majority because the chief plank of the Democratic platform was the maintenance of the Compromise of 1850. This calm was unstable, to be sure; but it permitted Emerson to regain self-control and, once escaped from the intrusive pressure of events, to formulate both for himself and for his public a philosophy to make sense of their recent experiences. It was during this period that from lecture to lecture he polished the texts he was to assemble in 1860 under the title of *The Conduct of Life*.[6] He thus remained faithful to what one might call his alluvial method of composition, which gives the book its fullness and charm;[7] but more than than ever it also consigns the critic to the investigation of insoluble questions. For example, is any one of the observers placed in control as chapter succeeds chapter truer or more central than the others? Does the honest man of "Culture," say, have more substance than the extremist of "Considerations by the Way"? And how is one to reconcile the gospel of success preached in "Power" or "Wealth" with the comedy of the iridescent, almost Shakespearean world of "Illusions"? The fact is that a reader's impression of the book will vary with his angle of vision; this one will chiefly retain the dark images of fatality with which the book

[5] See Harold Schwartz, "Fugitive Slave Days in Boston," NEQ 27 (June 1954), pp. 191–212). Despite a more resolute opposition than the populace had offered in 1851, the escaped slave Anthony Burns was returned to his Virginia owner. Whitman denounced the betrayal in the bitterly satiric "A Boston Ballad" (from the 1855 *Leaves of Grass*).

[6] The correspondence permits an approximate reconstruction of the book's development. "Power" was given separately, it seems, early in 1851 (see the letter to W. P. Atkinson of January 19, 1851 (L 4.241); then, in March and April of the same year, Emerson offered Pittsburgh audiences a series comprising "Laws of Success," "Wealth," "Economy," "Culture," and "Worship" (see L 4.246, n. 20). "Fate" was first given in December 1851 (see L 4.270, n. 98), but Emerson continued to tinker with it for some time (see letter to Carlyle of April 19, 1853 [CEC 485–487]). The other chapters of *The Conduct of Life* were written afterward, in 1855 or even later (see letter to Lidian Emerson of February 22, 1855 [L 4.494–495]).

[7] Cf. Robert Spiller, *The Cycle of American Literature* (New York, 1955), p. 57: "More settled in its inconsistencies than in its system, the matured Emersonian view of life presented a suspended judgment, a calm of soul obtained by the balance between forces, an admission of both fate and free will, of both divine and human sanctions. The strict philosophical mind has difficulty in accepting so relative a position; the literary mind requires it."

begins, that one the Turneresque luminosity of background in which conflicts are finally abolished. But perhaps this diversity is the most accurate measure of the book's greatness; our critical task is to show by what deep movement two so contradictory visions of the world not only are successively summoned to reside in the same consciousness but also become each other's sign and pledge of authenticity.

In a number of respects it is the initial essay, "Fate," the slow maturation of which has already been discussed, that is the most important. In it Emerson poses the central question from the beginning: how should one live? And because he intends to answer the question in entire sincerity, extending the field of his inquiry step by step, the result of his careful ordering of arguments is a search for the equation of the human condition, with all that expression's connotations for a mind like Emerson's of fluidity and radical indeterminateness. Carl Strauch is right to claim that in the term "fate" Emerson realizes "a grand synthesis of diverse elements that he kept in the mainstream of his thought in his richest period"[8]—a synthesis made possible, Strauch adds, by German Romantic philosophy, notably that of Schelling, which postulates the metaphysical identity of human liberty and universal necessity. Indeed, despite some fluctuations, the essay follows the dialectical pattern determined by that equivalence: if at first Emerson does full justice to the limits on liberty he comes up against (the determinism of heredity, the devastating power of circumstance, the statistical leveling of intelligences and talents), he is also quick to argue from our power of reflection that these limits are provisional, that a stoical acquiescence in the order of the world releases us from them, and that finally our spiritual growth is measured by our capacity for recognizing that order. We will have attained our full stature, he says, when we understand that the fate by which we feel oppressed is only the crude mask of beneficent necessity.[9]

The psychological pivot of this reorientation is the individual's becoming aware that we are free, effectually free, even at the moment we seem to succumb beneath "this mountain of Fate."[10] This paradox troubled Emerson for a long time, because he had learned to scent the snares

[8] In his important "Emerson's Sacred Science," PMLA 73 (June 1958), p. 245.

[9] Emerson's praise of Kossuth as a hero of liberty, in a speech welcoming him to Concord, proceeds from just the same sequence of thought: "We have seen, with great pleasure, that there is nothing accidental in your attitude. We have seen that you are organically in that cause you plead. The man of Freedom, you are also the man of Fate. You do not elect, but you are elected by God and your genius to the task" ("Address to Kossuth," May 11, 1852 [W 11.399]).

[10] From "Fate" (W 6.12).

of idealism, but in the end he committed himself to the carefully monitored testimony of his own intuition; and he makes this clear in a remarkable letter, in which the philosophical and intimately lived problem is organized into richly modulated metaphors:

> Friends are few, thoughts are few, facts few—only one; one only fact, now tragically, now tenderly, now exultingly illustrated in sky, in earth, in men & women. Fate, Fate. The universe is all chemistry, with a certain hint of a magnificent *Whence* or *Whereto* gilding or opalizing every angle of the old salt-acid acid-salt, endlessly reiterated & masqueraded thro' all time & space & form. The addition of that hint everywhere, saves things. Heavy & loathsome is the bounded world, bounded everywhere. An immense Boston or Hanover Street with mountains of ordinary women, trains & trains of mean, leathern men all immoveably bounded, no liquidity of hope or genius. But they are made chemically good, like oxen. In the absence of religion, they are polarized to decorum, wh. is its blockhead: —thrown mechanically into parallelism with the high *Whence* & *Whither*, wh. makes mountains of rubbish reflect the morning sun & the evening star. And we all are privy counsellors to that Hint wh. homeopathically doses the system, & can cooperate with the slow & secular escape of these oxen & semi-oxen from their quadruped estate, & invite them to be men & hail them such. I do not know—now that Stoicism & Christianity have for two milleniums preached liberty, somewhat fulsomely—but it is the turn of Fatalism. And it has great conveniences for a public creed. Fatalism, foolish & flippant, is as bad as Unitarianism or Mormonism. But Fatalism held by an intelligent soul who knows how to humour & obey the infinitesimal pulses of spontaneity, is by much the truest theory in use. All the great would call their thought fatalism, or concede that ninetynine parts are nature & one part power, tho' that hundredth is elastic, miraculous, &, whenever it is in energy, dissolving all the rest.[11]

Faced with this text, one is slow to decide whether it is continued faith or new renunciation that emerges victorious. Emerson affirms with all his old conviction the ultimate power of mind, though in his imagination its effect on its environment is purely "homeopathic."[12]

[11] Letter to Caroline Sturgis Tappan of July 22, 1853 (L 4.376–377).

[12] A further example of Emerson's quickness in transferring contemporary scientific notions to the domain of philosophical speculation. The name of Samuel Hahnemann, the founder of homeopathy, is, moreover, juxtaposed in *English Traits* to those of Swedenborg and Fourier, through the mediation of one Wilkinson who was an admirer of them all (see W. 5.250).

That creative liberty which remains the privilege of humankind rather crowns progress than sets it in motion; in the lower levels of creation the law of amelioration operates within the unconscious. Emerson's vision thus becomes that of a world patiently but irresistibly delivered from its original brutality, gradually emerging from the night of instincts, and reaching its fullness at the moment it discovers itself not only as thought but also as power. Constrained to abandon certain extreme hopes, Emerson finds the spectacle of this cosmic surge some compensation and seeks to understand its origins as the explorer adds to his visual image of the ice floe the idea of the glacial mass beneath it.

But compensation is perhaps not the right word here. Rather one should speak of a second manner, objective and historical, of arriving at the same original truth. As Strauch has shown in an article the present argument is much indebted to,[13] to the extent that it was detached from Transcendentalist postulates Emerson's thought tended to employ two distinct modes of knowledge concurrently—namely, myth and science—but without losing its inward coherence. This was possible because Emerson's monist faith remained unchanged. If he had become more prudent, and had come to appreciate the role played in certain ecstasies by illusion, he continued nonetheless to seek for the signs that manifest the essential unity of things, convinced that a perfectly free intelligence would see all the data of experience organize themselves into a coherent beam of light. "Science is false by not being poetic," one reads in *English Traits*, and criticism has used this formula to denounce the reactionary turn of mind it is said to express. But in reality, as Philip Nicoloff reminds us,[14] Emerson had no wish to rob science to pay poetry; he attacked scientists' subjection to the facts they catalog, but he respected scientific discipline and thought it fertile in insights into the structure of the world if only one could rise to "the connection which is the test of genius."[15] His own ambition was precisely to pass beyond the limits of the specialist, to make a specialty of generalities in the manner of Comte's philosopher. Borrowing in turn from the geologist, the biologist, the anthropologist, the geographer, and the historian, fusing together the results of their discoveries in the context of his monist faith, he strove to construct what one might call a poetic or mytho-scientific image of human history, aiming thereby to reveal the complex advances of fate. We are just beginning to see, thanks to Strauch and also to Nicoloff, that the work in which Emerson realizes that philosophy of his-

[13] In "Emerson's Sacred Science."

[14] *Emerson on Race and History*, chapter 5, "The Scientific Sources," particularly pp. 103–106.

[15] W. 5.53 (*English Traits*, chapter 14, "Literature").

tory is none other than the modestly titled *English Traits*. We need not here restate Nicoloff's analysis in detail; rather we shall linger over a concept that Emerson has set at the book's center and that in the perspective of this study calls for considerable commentary, namely, the concept of race, and in particular the application of that concept to the case of the Anglo-Saxons.

Under the influence of Sharon Turner, Emerson had begun to discuss the "Permanent Traits of the English National Genius" as early as 1835; but the process by which the barbarism of the race's ancestors had been transformed in their descendants into "refinement" and "virtue" had remained mysterious, for lack of a philosophy able to take cognizance of the creative power of time.[16] During the ensuing decade Emerson's allusions to theories of race, whether his own or someone else's, remained infrequent. He was gradually coming to see the world as suffused by a law of universal amelioration; but he saw no middle term between the immensity of geological periods and their culmination in the present moment. Only movement interested him; the individual phases, each in its turn withering and falling away, could not long retain a mind as Heraclitean as his own. It was only in 1847 that the journals and letters manifested an increase of interest in the idea of race; and that curiosity by Emerson's own account was to a large extent a consequence of the intellectual climate of the period.[17] In Germany, in England, in America, genuine and fraudulent scientists alike were investigating the rise and distribution of different human types. There was much enthusiasm for craniology and for measuring the facial angles; prognathous skulls were contrasted to orthognathous; and the word "Caucasian" was much in the air, having been applied by a German professor of anatomy, one Blumenbach, to a race hypothesized as the original source of the Anglo-Saxons.[18] Emerson had too much common sense to accept such theories blindly, which were proclaimed as final while founded on data sometimes unverifiable and at best approximate: "I believe, the races . . . must be used hypothetically or

[16] "Permanent Traits of the English National Genius" (EL 1.242).

[17] In an 1847 lecture on the superlative given in Manchester, Emerson classifies the various intentions or attitudes of thought that are expressed by that grammatical form by reference to racial criteria, and in so doing uncharacteristically claims the patronage of contemporary opinion: "The attention of Scholars has been much drawn, of late, to the study of races" (H.199.12).

[18] There are interesting details about the vogue of this idea in the unjustly unpublished thesis of Thomas Franck Gossett, "The Idea of Anglo-Saxon Superiority in American Thought" (University of Minnesota, 1953). The American Immigration Service still uses forms with the word "Caucasian" on them; clearly the pseudo-scientific vocabulary of the mid-nineteenth century is holding its own.

temporarily," he wrote in his journal after reading an article by Renan in opposition to the theories generally accepted in England and America,

> as we do by the Linnaean classification, for convenience simply, & not as true & ultimate. For, otherwise, we are perpetually confounded by finding the best settled traits of one race, claimed by some more acute or ingenious partisan as precisely characteristic of the other & antagonistic. It is with national traits as with virus of cholera or plague in the atmosphere, it eludes the chemical analysis.[19]

Clearly, then, Emerson was wary of a theory that claimed more than its rightful share of public belief and risked becoming deformed by the crowd into a modern superstition;[20] but would he have thought it necessary to denounce the error if he had not to some extent thought himself prone to succumb to it?

The fact is that the concept of race had acquired a new importance in his eyes, one far greater than the methodological convenience it had offered him earlier.[21] Now it suggested and comprehensively defined an organic community endowed with permanence, within which individuals not only could control their selfishness but could also learn to transcend their own limits, to savor a duration and power far beyond their particular destinies. Once more the devil of theology, whom one might have thought decisively exorcised, showed his cloven foot. Seeking a fallback position from which to safeguard the essential part of the Transcendentalist conquests, and ascribing to race—to *his* race—the triumphs he had once dreamed of for himself, Emerson resembled more than he knew the Puritan ministers of the seventeenth century who described their country as a sort of post-Christian Israel, chosen by God for the accomplishment of his kingdom[22]—though this implicit postulate of election is the only exact parallel. By his methods and by his care to gather the information that an age of constantly increasing curiosity

[19] JMN 13.288 (1854). The article by Renan Emerson must be referring to here appeared in February 1854 in the *Revue des deux mondes* as "La poésie dans des races celtiques," pp. 473–506.

[20] I borrow the title of Jacques Barzun's *Race: A Study in Modern Superstition* (New York, 1937).

[21] Vide supra, chapter 6.

[22] Here as elsewhere Emerson's thought is flexibly eclectic; a passage of the journal shows that one contribution to this theory of the white race's special destiny was made by the eugenicism of Plato (JMN 13.288). The same passage recounts a conversation between Emerson and Alcott in which the latter, showing himself a far more intemperate defender of racial prerogative than was Emerson, calls for polygamy among whites and castration for blacks!

put at his disposal, Emerson showed himself distinctly a man of the nineteenth century, who if he had lost nothing of his respect for the unifying power of ideas nonetheless did not intend to base them upon ignorance or arbitrary decision. The passages devoted to the question of race (which reveal a consistent concern with the matter, scattered as they are through the journals, the lectures, the first chapters of *English Traits* , and even certain places in "Fate"), thus offer a typically Emersonian blend of speculation and experience, of generalization and precise observation, which though conferring no scientific value makes for considerable vividness and energy.

One of the results of this new orientation—and, one has to admit, not the least troubling of them—was that Emerson now denied the races he judged inferior at least some of the qualities that he had formally accorded them a few years earlier. In analyzing the 1844 speech on British West Indian emancipation, this essay stressed the passage in which Emerson affirmed the blacks' spiritual vocation. In 1853, perhaps under the influence of the debate between monogenism and polygenism—which made scientists like Agassiz the more-or-less knowing accomplices of the slave-holding plantation owners[23]—the journal reveals an altogether different point of view: the black slave is now identified with the worst elements in the moral nature of his owner, and their common degradation establishes between slave and master a sort of monstrous solidarity:

> But the secret, the esoterics of abolition,—a secret, too, from the abolitionist,—is, that the negro & the negro-holder are really of one party, & that, when the apostle of freedom has gained his first point of repealing the negro laws, he will find the free negro is the type & exponent of that very animal law; standing as he does in nature below the series of thought, & in the plane of vegetable & animal existence, whose law is to prey on one another, and the strongest has it.[24]

And lest one might hope this hardening of disdain would soon reach its limit, Emerson returns to the charge in his journal a few days later:

> The abolitionist (theoretical) wishes to abolish slavery, but because he wishes to abolish the black man. He considers that it is violence, brute force, which, counter to intellectual rule, holds property in Man: but he thinks the negro himself the very representative & exponent of that brute base force; that it is the negro in the white man

[23] See Nicoloff, *Emerson on Race and History*, pp. 121–123.
[24] JMN 13.35.

which holds slaves. He attacks Legree, Macduffie, & slaveholders north & south generally, but because they are the foremost negroes of the world, & fight the negro fight. When they are extinguished, & law, intellectual law prevails, it will then appear quickly enough that the brute instinct rallies & centres in the black man. He is created on a lower plane than the white, & eats men & kidnaps & tortures, if he can.[25]

Yet one should not conclude that Emerson is abjuring the cause of abolitionism; rather he is fighting for a moral principle, and what he is first thinking of in denouncing slavery is its pernicious effects on the whites.[26]

Nor, moreover, ought one on the basis of a few lines that Emerson himself would never have published see him as a sort of American Gobineau. He had neither Gobineau's intellectual arrogance nor his taste for systematization. He was aware, as were all his contemporaries, of the astonishingly rapid progress of science; he nonetheless strove to take in and interpret science's lessons with a free intelligence. But he retained too much allegiance to his milieu and race to distinguish consistently between truth and prejudice, between receptivity to new ideas and self-indulgence. If the lecture he gave in 1854 on France (aimed, it is true, at a lyceum audience) were to be published,[27] readers would encounter a pungent but unreliable hodgepodge of observations, flashes of wit, clichés, brilliant generalizations, preconceptions, and unbelievably erroneous and obtuse judgments—notably on French literature. France is Emerson's ideal foil. Whereas the condition of the blacks has an element

[25] "The Sad Side of the Negro Question," JMN 13.198. The names Emerson mentions (the first probably a faulty spelling of Legare) are those of southern politicians from the first half of the nineteenth century. Cabot reproduces these two paragraphs (*Memoir*, 2.429) but does not date them—hence certain errors of interpretation in recent criticism, noted in JMN 1.xxv.

[26] Thus in the crisis he suffers after the passage of the Fugitive Slave Law, he notes in the journal, "the absence of moral feeling in the white man is the very calamity I deplore. The captivity of a thousand negroes is nothing to me" (JMN 11.85). Whitman also, despite his proclamations of universal brotherhood, nourished an ill-disguised aversion for blacks; see Roger Asselineau, *L'évolution de Walt Whitman* (Paris, 1954), 2.188–191 (chapter 8, "Democracy and Racialism—Slavery"). One should also recall with Henry Nash Smith, *Virgin Land* (Cambridge, Mass., 1950), p. 193, that even the members of the free-soil party did not make abolitionism the mainspring of their political program: "Free-soil for them meant keeping Negroes, whether slave or free, out of the territories altogether. It did not imply a humanitarian regard for the oppressed black man."

[27] The manuscript at the Houghton Library (H.202.4) is well preserved, but Cabot's summary of it (*Memoir*, 2.755–757) is as usual unsatisfactory. A better idea of it can be obtained from Lestrois Parish's pamphlet, "Emerson's View of France and the French," Franco-American Pamphlet Series 5 (New York, 1955). See also Charles Cestre, "Emerson et la France," in *Harvard et la France* (Paris, 1936), pp. 41–73.

of tragedy that keeps him from rhetorical exploitation of it, French frivolity arouses and deserves the censure of the wise; at the same time its inferiority to the Anglo-Saxon race is not such that one cannot profit from a comparison of the two races' respective virtues and deficiencies. No less useful as a standard of comparison than as an example of national failure, France is thus subject in turn both to Emerson's compliments and to his taunts; and he never lets one forget the deep reservations the country inspires in him.[28]

But the lecture also exhibits a third tone and makes a third use of its subject; for here more than in the contemporary *The Conduct of Life* Emerson is inclined to amuse and divert . The text of the manuscript is studded with the jokes of an after-dinner speaker, dependent for their impact on the brilliance or the unexpectedness of a phrase but also on the unabashed cultivation of the commonplace. Thus, for example, Emerson alludes to the story that "the Methusalem of French Cupids did not live six days."[29] He also makes use, and not very tasteful use, of the image of Saint Denis stumbling behind his severed head to illustrate the French lack of balance—the French, Emerson says, employ all their intelligence in pleasure, and are giddy and light-hearted even in the most serious affairs. But beneath the spume of metaphor one can discern the operation of a deep and largely irrational antipathy. As with Carlyle, Emerson paid for his dazzled discovery of German genius with a hostility, or at the very least a stubborn mistrust, regarding France. In 1835 he was thanking God for not having made him a Frenchman;[30] ten years later, in writing to J. S. Dwight to decline his invitation to contribute to *The Harbinger*, Brook Farm's Fourierist periodical,[31] he condemned in Fourier the intellectual poverty of the French mind as a whole, for which, he claimed, nature had reserved no very large role in the history of civilization: "But if things come to a still worse pass, indignation will perhaps summon a deeper voiced and wiser muse than our cool New England has ever listened to. I am sure she will be native, and no immigrant, least of all will she speak French."[32] Finally, in the 1854 lecture under discussion, not content to have a dig at French national pride

[28] Certain critics, notably Cestre, "Emerson et la France," and Nicoloff, *Emerson on Race and History* (p. 285, n. 28), have noted that Emerson seems to evince a livelier sympathy for France and the French in his 1848 letters from Europe. It is as if when he returned to America he strove to forget a temporary straying—and to have others forget it also.

[29] "France or Urbanity," H.202–204.

[30] Vide supra, chapter 6, n. 72.

[31] On the four years' life of this periodical (1845–1849, or as long a life as the *Dial*), see Clarence Gohdes, *The Periodicals of American Transcendentalism* (Durham, N.C., 1931), pp. 101–131.

[32] Letter to John Sullivan Dwight of April 20, 1845, ESQ 22 (1961), pp. 95–96.

in passing ("I do not know anything so aggressive and importunate"), Emerson reveals the two linked faults from which all the others derive: poverty of imagination and lack of moral fiber.

Despite the interest he had taken for some years in the new science of anthropology, then, Emerson had not at all modified the criteria that ultimately determined his scale of values. Science could justify those values; it was not to be substituted for them. Should certain irrefutable facts threaten to jeopardize Emerson's classifications, he made the necessary adjustments and set the ideal order on its feet again: Rabelais, Montaigne, and Pascal were judged too profound to be entirely French and became exiles in their own country, mysterious incarnations of the virtues of Teutonic genius. As a German critic has observed, racial adjectives in Emerson end up by taking on connotations so exclusively moral and spiritual that they can be applied to all the lofty moments of history and all the great men that mark its course.[33] Here Emerson's ultimate didactic intention is made clear; and indeed it is present as a sort of embroidery work throughout the lecture, darkening the gradually emerging portrait of France and revealing by contrast the virtues of its neighbor. France, explains Emerson, is superior to other peoples in grooming, in cooking, in dancing, and in maintaining law and order. That is to say that it delights in cultivating appearances, in a refined nurturing of materialism, and that it has developed to an unprecedented degree the arts of hazing and espionage! England, on the other hand, possesses the virtues France is condemned for lacking, and it owes them the role of guide and leader to which recent history had decisively assigned it: "[The French] are inconsequent, light-headed; stung to revolt by some petulance, not marching to it like the logical English, year after year, through sun and shade, and never pausing until it is attained. As far as now appears, on the survey of the world, only the English race can be trusted with freedom. The French have taken the yoke again: Cagliostro."[34]

The final allusion to Napoleon III, whom Emerson detested, highlights the divergent paths France and England had followed since the Revolution of 1789.[35] Once again one had been prepared to believe that France was to lead subject peoples to their emancipation; and once

[33] See E. Baumgarten, *Der Pragmatismus: Ralph Waldo Emerson, William James, John Dewey* (Frankfurt, 1938), part 1, chapter 2, "Philosophie der Macht." Though flawed by its deficient sense of chronological sequence, Baumgarten's book was until the appearance of Nicoloff's the only coherent critical account of the concept of race in Emerson's thought.

[34] "France or Urbanity," H.202.4, p. 119.

[35] A note added to *English Traits* just at the moment of its publication expresses the mixture of disappointment and disdain with which Emerson responded to England's recent overtures toward Napoleon III: see W 5.350.

again the enterprise had ended in bloody repression and the restoration of tyranny. For those who could understand, Emerson argues, the failure of the continental revolutions of 1848, occurring precisely as England was beginning to recover itself and as the specter of civil discord was gradually withdrawing from its shores, seemed a proof that History did not advance everywhere at the same pace or everywhere seek the same ends. A critic for the *Revue des deux mondes* had written as much in 1852, in an article on the United States that Emerson probably saw: "England—and America also, I would venture to say—proceed towards democracy by liberty and individualism; the continent's route is by equality and monarchy."[36] Thus on both sides of the Atlantic people were inclined to stress the exceptional destiny of a race created for independence but protected against anarchy, as Tacitus had noted, by a sharp sense of collective interest.[37] The French critic in his conclusion goes still further: on the basis of the similarities in their forms of government, he predicts that the not very distant future will see England and America united. Emerson had himself given considerable thought to America's situation among the nations of the world, and drew from it alternately pride or distress as he felt himself its heir or its son still in bondage. But with the passage of time, his sensibility had grown less acutely reactive; and without renouncing any of his intransigent practicality ("Can we never extract this tape-worm of Europe from the brain of our countrymen?" he asks in *The Conduct of Life*[38]), he had ventured on a consideration of the historical process by which the destiny of the Anglo-Saxon race, having reached one peak in the England of Shakespeare and Bacon, had now resumed its upward movement on the other side of the Atlantic and was marching toward a second culmination whose harbingers he could already here and there discern.

Here I should once again express my indebtedness to Philip Nicoloff's work;[39] but I should also make clear what differentiates his perspective from the present one. Nicoloff is concerned with a particular

[36] Émile Montégut, "Les États-Unis en 1852," *Revue des deux mondes* 15, (July 1, 1852), p. 324.

[37] Montégut allies the British concept of democracy with "the pure barbaric, German, and feudal tradition." Emerson himself had reread Tacitus in 1850 (see W 5.48); a manuscript note dated 1853 gives the *comitatus* as the Anglo-Saxon essential institution, the one that has retained its power in crossing the Atlantic: "This makes the aptitude of the Americans to annex Texas, Mexico, Louisiana, California . . . that they can extemporize a government" ("Anglo-Saxon," H.202.1). Where the ellipsis occurs the manuscript contains the bracketed words "Cuba" and "Canada."

[38] The sentence occurs in the essay "Culture" (W 6.145), but Emerson seems rather to be using a journal passage written considerably earlier (JMN 7.493 [1840]).

[39] See in particular his summary (*Emerson on Race and History*, pp. 48–49) of the chief points of Emerson's thought in *English Traits*.

text; he traces its genesis and illuminates its every part. My focus is rather on the author and on the situation in which as a New Englander he saw himself inextricably involved. The argument of *English Traits* will in this perspective no doubt seem less serene, less sublimely free of selfish concern; but it will perhaps gain a force and a passion with which Emerson is even now seldom credited.

Despite their unusual vitality and their resistance to the wear and tear of time—which, says Emerson, must be acknowledged by every sincere historian[40]—the Anglo-Saxons are showing some signs of exhaustion in their country of origin. Bacon, Shakespeare, and the great Platonists of the seventeenth century have no rivals in the literature Emerson sees around him; the material successes official voices compete to celebrate cannot conceal the age's spiritual emptiness: "the critic hides his skepticism under the English cant of practical."[41] It is true that a Wordsworth and a Coleridge could rise, and recently, above the bleak horizons beloved of a Macaulay; but the descent the race has made is rather to be measured by the distance that separates a poet from his audience, by the general misunderstanding with which he must now contest. The contemporaries of Shakespeare, Emerson says, were so close to him that they acknowledged his genius almost as a matter of course; the great miracle is that they did not proclaim one.[42] Now Carlyle thought no better of his time than did Emerson, and the proof is the dark chapters in *Past and Present* that follow the portrait of medieval England. But Carlyle had begun in *Sartor Resartus* to work out a cyclical theory of history according to which periods of skepticism and unbelief alternated with periods of faith just as in the biological order diastole and systole succeed each other as parts of a single process. Carlyle, therefore, could reject the present without despairing of the future; a day would come when society, like the phoenix rising from its ashes, would once again exhibit the radiant countenance of youth. But the image of the phoenix is, as Nicoloff rightly notes, foreign to Emerson's thought, in which decay is never a pledge of renascence, and in which the declining phase of a people's destiny leads only to death, and seems a gradual obliteration of their genius beyond which there is only oblivion. England is subject to the disease of age, and thus headed down the fatal slope; no one can stay her course. Some critics in conservative circles reproached Emerson for the presumptuousness of these judgments; but on the

[40] "I say that Saxondom is tough & manyheaded, & does not so readily admit of absorption & being sucked & vampyrized by a Representative as fluider races. For have not the English stood Chaucer? stood Shakespeare? & Milton, & Newton?" (JMN 13.120 [1852]).

[41] *English Traits*, W 5.247 (chapter 14, "Literature").

[42] See the manuscript notes grouped under the heading "Result English" (H.201.2).

whole it is surprising that so disturbing an argument upset English readers so little.[43]

But all these reasons for fear and doubt are valid only for old England. As the author of *English Traits*, writing for a cosmopolitan public and dealing with a subject rich to the point of contradiction, Emerson abstains from abruptly wresting a philosophy of history from it; but as the lecturer newly returned from Europe, speaking to those lucky enough to have been born on the right side of the Atlantic, he makes clear that the foreseeable decline of the mother country is legitimate cause for optimism. In the Anglo-Saxon community, it is America that is the heir, the legitimate son, the inevitable receiver of the instruments of power.[44] Tocqueville had already described the majestic movement by which the new continent's center of gravity was moving continually toward the West; Emerson takes up the image and extends it to the whole of the race,

> For we know that the balance of power and numbers of the Saxon race which has so long rested on the European shore, that the balance now poised over the mid-Atlantic, already oscillates, and shortly must rest on this shore; that the Anglo-Saxon race with its sceptre must leave London for Washington (New York and Philadelphia) for Cincinnati and Saint Louis.[45]

What Emerson is gradually discovering, with an enthusiasm more often than not tempered with critical skepticism, is this new royal nation's particular traits, the raw materials from which Nature is fashioning another masterwork; what is going on is the "Jonathanization" of John Bull, as he writes to Carlyle after returning from a long lecture tour in the West,[46] and he finds the metamorphosis spectacular enough to press his old friend to come and witness it on the spot.

By a coincidence that feels like something more than an accident, Emerson's first voyage west of the Ohio River took place in 1850 in the months following Webster's "treason." He went on the invitation of a group of men from Cincinnati; but the pleasure he took in going on, in thrusting deeper into the West despite slow and uncertain means of transport reveal a freshness of sensibility one has to admire in a man whom the aristocracy of England had two years previously treated as so distinguished a guest. Nor was Emerson at all disappointed by this first

[43] See Nicoloff, *Emerson on Race and History*, pp. 262–270 ("The Critical Reception of *English Traits* in England and America").

[44] See particularly the manuscript notes used in preparing the lecture "England and America" (H.201.1), which Emerson gave in 1849.

[45] "England and America" (H.201.1).

[46] Letter of March 11, 1854 (CEC 497–499).

experience, or unwilling to repeat it. In 1850, he saw St. Louis and the nearby confluence of the Mississipppi and the Missouri; February 1851 found him in western New York, admiring the cool boldness with which the inhabitants of Rochester were setting up a university;[47] during the winter of 1852–1853 he made the acquaintance of the mud of Illinois, into which a man might sink out of sight if he left the path marked out for him;[48] then the Mississippi attracted him again, that miry and powerful stream that imposes its conditions on man and also teaches him the love of the open spaces, endowing his enterprises with a certain boldness and amplitude.[49] Reading Emerson's travel notes reveals a remarkably astute observer, quick to discern the pioneer's dignity beneath his coating of vulgarity, aware of his courage and passion for independence, no less aware of his shocking deceitfulness in matters of business. And already Emerson's imagination was captivated by the western taste for the tall tale, identifying in it a primitive form of poetical expression, a sort of first victory of the mind over the enormous material forces conspiring to strangle it.[50] In a continent still dominated by primal mud—something like the *Urschleim* that in Oken is the universal womb[51]—every farmer is a new Ulysses, constantly threatened by ruin

[47]

> They had bought a hotel, once a railroad terminus depot, for $8,500, turned the dining-room into a chapel by putting up a pulpit on one side, made the barroom into a Pythologian Society's Hall, & the chambers into the Recitation rooms, Libraries, & professors' apartments, all for $700. a year. They had brought an Omnibus load of professors down from Madison bag & baggage—Hebrew, Greek, Chaldee, Latin, Belles Lettres, Mathematics, & all Sciences, called in a painter, sent him up a ladder to paint the title "University of Rochester" on the wall, and now they had runners on the road to catch students. One lad came in yesterday; another, this morning; "thought they should like it first rate", & now they thought themselves ill used if they did not get a new student every day. And they are confident of graduating a class of Ten by the time green peas are ripe. (JMN 11.519–520)

This passage is taken from a notebook Emerson called "Journal at the West," which contains numerous vivid vignettes of the West as Emerson found it in his travels of 1850, 1851, and 1852–1853; often, as here, the episode is given a rough dramatic treatment that heightens its effect.

[48] See the letter to Lidian Emerson of January 11, 1853 (L 4.342–343).

[49] "I answer too swift anthropomorphism with the sensible horizon," he notes in the course of the same excursion (JMN 11.521).

[50] Thus one passage in "Journal at the West" recounts the metamorphoses undergone by the description of a tornado as it passed from one speaker to another; another notes the richly metaphorical meaning of "sucker," used in the West to indicate someone from Illinois: the first colonists there settled in the south, then when the weather was good ascended the Mississippi to work the mines around Galena, then came down again at the approach of winter—thus imitating the seasonal migrations of the suckerfish.

[51] Emerson knew the theories of the German philosopher Oken on the origins of organic life through a work of Stallo's; vide supra, chapter 12, n. 15.

but surviving by strength of wit. Wisconsin is in its heroic age, Emerson writes in 1854 to a number of his correspondents;[52] interestingly, the year before, Carlyle had spoken of "the *epic*" in alluding to Emerson's "glimpses of . . . the huge . . . Republic."[53]

A lecture Emerson gave in January 1853 called "Anglo-American"[54] is an attempt to arrange, or at least to put in perspective, the anecdotes and assessments the journals of the preceding years had recorded, notably those from the long trips west of the Appalachians. As in 1843, Emerson stresses his countrymen's craving for change, their lack of application and perseverance;[55] but the consequences of this instability now seem to him less grim. Recent experience has led him to realize the dangers of ossification intrinsic to institutions of great stability, and conversely to appreciate the resources of a country like America—in which both land and inhabitants are marvelously flexible, in which impatience with tradition takes the form of a series of creative surges, and in which the rapidity of evolution throws a light of unaccustomed clarity on the methods and power of destiny. If the discoveries of modern science ever attract the attention they deserve, Emerson thinks, our conceptions of history will undergo their own Copernican revolution, and no one will any longer seek to restrict the development of humanity to the few centuries separating us from the birth of Christ. But, he continues, who cannot see that the spectacle of America constructing itself is a magnificent illustration of that revolution and can already aid us in shaking off our antiquated habits of mind? "In America," Emerson notes in the journal for this same year of 1853,

> everything looks new & recent, our towns look raw, & the makeshifts of emigrants, & the whole architecture tent-like.
>
> But one would say, that the effect of geology so much studied for the last forty years must be to throw an air of novelty & mushroom speed over history. The oldest Empires, all that we have called venerable antiquity, now that we have true measures of duration, become things of yesterday; and our millenniums & Kelts & Copts become the first experimental pullulations & transitional meliora-

[52] See the letters to Henry James (February 8, 1854; Ralph Barton Perry, *The Thought and Character of William James*, 2 vols. [Boston, 1935], 1.76–77), to Carlyle (March 11, 1854; CEC 497–499), and to Furness (March 14, 1854; *Records of a Lifelong Friendship*, p. 92).

[53] Letter to Emerson of May 13, 1853 (CEC 489).

[54] The lecture remains unpublished (H.202.2), but numerous passages were used in the writing of the late essay "The Fortune of the Republic" (W 11.509–544 and, for the notes, 642–648). Often in the first half of the nineteenth century the term "Anglo-American" is used where we would say "Anglo-Saxon"; cf. Gosset, "Anglo-Saxon Superiority," p. 263.

[55] Vide supra, chapter 10.

tions of the Chimpanzee. It is yet all too early to draw sound conclusions.[56]

But if it is too early to determine humanity's final destiny, it is nonetheless possible to discern the conditions guaranteeing its triumphant progress. The previous section showed how Emerson came to see in physical power the ultimate best assurance of a truly spiritual existence.[57] By 1853 that conviction had taken on the consistency of a dogma, and it gave his optimism a certain dense, elemental, exalted robustness that seemed to anticipate the tone of Carl Sandburg: "Corn makes swine; swine is the export of all the land; and Saint-Louis, furiously, like some Elatis, vociferates: 'Men! men! more men! for I have more pork to pack.' "[58] A good portion of *The Conduct of Life* is entirely based on this brutal faith, notably the essay "Power," in which Emerson comes close to praising unjust violence[59]—on the ground that all virtue is in the last analysis founded on animal energy, whereas from weakness, however civilized, one can expect only subservience and the negation of self. In its western populations—"Hoosier, Sucker, Wolverine, Badger"[60]—America has found new blood to fulfill its youthful vocation—even, if one believes D. H. Lawrence on the subject, while it keeps its gaze directed at old Europe.[61] So when in *English Traits* Emerson compares the rough peoples of Illinois or Indiana with the Germans described by Tacitus[62] he is not simply recording a pictur-

[56] JMN 13.199.

[57] Vide supra, chapter 11.

[58] "Anglo-American." The Elatis Indians were a part of the Cherokee nation and lived chiefly on the prairies.

[59] "It is an esoteric doctrine of society that a little wickedness is good to make muscle" ("Power" [W 6.66]). Emerson draws here on an entry in the journal in which, referring to the physical appearance of the Indians, he notes that the muscles of the legs, constantly in use, are far more developed than are those of the arms (JMN 10.340 [1848]).

[60] See "Power" (W 6.63). In the colorful, rich language of the pioneers, these four words indicate the inhabitants of Indiana, Illinois, Arkansas, and Wisconsin, respectively. "Journal at the West" contains a list of these "Middle West Emblems" with their strong poetical savor (JMN 11.524). See also the letters to Edith Emerson of February 13 and 17, 1860 (L 5.199–200). Whitman also is sensitive to the roughly evocative force of such terms; see section 16 of *Song of Myself*.

[61] See the famous passage in D. H. Lawrence's *Studies in Classic American Literature* in which, discussing Cooper's Leatherstocking Tales, Lawrence defines the "true myth of America": "she starts old, old, wrinkled and writhing in an old skin. And there is a gradual sloughing of the old skin, towards a new youth" (from the edition of *Studies* in *Shock of Recognition*, ed. Edmund Wilson, 2d ed. [New York, 1955], p. 957). On the persistence of this myth in American literature, cf. H. B. Parkes, "Metamorphoses of Leatherstocking," in *Literature in America*, ed. Philip Rahv (New York, 1957), pp. 431–448.

[62] See *English Traits*, W 5.48 (chapter 4, "Race").

esque external resemblance. In the flexible temporal frame of his thought, the inhabitants of the West are to the America of tomorrow what the Vikings or the Normans were to the England of today. History demonstrates that there is no rupture of continuity between the bloody chieftains of the ninth century and the genius of Bacon; to what greatness, then, can America not attain when the same refining effect will have been felt on the coarse and generous natures of its pioneers? The comparison defines the book's didactic purpose; addressing himself more particularly to his compatriots than he may seem to, Emerson is inviting them to take support from the English example to trace the energetically rising line of their destiny.

If one then turns back to the introductory lecture, one discovers that the ambitions Emerson cherishes for his country's future are immense. Inhabited by "a pushing versatile victorious race, with wonderful powers of absorption and appropriating," the United States will continue to extend its boundaries, will annex Cuba and South America, will turn its eyes toward Japan and far-off Asia.[63] No more than Parker before him or Whitman some years after does Emerson distinguish between material conquest and spiritual liberation; the United States is the hope of humanity, and its triumphs serve the race as a whole. While the Englishman is cramped in habits, which for him take the place of principles, and cannot rise to the contemplation of ideas, the American shares with the German a remarkable power of speculation that affects all areas of national life and gradually comes to affect "the gladiators at Washington" themselves. The government of the United States is thus both the most spiritual and the most moral in the world. It is also the most pacific, because it substitutes for the arbitrary decrees of a tyrant or monarch the decisions of the people, periodically expressed by vote ("every election is a revolution," Emerson boldly writes[64]). It is also the most just, because, to use the terms suggested by an image in the journal, the mountain of inequality of rank has been leveled to make a vast plateau.[65] The government of America is finally that government in which the sense and taste for liberty have become a national passion; the Atlantic

[63] "Anglo-American." Whitman too before the Civil War attests to the same expansionist passion; cf. Asselineau, *Walt Whitman*, pp. 129ff. (chapter 6, " 'These States'—Egocentrism and Patriotism"). Such dreams were, in fact, less vague and innocent than they seem; 1853 was the year in which Matthew Perry in the command of an armed squadron cast anchor very near the capital of Japan. There were also enthusiastic supporters, chiefly southerners, of a plan to make the Gulf of Mexico an American Mediterranean; see Smith, *Virgin Land*, pp. 175–176.

[64] "Anglo-American." The idea was first stated in the journal for 1851 (JMN 11.386) and was still present in "The Fortune of the Republic" (W 11.647–648).

[65] See JMN 14.24 (December 1855).

has retained the more fearful on the shores of the Old World, and the American continent has been peopled by an intrepid race preferring sacrifice to servitude. That Emerson's voice could make itself persuasive and stimulating along this line is sufficiently demonstrated in a letter sent him by the elder Henry James just as the latter was preparing once again to depart for Europe:

> For clearly the whole strain of your influence is to translate patriotism into humanity, and make one feel one's country to be that which harbours only the best men. You are the best and most memorable man to me here, whether the computation begin from my heart or my head, and your life has made clear to me many things in our future—or rather present and future.[66]

The homage is particularly vivid when one remembers that James was capable of expressing irritation and indeed resentment at his friend's stubbornly elusive personality.[67]

A witness of the prodigiously rapid and apparently anarchic growth of young America might, then, if he would only stand back a distance, see it set in the twofold philosophical perspective I have attempted to define. As England's heir, America continues the ascending course of the human race, which has itself issued from some enormous creative evolution. America is the last-born of the nations in both the senses of the term—that is, it is the most recent and is also that in which the evolutionary process reaches its culmination. But on another level it symbolizes the defeat of the evil and dark forces within us. It ushers in the reign of liberty and proclaims the ultimate spiritual advancement of humankind. It moves irresistibly, though as yet obscurely, toward its beneficent destiny. These two interwoven themes, that of the chosen race and that of the final flowering of humanity, find their most precise expression in a speech on slavery that Emerson gave on several occasions early in 1855, which appears to have attracted little critical attention.[68] "As the State is a reality," he declares in it, "so it is certain that societies of men, a race, a people, have a public function, a part to play

[66] Letter of June 18, 1855 (in Perry, *William James*, 1.80).

[67] See for example the letter of October 3, 1843, in which James vividly addresses Emerson as "Oh you man without a handle!" (Perry, *William James*, 1.51). And twenty-five years later, in a letter to his son William, James was still complaining of Emerson's "unreality" (1.96).

[68] The speech has not been published but is preserved in manuscript at the Houghton Library under the title of "American Slavery, January 26, 1855" (H.202.7). Cabot, *Memoir*, 2.588–593, gives plentiful excerpts, but Rusk's biography makes no mention of it. As noted (supra, chapter 13), it is the conclusion of this speech that the editor of W substitutes for that of the Fugitive Slave Law speech of 1851.

in the history of humanity. . . . The theory of our government is Liberty."[69] And soon afterward, defining the proper vocation of the Anglo-Saxon race amidst the rich diversity of ethnic groups, he adds: "that of our race is to eliminate liberty. So, it has public actions which it performs with electric energy."[70] It is not the least interesting aspect of this concept that it applies to a collective personality, identifiable by unique traits, the benefit of a privilege hitherto reserved for individuals alone. It is as if Emerson were restating one of his most cherished ideas, already developed at the time of his ministry, but were now exposing it to a different light, so as to incorporate it into the context of thought sanctioned by contemporary science—thereby manifesting once again that intellectual flexibility that seems to be one of his most remarkable qualities.[71]

But the interval of quiet that had followed the adoption of the Compromise of 1850, and that Emerson had profited from to pursue his thought along relatively new paths, was now over. The 1855 speech on slavery, following the second speech on the Fugitive Slave Law, bears clear witness that the danger was again present. The wind had changed early in 1854, when Stephen Douglas, then a senator from Illinois, introduced a bill to organize the Nebraska territory. Hoping to gather southern votes, Douglas had devised what he called the principle of popular sovereignty, by which the inhabitants of the new territory were to decide on the legality of slavery themselves. But Nebraska lay to the north of 36° 30′, which the Missouri Compromise had made the boundary of the slave territory; thus to follow Douglas' advice was at least implicitly to declare the Compromise abolished and to call into question a state of affairs accepted by both camps for more than thirty years. Douglas himself tried to ward off the deadly effects of his proposal by suggesting that Nebraska be divided into two states, Nebraska in the north and Kansas in the south, so that both camps might be satisfied. But it was too late. Passions had been rekindled; the South could not bear having its rights subjected to discussion, and the North was alarmed at the

[69] "American Slavery."

[70] Ibid. In support of Emerson's use of "eliminate," the 1843 *Webster's* gives: "incorrectly used for: 'to disengage, isolate, disentangle'—hence 'to elicit, to deduce.' "

[71] Sampson Reed's *Observations on the Growth of the Mind*, published in 1826, had already put forth the idea that every nation must take a distinctive and original part in the "regeneration" of the world; see Kenneth Cameron, *Emerson the Essayist*, 2 vols. (Raleigh, N.C., 1945), 1.275, for a transcription of the passage. For Victor Cousin also, the function of each individual nation was to illustrate and vivify the content of an idea. What is new here is Emerson's emphasis on the concept of race: even if a nation has devoted itself, as America has, to goals essentially moral and spiritual, it does so in virtue of a certain organic disposition imprinted on the whole of its history.

resurgence of southern imperialism. "What effrontery," exclaimed Emerson in his journal, "it required to fly in the face of what was supposed settled law & how it shows that we have no guards whatever, that there is no proposition whatever, that is too audacious to be offered us by the southerner."[72] The outrage here acknowledged was to constrain Emerson to attend once again to the present. The development of events certainly justified all anxieties; on May 25, 1854, Douglas' proposal was adopted, and the western territories were abandoned to the fierce rivalry of the opposing parties.

In assessing this situation, Emerson was quick to remind his countrymen of the virtue of patience. Liberty, he asserted in his second Fugitive Slave Law speech, measures precisely the progress made in persons and in nations[73]—which is to say that this world is still far from its perfection, and also that we must accommodate ourselves to the "delay of the Divine Justice."[74] But this point of view, which overlaps with Emerson's general evolutionist attitude defined before, remains just as unsatisfactory as before when Emerson tries to find some fit between the behavior of the North and the moral principles that shine in every human mind. He continued to pose this question of how to explain the betrayal of one's peers and make sense of their intellectual rout in 1854 and 1855. He found no definitive answer; but he did find a tentative one, which he advanced in a lecture delivered at Williams College[75] and repeated the following year in the speech on slavery: that the world, and America in particular, are in a period of eclipse; that the men of the nineteenth century are prisoners of their sensuality; and that they have forgotten the existence of the sun, and mistaken for it the poor wan gleams of their gas jets. "The scholar is worldly, the times are unspiritual, . . . this great Ocean which, in itself always equal and full, in regard to men ebbs and flows, —is now, for us, in ebb. . . . It is the vulgarity of this country . . . it is the vulgarity of England to believe that naked wealth, unrelieved by any use or design, is merit."[76] The French Revolution had already given an example of such a disastrous confusion of values in choosing a prostitute to embody the goddess of Reason.[77] At these mo-

[72] JMN 13.283 (1854).

[73] See "The Fugitive Slave Law, Lecture Read in the Tabernacle, New York City, March 7, 1854" (W 11.229).

[74] Ibid.

[75] "The Scholar, address to the Adelphi Union of Williamstown College, August 15, 1854." The manuscript is in excellent condition at the Houghton (H.202.6). Cabot, *Memoir*, 2.757–759, gives an unusually accurate summary.

[76] "The Scholar."

[77] See "American Slavery."

ments of "total eclipse," Emerson feels, it seems that humanity takes pleasure in shameful mockeries of the foundations of its dignity.

But clearly we should not see Emerson's crisis in 1850 and his distress over the Kansas affair as parallel. Douglas had neither Webster's prestige nor his antecedents; for him to ally himself with the oppressors could only confirm Emerson in his disdain for politicians and restore him with new impetuosity to the militant individualism of the first series of essays. That, no doubt, is why the first few pages of "Considerations by the Way," based on remarks from the journals of 1854 and 1855,[78] recall more than do the other chapters of *The Conduct of Life* the manner, the themes, and even the excesses of "Self-Reliance." In them Emerson recovers his youthful freshness in chastising American society—or rather the "masses," a term which he angrily notes is now the subject of much hypocritical prating.[79] He withholds neither sarcasm nor invective; but beneath this verbal violence is an evolutionist perspective that the early essays lack. The conflict within each human group between an enlightened elite and ignorant crowd is, it turns out, only a regrettable phase in the law of progress: "the mass are animal, in pupilage and near chimpanzee."[80] Far from indulging in the feeling of his own superiority, Emerson would like to hasten the process of emancipation, and persuade his fellow citizens that they can break free from the enormous mass that holds them captive. If he seems hostile to democracy it is only because it betrays its own ends, flatters popular weaknesses rather than opposes them, and practices a fraudulent charity concealing a far more rigid disdain than his own. Till the beginning of the Civil War Emerson's obsession was to form men—to make them courageous and resolute and without illusions—because liberty must be earned and won daily.[81]

In confronting this difficult task, Emerson continued to depend on the resources of inspiration; but he was more eager than before to suggest particular methods and means. In his famous letter to Whitman he acknowledges the "wonderful gift of *Leaves of Grass*," and thanks the author for writing a "fortifying" book in which a "free and brave"

[78] For example, the vivid, disdainful list of useless people (W 6.248) appears in a notebook for 1855 (JMN 13.440). The stupidity of a system permitting two political adversaries to agree not to vote is denounced in a paragraph of the journal for 1854 (JMN 13.304; see also W 6.250).

[79] See particularly W 6.249.

[80] W 6.251. The sentence is taken from the journal for 1854 (JMN 13.302).

[81] "We know the austere law of liberty, —that it must be reconquered day by day, that it subsists in a state of war, that it is always slipping away from those who boast it, to those who fight for it" (JMN 13.426 [1855]).

thought is affirmed on every page, [82] He pays extended tribute during the same period to the nature of women considered as the spontaneous ally of the forces of civilization;[83] but he also reveals considerably less confidence in the creative upwelling of the Spirit. It seems that a certain discipline is taking hold of him, compensating for an impoverishment of his experience; habit and memory, roughly abused by the author of the *Essays*, now find grace in his eyes and become considerable aids in the daily struggle;[84] the irreducible diversity of temperaments and talents having been posited once and for all,[85] one should no longer try to embrace the whole of the human condition; what is at issue now is the more modest enterprise of constructing each personality around a point of strong resistance. The law of infinite expansion yields to a less glorious law of concentration; a knowledge of man and his psychology is substituted, partly at least, for the poetical exaltation of his faculties; self-reliance is no longer the first virtue—or rather it is now obliged to protect its rear, basing itself upon a previously attained "self-possession."[86] Reading the prudent, solid, almost tight-fisted bits of wisdom scattered here and there through *The Conduct of Life*,[87] one wonders whether the Transcendentalist has not been entirely displaced, almost in the chemical sense of the term, by the practical moralist. But other passages of the book are at odds with such an interpretation. Emerson had reached the threshold of old age; and the sense of economy now comes to the aid of a faith made all the more tenacious by having learned to see the obstacles to be passed and to assess the difficulty of the effort.

Thus we see Emerson virtually repudiate the theory of education he had formerly developed under the influence of Alcott.[88] Intuition is not

[82] The letter is dated July 21, 1855 and has been often printed. A partial facsimile is in *The Bookman* 7 (January 1898), 495, a recent and readily available transcription in *Shock of Recognition*, ed. Wilson, pp. 247–248.

[83] See the speech he gave on September 20, 1855 to a Woman's Rights Convention at Boston (W 11.402–426, esp. 405, 409, 416, 420, and 422). It is significant that though Emerson supports most of the proposals the convention calls for (the right to education, legal access to property, etc.), he adopts a cautious and qualified attitude toward political rights. If women wish to vote, one might sum him up as saying, society has no good reason to oppose them; but the fair sex is not to take part in the debate. Similar reservations regarding marketplace feminism had already been stated in a letter from 1850 (L 4.229–230).

[84] See for example in "Courage" (W 7.263) the passage in which this virtue is described as the result of a long acquaintance with danger.

[85] See on this point the unpublished lecture (H.205.6) given in 1860 under the title "Classes of Men." Cabot, *Memoir*, 2.771, gives some vivid excerpts.

[86] This is the title of an unpublished lecture given in 1858 (H.203.7). Cabot's summary, *Memoir*, 2.765–766, is very unsatisfactory.

[87] Particularly in chapter 2, "Power" (W 6.73–80).

[88] Vide supra, chapter 8.

the panacea he had thought it; it often covers a voluntary ignorance and excuses idleness, presenting it in too flattering a light.[89] It is true that he is still severe toward universities, finding them gravely impaired by adherence to conformity and routine; but he now thinks that judicious treatment could revivify them and set them on the proper path while leaving their foundations intact. Why, for example, could examinations not take the form of true competitions and offer substantial prizes?[90] Why could one not accord physical exercise—running, climbing, jumping, hunting, riding—the place that in a harmonious education it should have?[91] As he writes in "Culture," the chapter of *The Conduct of Life* in which he gives a broad sketch of his own humanism—halfway between Montaigne's and Goethe's—men will some day have to replace politics by education if they really wish to root up their troubles—"slavery, war, gambling, intemperance"[92]—but clearly that goal will not be achieved by pure spirit. The fulfilled man as Emerson now saw him would have no less muscle than brain; his force would derive both from an intelligence open to the principle of the Good and from a hardened body.

Still, for a citizen of Massachusetts, to abandon oneself to that prophetic image was to dream, and perhaps to dream dangerously. If the North, in which support for the abolitionists was daily growing, could argue with some plausibility that it served a just cause, its physical weakness was painful to see. One day in May 1856, with the Senate in full session, Charles Sumner of Massachusetts had been savagely beaten with a walking stick by Preston Brooks of South Carolina, who sought to avenge a speech he had found insulting. The other senators, Douglas among them, had looked on impassively. On his return to South Carolina, Brooks had been received as a conquering hero; fanatical admirers had offered him sticks in celebration. Such insolence directed at a man of unusual probity—and one who, like Samuel Hoar, was known to him personally[93]—provoked Emerson's indignation. In a short speech at the Concord City Hall, anticipating Lincoln's own words by two years, he described the fearsome conclusion to which such episodes were leading:

> I do not see how a barbarous community and a civilized community can constitute one state. I think we must get rid of slavery, or we

[89] Cf. JMN 14.133–134 (1857).

[90] See JMN 14.22 (1855).

[91] See JMN 14.87–88 (1856).

[92] W 6.140–141.

[93] Emerson's correspondence contains numerous letters to Sumner, the first of them from 1837 (L 2.102–103). Here as often in Emerson's career one sees the living bond between the private life and the public.

> must get rid of freedom. Life has not parity of value in the free state and in the slave state. In one, it is adorned with education, with skilful labor, with arts, with long prospective interests, with sacred family ties, with honor and justice. In the other, life is a fever; man is an animal, given to pleasure, frivolous, irritable, spending his days in hunting and practising with deadly weapons to defend himself against his slaves and against his companions brought up in the same idle and dangerous way. Such people live for the moment, they have properly no future, and readily risk on every passion a life which is of small value to themselves or to others.[94]

It is not the analysis of the traits particular to each section that is new here (essentially the same account is sketched in a lecture from 1843[95]); rather it is the alarmed acknowledgment that North and South in fact share a common destiny, both elementary and profound. The life of the law-abiding citizen is no longer secure when his neighbor is a "desperado" resolved to impose his own law even at the cost of his own life. The Sumner affair thus continues and amplifies the scandal of the Fugitive Slave Law; moral constraint is now supplemented by physical intimidation, as in the darkest periods of human history; there seems in fact no difference between Europe and America, in which liberty after short-lived victories is engulfed in the night of tyranny.

But for those who, like Emerson, refused to confuse the ideal America with that political construction stained with injustices called the Union,[96] the South's effrontery could only be the signal for active resistance. As of 1856, in the journal, in the speeches called forth by particular occasions, and sometimes even in the lectures he continues to give all across the country, Emerson expressed himself more and more often with the concrete and precise firmness of the strategist. He had very early offered his financial support to the young northerners heading off for Kansas;[97] now, in September 1856, he agreed to aid the raising of funds for that enterprise with the authority of his eloquence. Nor on this occasion did he limit himself to recalling the moral principles that these farmer-missionaries were prepared, if necessary, to defend by force of arms; rather he went as far as to invite his compatriots to form

[94] "The Assault upon Mr. Sumner, Speech at a Meeting of the Citizens in the Town Hall, in Concord, May 26, 1856" (W 11.247).

[95] Vide supra, chapter 10.

[96] See the letter to Oliver Wendell Holmes of March 1856 (L 5.17–18), in which Emerson unsparingly denounces "the cant of Union."

[97] F. B. Sanborn, *Recollections of Seventy Years*, 2 vols. (Boston, 1909), 1.105, notes that in 1856 Emerson gave the Free State Men the sum of fifty dollars.

committees of public safety, and in passing exalted the principle of political decentralization, which had from 1835 on been the occasion of a good many fervent declamations:[98]

> I like the primary assembly. I own I have little esteem for governments. I esteem them only good in the moment when they are established. I set the private man first. . . . Next to the private man, I value the primary assembly, met to watch the government and to correct it. That is the theory of the American State, that it exists to execute the will of the citizens, is always responsible to them, and is always to be changed when it does not.[99]

One year before the war broke out, more discontented than ever with the government in Washington, Emerson returned to this idea; and this time he suggested that post-office head clerks be elected in town meeting and even that the responsibility for maintaining order and providing for local defense be entrusted to private enterprise,[100] so urgent did it seem to him in spineless America to tighten the bonds between the holders of public office and the men who elect them.

It is possible to set this concrete plea for greater decentralization in the context of Emerson's large effort to restore to his fellow citizens not only their taste for responsibility but also the sense of their real resources. Forced to recognize that material prosperity had not brought about the spiritual unfolding he had predicted it would,[101] Emerson retreated inward, as in 1840. In a paragraph of the journal so close to Thoreau in subject and in manner that it seems to have been written directly after a reading of *Walden*, he draws up a certificate of bankruptcy for Western civilization, seeing in it an enormous collective "mistake."[102] The judgment can partially be explained as a consequence of Thoreau's contagious ill-humor; but the slow worsening of the political situation was to make it seem less and less extreme. In April 1861, just as the war was beginning, Emerson restated the judgment in a lecture on art and accompanied it with an oddly optimistic comment on the Union's dissolution:

[98] Vide supra, chapter 5.

[99] "Speech at the Kansas Relief Meeting in Cambridge, Wednesday evening, September 10, 1856" (W 11.258).

[100] See JMN 14.350–351 (1860). A similar thesis had been advanced as early as "Politics"; vide supra, chapter 10, n. 117.

[101] Particularly in chapter 3, "Wealth," of *The Conduct of Life* (W 6.88–91).

[102] JMN 14.66 (1856). Thoreau's influence seems clear not only in the allusion to the cabin at Walden but also in the specific references to an auction and a purifying fire (see the passages of "Economy" on possessions).

> The facility with which a great political fabric can be broken, the want of tension in all ties which had been supposed adamantine, is instructive, and perhaps opens a new page in civil history. These frivolous persons with their fanaticism perhaps are wiser than they know, or indicate that the hour is struck, so long predicted by philosophy, when the civil machinery that has been the religion of the world decomposes to dust and smoke before the now adult individualism.[103]

This last formula well defines the climate of Emerson's thought during the five years before the war—one can hardly call them the last five years of peace. Emerson summoned individual energies to arms and denounced the torpor encouraged by comfort,[104] just as he had when he stirred up the Boston elite, drowsing with immaculate conscience. Even the economic crisis of 1857, in which a portion of Emerson's savings was lost,[105] enforces the parallel with this earlier period. But this time the tragedy was everywhere; and the same harsh tone, thus applied in a different historical context, was charged with disturbing resonances.

It was in the case of John Brown that Emerson for the first time found himself faced with violence put deliberately at the service of a sincere and disinterested ideal. One hundred years after the bloody raid on Harpers Ferry, the image of the sturdy farmer turned soldier (or gang leader, if one prefers) is still present to the national consciousness.[106] Emerson and Thoreau were among those whom Brown's personality and subsequently his tragic fate touched deeply. In 1857 Brown had made a short visit to Concord and been introduced to Emerson. Two years later he returned, aged and exhausted; his eyes burning fanatically, he spoke to the assembled people at the City Hall and showed them the chains used by the slave-holding colonists of Kansas to manacle the hands of his own son.[107] Emerson was so impressed at this rug-

[103] Cited by Cabot, *Memoir*, 2.603, who also (774–775) gives a summary of the lecture.

[104] See particularly the lecture given in 1857 called "Works and Days" (W 7.155–185), which today we might call "Being and Having."

[105] See the paragraph of the journal (JMN 14.171) in which he describes bankers as thieves in their Sunday best, and see also the letter to Mary Moody Emerson of December 10, 1857 (L 5.91–92).

[106] Of Civil War heroes, John Brown shares with Lincoln and Lee the honor of having given the richest nourishment to his countrymen's imagination; see particularly Stephen Vincent Benet's *John Brown's Body* (1928), which the author feared would be "the most colossal flop since Barlow's *Columbiad*" (letter to William Rose Benet of April 1927, in *Selected Letters of Stephen Vincent Benet*, ed. Charles Fenton [New Haven, Conn., 1960], p. 137).

[107] This anecdote too is recounted by Sanborn, *Recollections*, 1.150ff. A notorious abolition-

ged and indomitable courage that he transcribed Brown's argument into his journal with the docility of a schoolboy. "One of his good points was," he notes after the 1857 visit, "the folly of the peace party in Kansas, who believed, that their strength lay in the greatness of their wrongs, & so discountenanced resistance. He wished to know if their wrong was greater than the negro's, & what kind of strength that gave to the negro?"[108] Once more the spell of effective action had bewitched the thinker. Brown had a little in him of the inspired captain, the Yankee Cromwell whom Emerson had sought but not found in Thoreau; alone, or almost alone, in a nation consecrated to the idolatrous cult of outward forms, Brown had had the strength to put his conduct in accord with his principles. And so when the news of the attack on Harpers Ferry came north, and even abolitionist voices were raised to disavow the enterprise, Emerson refused to go along with them. His letters, it is true, reveal a certain perplexity;[109] but in public he hailed Brown's heroic action wholeheartedly and gave no hint that he disapproved of the violent methods to which Brown had recourse.[110] Indeed in a lecture composed during this bleak autumn, called—pertinently enough—"Courage," he comes near to comparing Brown's death with Christ's crucifixion,[111] thus forgetting or wishing to forget that the cross first illustrates a principle of meekness. But beyond the flight of rhetoric—or beneath it—was the stinging memory of the humiliations inflicted by the South on the defenseless North, as badly defended by the idealism of the antislavery societies as by the comfortable and cowardly indifference of the mass. It was true, after all, that only Brown's language of violence could touch such men as the assailant of Senator Sumner.

Between 1855 and 1860, then, Emerson was growing so inured to the idea of a violent confrontation that he was not far from desiring one.

---

ist, suspected of complicity in the raid on Harpers Ferry, Sanborn himself had twice to flee to Canada.

[108] JMN 14.125–126. The passage is used again in "Courage" (W 7.260).

[109] Cf. the letters of October 23, 1859 (to William Emerson) and October 26, 1859 (to Sarah Forbes) (L 5.178 and 179–180). Emerson admits that Brown has "lost his head," has committed "a fatal blunder."

[110] See his two speeches, one after Brown's arrest and the other after his execution: "Remarks at a meeting for the relief of the family of John Brown, at Tremont Temple, Boston, November 18, 1859" (W 11.265–273), and "John Brown, Speech at Salem, January 6, 1860" (W 11.275–281).

[111] "Look at that new saint, than whom none purer or more brave ever was led by love of men into conflict; and death, the new saint awaiting his martyrdom, and who, if he shall suffer, will make the gallows glorious like the cross" (cited in a note, W 7.434). Hawthorne was to experience a deep and almost incredulous repulsion on reading these lines; cf. Jay Hubbell, *The South in American Literature* (Durham, N.C., 1954), pp. 378–379.

This evolution is important in itself, in the history of a mind constantly striving not to be caught and held inert; but it also reflects a significant change in the social and political climate. In 1855, Emerson still believed that the tensions between North and South could be settled peacefully, and he would end his speech on slavery by inviting all men of goodwill, northerners and southerners alike, to join in formulating the terms of a just solution.[112] But as the South increased its pressure—waging a disguised war against northern farmers in the western territories, exercising a decisive influence not only on the administration but also on the judges of the Supreme Court, as the Dred Scott case established[113]—Emerson became convinced that the slave owners did not deserve the wide-ranging indulgence he had so long accorded them. Virulent denunciations accumulated in his journal till the day they exploded in public, precisely in this lecture called "Courage," given after Brown had been sentenced to death:

> the shooting complexion, like the cobra capello and scorpion, abounds mostly in warm climates. It has no wisdom, no capacity of improvement, is a dull scholar, a bad merchant, or administrator—it is only a disguised cat,—puss in boots and frock-coat taught to say "how dye do" and to swear vigorously, but for the rest pure grimalkin still,—small brain, running to claws and spitting. It looks in every landscape only for partridges, in every society for duels; in all personal history, the one question is: who fought, and which whipt? And as it threatens life, all wise men, brave or peaceable, keep out of the way of the spiderman, as they keep out of the way of a black spider, his type; since life is real and rich, and not to be risked on any curiosity to know whether the spider or spider-man can bite mortally, or only make a poisonous wound. With a nation of these, or a nation with a predominance of this complexion, war is the safest terms.
>
> That marks them, and if they cross the lines, they can be dealt with as all fanged animals must be. The yellow fever is only dan-

[112] See "American Slavery," It is in this context that Emerson suggests a plan of compensation inspired by the example of the British West Indies: the planter would receive a substantial sum in exchange for his slaves' liberty, and the North would subscribe the necessary funds; vide supra, chapter 12, and W 11.208–209. Emerson is clearly attempting to maintain an equal balance, to divide tasks if not responsibilities evenly between the two parties.

[113] Dred Scott was a Missouri slave who had accompanied his master on trips to Illinois and some of the western territories. On returning to Missouri, Scott claimed his freedom on the ground that he had twice resided in areas in which slavery was illegal. In March 1857 the Supreme Court rejected his claim; one of the considerations was that as a slave Scott was not a citizen and that in consequence his suit was not admissible.

gerous when the sick are scattered in the city. We intend to keep a cordon sanitaire all around the infected district, and by no means suffer the pestilence to spread.[114]

Composed eight or nine years after Emerson's fulminations against Webster, the passage reveals that indignation raised to a certain pitch could still stimulate in Emerson not only a formidable satiric energy but also a vivid power of imagination. Here as in the Ode to Channing, he draws the references he needs from a savage bestiary; the animals all belong to the inferior stages of creation, in which brutality—principled brutality, one might venture to call it—graphically expresses the failure of intellect.[115] In thus placing southerners at the bottom of the human scale, Emerson was cutting the last bonds of his sympathy with them. The antagonism opposing the two halves of the nation now seemed to him to express a natural law and gave a semblance of reasonableness even to war.

Henceforth Emerson's thought was pretty much fixed in a partisan intransigence, in which a sense of moral obligation was strengthened by a sense of the inevitable: "every principle is a war-note," he writes in his journal in 1859, and "whoever attempts to carry out the rule of right & love & freedom must take his life in his hand."[116] Speaking to Theodore Parker's congregation in 1861, some months after Parker's death, he is chiefly concerned with giving the imminent conflict a justification:

> Here are threats of invasion; they are calls to duty. If a number of malcontents will disturb the government and union of the States, it may easily become the duty of every able-bodied citizen to go directly to the spot where the burglar breaks in. If that is our duty, war, violence can be no impediment. Run all the risks of war: it may become necessary to take life, or to lose life—that is neither here nor there.[117]

It was no longer a time for scruples; and so when Wendell Phillips asked Emerson to speak at an antislavery meeting, Emerson acceded to the wish of the man he thought the best defense and almost sole bul-

[114] "Courage" (H.204.9). The passage was too dated and too polemical to be included in W; but one can find a sketch of it in two passages of the journal (JMN 14.169–170 and 197 [1857 and 1858]).

[115] Thus in "Classes of Men" Emerson describes the "contrary" temperament by comparing it to the snapping turtle, which starts biting even before opening its eyes. Cf. Cabot, *Memoir*, 2.771–772.

[116] JMN 14.335.

[117] "Cause and Effect," January 6, 1861 (H.205.7). Cabot, *Memoir*, 2.772–773, gives a number of extracts that diverge somewhat from the manuscript.

wark of northern rights. The meeting was stormy, as the *Liberator* itself reported;[118] Emerson was repeatedly interrupted by shouts and hisses, and had to retire before saying all that he had intended. But the content of his words counted less than the witness he had borne in standing publicly at Phillips' side. He was now at the extreme point of militant abolitionism.

We have almost reached the conclusion of this long chapter; but because we are after all dealing with Emerson, it still seems in order to furnish the image of the citizen, the patriot, the public man caught up in the whirl of public events with its necessary corrective. In May 1859, hardly six months before delivering his encomium on Brown, he wrote to Carlyle:

> I am fooled by my young people & grow old contented. I am victim all my days to certain graces of form & behavior, & can never come into equilibrium. The children suddenly take the keenest interest in life, & foolish papas cling to the world on their account, as never on their own. Out of sympathy we make believe to value the prizes of their hope & ambition.[119]

Such is the power of Emersonian optimism as stimulated by the pleasantly soothing atmosphere of Concord.[120] And in fact it takes some effort to imagine the imperiously exhortatory orator of the speech on Kansas as being also, and indeed chiefly, the respected gentleman-farmer leading an orderly life in a tranquil setting. Emerson had since he moved to Concord gradually increased the extent of his holdings; in 1859 he was proudly growing the most distinguished breeds of pears there and received chance visitors with generous hospitality.[121] For the rest, he participated willingly in town ceremonies,[122] sitting on the li-

[118] The account of this meeting, published February 1, 1861, is the subject of Rollo Silver's "Emerson as an Abolitionist Orator," NEQ 6 (March 1933), 154–158.

[119] Letter of May 1, 1859 (CEC 528).

[120] See VanWyck Brooks, *The Flowering of New England* (New York, 1936), particularly chapter 23, "Concord in the Fifties" (pp. 433–452), a felicitous evocation of the peaceful small town, in which the shock of national events was considerably diminished.

[121] See the letter in which the older Henry James describes the reception given him by Emerson, "the cordial Pan himself in the midst of his household," on a day in 1860 when he visited Emerson in Concord (Perry, *William James*, 1.90).

[122] Abundant information on Emerson's local political activity is in H. H. Hoeltje, "Emerson, Citizen of Concord," AL 11 (January 1940), pp. 367–378. See also F. B. Dedmond, "A New Note on Ralph Waldo Emerson, Public Official," *Notes & Queries* 195 (June 24, 1950), pp. 278–279, and "A Further Note on Emerson's Interest in Concord Libraries," *Notes & Queries* 197 (August 16, 1952), pp. 367–368. The first of Dedmond's notes indicates that in 1859 Emerson was made a member of the Cemetery Committee.

brary committee and delivering the official speech at the consecration of Sleepy Hollow Cemetery in September 1855.[123] Nearby farmers remained his friends and indeed his models. He had none of the city dweller's amused disdain for country fairs, and when he was invited in 1858 to honor the annual cattle-show of the Middlesex Agricultural Society with a speech, he took the invitation as an occasion not only to assure farmers of the affectionate sympathy he bore them but also to show how Malthus and Ricardo had erred in their pessimistic prophecies; taking over a thought of his compatriot Henry Carey (whom he cited explicitly by name), he celebrated the progress in methods of cultivation by which a better condition was promised even to a constantly increasing population: "The last lands are the best lands. It needs science and great numbers to cultivate the best lands, and in the best manner. Thus true political economy is not mean, but liberal, and on the pattern of the sun and sky."[124] On the eve of the war that was to shake his country's economy, then, Emerson imagined nothing of the revolution in preparation. The farmer's vocation remained in his eyes the fundamental vocation—the most solid, the most honorable and honest, the most philosophical—in any healthy society.

At the same time (and this trend is to some extent at odds with the preceding one), Emerson the resident of Concord was feeling a growing attraction toward the resources of the city. Since 1840, Emerson had at certain moments of spiritual ebbing recognized the need to turn toward his fellow men and to seek from them the inspiration, or at least the stimulation, that solitude denied him.[125] Further, he had in 1849 briefly belonged to a club aimed at promoting the intellectual exchange between city and country.[126] But these fits of sociability had quickly passed; and on each occasion the desire for independence had won out. But as of 1855—that is, as of the formation of the celebrated Saturday Club, of which he was one of the first members[127] Emerson took an un-

[123] The speech is printed in W 11.427–436; it is in reality a meditation on death, and in it one finds the oceanic feeling tempered with resignation that gives "Illusions," the last chapter of *The Conduct of Life*, its curiously nostalgic grandeur.

[124] W 7.152. Originally given as "The Man with the Hoe" (see W 7.383–384), the speech was somewhat modified before being published in *Society and Solitude* as "Farming." The most interesting modifications are set out in W 7.385–393. On Henry Carey (1793–1875), an economist and sociologist whom Emerson admired, author of *The Past, the Present, and the Future* and *Principles of Social Science*, see Kenneth Cameron, "Emerson's Second Merlin Song and H. C. Carey," ESQ 13 (1958), pp. 65–83; also John G. Gerber, "Emerson and the Political Economists," NEQ 22 (September 1949), esp. pp. 351–352.

[125] Vide supra, chapter 9.

[126] Vide supra, chapter 12.

[127] The "Saturday Club" was so named because its members agreed to dine together the last

interrupted pleasure in meeting regularly, and around a well-furnished table, with an intellectual circle of cultivated bankers and lawyers, scientists like Agassiz, and men of letters like Longfellow, Lowell, and Holmes. Though persuading himself that such encounters only "whipped his top," setting it spinning for new creative efforts,[128] he was imperceptibly won over by the charm of remarks exchanged in a haze of cigar smoke; his receptiveness to that charm ceased to yield any energy for literary creation; and the means became an end and needed no justification outside itself. One has only to read the letter—gravely frivolous, weightily jovial—that Emerson sent his young friend Cabot to announce Cabot's election to the club[129] to measure the distance Emerson had come since the Divinity School address.

In sum, then, Emerson had acquired something of the mellowness that sometimes comes with age—as he himself aptly explained in a lecture given in 1860[130]—and that change would be no cause for regret if it had done no more than allow him to enjoy the charms of society more fully; to take only one example, the excursion to the Adirondacks that he took part in with several other members of the club in August 1858 and subsequently commemorated in a long poem[131] has given us, if not any great work of literature, at least a supply of amusing and picturesque anecdotes. [132] But Emerson's strength had always been rooted precisely in his capacity for isolation; it was through his having been able to separate from others, to maintain his judgment in independence of and, if need be, in opposition to them that he had succeeded in seeing

---

Saturday of each month; it was founded by the Boston lawyer Horatio Woodman, but it was Emerson, if one is to believe Oliver Wendell Holmes (see W 7.416), who was its "nucleus of crystallization." For the history of the institution and an account of its most celebrated members see E. W. Emerson, *The Early Years of the Saturday Club, 1855–1870* (Boston, 1918).

[128] As noted (supra, chapter 9), this image is taken from the essay "Society and Solitude." The same argument is made also in the essay "Clubs" (W 7.223–250), based on a lecture given in 1859.

[129] Letter of November 28, 1860 (L 5.231–232).

[130] "We may outlive our faults of temper, and after being tart, testy, uncomfortable companions in all the years of strength, may pass in our old chair-days through the acetons into the saccharine fermentations, and at last, when we can no longer bite nor scratch, and no longer command, we can let go, and keep quiet, and say: 'Well! yours is not my way, but suit yourself' " ("Classes of Men," H.205.6). Though evidently exaggerated at the time the lecture was given, this portrait of a smiling and placid old age is an astonishingly vivid depiction of what Emerson was later to become.

[131] "The Adirondacs, a Journal dedicated to my fellow travellers" (W 9.182–194).

[132] Cf. Paul F. Jamieson, "Emerson in the Adirondacks," *New York History* 39 (July 1958), pp. 215–237. In particular Jamieson shows that Emerson's poem takes considerable liberties with geography. "The truth is," he writes, "that Emerson, surveyor and cartographer of the Infinite, was lost in the Adirondack woods."

further and more accurately than they had. Such was the law of his nature; in this respect age changed nothing, and the history of his tergiversations over Whitman and *Leaves of Grass* is painful proof of the fact. The Boston intelligentsia he now kept company with judged Whitman's excesses and vulgarities harshly, and so Emerson tempered his first enthusiasm even to the point that in his later assessments the reservations almost outweighed the remaining praise.[133] A certain idea of decorum, the restricted product of a class and a milieu, had eroded the vital sense of the universal.

One may object that such an erosion could not have taken place without inward complicities. And it is true, as has repeatedly been noted, that Emerson had had to defend himself all his life long from the attraction—the powerful attraction, as it seemed to him—of a form of civilization more attentive to manners than to reality. But defended himself he had, so much so that the journal of his youth resembles a dueling ground to which the future victor has come to hone his weapons: deliberately recording contradictory points of view, passing from one to the next without any thought of transition, emphasizing oppositions so as better to reveal relations. The vigor of his thought was in large part the consequence of this oscillatory play, which submitted it to severe tension and tested every element of it in turn. The episode of Emerson's halfway renunciation of Whitman reveals that he now had neither the same intellectual elasticity nor, in consequence, the same spiritual integrity.[134] And now perhaps more than at any previous time, contradictions were thick around him to be resolved: America seemed to him destined for a future of unprecedented innovation, coincident with the triumph of man over the forces of nature, yet the patriarchal life of the farmer was still the example Emerson most willingly offered the rising generation; he was aware of an irresistible concentration of political energy at the two poles of the nation, but remained attached to the traditions of his state and preached radical decentralization;[135] above all he

[133] See particularly his letter to Carlyle of May 6, 1856 (CEC 508–510), in which he explains the moral reasons that make him decline to send Carlyle that "nondescript monster which yet has terrible eyes & buffalo strength." The following year he speaks of Whitman's "real inspiration" as "choked by Titanic abdomen" (letter to Caroline Sturgis Tappan of October 13, 1857 [L 5.87]). A number of studies have attempted to trace the murky, sometimes controversial history of the relations between the two men; see particularly Clarence Gohdes, "Whitman and Emerson," *Sewanee Review* 37 (January 1929), pp. 79–93, and Carlos Baker, "The Road to Concord," *Princeton University Library Chronicle* 7 (April 1946), pp. 100–117.

[134] In 1859, with clouds of war gathering overhead—likely, one might have thought, to prompt the philosopher to reflection—Emerson noted that for the past year his writing in his journal had pretty much stopped; see JMN 14.428.

[135] It would be interesting here to compare Emerson's thought to that of Aldous Huxley,

had come to pray for a violent confrontation between North and South even as he was giving hostages to conformity and slackly yielding to its law. In every respect the gulfs between the man and his time, between his temperament and his philosophy, had widened. But Emerson nearing his sixtieth birthday no longer had the resources for a new molting; his thought could only harden, and the war, in its ironic guise of victory, could only hasten the process.

---

notably with respect to the latter's biographical novel *Grey Eminence*. Father Joseph's fault is his desire to extend his spiritual influence by impure means; and it seems that to Huxley greatness in politics is a contradiction in terms, since the nature of power inevitably perverts the justest intentions from the beginning.

14

~ ~ ~ ~

THE LAST STRUGGLE

ANY ATTEMPT at criticism of Emerson's last writings runs up against two obstacles. There is first a dissipation, an extreme fragmentation of the literary material. Despite certain inconsistencies, *The Conduct of Life* has to be considered Emerson's last real book;[1] *Society and Solitude* and *Letters and Social Aims*, though published during his lifetime, are simply collections of essays, without a trace of even the most rudimentary organizing idea. The unpublished lectures written after 1861 are numerous and to some extent original, but have undergone much revision—it may be Emerson's own, in a recasting of his notes for a new approach to the subject, or it may be that of his heirs, cutting and shaping for the sake of posthumous publication—so that it is difficult now, and probably ill-advised, to speculate about their original content.[2] There remain the two sources to which this study has so often had recourse: the correspondence, copious, detailed, and singularly barren in interest if one excepts a handful of letters long noted and often cited; and the journal, equally copious and far more interesting. But here the second obstacle emerges. The published journal is far from meeting current

[1] Vide supra, chapter 13.

[2] The most striking example in this respect is "The Fortune of the Republic," published in the eleventh volume, *Miscellanies*, of the Centenary Edition (pp. 509–544). The lecture was first given in December 1863 but was still being presented in March 1878, having in the meantime, as the editor's notes indicate (ibid., pp. 642–648), undergone considerable changes. Our practical inability to reconstruct the text of the late lectures is one of the reasons for which Whicher and Spiller decided not to include in their edition any work later than 1847; see EL 1.xxii-xxiv, "Introduction."

scholarly standards of precision and reliability. The chronology is dubious,[3] and the ordering of paragraphs is somewhat arbitrary—two defects hardly to be avoided, since Emerson habitually used several notebooks at once—but one would like to know more of the data.[4] With disorder thus compounding the effects of dissipated energy, one is hardly surprised that critics have generally been slow to inspect this last period of Emerson's work. And if one adds that the thought expressed in most of it is relatively banal (the representative man having pretty much yielded to the run-of-the-mill abolitionist), and that Emerson's imagination survives in them only in brief illuminations piercing the gray background of complaisant indulgent rhetoric, one may wonder whether any more needs to be said about this period than the single page devoted to it by Stephen Whicher.[5] It turns out, however, that certain changes—in sensibility no less than in thought—still can be discerned, and they attest to the intensity with which Emerson experienced the bloody trial inflicted on his country; and while similar changes did take place in several of his contemporaries, notably Whitman, Emerson's retain a particular significance by reason of the relation they bear to the whole body of work to which they seek to bring a glorious conclusion. This last chapter will be devoted to an elucidation of that relation.

It was only a few days before Emerson was saluting the Union's entry into the war with enthusiasm. The news of the bombardment of Fort Sumter had caught him by surprise in the middle of a series of lectures (the first of which, as noted earlier, breathed an extreme, anarchic, and almost despairing individualism[6]). Emerson at once resolved not to go ahead with his announced program, and feverishly wrote a text he de-

[3] For example, the editor of J attributes the notes used in preparing "American Nationality" to 1862 rather than 1861 (J 9.460–465).

[4] Thus the observations gradually collected in a notebook titled "War" are grouped in J under a single and thus necessarily inexact date; see J 9.362–371 and 441–445. Reference to the lectures in which these same observations are used reveals chronological incompatibilities in abundance. (The publication of "War" in its entirety [JMN 15.169–233] alleviates these difficulties but does not eliminate them.)

[5] See *Freedom and Fate*, pp. 169–170.

[6] See particularly his lecture on art, one passage of which is quoted earlier, chapter 13. In his otherwise exact and well-documented "Emerson and the Problem of War and Peace," W. A. Huggard errs somewhat in citing this lecture as evidence that in Emerson's eyes war was the enemy of art and civilization. The pessimistic tone derives rather from Emerson's response to the continuation of a dishonorable peace, gradually eating away at the moral fiber of the country. The manuscript is dated April 17; if, as that date seems to indicate, Emerson gave the lecture after the attack on Fort Sumter, one can only conclude that he needed several days to effectuate the conversion of thought that was now becoming necessary.

livered on April 23, 1861 under the title of "Civilization at a Pinch."[7] Like many others, the manuscript of this lecture has been reworked, and no systematic assessment of it is possible; but a note of joy sounds high and clear in it that the previous lectures entirely lacked. In a few days, war had swept away the miasmas fouling the air; the populace in its new unity had rediscovered a sense of, and a taste for, liberty; emerging from its long eclipse, the sun shone more brilliantly than ever, exposing to public opprobrium those prophets of doom who had not reckoned with this upsurging of Providence. In the course of his wartime lectures, Emerson was to develop unwearyingly the theme of war as reconciler and purifier, as testing ground, as the prober of character and the disspeller of hypocrisy and sham; war was seen as a benefactor, to which society owed its freedom from lies and despair and its experience of the fullness of a "poetical" condition.[8] Every town in the Union had felt the thrill of heroism and seen its inhabitants as the protagonists of a new *Iliad*, as simple and as beautiful as Homer's.[9]

One of the better critics of Emerson's thought and art, Oscar W. Firkins, has seen in this attitude the effect of a romantic impulse comparable to that which once made Emerson an admirer of Scott. W. A. Huggard has entered the lists against such an argument, which seems to him too superficial and too purely "esthetic."[10] But perhaps the problem lies in the terms in which the argument is being conducted. The Waverley novels do not exhaust the concept of Romanticism, nor does an aesthetic reaction necessarily exclude philosophical or moral commitment. If one remembers that Emerson had in his most richly receptive period been subject to the influence of German Romanticism,[11] both critics must be judged both right and wrong. In 1861, in "Civilization at a Pinch" and

[7] H.206.3. It is Cabot who tells us of the substitution and also prints several extracts from the speech (*Memoir* 2.599–601).

[8] In 1862, Emerson called the Emancipation Proclamation a "poetic act" (W 11.315).

[9] See for example the description Emerson gives in a letter to Edith Emerson (April 20, 1861 [L 5: 246]) of the first group of soldiers to depart from Concord for the battlefront: "Judge Hoar made a speech to them at the Depot, Mr Reynolds made a prayer in the ring the cannon which was close by us making musical beats every minute to his prayer. And when the whistle of the train was heard, & George Prescott (the commander) who was an image of manly beauty, ordered his men to march, his wife stopped him & put down his sword to kiss him, & grief & pride ruled the hour."

[10] See Oscar W. Firkins, *Ralph Waldo Emerson* (Boston, 1915), p. 140, and Huggard, "War and Peace," p. 65. F. I. Carpenter, *Emerson Handbook* (New York, 1953), p. 149, also alludes to this debate.

[11] Vide supra, chapter 7, for certain passages revelatory of Emerson's early fascination with the idea of organic totality, of *das Ganze*.

a few months later in "American Nationality,"[12] what is affirmed in fact is the vision of a people guided by an infallible instinct, marching to battle in unanimity of heart. As during the French Revolution—and the current political situation enabled Emerson to assess the stature of that event more justly—an alliance has been concluded between the masses and their leaders, under the banner of justice. Professional intellectuals must renounce their claims to be heard over the clamor of the mob; but what does their silence matter, now that Leviathan has a soul? "Do you know what makes the pure delight of the sentiment of the North? It is that patriotism has now become possible. We now have a country again."[13] Once redirected to its proper goal, which is the triumph of morality, the government has instantaneously attracted to itself a wide variety of latent energies, through a phenomenon of spontaneous crystallization comparable to those exhibited in nature.[14]

This comparison once again emphasizes the aesthetic character of Emerson's thought; but that does not impugn its seriousness. It is simply that after a long wait marked by disorder and confusion, the sight of a harmoniously reconstituted nation satisfied the imagination no less than it did the reason. At the same time as it was recovering its organic unity—a matter not of geography but of affinity between the world of objects and the world of souls—America was also becoming a repository of directly accessible and efficacious symbols: "By the magic of a shout and the unfurling of a flag, he who was alone, caring for nobody and for whom none cared, is surprised with the delight of feeling himself one in the ring of a vast brotherhood."[15] The period of occultation

[12] "American Nationality," H.206.9, first delivered on November 12, 1861. Given the present state of the manuscripts, no account of the two lectures' original content is possible.

[13] "Civilization at a Pinch," H.206.3.

[14] During the crucial weeks of 1861, this metaphor seems to have haunted Emerson. On March 29, when the secession of the South had been declared but hostilities had not yet broken out, Emerson writes to the elder Henry James, "What absence of men! It looks as if a single will might be a nucleus that would crystallize the entire population into a cube, were it great and wise—but now the pulverization has gone almost through" (quoted in Ralph Barton Perry, *The Thought and Character of William James*, 2 vols. [Boston, 1935], 1.93). A few months later, in "American Nationality," Emerson took up the image again, but gave it, so to speak, the opposite charge; when the Fort Sumter flagpole broke under the fire of the rebels and fell into the sea, it became, Emerson explains, the kernel around which the precious stone of national unity could at last be formed (H.206.9; Cabot, *Memoir*, 2.738, gives an abbreviated version of the passage).

[15] "Moral Forces," H.207.5. This lecture remains unpublished and was first given in April 1862. Cabot, *Memoir*, 2.786–787, gives a summary of it but ignores the remarks in the last part on the dynamic properties of symbols: "the power of victory is in the imagination," writes Emerson.

was over; once again the time was auspicious for poets, and the gap that had so long dissociated appearance and reality had closed, leaving the imagination free play over the infinite field of correspondences. Several sketches and a few undistinguished publications reveal that Emerson sought to avail himself of this auspicious change;[16] but it was too late. Perhaps the public role into which he henceforth projected himself imposed on his art a constraint it could not tolerate; perhaps he simply had ceased to see the irreconcilable conflict between his philosophy and the experience of daily life. In any case, the poems of this last period lack the force and enigmatic beauty of "Days," of "Brahma," even of "Uriel," though that also was written under the pressure of circumstances. The images are often ingenious—that of the banner starred with snowflakes, for example[17]—but they are not integrated into a larger structure. What is most often in control is a purely formal oratory, bringing in its train a crowd of personifications, allegories, rhetorical questions, parallelisms, and antitheses. Only a reader insensitive to the spell of true poetry could admire these flat cadences, these bright words unattended by the shadow of any mystery. Nothing, probably, measures so sadly the decline in Emerson's creative faculties as does this inability to rise to authentic poetical expression just when his countrymen seem to him transfigured by "the poetry of War."[18]

By a compensation in which one may see a certain irony, Emerson's stature as a public man, an official personage, grew continuously as his poetic stature diminished. When Whitman became a candidate for a federal job, and needed to be recommended to two cabinet ministers, he turned to Emerson.[19] The correspondence also shows Emerson recommending Americans on official business to English friends—and

[16] Indeed only two of the poems, "Boston Hymn" and "Voluntaries" (W 9.201–209), ever saw publication. We know that the composition of the former piece cost Emerson considerable effort; see Carl Strauch, "The Background for Emerson's Boston Hymn," AL 14 (March 1942), pp. 36–47. The second was conceived as a tribute to one of the first black regiments, but no more than the first could it pass as the expression of spontaneous feeling. Most of the unpublished sketches are in notebook EL (H.126).

[17] Cf. "Voluntaries," part 2 (W 9.206). Emerson plays on the similarity between snowflakes and the stars in the American flag so as to make a metaphorical connection between liberty and the roughness of northern climates.

[18] "The coldest of us must believe that the poetry of War, the picture before the regiments engaged of the general brandishing his sword, is too much for prudence, or reasoning, or terror: down goes discretion or arithmetic, and the youth who was lately fresh from a school makes a leap into the thick of bayonets" ("Moral Forces").

[19] See L 5.302–303 (1863). The letter, long considered lost, in which Emerson recommended Whitman to Secretary of the Treasury Salmon P. Chase was published by Carlos Baker in "The Road to Concord."

once, oddly, intervening on behalf of a disgraced general.[20] Invited to lecture in Washington in 1862, he was the guest of several important people, notably William Henry Seward, the secretary of state, and Charles Sumner, chairman of the Senate Foreign Affairs Committee, who procured him an interview with Lincoln. A few months later he was named to a committee charged with investigating pedagogical methods at West Point; and not only did he acquit himself of his task conscientiously, he also—and it is he himself who says as much[21]—derived a lively pleasure from it. We also have the journal's record of the Washington visit,[22] in which his satisfaction at these meetings with the nation's leaders is expressed by the care he takes in reconstructing the sequence of his activities and the uninspired docility with which he records conversational exchanges. One has only to compare these passages—more trivial, finally, than they are charming—with the shattering descriptions of *Specimen Days* to discover that Whitman and Emerson were not living the same war.

But one ought not to paint Emerson as a society lecturer, incisive and assured simply because he spared himself the experience of nights of battle. In 1863 no less than in 1852,[23] Emerson believed that his chief obligation was to reveal to the people the exigencies of the moral law.[24] Who can say whether in his irritation at the timidity of intellectuals he did not dream of playing the role of a modern Demosthenes? His classical training, his love of oratory could hardly have failed to suggest that model, and it is from that model that he seems to take his rough, passionate frankness[25] when in a lecture at Washington to a gallery of notables he subjects the delays and hesitations of Lincoln's administration to a stinging rebuke:

> In this national crisis, it is not argument that we want, but that rare courage which dares commit itself to a principle. . . . The existing administration is entitled to the utmost candor. It is to be thanked for its angelic virtue, compared with any executive experiences

[20] See L 5.322–325 (April–May 1863) and the letter to Charles Sumner of May 7, 1864 (L 5.375–376).

[21] See JMN 15.215–216.

[22] See JMN 15.187–200.

[23] Cf. JMN 13.80, quoted earlier.

[24] This reminder of the scholar's mission, whatever the political circumstances and imminent dangers, was the theme of a lecture Emerson gave on April 10, 1861 to the students of Tufts College (H.206.7). It is also the substance of an essay called "The Celebration of Intellect" (W 12.113–128).

[25] Demosthenes' "realism of Genius" is invoked in the Tufts College lecture (see also W 12.120).

> with which we have been familiar. But the times will not allow us to indulge in compliment. I wish I saw in the people that inspiration which, if government would not obey the same, would leave the government behind and create on the moment the means and executors it wanted.[26]

This is neither the tone nor the manner of a cultural dilettante.

One could easily cite other passages contemporary with this, chiefly drawn from the journal, in which Emerson expressed still more trenchantly his disappointment, his impatience, his irritation at human incompetence and the procrastinations of men in power. The hope of a swift victory vanished after Bull Run, in July 1861; from that time Emerson's attention was constantly drawn toward northern weaknesses. Not the least of them was that he had to cope with the slackness of the national capital itself, too close to the slave-holding south not to have been gravely and lastingly contaminated by it.[27] There were also the war's tactical necessities, which obliged the nation to delegate the conduct of operations to a very few people;[28] the generals were often criminally incompetent, as Emerson straightforwardly confesses in a letter to Carlyle,[29] and the real leaders encountered innumerable difficulties in imposing their will amidst political machinations.[30] Elsewhere, as always happens, unscrupulous men were building fortunes upon universal misery; and to these adventurers, embodiments of the lamentably universal type of the "genteel gilded felon,"[31] Emerson promises their just

[26] "American Civilization" (W 11.302–303). Published with some modifications in the *Atlantic Monthly* for April 1862, the text of the Washington lecture was later divided up, and is printed in W partly as "Civilization" (W 7.17–34) and partly as "American Civilization" (W 11.295–311).

[27] Emerson's hostility to Washington grew with his abolitionist sympathies; see a journal entry as early as 1847 (JMN 10.29). In 1861, Emerson declares that the capital could easily be moved to Harrisburg or Chicago, since no deep feeling is attached to its present location (JMN 15.143). The same year he notes ironically that "everything shines with us but the Washington news" (letter to A. L. Adams of July 24, 1861 [L 5.251]).

[28] See JMN 15.141 (1861).

[29] "Here we read no books. The war is our sole & doleful instructer. All our bright young men go into it, to be misused & sacrificed hitherto by incapable leaders" (letter of December 8, 1862 [CEC 536]).

[30] See JMN 15.96–97 (1862).

[31] Recalling the history and reputation of two expressions formulated somewhat later, Santayana's "genteel tradition" and Twain's (or Charles Dudley Warner's) "Gilded Age," which describe certain oddly complementary realities at the end of the nineteenth century, one may well find Emerson's juxtaposition of the two epithets remarkable. The passage has not been published; it is part of a discussion attached to the manuscript of "American Civilization" (H.207.3) that deals with the difficulties of the abolitionist cause in the North.

punishment, late if not early, but the vigor of his attack suggests that the size and seriousness of the problem genuinely alarmed him.

Still, disquieting as they were, these flaws in the northern armor never troubled Emerson as much as did what he judged the shirking, almost the treason, of England. England recognized the southern rebellion as of May 13, 1861, and subsequently accorded it her more or less avowed support and protection; to Emerson it thus seemed to have grossly denied the traditions of justice and liberty that had always distinguished it among the nations of the world.[32] It is true that the last chapters of *English Traits* reveal certain misgivings about England's future; but Emerson had not foreseen that moral decay would be felt so soon:

> It is mortifying that all events must be seen by wise men even, through the diminishing lens of a petty interest. Could we have believed that England should have disappointed us thus? that no man in all that civil, reading, brave, cosmopolitan country, should have looked at our revolution as a student of history, as philanthropist, eager to see what new possibilities for humanity were to begin, — . . . No, but every one squinted; Lords, Ladies, statesmen, scholars, poets, all squinted—like Borrow's gipsies when he read St. John's Gospel.[33]

Emerson's disdain and distress here are understandable; but perhaps they would not have the deep, inward resonance characteristic of many texts of that period if he had not had to count among the infidels the person of his old friend Carlyle. Such a desertion shattered him, as had once that of Webster. Now during the first months of the war, as the Confederates inflicted defeat after defeat upon the Union troops and Lincoln

[32] Emerson was not the only one to be surprised, and certainly not the only New Englander. Henry Adams, whose father Charles Francis had just been chosen by Lincoln as United States minister in London, experienced the same painful disappointment. Describing himself in chapter 8, "Diplomacy," of the *Education*, he writes, "he thought on May 12 that he was going to a friendly Government and people, true to the anti-slavery principles which had been their steadiest profession. . . . he was, like all Bostonians, instinctively English. He could not conceive the idea of a hostile England. He supposed himself, as one of the members of a famous anti-slavery family, to be welcome everywhere in the British Islands" (*The Education of Henry Adams*, ed. Ernest Samuels [Boston, 1973], p. 114).

[33] JMN 15.433 (1864). The lectures of the period do not at all avoid the subject, indeed they contain a number of violent diatribes against England, the "stepmother" of the young American nation; see particularly the manuscript notes (H.207.11) used in preparing "The Fortune of the Republic." One of the odd results of this reversal was a partial reevaluation of France; see specifically "The Fortune of the Republic" and a lecture on the scholar given in August 1863 at Waterville College (H.207.10).

hesitated to free the slaves, from England's viewpoint the situation may well have seemed confusing.[34] But then the Emancipation Proclamation had come, shedding the pure light of principle over the conflict, and Carlyle remained as hostile and sarcastic as before. The day he gave *Macmillan's Magazine* a short pamphlet containing a parable mocking the North,[35] Emerson was stung to the quick; and yet he had so much respect for his friend's spiritual integrity that he controlled his resentment and excused the insult:

> I suppose that it did not come so much from study of the existing parties at the moment, of which he is badly informed, but from his observation of America and Americans in many years. He is a severe realist, standing for severe truth and justice, hating a superficial enthusiasm and the bombast with which we, Americans, are wont to speak of our country where we dare to—that is among liberal men. You may be sure he separated instantly the talker, from the serious hero who will do all he says; and he marked his detection by scorn, and says substantially: "I believe you have no object at heart, that you are at the mercy of events, did not really make this war, but have been floated into it, and, finding that here, in England, men know a sacrifice for freedom, you pretend to it to win some sweet voices here."[36]

In September 1864, without any apparent agitation, Emerson returned to the divisive issue: ten days spent in America, he is sure, would have convinced Carlyle of his error, indeed would have persuaded him not only that the North served the juster cause but also that it was simply an instrument in the hands of providence: "Our Census of 1860, and the War, are poems, which will, in the next age, inspire a genius like your own."[37] As directed toward Carlyle, the argument was deficient neither in skill nor in elegance; but it also expressed Emerson's inmost thought, with the teleological cheerfulness that increased continually as the conflict neared its end.

If one stands back so as to see the whole range of Emerson's judgments on the political situation at a single glance (those bearing on the

[34] Cf. the faltering discouragement still evident in Emerson's letter of December 8, 1862 (CEC 536).

[35] Called "Ilias (Americana) in Nuce," the pamphlet accused the abolitionist cause of hypocrisy and dismissed both of the contending economic systems with equal severity. It is printed in Julian Symons, *Thomas Carlyle* (New York, 1952), p. 271.

[36] The text occurs in a notebook (H.200.4) recording a number of comments and judgments on Carlyle; the date cannot be exactly ascertained.

[37] Letter of September 26, 1864 (CEC 542).

war's beginning excepted), one cannot but be struck with how decisive for him was the role played by the Emancipation Proclamation. Before 1863, and despite the evident probity of Lincoln's administration, Emerson's dominant tone was impatience, tempered by a vague sense of personal guilt for the country's inertia. After 1863, by contrast, optimism and confidence dominated more and more distinctly. Emerson knew, of course, that the Emancipation Proclamation had no immediate practical effect, except perhaps as a new stimulus to southern bellicosity; but this risk and this momentary powerlessness seemed to him contemptible in comparison with the advantage of which the North assured itself by allying itself with a great moral principle: "This act," he explains in his speech paying tribute to Lincoln's decision,

> makes that the lives of our heroes have not been sacrificed in vain. It makes a victory of our defeats. Our hurts are healed; the health of the nation is repaired. With a victory like this, we can stand many disasters. It does not promise the redemption of the black race; that lies not with us; but it relieves it of our opposition. . . . it relieves our race once for all of its crime and false position.[38]

In extending the right of liberty to all men regardless of color, the nation was finally in harmony with itself, and its soul was reflected in its laws.

A watershed in the history of the war, the Emancipation Proclamation necessarily appeared to Emerson also as a touchstone by which to judge men in power, and notably the president. In this respect, there are few pages in the journal so human, so attractive in what they reveal of repulsion and benevolence mixed, as those in which Emerson seeks to limn the personality of Lincoln. At first a considerable distance separated Emerson from this gangling, awkward westerner, a politician to his fingertips and lamentably indifferent to good manners.[39] But during his Washington stay in the winter of 1862, Emerson had come to see the candor and uprightness concealed beneath the lawyer's prudence[40]—moderation, it seemed, need be no mark of cowardice in a

[38] "The Emancipation Proclamation, an Address Delivered in Boston in September 1862" (W 11.319–320).

[39] "You cannot refine Mr Lincoln's taste, or extend his horizon; he will not walk dignifiedly through the traditional part of the President of America, but will pop out his head at each railroad station & make a little speech, & get into an argument with Squire A. & Judge B.; he will write letters to Horace Greeley, and any Editor or Reporter or saucy Party committee that writes to him, & cheapen himself" (JMN 15.218). The assigned date of 1863 seems dubious, particularly because of Emerson's allusion to a letter of Lincoln's to Horace Greeley; this is probably the letter of August 22, 1862, in which Lincoln declared his supreme political goal to be the preservation of the Union.

[40] See JMN 15.187.

man bearing such heavy responsibilities. The Emancipation Proclamation retrospectively justified all the delayings, all the indirections of the statesman—and Emerson made amends in a public speech, thanking Lincoln for having done more for America than had any other American.[41] The loftiest homage, however, came after the assassination. Shattered like all his countrymen by the news of Lincoln's death, Emerson spoke at Concord while the funeral procession was traveling toward Illinois[42] and evoked the figure of Lincoln with an aptness, a perceptiveness, a simplicity that time has not withered. Perhaps the passion of the portrayal is the consequence of Lincoln's having been for Emerson the perfect antithesis of Webster. Handicapped by his education, by his lack of personal presence, by his long and humble legislative career, he had slowly overcome all the obstacles these disadvantages created without being corrupted by opportunism or ambition. At the moment of trial, he had risen to an admirable height, yet had remained the affable, modest, humorous man everyone could approach. He was the quintessential democratic leader, adjusting his course to that of the people, "slow with their slowness, quickening his march by theirs." As a recent critic has remarked, the qualities Emerson celebrates here—simplicity, rectitude, an almost heroic sense of duty—were precisely those he had always admired in the heroes of Plutarch.[43]

One should not, however, deduce from this posthumous tribute, sincere as it clearly is, that in the end the gulf between the philsosopher and the politician was solidly bridged. Lincoln had directed the war to its necessary end of a northern victory by way of a series of painful inward debates; he did not have recourse to the Emancipation Proclamation until he was persuaded that any less radical measure would in weakening the North only prolong the conflict and increase the general suffering. In 1864, alluding to the history of this bloody time, he was to say, "I claim not to have controlled events but confess plainly that events have controlled me."[44] Emerson might well have approved of the fatalism Lincoln expresses here, but the feelings of sadness and resignation with which it was accompanied would have seemed to him impious. If there is, in fact, one trait that strikes the reader following Emerson's

[41] "Emancipation Proclamation Address." See W 11.316–317.

[42] See "Abraham Lincoln, remarks at the funeral services held in Concord, April 19, 1865" (W 11.327–328). It is striking that Emerson's introduction lingers overs the image of Lincoln's mortal remains in their passage across the continent in much the same way as does Whitman's "When Lilacs Last in the Dooryard Bloom'd."

[43] See E. G. Berry, *Emerson's Plutarch* (Cambridge, Mass., 1961), pp. 261–262.

[44] Quoted in Richard Hofstadter, *The American Political Tradition* (New York, 1948), p. 132 (chapter 5; "Abraham Lincoln and the Self-Made Myth").

course through the war, it is less his insensitivity to the accumulation of misery than his joy in recognizing precisely in the extremity of his country's trial the clearest manifestation of providence. Paradoxically, this fratricidal combat fostered in the author of *Nature* a last flare of mysticism, which throws a disquieting light on certain deep characteristics of his genius.

The outbreak of hostilities stimulated Emerson as it did only because it reawakened in him a somewhat somnolent faith in the infinitude of divine wisdom. In the lectures from 1861 on, he expressed a joyful wonder at the strategy destiny was employing—has it not, he thinks, allowed the South to sustain its bold claims to such an intolerable extent that the North found itself irresistibly drawn into combat? Those whom the gods wish to destroy they first make mad.[45] A year after the war's beginning, in a lecture meaningfully titled "Moral Forces," Emerson took up the same theme again, this time opposing the sovereign power of providence to the impotence of human striving:

> See how we have plotted against slavery, compromised, made state-laws, invented Colonization Societies, proposed Hayti, Underground Railroads etc. . . . but we have not done much. Abolitionists fell out with one another and could not agree. Those who could were a handful, too feeble for action. Moreover the action of the slave's friend roused counteraction not only in the State, but in this and in all the free States. See what a formidable opposition was at last combined: the Church, the Universities, the Democratic Party, the Whig Party, the rich for the most part, and all ambitious young men, who were eager to push their fortune to a worldly success, threw themselves against this philanthropy on some one or other plea. Plainly the man-way did not much prosper.[46]

The war was the cruel but inevitable price of the nation's recovery of moral health. To refuse to yield to that truth was to cultivate the skepticism that had already cost the nation so dear. In 1863, with the war dead already numbering hundreds of thousands, Emerson did not hesitate to declare to an audience of students that the crusade against slavery would have to be prosecuted till the accursed institution was eliminated, even if at the cost of the young men of an entire generation.[47]

[45] See particularly "Civilization at a Pinch."

[46] "Moral Forces."

[47] See "Address at Waterville College," August 1863. It was this passionate sense of universal justice in the process of establishing its kingdom that permitted Emerson to speak in similar terms to a husband and wife whose son had just been killed in battle (see the letter to Benjamin and Susan Morgan Rodman of June 17, 1863 [L 5.331–332]).

The Civil War was thus for Emerson an ideological war, a holy war[48]—as it also was, as has often been shown, for a good many of the North's supporters, for whom abolitionism, long powerless and mocked, had become something of an obsession. But there is more; here and there in Emerson is the hint of a fascination not only with the providential aspects of the confrontation but with war itself in the absolute. "War is the father of all things," writes Emerson for the epigraph to one of his notebooks,[49] quoting Heraclitus and heralding Nietzsche, who also admired the healthy roughness of the pre-Socratics. War restores us—or leads us—to bare principles, Emerson argues, and that is why in the last analysis it is of benefit less to the nation than to the individuals on whom its iron hand is laid:

> My interest in my Country is not primary, but professional. I wish that war as peace shall bring out the genius of the men. In every company, in every town, I seek intellect & character; & so in every circumstance. War, I know, is not an unmitigated evil: it is a potent alterative, tonic, magnetiser, reinforces manly power a hundred & a thousand times. I see it come as a frosty October, which shall restore intellectual & moral power to these languid and dissipated populations.[50]

The last image has the force of an aphorism from *Thus Spake Zarathustra*. As he began to yield to the torpor of old age, it seems, Emerson gave himself up with delight to the bitter wind by which his country was desolated.

Here a brief step backward is necessary to see where the roots of this delight lie. Mention has already been made of Emerson's longing for action and physical danger, for the sake of the dignity man gains from overcoming fear.[51] The great texts on which Emerson's reputation rests, notably "The American Scholar" and "Self-Reliance," themselves represent an oddly aggressive sort of idealism.[52] As for the first chapters

[48] See particularly JMN 15.299–302.

[49] See JMN 15.170 (1862). He expands on the formula in "Harvard Commemoration Speech" (W 11.341–342), a talk Emerson gave just after the war's end.

[50] JMN 15.379–380 (1863). The paragraph is part of a discussion titled "Uses of the War."

[51] Vide supra, chapter 6.

[52] Emerson chose as the epigraph to his essay on heroism (first series of *Essays*, 1841) an aphorism of Mohammed's: "Paradise is under the shadow of swords" (W 2.243). The same expression is used in the 1854 Fugitive Slave Law speech (W 11.236). But it is perhaps "Prospects," the eighth lecture in the series "The Times" from the winter of 1841–1842, (EL 3.366–385), that most boldly celebrates the Dionysian power of absorption by which great destinies are distinguished. A curious coincidence is that in the introduction to this lecture, so strikingly Nietzschean in its tone, Emerson defines the scholar faithful to his mission as a "pro-

of *English Traits* and *The Conduct of Life*, with their eulogy of force—they, too, clearly proceed from the same deep inclination. Disguised in most cases by the intuitions of his philosophy, refined by an enormously wide reading, there was nonetheless in Emerson the germ of a very real desire for power. If for the sake of an alluring metaphysical theory his habit of moral reflection was once set in abeyance, he found himself unresistingly yielding to the instincts of his own deeper nature—as, after all, Melville had indirectly warned him he would.[53] And that is what happened in 1845, as Emerson was developing the notion of "beneficent necessity"[54] as the central pillar of his philosophy. As sublime as it may appear to pure intelligence, the identity asserted in "Brahma" between the slayer and the slain[55] cannot help men better to live together, cannot further mutual understanding or respect. In strictly denying personal responsibility, Emerson had condemned himself to live in his community as a stranger. Thus when the war came, he was incapable of seeing its tragic ambiguity,[56] or of measuring, as could Hawthorne,[57] the complexity of the causes pitting the two halves of the nation against each other. He felt neither the cruelty nor the often nihilistic violence of events, so entirely was he bent on deciphering their ideal abstract significance.

---

fessor of the Joyous Science"; and it is precisely in his *The Joyous Science*, that is, his *Fröhliche Wissenschaft*, that Nietzsche first praises Emerson. See Hermann Hummel, "Emerson and Nietzsche," NEQ 19, (March 1946), pp. 63–84.

[53] Vide supra, chapter 11.

[54] It is striking that two poems like the Ode to Channing and "Voluntaries" (W 9.75–79 and 205–209), written fifteen years apart but both responding to a similar striving for political understanding, should also both exhibit the same ascending movement and both end in an exaltation of the mysterious ways of destiny.

[55] See W 9.195.

[56] See the remark of Max Scheler's that Irving Howe uses as an epigraph to his *Politics and the Novel* (New York, 1957): true tragedy arises "when the idea of 'justice' appears to be leading to the destruction of higher values."

[57] To compare the two men's attitudes, see the letter cited by Moncure D. Conway in *Emerson at Home and Abroad* (Boston, 1882), pp. 273–275. Hawthorne cannot keep from feeling an immense pessimistic despondency. France, he recalls, once declared it was fighting for liberty; and Americans have inherited that fanaticism, though in accord with their different geographical situation they appeal to different principles: "all are thoroughly in earnest," he adds with a tone of mournful irony, "and all pray for the blessing of heaven to rest upon the enterprise. The appeals are so numerous, fervent, and yet so contradictory, that the Great Arbiter to whom they so piously and solemnly appeal must be sorely puzzled how to decide." The only certainty is the enthusiasm of the young recruits going off to war, an enthusiasm that he would share "were it not for certain silvery monitors hanging by my temples suggesting prudence." The conclusion of the letter might well seem an attack directed against Emerson personally: "I apprehend that no people ever built up the skeleton of a warlike history so rapidly as we are doing. What a fine theme for the poet!"

Thus reduced to tracing and retracing the same furrow over and over—though a little more deeply each time—Emerson's thought could in the end receive from the war only a confirmation of its faith in America's privileged vocation. Once his first distresses at the behavior of the Washington government were quieted, Emerson had no difficulty in persuading himself that this time his country had set out on the just path and would not desert it. The crisis of slavery had indissolubly joined within every American mind the idea of liberty and the idea of labor, and in making the connection had established the basis of a true civilization.[58] One should look closely at "The Fortune of the Republic," that political testament in which Emerson sketches in glowing traits the image of the America to come: generously open to the unfortunate, offering to all without distinction of color or creed the infinite variety of its natural resources, America represents "the great charity of God to the human race."[59] At the same time, Emerson goes on, the madness of the South, unleashing the war in its attempt to oppose a law of progress written in the texture of the universe, showed that obscurantism and violence are fit partners, even if the language of the day does not recognize their affinity:

> Washington & Cromwell, —one using a moral, the other a revolutionary policy. The Govt. of Algiers & of Turkey is, tho' it last for ages, revolutionary. If we continued in Boston to throw tea into the bay at pleasure, that were revolutionary. But our *revolution* was in the interest of the moral or anti-revolutionary. Slavery is Algiers or perpetual revolution. Society upside down, head over heels, & man eating his breakfast with pistols by his plate. . . . Thus a violent conservatism is more revolutionary than abolition or freedom of speech & of press. 'Tis like shutting your window when you have lighted a pan of coals in the unchimneyed apartment.[60]

[58] Just before the war Emerson was in despair over the prospects of civilization; now he sought to show that America would, once peace had been restored, embody a stage of civilization superior to any the world had ever seen. Such is in particular the sense of the lecture series called "American Life" (see Cabot, *Memoir*, 1.788–791), delivered during the winter of the war's last year. As it happens, the establishment of a society as nearly perfect as human nature would admit, founded on a recognition of the dignity of labor and the abolition of all legal coercion, was already Emerson's theme as early as "Boston Hymn," a poem written to celebrate the enactment of the Emancipation Proclamation.

[59] "The Fortune of the Republic" (W 11.540). See also the essay "Resources" (W 8.135–154), the central pages of which are taken from the lecture of the same title in the series "American Life." Dithyrambically celebrating the discovery of oil in Pennsylvania, Emerson cites Saint-Simon's remark, "The Golden Age is not behind, but before you." (p. 142).

[60] JMN 15.391 (1863).

One of the distinctive traits of American democracy was precisely its flexibility, its adaptiveness, its capacity to advance in accord with the rhythms of the universe, registering its impressions without succumbing to a fatal shock.[61] The great reconciliation Emerson had always sought between a principle of order to which he was attached by temperament and a need for change enjoined by both his philosophy and his nationality was visible in outline, luminous, on the horizon he contemplated unwearyingly. America was approaching the goal that providence had assigned it; it was entering the promised land of "pure Christianity & humanity."[62]

With the dubious superiority over Emerson granted us by our experience of a historical reality considerably less beautiful than his vision, we can hardly keep from impatience, hardly not consider these last variations on the theme of the American dream as simple triflings, superficial and yet dangerous. Where is the freely ironic lucidity with which Emerson had once regarded the experiment at Brook Farm? And how is one to excuse Emerson's recantation when after the war he asks the poet of the new America to anathematize on all violence?[63] Indeed, as one of the most sensitive interpreters of Emerson's thought has shown, the victory of the North—prophesied, awaited, and celebrated with a believer's fervor—seemed to Emerson the dawn of a new religious era, the last and richest of human history.[64] The blossoming of humanity that Transcendentalists and Puritans had for different and in a

[61] Cf. this passage from the first version of "The Fortune of the Republic" (W 11.647–648): "Americans—not girded by the iron belt of condition, not taught by society and institutions to magnify trifles, not victims of technical logic, but docile to the logic of events; not, like English, worshippers of fate; with no hereditary upper house, but with legal, popular assemblies, which constitute a perpetual insurrection, and by making it perpetual save us from revolutions." A sketch of this theory appeared twelve years earlier in the journal (JMN 11.386), but at that time Emerson had not yet fully worked out his definition of revolution. The lecture "Books" (H.208.6) in the series "American Life" has an interesting analysis of the Constitution, which one might profitably compare with the present passage; Emerson distinguishes between the document's permanent and transient elements and sees the preamble, with its "blazing ubiquities," as the indestructible kernel.

[62] JMN 15.404–405 (1863). This passage seems to have been incorporated into the first version of "The Fortune of the Republic" (H.207.11).

[63] "Science shall not be abused to make guns. The poet shall bring out the blazing truth, that he who kills his brother commits suicide" (JMN 16.88 [1868]). At the beginning of the war, Emerson copied into his journal a letter of Cicero's on the calamity of civil war (JMN 15.171); its pain and grief strikingly contrast with the abstract passion of Emerson's own remarks.

[64] Ernest E. Sandeen, in chapter 6, "Beneficent Necessity and the Future of American Culture," of his *Emerson's Americanism*, University of Iowa Studies: Humanistic Studies 6.1 (Iowa City, 1942).

way complementary reasons (the former bereft of equilibrium by their intoxication with speculation, the latter held inert in the wrappings of their theology) been unable to bring about was again within our reach, more accessible than ever, at the conflux of the two great currents of liberation constituted for the nineteenth century by the progress of science and the movement of history. A man of his time and of his country even—perhaps chiefly—in his dreams, Emerson was doing little more than fitting to his temperament an image in which his contemporaries could, for a few brief moments, find their reflection.

Hence the interest, as well as the vaguely pathetic quality, of this portrait of an ideal America destined to fulfill the boundless hopes the war had evoked. Except when the hostile attitude of England arouses Emerson's pride as an American citizen, he is wary of a strutting, boastful nationalism: "We have much to learn, much to correct, —a great deal of lying vanity. The spread eagle must fold his foolish wings and be less of a peacock."[65] Thanks to the almost spiritual nature of its politics, America is not one nation among others; it is rather the culmination and recapitulation of all nations. If once Emerson had sung with perhaps excessive passion the extraordinary virtues of the Anglo-Saxon, the issues involved in the recent conflict had by now depreciated the value of that concept, had shown it to be flawed by provincialism. Henceforth humanity could only be conceived in its universal form;[66] and Emerson must be given credit for the inclusiveness of his views, because during the last decades of the nineteenth century they were in striking contrast with those of most Americans.[67] Invited to speak during an 1868 reception for the Chinese ambassador, Emerson heralded the influx of Asian immigrants on the West Coast with wholehearted acclaim, saying that "their power of continuous labor, their versatility in adapting themselves to new conditions, their stoical economy are unlooked-for virtues"[68] sure to benefit the entire community.

65 "The Fortune of the Republic" (W 11.530).

66 "When Renan speaks of France, or Macaulay of England, or any American of America, I feel how babyish they are. I suppose hardly Newton, or Swedenborg, or Cervantes, or Menu, can be trusted to speak of his nationality" (JMN 15.421 [1864]). This attitude is developed in "Table-Talk," the fourth lecture of "American Life."

67 See particularly here Richard Hofstadter, *Social Darwinism in American Thought* (Philadelphia, 1944), especially chapter 9, "Racism and Imperialism."

68 "Speech at Banquet in Honor of the Chinese Embassy, Boston, 1868" (W 11.474). This desire for cosmopolitanism led Emerson to emphasize the beneficent result of racial intermixture wherever he could; see for example his comments on the crusades in "Chivalry" (H.211.1–1869). Moreover, the interpenetration of even the most diverse peoples seemed to Emerson sure to increase at a constantly growing rate because of the discoveries of science (the

In this portrait of the human assembly, to which each people is summoned to be enriched by the particular merits of all the others, what in fact Emerson was aiming at, once again, was the full realization of the individual destiny: "Here let there be," he cries out in "The Fortune of the Republic," "what the earth waits for, —exalted manhood. What this country longs for is personalities, grand persons, to counteract its materialities."[69] He is not interested in a vague eclecticism, in which virtues would be accumulated as are marbles by children; rather it is each person's obligation to achieve his own identity by conquest, and America's role in leading humanity to its final perfection is not distinguished from its offering each of its inhabitants a greater autonomy than could have been furnished by any nation of the Old World. "The paucity of population, the vast extent of territory, the solitude of each family & each man, allow some approximation to the result that every citizen has a religion of his own, —is a church by himself, —& worships & speculates in a new quite independent fashion."[70] Thus in its last phase Emerson's thought experienced a curious resurgence of Transcendentalism, which is most clearly indicated in his two speeches to the Free Religious Association, in 1867 and 1869.[71] The moral sentiment remained the link between man and divinity, the source of all progress and of all profound life, provided one yield to it without seeking to direct it;[72] it was at the strategic center of both speeches just as once it had been the moving force behind the Divinity School address. But the obstacle Emerson's earlier emancipatory passion had run up against no longer existed. Purified by the war, restored to the straight and narrow road of the ideal, America had in a single gesture freed itself of Europe and consecrated itself to the service of liberty. It had become the political projection of the highest human ambitions and had given them a new attractive power; its new mission was to demonstrate that morality is the only thing necessary to the success of a government.[73] The Jeffersonianism

---

steamship, the telegraph etc.); see the manuscript notes assembled for the lecture "Natural Religion" (H.211.9–1869).

[69] W 11.535.

[70] JMN 16.211.

[71] See "Remarks at the Meeting for Organizing the Free Religious Association, Boston, May 30, 1867" (W 11.475–481) and "Speech at the Second Annual Meeting of the Free Religious Association, at Tremont Temple, Friday, May 28, 1869" (W 11.483–491).

[72] When in 1871 Bret Harte disputed in Emerson's presence the optimistic theory the latter had expounded in "Civilization" (W 8.21) and asserted that in fact the West had been settled by unscrupulous speculators and prostitutes, Emerson contented himself with replying that he himself spoke as the son of a pioneer and "knew on good grounds the resistless culture that religion effects" (JMN 16.247).

[73] See "American Politics" (JMN 16.9).

of the essay "Politics," born of a tenacious distrust of power, was here less denied than passed over. The goals served by the state were no longer incompatible with the demands of the moral sense; indeed, by the only acceptable definition of the word democracy, they had become indistinguishable from them.[74]

Emerson's biographers have discretely noted the sluggishness, almost the torpor that imperceptibly crept over his thought from 1865 on—considerably earlier, one should note, than the onset of senility. It is difficult not to agree with Whicher that the chief factor in this premature decline was the war.[75] Not only did the war put Emerson's moral idealism to a severe test, compelling it to accept disturbing allies if it was to survive; in Emerson's eyes the war became nearly identical with the grand cosmic operation of providence, so that when the north had won he found himself incapable of recovering his independence of judgment. With its hopes too abundantly gratified, his thought could not resist the illusion of security; it relaxed, and as it were withdrew itself from service.[76] The few criticisms Emerson made of his country subsequently do not at all suggest the cynical and brutal political atmosphere of Reconstruction;[77] confronted with the emergence of that powerful class of schemers and speculators that was to impress its sinister coloring on the last decades of the century, Emerson immediately minimized its threat by asserting that universal law, and in particular

[74] Vide supra, chapter 10.

[75] See *Freedom and Fate*, p. 170.

[76] One of the most interesting comments we have along this line (and one that happily contrasts with the unqualified encomia offered to the aging Concord sage throughout America) is that which the young Charles Eliot Norton recorded in his journal in 1873, after a transatlantic crossing in Emerson's company: "Emerson was the greatest talker in the ship's company. He talked with all men, and yet was fresh and zealous for talk at night. His serene sweetness, the pure whiteness of his soul, the reflection of his soul in his face, were never more appparent to me; but never before in intercourse with him had I been so impressed with the limits of his mind. His optimistic philosophy had hardened into a creed, with the usual effects of a creed in closing the avenues of truth. He can accept nothing as fact that tells against his dogma. His optimism becomes a bigotry, and, though of a nobler type than the common American conceit of the preemineent excellence of American things as they are, has hardly less of the quality of fatalism. To him this is the best of all possible worlds, and the best of all possible times" (*Letters of Charles Eliot Norton*, 2 vols. [London, 1913] 1.503–504).

[77] He acknowledges, for example, that the war has not led to the "great expansion" he hoped for; see JMN 15.77–78 (November 5, 1865) and the letter to Carlyle of January 7, 1866 (CEC 546–548). He recognizes, though grudgingly, the fact of grave political scandals in the state and city of New York; see the letter to Carlyle of January 1871 (L 6.97–98). Chiefly he deplores the absence of competent and courageous men in the influential circles in Washington; he is thus led to press Wendell Phillips to run for election in 1866 (see his letter of September 23, 1866, printed in William White, "Thirty-Three Unpublished Letters of Ralph Waldo Emerson," AL 33 [May 1961], p. 172). As it happened, Phillips refused.

the law of death, will make quick work of any excessive vagaries of fortune.[78] If one declines to measure time by Emerson's geological scale, one has to admit that such arguments to some extent justify Emerson's tenacious reputation for facile optimism. By an unfortunate coincidence—from which other authors also have suffered—much renown came to him in these last years of his life, with his genius only a shadow of itself; and it is too often the remarks of an old, weakened man that his undiscerning admirers strove to propagate in their articles and books.[79]

The end of Emerson's career, as poor in genuine literary production as it was rich in social activity, in travel, and in honor, can interest only the biographer.[80] The one area in which his thought was vigorously exercised was that of education. Elected an overseer of Harvard in 1867, he took a lively interest in the reforms proposed by a new generation of educators who made no secret of their sympathy with his ideas,[81] and thus contributed to shaping a course of study that was to remain in force for at least half a century. As is well known, old age treated Emerson kindly. This was, one may say, the last gift of providence; but like most of those he had received, he knew how to acknowledge it.

> Old age brings along with its uglinesses the comfort that you will soon be out of it, —which ought to be a substantial relief to such discontented pendulums as we are. To be out of the war, out of debt, out of the drouth, out of the blues, out of the dentist's hands, out of the second thoughts, mortifications & remorses that inflict such twinges & shooting pains, —out of the next winter, & the high prices, & company below your ambition, —surely these are soothing hints.[82]

By a meaningful paradox, only in addressing the miseries of age could Emerson now recover the grace and freshness of his youthful utterance.

[78] See JMN 16.87 (1868).

[79] Cf. for example J. B. Thayer, *A Western Journey with Mr. Emerson* (Boston, 1884), and Charles J. Woodberry, *Talks with Ralph Waldo Emerson* (London, 1890). One thinks necessarily of Whitman, also a victim in his old age of clumsy hagiography, though unlike Emerson he contributed to it.

[80] See the last three chapters, admirably exact and full, of Rusk's *Life*.

[81] Charles W. Eliot, the president of Harvard who promulgated the elective system, often acknowledged that the influence of Emerson's thought on him had been decisive; see H. C. Carpenter, "Emerson, Eliot, and the Elective System," NEQ 24 (March 1951), pp. 13–34.

[82] JMN 15.428 (1864). The essay "Old Age" (W 7.313–336), probably composed late in 1861, might for the smiling and serene wisdom expressed in it be quoted here in its entirety.

BIBLIOGRAPHY OF EMERSON'S WRITINGS

ONE SHOULD distinguish between Emerson's *works*, the texts intended for the public, and his journals and letters. His poetry in some sense occupies an intermediate position, since not all the poems we have were intended for publication; for reasons of convenience they are here joined with the former group of writings.

PUBLISHED TEXTS

1. Works

When completed, the standard edition will be *The Collected Works of Ralph Waldo Emerson*, ed. Alfred R. Ferguson et al. (Cambridge, Mass., 1971–). As of the moment, the most comprehensive collection of Emerson's works is still the Centenary Edition: *The Complete Works of Ralph Waldo Emerson*, 12 vols. (Boston 1903–1904); it has valuable notes, and the last volume contains a general index.

To it should be added the following:

Uncollected Writings: Essays, Addresses, Poems, Reviews and Letters by Ralph Waldo Emerson. ed. Charles Bigelow (New York, 1912); fifty-four pieces, mostly short, many taken from the *Dial*.

Emerson, Essays and Lectures, ed. Joel Porte (New York, 1983); the sermon on the Lord's Supper and all of Emerson's signed or identified contributions to the *Dial*.

Also, in order of composition:

Two of Emerson's college themes: *Two Unpublished Essays: "The Character of Socrates," "The Present State of Ethical Philosophy,"* ed. Edward Everett Hale (Boston, 1896).

An early poem: " *'Indian Superstition,'* " *with a Dissertation on Emerson's Orientalism at Harvard*, ed. Kenneth Cameron (Hanover, N.H., 1954).

"Thoughts on the Religion of the Middle Ages," *The Christian Disciple* 4 (November–December 1822), pp. 401–407; unsigned.

Young Emerson Speaks, ed. Arthur Cushman McGiffert, Jr. (Boston, 1938); a selection of twenty-five sermons.

Sermon on the Death of George Adams Sampson, 1834 (Boston, 1903).

The Early Lectures of Ralph Waldo Emerson, ed. Stephen Whicher and Robert Spiller, 3 vols. (Cambridge, Mass., 1959–1972).

"Phi-Beta-Kappa Poem," 1834, ed. Carl Strauch, *New England Quarterly* 23 (March 1950), pp. 65–90.

Preface to Thomas Carlyle, *Sartor Resartus* (Boston, 1836).

Preface to Thomas Carlyle, *Critical and Miscellaneous Essays* (Boston, 1838).

Numerous unsigned contributions to the *Dial*, identified by G. W. Cooke in *The Journal of Speculative Philosophy* 19 (July 1885), pp. 261–265. Cabot, *Memoir*, 2.695–696 (Appendix C), gives a slightly different list. The copy of the *Dial* in the British Museum has marginal annotations in Emerson's hand verifying these identifications; the poems and reviews, however, have for the most part not been authoritatively attributed.

Poem: "The Skeptic," 1842, in Carl Strauch, "The Importance of Emerson's Skeptical Mood," *Harvard Library Bulletin* 11 (1957), 117–141.

Poem: "New England Capitalist," 1843, ed. Carl Strauch, *Harvard Library Bulletin* 10 (1956), pp. 245–253.

Dante's "Vita Nuova" Translated by Ralph Waldo Emerson, ed. J. Chesley Mathews (Chapel Hill, 1960).

Memoirs of Margaret Fuller Ossoli, 2 vols. (Boston, 1852); a collective work, of which Emerson wrote 1.199–351.

Poem: "To Lowell, on his 40th Birthday," 1859, *The Century* 47 (November 1893), pp. 3–4.

"Saadi," preface to *The Gulistan, or Rose-Garden*, trans. Francis Gladwin (Boston, 1865); also in *Atlantic Monthly* 14 (July 1864), pp. 33–37.

Address given in New York for the Pilgrim Celebration, 1870; in *The New England Society Orations*, ed. Cephas Brainerd and Evelyn Brainerd, 2 vols. (New York, 1901), 2.371–396.

Address for the hundredth anniversary of the "Concord Fight," April 19, 1875; in G. W. Cooke, *Ralph Waldo Emerson: His Life, Writings and Philosophy* (Boston, 1881), pp. 182–183.

2. *Journal*

The standard edition is now the magisterial *Journals and Miscellaneous Notebooks of Ralph Waldo Emerson*, ed. William H. Gilman et al., 16 vols. (Cambridge, Mass., 1960–1982). This work has largely supplanted *The Journals of Ralph Waldo Emerson*, ed. Edward Waldo Emerson and Waldo Emerson Forbes, 10 vols. (Boston, 1909–1914), though the latter occasionally prints texts (for example, letters to Mary Moody Emerson) not included in the former.

3. *Letters.*

The chief collection is *The Letters of Ralph Waldo Emerson*, ed. Ralph L. Rusk, 6 vols. (New York, 1939). It contains some two thousand letters not previously printed, and in addition corrects numerous faulty readings in previous transcriptions and includes in chronological sequence an account of all the letters Rusk had established the existence of but not been able to recover.

To Rusk's work should be added the following:

The Correspondence of Emerson and Carlyle, ed. Joseph Slater (New York, 1964).

"The Emerson–Thoreau Correspondence," ed. Franklin Benjamin Sanborn, *Atlantic Monthly* 69 (1892), pp. 577–596 and 736–753.

A Correspondence Between John Sterling and Ralph Waldo Emerson, ed. Edward Waldo Emerson (Boston, 1897).

Letters from Ralph Waldo Emerson to a Friend, ed. Charles Eliot Norton (Boston, 1899).

"Correspondence Between Ralph Waldo Emerson and Hermann Grimm," ed. Frederick W. Holls, *Atlantic Monthly* 91 (1903), pp. 467–479.

Records of a Lifelong Friendship, 1807–1882: Ralph Waldo Emerson and William Henry Furness, ed. H. H. Furness (Boston, 1910).

Emerson–Clough Letters, ed. Howard F. Lowry and Ralph L. Rusk (Cleveland, 1934).

The correspondence between Emerson and Henry James, Sr., in Ralph Barton Perry, *The Thought and Character of William James*, 2 vols. (Boston, 1935), is scattered through chapters 3–5 of volume 1.

We should note also some smaller collections; such will doubtless continue to be published for some time:

A letter to Mrs. Drury, ed. B. D. Simison, *Modern Language Notes* 55 (June 1940), p. 427.

"A Sheaf of Emerson Letters," ed. Kenneth Cameron, *American Literature* 24 (January 1953).

"Five Emerson Letters," ed. Howard M. Fisk, Jr., *American Literature* XXVII, March 1955).

"More Uncollected Emerson Leters," ed. Walter Harding, *Emerson Society Quarterly* 13 (1958), p. 4.

"A Bundle of Emerson Letters," ed. Kenneth Cameron, *Emerson Society Quarterly* 22 (1961), p. 1.

"Thirty-Three Unpublished Letters of Ralph Waldo Emerson," ed. William White, *American Literature* 33 (May 1961).

Manuscripts

Aside from the letters, most of the manuscripts are in the Houghton Library of Harvard University.

1. Works
(chiefly the poems, sermons, and lectures)

Carl Strauch has been working for some years on a comprehensive edition of Emerson's poems.

Arthur McGiffert, *Young Emerson Speaks*, pp. 263–271, gives a list of 173 sermons in manuscript; to this should be added at least one, not dated, "The Freedom of Enquiry" (H.387), and some fragments of varied length and importance collected in a notebook titled "Sermons and Journals" (H.21A—Cabot's TUV). Of all these less than thirty have been published. The manuscripts are mostly in excellent condition and have been carefully cataloged and labeled; a complete edition would not, it seems, be an insuperably difficult task.

The situation regarding the lectures is very different. The manuscripts up until seven or eight years after Emerson left his church are in reasonably good condition. After that time, however, difficulties both of transcription and of interpretation are occasioned both by Emerson's countless revisions and by those of his posthumous editors, and the difficulties only increase from year to year. It is this consideration that led the editors to limit *The Early Lectures* to the years between 1832 and 1842 (see EL 1.xiii–xiv).

Cabot, *Memoir*, 2.710–803 (Appendix F) gives a chronological list of Emerson's lectures and addresses through his career. The brief résumé following each title is composed of separate passages selected from the manuscripts; it is not, that is, a summary of the work, and does not give an accurate idea of the work's content.

In some cases it has been possible to work from newspaper reviews so as to reconstitute individual lectures or addresses. See particularly:

"Three Unpublished Lectures of Ralph Waldo Emerson," ed. Jeanne Kronman, *New England Quarterly* 19 (March 1946), pp. 98–110. The lectures are "Prospects" (subsequently published in EL 3); "The Spirit of the Age" (January 1850); and "Economy" (February 1852; second of four lectures making up a series constituting a first version of *The Conduct of Life*).

"Emerson's Second West India Emancipation Address," ed. Louis Ruchames, *New England Quarterly* 28 (September 1955), pp. 382–388.

"Two Forgotten Addresses by Ralph Waldo Emerson," ed. Louis Ruchames, *American Literature* 28 (January 1957), pp. 425–433; these were delivered July 4, 1846 and August 3, 1849, both on the anniversary of West Indian Emancipation, celebrated annually by the Massachusetts Antislavery Society.

"Emerson as an Abolitionist Orator," ed. Rollo L. Silver, *New England Quarterly* 6 (1933), pp. 154–158: an address delivered on January 24, 1861, at a meeting of the Massachusetts Antislavery Society.

Uncollected Lectures by Ralph Waldo Emerson, ed. Clarence Gohdes (New York, 1938); these include a series of six lectures titled "American Life," given in 1864–1865, and a single lecture titled "Natural Religion," given April 4, 1869.

2. *Journal*

JMN 1.403–415 contains a list of all the Emerson notebooks in the Houghton Library; many exist also in typed transcriptions.

3. *Letters*

The work of classifying and editing continues. The *Emerson Society Quarterly* has published several descriptive lists of manuscripts in various libraries and institutions; many of these manuscripts are letters. The same journal also publishes lists of letters, sometimes unpublished, offered for sale by various specialized libraries. See particularly:

"Opening Pandora's Box: Some Collections of Emerson Manuscripts," ed. Kenneth Cameron (as are all the items in this category), *Emerson Society Quarterly* 3 (1956), pp. 1–3.

"Some Emerson Letters, Ungathered and Migrant," *Emerson Society Quarterly* 3 (1956), pp. 4–6.

"Some Collections of Emerson Manuscripts (Part Two)," *Emerson Society Quarterly* 5 (1956), pp. 20–21.

"Some Collections of Emerson Manuscripts (Part Three)," *Emerson Society Quarterly* 6 (1957), pp. 21–23.

"Emerson Manuscripts, Ungathered and Migrant (Part Two)," *Emerson Society Quarterly* 6 (1957), pp. 26–27.

"Emerson Manuscripts, Ungathered and Migrant (Part Three)," *Emerson Society Quarterly* 13 (1958), pp. 36–41.

INDEX

Translator's Note: The following index covers both text and notes (indicated by "n" following the page number), and for both text and notes covers not only Professor Gonnaud's own exposition but also the passages he quotes—thus, if Emerson is quoted as referring to Marcus Aurelius, the reference will turn up in the index.

Library of Congress Cataloging-in-Publication Data

Gonnaud, Maurice.
An uneasy solitude.

Translation of: L'individu et société dans l'oeuvre de R. W. Emerson.
1. Emerson, Ralph Waldo, 1803–1882—Political and
social views. 2. Social problems in literature.
3. Individualism in literature. I. Title.
PS1642.S58G66 1987 814'.3 87–45519
ISBN 0–691–06718–X

MAURICE GONNAUD is Professor of American Literature and Civilization at the University of Lyon. The translator, Lawrence Rosenwald, is Associate Professor of English at Wellesley College.